The

Doctrines

of

Grace and Justice

I0161082

The Doctrines of Grace and Justice

By

John Fletcher

Compiled and edited by
Jeffrey L. Wallace

This edition copyright © 2014 by Apprehending Truth.
All Rights Reserved.

ISBN-10: 0692227970

ISBN-13: 978-0692227978

A *Heritage of Truth* Book
Reclaiming the Wisdom of the Past

Heritage of Truth
Reclaiming the Wisdom of the Past

Published by:
Apprehending Truth Publishers
Brookfield, Missouri
2014

Buy the Truth and sell it not. ~Proverbs xxiii, 23

AT 10 9 8 7 6 5 4 3 2 1
060114

Other Titles published by Apprehending Truth:

Defining Biblical Holiness

The Works of John Fletcher:
Volume One: Five Checks To Antinomianism
Volume Two: Creeds and Scripture Scales
Volume Three: Doctrines of Grace and Justice
Volume Four: Portrait of Paul & An Appeal (forthcoming)
Volume Five: A Vindication of the Faith (forthcoming)
Volume Six: Outlines & Miscellany (forthcoming)

Adam Clarke's Christian Theology

What the Bible Really Teaches About Divorce and Remarriage

Did Jesus Correct Moses?

God's Crucible: Life in a Biblical Church

Antinomianism and the Gospel

The Way To Life: Understanding the Gospel Message

The Ageless Conflict

-----

www.ATPublishers.net

Jean Guillaume de la Flechere

The Works

of

John Fletcher

Volume Three

Doctrines of Grace and Justice

Apprehending Truth Publishers

Brookfield, Missouri

2014

CONTENTS

THE DOCTRINES OF GRACE AND JUSTICE

SECTION I. A plain account of the Gospel, and its various dispensations—It holds forth the doctrines of justice as well as those of grace,   - 3 -

II. Remarks on the two Gospel axioms upon which the doctrines of grace and justice are founded,   - 9 -

III. By whom chiefly the Gospel axioms were systematically parted,   - 13 -

IV. Luther and Calvin did not restore the balance of the Gospel axioms; but Cranmer did,   - 14 -

V. The two modern Gospels, and their dreadful consequences.   - 18 -

THE RECONCILIATION; OR, AN EASY METHOD TO NITE THE PEOPLE OF GOD.

SECTION I. The sad consequence of the division of those who make a peculiar profession of faith in Christ,   - 27 -

II. Moderate Calvinists and Arminians may be easily reconciiled to each other,   - 32 -

III. Eight pair of opposite propositions on which the opposite doctrines of grace and justice are founded,   - 38 -

IV. Bible Calvinism and Bible Arminianism stated in two essays,   - 41 -

V. Inferences from the two essays,   - 75 -

VI. A plan of general reconciliation and union between moderate Calvinists and Arminians,   - 81 -

VII. Directions how to secure the blessings of peace and brotherly love,   - 89 -

VIII. Farther motives to a speedy reconciliation,   - 95 -

REMARKS ON MR. TOPLADY'S SCHEME OF CHRISTIAN AND PHILOSOPHICAL NECESSITY.

INTRODUCTION.   - 105 -

SECTION I. A view of Mr. Toplady's scheme—It represents God as the first cause of all sin and damnation,   - 106 -

II. His error is overthrown by fourteen arguments,   - 112 -

III. Twelve keys to open the passages of Scripture on which he founds his scheme,   - 122 -

IV. The capital objections of the necessitarians to the docrine of liberty answered,   - 136 -

V. The doctrine of necessity is the capital error of the Calvinists, and the foundation of the most wretched schemes of philosophy and divinity,   - 142 -

ANSWER TO MR. TOPLADY'S VINDICATION OF THE DECREES.

INTRODUCTION. - 149 -

SECTION I. The Calvinian scheme evidently implies that some men shall be saved, do what they will; and others damned, do what they can, - 151 -

II. Calvinism upon its legs: or a full view of the arguments by which Mr. Toplady attemps to reconcile Calvinism with God's holiness, - 154 -

III. Mr. Toplady appeals in vain to Scripture and reason to support the absoluteness and holiness of the Calvinian decrees, - 162 -

IV. Calvinian reprobation cannot be reconciiled with Divine justice, - 165 -

V. Much less can it be reconciled with Divine mercy, - 176 -

VI. A view of the manner in which Mr Toplady attempts to prove Calvinian reprobation from the Scriptures, - 179 -

VII. The arguments answered by which Mr. Toplady tries to reconcile Calvinism with a future judgment, and absolute necessity with moral agency, - 184 -

VIII. Mr. Toplady's arguments from God's prescience answered, - 193 -

IX. An answer to the charges of robbing the trinity, and encouraging Deism, - 198 -

X. Mr. Toplady attempts in vain to retort the charge of Antinomianism, and to show that Calvinism is more conducive to holiness, than the opposite doctrine, - 200 -

XI. A caution against the tenet, "Whatever is, is right," - 204 -

XII. Some encouragements for those who, from a principle of conscience, bear their testimony against absolute election and reprobation, - 210 -

POLEMICAL ESSAY

PREFACE. Reasons of the title given to this tract—The doctrines of the heathens, the Papists, and Calvinists, concerning the purgation of souls from the remains of sin—The purgatory recommended in this book, - 214 -

SECTION I. The doctrine of Christian perfection placed in a Scriptural light, - 219 -

II. Pious Calvinists dissent from us chiefly because they confound the law of innocence, and the law of liberty, or Adamic and Christian perfection, - 223 -

III. Objections against this doctrine solved merely by considering the nature of Christian perfection, - 228 -

IV. The ninth and fifteenth articles of our Church, properly understood, are not against the doctrine of Christian perfection—That our Church holds it, is proved by thirteen arguments, - 233 -

V. St. Peter and St. James declare for Christian perfection, - 243 -

VI. St. Paul preached Christian perfection, and professed to have attained it, - 247 -

VII. St. Paul was not carnal, and sold under sin—The true meaning of Galatians 5:17, and of Romans 7:14 - 254 -

VIII. An answer to the arguments by which St. Paul's supposed carnality is generally defended, - 264 -

IX. St. Paul presents us with a striking picture of a perfect Christian, by occasionally describing his own spirituality, - 271 -

X. St. John is for Christian perfection, and not for a death purgatory, - 276 -

XI. Why the privileges of believers under the Gospel cannot be justly measured by the experience of believers under the law of Moses, - 282 -

XII. A variety of arugments to prove the absurdity of the twin doctrines of Christian imperfection and a death purgatory, - 287 -

XIII. A variety of arguments to prove the mischievousness of the doctrine of Christian imperfection, - 294 -

XIV. The arguments answered, by which the imperfectionists support the doctrine of the necessary indwelling of sin till death, - 300 -

XV. The doctrine of Christian perfection is truly evangelical—A recapitulation of the Scripture proofs whereby it is maintained, - 314 -

XVI. The distinction between sins and infirmities is truly Scriptural—An answer to Mr. Henry's grand argument for the continuance of indwelling sin, - 321 -

XVII. An address to perfect Christian Pharisees, - 330 -

XVIII. To prejudiced imperfectionists, - 335 -

XIX. To imperfect believers, who embrace the doctrine of Christian perfection, - 344 -

XX. Address to perfect Christians, - 373 -

THE DOCTRINES

OF

GRACE AND JUSTICE,

EQUALLY

ESSENTIAL TO THE PURE GOSPEL;

WITH

SOME REMARKS

ON THE MISCHIEVOUS DIVISIONS CAUSED AMONG
CHRISTIANS BY PARTING THOSE DOCTRINES.

BEING

AN INTRODUCTION TO A PLAN OF RECONCILIATION

BETWEEN THE DEFENDERS OF THE DOCTRINES OF PARTIAL GRACE,
COMMONLY CALLED CALVINISTS; AND THE DEFENDERS OF THE DOCTRINES
OF IMPARTIAL JUSTICE, COMMONLY CALLED ARMINIANS.

The Works of John Fletcher

THE DOCTRINES OF GRACE AND JUSTICE.

SECTION I.

A plain account of the Gospel in general, and of the various dispensations into which it branches itself — The Gospel holds forth the doctrines of justice, as well as the doctrines of grace — An opposition to this capital truth gave rise to the controversy about the Minutes — An answer to an objection of those who suppose that the Gospel consists only of doctrines of grace.

IF a judicious mariner, who has sailed round the world, sees with pleasure and improvement a map, which exhibits, in one point of view, the shape and proportion of the wide seas, in crossing of which he has spent some years; a judicious Protestant may profitably look upon a doctrinal map, (if I may be allowed the expression,) which places before him in diminutive proportion, the windings of a controversy, which, like a noisy, impetuous torrent, has disturbed the Churches of Christ for fourteen hundred years, and carried religious desolation through the four parts of the globe; but more especially if this map exhibits, with some degree of accuracy, the boundaries of truth, the crooked shores of the sea of error, the haven of peace, and the rocks rendered famous by the doctrinal wrecks of myriads of unwary evangelists. Without any apology, therefore, I shall lay before the reader a plain account of the *primitive catholic Gospel*, and its various dispensations.

THE GOSPEL, in general, is a Divine system of truth, which, with various degrees of evidence, points out to sinners the way of eternal salvation, agreeable to the mercy and justice of a holy God; and therefore the Gospel, in general, is an assemblage *of holy doctrines of* GRACE, *and gracious doctrines of* JUSTICE. This is the idea which our Lord himself gives us of it, Mark 16:16. For though he speaks there of the peculiar Gospel dispensation, which he opened, his words may, in some sense, be applied to every Gospel dispensation. "Preach the GOSPEL. He that believeth [in the light of his dispensation, supposing he does it *'with the heart unto righteousness'*] shall be saved," according to the privileges of his dispensation: here you have a holy doctrine of *grace*. "But he that believeth not shall be damned:" here you have a gracious doctrine of *justice*. For, supposing man has a gracious capacity to believe in the light of his dispensation, there is no Antinomian grace in the promise, and no free wrath in the threatening, which compose what our Lord calls the Gospel; but the conditional promise exhibits a righteous doctrine of grace, and the conditional threatening displays a gracious doctrine of justice.

THE GOSPEL *in general* branches itself out into four capital dispensations, the last of which is most eminently called *the Gospel*, because it includes and perfects all the preceding displays of God's grace and justice toward mankind. Take we a view of these four dispensations, beginning at the lowest, viz. *Gentilism*.

I. GENTILISM, which is frequently called *natural religion*, and might with propriety be called, *the Gospel of Gentiles*. Gentilism, I say, is a dispensation of grace and justice, which St. Peter preaches and describes in these words: — "In every nation he that feareth God, and worketh righteousness [according to his light] is accepted of him." These words contain a holy doctrine of grace; which is inseparably connected with this holy doctrine of justice, *In every nation he that feareth* NOT *God, and worketh* NOT *righteousness,* [according to his light,] *is* NOT *accepted of him.*

II. JUDAISM, which is frequently called the *Mosaic dispensation*, or the law, (that is, according to the first meaning of the Hebrew word תורת, *the doctrine*, or *the instruction*,) and which might with propriety be called *the Jewish Gospel*. Judaism, I say, is that particular display of the doctrines of grace and justice, which was chiefly calculated for the meridian of Canaan, and is contained in the Old Testament; but especially in the five books of Moses. The Prophet Samuel sums it all up in these words: — "Only fear the Lord, and serve him in truth with all your heart, [according to the law, i.e. doctrine of Moses,] for consider how great things he hath done for you, [his peculiar people:] but if ye shall still do wickedly, ye shall be consumed," Samuel 12:24. In this Gospel dispensation, also, the doctrine of grace goes hand in hand with the doctrine of justice. Every book in the Old Testament confirms the truth of this assertion.

III. THE GOSPEL of John the Baptist, which is commonly called the baptism of John, in connection with *the Gospel*, or baptism, which the apostles preached, before Christ opened the glorious baptism of his own Spirit on the day of pentecost; this Gospel dispensation, I say, is the Jewish Gospel improved into *infant Christianity*. Or, if you please, it is Christianity falling short of that "indwelling power from on high," which is called "the kingdom of God come with power." This Gospel is chiefly found in the four Gospels. It clearly points out the person of Christ, gives us his history, holds forth his mediatorial law; and, leading on to the perfection of Christianity, displays, with increasing light, (1.) The doctrines of *grace*, which kindly call the chief of sinners to eternal salvation through the practicable means of repentance, faith, and obedience. And, (2.) The doctrines of *justice*, which awfully threatens sinners with destruction, if they finally neglect to repent, believe, and obey.

The capital difference between this Gospel dispensation and the Jewish Gospel, consists in this: the Jewish Gospel holds forth Christ *about to come*, in types and prophecies; but this Gospel displays the fulfilment of the Jewish prophecies, and without a typical veil points out Christ *already come*. Again: the *political* part of the Jewish Gospel admits of some temporary indulgences, with respect to divorce, a plurality of wives, &c, which indulgences are repealed in the Christian institution, where morality is carried to the greatest height, and enforced by the strongest motives. But, on the other hand, the *ceremonial* part of the Gospel of Christ grants us many indulgences with respect to Sabbaths, festivals, washings, meats, places of worship, &c. For it binds upon us only the two unbloody significant rites, which the Scriptures call *baptism* and *the Lord's Supper;* freeing us from shedding human blood in circumcision; and the blood of beasts in daily sacrifices; an important freedom this, which St. Paul calls "the *ceremonial* liberty wherewith Christ hath made us free," and for which he so strenuously contends against the Judaizing preachers, who would have brought his Galatian converts under the bloody yoke of circumcision and Jewish bondage.

IV. *The perfect Gospel* of CHRIST is frequently called THE GOSPEL only, on account of its fulness, and because it contains whatever is excellent in the above-described Gospel dispensations. We may truly say, therefore, that *perfect Christianity,* or the *complete Gospel of Christ,* is *Gentilism, Judaism,* and *the baptism of John,* arrived at their full maturity. This perfected Gospel is found then, initially, in the four books, which bear the name of Gospels, and perfectively in the *Acts of the Apostles* and the *epistles.* The difference between this perfected Gospel and the Gospel which was preached before the day of pentecost, consists in this capital article: — Before that day, our Lord and his forerunner, John the Baptist, foretold that Christ "should baptize with the Holy Ghost;" and Christ promised the indwelling Spirit. He said, "He dwelleth with you, and shall *then* be in you. Ye shall be baptized with the Holy Ghost, not many days hence." But the full Gospel of Christ takes in the full dispensation of Christ's Spirit, as well as the full history of Christ's life, death, and resurrection; comprehending the glad news of the descent of the Holy Ghost, as well as the joyful tidings of the ascension of the Son; and therefore its distinguishing character is thus laid down by St. Peter, "Jesus, being by the right hand of God EXALTED, and having received of the Father the promise of the Holy Ghost, he hath shed forth this, which ye now see and hear. This promise is unto you [that repent and believe.] We are his witnesses of these things, and so is also the Holy Ghost, whom God [since the day of pentecost] hath given to them that obey him:" for, before Christ's ascension, the evangelists could say, "The Holy Ghost is not yet given, [in its Christian fulness,] because Christ is not yet GLORIFIED:" compare Acts 2:33, &c, with Acts 5:22, and John 7:39.

This Gospel is the richest display of Divine grace and justice which takes place among men in the present state of things. For Christ's sake "the Holy Ghost is given" as an indwelling, sanctifying comforter. Here is the highest doctrine of grace! He is thus given "to them that obey;" and of consequence he is refused to the disobedient. Here is the highest doctrine of justice, so far as the purpose of God, according to the elections of grace and justice, actually takes place in this life, before the second coming of Christ. These two last clauses are of peculiar importance.

1. I say *in this life,* because, after death, two great dispensations of grace and justice will yet take place, with respect to every man: the one in the day of *death,* when Christ will say to each of us, "Thou shalt be with me in paradise;" or, "Thou shalt go to thy own place:" and the other in the day of *judgment,* when our Lord will add, "Come, ye blessed," or, "Go, ye cursed." Then shall the "Gospel mystery of God," which equally displays the doctrines of grace and of justice, be fully accomplished.

2. I have added the clause, *before the second coming of Christ* because in the Psalms, Prophets, Acts, Epistles, and especially in the Revelation, we have a variety of promises, that "in the day of his *displayed* power, *Christ will* come in his glory, to judge among the heathen, to wound even kings in the day of his wrath, to root up the wicked, to fill the places with their dead bodies, *to* smite in sunder *antichrist, and* the heads over divers countries, *and* to lift up his *triumphant* head," on this very earth, where he once "bowed his *wounded* head, and gave up the ghost:" compare Psalm 110, with Acts 1:11; 2 Thessalonians 1:10; Rev. 19, &c. In that great day, another Gospel

dispensation shall take place. We have it now in prophecy, as the Jews had the Gospel of Christ's first advent; but when Christ shall "come to destroy the wicked, to be *actually* glorified in his saints, and admired in all them that believe: in that day," ministers of the Gospel shall no more prophesy, but, speaking a plain, historical truth, they shall lift up their voices, as "the voice of many waters and mighty thunderings, saying, Allelujah, for the Lord God omnipotent reigneth; the marriage of the Lamb is come; his wife [the Church of the first born] has made herself ready: blessed and holy is he that has part in the first resurrection: he REIGNS with Christ a thousand years. Blessed are the meek, for they DO inherit the earth. The times of refreshing ARE come, and he HAS SENT Jesus Christ, who before was preached unto us; whom the heaven DID receive" till this solemn season. But now are come "the times of restitution of all things, which God hath spoken by the mouth of all his holy prophets, since the world began," Rev. 19, 20; Matthew 5:5; Acts 3:19, &c. May the Lord hasten this Gospel dispensation! And, till it take place, may "the Spirit and the bride say, Come!"

This being premised, it will not be difficult to give the reader a just idea of the grand controversy which has torn the Churches of Christ, from the days of Augustine and Pelagius, and which has lately been revived among us, on the following occasion.

In the year 1770, Mr. Wesley (in the Minutes of a conference, which he held with the preachers in his connection) advanced some propositions, the manifest tendency of which was to assert that the doctrines of justice are an essential part of the Gospel; and that, when we have been afraid to preach them, as well as the doctrines of grace, we have been partial dispensers of the truth, and have leaned too much toward Calvinism; that is, toward a system of doctrine, which, in a great degree, explains away the doctrines of *justice*, to make more room for the doctrines of *grace*.

Some good people, who imagined that the doctrines of *impartial justice* have little or nothing to do with the Gospel, were not only highly displeased with Mr. Wesley's propositions, but very greatly alarmed at the word *merit*, which he warily used in one of them, to intimate that the doctrines of justice and the day of judgment must fall to the ground, if *every kind* of merit or desert is banished from the Gospel; justice being a virtue which, from an impartial tribunal, "renders to every man according to his WORKS," that is, according to his worthiness or unworthiness, or, as some express it, according to his merit or demerit.

A regard for the doctrines of justice, and a fear lest Antinomian doctrines of grace, and dreadful doctrines of free wrath, should be still entertained by my friends as the genuine doctrines of grace, engaged me to vindicate those obnoxious propositions, or rather, the doctrines of justice held forth therein. And this, I hope, I have done in a series of *Checks to Antinomianism*, or of tracts against an unscriptural doctrine of grace, a doctrine of *grace* torn from the Scripture doctrine of *justice*. In order to rescue the doctrine of justice, I have endeavoured to prove that no man is born an absolute reprobate in Calvin's sense of the word; that "God is loving to every man" for Christ's sake; and that, of consequence, there is a Gospel dispensation for every man, though it should be only that which is called Gentilism. I have shown the cruelty of those opinions which directly or indirectly doom to eternal perdition all the heathens, who never read the law of Moses, or heard the Gospel of Christ. I have evinced, by a variety of arguments, that nothing can be more unscriptural than to represent the law of Moses (i.e. the Jewish Gospel) as a *graceless* doctrine of justice;

and the law of Christ (or the Christian Gospel) as a *lawless* doctrine of grace. By these means I have defended, so far as lay in me, both the Jewish doctrines of grace and the Christian doctrines of justice. And by demonstrating that the Scripture doctrines of *grace* are inseparably connected with the Scripture doctrines of *justice*, I flatter myself to have opened the way for the reunion of the two partial gospels of the day; the capital error of which consists either in excluding the doctrines of grace from the doctrines of justice, which is the error of all rigid free willers; or in excluding the doctrines of justice from the doctrines of grace, which is the mistake of all rigid bound willers.

"What," says one of these partial defenders of the doctrines of grace, "will you still persist to legalize the Gospel? Do you not know that the word GOSPEL, in the original, means GOOD *news*, or a GOOD *message*, and therefore must denote doctrines of *grace* abstracted from all the severity of what you call the doctrines of *justice*?" To this plausible objection, which has deluded thousands of simple souls, I answer: —

(1.) A royal proclamation may be called a GOOD *proclamation*, though it does not turn the king's subjects into lawless favourites, and the LAWS of the realm into *rules of life*, as insignificant in judgment as rules of grammar. And the statutes of parliament may be GOOD *statutes*, though they may secure the righteous punishment of offenders as well as the gracious privileges of loyal subjects. (2.) If the hand of God is a GOOD *hand* when it "resists the proud," as well as when it "gives grace to the humble;" and if his arm was a *merciful* arm when it "overthrew daring Pharaoh and his host in the Red Sea," as well as when it "made *obedient* Israel to pass through the midst of it," see Psalm 136, why may not a message from God, which requires practical obedience, and is enforced by promises of gracious rewards in case of compliance, and by threatenings of righteous punishments in case of non- compliance; why may not, I say, such a message be called a GOOD *message* or *Gospel*? (3.) Why should not a revelation from God be a GOOD *revelation* or a *Gospel*, when it displays the severity of his justice toward those who reject his gracious offers, as well as the tenderness of his compassion toward those who accept them; especially if we consider that the first intention of the denunciations of his vindictive justice is to excite the godly fear which endears offers of mercy to sinners, and is in them "the beginning of wisdom?" (4.) If, in the Old Testament, the sweetest and most joyful messages of God's grace are called *law*, and if, in the New Testament, the most terrible denunciations of indignation and wrath, tribulation and anguish, are called *Gospel*, nothing in the world can be more unscriptural and absurd than the Antinomian Babel erected by some zealous evangelists, who teach that *the law of God* is nothing but the doctrine of *merciless justice;* and that *the Gospel of Christ* is nothing but the doctrine of *lawless grace*.

That the word LAW, in the Old Testament, frequently means the sweetest Gospel promises, I prove, *first*, from these sayings of David: "The law of thy mouth is better to me than thousands of gold and silver," Psalm 119:72. "He hath remembered his Gospel covenant for ever, — which covenant he made with Abraham, and his oath to Isaac, and confirmed the same unto Jacob for a law," Psalm 105:8, &c. Here the Gospel covenants made with the three chosen patriarchs, are called a law. Hence it is that when Isaiah speaks of the brightest display of Gospel grace at the time that "the mountain of the Lord's house shall be established on the top of the mountains," he says, "Out of Sion shall go forth the law," Isaiah 2:2, 3. Agreeably to this view of things we read in Nehemiah, that "all the people gathered themselves together as one man, and spake to Ezra to bring the book of the law of Moses: *that* the ears of all the people were attentive to the book of the law: *that* the Levites did read in the law of God distinctly, and gave the sense: *and that* all the people went their way, &c, to make great mirth, because they had understood the words that were declared to them: and there was a very great gladness, — the joy of the Lord being *their* strength," Nehemiah 8:1, 3, 8, 10, 12, 17. Now, if *the law*, which was read and explained to them, contained only the impracticable sanctions of a merciless, thundering justice; were not all the people out of their senses when they "went their way with great gladness" after hearing *the law* expounded?

The New Testament confirms this account of the doctrines of grace and justice, and of the words law and Gospel. When our Lord (who undoubtedly knew the exact meaning of the word Gospel) sent his disciples to "preach the Gospel to every creature," he charged them to declare, that "he who believeth not shall be damned," as well as that "he who believeth shall be saved," Mark 16:16. Whence it evidently appears that our Lord meant by *the* GOSPEL the severe doctrines of justice, as well as the comfortable doctrines of grace.

St. Paul gives us exactly the same idea of the Gospel. In the Epistle to the Romans, where he contends most for the gratuitous election of distinguishing love, he expostulates with those who "despise the riches of God's goodness, and treasure up unto themselves wrath against the day of wrath, and revelation of the righteous judgment of God; who will render to every man according to his deeds, — eternal life to them, who, by patient continuance in well doing, seek for glory; but indignation and wrath to them that obey not the truth." If you ask St. Paul when God will thus display his merciful goodness and tremendous justice, he directly answers, "When God shall judge the secrets of men according to my Gospel," that is, according to the promises and threatenings, — the doctrines of grace and the doctrines of justice, which compose the Gospel I preach, Romans 5, 4-16.

Hence it is that the apostle calls the Mosaic dispensation sometimes the law, and sometimes the Gospel, while he styles the Christian dispensation sometimes *the law of Christ*, and sometimes *the Gospel of Christ*.

That St. Paul indifferently calls the Mosaic dispensation law and Gospel, is evident from the following texts: "Every man that is circumcised is a debtor to the whole law," Galatians 5:3. Here the word law undoubtedly means the Mosaic dispensation. Again: "To us was the Gospel preached, as well as to them," the Israelites who perished in the wilderness, for not believing Moses, Hebrews 4:2. Whence it follows, that "to THEM [the Israelites, who perished] the Gospel [i.e. the doctrines of grace and justice] was preached as well as to US," Christians, who are saved by obedient faith. Once more: that what Moses preached to them was a doctrine of grace and of justice, is evident from this consideration: had the Mosaic Gospel been a doctrine of mere justice, it could not have been a Gospel like our gracious Gospel; and had it been a mere doctrine of grace, the apostle could never have excited us not to neglect our Christian Gospel, and great salvation, by pointing out to us the fearful destruction of the Israelites, who neglected their Jewish Gospel and salvation; "lest any *Christian* should fall after the same example of unbelief," Hebrews 4:11.

With respect to the Christian dispensation, the apostle calls it sometimes the law: "The doers of *the law* [i.e. of the *preceptive* part of the Gospel] shall be justified, when

God shall judge the secrets of men according to my Gospel," Romans 2:13, 16, compared with Matthew 12:36, 37. Sometimes he calls it *the law of Christ:* "Bear ye one another's burdens, and so fulfil the law of Christ," Galatians 6:2: sometimes *the laws of God:* "I will write my laws [i.e. my evangelical precepts and promises] in their hearts," Hebrews 8:10; 10:16: sometimes *the law of the Spirit,* Romans 8:2: and sometimes *the Gospel of Christ,* Romans 1:16.

Hence it is that to be a Christian believer, in St. Paul's language, is "to be under the law of Christ," 1 Corinthians 9:21. As for St. James, he never calls the Christian dispensation *Gospel;* but he simply calls it either *the law,* James 4:11, 12; 2:10, *the law of liberty,* James 2:12, or, *the perfect law of liberty,* James 1:25. St. John uses the same language in his epistles, in which he never mentions the word Gospel, and in which, speaking of the sins of Christian believers, he says, that "sin is the transgression of the law;" whence it follows, that the sin of Christians is the transgression of the law of Christ, or of the holy doctrines of justice preached by Jesus Christ. To deny it, would be asserting we cannot sin; for St. Paul informs us that the Mosaic law is done away, 2 Corinthians 3:11. Now, if no Christian is under the law of Moses, and if Christ never adopted the law of our nature, and never grafted the moral part of the Mosaic law into the Christian dispensation; or, in other terms, if Christ's Gospel is a lawless institution, it necessarily follows that no Christian can sin: for sin is not imputed or charged, (that is, there is no sin,) "where there is no law," Romans 5:13. Hence it is that Antinomian doctrines of grace represent fallen, adulterous, bloody believers as spotless, or sinless before God, in all their sins. Such is the necessary consequence of a lawless Gospel armed with pointless "rules of life!" Such the dreadful tendency of doctrines of *grace* torn away from the doctrines of *justice.*

SECTION II.

Remarks on the two Gospel axioms, or capital truths, upon which the doctrines of grace and justice are founded — Augustine himself once granted both those truths — Rigid Arminians indirectly deny the one, and rigid Calvinists the other — How the partial defenders of the doctrines of justice and grace try to save appearances, with respect to the part of the truth which they indirectly oppose.

So noble and solid a superstructure as the Gospel, i.e. the Scripture doctrines of grace and justice, undoubtedly stands upon a noble and sure principles, the one theological and the other moral. These two principles, or, if you please, these two pillars of Gospel truth, may, for distinction sake, be called Gospel axioms; at least, I beg leave to call them so. Nor will the candid reader deny my request, if he consider the following definitions:—

I. AN AXIOM is a self-evident truth, which at once recommends itself to the understanding, or the conscience of every unprejudiced man. Thus, *two and two make four,* is an AXIOM in every counting house. And that "the absolute necessity of all human actions is incompatible with a moral law and a day of judgment," is an axiom in every unprejudiced mind.

II. The two Gospel axioms are the two principles, or capital self-evident truths, on which the primitive Gospel, that is, the Scripture doctrine of grace and justice is founded.

III. The first Gospel axiom bears up the holy doctrines of grace, and when it is cordially received, is equally destructive of proud Pharisaism and the unholy doctrines of lawless grace. This axiom is the following self-evident truth, which recommends itself to the mind and conscience of every candid Bible Christian: — "Our first talent or degree of salvation is merely of God's free grace in Christ, without any work or endeavour of our own; and our eternal salvation is originally, capitally,* and finally† of God's free grace in Christ; through our not neglecting that first talent or degree of salvation. I say through our not neglecting, &c, to secure the connection of the two Gospel axioms, and to leave Scripture room for the doctrines of remunerative justice.

IV. The second Gospel axiom bears up the doctrines of justice, and extirpates the doctrine of free wrath. It is the following proposition, which, I believe, no candid Bible Christian will deny: — "Our eternal damnation is originally‡ and principally of our own personal free will, through an obstinate and final neglect of the first talent or degree of salvation."

These two Gospel axioms may be thus expressed: (1.) *Our salvation is of God:* or, *there is free grace in God,* which, through Christ, freely places all men in a state of temporary redemption, justification, or salvation, according to various Gospel dispensations, and crowns those who are faithful unto death with an eternal redemption, justification, or salvation. (2.) *Our damnation is of ourselves:* or, *there is free will in man,* by which he may, through the grace freely imparted to him in the day of temporary salvation, work out his own eternal salvation: or he may, through the natural power which angels had to sin in heaven, and our first parents in paradise,

---

* A Solifidian would say *entirely,* and by this means he would leave no room for the second Gospel axiom, for the rewardableness of the works of faith, and for the doctrine of remunerative justice. But by saying *capitally,* we avoid this threefold mistake, we secure the honour of holy free grace, and shut the door against its counterfeit.

† By adding *finally,* we show that the top stone, as well as the foundation stone of our eternal salvation, is to be brought with "shouting, Grace! grace! unto it;" because if God had honoured his obedient saints with a sight of his heavenly glory for half an hour, and then suffered them to fall gently asleep in the bosom of oblivion, or to slide into a state of personal non-existence, he would have demonstrated his remunerative justice, and amply rewarded their best services. Hence it appears that God's giving eternal rewards of glory for a few temporary services, done by his own grace, is such an instance of free grace as nothing but eternal shouts of "Grace! grace!" can sufficiently acknowledge. We desire our mistaken brethren to consider this remark; otherwise they will wrong the truth and us, by continuing to say that our doctrines of grace allow indeed free grace to lay the foundation, but that they reserve to the works of our rectified free will the honour of bringing the top stone of our eternal salvation, with saying, "Works! works! unto it:" a Pharisaic doctrine this, which we abhor; loudly asserting that although our free, unnecessitated obedience of faith intervenes, yet God in Christ is the Omega as well as the Alpha, — the end, as well as the beginning, of our eternal salvation.

‡ I add the word *originally,* to cut off the self-excusing opinion of those men who charge their eternal damnation upon an absolute decree of reprobation, or upon Adam's first transgression. *As* for the word *principally,* it secures the part in the damnation of the wicked, which the Scriptures ascribe to the righteous God: it being certain, (1.) That God judicially hardens his slothful and unprofitable servants, by taking from them, at the end of their day of grace, the talent of softening grace, which they have obstinately buried. And, (2.) That he judicially reprobates or damns them, by pronouncing this awful sentence, "Depart, ye cursed," &c. A flame of vindictive justice belongs to the Gospel of Christ, Hebrews 12:29, but not a single spark of free wrath.

choose to sin away the day of temporary salvation. And by thus working out his damnation, he may provoke just wrath, which is the same as despised free grace, to punish him with eternal destruction.

These two truths, or axioms, might be made still plainer, thus: (1.) Our gracious and just God, in a day of salvation begun, sets life or death before us. (2.) As free-willing, assisted creatures, we may, during that day, choose which we please: we may "stretch out *our* hand to the water, or to the fire." Or thus: (1.) There is holy, righteous, and partial free grace in God. (2.) There is free will in redeemed, assisted man, whereby he is capable of obeying or disobeying God's holy, righteous, and partial free grace. For conveniency's sake, these axioms may be shortened thus: (1.) The doctrine of holy free grace and partial mercy in God is true. (2.) The doctrine of rectified, assisted free will in man, and of impartial justice in God, is true also.

This lovely pair of evangelical propositions appears to me so essential to the fulness and harmony of the Gospel, that I believe if Pelagius and Augustine themselves were alive, neither of them would dare directly to rise against it. Time, or envy, has destroyed the works of Pelagius, the great asserter of free will and the doctrines of justice; we cannot therefore support the doctrines of free grace by his concessions: but we have the writings of Augustine, the great defender of God's distinguishing love, and the doctrine of free grace; and yet, partial as he was to these doctrines, in a happy moment, he boldly stood up for free will and the doctrines of justice. This appears from the judicious and candid questions which he proposes in one of his epistles: — *Si non est gratia Dei, quomodo salvat mundum? Si non est liberum arbitrium, quomodo judicat mundum?* If there be not free grace in God, how does he *graciously* save the world? If there be not free will *in men*, how does he *righteously* judge the world?"

To conclude: whoever holds forth these two Bible axioms, "There is free grace in God, whence man's salvation graciously flows in various degrees;" and, "There is free will in every man, whence the damnation of all that perish justly proceeds:" whoever, I say, consistently holds forth these two self-evident propositions, is, in my humble judgment, a Gospel minister, who "rightly divides the word of truth." He is a friend to both the doctrines of partial grace and impartial justice, of mercy and obedience, of faith and good works: in short, he preaches the primitive Gospel, reunites the two opposite gospels of the day, and equally obviates the errors of Honestus and Zelotes, who stand up for these modern gospels.

If you ask what those errors are, I answer, as follows: — Honestus, the Pelagian, seldom preaches free grace, and never dwells upon the absolute sovereignty with which God at first distributes the various talents of his grace: and when he preaches free will, he seldom preaches free will initially rectified and continually assisted by free grace; rarely, if ever, deeply humbling his hearers by displaying the total helplessness of unrectified and unassisted free will: and thus he veils the delightful doctrine of God's free grace, clouds the evangelical doctrine of man's free will, and inadvertently opens the door to self-conceited Pharisaism. On the other hand, Zelotes, the Solifidian, or rigid Calvinist, seldom or never preaches rectified, assisted free will; he harps only on the doctrines of absolute necessity; and when he preaches free grace, he too often preaches, (1.) A cruel free grace, which turning itself into free wrath, with respect to a majority of mankind, absolutely passes them by, and consigns them over to everlasting, infallible damnation, by means of necessary, foreordained sin;

and, (2.) An unscriptural free grace, which turning itself into lawless fondness, with respect to a number of favourite souls, absolutely insures to them eternal redemption, complete justification, and finished salvation, be they ever so unfaithful.

By these means Zelotes spoils the doctrine of free grace, undesignedly injures the doctrine of holiness, and utterly destroys the doctrine of justice. For when he denies that the greatest part of mankind have any interest in God's redeeming love; when he intimates that the doctrines of an absolute, necessitating election to eternal life are true; and that God's reprobates are not less necessitated to sin to the end and be damned, than God's elect are to obey to the end and be saved; does he not pour contempt upon the throne of Divine justice? Does he not make the supreme Judge, who fills that throne, appear as unwise when he distributes heavenly rewards, as cruel, when he inflicts infernal punishments? Honestus and Zelotes will probably think that I misrepresent them. Honestus will say that he cordially believes God is full of free grace for all men, and that he only thinks it would be unjust in God to be partial in the distribution of his free grace. But when Honestus reasons thus, does he not confound grace and justice? Does he not sap the foundation of the throne of grace, under pretence of establishing the throne of justice? If God cannot do what he pleases with his grace, and if justice always binds him in the distribution of his favours, does not his grace deserve the name of impartial justice, far better than the appellation of free grace?

As Honestus tries to save appearances with regard to the doctrines of grace, so does Zelotes with regard to the doctrines of justice. "The Gospel I preach," says he, "is highly consistent with the doctrines of justice. I indeed intimate that the elect are necessitated to believe and be eternally saved; and the reprobates to continue in sin and be lost: but both this salvation of the elect, and damnation of the reprobates, perfectly agree with Divine equity. For Christ, by his obedience unto death, merited the eternal salvation of all that shall be saved: and Adam, by his first act of disobedience, deserved the absolute reprobation of all that shall be damned. Our doctrines of grace are therefore highly consistent with the doctrines of justice." This argument appears unanswerable to Zelotes: but I confess it does not satisfy me. For if the doctrine of absolute necessity be thus foisted into the Gospel, and if Christ make his elect people absolutely and unavoidably willing to obey and go to heaven, while Adam makes his reprobate people absolutely and unavoidably willing to sin and go to hell; I should be glad to know how the elect can be wisely judged according to, and rewarded for their faith and good works; and how the reprobates can be justly sentenced according to, and punished for their unbelief and bad works. I repeat it, the doctrine of absolute predestination to life or death eternal, which is one and the same with the doctrine of an absolute necessity to believe or disbelieve, to obey or disobey, to the last, — such a doctrine, I say, is totally subversive of the doctrines of justice. For reason deposes that it is absurd to give to necessary agents a law, or rule of life, armed with promises of reward, and threatenings of punishment. And conscience declares that it is unjust and cruel to inflict fearful, eternal punishments upon beings that have only moved or acted by absolute necessity: whether such beings are running streams, aspiring flames, falling stones, turning wheels, mad men, bound thinkers, bound willers, or bound agents; supposing such bound thinkers, bound willers, and bound agents, did think, will, and act, as unavoidably as the wind raises a storm, and as necessarily as a fired cannon pours forth flames and destruction. Absolute necessity and a righteous judgment are absolutely incompatible. We must renounce the mistakes of rigid Calvinists, or give up the doctrines of justice.

SECTION III.

By whom chiefly the Gospel axioms were systematically parted; and under what pretences prejudiced, good men tore asunder the doctrines of grace and justice; and rent the one primitive, catholic Gospel, into the two partial gospels of the day.

FROM the preceding section it appears, that to preach the Gospel in its primitive purity, is so to hold forth and balance the two Gospel axioms as to allow both the doctrines of grace and the doctrines of justice the place which is assigned them in the word of God: it is so to preach holy free grace, and rectified, assisted free will, as equally to grind Pharisaism and Antinomianism (the graceless and the lawless gospel) between these two evangelical mill stones. And thus the Gospel was, in general, preached by good men for above three hundred years after Christ's ascension. If ever the tempter put successfully in practice his two capital maxims, "Confound and destroy, — Divide and conquer," it was in the fourth century, when he helped Pelagius and Augustine, two warm disputants, openly to confound what should have been properly distinguished, and systematically to divide what should have been religiously joined; by which means they broke the balance of the doctrines of grace and justice. Nor did they do it out of malice; but through an immoderate regard for one part of the Gospel; an injudicious regard this, which was naturally productive of a proportionable disregard for the other part of God's word.

Pelagius (we are told by Augustine) preached free will; but, confounding natural free will with free will rectified and assisted by grace, he made too much of natural free will, and too little of God's free grace. The left leg of his Gospel system grew gigantic, while the right leg shrunk almost to nothing. And, commencing a rigid free willer, he insisted upon the sufficiency of our natural powers, and dwelt on the second Gospel axiom, and the doctrines of justice in so partial a manner, that he almost eclipsed the first Gospel axiom and the doctrines of grace.

Augustine, his cotemporary, under pretence of mending the matter, was guilty of an error exactly contrary. He so puffed up the right leg of his Gospel system, as to make it monstrous; while the left grew as slender and insignificant as a rotten stick. To bring this unhappy change about, in his controversial heats he confounded lawful, righteous free grace, with lawless, unscriptural, overbearing free grace; and, to make room for this latter, imaginary sort of grace, he sometimes turned free will out of its place, to give that place to necessity. Thus he commenced a rigid bound willer. The irresistible free grace, which he preached, bound the elect by the chains of an unconditional election to life, absolutely necessitating them to repent, believe, and be eternally saved: while the irresistible free wrath, which secretly advanced behind that overbearing grace, bound the nonelect in chains of absolute reprobation, and necessitated them to continue in sin, and be unavoidably damned. By these means, new, unholy doctrines of grace and wrath jostled the holy, ancient doctrines of grace and justice out of their place. The two Gospel axioms did no longer agree; but the first axiom, becoming like Leviathan, swallowed up the second. For the moment irresistible, lawless free grace, and despotic, cruel free wrath, mount the throne, what room is there for holy, righteous free grace? What room for free will? What room for the doctrines of justice? What room for the primitive Gospel? Absolutely none; unless it be a narrow room indeed, artfully contrived under a heap of Augustinian contradictions, and Calvinian inconsistencies.

From this short account of Pelagianism and Augustinianism, it is evident that heated Pelagius (if the account given us be true) gave a desperate thrust to the right side of primitive Christianity; and that heated Augustine, in his hurry to defend her, aimed a well-meant blow at Pelagius, but by overdoing it, and missing his mark, wounded the left side of the heavenly woman, who from that time has lain bleeding between these two rash antagonists. "The beginning of strife is as when one letteth out water," says the wise man. These "waters of strife," which Pelagius and Augustine let in upon the Church, by breaking the flood gates of Gospel truth, soon overflowed the Christian world, and at times, like the waters of the overflowing Nile, have almost been turned into blood. When streams of self-justifying, rigid, Pelagian free will, have met with streams of selfelecting, lawless, Augustinian free grace, the strife has been loud and terrible. They have foamed out their own shame, and frighted thousands of persons, travelling to Sion, out of the noisy ways of a corrupted gospel, into the more quiet paths of infidelity.

For above a thousand years these "waters of strife" have spread devastation through the Christian world; I had almost said also through the Mohammedan world: for Mohammed, who collected the filth of corrupt Christianity, derived these errors into his system of religion: Omar and Hali, at least, two of his relations and successors, became the leaders of two sects, which divide the Mohammedan world. Omar, whom the Turks follow, stood up for bound will, necessity, and a species of absolute Augustinian predestination. And Hali, whom the Persians revere, embraced rigid free will and Pelagian free agency. But the worst is, that these muddy waters have flowed through the dirty channel of the Romish Church, into all the Protestant Churches, and have at times deluged them; turning, wherever they came, brotherly love into fierce contention. For, breaking the evangelical balance of the Gospel axioms is as naturally productive of polemical debates in the Church, as breaking the parliamentary balance between the king and the people is of contention and civil wars in the state. How the plague first infected Protestantism will be seen in the next section.

SECTION IV.

Luther and Calvin do not restore the balance of the Gospel axioms — That honour was reserved for Cranmer, the English reformer, who modelled the Church of England very nearly according to the primitive Gospel — How soon the Augustinian doctrines of lawless grace preponderated — How the Pelagian doctrine of unassisted free will now preponderates.

WHEN the first reformers shook off the yoke of Papistical trumperies, they fought gallantly for many glorious truths. But it is to be wished, that while they warmly contended for the simple, Scriptural dress of the primitive Gospel, they had not forgotten to fight for some of its very vitals, I mean the doctrines of holy free grace, and rectified, assisted free will. They did much good in many respects; so much indeed, that no grateful Protestant can find fault with them without reluctance. But, after all, they did not restore the balance of the doctrines of grace and justice. Luther, the German reformer, being a monk of the order of Augustine, entered upon the reformation full of prejudices in favour of Augustine's Solifidian mistakes. And he was so busy in opposing the pope of Rome, his indulgences, Latin masses, and other monastic fooleries, that he did not find time to oppose the Augustinian fooleries of fatalism, Manichean necessity, lawless grace, and free wrath. On the contrary, in one of his heats, he broke the left scale of the Gospel balances, denied there was any such thing as free will, and by that means gave a most destructive blow to the doctrines of justice: a rash deed, for which Erasmus, the Dutch reformer, openly reproved him, but with too much of the Pelagian spirit.

Calvin, the French reformer, who, after he had left his native country, taught divinity in the academy of Geneva, far from getting light, and learning moderation by the controversy of Luther and Erasmus, rushed with all the impetuosity of his ardent spirit into the error of heated Augustine, and so zealously maintained it, that, from that time, it has been called Calvinism.

If Calvin did not grow wiser by the dispute of Luther and Erasmus, Melancthon, another German reformer, did; and our great English reformer, Cranmer, who in wisdom, candour, and moderation, far exceeded the generality of the reformers on the continent, closely imitated his excellent example. Nay, to the honour of this favoured island, and of perfect Protestantism, in a happy moment he found the exact balance of the Gospel axioms. Read, admire, and obey his anti-Augustinian, anti-Pelagian, and apostolic proclamation. "All men be also to be monished, and chiefly preachers, that, in this high matter, they, looking on both sides, [i.e. looking both to the doctrines of grace and the doctrines of justice] so attemper and moderate themselves, that neither they so preach the grace of God, [with heated Augustine] that they take away thereby free will, nor on the other side so extol free will, [with heated Pelagius,] that injury be done to the grace of God." (*Erud. of a Christian Man, sec. on free will,* which was added by Cranmer.) Here you see the balance of the doctrines of grace and justice, which Augustine and Pelagius had broken, and which Luther and Calvin had ground to dust in some of their overdoing moments, — you see, I say, that important balance perfectly restored by the English reformer. With this short valuable quotation, as with a shield of impenetrable brass, all men, and chiefly preachers, may quench all the fiery darts cast at the primitive Gospel by the preachers of the partial gospels of the day; I mean the abettors of the Augustinian or of the Pelagian error.

Mankind are prone to run into extremes. The world is full of men who always overdo or underdo. Few people ever find the line of moderation, the golden mean; and of those who do, few stay long upon it. One blast or another of vain doctrine soon drives them east or west from the meridian of pure truth. How happy would it have been for the Church of England if her first members had steadily followed the light which our great reformers carried before them. But alas, not a few of them had more zeal than moderation. Cranmer could not make all his fellow reformers to see with his eyes. In the time of their popish superstition many of them had deeply imbibed the errors of St Augustine, whom the Church of Rome reveres as the greatest of the fathers, and the holiest of the ancient saints. These good men, finding that his doctrine was countenanced by Luther, Calvin, Peter Martyr, Bucer, and others, whom they look upon as oracles, soon relapsed into the Augustinian doctrines of lawless grace, from which some of them had never been quite disentangled. Even during Cranmer's confinement (but much more after his martyrdom) they began to renounce the doctrines of justice, which were only indirectly secured in the seventeenth article of our Church; warmly contending for the doctrines of necessitating grace, which are always destructive of the doctrines of justice. Thus, while some of them erected the canopy of a lawless, Solifidian free grace over some men, elected according to Calvin's notion of an absolute election to eternal life; others cast the sable net of free wrath over the rest of mankind; imagining that from all eternity most men were absolutely predestinated to eternal death, according to the Calvinian doctrine of absolute, unconditional reprobation. Thus the balance of the Gospel axioms, which Cranmer (considering the times) had maintained to admiration, was again broken. Rigid Calvinism got the ascendancy; the doctrines of justice were publicly decried as popery and heresy, almost all England over. All the reprobates were exculpated. By the doctrine of necessity, their unavoidable continuance in sin, and their damnation, were openly charged upon God and Adam. Decrees of absolute predestination to necessary holiness and eternal salvation, and statutes of absolute appointment to necessary sin and eternal damnation began currently to pass for Gospel. And the doctrines of justice were swept away, as if they had been poisonous cobwebs spun by popish spiders. Hence it is that the Rev. Mr. Toplady, describing the triumphs of rigid Calvinism in the days of Queen Elizabeth, says, in his letter to Dr. Nowell, p. 45, that "those who held this opinion of God's not being any cause of sin and damnation, were at that time mightily cried out against by the main body of our Reformed Church, as *fautors of false religion*," and "that to be called *a free-will man*, was looked upon as a shameful reproach, and opprobrious infamy; yea, and that a person so termed was deemed heretical." A proof this, that Dr. Peter Heylin speaks the truth when he says, "It was safer for any man in those times to have been looked upon as a heathen or publican, than an anti-Calvinist."

Should the judicious reader ask how it happened that the doctrines of unscriptural grace, free wrath, and necessity were so soon substituted for the doctrines of genuine free grace, and rectified, assisted free will, which Cranmer had so evangelically maintained; I answer, that although Thomas Aquinas and Scotus, the leading divines of the Church of Rome, through their great veneration for Augustine, leaned too much toward the lawless, wrathful doctrines of grace; yet Luther, Calvin, and Zuinglius leaned still more toward that extreme. This was soon observed by some of the popish doctors; and as they knew not how to make a proper stand against the genuine doctrines of the reformation, they were glad to find a good opportunity of opposing the reformers, by opposing the Augustinian mistakes which Luther and Calvin carried to the height. Accordingly, leaving the extreme of Augustine, to which they had chiefly leaned before, many of the popish divines began to lean toward the extreme of Pelagius, and commenced rigid and partial defenders of the doctrines of justice, which the German, French, and Swiss reformers had indirectly destroyed, by overthrowing the doctrine of free will, which is inseparably connected with the doctrine of a day of just judgment. Hence it is, that, at the council of Trent, which the

Doctrines of Grace and Justice

pope had called to stop the progress of the reformation, the Papists took openly the part of the second Gospel axiom; and in the spirit of contradiction began warmly to oppose Augustine's mistakes, which the first Jesuits had ardently embraced, Bellarmine himself not excepted. Party spirit soon blew up the partial zeal of the contending divines. Protestant bigotry ran against popish bigotry; and the effect of the shock was a driving of each other still farther from the line of Scripture moderation. Thus many Papists, especially those who wrote against the Calvinian Protestants, became the partial supporters of the doctrines of justice, while their opponents showed themselves the partial vindicators of the doctrines of grace. Hence it is, that, in the popish countries, those who stood up for faith and distinguishing free grace began to be called heretics, Lutherans, and Solifidians: while, in the Protestant countries, those who had the courage to maintain the doctrines of justice, good works, and unnecessitated obedience, were branded as Papists, merit mongers, and heretics.

Things continued in this unhappy state till oppressed truth made new efforts to shake off the yokes put upon her. For the scales, which hold the weights of the sanctuary, (the two Gospel axioms,) hover and shift till they have attained their equilibrium; just as the disturbed needle of a compass quivers and moves till it has recovered its proper situation, and points again due north. This new shifting happened in the last century, when Arminius, a Protestant divine, endeavoured to rescue the doctrines of justice, which were openly trampled under foot by most Protestants; and when Jansenius, a popish bishop, attempted to exalt the doctrines of distinguishing grace, which most divines of the Church of Rome had of late left to the Protestants. Thus Jansenius, overdoing after Augustine, brought the doctrines of unscriptural grace and free wrath with a full tide into the Church of Rome: while Arminius (or, at least, some of his followers) drove them with all his might out of the Protestant Churches.

Many countries were in a general ferment on this occasion. A great number of Protestant divines, assembled at Dort in Holland, confirmed Calvin's indirect opposition to the doctrines of justice, and condemned Arminius after his death; for during his life none dared to attack him; such was the reputation he had, even through Holland, both for learning and exemplary piety! On the other hand, the pope, with his conclave, imitating the partiality of the synod of Dort, injudiciously condemned Jansenius and his Calvinism, and thus did an injury to the doctrines of grace, which Jansenius warmly contended for. But truth shall stand, be it ever so much opposed by either partial Protestants or partial Papists. Therefore, notwithstanding the decisions of the popish conclave, Jansenism and the doctrines of grace continued to leaven the Church of Rome: while, notwithstanding the decisions of the Protestant synod, Arminianism and the doctrines of justice continued to spread through the Protestant Churches.

Archbishop Laud, in the days of King James and Charles the First, caused in the Gospel scales the turn which then began to take place in our Church in favour of the doctrines of justice. He was the chief instrument, which, like Moses' rod, began to part the boisterous sea of rigid Calvinism. He received his light from Arminius: but it was corrupted by a mixture of Pelagian darkness. He aimed rather at putting down absolute reprobation and lawless grace, than at clearing up the Scripture doctrine of a partial election, doing justice to the doctrines of grace, and reconciling the contending parties, by reconciling the two Gospel axioms. Hence, passing beyond the Scripture meridian, he led most of the English clergy from one extreme to the other. For now it is to be feared that the generality of them are gone as far west as they were before east, in the reign of Queen Elizabeth. The *first* Gospel axiom formerly preponderated, and now the *second* goes swiftly down. Free will is, in general, cried up in opposition to free grace, as excessively and Pelagianistically (if I may use the expression) as, in the beginning of the last century free grace was unreasonably and Calvinistically set up in opposition to free will. I say *in general,* because although most of our pulpits are filled with preachers, who Pelagianize as well as Honestus, there are still a few divines, who, like Zelotes, strongly run into the Calvinian extreme.

But however, sooner or later, judicious, moderate men will convince the Christian world that the Gospel equally comprises the doctrines of grace and of justice; and that it consists of promises to be believed, and precepts to be observed; gracious promises and holy precepts, which are armed with the sanction of proper rewards or punishments, and are as incompatible with Pelagian self sufficiency, as with the Calvinian doctrines of lawless grace and free wrath. And as soon as this is clearly and practically understood by Christians, primitive unity and harmony will be restored to the partial gospels of the day.

SECTION V.

What the two modern gospels are — Their dreadful consequences — Arminius tried to find the way of truth between these two gospels, but perhaps missed it a little — The rectifying of his mistakes lately attempted.

BY the two modern gospels, I mean Pelagianism or rigid Arminianism, and the doctrine of absolute necessity or rigid Calvinism. The former is a gospel which so exalts the doctrines of justice, as to obscure the doctrines of partial grace: a gospel which so holds forth the second Gospel axiom, as to hide the glory of the first, either wholly or in part. Rigid Calvinism, on the other hand, is a gospel which so extols the doctrines of distinguishing grace, as to eclipse the doctrines of justice: a gospel which so holds forth the first Gospel axiom as to hide the glory of the second, in whole or in part. The fault of these two systems of doctrine consists in parting, or in not properly balancing the doctrines of grace and of justice.

The confusion which this error has occasioned in the Churches of Christ for above a thousand years should, one would think, have opened the eyes of all overdoing and underdoing divines, and made them look out for a safe passage between the Pelagian and the Calvinian rocks. That any good men should continue unconcernedly to run the bark of their orthodoxy against those fatal rocks of error, is really astonishing; especially if we consider that nobody can look into ecclesiastical history without seeing the marks of the numerous wrecks of truth and love which they have caused. Wide, however, as the empire of prejudice is, candour is not yet turned out of the world. In all the Churches of Christ, there are men who will yet hear Scripture and reason. But many of them, through a variety of avocations, through an indolence of disposition, or through despair of finding the exact truth, tamely submit to what appears to them a remediless evil. They are sorry that Christians should be so divided: but not seeing any prospect of ending our deplorable divisions, they quietly walk in Pelagian or Calvinian ways, without seeking the unbeaten path of truth which lies exactly between those two frequented roads. One of the reasons why they take up so readily with the Pelagian or Calvinian system, is, their not considering the dreadful evils which flow from each, some of which I shall set before the reader. I have already observed that the error of Pelagius (if St. Augustine and his votaries do not wrong him) consists in exalting free will and human powers, so as to leave little or no room for the exertion of free grace and Divine power; and that, on the other hand, the error of Augustine and Calvin consists in so exalting irresistible free grace openly, and irresistible free wrath secretly, that there is no reasonable room left for the exertion of faithful or unfaithful free will, or indeed for any free will at all. Now in the very nature of things, these two opposite extremes lead to the most dangerous errors. I begin with enumerating those which belong to the Pelagian extreme.

Reason and experience show that when the Pelagian error rises to its height, it leads men into *Arianism, Socinianism, Deism,* and, sometimes, into *avowed fatalism,* or *popish Pharisaism.*

1. By ARIANISM I mean the doctrine of Arius, a divine of Alexandria, who lived about the time of Pelagius, and not only insinuated that man was not so fallen as to need an omnipotent Redeemer, whose name is "God with us;" but openly taught that Christ was only an exalted, super-angelical creature.

2. SOCINIANISM is the error of Socinus, a learned, moral man, who lived since the reformation, and had such high notions of man's free will and powers, that he thought man could save himself, even without the help of a super-angelical Redeemer. And accordingly he asserted that Christ was a mere man like Moses and Elias, and that his blood had no more power to atone for sin, than that of Abel or St. Paul.

3. DEISM is the error of those who carry matters still higher, and think that man is so perfectly able, by the exertions of his own mere free will and natural powers, to recommend himself to the mercy of the Supreme Being, that he needs no Redeemer at all. Hence it is, that, although the Deists still believe in God, and on that account assume the name of Theists or Deists, they make no more of Christ and the Bible, than of the pope and his mass book, and look upon the doctrines of the incarnation and the trinity as wild and idolatrous conceits.

4. AVOWED FATALISM is the error of those who believe that "whatever is, is right;" and that all things happen (and of consequence that all sins are committed) of *fatal,* absolute necessity. This is an error into which immoral Deists are very apt to run: for, when they feel guilt upon their consciences, as they have no idea of a Mediator to take it away, they wish that their bad actions had been necessary, that is, absolutely brought on by the stars, or caused by God's decrees, which would fully exculpate them. And as this doctrine eases their guilty consciences, they first desire that it may be true, and by little and little persuade themselves that it is so, and publicly maintain their error. Hence it is that immoral Deists, such as Voltaire, and many of his followers, are avowed fatalists.

5. JEWISH PHARISAISM is the error of those who are such strangers to the doctrines of grace, as to think they have no need of the rich mercy which God

extends to poor publicans. Fancying themselves righteous, they thank God for their supposed goodness, when they should smite upon their breasts on account of their real depravity. POPISH PHARISAISM is an error still more capital. Those who are deep in it not only take little notice of the doctrines of grace, but carry their ideas of the doctrines of justice to such unscriptural and absurd lengths as to imagine that their penances can make a proper atonement for their sins; that God is, strictly speaking, their debtor on account of their good works; and that they can not only merit the reward of eternal life for themselves by their good deeds, but deserve it also for others by their works of supererogation, and through their superabundant obedience and goodness; a conceit so detestable, that one would think it need only be mentioned to be fully exploded and perfectly abhorred.

Dreadful as are these consequences of Pelagianism carried to its height, the consequences of Augustinianism, or Calvinism, carried also to its height, are not at all better. For the demolition of free will, and the setting up of irresistible, electing free grace, and absolute, reprobating free wrath, lead to *Antinomianism, Manicheism, disguised fatalism, widely reprobating bigotry, and self-electing presumption* or *self-reprobating despair*. The four first of these errors need explanation.

I. ANTINOMIANISM is the error of such rigid Calvinists as exalt free grace in so injudicious a manner, and make so little account of free will, and its startings aside out of the way of duty, as to represent sin, at times, like a mere bugbear, which can no more hurt the believer, who now commits it, than scarecrows can hurt those who set them up. They assert that if a sinner has once believed, he is not only safe, but eternally and completely justified from all future as well as past iniquities. The pope's indulgences are nothing to those which these mistaken evangelists preach. I have heard of a bishop of Rome who extended his popish indulgences, pardons, and justifications, to any crime which the indulged man might commit within ten years after date: but these preached finished salvation in the full extent of the word, without any of our own works, and by that means they extend their Protestant indulgences to all eternity — to all believers in general — and to every crime which each of them might choose to commit. In a word, they preach the inamissible, complete justification of all fallen believers, who add murder to adultery, and a hypocritical show of godliness to incest. Antinomianism, after all, is nothing but rigid Calvinism dragged to open light by plain-spoken preachers, who think that truth can bear the light, and that no honest man should be ashamed of his religion.

II. MANICHEISM is the capital error of Manes, a Persian, who, attempting to mend the Gospel of Christ, demolished free will, made man a mere passive tool, and taught that there are two principles in the Godhead, the one good, from which flows all the good, and the other bad, from which flows all the evil in the world. Augustine was once a Manichee, but afterward he left their sect, and refuted their errors. And yet, astonishing! when he began to lean to the doctrine of absolute predestination, he ran again, unawares, into the capital error of Manes. For if all the good and bad actions of angels, devils, and men, have their source in God's absolute predestination, and necessitating decrees, it follows that vice absolutely springs from the predestinating God, as well as virtue; and, of consequence, that rigid Calvinism is a branch of Manicheism, artfully painted with fair colours borrowed from Christianity.

III. DISGUISED FATALISM is nothing but an absolute necessity of doing good or evil, according to the overbearing decrees, or forcible influences of Manes' God, who

Doctrines of Grace and Justice

is made up of free grace and of free wrath, that is, of a good and bad principle. I call this doctrine *disguised fatalism:* **(1.)** Because it implies the absolute *necessity* of our actions; a necessity this, which the heathens called *fate:* and, **(2.)** Because it is so horrible, that even those who are most in love with it, dare not look at it without some veil, or *disguise.* As the words *fatalism, evil god, good devil,* or *Manichean deity,* are not in the Bible, the Christian fatalists do what they can to cover their error with decent expressions. The *good principle* of their Deity they accordingly call free grace, or everlasting, unchangeable love. From this good principle flow their absolute election and finished salvation. With respect to the *bad principle,* it is true they dare not openly call it free wrath, or everlasting, unchangeable hatred, as the honest Manichees did; but they give you dreadful hints that it is a sovereign something in the Godhead, which necessitates reprobated angels and men to sin; something which ordains their fall, and absolutely passes them by when they are fallen; something which marks out unformed, unbegotten victims for the slaughter, and says to them, according to unchangeable decrees productive of absolute necessity, "Depart, ye cursed, into everlasting fire; for I passed you by: my absolute reprobation eternally secured your sin, and your continuance in sin; and now, my unchangeable, everlasting wrath absolutely secures your eternal damnation. Go, ye absolutely reprobated wretches, — go, and glorify my free wrath, which flamed against you before the foundation of the world. My curses and reprobation are without repentance." There is not a grain of equity in all this speech: and yet it agrees as truly with rigid Calvinism as with the above-described branch of Manicheism; it falls in as exactly with the necessitating, good-bad principles of Manes, as with the necessitating, good-bad principle of lawless free grace, and absolute sovereignty — the softer name which some Gospel ministers decently give to free wrath.

IV. WIDELY REPROBATING BIGOTRY is the peculiar sin of the men who make so much of the doctrines of partial grace, as to pay little or no attention to the doctrines of impartial justice. This detestable sin was so deeply rooted in the breasts of the Jews, that our Lord found himself obliged to work a miracle, that he might not be destroyed by it before his hour was come. Because the Jews were the peculiar, and elected people of God, they uncharitably concluded that all the heathens, i.e. all the rest of mankind were absolutely reprobated, or at least that God would show them no mercy, unless they became proselytes of the gate, and directly or indirectly embraced Judaism. And therefore, when Christ told them that many Gentiles would come from the east and west, and sit with Abraham in the kingdom of God, while many of the Jews would be cast out; and when he reproved their bigotry, by reminding them that in the days of Elijah God was more gracious to a heathen widow, than to all the widows that dwelt in Judea, they flew into a rage, and attempted to throw him down from the top of the craggy hill off which the town of Nazareth was built. It is the same widely reprobating bigotry, which makes the rigid Romanists think that there is no salvation out of their Church. Hence also the rigid Calvinists imagine that there is no saving grace but for those who share in their election of grace. It is impossible to conceive what bad tempers, fierce zeal, and bloody persecutions this reprobating bigotry has caused in all the Churches and nations where the privileges of electing love have been carried beyond the Scripture mark. Let us with candour read the history of the Churches and people who have engrossed to themselves all the saving grace of God, and we shall cry out, From such a fierce election, and such reprobating bigotry, good Lord deliver us!

I make no doubt but this sketch of the dangerous errors to which *rigid* Pelagianism and *rigid* Calvinism lead unwary Christians, will make the judicious reader afraid of these partial gospels, and will increase his thankfulness to God for the primitive Gospel, which by its doctrines of grace guards us against rigid Pelagianism and its mischievous effects; and, by its doctrines of justice, arms us against rigid Calvinism and its dangerous consequences.

Among the divines abroad, who have endeavoured to steer their doctrinal course between the Pelagian shelves and the Augustinian rocks, and who have tried to follow the reconciling plan of our great reformer Cranmer, none is more famous, and none came nearer the truth than Arminius. He was a pious and judicious Dutch minister, who, in the beginning of the last century, taught divinity in the university of Leyden in Holland. He made some noble efforts to drive Manicheism and disguised fatalism out of the Protestant Church, of which he was a member; and, so far as his light and influence extended, (by proving the evangelical union of redeeming grace and free will,) he restored Scripture harmony to the Gospel, and carried on the plan of reconciliation which Cranmer had laid down. His sermons, lectures, and orations made many ashamed of absolute reprobation, and the bad principled God, who was before quietly worshipped all over Holland. Nevertheless, his attempt was partly unsuccessful; for, attacking free wrath, (or the bad principle of the Manichean god,) without setting free grace in its full Gospel light, and without properly granting the election of grace which St. Paul contends for, he gave the Calvinists just room to complain. They availed themselves so skilfully of his embarrassment about the doctrine of election, and they pleaded so plausibly for the sovereignty of the good-principled God, as to keep their absolute reprobation, and the sovereignty of the bad-principled God partly out of sight. In short, implacable free wrath escaped by means of Antinomian free grace. The venomous scorpion concealed itself under the wing of the simple dove; and the double-principled Deity, the sparingly electing and widely reprobating God, was still held forth to injudicious Protestants as the God of all grace, the God of love, the God in whom is no darkness at all. For, as I have already observed, a number of divines, after the heart of Calvin, assembled at Dort in Holland, and openly condemned there the efforts that Arminius had made to reconcile the doctrines of justice and the doctrines of grace: the clergy who had espoused his sentiments were deprived of their livings; he himself was represented as the author of a heresy almost as dangerous as that of Pelagius; and from that time the rigid Calvinists have considered all those who stand up for the two Gospel axioms with any degree of consistency, as semi-Pelagian, or Arminian heretics.

And if Mr. Bayle be not mistaken, the Calvinists did not complain of Arminius' doctrine altogether without reason; for although he went very far in his discovery of the passage between the Pelagian and the Augustinian rocks, yet he did not sail quite through. Election proved a rock on which his doctrinal bark stuck fast; nor could he ever get entirely clear of that difficulty.

Among our English divines several have greatly distinguished themselves by their improvements upon Arminius' discoveries, Bishop Overal, Bishop Stillingfleet, Bishop Bull, Chillingworth, Baxter, Whitby, and others. But if I am not mistaken, they have all stuck where Arminius did, or on the opposite rock. And thereabouts we stuck too, when Mr. Wesley got happily clear of a point of the Calvinian rock which had retarded our course, and (so far as he appeared by us to be governed by the Father of lights) we began to sail on with him through the straits of truth. When we left our moorings, the partial defenders of the doctrines of grace hung out a signal of distress, and cried to us that our doctrinal ark was going to be lost against the same cliff where Pelagius' bark went to pieces. Their shouts have made us wary. The Lord has, we humbly hope, blessed us with an anchor of patient hope, a gale of cheerful love of truth, and a shield of resignation to quench the fiery darts which some warm men, who defend the barren rock of absolute reprobation, have thrown at us in our passage. We have sounded our way as we went on; and looking steadily to our theological compass, the Scriptures, to the Sun of righteousness, the Lord Jesus Christ, and to the stars which he holds in his right hand, the apostles and true evangelists, after sailing slowly six years through straits, where strong currents of error and hard gales of prejudice have often retarded our progress, we flatter ourselves that we have got quite out of those narrow and rocky seas, where most divines have been stopped for a long succession of ages. If we are not mistaken, the ancient haven of Gospel truth is in sight; and, while we enter in, I take a sketch of it, which the reader will see in a *Plan of Reconciliation* between the Calvinists and Arminians, which these sheets are designed to introduce.

THE RECONCILIATION:

OR

AN EASY METHOD

TO

UNITE THE PROFESSING PEOPLE OF GOD.

BY PLACING THE DOCTRINES OF GRACE AND JUSTICE IN SUCH A LIGHT AS TO MAKE THE CANDID ARMINIANS BIBLE CALVINISTS, AND THE CANDID CALVINISTS BIBLE ARMINIANS.

Vestra solum legitis; vestra amatis; coeteros, incognita causa, condemnatis. —CICERO.
"Follow peace with all men. Look not every man on his own things [and favourite doctrines only;] but every man also on the things [and favourite doctrines] of others." "The wisdom that is from above is peaceable, and without partiality," Hebrews 12:14; Philippians 2:4; James 3:17.

THE RECONCILIATION, &c.

SECTION I.

The sad consequences of the divisions of those who make a peculiar profession of faith in Christ — It is unscriptural and absurd to object that believers can never be of one mind and heart.

UNSPEAKABLE is the mischief done to the interests of religion by the divisions of Christians: and the greater their profession is, the greater is the offence given by their contests. When the men who seek occasion against the Gospel, see them contending for the truth, and never coming to an agreement, they ask, like Pilate, "What is truth?" and then turn away from Christianity, as that precipitate judge did from Christ.

Of all the controversies which have given offence to the world, none has been kept up with more obstinacy than that which relates to Divine grace and the nature of the Gospel. It was set on foot in the fourth century by Augustine and Pelagius, and has since been warmly carried on by Godeschalchus, Calvin, Arminius, and others. And it has lately been revived by Mr. Whitefield, and Mr. Wesley, and by the author of *Pietas Oxoniensis,* and the orator of the university of Oxford. This unhappy controversy has brought more contempt upon the Gospel for above twelve hundred years, than can well be conceived. Preachers entangled therein, instead of agreeing to build the temple of God, think themselves obliged to pull down the scaffolds on which their brethren work. Shepherds, who should join their forces to oppose the common enemy, militate against their fellow shepherds: and their hungry followers are too frequently fed with controversial chaff, when they should be nourished with the pure milk of the word. After the example of their leaders, the sheep learn to butt, and wounds or lameness are the consequences of the general debate. The weak are offended, and the lame turned out of the way. The godly mourn, and the wicked triumph: bad tempers are fomented; the hellish flame of party zeal is blown up, and the souls of the contenders are pierced through with many sorrows.

This is not all: the Spirit of God is grieved, and the conversion of sinners prevented. How universally would the work of reformation have spread if it had not been hindered by this growing mischief! How many thousands of scoffers daily say, Can these devotees expect we should agree with them, when they cannot agree among themselves? And indeed how can we reasonably hope that they should give us the right hand of fellowship, if we cannot give it one another? "By this," saith our Lord, "shall all men know that you are my disciples, if ye love one another." Continual disputes are destructive of love; and the men of the world, seeing us cherish such disputes, naturally conclude that we are not the disciples of Christ, that there are none in the world, that the Gospel is only a pious fraud or a fine legend, and that faith is nothing but fancy, superstition, or enthusiasm.

Nor will such men be prevailed upon cordially to believe in Christ, till they see the generality of professors "made perfect in one," by agreeing in doctrine, and "walking in love." We may infer this from our Lord's prayer for his Church: "Neither pray I for these alone, but for them also who shall believe on me through their word: that they all may BE ONE, as thou, Father, art in me, and I in thee, that they also may be one in us: that THE WORLD MAY BELIEVE," John 17:20, 21. Christ intimates, in these words, the men of the world will never generally embrace the Gospel, till the union he prayed for take place among believers. To keep up divisions, therefore, is one of the most effectual methods to hinder the conversion of sinners, and strengthen the unbelief which hardens their hearts.

The destructive nature of this sin appears from the severity with which St. Paul wrote to the Corinthians and Galatians, who were divided among themselves. The former he could not acknowledge as "spiritual men," but called them "carnal," and affirmed that "to their shame, some of *them* had not the knowledge of God." And the latter he considered as persons almost "fallen from Christ;" intimating, that if they continued to "bite each other," (an expression which is beautifully descriptive of the malignity, with which most controvertists speak and write against their antagonists,) they would "be consumed one of another," Galatians 5:15.

In families and civil societies divisions are truly deplorable; but in the Churches of Christ they are peculiarly pernicious and scandalous: (1.) *Pernicious:* to be persuaded of it, we need only consider these awful words of St. James: — "If ye have bitter envying and strife in your hearts, glory not, and lie not against the truth. This wisdom is devilish. For where envying and strife is, there is confusion and every evil work," James 3:14, &c. (2.) *Scandalous:* if Christ be the Prince of Peace, why should his subjects be sons of contention? If he came to reconcile Jews and Gentiles, "by breaking down the middle wall of partition between them;" if he "made in himself, of twain [of those two opposed bodies of men] one new man," that is, one new body of men, "all of one heart and of one soul;" if he has "slain the enmity, so making peace;" if "it pleased the Father to reconcile all things unto himself by him;" and if "in the dispensation of the fulness of times [the Christian dispensation] he gathers together all things in him:" if this, I say, is the case, what can be more contrary to the Gospel plan than the obstinacy with which some Protestants refuse to be "gathered together" with their fellow Protestants, under the shadow of their Redeemer's wings? And what can be more scandalous than for Christ's followers, yea, for the strictest of them to spend their time in building "middle walls of partition" between themselves and their brethren, or in "daubing over with untempered mortar" the walls which mistaken men have built in former ages?

Many Jews refused to be saved by Christ, because he came to save the Gentiles as well as themselves. And it is to be feared that some Christians, from a similar motive, refuse the Divine favour, or the eminent degrees of it, to which they are called in the Gospel. Christ says to these bigots, "How often would I have gathered you together, as a hen gathers her *scattered* brood under her wings! but ye would not:" ye were afraid of your Calvinian or Arminian brethren, and preferred the selfish heat of party spirit, to the diffusive warmth of Divine and brotherly love. I say Divine, as well as brotherly love; for he "that loveth not his brother, whom he hath seen, how can he love God, whom he hath not seen?"

My regard for unity revives my drooping spirits, and adds new strength to my wasted body.* I stop at the brink of the grave over which I bend: and, as the blood, oozing from my decayed lungs, does not permit me vocally to address my contending brethren, by means of my pen I will ask them if they can properly receive the holy communion while they wilfully remain in disunion with their brethren from whom controversy has needlessly parted them? For my part, if I felt myself unwilling to be reconciled on Scripture terms, either with my Calvinian or Arminian neighbours, I would no more dare go to the Lord's table, than if I had harboured murder in my heart; and this scripture would daily haunt my conscience, "Whosoever shall say to his brother, Thou fool, [thou silly free willer, thou foolish bound willer, thou heretic!] shall be in danger of hell fire. Therefore, if thou bring thy gift before the altar, and there rememberest that thy [Calvinian or Arminian] brother hath aught against thee; leave thy gift and go thy way, first be reconciled to thy brother, and then come and offer thy gift. Agree with thine adversary quickly" — thy religious as well as thy civil adversary — him with whom thou differest about the gold of the word; as well as him with whom thou contendest about the gold of this world.

Not to be reconciled when we properly may, is to keep up divisions; and to keep up divisions is as bad as to cause them. And what a dreadful thing it is to cause divisions, appears from St. Paul's charge to the Romans: "I beseech you, brethren, mark them who cause divisions and offences, contrary to the doctrine which ye have learned, and avoid them," Romans 16:17. Avoid them, for those who have the itch of contention, and the plague of party spirit, are not only in a dangerous case themselves; but they carry about a mortal infection, which they frequently communicate to others. Should party men exclaim against my reconciling attempt, and say that "there always were, and always will be divisions among the children of God, and that to aim at a general reconciliation, is to aim at an absolute impossibility;" I reply, —

(1.) This plea countenances the lusts of the flesh. "Walk in the Spirit," saith St. Paul, "and ye shall not fulfil the lusts of the flesh:" and among these lusts he immediately numbers "debate, emulations, wrath, contentions, and such like," observing, at the same time, that "the fruit of the Spirit is love, peace, gentleness, meekness," &c. Now when party men insinuate that we can never live in peace and harmony with our Christian brethren, do they not indirectly teach that "debate, emulations, contentions, and such like, must" still waste our time, disturb our minds, and impair our love? And is not this an underhand plea for a wretched obligation to neglect "the fruit of the Spirit," and for an Antinomian necessity to bring forth the "fruit of the flesh?"

(2.) It militates against St. Paul's conflict for believers: "I would," says he to the Colossians, "that ye knew what great conflict I have for you, for them at Laodicea, and for as many as have not seen my face in the flesh, that their hearts might be comforted; being knit together in love, and unto all riches of the full assurance of understanding, to the acknowledgment of the mystery of God," Colossians 2:1, 2. It

---

* Mr. Fletcher was judged to be now in the last stage of a consumption.

opposes also the end of the apostle's prayer for the Romans: "The God of patience and consolation grant you to be like minded, &c, that you may with one mind and one mouth glorify God, &c. Wherefore receive you one another, as Christ also received us," Romans 15:5, &c. But what is far worse, it directly contradicts Christ's capital prayer, which I have already quoted: "I pray," says he, "that they [believers] may be one, as thou, Father, art in me, and I in thee: that they also may be one in us: that they may be one, even as we are one: I in them and thou in me, that they may be made perfect in one: that the [unbelieving] world may know that thou hast sent me," John 17:20, &c. Now if our Lord asked for an absolute impossibility, when he asked for the perfect union of believers in this life, where was his wisdom? And if he cannot make us one in heart and mind (supposing we are willing to abide by his reconciling word) where is his power?

(3.) It strikes at the authority of these evangelical entreaties, exhortations, and commands: — "Be of the same mind," Romans 12:16. "I beseech you, brethren, by the name of our Lord Jesus Christ, that ye all speak thesame thing, and that there be no divisions among you; but that ye be perfectly joined together in the same mind, and in the same judgment," 1 Corinthians 1:10. "Finally, brethren, be perfect, be of good comfort, be of one mind; live in peace, and the God of love and peace shall be with you," 2 Corinthians 13:11. "Let your conversation be as it becometh the Gospel of Christ: that I may hear ye stand fast in one spirit, with one mind; striving together for the faith of the Gospel. Fulfil ye my joy that ye be like minded — being of one accord, of one mind. I beseech Euodias and Syntyche, that they be of the same mind in the Lord," Philippians 1:27; 2:2; 4:2. "Finally, be ye all of one mind, &c. Love as brethren, be courteous. For he that will see good days, &c, let him seek peace [with his enemies, much more with his brethren;] and let him pursue it," 1 Peter 3:8, &c. "Let us walk by the same rule, let us mind the same things," Philippians 3:16. "With all lowliness and meekness, with long suffering, forbearing one another in love: endeavouring to keep the unity of the Spirit in the bond of peace. For there is one body and one Spirit, even as ye are called in one hope of your calling; one Lord, one faith, one baptism, one God and Father of all," Ephesians 4:2, &c. The same apostle, writing to the divided Corinthians, tries to reconcile them by comparing again the body of believers to the human body, and drawing a suitable inference: "The body is one," says he, "though it hath many members; that there should be no schism, [no division] in the body; but that the members should have the same care one for another; all suffering when one member suffers, and all rejoicing when one member is honoured," 1 Corinthians 12:12-26. Hence it follows that to plead for the continuance of schisms and divisions in Christ's mystical body, is evidently to plead for a breach of "the bond of peace," and for the neglect of all the above-mentioned apostolic injunctions.

(4.) It gives the lie to the following promises of the God of truth. "The hatred to Ephraim shall depart, &c. Ephraim shall not envy Judah, neither shall Judah vex Ephraim," Isaiah 11:13. "I will give them one heart and one way, that they may fear me for ever, for the good of them and of their children," Jeremiah 32:39. "I will give them one heart, and I will put a new spirit within them," Ezekiel 11:19. "I will turn to the people a pure language, that they may all call upon the name of the Lord, to serve him with one consent, &c. Other sheep I have, which are not of this fold. Them also

I must bring, and they shall hear my voice; and there shall be one fold and one shepherd," John 10:16.

(5.) It contradicts the following accounts of God's faithfulness in the initial accomplishment of the preceding promises: — "They were all with one accord in one place; continuing daily with one accord in the temple," Acts 2:1, 46. "The multitude of them that believed were of one heart, and of one soul," Acts 4:32. "If we walk in the light, &c, we have fellowship one with another. For he that loveth his brother abideth in the light, and there is in him no occasion of stumbling:" nothing in his heart will either cause or keep up divisions, 1 John 1:7; 2:10. "We are bound to thank God always for you, brethren, because your faith growth exceedingly, and the charity of every one of you all toward each other aboundeth," 2 Thessalonians 1:3. "By one Spirit, all *complete Christians* are baptized into one body, whether *they* be Jews or Gentiles, whether *they* be bond or free; and have been all made to drink into one Spirit" — the Spirit of truth and love; and (unless they leave their first love as the Corinthians did) they sweetly continue to "keep the unity of the Spirit in the bond of peace," 1 Corinthians 12:13; Ephesians 4:3. From these accounts of the unity of the primitive Christians before they "left their first love," I infer, that unity is attainable, because it was attained. The arm of the Lord is not shortened; "the same Lord over all *is* rich unto all that call upon him;" and if we be not obstinately bent upon despising the "wisdom from above, which is peaceable, gentle, easy to be entreated, full of good fruits and without partiality;" we shall find that "the fruit of righteousness is sown in peace of them that make peace;" and we shall evidence that all the sincere followers of Christ can yet "continue steadfastly in the apostles' doctrine and fellowship," instead of perversely continuing in their own mistakes and in the spirit of discord.

Lastly: the objection I answer has a tendency to stop the growth of Christ's mystical body, and opposes God's grand design in sending the Gospel: for "he gave apostles, evangelists, and pastors, for the perfecting of the saints, and the edifying of the body of Christ; till all come, in the unity of the faith, and of the knowledge of the Son of God, unto a perfect man, unto the measure of the stature of the fulness of Christ: that we be no more carried about with every wind of doctrine, &c, but speaking the truth in love, may grow up in all things into him who is the head, even Christ; from whom the whole body fitly joined together, and compacted by that which every joint supplieth, according to the effectual working in the measure of every part, maketh increase of the body, unto the edifying of itself in love," Ephesians 4:11, 17. No believer can I think, candidly read these words of the apostle, without being convinced that union and growth are inseparable in the Church of "Christ, from whom all the body, by joints and bands having nourishment [or help] ministered, and being knit together, increaseth with the increase of God," Colossians 2:19.

From these observations, I hope, it appears, that whether we consider the earnest entreaties of the apostles; their conflicts and pious wishes for their converts; the wisdom of our Lord's address to his Father for the union of believers; the repeated commands of the Gospel to be of "one mind and one judgment;" the promises which God has made to help us to keep these commands; the Divine power, by which the primitive believers were actually enabled to keep them, so long as they walked in the Spirit; or whether we consider the end of evangelical preaching, and the unity and growth of Christ's mystical body; nothing can be more unscriptural than to say that believers can never be again of one heart and of one mind.

And as this notion is unscriptural, so it is irrational; inasmuch as it supposes that the children of God can never agree to serve him, as the children of the wicked one do to honour their master; for St. John informs us that "these have one mind to give their power and strength unto the beast," Revelation 17:13. And experience daily teaches that when the men of the world are embarked in the same scheme, they can perfectly agree in the pursuit of wealth, pleasure, and fame, or in the performance of duty. If ships that sail under the command of the same admiral do not give each other a broadside, because they have different captains, and are employed in different services; if soldiers, who follow the same general, do not quarrel because they belong to different regiments, because their coats are not turned up alike, or because they do not defend the same fort, fight in the same wing of the army, hear the same drum, and follow the same pair of colours: and if the king's faithful servants can unanimously promote his interests, and cheerfully lend each other a helping hand, though their departments are as different as the fleet is different from the army, is it not absurd to suppose that Christ's faithful soldiers and servants, who are the meekest, the humblest, the most disinterested, and the most loving of all men, can never live in perfect union, and sweetly agree to promote the interests of their Divine Master? I conclude, therefore, that the objection which supposes the contrary, is not less contrary to reason than to the word of God.

SECTION II.

Pious, moderate Calvinists, and pious, moderate Arminians in particular, may be easily reconciled to each other; because the doctrines of grace and justice, about which they divide, are equally Scriptural, and each party contends for a capital part of the Gospel truth; their grand mistake consisting in a groundless supposition that the part of the truth they defend is incompatible with the part which is defended by their brethren.

SOME persons will probably make a more plausible objection than that which is answered in the preceding pages. They will urge, "that truth should never be sacrificed to love and peace; that the Calvinists and the Arminians holding doctrines diametrically opposite, one party at least must be totally in the wrong; and as the other party ought not to be reconciled to error, the agreement I propose is impossible: it will never take place, unless the Calvinists can be prevailed upon to give up unconditional election, and their favourite doctrines of partial grace; or the Arminians can be persuaded to part with conditional election, and their favourite doctrines of impartial justice; and as this is too great a sacrifice to be expected from either party, it is in vain to attempt bringing about a reconciliation between them."

This objection is weighty: but far from discouraging me, it affords me an opportunity of laying before my readers the ground of hope I entertain, to reconcile the Calvinists and Arminians. I should indeed utterly despair of effecting it, were I obliged to prove that either party is entirely in the wrong. But I may without folly expect some success, because my grand design is to demonstrate that both parties have an important truth on their side; both holding opposite doctrines, which are as essential to the fullness of Christ's Gospel, as the two eyes, nostrils, and cheeks, which compose our faces, are essential to the completeness of human beauty.

"The language of Scripture seems to favour the one as well as the other," says Dr. Watts on a similar occasion: "but this is the mischief that ariseth between Christians who differ in their sentiments or expression of things; they imagine that while one is true, the other must needs be false: and then they brand each other with error and heresy: whereas, if they would but attend to Scripture, that would show them to be both in the right, by its different explication of their own forms of speaking. In this way of reconciliation I cannot but hope for some success, because it falls in with the universal, fond esteem that each man has of his own understanding: it proves that two warm disputers may both have truth on their side. Now, if ten persons differ in their sentiments, it is much easier to persuade all of them that they may be all in the right, than it is to convince one that he is in the wrong."

I shall illustrate this quotation by a remark, which occurs in the beginning of my Scripture Scales; only taking the liberty of applying to pious Calvinists and pious Arminians what I said there of pious Solifidians and pious moralists: — "The cause of their misunderstanding is singular. They are good men upon the whole; therefore they never can oppose truth as truth: and as they are not destitute of charity, they cannot quarrel merely for quarreling's sake. Whence then spring their continual disputes? Is it not from inattention and partiality? They will not look truth full in the face: determined to stand on one side of her, they seldom see above one half of her beauty. The rigid Calvinians gaze upon her side face on the right hand, and the rigid Arminians contemplate it on the left. But her unprejudiced lovers, humbly sitting at her feet, and beholding her in full, admire the exquisite proportion of all her features: a peculiar advantage this, which her partial admirers can never have in their present unfavourable position."

To be more explicit: a rigid Calvinist has no eyes but for God's sovereignty, unconditional election, and the doctrines of partial grace; while a rigid Arminian considers nothing but God's equity, conditional election, and the doctrines of impartial justice. And therefore, to unite these contending rivals, you need only prevail on the Arminians to bow to God's sovereignty, to acknowledge an unconditional election, and to receive the doctrines of partial grace; and as soon as they do this, they will be reconciled to Bible Calvinism and to all moderate Calvinists. And, on the other hand, if the Calvinists can be convinced that they should bow to God's equity, acknowledge a conditional election, and receive the doctrines of impartial justice, they will be reconciled to Bible Arminianism, and to all moderate Arminians. Should it be said that it is impossible to convince the Arminians of the truth of an unconditional election, &c, and that the Calvinists will never receive the doctrine of a conditional election, &c, I answer, that bigots of either party will not be convinced, because they all pretend to infallibility, though they do not pretend to wear a triple crown. But the candid, on both sides of the question, lie open to conviction, and will, I hope, yield to the force of plain Scripture and sound reason, the two weapons with which I design to attack their prejudices.

But before I open my friendly attack, I beg leave, candid reader, to show thee the ground on which I will erect my Scriptural and rational batteries. It is made up of the following reasonable propositions: —

(1.) When good men warmly contend about truth, you may in general be assured that, if truth can be compared to a staff, each party has one end of the staff, and that to have the whole you need only consistently hold together what they inconsiderately pull asunder. (2.) The Gospel contains doctrines of partial grace and unconditional election, as well as doctrines of impartial justice and conditional election. Nor can we embrace the whole truth of the Gospel, unless we consistently hold those seemingly contrary doctrines. (3.) Those opposite doctrines, which rigid Calvinists and Arminians suppose to be absolutely incompatible, agree as well together as the following pair of propositions: God has a throne of grace and a throne of justice; nor is the former throne inconsistent with the latter. God, as the Creator and Governor of mankind, sustains the double character of sovereign Benefactor, and righteous Judge: and the first of these characters is perfectly consistent with the second. This is the ground of my reconciling plan: and this ground is so solid, that I hardly think any unprejudiced person will ever enter his protest against it. Were divines to do it, they would render themselves as ridiculous as a pilot, who should suppose that the head and stern of the vessel he is called to conduct, can never be two essential parts of the same ship.

If Christianity were compared to a ship, the doctrines of grace might be likened to the fore part, and the doctrines of justice to the hinder part of it. This observation brings to my remembrance a quotation from Dr. Doddridge, which will help the reader to understand how it is possible that an election of grace, maintained by moderate Calvinists, and an election of justice, defended by moderate Arminians, may both be true: "I have long observed," says the judicious doctor, "that Christians of different parties have eagerly been laying hold on particular parts of the system of Divine truths, and have been contending about them as if each had been all; or as if the separation of the members from each other, and from the head, were the preservation of the body, instead of its destruction. They have been zealous to espouse the defence, and to maintain the honour and usefulness of each part; whereas their honour as well as usefulness seems to me to lie much in their connection: and suspicions have often arisen between the respective defenders of each, which have appeared as unreasonable and absurd as if all the preparations for securing one part of a ship in a storm, were to be censured as a contrivance to sink the rest." In the name of God, the God of wisdom, truth, and peace, let then the defenders of the doctrines of grace cease to fall out with the defenders of the doctrines of justice, and let both parties seek the happy connection which Dr. Doddridge speaks of, and rejoice in the part of the truth peculiarly held by their brethren, as well as in that part of the Gospel to which they have hitherto been peculiarly attached.

Many good men, on both sides of the question, have at times pointed out the connection of the opposite doctrines, which are maintained in these sheets. Mr. Henry, a judicious Calvinist, does it in his notes on the parable of the talents, where he contends for the doctrines of partial grace and impartial justice, and exalts God both as a sovereign Benefactor, and a righteous Judge. Commenting upon these words, "Take therefore the talent from him" [the slothful servant] says he, "The talents were first disposed of by the master as an absolute owner, [that is, a sovereign benefactor, who does what he pleases with his own.] But this was now disposed of by him as a judge; he takes it from the unfaithful servant to punish him, and gives it to him that was eminently faithful to reward him." This is "rightly dividing the word of truth," and wisely distinguishing between the throne of grace and that of justice.

Dr. John Heylin, a judicious Arminian, in his discourse on 1 Timothy 4:10, is as candid as Mr. Henry in the above-quoted note; for he stands up for God's sovereignty and the doctrine of partial grace, as much as Mr. Henry does for God's equity and the doctrine of impartial justice, After pointing out in strong terms the error of those who, by setting aside the doctrines of justice, "sap[*] the foundation of all religion, which is the moral character of the Deity," he adds: —

"Nor, on the other hand, do[†] they less offend against the natural prerogative, I mean the absolute sovereignty of God, who deny him the free exercise of his bounty, as they seem too much inclined to do who are backward to believe the great disparity among mankind with regard to a future state, which revelation always supposes. His mercy is over all his works, but that mercy abounds to some *much more* than to others, according to the inscrutable 'counsel of his own will.' Nor is there a shadow of injustice in such *unequal* distribution of his favours. The term favours implies freedom in bestowing them; else they were not favours, but debts. The almighty Maker is master of all his productions. Both matter and form are his: all is gift, all is bounty; nor may the lizard complain of his size, because there are crocodiles; nor is the worm injured by the creation of an eagle."

I shall conclude this section by producing the sentiments of two persons, whose authority is infinitely greater than that of Mr. Henry and Dr. Heylin. Who exceeds St. Paul in orthodoxy? And yet what Calvinist ever maintained the doctrines of grace more strongly than he does? "By the grace of God," says he, "I am what I am," 1 Corinthians 15:10. "By grace you are saved [that is, admitted into the high state of Christian salvation] through faith, and that not of yourselves, it is the gift of God:" [a special gift, which God has kept back from far the greatest part of the world;] "not of works, lest any man should boast," Ephesians 2:8. "At this time also there is a remnant according to the election of grace. And if by grace, then it is no more of works, otherwise grace is no more grace," Romans 11:5, 6. "Not by works of righteousness which we have done, but according to his mercy he saved us," or made us partakers of the glorious privileges of Christians, which he has denied to millions of the human race," Titus 3:5. "He is the Saviour of all men, especially of those that believe;" for he saves "Christians with" a special salvation, which is called "the great salvation," 1 Timothy 4:10; Hebrews 3:3. Christ indeed "is not the propitiation for our sins only, but also for the sins of the whole world," 1 John 2:2. Nevertheless, he is especially our Mediator, our passover or paschal Lamb, and "the High Priest of our *Christian* profession, in whom God hath chosen us *Christians* before the foundation of the world, that we should be holy" above all people: "having predestinated us unto the adoption of children by Jesus Christ, to the praise of the glory of his grace:" a high adoption, which is so superior to that to which the Jews had been predestinated in Abraham, Isaac, Jacob, and Moses, that St. Paul spends part of his Epistle to the Ephesians in asserting the honour of it, and in extolling the glory of the peculiar grace

---

[*] He means the rigid Calvinists.

[†] He means the rigid Arminians.

given unto us in Christ. And if you exclaim against this Divine partiality, the apostle silences you by a just appeal to God's sovereignty: see Romans 9:20.

But was St. Paul Calvinistically partial? Did he so contend for the doctrines of grace, as to cast a veil over the doctrines of justice? Stands he not up for the latter, as boldly as he does for the former? What Arminian ever bowed before the throne of Divine justice more deeply than he does in the following scriptures? "God is not unrighteous to forget your work and labour of love," Hebrews 6:10. "I have fought the good fight, &c. Henceforth there is laid up for me a crown of righteousness, which the Lord, the righteous Judge, shall give me at that day, 2 Timothy 4:7, 8. These passages strongly support the doctrines of justice, but those which follow may be considered as the very summit of Scripture Arminianism. "Knowing that whatsoever good thing any man doth, the same shall he receive of the Lord," Ephesians 6:8. "Whatsoever ye do, do it heartily, &c, knowing that of the Lord ye shall receive the reward of the inheritance: for ye serve the Lord Christ. But he that does wrong shall receive [adequate punishment] for the wrong which he hath done," Colossians 3:23, &c. "We must all appear before the judgment seat of Christ, that every one may receive the things done in his body, according to that which he hath done, whether it be good or bad," 2 Corinthians 5:10. "In the day of wrath and revelation of his righteous judgment, God will render to every man according to his deeds; eternal life to them who, by patient continuance in well doing, seek for glory, honour, and immortality; but indignation and wrath to them that are contentious, and do not obey the truth, but obey unrighteousness, &c; for [before the throne of justice] there is no respect of persons with God," Romans 2:5, &c.

Should it be asked how these seemingly contrary doctrines of grace and justice can be reconciled, I reply, They agree as perfectly together as the first and second advent of our Lord. At his first coming he sustained the gracious character of a Saviour; and at his second coming he will sustain the righteous character of a Judge. Hear him explaining the mystery, which is hid from the rigid Calvinists and the rigid Arminians. Speaking of his first coming, he says: — "I came not to judge the world, but to save the world," by procuring for mankind different talents of initial salvation: a less number for the heathens, more for the Jews, and most for the Christians, who are his most peculiar people: "for God sent not his Son into the world to condemn the world; but that the world through him might be saved," John 12:47; 3:17. "The Son of man is come to seek and to save that which was lost," Luke 19:10. "Ye have not chosen me, but I have chosen you, and ordained you, that you should go and bring forth fruit, and that your fruit should remain," John 15:16. Here are doctrines of grace!

But did our Lord so preach these doctrines as to destroy those of justice? Did he so magnify his coming to save the world, as to make nothing of his coming to judge the world? No: hear him speaking of his second advent:" When the Son of man shall come in his glory, then shall he sit upon the throne of his glory, and before him shall be gathered all nations, and he shall separate them one from another, [them that have done good from them that have done evil,] and these shall go away into everlasting punishment, but the righteous into life eternal," Matthew 25:31, 32, 46. "Behold I come quickly, and my reward is with me, to give every man according as his work shall be," Revelation 22:12. "For the hour is coming, in the which all that are in the graves shall hear his [the Son of man's] voice, and shall come forth: they that have done good unto the resurrection of life: and they that have done evil unto the resurrection of damnation," John 5:28, 29. Here are doctrines of justice! And the man who says that such doctrines are not as Scriptural as the above-mentioned doctrines of grace, may as well deny the succession of day and night.

Dr. Watts, in his excellent book entitled, *Orthodoxy and Charity United*, gives us a direction which will suitably close the preceding appeal to the Scriptures: — "Avoid," says he, "the high flights and extremes of zealous party men, &c. You will tell me, perhaps, that Scripture itself uses expressions as high upon particular occasions, and as much leaning to extremes as any men of party among us. But remember, then, that the Scripture uses such strong and high expressions not on one side only, but on both sides, and infinite wisdom hath done this more forcibly to impress some present truth or duty: but while it is evident the holy writers have used high expressions, strong figures of speech, and vehement turns on both sides, this sufficiently instructs us that we should be moderate in our censures of either side, and that the calm, doctrinal truth, stript of all rhetoric and figures, lies nearer to the middle, or at least that some of these appearing extremes are more reconcilable than angry men will generally allow. If the apostle charges the Corinthians, 'So run that ye may obtain,' 1 Corinthians 9:24; and tells the Romans, 'It is not of him that willeth, nor of him that runneth, but of God who showeth mercy,' Romans 9:16; we may plainly infer that our running and his mercy — our diligence and Divine grace are both necessary to salvation."

From all these scriptures it evidently follows: (1.) That as God is both a Benefactor and a Governor, a Saviour and a Judge, he has both a throne of grace, and a throne of justice. (2.) That those believers are highly partial who worship only before one of the Divine thrones, when the sacred oracles so loudly bid us to pay our homage before both. (3.) That the doctrines of grace are the statutes and decrees issuing from the former throne: and that the doctrines of justice are the statutes and decrees issuing from the latter. (4.) That the principal of all the doctrines of grace is, that there is an election of grace: and that the principal of all the doctrines of justice is, that there is an election of justice. (5.) That the former of those elections is unconditional and partial; as depending merely on the good pleasure of our gracious Benefactor and Saviour: and that the latter of those elections is conditional and impartial; as depending merely on the justice and equity of our righteous Governor and Judge: for justice admits of no partiality, and equity never permits a ruler to judge any men but such as are free agents, or to sentence any free agent, otherwise than according to his own works. (6.) That the confounding or not properly distinguishing those two elections, and the reprobations which they draw after them, has filled the Church with confusion, and is the grand cause of the disputes which destroy our peace. And (lastly) that to restore peace to the Church, these two elections must be fixed upon their proper Scriptural basis, which is attempted in the following section.

SECTION III.

Eight pair of opposite propositions, on which the opposite doctrines of grace and justice are founded, and which may be considered as the basis of Bible Calvinism and Bible Arminianism, and as a double key to open the mysteries of election and reprobation.

Scripture ground of CALVINISM, *and the doctrines of* GRACE.

PROPOSITION I.

GOD is original, eternal, and unbounded life, light, love, and purity; and therefore, wherever these blessings are found, in any degree, they originally come from him, the overflowing fountain of all that is excellent in the natural, moral, and spiritual world.

II. God is an infinitely wise Benefactor, full of goodness and GRACE.

III. It seems highly inconsistent with the wisdom of a Creator and Benefactor, to make all his creatures of the same size and rank, and to deal out his bounties to them in the same measure. To say that he should do it, is as absurd as to affirm that his goodness requires him to make every insect as big as an elephant, and every spire of grass as tall as an oak.

IV. For want of considering the preceding, self-evident propositions, and their necessary consequences, the heated advocates for the doctrines of justice have erred, either by denying, or by not fully granting these two undeniable truths: **(1.)** All good comes originally from God's free grace and overflowing

Scripture ground of ARMINIANISM, *and the doctrines of* JUSTICE.

PROPOSITION I.

THERE is no death, darkness, free wrath, or sin in God: and therefore these evils, wherever they are found, originally flow from inferior agents, whose free will may become the fountain of all evil: for when free agents choose first the evil of *sin,* God is obliged in justice to choose next the evil of *punishment.* Thus *moral* evil draws *natural* evil after it.

II. God is an infinitely wise Governor, full of equity and JUSTICE.

III. It seems highly inconsistent with the equity of a Governor and a Judge to decree that millions of rational creatures shall be born in a graceless, sinful, and remediless state, that he may display his righteous sovereignty by passing a sentence of death and eternal torments upon them, for being found in the state of remediless corruption, in which his irresistible decree has placed them.

IV. For want of considering the preceding, self-evident propositions, and their unavoidable consequences. The heated advocates for the doctrines of grace have erred, by directly or indirectly maintaining these two capital untruths: **(1.)** Some real evil can originally flow from that part of God's predestination fulness. **(2.)** God, as a sovereign benefactor, may do what he pleases with his own. Nor should our "eye be evil because he is good," and displays his superabounding goodness toward some men, more than he does toward others.

V. The grand mistake of the rigid Arminians consists then in not frankly ascribing to God all the original goodness, and gracious sovereignty which belong to him as the sovereign author and first parent of all good.

VI. Would you get clear of the error, of rigid Arminians, not only assert God's *grace* and *goodness*, insisting that he is the first cause and eternal parent of ALL good, natural and spiritual, temporal and eternal, but boldly stand up also for his free grace and exuberant goodness; maintaining that he has the most unbounded right to dispense the peculiar bounties of his grace, without any respect to our works. For the children [Esau and Jacob] not being yet born, neither having done any good or evil, that the purpose of God according to [the] election [of superior grace] might stand, not of works, but of him that [arbitrarily chooseth and] calleth; it was said, [not the one is absolutely ordained to eternal death, and the other absolutely ordained to eternal life; but] "the elder shall serve the younger:" the younger shall have a superior blessing. And in this respect "it is not *at all* of him that willeth, nor of him that runneth, but of God, who most *freely and absolutely* showeth mercy, or favour," Romans 9:11, 12, 16. Hence it appears, that to deny a PARTIAL election of distinguishing grace, is equally to fly in the face of St. Paul and of reason.

which is generally called "absolute reprobation," or "predestination to eternal death." **(2.)** God, as a sovereign, may absolutely ordain some of his rational creatures to eternal death, before they have personally deserved it: or, which is all one, he may so pass by unborn children as to insure their continuance in sin, and their everlasting damnation.

V. The grand mistake of the rigid Calvinists consists then in directly ascribing to God some original evil, and a reprobating sovereignty, which is irreconcilable with the *goodness* of a Creator, and the *equity* of a Judge.

VI. Would you, on the other hand, get clear of the error of rigid Calvinists, not only maintain in general that God is just, but confidently assert that he utterly disclaims a sovereignty which dispenses *rewards* and *punishments* from a throne of justice, otherwise than according to works: witness his own repeated declarations: — "I said indeed that thy house, &c, should walk before me for ever: but now be it far from me: for them that honour me, I will honour; and they that despise me shall be lightly esteemed," 1 Samuel 2:30. Again: "If the wicked man will turn from all his sins, he shall surely live, &c. But when the righteous man turneth away from his righteousness, &c, in his sin that he hath sinned shall he die. Yet ye say, The way of the Lord is not equal. O house of Israel, are not my ways equal? Are not your ways unequal? Therefore I will judge you, every one according to his ways, saith the Lord. Repent, &c, for I have no pleasure in the death of him that dieth," Ezekiel 18:21, &c. Hence it appears, that with respect to the election and reprobation of justice, God's decrees, so far as they affect our personal salvation or damnation, are regulated according to our personal righteousness or sin, that is, according to our works.

VII. When we consider the election of *partial* grace, and the harmless reprobation that attends it, we may boldly ask, with St. Paul, "Hath not the potter power over the clay, of the same lump to make one vessel unto [superior] honour, and* another unto [comparative] dishonour?" Cannot God ordain, that of two unborn children, the one (as Jacob) shall be appointed to superior blessings, and (in this sense) shall be *more loved;* while the other (as Esau) shall be deprived of those blessings, and in this sense shall be *less loved,* or comparatively *hated?* "As it is written, Jacob have I loved, and Esau have I hated," Romans 9:13. When we speak of the same election, we may say, as the master of the vineyard did to the envious labourer, "Is thine eye evil, because *the Master of the universe* is good?" Matthew 20:15.

VII. When we consider the election of *impartial* justice, and the fearful reprobation that answers to it, we may say, with St. Peter, "If ye call on the Father, who without respect of persons judgeth according to every man's work, pass the time of your sojourning here in fear," 1 Peter 1:17. "God is no respecter of persons: but in every nation he that feareth him and worketh righteousness, is accepted of him," Acts 10:34. We may add with Christ, "In the day of judgment, men shall give account of their words. For by thy words thou shalt be justified, and by thy words thou shalt be condemned," Matthew 12:36, 37. And we may humbly expostulate with God, as Abraham did: "That be far from thee to do after this manner, to slay the righteous with the wicked: and that the righteous should be as the wicked, that be far from thee: shall not the Judge of all the earth do right?" Genesis 18:25.

VIII. From the preceding propositions it evidently follows, that when God is considered as electing and reprobating the children of men from his throne of grace, his election and reprobation are *partial* and *unconditional.*

VIII. From the preceding propositions it evidently follows, that when God is considered as electing and reprobating the children of men from his throne of justice, his election and reprobation are *impartial* and *conditional*

---

* To understand Romans 9, we must remember that the apostle occasionally speaks of the election and reprobation of justice; although his first design is to establish the election of grace, and the harmless reprobation which answers to it. When he speaks of Jacob and Esau, he contends for the election of grace: and when he brings in Pharaoh and "the vessels of wrath," who, by their obstinate unbelief, have provoked vindictive wrath to harden them, or to give them up to the hardness of their hearts, he speaks of the election of justice. The passage to which this note refers, is the apostle's transition from the one election to the other, and may be applied to both: I have applied it here to the election of grace. But if you apply it to the election of justice, the meaning is: hath not the Governor and Judge of all the earth authority over all mankind, as being their sovereign and lawgiver? Can he not fix the terms on which he will reward or punish his subjects? The terms on which he will give them more grace, or take from them the talent of grace which they have buried, and leave them to the rigour of his law? Can he not appoint that obedient believers shall be saved, or elected to eternal salvation; and that his mark of judicial reprobation shall be fixed upon all obstinate unbelievers, as Pharaoh and his host certainly were?

Having thus laid down the rational and Scriptural ground of Bible Calvinism, which centres in the PARTIAL election of grace, — and of Bible Arminianism, which centres in the IMPARTIAL election of justice, I shall show the nature, excellence, and agreement of both systems in the following essays, which, I trust, will convert judicious Arminians to Scripture Calvinism, and judicious Calvinists to Scripture Arminianism.

SECTION IV.

Bible Calvinism and Bible Arminianism are plainly stated and equally vindicated in two essays, the first on the doctrines of partial grace, and the second on those of impartial justice — Those opposite doctrines are shown to be highly agreeable to reason and Scripture, and perfectly consistent with each other.

ON the eight pair of balanced propositions, which are produced in the preceding section, I rest the two essays which follow. I humbly recommend the *first* to rigid Arminians; because it contains a view of Bible Calvinism, of the doctrines of grace, and of the absolute, unconditional, and partial election, to which they perpetually object. And I earnestly recommend the SECOND essay to rigid Calvinists, because it contains a view of Bible Arminianism, of the doctrines of justice, and of the judicial, conditional, and impartial election, against which they are unreasonably prejudiced.

BIBLE CALVINISM.

ESSAY THE FIRST.

Displaying the doctrines of partial grace, the capital error of the Pelagians, and the excellence of Scripture Calvinism.

THE doctrines of partial grace rest on these scriptures: — "I will be [peculiarly] gracious to whom I will be [peculiarly] gracious; and I will show *special* mercy, on whom I will show *special* mercy," Exodus 33:19. "Is it not lawful for me to do what I will with mine own?" Matthew 20:15.

These precious doctrines subdivide themselves into a *partial* election, and a *partial* reprobation; both flowing from a free, wise, and sovereign grace, which is notoriously respective of persons.

The partial election and reprobation of free grace is the gracious and wise choice, which God (as a sovereign and arbitrary benefactor) makes, or refuses to make, of some persons, Churches, cities, and nations, to bestow upon them, for his own mercy's sake, more favours than he does upon others. It is the partiality with which he imparts his talents of nature, providence, and grace, to his creatures or servants; giving five talents to some, two talents to others, and one to others; not only without respect to their works, or acquired worthiness of any sort, but frequently in opposition to all personal demerit. Witness the thieves, between whom our Lord was crucified, who were the only dying men that Providence ever blessed with the invaluable talents or gracious opportunities of the company and audible prayers of their dying Saviour. From this doctrine of election it follows, that when God freely elects a man to the receiving of one talent only, he freely reprobates him with respect to the receiving of two, or five talents.

According to this election, although God never leaves himself without the witness of some favour, by which the basest and vilest of men, who have not yet sinned out their day of salvation, are graciously distinguished from beasts and devils; and although, therefore, he is really gracious to all; yet he is not equally gracious: for he gives to some persons, families, Churches, and nations, more power and opportunity to do and receive good, more means of grace, yea, more excellent means, more time to use those means, and more energy of the Spirit in the use of them, than he gives to other persons, families, Churches, and nations. With respect to the election of grace, therefore, there is great partiality in God, and so far is this partiality from being in any degree caused by any natural or evangelical worth, that it is itself the first cause of all natural excellences, and evangelical worthiness. Hence it appears, that the doctrine of the Pelagians destroys the doctrines of partial grace: the capital error of those who inconsiderately oppose Calvinism, consisting in denying the gracious, electing, and reprobating partiality of God; and in supposing that the reasons of God's election and reprobation are always taken from ourselves; that God never elected some men in Christ, merely "after the counsel of his own *absolute* will;" and that the doctrine of a gratuitous election and reprobation is both unscriptural and horrible.

Having thus stated the doctrine of grace, and the opposite error of Pelagius, I encounter that famous champion of the rigid free willers, not with a sling and a few stones, but with the Bible and some plain quotations from it, which will establish and illustrate the gratuitous election and reprobation, into which the doctrine of partial grace is subdivided.

I have already observed, in the Scripture Scales, that "the election of [partial] grace" is taught in that part of the parable of the talents, where it is said, that the master chose and "called his own servants, and delivered unto them HIS [not THEIR] goods; *freely* giving to one FIVE talents, to another TWO, and to another ONE," Matthew 25:14, 15. In this free distribution of the master's goods to the servants, we see a striking emblem of God's partiality.

Should a Pelagian deny it, and say that God does not deal out his talents of grace with Calvinian freeness, but *according to the several abilities of his servants,* I reply, by asking the following questions: **(1.)** How came these servants to *be?* **(2.)** How came they to be *his* servants? And, **(3.)** How came they to have *every one* HIS *several ability?* Was this several ability acquired merely by dint of unassisted, personal industry? If you reply in the affirmative, you absurdly hold that God casts all his rational creatures in the same mould, that they are all exactly alike both by nature and by grace, and that they alone "make themselves to differ," as often as there is any difference. If you reply in the negative, you give up the ground of Pelagianism, and grant that God of his rich, undeserved goodness, gives to "every one his several *primary* abilities" of nature and grace: and when he does this, what does he do, but display a primary election and reprobation of grace; seeing he distributes these natural and gracious abilities in as distinguishing a manner as five are distinguished from one; arbitrarily reprobating from four talents the persons, families, Churches, and nations which he elects only to one talent.

This scripture, "Learn not to think of men above what is written, that not one of you be puffed up: for who maketh thee to differ," with respect to the first number of thy talents? "Which *of them* is it that thou didst not receive? Now if thou didst receive it, why dost thou glory as if thou hadst not received it?" 1 Corinthians 4:6, 7. This one scripture, I say, like the stone which sunk into Goliah's forehead, is sufficient, one would think, to bring down the gigantic error of Pelagius. But if that stone be not heavy enough to do the wished-for execution, I will choose two or three more out of the brook of truth, which flows from the throne of God. St. James points me to the first: "Every good gift is from above, and cometh down from the Father of lights," James 1:17. I am indebted for the others to our Lord's forerunner, and to our Lord himself. "John said, A man can receive nothing, except it be given him from heaven. Jesus answered, Thou couldest have no power at all, except it were given thee from above," John 3:27; 19:11.

If the Pelagian error stands it out against these weighty declarations, I shall draw "the sword of the Spirit," and aim the following strokes at that fashionable and dangerous doctrine: —

Why was Adam elected to the enjoyment of human powers? Was it not God's free electing love which raised him to the sphere of a rational animal; that exalted sphere, from which all other animals are reprobated? Was it not distinguishing favour which "made him but a little lower than the angels?" Let the Pelagians tell us what uncreated Adam did to merit the election which raised him above the first horse? Or what the first horse had done to deserve his being everlastingly shut out of heaven, and reprobated from all knowledge of his Creator? Why was the lark elected to the blessing of a towering flight, and of sprightly songs, from which the oyster is so abundantly reprobated;— the poor oyster, which is shut up between two shells, without either legs or wings, and so far as we know equally destitute of ears and eyes?

If a disciple of Pelagius think that I demean my pen by proposing these questions, to prove the gratuitous and absolute election and reprobation, which are so conspicuous in the world of nature; I will rise to his sphere, and ask him what he did to deserve the honour of being elected to the superiority of his sex — an honour this, from which his mother was absolutely reprobated; and if he has a rich father, who gave him a liberal education, I should be glad to know what good works he had done, before he was providentially elected to this blessing, from which the bulk of mankind are so eminently reprobated.

Can we not trace the footsteps of an electing or reprobating Providence all the earth over, with respect to persons and places? Why is one man elected to sway a sceptre, when another is only elected to handle an axe, a spade, a file, or a brush? Why were Abraham, Job, and the rich man, mentioned Luke xvi, elected to a plentiful fortune, when poor Lazarus, a notorious reprobate of Providence, lay starving at the door of merciless plenty? Why does a noble sot idle away his life in a palace, while an industrious, sober mechanic, with all his care, can hardly pay for a mean lodging in a garret? Why is one man elected to enjoy the blessings of the five senses, the advantage of a strong constitution, and the prerogative of beauty; while another is born blind or deaf, sickly, or deformed? What have these poor creatures done to deserve this misfortune? And if God can dispense his providential blessings with such apparent partiality, why should it be thought strange that he should be partial in the distribution of his spiritual favours? May not our heavenly Benefactor have daisies and crocuses, as well as tulips and roses, in the garden of his Church? May he not, in the building of his temple, use plain free stone, as well as sapphires, amethysts, and pearls? And why should we think that it is unjust in God to have moral instruments of a different shape and sound in his grand, spiritual concert, when David could (without violation of any right) predestinate some of his musicians to praise God with trumpets, shawms, and loud cymbals, when others were appointed to do it only upon a harp, a lute, and a pipe?

St. Paul compares believers, who are the members of Christ's mystical body, to the various parts which compose the human frame; and wisely observes, that though our uncomely parts (the feet for example) are reprobated from the honour put upon the head, they are, nevertheless, all useful in their places. His illustration is striking, and would help Pelagian levellers to see their mistakes, if they would consider it without prejudice. "There are diversities of gifts" under all the inferior dispensations of God's grace, as well as under the Gospel of Christ, to which the apostle's simile immediately refers: "The manifestation of the Spirit is given to every man to profit withal. For the Spirit divides *his gifts of partial grace* to every man severally as he will. The body is not one member, but many. If the foot shall say, Because I am not the hand *or the eye,* I am not of the body, is it therefore not of the body?" Is it absolutely reprobated from the bodily system? On the other hand, "if the whole body were an eye, where were the ear? And if the whole were ear, where were the nose? But now hath God set the members every one of them in the body, as it hath pleased him," that is, according to the good pleasure, counsel, and wisdom of his electing or reprobating will.

If the Pelagians will contend for their error on a religious ground, I meet them there, and ask, What good thing did Adam to deserve that God should plant for him "the tree of life in the midst of the garden," and should lay upon him no other burden for his trial, than abstaining from eating of the fruit of one tree? Would not God have been gracious, if he had suspended the judicial reprobation of our first parents on their refusing to abstain from all food every other day, for a thousand years? Who does not see free grace in the appointment of so easy a term, by submitting to which he might have made his gratuitous election sure, and secured the remunerative election of justice? Again: when judicial reprobation had overtaken the guilty pair, what did they do to deserve that the execution of the sentence should not instantly take place in all the fierceness of the threatened curse? And how many good deeds did they muster up, to merit the Gospel of redeeming grace? the precious promise that "the seed of the woman should bruise the serpent's head?" "Verily," says the apostle, "he [the Redeemer] took not on him the nature of angels: but he took on him the seed of" a man, viz. Abraham, and became "the son of man," though he is "the everlasting Father." Is there no partiality of grace in the mystery of the incarnation? Was it mere equity, which dictated that the Son of God should come "in the likeness of sinful flesh," to save sinful man; and not "in the likeness of sinful" spirit, to save fallen angels?

But supposing (not granting) that this partiality in favour of mankind, sprang merely from the peculiar excusableness of their case; I ask, Why did the sons of Cain deserve to be begotten of a marked murderer, who brought them up as sons of Belial; while the children of Seth were providentially elected into the family of a pious man, who brought them up as sons of God?

But if we will see the election and reprobation of partial grace, together with the glory of distinguishing predestination, shining in their greatest lustre, we must take a view of the "covenants of promise," which God made at different times with favoured men, families, Churches, and nations; peculiar covenants, which flowed every one from a peculiar election of grace.

Was it not of free, distinguishing grace, that God called Abraham, and raised himself a Church in a branch of his numerous family? Could he not as well have called to this honour Abimelech, king of Gerar, Melchisedec, king of Salem, or Job, the perfect man in the land of Uz? Or could he not have said to the father of the faithful, Not in Isaac, but in Ishmael, or in the sons of Keturah, thy last wife, "shall thy" peculiarly covenanted "seed be called?"

Nay, what did Abraham do to be justified as a sinner? Was he not fully justified in this sense, merely by receiving God's free gift through faith? The point is important, for it respects not only Abraham's gratuitous justification as a sinner, but also the free justification of every other sinner, who does not spurn the heavenly gift. Dwell we then a moment upon St. Paul's question, concerning Abraham's justification as a sinner. "What shall we say then? If Abraham were justified by works [as a sinner] he hath whereof to glory;* but not before God. For what says the Scripture? Abraham

---

* "With fear" of offending any of my brethren, "and with trembling," lest I should injure any doctrine of grace, I will venture to propose here a few questions, the decision of which I leave to the candour of those who are afraid of making one part of the Scripture contradict another. Granting that a sinner, as such, can never have any thing to glory in, unless it be his sin, his shame, and condemnation, I ask, Is there not a sense, in which a believer may rejoice or glory in his works of faith? And may not such a rejoicing or glorying be truly evangelical? What does St. Paul mean, when he says, "Let every [believing] man prove his own work, and then shall he have rejoicing [or] glorying in himself, and not in another?" Galatians 6:4. Did St. John preach self righteousness, when he wrote, "Hereby [by loving our neighbour in deed and in truth] we shall assure our hearts before him," that is, before God? "For if our heart condemn us, God is greater than our heart, and knoweth all things, [that make for our condemnation, better than we do.] Beloved, if our heart [or conscience] condemn us not, then have we confidence toward God, [that is, before God.] And whatsoever we ask we receive of him, because we keep his commandments, and do those things which are pleasing in his sight," 1 John 3:9, &c. If all such glorying is Pharisaical, who was, to the last, a greater Pharisee than the great apostle, who said, "Our rejoicing [or glorying] is this, the testimony of our conscience, that in godly sincerity, &c, we have had our conversation in the world?" 2 Corinthians 1:12. If St. Paul was guilty for living, how much more for dying full of this glorying? And is it not evident he did, from his own dying speech? "I am now ready to be offered, and the time of my departure is at hand. I have fought — I have finished — I have kept — henceforth there is laid up for me a crown of righteousness, which the Lord, the righteous Judge, shall give me at that

day," 2 Timothy 4:7, 8. Does not St. John exhort us to attain the height of the confidence in which St. Paul died, when he says, "Look to yourselves, that we lose not those things which we have wrought, but that we receive a full reward?" 2 John 1:8. Does not St. Paul represent spiritual men as persons who have "God's Spirit bearing witness together with their spirit, [and 'vice versa,' who have their spirit or conscience, bearing witness together with God's Spirit] that they are the children of God?" Romans 8:16. And is it right to abolish the office of conscience, by turning out of the world all comfortable consciousness of having done that which is right in the sight of God, and by discarding all tormenting consciousness of having done the contrary, under the frivolous pretence that our Lord, in his parabolical account of the day of judgment, represents the generality of good and wicked men as not being yet properly acquainted with this Christian truth, that whatever good or wrong we do to the least of our fellow creatures, Christ will reward or punish, as if it were done to himself? Alas! if the generality of Christians do not yet properly know this important truth, which is so clearly revealed to them, is it surprising to hear our Lord intimate that the Jewish, Mohammedan, and heathen world will wonder when they shall see themselves rewarded or punished according to that deep saying of St. Paul, "The head of every man is Christ?" Whence it follows, that whatever good or evil is done to any man, (but more especially to any Christian) is done, in some sense, to a member of Christ, and consequently to Christ himself! How deplorable is it to see good men cover an Antinomian mistake by an appeal to a portion of Scripture, which our Lord spoke to leave Antinomianism no shadow of covering!

Should it be said that the evangelical glorying, for which I plead after St. Paul, is subversive of his own doctrine, because he says, "He that glorieth, let him glory in the Lord:" I answer, That we keep this Gospel precept, when we principally glory in the Lord himself, and when we subordinately glory in nothing but what is agreeable to the Lord's word, and in the manner, and for the ends which the Lord himself has appointed. When the apostle says, "He that glorieth, let him glory in the Lord," he no more supposes that it is wrong to glory, as he did, "in the testimony of a good conscience," than he supposes that it is wrong in a woman to be married to a man as well as to Christ, because he says, "If she marrieth, let her marry in the Lord." Such a conclusion would be as absurd as the following Antinomian inferences: — "God will have mercy and not sacrifice, and therefore we must offer him neither the sacrifice of our praises, nor that of our persons." "Christ said to Satan, 'The Lord thy God only shalt thou serve;' and therefore it is a species of idolatry in domestics to serve their masters." May God hasten the time when such sophistry shall no more pass for orthodoxy!

Should it be farther objected, that St. Paul says, "God forbid that I should glory, save in the cross of Christ!" Galatians 6:14: I reply, That it is unreasonable not to give evangelical latitude to that expression, because, if it be taken in a literal and narrow sense, it absolutely excludes all glorying in Christ's resurrection, ascension, and intercession; a glorying this, which the apostle himself indulges in, Romans 8:34. However, that he could, in a subordinate sense, glory in something beside the cross of Christ, appears from his own glorying in his labours, sufferings, infirmities, revelations, and converts; as well as in his preaching the Gospel in Achaia without being burthensome to the people. But all this subordinate glorying was "in the Lord, through whom" he did and bore all things, and "to whom" he referred all inferior honours, And therefore when he said, that "the righteous Judge" would give him "a crown of righteousness" for having "so run as to obtain it," he, no doubt, designed to cast it at the feet of Him, in whose cross he principally gloried, and whose person was his "all in all." "But all this glorying was before men, and not before God." So it is said: but I prove the contrary by reason and Scripture: **(1.)** By "reason." Next to the cross of Christ, what St. Paul chiefly gloried or rejoiced in, was "the testimony of his conscience," 2 Corinthians 1:12. Now I ask, Had the apostle this joy and glorying only when he was in company? Did he not enjoy it when he was alone? If you say that he had it only in company, you represent him as a vile hypocrite, who could change the testimony of his conscience, as easily as he did his coat or company. And if you grant that he believed God [when God freely called him to receive grace, or more grace] and it was counted to him for righteousness," Romans 4:1, &c.

Now, if "Abraham believed God," it is evident that God offered himself first to Abraham, that Abraham might believe in him. Therefore a free election, calling, and gift (for an offer from God is a gift on his part, whether we receive what he offers or not) a *free gift*, I say, preceded Abraham's faith. His very belief of any justifying and saving truth proves that this truth, in which he believed, was *freely* offered and given him, that he might believe in it; yea, before he possibly could believe in it. To deny this is as absurd as to deny that God freely gives us eyes and light before we can see. Abraham, therefore, who was so eminently justified by the works of faith as an obedient believer, was initially accepted or justified as a sinner of the Gentiles by mere grace, and before he could make his calling and acceptance sure by believing and obeying: for the power to believe and obey always flows from the first degree of our acceptance, a *free gift* this, which is "come upon all men to justification," Romans 5:13, though, alas! most men refuse it through unbelief, or throw it away through an obstinate continuance in sin. Abraham, therefore, by receiving this *free gift* through faith, was *fully justified as a sinner*, and went on from faith to faith, till, by receiving and embracing the special grace, which called him to a covenant of peculiarity, he became the father of all those who embrace the special callings and promises of God, under the patriarchal, Mosaic, and Christian dispensations of Divine grace.

I have said that through faith Abraham was *fully justified as a sinner*, because our *full justification* as sinners implies two things: (1.) God's freely justifying us; and, (2.) Our freely receiving his justifying grace. Just as being *fully knighted* implies two things: (1.) The king's condescending to confer the honour of knighthood upon a gentleman; and, (2.) That gentleman's submitting to accept of this honour.

To conclude this digression: the *free and full* justification of a sinner by faith alone, or by a mere receiving of the gratuitous, justifying mercy of God, is a most comfortable, reasonable, and Scriptural doctrine, which St. Paul strongly maintains, where he says, "To him that worketh not, but believeth on him that justifieth the ungodly, his faith is counted for righteousness," Romans 4:5. When Luther therefore held forth this glorious truth, which the Church of Rome had so greatly obscured, he did the work of a reformer, and of an apostle. Happy would it have been for the

---

had this rejoicing when he was alone, you give up the point; for reason tells us, that all the rejoicing and glorying, which an enlightened man has in his own conscience, when he is alone, must be before God; because an enlightened conscience is a court, at which none is present but God, and where God always presides.

2. By "Scripture." Paul himself exhorts the Thessalonians so to "walk" as to "please God," 1 Thessalonians 4:1. Now the joyous testimony of our conscience that we walk so as to please God, must, in the nature of things, be a testimony "before" God. St. Peter represents our present salvation as consisting in "the answer of a good conscience toward God," that is, "before God," 1 Peter 3:21. And St. John cuts up the very root of the objection, where he declares, that, by the consciousness of our love to our neighbour, "we assure our hearts before God," that "if our hearts condemn us not, then we have confidence toward God;" and that if we abide in Christ by walking as he also walked, "we shall have confidence, and not be ashamed before him at his coming," 1 John 2:6, 28; 3:18, &c: How surprising is it, that an objection, which is so contrary to reason, Scripture, and the experience of the apostles, should be as confidently produced by Protestants, as if it contained the marrow of the Gospel!

Protestant world, if he had always done it as St. Paul and St. James; and if, adding the doctrines of justice to the doctrines of grace, he had as impartially enforced the judicial justification of a believer by the works of faith, as the apostle does in these words, "Not the hearers of the law [of nature, of Moses, or of Christ] are just before God, but the doers shall be justified — in the day when God shall judge the secrets of men, according to my Gospel," Romans 2:13, 16, yea, and in the day when God shall try the faith of believers, that he may justly praise or blame them, reward or punish them. And how can he do this justly, without having respect to their own works, that is, to their tempers, words, and actions, which are the works of their own hearts, lips, and hands? This important doctrine Luther sometimes overlooked, although St. James strongly guards it by these anti- Solifidian words, "Was not Abraham our father justified by works, when he had offered Isaac, &c? Ye see then how that by works a *believing* man is justified, and not by faith only," James 2:21, 24.

But a sinner, considered as such, can never be justified otherwise than by mere favour. Nor can St. Paul's doctrine be too strongly insisted upon to "the praise of the glory of God's grace," and to the honour of "the righteousness of God, which is by faith of Jesus Christ, unto all and upon all them that believe; for there is no difference: for all have sinned and come short of the glory of God; being justified freely by his grace, through the redemption that is in Jesus Christ," Romans 3:21, &c. Here we see that, to the complete justification of a sinner, there go three things: (1.) Mercy or free grace on God's part, which mercy, (together with his justice satisfied by Christ, and his faithfulness in keeping his Gospel promises,) is sometimes called "the righteousness of God." (2.) Redemption on the Mediator's part. And, (3.) Faith on the sinner's part. And if an interest in the "redemption that is in Jesus Christ," namely, in his meritorious incarnation, birth, life, death, resurrection, ascension, and intercession, is what is commonly called "Christ's imputed righteousness," I do not see why any Christian should be offended at that comprehensive phrase. In this Scriptural sense of it, nothing can be more agreeable to the tenor of the Gospel than to say, "All have sinned," and all sinners who are received to Divine favour, "are justified freely by God's grace" or mercy, through Christ's merits and satisfaction; or (if you please) through his imputed righteousness; or to speak in St. Paul's language, "through the redemption that is in Jesus Christ." For my part, far from finding fault with this comfortable, evangelical doctrine, I solemnly declare, that to all eternity I shall have nothing to plead for my justification as a sinner — absolutely nothing, but, (1.) God's free grace m giving his only begotten Son "to save sinners, of whom I am chief." (2.) Christ's meritorious life, death, and intercession, which abundantly avail for the chief of sinners. And, (3.) The Gospel charter, which graciously offers mercy through Christ to the chief of sinners, and according to which I am graciously endued with a power to forsake sin by repentance, and to receive Christ and his salvation by faith. And therefore to all eternity I must shout, Free grace! and make my boast of imputed righteousness.*

---

* Some of my readers will possibly ask why I plead here for the good sense of that much controverted phrase, "The imputed righteousness of Christ," when, in my Second Check to Antinomianism, I have represented our Lord as highly disapproving, in the day of judgment, not only the plea of a wicked Arminian, who urges that "God is merciful, and that Christ died for all;" but also the plea of a wicked Solifidian, who begs to be justified merely by the imputed

Doctrines of Grace and Justice

And, indeed,

> While Jesus' blood, through earth and skies,
> Mercy, free, boundless mercy cries,

What believer can help singing,

> "Jesus, thy blood and righteousness,
> My beauty are, my glorious dress;
> 'Midst flaming worlds, in these array'd,
> With joy shall I lift up my head."

To return: the same grace which called Abraham, rather than Terah his father, or Lot his nephew; this same distinguishing grace, I say, chose and called Isaac to the covenant of peculiarity, from which Ishmael, his elder brother, was reprobated: a special calling, which had been fixed upon before the birth of Isaac, and therefore could no ways be procured by his obedience. In full opposition to Isaac's design, the same distinguishing grace called Jacob rather than Esau, to inherit the promises of the peculiar covenant made with Abraham and Isaac. "For the children not being yet born, neither having done any good or evil, that the purpose of God, according to election, [to merely gratuitous favours,] might stand, not of works, but of him that calleth, [of arbitrary and partial grace,] it was said, The elder shall serve the younger." Nor can it be said that this partial preferring of Jacob had its rise in God's foreseeing that Esau would sell his birthright, for the above-quoted passage is flatly contrary to this notion: beside, Jacob himself, by Divine appointment, transferred to Joseph's youngest son the blessing which naturally belonged to the eldest. "Joseph said to his

---

righteousness of Christ, without any good works. I answer: (1.) I no more designed to ridicule the above-stated doctrine of *imputed righteousness,* than to expose the doctrine of God's *mercy,* or that of *general redemption.* And I am truly sorry, if by not sufficiently explaining myself I have given to my readers any just occasion to despise these precious doctrines of grace, or any one of them. (2.) I only wanted to guard against the abuse of evangelical principles, and to point out the absurd consequences of the spreading opinion, that "God will justify us in the great day merely by Christ's imputed righteousness, without the works of faith, or without any regard to personal righteousness and inherent holiness." This tenet, which as the very soul of speculative Antinomianism, leaves the doctrine of justice neither root nor branch. At this unscriptural notion only I levelled the blow, which has given so much groundless offence to so many persons, whom I honour for their piety, love for the resemblance they bear to the holy Jesus, and commend for their zeal in maintaining the doctrines of grace, so far as they do it without injuring the doctrines of godliness and justice. And I am glad to have this opportunity of explaining myself, and assuring my Calvinist brethren that I would lose a thousand lives, if I had them, rather than asperse the blood and righteousness of my Saviour, or ridicule the Christian covenant, which is ordered in all things and sure, and on the gracious terms of which (as well as on the Divine mercy which fixed them, the infinitely meritorious obedience which procured them, and the atoning blood which seals them) I entirely rest all my hopes of salvation in time, in the day of judgment, and to all eternity. And that this is Mr. Wesley's sentiment, as well as mine, is evident from his reconciling sermon on *imputed righteousness.*

father, Not so, my father:" be not partial to my younger son. "This is the first-born, put thy right hand upon his head:" he hath not sold his birthright like Esau. "But his father refused, and said, I know it, my son. He [Manasses] shall be great; but truly his [younger] brother [Ephraim] shall be greater than he," Genesis 48:18, 19. A clear proof this, that the reprobation of grace is quite consistent with an election to inferior blessings.

Nor was the calling of Moses less special than that of Abraham, Isaac, and Jacob. Was it not God's free, predestinating grace which so wonderfully preserved him in his infancy, and so remarkably ordained him at Mount Horeb to be the deliverer of the Israelites, and the visible mediator of the Jewish covenant? Can we help seeing some distinguishing grace in the following declaration: "I will do what thou hast spoken: for thou hast found grace in my sight, and I know thee by name: I will make all my goodness pass before thee, and I will proclaim the name of the Lord before thee?"

I cannot conceive with what eyes Pelagius could read the Scriptures. For my part, I see a continued vein of distinguishing favour running through the whole. Does the Lord want a man of peculiar endowments to finish the tabernacle? He says to Moses, "See, I have called by name Bezaleel, the son of Uri, of the tribe of Judah, and I have filled him with the Spirit of God," Exodus 31:2, 3. Does he want a captain for his people, and a man to be Moses' successor? Caleb himself is reprobated from that honour, and the Lord says, "Take thee Joshua, the son of Nun." The same distinguishing grace manifests itself in the special calling of Barak, Gideon, Samson, Samuel, Saul, David, Solomon, Elisha, Jehu, Daniel, Cyrus, Nehemiah, Esther, Esdras, Judas Maccabeus, and all the men whom the Lord, by his special grace and power, raised up to instruct, rule, punish, or deliver his people.

I have observed that, in the very nature of things, a gratuitous and personal reprobation follows the gratuitous and personal election which I contend for. Is not this assertion incontestable? While Jacob and the Israelites were peculiarly loved, were not Esau and the Edomites comparatively hated? When God will show a special, distinguishing favour, can he show it to all? Does not reason dictate that if he showed it to all, it would cease to be special and distinguishing? If God had made his covenants of peculiarity with all mankind, would they not have ceased to be peculiar? Once more: if God could, without impropriety, show more favour to the Jews than to the Gentiles, and to the Christians than to the Jews; I ask, Why cannot he also, without impropriety, show more favour to one Jew, or to one Christian, than he does to another? By what argument can you prove that it is wrong in God to do personally, what it is granted on all sides he does nationally? If you can, without injustice, give a crown to an English beggar, while you give only sixpence to a poor Irishman; why may you not give ten shillings to another English beggar, supposing your generosity prompts you to show him that special favour? And may not God, by the rule of proportion, give you ten talents of grace to improve, while he gives your Christian brother only five; as well as he can bestow five talents upon your fellow Christian, while he gives a poor Mohammedan one talent only?

Can any thing be more glaring than the partiality which our Lord describes in these words: "Wo unto thee, Chorazin; wo unto thee, Bethsaida; for if the mighty works had been done in Tyre and Sidon, which have been done in thee, they had a great while ago repented, sitting in sackcloth and ashes?" Luke 10:13. Who can read these words with a grain of candid attention, and refuse his assent to the following proposition? (1.) God was notoriously partial to Chorazin and Bethsaida; for he granted them more means of repentance, and more powerful means, and for a longer season, than he did to Tyre and Sidon. (2.) If God had been as gracious to the two heathenish cities as he was to the two Jewish towns, Tyre and Sidon "would have repented — a great while ago" — in the deepest and most solemn manner, "sitting in sackcloth and ashes." And, (3.) The doctrine of *necessity*, or *irresistible grace*, is unscriptural; and the doctrines of impartial justice are never overthrown by the doctrines of partial grace; for notwithstanding God's distinguishing favour, which wrought wonders to bring Chorazin and Bethsaida to repentance, they repented not; and our Lord says in the next verse, "But it shall be more tolerable for Tyre and Sidon at the day of judgment, than for you," who have resisted such distinguishing grace.

For want of understanding the partiality of Divine grace, and the nature of the harmless reprobation, which flows from this harmless partiality, some of God's faithful servants, who have received but one or two talents, are tempted to think themselves absolute reprobates; as often, at least, as they compare their case with that of their fellow servants, who have received more talents than they: while others, who have been indulged with peculiar favours, and have sinned, or idled them away, consider themselves as peculiar favourites of Heaven, upon whom God will never pass a sentence of judicial reprobation. Hence arise the despairing fears of some believers, the presumptuous hopes of others, and the spread of the mistaken doctrines of grace. By the same mistake, rash preachers frequently set up God's peculiar grants to some of his upper servants, as a general standard for all the classes of them, and pass a reprobating sentence upon every one who does not yet come up to this standard; to the great offence of the judicious, to the grief of many sincere souls, whom God would not have thus grieved, and to the countenancing of Calvinian reprobation.

A plain appeal to matter of fact will throw light upon all the preceding remarks. Are not many true Christians evidently reprobated, with respect to some of the special favours which our Lord conferred on the woman of Samaria, Zaccheus, Levi, (afterward St. Matthew,) and St. Paul? How few have been called in so extraordinary, abrupt, and cogent a manner as they were! Nay, how many strumpets, extortioners, busy worldlings, and persecutors in all ages, have been hurried into eternity, without having received the special favours, from which we date the conversion of those four favourites of free grace!

Has not God in all ages shown the partiality of his grace, by giving more of it to one man than to another? — to persecuting Saul, for example, than to thousands of other sincere persecutors, who thought, as well as he, that they did God service in dragging his saints to prison and to death? Did not the Lord show less distinguishing mercy to Zimri and Cosbi than to David and Bathsheba? Less to Onan than to the incestuous Corinthian, and the woman caught in adultery? Less to the forty-two children, who mocked the bald prophet, than to the more guilty sons of Jacob, who went about to kill their pious brother, sold him into Egypt, and covered their cruelty with hypocrisy and lies? Did he not give less time to repent to drunken Belshazzar than he did to proud Nebuchadnezzar? Did he not hurry Ananias and Sapphira into eternity, with a severity which he did not display toward Cain, Solomon, Peter, and Judas? Did he show as much long suffering to Eli and his sons, or to King Saul and his unfortunate family, as he did to David and his ungodly house? Was he as gracious to the man who gathered sticks on the Sabbath, or to him who conveyed the Babylonish garment into his tent, as he was to Gehazi, and to King Ahab, whom he spared for years after the commission of more atrocious crimes? Did not Christ show less distinguishing love to Zebedee than to his sons? Less to the woman of Canaan than to Mary Magdalene? Less to Jude, Bartholomew, and Lebbeus, than to Peter, James, and John? How soon, how awfully did God destroy Nadab and Abihu, for offering strange fire? Korah, Dathan, and Abiram, for resisting Moses? Uzzah, for touching the ark? And the prophet of Judah, for eating bread in Bethel; when nevertheless he bore for months or years with the wickedness of Pharaoh, the idolatry of Solomon, the witchcrafts of bloody Manasses, and the hypocrisy of envious Caiaphas? Is not this unequal dealing of Divine patience too glaring to be denied by any unprejudiced person?

Does not this partiality extend itself even to places and cities? Why did God reprobate Jericho, and elect Jerusalem? "Jerusalem, the city which the Lord did choose out of all the tribes of Israel to put his name there," 1 Kings 14:21. Do we read less than nineteen times this partial sentence, "The place which the Lord shall choose," even in the book of Deuteronomy? Could not God have chosen Babylon, Bethlehem, or Bethel, as well as the city of the Jebusites? Why did he make "Mount Zion his holy hill?" Why did he "love the gates of Zion, more than all the dwellings of Jacob?" Is there neither election nor reprobation in these words of the psalmist? "Moreover he refused [reprobated] the tabernacle of Joseph, and chose not [passed by] the tribe of Ephraim: but chose the tribe of Judah, the Mount Zion, which he loved," Psalm 78:67, 68. Again: Why did the angel, who troubled the pool of Bethesda, pass by all the other pools of Jerusalem? Why did our Lord send the lepers to the pool of Siloam, rather than to any other? And why were Abana and Pharpar, the rivers of Damascus, reprobated with respect to the power of healing Naaman's leprosy, when Jordan was elected to it? Was it not because God would convince the Syrians of his partiality to his peculiar people, and to their country?

But is this partiality confined to Judea and Syria? Or to Egypt and Goshen? May we not see the footsteps of an electing, partial providence in this favoured island? Why is it a temperate country? Could not God have placed it under the heaps of snow which cover Iceland; or in the hot climates, where the vertical sun darts his insufferable beams upon barren sands? Could he not have suffered it to be enslaved by the Turks, as the once famous isle of Crete now is? And to lie in popish darkness, as Sicily does? Or in heathenish* superstitions, as the large islands of Madagascar and Borneo do?

---

* Mr. Addison gives us this just view of our gratuitous election, in one of the Spectators. I shall transcribe the words of that judicious and pious writer: — "The sublimest truths, which among the heathens only here and there one, of brighter parts, and more leisure than ordinary, could attain to, are now grown familiar to the meanest inhabitants of these nations. Whence came this surprising change: that regions formerly inhabited by ignorant and savage people, should now outshine ancient Greece in the most elevated notions of theology and morality? Is it the effect of our own parts and industry? Have our common mechanics more refined understandings than the ancient philosophers? It is owing to the God of truth, who came

Doctrines of Grace and Justice

Who does not see the partiality of sovereign grace in the sparing of some nations, cities, and Churches? Did not God reprobate the disobedient Amalekites sooner than the disobedient Jews? Why are the former utterly destroyed, when the latter are yet so wonderfully preserved? Did not God bear less with Ai, Nineveh, and Carthage, than he does with London, Paris, and Rome? Less with the ten tribes, which formed the kingdom of Israel, than with the two tribes which formed the kingdom of Judah? Why does the Lord bear longer with the Church of Rome than he did with the Churches of Laodicea and Constantinople? Is it merely because the Church of Rome is less corrupted? Nay, why does he bear so long with this present evil world, when, comparatively speaking, he destroyed the antediluvian world so soon? And why are the Europeans, in general, elected to the blessings of Christianity, from which the rest of the world is generally reprobated; most nations in Asia, Africa, and America, being indulged with no higher religious advantages than those which belong to the religions of Confucius, Mohammed, or uncultivated nature?

If God's partiality in our favour is so glaring, why do not all our Gospel ministers try to affect us with a due sense of it? May I venture to offer a reason of this neglect? As the sins forbidden in the seventh commandment by their odious nature frequently reflect a kind of unjust shame upon a pure marriage bed, which, according to God's own declaration, is truly honourable; so the wanton election and horrid reprobation, that form the modern doctrines of grace, have, I fear, poured an undeserved disgrace upon the pure election, and the wise reprobation, which the Scriptures maintain. Hence it is, that even judicious divines avoid touching upon these capital doctrines in public, lest minds defiled with Antinomianism should substitute their own unholy notions of election, for the holy notions which the Scriptures convey. This evil shame is a remain of Pelagianism, or of false wisdom. The abuse of God's favours ought not to make us renounce the right use of them. Far then from being wise above what is written, let us with the prophets of old make a peculiar use of the doctrine of partial grace, to stir up ourselves and others to suitable gratitude. How powerful is the following argument of Moses! "The Lord thy God hath chosen thee, to be a special people to himself, above all people that are upon the face of the earth. The Lord thy God did not set his love upon thee, nor choose thee, because ye were more in number than any people, (for ye were the fewest of all people,) but because the Lord loved you, &c. He had a delight in thy fathers to love them, and he chose their seed after them, even you above all people, as it is this day, &c. He is thy praise, and he is thy God, who hath done for thee these great and wonderful things," Deuteronomy 7:6, &c; 10:15, 21. "For what nation is there so great, who have God so nigh unto them as the Lord our God is in all things which we call upon him for? Ask now of the days that are past: ask from the one side of heaven to the other, whether there hath been any such thing as this great thing is. Did ever people hear the voice of God speaking out of the midst of the fire, as thou hast heard? Or hath God assayed to take him a nation from the midst of another nation, by signs and wonders, &c? Unto thee it was showed that thou mightest know [with peculiar certainty] that the Lord he is God," Deuteronomy 4:7, 32, &c.

---

down from heaven, and condescended to be himself our teacher. It is as we are Christians, that we possess more excellent and Divine truths than the rest of mankind."

Does not the psalmist stir up the Lord's chosen nation to gratitude and praise, by the same motive of which the anti-Calvinists are ashamed? "He showeth his word to Jacob, his statutes to Israel. He hath not dealt so with any nation. As for his judgments, they [the heathen] have not known them. Praise ye the Lord, O ye seed of Abraham, ye children of Jacob his chosen," Psalm 142:19, 20; 105:6.

Nay, does not God himself stir up Jerusalem, (the holy city become a harlot,) to repentance and faithfulness, by dwelling upon the greatness of his distinguishing love toward her? How strong is this expostulation! How richly descriptive of God's partiality toward that faithless city! "Thus says the Lord God to Jerusalem, Thy birth and thy nativity is of the land of Canaan. Thy father was an Amorite, and thy mother a Hittite. Thou wast cast out in the open field to the loathing of thy person in the day that thou wast born; and when I passed by thee, and saw thee polluted in thy blood, I said to thee, Live. I entered into a covenant with thee: I put a beautiful crown upon thy head: thou didst prosper into a kingdom, and thy renown went forth among the heathen for thy beauty, for it was perfect through my comeliness which I had put upon thee, saith the Lord," Ezekiel 16:3, &c, If this could be said to Jewish Jerusalem, how much more to Protestant London!

Should rigid Arminians still assert that there is absolutely no respect of places and persons with God, I desire the opposers of God's gracious partiality to answer the following questions: — When the apostle says, "The time of *heathenish* ignorance God winked at, but now *explicitly* commandeth [by his evangelists] all men every where to repent," Acts 17:30, does he not represent God as being partial to all those men, to whom he sends apostles, or messengers, on purpose to bid them repent? And does not the Lord show us more distinguishing love, than he did to all the nations, which he "suffered to walk in their own ways, without *the Gospel of* Christ, aliens from the commonwealth of Israel, *and* strangers to the covenants of promise, having no hope, [founded upon a special Gospel message,] and being without God in the world? Acts 14:16; Ephesians 2:12.

Again: when St. Paul observes that "God spake in time past to the fathers by the prophets; but hath, in these last days, spoken to us by his Son," Hebrews 1:1, 2; is it not evident that he pleads for the partiality of distinguishing grace; intimating that God has favoured us more than he did the fathers? And has not our Lord strongly asserted the same thing, where he says, "Blessed are your eyes, for they see; and your ears, for they hear: for verily I say unto you, that many prophets and righteous men have desired to see those things which ye see, and have not seen them; and to hear those things which ye hear, and have not heard them?" Matthew 13:16, 17.

Once more: what is the Gospel of Christ, from first to last, but a glorious blessing flowing from distinguishing, grace; a blessing from which all mankind were reprobated for four thousand years, and from which the generality of men are to this day cut off by awful, providential decrees? When the Pelagians, and rigid Arminians, therefore, are ashamed to shout the partiality of God's free, distinguishing grace toward us, (Christians,) are they not "ashamed of the Gospel of Christ," and of the election of peculiar grace, by which we are raised so far above the dispensations of the Jews and heathens? A precious and exalted election or predestination, in which St. Paul and the primitive Christians could never sufficiently glory, (as appears by Ephesians i, ii, iii,) and of which it is almost as wicked to be ashamed, as it is to be ashamed of Christ himself. Nay, to slight our election of grace, — our election in

Christ, is to be ashamed of our evangelical crown, which is more inexcusable, than to blush at our evangelical cross.

Hence it appears that the genuine tendency of Pelagius' error, toward which rigid Arminians lean too much, is to make us (Christians) fight against God's distinguishing love to us; or, at least, to hide from us "the riches of the *peculiar* grace, wherein God hath abounded toward us in all wisdom and prudence, having made known to US the mystery of his will, according to his good pleasure, which he purposed in himself, when he predestinated US, according to the counsel of his grace, and the good pleasure of his will, to the praise of the glory of his *peculiar* grace, wherein he made US accepted in the Beloved, [and his dispensation,] that WE should be to the praise of his glory;" that is, that WE (Christians) should "show forth the praises" of his distinguishing mercy, and glorify him for bestowing upon US those evangelical favours, from which he still reprobates so many myriads of our fellow creatures.

O Pelagianism, thou wretched levelling system, how can we, Christians, sufficiently detest thee, for thus robbing us of the peculiar comforts arising from the election of grace, which so eminently distinguishes us from Jews, Turks, and heathens! And how can we sufficiently decry thee, for robbing, by this means, our sovereign Benefactor of "the praise of the glory of his grace!" Were it not for Pelagian unbelief, which makes us regardless of the comforts of our gratuitous election in Christ, and for whims of Calvinian reprobation, which damp or destroy these comforts, many Christians would triumph in Christ; and, "rejoicing with joy unspeakable and full of glory, in the vocation wherewith they are called, they would thank God for his unspeakable gift." They would shout electing love as loudly as Zelotes, but not in the unnatural, unscriptural, barbarous, damnatory sense in which he does it. They would not say, "Why *me,* Lord? Why *me?* Why am I absolutely appointed to eternal justification and finished salvation, while most of my neighbours (poor creatures!) are absolutely appointed to eternal wickedness, and finished damnation?" But with charitable and wondering gratitude, they would cry out, "Why *us,* Lord? Why *us?* Why are *we* (Christians) predestinated and elected to the blessings of the full Gospel of Christ, from which Enoch, the man who walked with thee, Abraham, the man whom thou calledst thy friend, Moses, the man who talked with thee face to face, David, the man after thy own heart. Daniel, the man greatly beloved, and John the Baptist, the man who excelled all the Jewish prophets, were every one reprobated?

In such evangelical strains as these should Christians express before God their peculiar gratitude for their peculiar election and calling: and then running to each other, with hearts and mouths full of evangelical congratulations, they should say as the apostle did to Timothy, "God hath saved US [Christians] and called US with a holy [Christian] calling; not according to our works, but according to his own purpose and grace, which was given US [Christians] in Christ Jesus before the world began, [when God planned the various dispensations of his grace,] but is now made manifest by the appearing of our Saviour Jesus Christ, who hath abolished death, and hath brought life and immortality to light through the Gospel of Christ — a precious, perfect Gospel, with which God hath blessed *us,* as well as our neighbours, who are ungrateful enough to "put it from them," 2 Timothy 1:9, 10. In a word, they should all say to their brethren in the election of [Christian] grace, "Blessed be the Father of our Lord Jesus Christ, who, according to his abundant mercy, hath begotten US again to a lively hope by the resurrection of Christ, in whom, though now ye see him not, yet believing, ye rejoice; receiving the end of your [Christian] faith, even the [Christian] salvation of your souls: of which salvation the prophets inquired, and searched diligently, who prophesied of the [Christian] grace that should come unto you: unto whom it was revealed, that not unto themselves, but unto US [Christians] they did minister the things which are now reported unto you, by them that have preached the Gospel unto you, with the Holy Ghost sent down from heaven; which things the angels desire to look into," 1 Peter 1:8, &c. "Unto him," therefore, that so peculiarly" loved us," as to elect and call us into his Christian reformed Church, "which he hath purchased with his own blood;" peculiarly redeeming it from heathenish ignorance, Jewish bondage, and popish superstition — "unto him," I say, that thus "loved US, [reformed Christians,] and washed us from our sins," not by the blood of lambs and heifers, as Aaron washed the Jews, "but by his own blood, and hath made US [who believe] kings and priests to God and his Father, to him be glory and dominion for ever and ever!" Revelation 1:5, 6; Acts 20:28.

But while reformed Christians express thus their joy and gratitude for their election to this peculiar salvation, they should not gorget to guard this comfortable doctrine in as anti-Solifidian a manner as St. Paul and St. Peter did, when they said to their fellows elect, "If every transgression and disobedience [against the Gospel of Jewish salvation] received a just recompense of reward; how shall WE escape if WE neglect so great salvation, *as that* which at the first began to be spoken by the Lord Jesus," and his apostles! "Wherefore the rather, brethren, partakers of the heavenly calling" in Christ, who is "the Apostle and High Priest of our profession" or dispensation, "give diligence to make your [high] calling and [distinguishing] election sure; for, if ye do these things, ye shall never fall" into the aggravated ruin which awaits the "neglecters of so great salvation," Hebrews 2:2, 3; 3:1; 2 Peter 1:10.

Should a rigid Arminian say, "I cannot reconcile your doctrine of partial grace with Divine goodness and equity, and therefore I cannot receive it; why should not God bear with all men as long as he did with Manasses? With all nations as long as he did with the Jews? And with all Churches as long as he does with the Church of Rome?" I answer: —

Mercy may lengthen out her cords on *particular* occasions to display her boundless extent. But if she did so on *all* occasions, she would countenance sin, and pour oil on the fire of wickedness. If God displayed the same goodness and long suffering toward all sinners, Churches, and nations, then all sinners would be spared till they had committed as many atrocious crimes as Manasses, who filled Jerusalem with blood and witchcraft. All fallen Churches would be tolerated, till they had poisoned the Gospel truth with as many errors as the Church of Rome imposes upon her votaries. And all corrupted nations would not only be preserved till they had actually "sacrificed their sons and daughters to devils;" but also till they had an opportunity to "kill the Prince of life," coming in person to "gather them as a hen gathers her brood under her wings." So universal a mercy as this would be the greatest cruelty to myriads of men, and instead of setting off Divine justice, would for a time lay it under a total eclipse.

Beside, according to this impartial, this levelling scheme, God would have been obliged to make all men kings, as Manasses; all Churches Christian, as the Church of Rome; and all people his peculiar people, as the Jewish nation. But even then distinguishing grace would not have been abolished: unless God had made all men archangels, all Churches like the triumphant Church, and all nations like the glorified nation which inhabits the heavenly Canaan. So monstrous are the absurdities which result from the leveling scheme of the men who laugh at the doctrine of the Gospel dispensations; and of those who will not allow Divine sovereignty and supreme wisdom to dispense unmerited favours as they please; and to deal out their talents with a variety which, upon the whole, answers the most excellent ends; as displaying best the excellency of a government, where sovereignty, mercy, and justice wisely agree to sway their common sceptre!

Should a Pelagian leveller refuse to yield to these arguments, under pretence that "they lead to the Calvinian doctrines of lawless grace, free wrath, and absolute reprobation;" I answer this capital objection five different ways: —

1. The objector is greatly mistaken: for, holding forth the gratuitous reprobation of partial grace, as the Scriptures do, is the only way to open the eyes of candid Calvinists, to keep the simple from drinking into their plausible error, and to rescue the multitude of passages, on which they found their absolute, gratuitous predestination to eternal life and eternal death. I say it again, rigid Calvinism is the child of confusion, and lives merely by sucking its mother's corrupted milk. Would you destroy the brat, only kill its mother: destroy confusion: "divide the word of God aright:" and thus lead the rigid Predestinarians to the truth — the delightful truth, whence their error has been derived "by the *mistake or* sleight of men, and by the cunning craftiness whereby *the spirit of error* lies in wait to deceive," and you will destroy the Antinomian election, and the cruel reprobation which pass for Gospel. In order to this, you strike at those serpents with the swords of your mouths, and cry out, "Absurd! unscriptural! horrible! diabolical!" But, by this means, you will never kill one of them: there is but one method to extirpate them: hold out the partial election and reprobation maintained by the sacred writers. Throw your rod, like Moses, amidst the rods of the magicians. Let it first become a serpent, which you can take up with pleasure and safety: display the true partiality of Divine grace: openly preach the Scripture election of grace; and boldly assert the gratuitous reprobation of inferior grace. So shall your harmless serpent swallow up the venomous serpent of your adversaries. The true reprobation shall devour the false. Bigoted Calvinists will be confounded, hide themselves for fear of the truth: and candid Calvinists will see the finger of God, and acknowledge that your rod is superior to theirs, and that the harmless reprobation of inferior grace, which we preach, has fairly swallowed up the horrible reprobation of free wrath which they contend for.

Be neither ashamed nor afraid of our serpent — our reprobation. Like Christ, it has not only the "wisdom of the serpent," but also the "innocency of the dove:" you may handle it without danger: nay, you may put it into your bosom: and, instead of stinging you with despair, and filling you with chilling horrors, it will warm your soul with admiration for the manifold wisdom and variegated goodness of God: it will make you sharp sighted in the truth of the Gospel, and in the errors of overdoing evangelists. In the light of this truth you will, every where, see a glorious rainbow, where before you saw nothing but a dark cloud.

When our serpent has had this blessed effect, you may take it out of your bosom for external use, and it will become a rod fit to chastise the errors of Pelagius and Augustine — of Calvin and Socinus. But use it with such gentleness and candour that all the spectators may see you do not deal in free wrath, and that there is as much difference between the gratuitous reprobation, which Calvin and Zanchius hold forth, and the gratuitous reprobation, which our blessed Lord and St. Paul maintain, as there is between the blasted dry rod of Korah, and the blossoming, fragrant rod of Aaron; between a fire which gently warms your apartment, and one which rapidly consumes your house; between the bright morning star, inferior in light to the sun, and a horribly glaring comet, which draws its fiery tail over the earth to smite it with an eternal curse, and to drag, with merciless necessity, a majority of its frightened inhabitants to everlasting burnings.

2. Our gratuitous reprobation is not a reprobation from all saving grace, as that of the Calvinists, but only from the superior blessings of saving grace. It is therefore as contrary to Calvinian reprobation, as initial salvation is contrary to insured damnation. It is perfectly consistent with the "free gift which is to come," in various degrees, "upon all men to justification." We steadily assert, with Christ and St. Paul, that "the saving grace of God hath appeared to all men," and that all the reprobates of superior grace, that is, all who are refused three, four, or five talents of grace receive two, or at least one talent of true and saving grace. There never was a spark of Calvinian free wrath in God against them. They are all redeemed with a temporal redemption. They have all an accepted time, and a day of initial salvation, with sufficient means and helps to "work out their own *eternal* salvation," according to their Gospel dispensation. We grant that God does not bestow upon them so many of his gratuitous favours as he does on his peculiar people. But if he give them less, he requires the less of them; for he is too just to insist upon the improvement of five talents from the servants on whom he has bestowed but one talent.

To understand this perfectly, distinguish between the two Gospel axioms, or, if you please, between the doctrines of *grace,* and the doctrines of *justice.* According to the *former,* God, with a *partial* hand, bestows upon us *primary* and merely *gratuitous* favours. And, according to the *latter,* he, with an *impartial* hand, imparts to us *secondary* and *remunerative* favours. God's primary, and merely gratuitous favours, depend entirely on his partial grace: so far all Christians should agree with Calvin, and hold with him the doctrine of grace. But God's secondary, remunerative favours depending on his rewarding grace, conditional promise, and distributive justice, depend of consequence in some degree on our free agency; for our free will, by making a bad or good use of God's primary favours, secures to us his righteous punishments, or gracious rewards, that is, his secondary favours. And herein all Christians should agree with Arminius. By thus joining the peculiar excellencies of Calvinism and Arminianism, we embrace the whole Gospel, and keep together the doctrines of grace and justice, which the partial ministers of the two modern gospels rashly tear asunder.

3. Many of the persons who have been reprobated from superior favours by partial grace, have been eternally saved by improving their one talent of inferior favour; while some of those who had a large share in the election of distinguishing grace, are condemned for the non-improvement or abuse of the five talents which that grace had richly bestowed upon them. Who, for example, will dare say that Melchisedec, Esau, Jonathan, and Mephibosheth, are damned because they were reprobated with respect to the peculiar favours which God bestowed upon Abraham, Jacob, David, and Solomon? Or that Judas, Ananias, and Sapphira are saved, because

they were all three chosen and called to the highest blessings which distinguishing grace ever bestowed upon mortals, — the blessings of the new covenant, which is the best covenant of peculiarity; and because Judas was even chosen and called to the high dignity of the apostleship, in this excellent covenant?

4. We all know how fatal Calvinian reprobation must prove to those who are its miserable subjects. A man may be seized by the plague and live. But if that fatal decree, as drawn by some mistaken theologians, seize on ten thousand souls, not one of them can escape: their hopes of salvation are sacrificed for ever. But the gratuitous election and reprobation, which the Scripture maintains, are attended with as favourable circumstances, as the elections and reprobations mentioned in the following illustrations: —

While the sun is alone elected to gild the day, the moon, though reprobated from that honour, is nevertheless elected to silver the night, in conjunction with stars of different brightness. The "holy place" of the temple was reprobated, with respect to the glory of the "holy of holies:" it contained neither the cherubim, nor the mercy seat, nor the ark of the covenant; but yet it was elected to the honour of containing the golden altar, on which the incense was burned. The "court of the priests" was reprobated from the honour of containing the *golden altar*, but yet it was freely elected to the honour of containing *the brazen* altar, on which the sacrifices were offered. As for the "court of the Gentiles," though it was reprobated from all these honourable peculiarities, yet it was elected to the advantage of leading to the brazen altar: and the Gentiles, who worshipped in this court, not only heard at a distance the music of the priest, and discovered the smoke, which ascended from the burnt offerings; but, when they looked through the open gates, they had a distant view of the brazen altar, of the fire which descended from heaven upon it, and of the lamb, which was daily consumed in that fire. And therefore they were no more absolutely reprobated from all interest in the daily sacrifice, than Caiaphas was absolutely elected to an inamissible interest in the daily oblation, in which his near attendance at the altar gave him the first right. Once more: the tribe of Levi was elected to the honour of doing the service of the sanctuary; an honour from which eleven tribes were reprobated. And, in that chosen tribe, the family of Aaron was elected to the priesthood and high priesthood: peculiar dignities, from which the sons of Moses himself were all reprobated. Now if it would be absurd to deduce Calvinian reprobation, and unavoidable damnation, from these elections; is it reasonable to deduce them, as the Calvinists do, from a gratuitous election to the distinguishing blessings of the Jewish and Christian covenant?

5. The difference between the partial reprobation which the Holy Ghost asserts, and that which Calvin maintains, is so important, that I beg leave to make the reader sensible of it by one more illustration. God's partial reprobation, which flows from his inferior favour, and not from free wrath, may be compared, (1.) To the king's refusing a regiment of foot the advantage of riding on horseback — a free prerogative, which he grants to a regiment of dragoons. And, (2.) To his denying to common soldiers the rank of captains; and to captains, the rank of colonels. But Calvin's partial reprobation, which flows from free wrath, and has nothing to do with any degree of saving grace, may be compared to the king's placing a whole regiment of marines in such dreadful circumstances by sea and land, that all the soldiers, and officers, shall be sooner or later necessitated to desert, and to have their brains blown

out for desertion; a distinguishing severity this, which will set off the distinguishing favour which his majesty bears to a company of favourite grenadiers, on whom he has absolutely set his everlasting love, and who cannot be shot for desertion, because they are tied to their colours by necessity, — an adamantine chain, which either keeps them from running away, or irresistibly pulls them back to their colours as often as they desert. Thus all the marines wear the badge of absolute free wrath; not one of them can possibly escape being shot; and the grenadiers wear the badge of absolute free grace; not one of them can possibly be shot, let them behave in ever so treacherous a manner for ever so long a time. But, alas! my illustration fails in the main point. When a soldier, who has been necessitated to desert, is shot, his punishment is over in a moment: but when a reprobate, who has been necessitated to continue in sin, is damned, he must go into a fire unquenchable, where "the smoke of his torment shall ascend for ever and ever."

By these various answers candid Arminians will, I hope, be convinced, that, although Calvinian reprobation is unscriptural, irrational, and cruel, the gratuitous election and reprobation maintained in the preceding pages is truly evangelical, and, of consequence, perfectly consistent with the dictates of sound reason and pure morality.

BIBLE ARMINIANISM.

ESSAY THE SECOND.

Displaying the doctrines of impartial justice, the capital error of the Calvinists, and the excellence of Scripture Arminianism.

THE doctrines of *impartial justice* rest on these scriptures: — "I say unto you, that to every one who hath [to a good purpose] more shall be given: and from him [the slothful servant] who hath not [to a good purpose] even that he hath shall be taken away from him," Luke 19:26. "Cursed is he that perverteth judgment," Deuteronomy 27:19.

These awful doctrines subdivide themselves into an *impartial election*, and an *impartial reprobation;* both flowing from Divine justice, which is always irrespective of persons.

The impartial election and reprobation of justice is the righteous and wise choice, which God, as an equitable and unbribed JUDGE, makes, or refuses to make, of some persons, Churches, cities, and nations, judicially to bestow upon them, for Christ's sake, gracious rewards according to his evangelical promises: or judicially to inflict upon them, for righteousness' sake, condign punishments, according to his reasonable threatenings; solemn promises and threatenings these, which St. Paul sums up in these words: — "God, in the revelation of his righteous judgment, will render to every man according to his deeds. To them who, by patient continuance in well doing, seek for glory, &c, eternal life: but to them that do not obey the truth, but obey unrighteousness, *he will render* indignation and wrath: tribulation and anguish, upon every soul of man that doth evil, of the Jew [and Christian] first," as having received more talents than others; "and also of the Gentile; [or heathen:] but glory, honour, and peace, to every man that worketh good, to the Jew [and Christian] first," as being God's peculiar people, "and also to the heathens. For," with regard to the doctrines of justice, "there is no respect of persons with God. For as many as have sinned without the law, [of a peculiar covenant,] shall also perish without the law, [of a peculiar covenant:] and as many as have sinned under the law, [of a peculiar covenant,] shall be judged by the law," of the peculiar covenant they were under, whether it were "the law of Moses, *or* the law of Christ. For not the hearers, but the doers of the law shall be justified in the day when God shall judge the secrets of men according to my Gospel." And lest some should object that the heathens, having neither the law of Moses nor that of Christ, cannot be judged according to their works, the apostle intimates that they are under the law of the human nature, which law is written upon every man's conscience, by a beam of "the true light, that enlightens every man that comes into the world. For when the heathens," says he, "which have not the law, do by nature, [assisted by the general light above mentioned,] the things contained in the *written* law [of Moses or of Christ,] these, having not the *written* law, are a law unto themselves; and show the work of the law written in their hearts, their consciences also bearing witness, and their thoughts the mean while accusing or else excusing one another," as a pledge and earnest of the condemnation or justification which awaits them before the throne of justice, Romans 2:5, 16.

And let none say that this is St. James' legal doctrine, into which St. Paul had slided unawares, through "the legality which cleaves to our nature;" for the evangelical prophet is as deep in it as the herald of free grace. Hear Isaiah: — "Say ye to the righteous, that it shall be well with them; for they shall eat the fruit of their doings: wo to the wicked, it shall be ill with him; for the reward of his hands shall be given him," Isaiah 3:10, 11. If Isaiah be accused of having imbibed this anti-Solifidian doctrine, like legal Ezekiel, I reply, that our Lord himself was as deep in it as Ezekiel and St. James; witness his last charge: — "Behold, I come quickly; and my reward is with me, to give every man according as his work shall be. Blessed are they that do his commandments, that they may have a right to the tree of life, and may enter into the *heavenly* city *of God:* for without are dogs, &c, [all manner of evil workers,] and whosoever loveth or maketh a lie," Revelation 22:12, 15. The "few names in Sardis which have not defiled their garments, shall walk with me in white, for they are worthy," Revelation 3:4. "Watch ye, &c, that you may be counted worthy to escape all these things that shall come to pass, and to stand before the Son of man," Luke 21:37.

The *election* of justice is then nothing but the impartiality with which God makes *choice* of his good and faithful servants, rather than of his wicked and slothful servants, to bestow upon them the temporal and eternal rewards of goodness and faithfulness, according to their works; when he "cometh and reckoneth with them," about the talents which his free grace hath bestowed upon them, Matthew 25:19. Nor is the *reprobation* of justice any thing but the impartiality with which God, as a righteous dispenser of his punishments, *reprobates* from his rewards of grace and glory his wicked and unfaithful servants, who do not use, or who vilely abuse the talents which his free grace hath entrusted them with.

When God "commands the servants, to whom he hath given his pounds, to be called to him, that he may know how much every man has gained by trading," in order to bestow his evangelical rewards with equity; according to the election of justice, he makes choice of the servants who have gained something with their pounds, rather than of the servant who has slothfully "laid up his pound in a napkin." And according to the reprobation of justice, he reprobates from all rewards, and appoints to a deserved punishment the unprofitable and slothful servant, rather than the faithful and diligent servants, who have improved their Lord's gifts. Once more: according to the election of justice, God elects and calls to a *double* reward his servants who have given *double* diligence to make their gratuitous election sure. Thus he elects to the honour of "being ruler over TEN cities," the man whose pound "had gained TEN pounds," rather than the man whose pound had only gained *five* pounds, and who, by the rule of equitable proportion, is only placed over *five* cities, Luke 19:15, &c. And, according to the reprobation of justice, in the day of judgment it shall be more intolerable for unbelieving Chorazin and Bethsaida, than for Sodom and Gomorrah; and for unbelieving London and Edinburgh, than for Chorazin and Bethsaida; because they bury more talents, resist brighter light, and sin against richer dispensations of Divine grace, Matthew 10:15.

With regard to the election and reprobation of justice, "there is *absolutely* no respect of persons with God:" and evangelical worthiness, which dares not show its head before the throne of God's partial grace, may lift it up with humble confidence before the throne of Christ's remunerative justice. Hence it is that St. Paul, who so strongly asserts in Romans 9. that, before the throne of partial grace, "it is not of him that willeth, nor of him that runneth, but of God who showeth mercy," or favour, when, and in what degree he pleases, does not scruple to say, when he is going to appear before the mediatorial throne of Divine justice, "The time of my departure is at hand: I have fought a good fight, I have finished my course, I have kept the faith. Henceforth there is laid up for me a crown of righteousness, which the Lord, the righteous Judge, shall give me at that day: when he shall render eternal life to them who seek for glory, by patient continuance in well doing," 2 Timothy 4:6, &c; Romans 2:7.

The doctrine of *proper merit,* or merit of *condignity,* is unscriptural, irrational, and wild. The bare thought of it might make an *innocent* angel blush before his Creator, and should fill a *reprieved* sinner with the greatest detestation. And yet the doctrine of improper or *evangelical* worthiness is of so great importance, that if you take it away, you eclipse God's distributive justice; you destroy the law of Christ, and all the conditional promises and threatenings in the Bible; you demolish all the doctrines of personal rewards and punishments, together with the judgment seat of Christ; and upon their ruins you raise an Antinomian Babel, whose dreadful foundation is finished, or necessary damnation for the millions of Calvin's absolute reprobates; while its airy top is finished, or necessary salvation for all his absolute elect.

Hence it appears that the mistake of heated Calvin is exactly contrary to that of heated Pelagius. Pelagianism throws down the throne of God's partial grace, and rigid

Doctrines of Grace and Justice

Calvinism leaves no foundation for the throne of his impartial justice. The former of these modern gospels shackles God our Benefactor; and the latter pours infamy upon God our Judge. It fixes upon him the astonishing inconsistency of finally judging men according to their works, and yet of finally justifying them without any regard to their works; and by this mean it indirectly gives the lie to our Lord himself, who says, "In the day of judgment by thy words thou shalt be justified or condemned."

Having thus described the impartial election and reprobation of justice, for which the Calvinists substitute a partial election of lawless grace in Christ, and a partial reprobation of free wrath in Adam; I support the doctrines of justice by the following appeals to Scripture and matter of fact: —

Search the Scriptures, for they bear testimony to the equity of God, our rewarder and punisher. If he praises and rewards one man rather than another, this difference flows from the holiness of his nature, which makes "his *judicial* ways equal." He "loves righteousness and hates iniquity;" and therefore he judicially "chooses the man that is godly," while he judicially reprobates the man that is ungodly. If a veil, as thick as that which is upon the Jews, were not upon us when we read the Scriptures, would we not confess that God's judicial reprobation impartially turns upon our not receiving the truth, and not living up to it, that is, upon our voluntary unbelief, and the unnecessitated disobedience which flows from it?

Does not the experience of all ages confirm this assertion? When creating grace had gratuitously elected and called Adam to the enjoyment of a paradisiacal kingdom, did not impartial and remunerative justice put the stamp of Divine approbation upon his faith and obedience, by equitably continuing him in that kingdom till he sinned? And did not impartial justice seal him with the seal of reprobation, when he had sinned? Hear the reprobating decree: — "BECAUSE thou hast hear-kened to the voice of thy wife, &c, cursed is the ground for thy sake. THEREFORE the Lord God sent him forth from the garden," Genesis 3:17, 23.

When redeeming grace had reprieved him, and his posterity, did Divine approbation and reprobation Calvinistically fasten upon their children? Did not the judicial difference, which God made between Cain and Abel, spring merely from the personal faith of Abel, and the excellence of his sacrifice? Hear Moses and St. Paul:— "The Lord had respect to Abel and his offering: but to Cain and his offering he had not respect. For by FAITH Abel offered a more excellent sacrifice than Cain." Thus the Lord had respect to Cornelius and his charity. "His prayers and alms came up for a memorial before God:" but to the Pharisees, their prayers and alms "he had not respect:" for, by faith in his light, Cornelius offered more excellent prayers and alms than the Pharisees. "By which he," like Abel, "obtained witness that he was righteous and accepted:" God, by the angel, "testifying" of his gifts. "And, by it, he, being dead, yet speaketh" to all Solifidians, who would banish the election and reprobation of justice out of the world.

Righteous Seth succeeds righteous Abel: his children do the works of God, and are, of consequence, the elect of his justice, as well as of his grace. But as soon as these pious sons of God begin to draw back, and to follow the worldly ways of the daughters of men, they begin to rank among the reprobates of justice, and are involved in their dreadful punishment. Through the apostasy of these sons of God, "the earth was soon corrupt before God:" and yet "Noah was a just man, perfect in his generation, and Noah walked with God." Therefore when a decree of judicial reprobation went forth against "the world of the ungodly," a decree of judicial election was made in his favour: "and the Lord said to Noah, Come thou, and all thy house, into the ark; for thee I have seen righteous before me in this generation," Genesis 8: 1. Ham, the father of Canaan, shared in the election which saved Noah; but, by his flagrant violation of the fifth commandment, he soon brought upon himself a judicial reprobation.

A degree of vindictive reprobation passes against Sodom, but the sacred historian, who informs us of it, sets his pen, like a bar of brass, against the Calvinian doctrine of free wrath: nay, God himself condescends to speak in our language on that awful occasion. "The Lord said, Because the cry of Sodom is great, I will go down now, and, [before I judicially reprobate it,] I will see whether they have done altogether according to the cry of it, and if not, I will know," Genesis 18:20. So far is the Lord from judicially reprobating his creatures otherwise than according to works, that is, according to evangelical worthiness or unworthiness.

Agreeably to the same doctrine of justice, God showed favour to righteous Lot, rather than to the wicked inhabitants of Sodom. For "it came to pass, when God destroyed the cities of the plain, that God remembered Abraham," and his cogent plea: ("Wilt thou [reprobate and] destroy the righteous with the wicked? That be far from thee, to do after this manner! Shall not the Judge of all the earth do right?") "And *accordingly* God sent Lot out of the midst of the overthrow."

His wife shared in this election of justice, for the angels "laid hold upon her hand," and extended to her the same favour which they did to her husband. But as soon as she looked back, and broke the commandment, "Look not behind thee," she forfeited her election: reprobation laid hold on her, and she became a monument of God's judicial impartiality.

Although God's distinguishing grace shines in his calling Abraham to be a father of his peculiar people; yet the election of justice soon goes hand in hand with the election of grace. How striking are these anti-Solifidian passages! "I will perform the oath which I sware to Abraham thy father, &c, BECAUSE that Abraham obeyed my voice, and kept my charge, my commandments, my statutes and my laws," Genesis 26:3, 5. Did not God judicially elect that faithful patriarch to the rewards of grace, when he said, "By myself have I sworn; BECAUSE thou hast done this thing, and hast not withheld thine only son, that in blessing I will bless thee, because thou hast obeyed my voice?" Genesis 22:16, 18. Do not these scriptures prove that if Abraham had not made his election of peculiar favour sure, by
obeying God's voice, he would have forfeited that election as well as Saul and Judas?

But to return to the election of justice: does not this election extend, m some degree, even to the children of the godly? When God had said to Abraham, according to the reprobation of inferior grace, "Cast out the bond woman and her son" Ishmael, did he not say also, according to the election of justice, "For Ishmael I have heard thee: behold, I have blessed him — because he is thy seed?" Genesis 17:20; 21:13. And is not the decree of this remunerative election openly written by David, where he says, "Blessed is the man that feareth the Lord: his seed shall be mighty upon earth: the generation of the upright shall be blessed?"

A striking instance of the impartial reprobation of justice we have in the Amorites and Israelites, the two nations to which God, according to the election of special favour, successively gave the good land of Canaan. God's justice would not absolutely reprobate the Amorites from it, till they had sinned out their day of national salvation, or squandered away all the time which he had allotted them for national repentance. "I brought thee out of Ur to give thee this land," said God to Abraham, but thy posterity shall not immediately inherit it, "for the iniquity of the Amorites is not yet full," Genesis 15:16. And God was exactly as equitable to the corrupted Israelites, as he had been to the corrupted Canaanites; for he would not drive the Jews out of the land of Canaan, till they were quite ripe for that national reprobation. Hence it is, that our Lord, by nationally sparing them, suffered them also to "fill up the measure of their iniquities," Matthew 23:32.

To return: God says to Abraham, "I will judge the oppressive nation, whom the Israelites shall serve;" and accordingly he judicially reprobates Rahab and the dragon — Egypt and Pharaoh. But is Rahab struck with any plague, is the river turned into blood, before its waters have been mixed with the briny tears, and tinged with the innocent blood of the children of God's people? Is Pharaoh drowned in the Red Sea, or hardened, before he has hardened his own heart, by setting his seal to the most cruel decrees, and by drowning the helpless posterity of Joseph, who had been the deliverer of his kingdom?

Proceed to the book of Numbers, and you see at large the awful account, which St. Jude and St. Paul sum up in these words: — "I will put you in remembrance that the Lord having saved the people out of the land of Egypt," through obedient faith, "afterward destroyed them that believed not," Jude 1:5. For "our fathers did all drink of the spiritual rock which followed them, and that rock was Christ." But, because they did not all secure the gracious rewards of justice, notwithstanding their election of grace, "with many of them God was not well pleased, for they were overthrown in the wilderness" by the plague, by serpents, by the destroyer. "Now all these things happened to them," the elect of distinguishing grace, "and they are written for our admonition," lest we should not make our election of justice sure by the works of faith: "Wherefore let him that thinketh he *sufficiently* standeth," by the election of partial grace," take heed lest he fall" into sin, which draws after it the reprobation of impartial justice, 1 Corinthians 10:1, &c.

As a proof that, with respect to the election of justice, God is no respecter of persons, I produce Moses and Aaron, the great prophet and the high priest of the Jewish dispensation. They are both elected and called to inherit the land of Canaan; but not making this calling and election sure, they are both reprobated with respect to that inheritance. The adult Israelites share their reprobation. Of several hundred thousand, none but Caleb and Joshua make their election to that favour sure.

Joshua and a new generation of Israelites obey; Jordan is parted: Jericho and her wicked inhabitants are destroyed. But Rahab and her friends, although they were Canaanites, are elected to partake of a peculiar deliverance, because "she had received the messengers" with hospitable kindness, James 2:25. On the other hand, Achan, one of those who were interested in the covenant of peculiarity, hides the wedge of gold, and the reprobation which Rahab's hospitality had averted lights on him for his covetousness. She is blessed as a daughter of Abraham, and he is destroyed as a cursed Canaanite.

After Joshua's death, God's chosen people corrupted themselves. "And the angel of the Lord came and said, I made you to go up out of Egypt, and have brought you into the land, which I sware to your fathers: and I said, I will never break my covenant with you." Here is the election of grace! "But ye have not obeyed my voice. Wherefore I also said, I will not drive out the inhabitants of the land before you. They forsook the Lord, and served Baal. And the anger of the Lord was hot against them: whithersoever they went out, the hand of the Lord was against them for evil, as the Lord had sworn unto them," Judges 2:1, 15. Here is the reprobation of justice!

I have already mentioned how Phinehas' zeal procured his election to the highest dignity in the Church militant, and how Eli's remissness caused his reprobation from that dignity, and entailed degradation and wretchedness upon his family. As for Saul, "when he was little in his own sight, God *gratuitously* made him the head of the tribes of Israel." But when he grew proud and disobedient, "God *judicially* rejected *or reprobated* him from being king." In his days the Kenites were predestinated to be delivered from death, "because they showed kindness to all the children of Israel, when they came up out of Egypt:" while the Amalekites, their neighbours, were appointed for utter destruction, because "they laid wait for Israel in the way, when he came up from Egypt," 1 Samuel 15:2, 6.

Although the Lord called David, rather than Jonathan, to the crown of Israel, according to the election of grace; he nevertheless preferred David to his brother Eliab according to the election of justice! "Samuel," says the historian, "looked on Eliab, and said, Surely the Lord's anointed is before him: but the Lord said, Look not on his countenance, or on the height of his stature, because I have refused [reprobated] him: for the Lord seeth not as man seeth, for the Lord looketh on the heart; to this man will I look, who is poor and of a contrite spirit, and trembleth at my word," 1 Samuel 16:6, 7, and Isaiah 66:2. And therefore when Saul was rejected, Samuel said to him, "God hath chosen a man after his own heart; a neighbour that is better than thou," 1 Samuel 15:28.

"Solomon loved the Lord, and said to him, Thou hast showed unto my father great mercy, according as he walked before thee in uprightness of heart, &c, and now, O Lord, I am but a little child, &c, give therefore thy servant an understanding heart. And the speech pleased the Lord: and God said to him, BECAUSE thou hast asked this thing, and not riches, &c, lo, I have given thee a wise and understanding heart, and I have also given thee [or elected thee to receive] that which thou hast not asked, both riches and honour," 1 Kings 3:3, &c. Here we see young Solomon, by the power of assisted free will, trading so wisely with his one talent of initial wisdom, as to increase in wisdom above all his contemporaries. And yet when he was old, and had got ten talents of wisdom, he "hid them," not indeed "in a napkin," but in the lap of the strange, idolatrous women whom he had collected. A demonstration this, that man is endued with freedom of will, and that, as free grace did not necessitate Solomon to choose wisdom in his youth, neither did free wrath necessitate him to choose folly in his old age.

To return: Divine mercy gently holds out her sceptre to some men whom the Calvinists generally consider as absolute reprobates, while Divine justice awfully brandishes her sword against other men whom the Calvinists consider as absolute elect. Take a proof or two of the former part of this proposition.

Cain's countenance falls; anger, the parent of murder, is conceived in his envious heart: but God addresses him with the gentleness of a father, and the mildness of a friend. The wretch, notwithstanding, imbrues his hand in his brother's blood: but the goodness and patience of God endure yet daily, and secure the frighted murderer a long day of grace, by threatening a sevenfold punishment to the man that should slay him. Wicked Ahab repents in part, and God in part reverses the decree of his judicial reprobation. "The word of the Lord came to Elijah, saying, Seest thou how Ahab humbleth himself before me? I will not bring the evil in his days upon his house." What is such a decree as this, but a judicial reprobation, tempered by a judicial election?

Take one or two proofs of the latter part of the proposition. David numbers the people to indulge his vanity, and God gives him the choice of the decrees of reprobation from his special favour. He sins in the matter of Uriah: a decree of death goes forth against his child, and of slaughter against his family. Hezekiah's heart is lifted up: he looks at his wealth with self complacence, and a decree of poverty and captivity is made against his house.

What were these severe judgments, but the marks and effects of a judicial reprobation from the peculiar favour which God had for these pious kings?

I have observed in the former Essay how partial grace favoured bloody Manasseh, in lengthening out his day of grace: but his election of grace did not hinder the election and reprobation of justice from having their free course. Take first an account of this reprobation: "And the Lord spake, &c, saying, Because Manasseh hath done these abominations, &c, therefore behold I am bringing such evil upon Jerusalem, that whosoever heareth it, both his ears shall tingle," &c. Take next an account of Manasseh's judicial election: "When he was in affliction, he besought the Lord his God, and humbled himself greatly before the God of his fathers, and prayed to him, and he heard his supplication, [reversed in part the decree of his judicial reprobation,] and brought him again to Jerusalem into his kingdom. His prayer also, and how God was entreated of him, &c, behold they are written, &c. Amon did evil as did Manasseh his father, but humbled not himself, as Manasseh had humbled himself," 2 Chronicles 33:12-23.

The New Testament gives us the same views of God's righteous reprobation. Judas, one of those whom "the Father had given to Christ," John 17:12, — Judas, whom Christ himself had chosen or elected, John 6:70, — Judas, for whom he designed one of the twelve brightest thrones in glory, Matthew 19:28, — Judas "by transgression fell," and was lost, or to speak according to the Hebrew idiom, became a "son of perdition," Acts 1:25; John 17:12. "He loved cursing more than blessing," and it judicially "entered like oil" into his bones. The decree of reprobation, which had prophetically gone forth, according to God's foresight of his crime, now goes forth judicially. He is his own executioner, and another fills his vacated throne. Herod does not give glory to God. A decree of reprobation overtakes him, and worms eat him up. Regardless of the starving poor, the rich farmer fills his barns, and the rich glutton his belly, and a decree similar to that which sealed drunken Belshazzar's doom is made against them. "The *Jewish* builders reject the corner stone," and Christ says, "The kingdom of God shall be taken from you, and given to a nation bringing forth the fruits thereof." The master of the vineyard comes three years to seek fruit on his fig tree: but, finding none, he judicially reprobates the barren nuisance at last. And patience, which suspends a year the execution of the sentence, offers to seal herself the decree of reprobation, if the tree continues barren to the end of the year of reprieve. The wicked servant beats his fellow servants: the foolish virgins provide no supply of oil: the uncharitable will not give drink to the thirsty; and therefore they all fall a righteous sacrifice to Divine justice. The Gospel feast is provided, and "all things are now ready." Multitudes of men are chosen and called to come to the feast, but their frivolous excuses engage the king to reprobate them. Hear the decree of their judicial reprobation, taken down by three sacred writers: — "I say unto you, that none of those men which were bidden [and refused to come in time] shall taste of my supper," Luke 14:24. "The wedding is ready, but they which were bidden were not worthy," Matthew 22:8. "I was grieved with that generation, and said, They do always err in their heart, &c. So I sware in my wrath, They shall not enter into my rest," Hebrews 3:10. These decrees breathe nothing but just wrath kindled by an obstinate contempt of free grace. From these, and the like Scripture examples, it is evident, that a personal reprobation of justice is an awful and true doctrine; and that a personal, Calvinian reprobation of free wrath is as unscriptural as it is cruel and absurd.

Who can read the Scriptures without prejudice, and not see that the election and reprobation of partial favour yield to the election and reprobation of impartial justice? Although God chose and called Abraham out of distinguishing grace, did he not extend his mercy far beyond the little circle of that narrow calling and election? Did he set his love upon the father of the faithful and his posterity in such a manner that there was nothing but blind mercy for the favoured seed of Abraham, Isaac, and Jacob, and nothing but free wrath, and Calvinian reprobation, for all who were reprobated with respect to that election? What shall we say of conscientious Abimelech, venerable Melchisedec, patient Job, and his pious friends, for whom "God was entreated?" What of Bethuel, Rebekah's father? What of Asenath, an Egyptian woman, the wife of Joseph? What of prudent Jethro, and his daughter, the wife of Moses? What of the submissive Gibeonites, whose part God so eminently took, against the children of Israel and the house of Saul? What of loving Ruth, a daughter of Moab? What of the inquisitive queen of Sheba, and the Sidonian widow, who had charity enough to share her last morsel with Elijah, a hungry and desolate stranger? What of grateful Naaman, the Syrian, whom the prophet sent away in peace, when he entailed a curse, upon Gehazi, the lying Israelite? What of humbled Nebuchadnezzar, who was restored to his former greatness, in as wonderful a manner as patient Job, and penitent Manasseh? What of the wise men, who came from the east; and the treasurer of queen Candace, who came from the south, to worship in Judea? What of the importunate woman of Canaan, the zealous woman of Samaria, and the charitable Samaritan, who had compassion on the wounded man, the "poor creature," whom the elect priest had reprobated, and whom the chosen Levite had passed by? Had God absolutely no respect to their repentance, faith, and charity? Was there never a "well done! thou good and faithful servant," for any of them? Shall "a cup of cold water," given in Christ's name, have its reward; and shall not the oil and the wine of the non-elect Samaritan, given in the name of humanity, divinity, mercy, love, truth, and righteousness, (six of Christ's sweetest names,) shall not, I say, that "wine and oil" have their reward? Hath God forgotten to be gracious? Hath he shut up his remunerative kindness in displeasure? Is there nothing but vindictive free wrath for all that are not interested in the peculiar "covenants of promise," made with Abraham, Moses, and "the High Priest of our profession?" And nothing but flaming love for Nadab, Abihu, Korah, Dathan, Abiram, Demas, Hymeneus, Philetus,

Doctrines of Grace and Justice

Alexander, and Diotrephes, who so eminently shared in the Jewish and Christian covenants of peculiarity?

If you say, with St. Paul, "All are not *true* Israelites who are of Israel," you grant what we contend for: you allow that all are not the elect of God's impartial justice, who are the elect of his partial favour; and that finally the scale will turn for the retribution of eternal life or eternal death, according to the election or reprobation of impartial justice, and not according to the election of partial grace, and the reprobation of free wrath. Who had ever a larger share in the election of partial grace than David? And yet, who ever maintained the election and reprobation of justice more strongly than he? Does he not still cry to all the world, from the walls of Jerusalem, "Verily, there is a reward for the righteous, [of whatever family, tribe, or religion he be:] doubtless there is a God that judgeth the earth?" Does not every body know, that to judge the earth is to justify, or condemn all its inhabitants, according to their works? And when God finally justifies or condemns, what does he do but declare that the godly are evangelically worthy of walking with him in white, and of following him to fountains of living water; and that the ungodly are every way worthy to depart with the devil, and follow him into the lake of fire?

I have observed that the election of partial grace extends to cities and nations; and so does the reprobation of impartial justice. Take one or two remarkable instances of it. According to the election of distinguishing favour, God "chose Jerusalem to put his name there." But when Jerusalem showed herself absolutely unworthy of his judicial election, he reprobated her in righteousness. Hear the awful decree: — "I will make Jerusalem heaps, and a den of dragons. The houses of Jerusalem shall be defiled as Tophet," Jeremiah 9:11; 19:13. The mild Jesus, after a last effort to "gather her children, as a hen gathers her brood," with a flood of tears, pronounces the final sentence of her judicial reprobation: "O Jerusalem, Jerusalem, thou that killest the prophets, — there shall not be left in thee one stone upon another, that shall not be thrown down."

The gratuitous election, and the judicial reprobation of Jerusalem, are typical of the gratuitous election of the Israelites, and of their judicial reprobation. An account of their gratuitous election is set before the reader in the Essay on Scripture Calvinism. Here follows an account of their righteous reprobation: — "And it shall come to pass, if thou shalt hearken diligently to the voice of the Lord thy God, to observe all his commandments, that the Lord will set thee on high: all these blessings shall overtake thee; the Lord shall establish thee a holy people to himself, as he hath sworn to thee. But it shall come to pass, if thou wilt not hearken, &c, that all these curses shall overtake thee, &c. The Lord shall send upon thee cursing, until thou be destroyed, and until thou perish quickly, because of all the wickedness of thy doings, whereby thou hast forsaken me," Deuteronomy 28:20. Again: "See, I have set before thee life and good, and death and evil, in that I command thee to love the Lord thy God, that thou mayest live. But if thine heart turn away, &c, I denounce unto you this day, that ye shall surely perish," Deuteronomy 30:15, &c. Here are the decrees of God's judicial election and reprobation. According to these decrees, David says to his elect son, "Solomon, my son, serve the God of thy father with a willing mind. If thou seek him, he will be found of thee: but if thou forsake him, he will cast thee off for ever. Take heed now, for the Lord hath chosen thee to build a house," &c, 1 Chronicles 28:9. According to these decrees, "Because of all the provocations, &c,

the Lord said, I will remove Judah also out of my sight, as I have removed Israel, and I will cast off this city Jerusalem, which I have chosen, and the house, of which I said, My name shall be there," 2 Kings 23:26, 27.

It is only to defend the election and reprobation of justice that St. Paul says, "God hath not cast away his [believing, obedient] people whom he foreknew," that is, foreapproved as believing, and obedient: for, as there were seven thousand believing and obedient Jews, upon whom impartial justice smiled in the days of Jezebel, under the Jewish election of partial grace; "even so at this present time," adds the apostle, "there is a remnant" of such Jews under the Christian election of partial grace. That is, a number of Jews make their Christian election sure, not by the works of the Mosaic law, but by obedient faith in Christ. And even these obedient believers, in conjunction with the convened Gentiles, the apostle keeps in their duty by threatening them with reprobation of impartial justice. "Because of unbelief," says he, "they [the unbelieving Jews] were broken off, [that is, judicially reprobated,] and thou [Christian believer] standest by faith. Be not high minded, but fear. For if God spared not the natural branches; [so inflexible is his justice!] take heed lest he also spare not thee. Behold, therefore, the goodness and severity of God: on them that fell [the Jews elected through distinguishing grace] severity; but toward thee [a Christian, elected by distinguishing favour] goodness, if thou continue in his goodness, by continuing in the faith of Christ; otherwise thou shalt also be cut off," notwithstanding thy Christian election of distinguishing grace. "And they," notwithstanding their present reprobation of justice, which is occasioned by their unbelief, "if they abide not still in unbelief, shall be grafted in:" that is, if they make their Christian calling and election of grace sure by the obedience of faith, they shall be numbered among the rewardable elect, the elect that do not perish, the elect of justice as well as of grace, Romans 11:1-23.

The apostle frequently speaks the same anti-Calvinian language: take one or two more instances of it: "The end of those things is death," that is, final reprobation from life. "But, &c, ye have your fruit unto holiness, and the end [of this fruit is a judicial election to] everlasting life: for the wages of sin is death," that is, a judicial reprobation from life, "but the gift of God is eternal life through Jesus Christ:" an invaluable gift, which the Redeemer has procured, and which shall be judicially bestowed upon obedient, persevering believers, as the king's purses and plates, which are the mere gifts of his majesty, are equitably bestowed upon them that so run as to obtain the prize. And, therefore, "so run," says the apostle, "that ye may obtain an incorruptible crown. Be followers of me: I so run, &c, lest I myself should be cast away," according to the reprobation of justice, 1 Corinthians 9:24, &c.

The election and reprobation of partial grace depend entirely upon the wisdom and sovereignty of God. The great "Potter hath power over the clay, to make of the same lump vessels to honour, or to *comparative* dishonour," just as he pleases. As a supreme Benefactor, he had a right to raise the Jews above all nations, by calling them at the third hour into his enclosed vineyard. He could, without injustice, call the Corinthians at the sixth hour, and the English at the ninth hour. And if he call the Hottentots at the eleventh hour, they shall be entitled to the blessings of the richest election of grace, which are represented by the penny of the parable, as much as if they had been called as early as Abraham was; and had borne the burden and heat of the day as long as St. Paul and Cranmer did. I repeat it, with respect to the privileges of the covenants of promise made with the Jews and the Christians, which privileges our Lord sometimes calls his pence, and sometimes his talents; they are ours as soon as we are called, if we do but answer the call by going into the Lord's vineyard or field. This is what Christ condescends to call our hire for going into his Church militant — our hire bestowed according to the election of prevenient grace. But our eternal reward shall be given according to a very different rule, namely, according to the election of impartial justice. To secure this reward, we must not only go into the Lord's field, when we are called; but we must sow as we are directed. "Be not deceived," says the apostle when he stands up for the doctrines of justice; as God does not necessitate man by Calvinian decrees of finished reprobation, and then mock him by Arminian offers of salvation: so he "is not mocked: for whatsoever a man soweth, that shall he also reap. For he that soweth to his flesh, shall of the flesh [naturally and judicially] reap corruption and destruction: [the word has this double meaning in the original.] But he that soweth to the Spirit, shall of the Spirit reap life everlasting," both by natural and judicial consequence. "For the *moral* earth, which bringeth forth herbs meet for them by whom it is dressed, receiveth blessing from God:" ("Come, ye blessed, inherit the kingdom, &c, for I was hungry, and ye gave me meat.") "But that which beareth thorns and briers is rejected [reprobated] and is nigh unto cursing, whose end is to be burned," according to the fearful sentence, "Depart, ye cursed, into everlasting fire, for I was hungry and ye gave me no meat," &c, Galatians 6:7; Hebrews 6:7; Matthew 25:34, &c.

Well then might our Lord and St. Paul charge us to escape the reprobation, and secure the election of justice. How awful and anti-Calvinian are their directions! "Watch and pray always, that ye may be accounted worthy to escape all these *terrible* things, and to stand *rewardable* before the Son of man," Luke 21:36. "Whatsoever ye do, do it heartily, as to the Lord: knowing that of the Lord ye shall receive the reward of the inheritance," Colossians 3:24.

From these and a multitude of such scriptures it appears, that when the Calvinists overlook the impartial election and reprobation of distributive justice, they betray as much prejudice as the rigid Arminians do, when they deny the partial election and reprobation of distinguishing grace. There is, however, some difference between the extensiveness of their errors. If rigid Arminianism rejects the partial election and reprobation of distinguishing grace, it strenuously maintains the righteous election and reprobation of impartial justice; and, by this means, it preserves one half of the doctrines of the Bible in all their purity, namely, the doctrines of justice. But rigid, downright Calvinism equally spoils the doctrines of grace and the doctrines of justice: for it turns the holy doctrines of special grace into Solifidian doctrines of lawless grace: and, with respect to the doctrines of impartial justice, it totally demolishes them by allowing but of one eternal, absolute, partial, and personal election, which necessarily binds Christ's righteousness, and finished salvation, upon some men; and of one eternal, absolute, partial, and personal reprobation, which necessarily fastens Adam's unrighteousness, with finished damnation, upon all the rest of mankind. Now, according to these doctrines of partial grace and free wrath, it is evident that justice can no more be concerned in justifying or condemning, rewarding or punishing men under such circumstances, than you could be equitably concerned in crowning some men for swimming, and in burning others for sinking; supposing you had first bound the elected swimmers fast to an immense piece of cork, and tied a huge mill stone about the neck of the sinking reprobates. Hence it appears, that, although a Bible Christian may hold Pelagius' election and reprobation of justice, he can neither hold Calvin's one election of lawless grace, nor his one reprobation of free wrath.

But, while I bear my plain testimony against rigid Calvinism, I beg the reader to make a difference between that system and the good men who have embraced it. With joy I acknowledge that many Calvinist ministers have done much good in their generation. But whatever good they have done, was not done by their errors, but by the Gospel truths which they inconsistently mixed with their errors, and by God's overruling their mistakes. The doctrines of *distributive justice* belong no more to rigid Calvinism, than to Nero's private system of policy: but as good magistrates, even under Nero's authority, steadily punished vice, and rewarded virtue; so good men, who have the misfortune to be involved in rigid Calvinism, inconsistently deter men from sin by preaching the terrors of a sin-revenging God, and by pointing out the rewards of grace and glory, which await the faithful. Add to this, that by still holding out the law of God to the unawakened, though that kind of preaching is absurd upon their system, yet they do good, because, so far, they preach the doctrines of justice. And by preaching a "rule of life" to believers, they now and then meet with professors ingenuous enough to follow that rule. For, as there are even in Billingsgate persons cleanly enough to wash their hands, although their neighbours should constantly assure them that they can never get one speck of dirt off; that the king must do it all away himself in the day of his power; that, in the meantime, his majesty sees no dirt upon their hands, because he looks at them only through the hands of the prince of Wales, which are as white as snow, and the cleanness of which his majesty is pleased to impute to their dirty hands; and beside, that dirt will work for their good; will display the strength of their constitution; will set off, by and by, the cleansing virtue of soap and water; and will make dirty people sing louder at court, when the king's irresistible power, and their own deadly sweats, shall have cleansed their hands: as there are cleanly persons, I say, who would wash their hands notwithstanding such dirty hints as these; so there are some sincere souls among every denomination of Christians, who hate sin, and depart from it, notwithstanding all that some mistaken theologists may *say*, to make them continue in sin, in order that the graces of humility and of faith in the atoning blood, may be abundantly exercised.

Again: the rigid Arminians are greatly deficient in exalting God's partial grace, and the rich election which flows to Christian believers from this grace. Now when the Calvinists preach to Christians a gratuitous election of distinguishing grace, though they do not preach it aright, yet they say many things which border upon the truth; and by which God sometimes raises the gratitude and comforts of some of his people; overruling Calvin's mistakes to their consolation, as he overruled to our comfort the high priest's dreadful sentence: "Ye know nothing at all, nor consider that it is expedient for us, that one man should die for the people." Never did a prophet preach the atonement more clearly than Caiaphas does in these words. Just so do pious Calvinists preach the election of grace, and in the same manner is their preaching overruled to the comfort of some.

But alas! if this confused method of preaching election be indirectly helpful to a few, is it not directly pernicious to multitudes, whom it tempts to rise to the presumption of "Mr. Fulsome," or to sink to the despair of Francis Spira? Beside, would not doubting Christians be sufficiently cheered by the Scriptural doctrine of our election, as it is held forth in the Essay on Scripture Calvinism? Are those liquors best, which are made strong and heady by intoxicating and poisonous ingredients? Cannot the doctrine of our gratuitous election in Christ be comfortable, unless it be adulterated with Antinomianism, fatalism, Manicheism, and a reprobation, which necessarily drags most of our friends and neighbours into the bottomless pit? And might we not so preach our judicial election by Christ, and so point out the greatness of the helps, which the Gospel affords us to make our election sure, as to excite the careless to diligence without driving them upon the fatal rocks, with which the Solifidian Babel is surrounded?

From the preceding remarks it follows, that the error of rigid Calvinists centres in the denial of that evangelical liberty, whereby all men, under various dispensations of grace, may, without necessity, choose life in the day of their initial salvation. And the error of rigid Arminians consists in not paying a cheerful homage to redeeming grace, for all the liberty and power which we have to choose life, and to work righteousness since the fall. Did the followers of Calvin see the necessary connection there is between the freedom of our will, and the distributive justice of God our Judge, they would instantly renounce the errors of Calvinian necessity, and rigid bound will. And did the rigid followers of Arminius discover the inseparable union there is, since the fall, between our free agency to good, and the free redeeming grace of God our Saviour, they would readily give up the errors of Pharisaical self sufficiency and rigid free will.

To avoid equally these two extremes, we need only follow the Scripture doctrine of free will restored and assisted by free grace. According to this doctrine, in order to repent, believe, or obey, we stand in need of a talent of power "to will and to do." God, of his good pleasure, gives us this talent for Christ's sake; and our liberty consists in not being necessitated to make a good or bad use of this talent, to the end of our life. But we must remember that, as this precious talent comes entirely from redeeming grace, so the right use of it is first of redeeming grace, and next of our own unnecessitated, though assisted free will; whereas the wrong use of it is of our own choice only; an unnecessitated choice, which constitutes us legally punishable, as our right, unnecessitated choice of offered life (through God's gracious appointment) constitutes us evangelically rewardable.

Hence it follows that our accepted time, or day of salvation begun, has but one cause, namely, the mercy of God in Christ: whereas our continued and eternal salvation has two causes. The first of which is a primary and proper cause, namely, "the mercy of God in Christ;" the second is a secondary or improper cause, or, if you please, a condition, namely, "the works of faith." Nor do some Calvinists scruple, any more than we, to call these works a cause, improperly speaking. Only, like physicians, who write their prescriptions in Latin, to keep their ignorant patients in the dark, they call it *Causa sine qua non;* that is, in plain English, a cause, which, if it be absent, absolutely hinders an effect from taking place. Thus a mother is not the primary cause of her child's conception, but *causa sine qua non;* that is, such a cause as, if it had been wanting, would have absolutely prevented his being conceived

If the Calvinists will speak the truth in Latin, I will speak it in plain English. And therefore, standing up still as a witness of the marriage between prevenient free grace, and obedient free will; (an evangelical marriage this, which I have proved in the Scripture Scales;) I assert, upon the arguments contained in these two Essays, that our eternal salvation depends, *first*, on God's free grace, and *secondly*, on our practical submission to the doctrines of grace and justice; or, if you please, on our making our election of grace and justice sure by faith and its works.

To be a little more explicit: our day of salvation begun is merely of free grace, and prevents all faith and works; since all saving faith, and all good works, flow from a beginning of free salvation. But this is not the case with our continued and eternal salvation: for this salvation depends upon the concurrence of two causes; the first of which is prevenient and assisting free grace, which I beg leave to call the father cause; and the second is submissive and obedient free will, which I take the liberty to call the mother cause. And I dare say that the Pelagians will as soon find on earth an adult man who came into the world without a father; and that the Calvinists will as soon find one who was born without a mother, as they will find an adult person in heaven, who came there without the concurrence of free grace and free will, which I beg leave to call the paternal and maternal causes of our eternal salvation. And therefore, while the rigid Arminians and the rigid Calvinists make two partial, solitary, barren gospels, by parting mercy and justice, free grace and free will, let Bible Christians stand up, in theory and practice, for the one entire Gospel of Christ. Let them marry preventing and assisting free grace with prevented and assisted free will; so shall they consistently hold the two Gospel axioms, and evangelically maintain the doctrines of grace and justice, which are all suspended on the partial election and reprobation of distinguishing grace, and on the impartial election and reprobation of remunerative justice.

Till we do this, we shall spoil the Gospel, by confounding the dispensations of Divine grace; we shall grieve those whom God has not grieved, and comfort those whom God would not have comforted; we shall involve the truth in clouds of darkness; and availing ourselves of that darkness, we shall separate what God has joined, and join what he has separated; causing the most unnatural divisions and monstrous mixtures, and doing in the doctrinal world what the fallen Corinthian did in the moral, when he tore his mother from his father's bosom, and made her his own incestuous wife. In a word, we shall tear the impartial election of justice from the partial election of grace; and according to our Pelagian or Augustinian taste, we shall espouse the one, and fight against the other. If we embrace only the election of impartial justice, we shall propagate proud, dull, and uncomfortable Pelagianism. And if we embrace only the election of partial grace, we shall propagate wanton Antinomianism, and wanton cruelty, or absolute election to, and absolute reprobation from eternal life. We shall generate the conceits of finished salvation and finished damnation, which are the upper and lower parts of the doctrinal syren, whom Dr. Crisp mistook for the Gospel; the head and the tail of the evangelical chimera, which Calvin supposed to have sprung from "the Lion of the tribe of Judah." But, if we equally receive the election of grace and that of justice, we shall have the whole truth, as it is in Jesus — the chaste woman, who stands "in heaven clothed with the sun, and having the moon [Pelagian changes and Calvinian innovations] under her feet." Nor will candid Christians be offended at her having two breasts, to give her children "the sincere milk of the word;" and two arms, to defend herself against Pelagianism and Calvinism, the obstinate errors which attack her on the right hand and on the left.

She has put forth her two arms in these two Essays; and, if her adversaries do not resist her, as the Jews did Stephen by stopping their ears, it is to be hoped that some of them will impartially renounce the errors of heated Pelagius and heated Augustine, and will honour Christ both as their Saviour and their Judge, by equally embracing the doctrines of grace and the doctrines of justice.

SECTION V.

Inferences from the two Essays.

IF the preceding Essays on Bible Calvinism and Bible Arminianism are agreeable to Scripture and reason, I may sum up their contents m some inferences, the justness of which will, I humbly hope, recommend itself to the reader's good understanding and candour: —

I. The doctrine of a *gratuitous, partial, and personal* election and reprobation is truly Scriptural. So far Calvinism is nothing but the Gospel. On the other hand, the doctrine of a *judicial, impartial,* and *conditional* election and reprobation is perfectly Scriptural also: and so far Arminianism is nothing but the Gospel. For, as light flows from the sun, so Bible Calvinism does from the first Gospel axiom, (our salvation is of God,) and as a river flows from its source, so Bible Arminianism does from the second Gospel axiom, (our destruction is of ourselves.) Confounding these two axioms and elections, or denying one of them, has greatly injured the doctrines of grace and justice, darkened all the Gospel dispensations, and bred the misunderstandings which formerly subsisted between the followers of Augustine and those of Pelagius, and now subsist between the Calvinists and the Arminians.

II. It is absurd to ridicule the doctrine of a twofold election, under pretence that it flows from what some people are pleased to call "the flights of my romantic pen;" since the full tide of Scripture evidently flows in two channels; an election of partial grace, according to which God grants or denies his primary favours, as a SOVEREIGN BENEFACTOR; and an election of impartial justice, according to which he bestows rewards or inflicts punishments, as a SUPREME JUDGE.

III. Nor does this doctrine deserve to be called *new*, since it is so manifestly found in the oldest book in the world. An objection drawn from the seeming novelty of these observations, would be peculiarly unreasonable in the mouth of a member of the Church of England; because she indirectly points out the distinction which I contend for. That our reformers had some insight into the doctrine of a partial election of grace in Christ, and of an impartial election of justice through Christ, appears, I think, from the standard writings of our Church. The beginning of her seventeenth article evidently countenances our unconditional election of grace in Christ, while the latter part secures the doctrines of our conditional election of justice through Christ. Few Calvinists will be so prejudiced as to deny that our Church guards the doctrines, and consequently the election of justice in this important paragraph: — "Furthermore, we must receive God's promises in such wise as they are generally set forth in Holy Scripture." Now the promises being generally set forth in a conditional manner in God's word, it is evident that our Church, in giving us this caution and charge, intends to secure the conditionality of the election of justice; the conditionality of this election being inseparably connected with the conditionality of

God's promises; just as the conditionality of the reprobation of justice is inseparably connected with the conditionality of God's threatenings.

In conformity to this doctrine our Church assures us, in her homily on good works, "If he [the elected thief] had lived, and not regarded faith and the works thereof, he would have lost his salvation again:" or, which comes to the same thing, he would have forfeited his election of partial grace, by losing the election of impartial justice. Our liturgy speaks the same language; witness that prayer in the office of baptism: "Grant that these children [or persons] now to be baptized, &c, may ever remain in the number of thy faithful and elect children, through Jesus Christ our Lord." That is, grant that these persons, who are now admitted into thy Christian Church, according to the election of grace in Christ, may so believe and obey, as never to forfeit the privileges of this election, but may ever share in the privileges of thy faithful children who are elect in every sense of the word; the obedient being the only persons who keep their part in the election of grace, and secure a share in the election of justice. Such complete elect are the "sheep" which "hear Christ's voice, and follow his" steps. "None shall pluck them out of his hands." The talent of their election of grace shall never be taken from them: they shall all hear these cheering words: "Well done, thou good and faithful servant!" They shall all "enter into the joy of their Lord," and eternally share in the double privileges of the election of grace and justice.

IV. The gratuitous, partial election and reprobation, which the Scriptures maintain, chiefly refer to the three grand covenants which God has made with man, and to the greater or less blessings which belong to these covenants. The first of these covenants takes in all mankind; for it was made with spared Adam after the fall, and confirmed to preserved Noah after the flood; and every body knows that Adam and Noah are the two general parents of all mankind. The second of these covenants was made with Abraham, ratified to Isaac and Jacob, ordained in the hands of Moses, and ordered in all things, and peculiarly insured to David. This covenant takes in the first peculiar people of God, or the Jewish nation; and includes more particularly David and his family, of which the Messiah was to be born. The third of these covenants was made with Christ, as "the Captain of our salvation," and "the High Priest of our profession," or dispensation; and takes in God's "most peculiar people," or the Christian Church. The first of these three covenants is general. The other two are covenants of peculiarity, the former of which is frequently called, in Scripture, the old covenant, or the Old Testament, while the latter is spoken of by the name of the new covenant, or New Testament. The two first of these covenants were sealed with the blood of sacrificed beasts or circumcised men, but the last was sealed with the blood of the Lamb of God. Hence our Lord termed it "the new covenant in my blood," Luke 22:20, calling his blood, "my blood of the New Testament," Matthew 26:28. Hence also the apostle observes, that "Jesus was made a surety of a better Testament," and that "he is the Mediator of the New Testament," which is far superior to that which "was ordained by angels in the hand of Moses," the mediator of the Old Testament: see Hebrews 7:22; 9:15; 12:24; 2 Corinthians 3:6; Galatians 3:19.

V. These three grand covenants give birth to *Gentilism, Judaism,* and *Christianity;* three Divine religions, or dispensations of grace, from the confounding of which partial divines have formed the schemes of religion, which I beg leave to call *rigid* Arminianism, and *rigid* Calvinism.

VI. The error of rigid Arminians, with respect to those three grand covenants, consists in not sufficiently distinguishing them, and in not maintaining, with sufficient plainness, that they are all covenants of redeeming grace; that Judaism is the old covenant of partial, redeeming grace; and that Christianity is the new covenant of partial, redeeming grace.

VII. The error of rigid Calvinists consists in confounding the covenants of creating and redeeming grace, and in reducing them all to two: the one a covenant of non-redemption, which they call "the law," and the other a covenant of particular redemption, which they call "the Gospel." To form the first of these unscriptural covenants, they jumble the Creator's law, given to innocent man in paradise, with the Redeemer's law, given to the Israelites on Mount Sinai. Nor do they see that these two laws, or covenants, are as different from each other, as a covenant made with sinless man, without a priest, a sacrifice, and a mediator, is different from a covenant made with sinful man, and "ordained in the hand of a Mediator," with an interceding priest, and atoning sacrifices, Galatians 3:19. Secondly, they suppose that all men now born into the world are under this imaginary law, that is, under this unscriptural, confused mixture of the Adamic law of innocence, and of the Mosaic law of Sinai: an error this, which is so much the more glaring, as no man, except Christ, was ever placed under the covenant of innocence, since the Lord entered into a mediatorial covenant with fallen Adam: and no man has been put under the law, or covenant of Moses, from the time that covenant was "abolished, and done away in Christ," 2 Corinthians 3:7, 14, which happened when Christ said, "It is finished," and when "the veil of the temple," a type of the Jewish dispensation, "was rent from top to bottom."

So capital an error, as that of the rigid Calvinists about the law, could not but be productive of a similar error about the Gospel. And therefore when they had formed the merciless covenant which they call the law, by confounding the precept and curse of the law of innocence, with the precept and curse of the law of Moses, abstracted from all mediatorial promises; when they had done this, I say, it was natural enough for them to mistake and confound the promises of the three grand covenants, which I have just mentioned; I mean the one general covenant of grace, made with Adam and Noah; and the two particular covenants of grace, the former of which was "ordained in the hands of Moses, the servant of God," and the latter in the hands of "Christ, the only begotten Son of God." Hence it is, that overlooking the promises of the general covenant of grace, and considering only the promises of Judaism and Christianity, which are two grand covenants of peculiar grace, the rigid Calvinists fancy that there is but* one covenant of grace: that this covenant is particular; that it was made with Christ only; that it was a covenant of unchangeable favour on the part of the Father, of eternal redemption on the part of the Son, and of irresistible sanctification on the part of the Holy Ghost; that some men, called the elect, are

---

* Zelotes will possibly laugh at the insinuation that there is more than one covenant of grace. If he does, I will ask him if a covenant of grace is not the same thing as a covenant of promise; and if St. Paul does not expressly mention "the covenants of promise," Ephesians 2:12, and a "better covenant," which was "established upon better promises" than the first [particular] covenant of promise? Hebrews 8:6, 7

absolutely and eternally interested in this covenant; that other men, called the reprobates, are absolutely and everlastingly excluded from it; that finished salvation, through Christ, is the unavoidable lot of the fortunate elect, who are supposed to be under the absolute blessing of a lawless Gospel; and that finished damnation, through Adam, is the unavoidable portion of the unfortunate reprobates, who are supposed to be, from their mother's womb, under the absolute, irreversible, everlasting curse of a merciless law, and of an absolutely Christless covenant.

VIII. We may say to rigid Calvinists, and rigid Arminians, what God said once to the Jewish priests: "Ye have been partial in the law," Malachi 2:9. Nor is it possible to reduce their two partial systems to the genuine and full standard of the Gospel, otherwise than by consistently guarding the Calvinian doctrines of grace, by the Arminian doctrines of justice; and the Arminian doctrines of justice, by the Calvinian doctrines of grace: when these two partial gospels are joined in a Scriptural manner, they do not destroy, but balance and illustrate each other. Take away from them human additions, or supply their deficiencies, and you will restore them to their original importance. They will again form the spiritual "weights of the sanctuary," which are kept for public use in the sacred records, as I humbly hope I have made appear in the Scripture Scales.

IX. To guard the Gospel against the errors of the rigid Calvinists, and the rigid Arminians, we need then only show that God, as Creator, Redeemer, and Sanctifier, has a right to be, and actually is partial in the distribution of grace; but that as Lawgiver, Governor, and Judge, he is, and ever will be, impartial in the distribution of justice: or, which comes to the same thing, we need only restore the doctrine of God's various laws, or covenants of grace, to their Scripture lustre. Rigid Calvinism will be lost in Bible Arminianism, and rigid Arminianism will be lost in Bible Calvinism, as soon as Protestants will pay a due regard to the following truths: (1.) God, for Christ's sake, dissolved, with respect to us, the covenant of paradisiacal innocence, when he turned man out of a forfeited paradise into this cursed world, for having broken that covenant. Then it was that man's Creator first became his Redeemer; then mankind were placed under the first mediatorial covenant of promise. Then our Maker gave to Adam, and to all the human species, which was in Adam's loins, a Saviour, who is called "the seed of the woman, — the Lamb slain from the foundation of the world," who was to make the paradisiacal covenant honourable by his sinless obedience. (2.) Accordingly, "Christ, by the grace of God, tasted death for every man;" purchasing for all men the privileges of the general covenant of grace, which God made with Adam, and ratified to Noah, the second general parent of mankind. (3.) Christ, according to the peculiar predestination and election of God, peculiarly tasted death for the Jews, his first chosen nation and peculiar people; purchasing for them all the privileges of the peculiar covenant of grace, which the Scriptures call the old covenant of peculiarity. (4.) That Christ, according to the most peculiar predestination and election of God, most peculiarly tasted death for the Christians, his second chosen nation and most peculiar people; procuring for them the invaluable privileges of his own most precious Gospel, "by which he has brought life and immortality to *meridian* light;" and has richly supplied the defects of the Noahic and Mosaic dispensations; the first of which is noted for its darkness; and the second for its veils and shadows. And lastly, that with respect to these peculiar privileges, Christ is said to have peculiarly "given himself for the

Christian Church, that he might cleanse it with the *baptismal* washing of water by the word," Ephesians 5:26; peculiarly "purchasing it by his own blood," Acts 20:28; and delivering it from heathenish darkness, and Jewish shadows, that it might be "redeemed from all iniquity," and that his Christian people might be a "peculiar people to himself, zealous of good works," even above the Jews who "fear God," and the Gentiles who "work righteousness," Titus 2:14.

X. As soon as we understand the nature of "the covenants of promise," and the doctrine of the dispensations of Divine grace, we have a key to open the mystery of God's gratuitous election and reprobation. We can easily understand, that when a man is elected only to the general blessings of Gentilism, he is reprobated from the blessings peculiar to Judaism and Christianity; and that when he is elected to the blessings of Christianity, he is elected to inherit the substance of all the covenanted blessings of God, because the highest dispensation takes in the inferior ones; as the authority of a colonel includes that of a lieutenant and a captain; or as meridian light takes in the dawn of day and the morning light.

XI. Our election from Gentilism or Judaism to the blessings of Christianity, is an election of peculiar grace. It is to be hoped, that few Arminians are so unreasonable as to think that God might not have deprived us of New Testament blessings, as he did Moses; and of Old Testament blessings, as he did Noah; leaving us under the general covenant of Gentilism, as he did that patriarch.

XII. When God gratuitously elected and called the Jews to be his peculiar people, and chosen nation, he reprobated all the other nations, that is, all the Gentiles, from that honour; an unspeakable honour this, which the Jews thought God had appropriated to them for ever. But when Christ formed his Church, he elected to its privileges the Gentiles as well as the Jews; insomuch that, to enter into actual possession of all the blessings of Christianity, when a Jew or Gentile is called by the preaching of the Gospel of Christ, nothing more is required of him, than to "make his *free* calling and election sure," by "the obedience of faith." That God had a right to extend his election of peculiar grace to the believing Gentiles, and to reprobate the unbelieving Jews, is the point which St. Paul chiefly labours in Romans 9. And that the privileges of this election, which God has extended to the Gentiles, are immensely great, is what the apostle informs us of in the three first chapters of his Epistle to the Ephesians.

XIII. Our election to Christianity, and its peculiar blessings, being entirely gratuitous, and preceding every work of Christian obedience; nothing can be more absurd and unevangelical, than to rest it upon works of any sort. Hence it is, that when St. Paul maintains the partial election of richest grace, he says, speaking of the Jews, "There is [among them] a remnant according to the election of grace." That is, "There is a considerable number of Jews, who, like myself, make their gratuitous calling and election to the blessings of Christianity sure through faith." For wherever there were Jews and Gentiles, the Jews had the honour of the first call: so far was God from absolutely reprobating them from his Christian "covenant of promise!" If you ask, why the apostle calls this election to the blessings of Christianity "the election of grace," I answer, that it peculiarly deserves this name, because it is both peculiarly gracious, and amazingly gratuitous. And therefore, adds the apostle, "if *this election* is by *mere* grace, then it is no more of works; otherwise grace is no more *mere* grace. But if it be of works, then it is no more of *mere* grace: otherwise work is no more work," Romans 11:5, 6.*

XIV. If the rigid Arminians are culpable for being ashamed of God's evangelical partiality, for overlooking his distinguishing love, and for casting a veil over his election of grace; the rigid Calvinists are not less blamable, for turning that holy election into an unscriptural and absolute election, which leaves no room for the propriety of making our "election sure," and is attended with an unscriptural and absolute reprobation, as odious as free wrath, and as dreadful as insured damnation. This merciless and absolute reprobation is the fundamental error of the rigid Papists, as well as of the rigid Calvinists. Take away this popish principle, "There is no salvation out of the Church: a damning reprobation rests upon all who die out of her pale;" and down comes persecuting popery. There is no pretext left to force popish errors upon men by fire, faggots, or massacres; and the burning of heretics gives place to the charity which hopeth all things. Again: take away this principle of the rigid Calvinists, "There is absolutely no redemption, no salvation, but for a remnant according to the new covenant, and the election of God's partial grace; an absolute reprobation, and an unavoidable damnation, rest upon all mankind beside;" take away, I say, this principle of the rigid Calvinists, and down comes unscriptural Calvinism, with all the contentions which it perpetually begets.

XV. The rigid Papists, who set up themselves as defenders of the doctrines of justice, and yet hold popish reprobation, are full as inconsistent as the rigid Calvinists, who come forward as defenders of the doctrines of grace, and yet hold Calvinian reprobation: for popish and Calvinian reprobation equally confound the Gospel dispensations, and leave Divine justice and grace neither root nor branch, with respect to all those who die unacquainted with Christianity, that is, with respect to far the greatest part of mankind.

XVI. To conclude: Milton says somewhere, "There is a certain scale of duties, a certain hierarchy of upper and lower commands, which for want of studying in right order, all the world is in confusion." What that great man said of the scale of duties and commands, may with equal propriety be affirmed of the scale of evangelical truths, and the hierarchy of upper and lower Gospel dispensations. For want of studying them in right order, all the Church is in confusion. The most effectual, not to say the only way of ending these theological disputes of Christians, and destroying the errors of levelling Pelagianism, Antinomian Calvinism, confused Arminianism, and reprobating popery, is to restore primitive harmony and fulness to the partial gospels of the day; which can be done with ease, among candid and judicious

---

* My light and theological accuracy have, I hope, increased since I wrote the sermon on these words. I did not then clearly see that the election of grace, of which the apostle speaks in this verse, is our gratuitous election to the blessings of Christianity as it is opposed to Judaism, and not merely as it is opposed to the Adamic covenant of works. I had not then sufficiently considered these words of St. John: — "The law [that is, the Jewish dispensation] came by Moses, but grace and truth [that is, a more gracious and brighter dispensation] "came by Jesus Christ." Hence it follows, that this expression, "the election of grace," when a sacred writer speaks of the Jewish and of the Christian dispensations, which St. Paul does throughout this part of his Epistle to the Romans, means our gratuitous election to Christianity, or to the peculiar blessings of the Gospel of Christ.

inquirers after truth, by placing the doctrine of the dispensations in its Scripture light; and by holding forth the doctrines of grace and justice in all their evangelical brightness. This has been attempted in the two Essays from which these inferences are drawn. Whether the well-meant attempt shall be successful with respect to one, is a question, which thy reason and candour, gentle reader, are called upon to decide.

SECTION VI.

The plan of a general reconciliation and union between the moderate Calvinists and the candid Arminians.

BY the junction of the doctrines of grace and justice, which, I hope, is effected in the two Essays on Bible Calvinism and Bible Arminianism, the Gospel of Christ recovers its original fulness and glory, and the two Gospel axioms are equally secured: for, on the one hand, the absolute sovereignty and partial goodness of our Creator and Redeemer shine as the meridian blaze of day, without casting the least shade upon his truth and equity: you have an election of free grace, without a reprobation of free wrath. And, on the other hand, the impartial justice of our Governor and Judge appears like an unspotted sun, whose brightness is perfectly consistent with the transcendent splendour of free grace and distinguishing love. The elect receive "the reward of the inheritance" with feelings of pleasing wonder and shouts of humble praise. Nor have the reprobates the least ground to say, that the Judge of all the earth does not do right, and that they are lost merely because irresistible power necessitated them to sin by Adam without remedy, that they might be damned by Christ without possibility of escape. Thus the gracious and righteous ways of God with man are equally vindicated, and the whole controversy terminates in the following conclusion, which is the ground of the reconciliation, to which moderate Calvinists and candid Arminians are invited.

Bible Calvinism and Bible Arminianism are two essential opposite parts of the Gospel, which agree as perfectly together as two wings of a palace, the opposite ramparts of a regular fortress, and the different views of a fine face, considered by persons who stand, some on the right and some on the left hand of the beauty who draws their attention. Rigid Calvinists* and rigid Arminians* are both in the wrong;

---

* Rigid Calvinists are persons who hold the Manichean doctrine of absolute necessity, and maintain both an unconditional election of free grace in Christ, and an unconditional reprobation of free wrath in Adam. Moderate Calvinists are men who renounce the doctrine of absolute necessity, stand up for the election of free grace, and are ashamed of the reprobation of free wrath. Rigid Arminians are persons who will not hear of an unconditional election, make more of free will than of free grace, oppose God's gracious sovereignty, deny his partiality, and condemn Calvinism in an unscriptural manner. Candid Arminians are people who mildly contend for the doctrines of justice, and are willing to hear with candour what the judicious Calvinists have to say in defence of the doctrines of grace. In my Preparatory Essay, I

the former in obscuring the doctrines of impartial justice, and the latter in clouding the doctrines of partial grace: but moderate Calvinists* and candid Arminians* are very near each other, and very near the truth; the difference there is between them being more owing to confusion, want of proper explanation, and misapprehension of each other's sentiments, than to any real, inimical opposition to the truth, or to one another. And therefore, they have no more reason to fall out with each other, than masons who build the opposite wings of the same building; soldiers, who defend the opposite sides of the same fortification; painters, who take different views of the same face; or loyal subjects, who vindicate different, but equally just claims of their royal master.

Since there is so immaterial a difference between the moderate Calvinists and the candid Arminians, why do they keep at such distance from each other? Why do they not publicly give one another the right hand of fellowship, and let all the world know that they are brethren, and will henceforth own, love, help, and defend each other as such? That no essential difference keeps them asunder, I prove by the following argument: —

If candid Arminians will make no material objection to my Essay on Bible Calvinism; and if judicious Calvinists will not condemn my Essay on Bible Arminianism as unscriptural, it is evident that the difference between them is not capital, and that it arises rather from want of light to see the whole truth clearly, than from an obstinate enmity to any material part of the truth.

Nor is this a sentiment peculiar to myself: I hold it in common with some of the most public defenders of the doctrines of grace and justice. The Arminians will not

---

have expressed myself as one, who sometimes doubts whether Arminius did see the doctrine of election in a clear light. It may be proper to account here for a degree of seeming inconsistency into which this transient doubt has betrayed me. Having been long ill, and at a distance from my books, I have not lately looked into Arminius' Works; nor did I ever read them carefully through, as every one should have done, who positively condemns or clears him. And if I have somewhere positively said, that he was not clear in the doctrine of election, I did it, (1.) Because I judged of Arminius' doctrine by that of the Arminians, who seem to me to be in general (as I had been for years) unacquainted with the distinction between the election of grace and that of justice. (2.) Because, at the synod of Dort, the Arminians absolutely refused to debate first the point of election, which the Calvinists wanted them to do. Whence I concluded that Arminius had not placed that point of doctrine in a light strong enough to expel the darkness which rigid Calvinists had spread over it. And, (3.) Because it is generally supposed that Arminius leaned to the error of Pelagius, who did not do justice to the election of grace. Mr. Bayle, for example, in his life of Arminius, says, "Arminius condemned the Supralapsarian Beza, and afterward acknowledged no other election than that which was grounded on the obedience of sinners to the call of God by Jesus Christ." If this account of Mr. Bayle be just, it is evident that Arminius, as well as Pelagius, admitted only the election of justice. However, a candid clergyman, who has read Arminius, assures me that in some parts of his writings, he does justice to the unconditional election of grace. And indeed this election is so conspicuous in the Scriptures, that it is hard to conceive it should never have been discovered by so judicious a divine as Arminius is said to have been. The difficulty in this matter is not to meet and salute the truth now and then, but to hold her fast, and walk steadily with her, across all the mazes of error. The light of evangelists should not break forth now and then, as a flash of lightning does out of a dark cloud; but it should shine constantly, and with increasing lustre, as the light of the eclipsed sun.

think that Mr. J. Wesley is partial to the Calvinists, and the professing world is no stranger to Mr. Rowland Hill's zeal against the Arminians. Nothing can be more opposite than the religious principles of these two gentlemen. Nevertheless, they both agree to place the doctrines which distinguish pious Calvinists from pious Arminians, among the opinions which are not essential to genuine, vital, practical Christianity. Mr. Wesley, in his thirteenth Journal, page 115, says, in a letter to a friend, "You have admirably well expressed what I mean by an opinion, contradistinguished from an essential doctrine. Whatever is compatible with love to Christ, and a work of grace, I term an opinion, and certainly the holding particular election and final perseverance is compatible with these." What he adds in the next rage is perfectly agreeable to this candid concession: "Mr. H —— and Mr. N —— hold this, and yet I believe these have real Christian experience. But if so, this is only an opinion: it is not subversive [here is clear proof to the contrary] of the very foundations of Christian experience. It is compatible with love to Christ, and a genuine work of grace; yea, many hold it, at whose feet I desire to be found in the day of the Lord Jesus. If then I oppose this with my whole strength, I am a mere bigot still." As Mr. Wesley candidly grants here that persons may hold the Calvinian opinions which Mr. Hill patronizes, and yet be full of love to Christ, and have a genuine work of grace on their souls; so Mr. Hill, in his late publication, entitled, *A Full Answer to the Rev. J. Wesley's Remarks,* page 42, candidly acknowledges that it is possible to hold Mr. Wesley's Arminian principles, and yet to be serious, converted, and sound in Christian experience. His words are: "As for the serious and converted part of Mr. Wesley's congregation, as I by no means think it necessary for any to be what are commonly called Calvinists, in order that they may be Christians, I can most solemnly declare, however they may judge of me, that I love and honour them not a little; as I am satisfied that many who are muddled in their judgments are sound in their experience." These two quotations do honour to the moderation of the popular preachers from whose writings they are extracted. May all the pious Arminians and Calvinists abide by their decisions! So shall they find that nothing parts them but unessential opinions; that they are joined by their mutual belief of the essential doctrines of the Gospel; and therefore, that if they oppose each other with their whole strength, they are "mere bigots still."

To conclude this reconciling argument: if there be numbers of holy souls, who are utter strangers to the peculiarities of rigid Calvinism and rigid Arminianism; if both the Calvinists and the Arminians can produce a cloud of witnesses, that their opinions are consistent with the most genuine piety, and the most extensive usefulness; if there have been many excellent men on both sides of the question, who (their opponents being judges) have lived in the work of faith, suffered with the patience of hope, and died in the triumph of love; and if, at this very day, we can find, among the clergy and laity, Calvinists and Arminians, who adorn their Christian profession by a blameless conduct, and by constant labours for the conversion of sinners, or the edification of saints, and who, the Lord being their helper, are ready to seal the truth of Christianity with their blood; if this, I say, has been, and is still the case, is it not indubitable that people may be good Christians, whether they embrace the opinions of Calvin, or those of Arminius; and by consequence, that neither rigid Calvinism nor rigid Arminianism are any essential part of Christianity?

And shall we make so much of nonessentials, as, on their account, to damp, and perhaps extinguish the flame of love, which is the most important of all the essentials of Christianity? Alas! what is all faith good for: yea, all faith adorned with the "knowledge of all *doctrines and* mysteries," if it be not attended by charity? It may indeed help us to "speak with the tongues of men and angels," to preach like apostles, and talk like seraphs; but, after all, it will leave us mere cyphers, or at best a "sounding brass," a pompous nothing in the sight of the God of love. And therefore, as we would not keep ourselves out of the kingdom of God, which consists in "love, peace, and joy;" and as we would not promote the interests of the kingdom of darkness, by carrying the fire of discord in our bosoms, and filling our vessels with the "waters of strife," which so many foolish virgins prefer to the "oil of gladness," let us promote peace with all our might. Let us remember, that, "in all Churches of the saints, God is the author of peace; that his Gospel is the Gospel of peace;" that "he hath called us to peace; and that the fruit of righteousness is sown in peace of them that make peace." Let us "study to be quiet; following peace with all men;" and "pursuing *especially* those things which make for peace in the household of faith:" nor let us turn from the blessed pursuit, till we have attained the blessing offered to peace makers.

"The kingdom" of love, peace, and joy, "suffereth violence:" it cannot be taken and kept, without great and constant endeavours. The violent alone are able to conquer it; for it is taken by the force of earnest prayer to God, for his blessing upon our overtures of peace; and by the vehemence of importunate requests to our brethren, that they would grant us an interest in their forgiving love, and admit us, for Christ's sake, to the honour of union, and pleasure of communion with them. It is an important part of "the good fight of faith working by love," to attack the unloving prejudices of our brethren, with a meekness of wisdom which turneth away wrath; with a patience of hope which a thousand repulses cannot beat off; with a perseverance of love which taketh no denial; and with an ardour of love which floods of contempt cannot abate. May God hasten the time when all the soldiers of Christ shall so learn and practise this part of the Christian exercise, as to overcome the bigotry of their brethren! Nor let us think that this is impossible: for if the love of Christ has conquered us, why should we despair of its conquering others? And if the unjust judge, who neither feared God, nor regarded man, was nevertheless overcome by the importunity of a poor widow, why should we doubt of overcoming, by the same means, our fellow Christians who fear God, rejoice in Christ, regard men, and love their brethren? Let us only convince them by every Christian method, that we are their brethren indeed, and we shall find most of them far more ready to return our love, than we have found them ready to return our provocations or indifference.

Should it be asked, What are those Christian methods, by which we could persuade our Calvinian or Arminian brethren, that we are their brethren indeed? I answer, that all these methods centre in these few Scriptural directions: — "Be not overcome of evil, but overcome evil with good." Love your opponents, though they should "despitefully use you." "Bless them," though they should "curse you." "Pray for them," though they should "persecute you." Wait upon them, and salute them as brethren, though they should keep at as great a distance from you, as if you were their enemies: "for if ye show love to them who show love to you, what reward have ye? Do not even the publicans the same? And if ye salute your brethren only," who kindly salute you, "what do ye more than others? Do not even the publicans so?" But treat them as God treats us: so shall you "be the children of your Father, who is in heaven, for he maketh his sun to rise, and sendeth his rain upon us all. Be ye therefore perfect, even as he is perfect." No bigot ever observed these Gospel directions. And it is only by observing them that we can break the bars of party spirit; and pass from the close confinement of bigotry, into the "glorious liberty" of brotherly love.

These scriptures were probably before the eyes of a laborious minister of Christ, when he drew up, some years ago, a plan of union among the clergymen of the Established Church, who agree in these essentials: "(1.) Original sin. (2.) Justification by faith. (3.) Holiness of heart and life; provided their life be answerable to their doctrines." This plan is as follows: — "But what union would you desire among these? Not a union of opinions. They might agree or disagree, touching absolute decrees on the one hand, and perfection on the other. Not a union in expression. These may still speak of the imputed righteousness, and those of the merits of Christ. Not a union with regard to outward order. Some may still remain quite regular; some quite irregular; and some partly regular, and partly irregular." Not a union of societies. Some who do not see the need of discipline, may still labour without forming any society at all: others may have a society, whose members are united by the bands of a lax discipline. And others, who have learned by experience that professors can never be kept long together without the help of a strict discipline, may strengthen their union with those who are like minded, by agreeing to observe such rules as appear to them most conducive to the purposes of Divine and brotherly love. "But these things being as they are, as each is persuaded in his own mind, is it not a most desirable thing that we should first remove hinderances out of the way? Not judge one another, not envy one another? Not be displeased with one another's gifts or success, even though greater than our own? Never wait for one another's halting; much less wish for it, or rejoice therein? Never speak disrespectfully, slightly, coldly, or unkindly of each other? Never repeat each other's faults, mistakes, or infirmities; much less listen for and gather them up? Never say or do any thing to hinder each other's usefulness, either directly or indirectly? Is it not a most desirable thing, that we should, secondly, love as brethren? Think well of, and honour one another? Wish all good, all grace, all gifts, all success, yea, greater than our own, to each other? Expect God will answer our wish, rejoice in every appearance thereof, and praise him for it? Readily believe good of each other, as readily as we once believed evil? Speak respectfully, honourably, kindly of each other? Defend each other's character: speak all the good we can of each other: recommend one another, where we have influence: each help the other on in his work, and enlarge his influence by all the honest means we can?"

I do not see why such a plan might not be, in some degree, admitted by all the ministers of the Gospel, whether they belong to, or dissent from, the Establishment. I would extend my brotherly love to all Christians in general, but more particularly to all Protestants, and most particularly to all the Protestants of the Established Church, with whom I am joined by repeated subscriptions to the same articles of religion, by oaths of canonical obedience, by the same religious rites, by the use of the same liturgy, by the same prerogatives, and by the fullest share of civil and religious liberty. But God forbid that I should exclude from my brotherly affection, and occasional assistance, any true minister of Christ, because he casts the Gospel net among the Presbyterians, the Independents, the Quakers, or the Baptists! If they will not wish me good luck in the name of the Lord, I will do it to them. So far as they cordially aim at the conversion of sinners, I will offer them the right hand of fellowship, and communicate with them in spirit. They may excommunicate me, if their prejudices prompt them to it: they may build up a wall of partition between themselves and me; but "in the strength of my God," whose love is as boundless as his immensity, and whose mercy is over all his works, "I will leap over the wall;" being persuaded that it is only daubed with untempered mortar, and made of Babel materials. Should not Christian meekness, and ardent love bear down party spirit, and the prejudices of education? The king tolerates and protects us all, the parliament makes laws to insure toleration and quietness, peace and mutual forbearance; and shall we, who make a peculiar profession of the "faith which works by love," and binds upon us the new commandment of laying down our lives for the brethren; shall we, I say, be less charitable and more intolerant than our civil governors, who, perhaps, make no such profession? Let bigoted Jews and ignorant Samaritans dispute whether God is to be worshipped on Mount Moriah, or on Mount Gerizim; let rigid Churchmen say, that a parish church is the only place where Divine worship ought to be performed, while stiff dissenters suppose that their meeting houses are the only bethels in the land; but let us, who profess moderation and charity, remember the reconciling words of our Lord, "The hour cometh, and now is, when true worshippers shall worship God every where, in spirit and in truth. For the Father seeketh such *catholic and spiritual persons* to worship him;" and not such partial and formal devotees as the Jews and Samaritans were in the days of our Lord.

But to return to our plan of reconciliation: might not some additions be made to Mr. Wesley's draught; for it is from a letter published in his thirteenth Journal, that I have extracted the preceding sketch of union. Might not good men and sincere ministers, who are bent upon inheriting the seventh beatitude, form themselves into a *society of reconcilers,* whatever be their denomination, and mode of worship? Interest brings daily to the royal exchange a multitude of merchants, ready to deal with men of the most opposite customs, dresses, religions, and countries; and shall not the love of peace, and the pursuit of love, have as great an effect upon the children of light, as the love of money, and the pursuit of wealth have upon the men of the world? There is a society *for promoting religious knowledge among the poor;* some of its members are Churchmen, and others dissenters: some are Calvinists, and others Arminians; and yet it flourishes, and the design of it is happily answered. Might not such a society be formed for promoting peace and love among professors? Is not charity preferable to knowledge? And if it be well to associate, in order to distribute Bibles and Testaments, which are but the letter of the Gospel, would it not be better to associate, in order to diffuse peace and love, which are the spirit of the Gospel? There is another respectable *society for promoting the Christian faith among the heathen;* and why should there not be a society for promoting unanimity and toleration among Christians? Ought not the welfare of our fellow Christians to lie as near our hearts as that of the heathen? There are in London, and other places, associations for the preventing and extinguishing of fires. As soon as the mischief breaks out, and the alarm is given, the firemen run to their fire engines; and without considering whether the house on fire be inhabited by Churchmen or dissenters, by Arminians or Calvinists, they venture their lives to put out the flames; and why should there not be associations of peace makers, who, the moment the fire of discord breaks out in any part of our Jerusalem, may be ready to put it out by all the methods which the Gospel suggests? Is not the fire of hell, which consumes souls, more to be guarded against than that fire which can only destroy the body?

Should it be asked what methods could be pursued to extinguish the fire of discord, and kindle that of love; I reply, that we need only be as wise as the children of this world. Consider we then how they proceed to gain their worldly ends; and let us go, and do as much to gain our spiritual ends.

Many gentlemen, some laymen and others clergymen, some Churchmen and others dissenters, wanted lately to procure the repeal of our articles of religion. Notwithstanding the diversity of their employments, principles, and denominations, they united, wrote circular letters, drew up petitions, and used all their interest with men in power to bring about their design. Again: some warm men thought it proper to blow up the fire of discontent in the breasts of our American fellow subjects. How did they go about the dangerous work? With what ardour did they speak and write, preach and print, fast and pray, publish manifestoes and make them circulate, associate, and strengthen their associations, and at last venture their fortunes, reputations, and lives, in the execution of their warlike project! Go, ye men of peace, and do at least half as much to carry on your friendly design. Associate, pray, preach, and print for the furtherance of peace. When ye meet, consult about the means of removing what stands in the way of a fuller agreement in principle and affection, among all those who love Christ in sincerity; and decide if the following queries contain any hint worthy of your attention: —

Might not moderate Calvinists send with success circular letters to their rigid Calvinian brethren; and moderate Arminians to their rigid Arminian brethren, to check rashness, and recommend meekness, and moderation, and love? Might not the Calvinist ministers, who patronize the doctrines of grace, display also the doctrines of justice, and open their pulpits to those Arminian ministers who do it with caution? And might not the Arminian ministers who patronize the doctrines of justice, make more of the doctrines of grace, preach as nearly as they can like the judicious Calvinists, admit them into their pulpits, and rejoice at every opportunity of showing them their esteem and confidence? Might not such moderate Calvinists and Arminians as live in the same towns, have from time to time a general sacrament, and invite one another to it, to cement brotherly love, by publicly confessing the same Christ, by jointly taking him for their common head, and by acknowledging one another as fellow members of his mystical body? Might not some of the ministers, on these occasions, preach to edification on such texts as these: — "Christ asked him, What was it that ye disputed about among yourselves by the way? But they held their peace;" for by the way they had disputed, "who should be the greatest:" and he said unto them, "If any man desire to be first, the same shall be last of all, and servant of all. Know ye what I have done to you? Ye call me Master and Lord: and ye say well; for so I am. If I then, your Lord and Master, have washed your feet, ye ought also to wash one another's feet. For I have given you an example, that ye should do as I have done unto you. Receive ye one another as Christ also received us. Yea, him that is weak in the faith receive you, but not to doubtful disputations. Let us not judge one another any more: but judge this rather, that no man put a stumbling block or an occasion to fall in his brother's way. Let us follow after those things which make for peace, and things wherewith one may edify another: holding the head, from which all the body having nourishment, and knit together, increaseth with the increase of God.

Behold, how good and how pleasant it is for brethren to dwell together in unity! It is like the precious ointment upon Aaron's head, and like the dew upon Mount Sion: for there the Lord commanded the blessing, and life for evermore." Could not the society have corresponding members in various parts of the kingdom, to know where the flame of discord begins to break out, that by means of those mighty engines, the tongue, the pen, or the press, they might, with all speed, direct streams of living water, floods of truth and kindness, to quench the kindling fire of wrath, oppose the waters of strife, and remove whatever stands in the way of the fire of love? And if this heavenly fire were once kindled, and began to spread, might it not, in a few years, reach all orders of professors in Great Britain, as the contrary fire has reached our brethren on the continent? If we doubt the possibility of it, do we not secretly suppose that Satan is stronger to promote discord and contention, than Christ is to promote concord and unity? And, in this case, where is our faith? And where the love which"thinketh no evil," and "hopeth all things?" If one or two warm men have kindled on the continent so great a fire, that neither our fleets nor our armies, neither the British nor the German forces employed in that service, have yet been able to put it out; what will not twenty or thirty men, burning with the love of God and of their neighbour, be able to do in England? We may judge of it by what twelve fishermen did one thousand seven hundred years ago. Arise then, ye sons of peace, ye sons of God, into whose hands these sheets may fall. Our Captain is ready to lead you to the conquest of the kingdom of love. Be not discouraged at the smallness of your number, nor at the multitude of the men of war, who are ready to oppose you. Jesus is on your side: he is our Gideon. With his mighty cross he has smitten the foundation of the altar of discord: pull it down. Break your narrow pitchers of bigotry. Hold forth your burning lamps: let the light of your love shine forth without a covering. Ye loving Calvinists, fall upon the necks of your Arminian opponents: and ye loving Arminians, be no more afraid to venture among your Calvinian antagonists. You will not find them cruel Midianites, but loving Christians: methinks that your mingled lights have already chased away the shades of the night of partiality and ignorance. You see that you are brethren; you feel it: and, ashamed of your former distance, you now think you can never make enough of each other, and testify too much your repentance, for having offended the world by absurd contentions, and vexed each other by inimical controversies. The first love of the Christians revives: you are "all of one heart and of' — but I forgot myself: I antedate the time of love, which I so ardently wish to see. The Jericho of bigotry, which I desire to compass, is strong: the Babylon of confusion and division, I would fain demolish, is guarded by a numerous garrison, which thousands of good men think it their duty to reinforce. It may not be improper therefore to make one more attack upon these accursed cities, and to insure the success of it by proper directions.

SECTION VII.

Some directions how to secure the blessings of peace and brotherly love.

"Do all things without disputings," says St. Paul, "that ye may be blameless and harmless, the sons of God without rebuke. Be at peace among yourselves; and if it be possible, as much as lieth in you, live peaceably with all men:" but especially with your brethren in Christ. "Nor quench the Spirit," by destroying its most excellent fruits, which are peace and love. And that we may not be guilty of this crime, the apostle exhorts us to "avoid contentions," and assures us, that God will "render indignation to them that are contentious, and do not obey the truth." It highly concerns us, therefore, to inquire how we shall escape the curse denounced against the contentious, and live peaceably with our fellow professors. And if we ought to do "all that lieth in us," in order to obtain and keep the blessing of peace; surely we ought to follow such directions as are agreeable to Scripture and reason. I humbly hope that the following are of this number.

DIRECTION I. Let us endeavour to do justice to every part of the Gospel; carefully avoiding the example of those injudicious and rash men, who make a wide gap in the north hedge of the garden of truth, in order to mend one in the east or south hedge. Let every evangelical doctrine have its proper place in our creed, that it may have its due effect on our conduct. Consideration, repentance, faith, hope, love, and obedience, have each a place on the scale of Gospel truth. Let us not breed quarrels by thrusting away any one of those graces, to make more room for another. While the philosopher exalts consideration alone; the Carthusian, repentance; the Solifidian, faith; the mystic, love; and the moralist, obedience; thou, man of God, embrace them all in their order, nor exalt one to the prejudice of the rest. Tear not Christ's seamless garment, nor divide him against himself. He demands our reverential obedience as our King, as much as he requires our humble attention as our Prophet, and our full confidence as our Priest. It is as unscriptural to magnify one of his offices at the expense of the others, as it would be unconstitutional to honour George III. as king of Ireland, and to insult him as king of England or Scotland. And it is as provoking to the God of truth and order to see the stewards of his Gospel mysteries make much of the dispensation of the Son, while they overlook the dispensation of the Father, and take little notice of the dispensation of the Holy Ghost, as it would be provoking to a parent to see the persons, whom he has entrusted with the care of his three children, make away with the youngest, and starve the eldest, in order to enrich and pamper his second son. Where moderation is wanting, peace cannot subsist: and where partiality prevails, contention will soon make its appearance.

II. Let us always make a proper distinction between essential and circumstantial differences. The difference there is between the Christians and the Mohammedans is essential: but the difference between us and those who receive the Scriptures, and believe in the Father, Son, and Holy Ghost, is in general about non-essentials: and therefore such a difference ought not to hinder union; although in some cases it may and should prevent a close communion. If we fancy that every diversity of doctrine, discipline, or ceremony, is a sufficient reason to keep our brethren at arm's length from us, we are not so much the followers of the condescending Jesus, as of the stiff and implacable professors, mentioned in the Gospel, who made much ado about mint, anise, and cummin; but shamefully neglected mercy, forbearance, and love.

III. Let us leave to the pope the wild conceit of infallibility; and let us abandon to bigoted Mohammedans the absurd notion that truth is confined to our own party, that those who do not speak as we do are blind, and that orthodoxy and salvation are plants, which will scarcely grow any where but in our own garden. So long as we continue in this error, we are unfit for union with all those who do not wear the badge of our party. A Pharisaic pride taints our tempers, cools our love, and breeds a forbidding reserve, which says to our brethren, "Stand by; I am more orthodox than you."

IV. Let us be afraid of a sectarian spirit. We may indeed, and we ought to be more familiar with the professors with whom we are more particularly connected; just as soldiers of the same regiment are more familiar with one another, than with those who belong to other regiments. But the moment this particular attachment grows to such a degree as to make a party in the army of King Jesus, or of King George, it breaks the harmony which ought to subsist between all the parts, and hinders the general service which is expected from the whole body. In what a deplorable condition would be the king's affairs, if each colonel in his army refused to do duty with another colonel: and if, instead of mutually supporting one another in a day of battle, each said to the rest, "I will have nothing to do with you and your corps: you may fight yonder by yourselves, if you please: I and my men will keep here by ourselves, doing what seems good in our own eyes. As we expect no assistance from you, so we promise you that you shall have none from us. And you may think yourselves well off if we do not join the common enemy, and fire at you; for your regimentals are different from ours, and therefore you are no part of our army." If so absurd a behavior were excusable, it would be among the wild, cruel men, who compose an army of Tartars or savages; but it admits of no excuse from men who call themselves believers, which is another name for the "followers of Him" who laid down his life for his enemies, and perpetually exhorts his soldiers to love one another as brethren, — yea, as he has loved us.

Let us then peculiarly beware of inordinate self love. It is too often the real source of our divisions; when love to truth is their pretended cause. If St. Paul could say of fallen believers in his time, "They all seek their own;" how much more may this be said of degenerate believers in our days? Who can tell all the mischief done by this ungenerous and base temper? Who can declare all the mysteries of error and iniquity, which stand upon the despicable foundation of the little words, I, me, and mine? Could we see the secret inscriptions which the Searcher of hearts can read upon the first stones of our little Babels, how often would we wonder at such expressions as these: — *My* church, *my* chapel, *my* party, *my* congregation, *my* connections, my popularity, *my* hope of being esteemed by my partisans, *my* fear of being suspected by them, *my* jealousy of those who belong to the opposite party, *my* system, *my* favourite opinions, *my* influence, &c, &c! To all those egotisms let us constantly oppose those awful words of our Lord, "Except a man deny himself, he cannot be my disciple."

Till we cordially oppose our inordinate attachment to our own interest, we "sacrifice to our own net," in our public duties; and even when we "preach Christ," it is to be feared that we do it more "out of contentions" than out of a real concern for his interest.

What Dr. Watts writes on this subject is striking: — "Have we never observed what a mighty prevalence the applause of a party, and the advance of self interest have over the hearts and tongues of men, and inflame them with malice against their neighbours? They assault every different opinion with rage and clamour: they rail at the persons of all other parties, to ingratiate themselves with their own. When they put to death [or bitter reproach] the ministers of the Gospel, they boast like Jehu, when he slew the priests of Baal, 'Come and see my zeal for the Lord.' And as he designed hereby to establish the kingdom in his own hands; so they to maintain the reputation they have acquired among their own sect. But, ah! how little do they think of the wounds that Jesus the Lord receives by every bitter reproach they cast on his followers!"

V. Let us be afraid of needless singularity. The love of it is very common, and leads some men to the wildest extremes. The same spirit which inclines one to wear a hat cocked in the height of the fashion, and influences another to wear one in full contrariety to the mode, may put one man upon minding only the first Gospel axiom, and the blood of Christ, while another man fancies that it becomes him to mind only the second Gospel axiom, and the law of Christ. Thus, out of singularity, the former insists upon faith alone, and the latter recommends nothing but morality and works. May we detest a temper, which makes men delight in an unnecessary opposition to each other! And may we constantly follow the example of St. Paul, whose charitable maxim was, to "please all men to their edification!" So shall "our moderation be known to all men:" nor shall we absurdly break the balance of the various truths which compose the Gospel system.

VI. Let us never blame our brethren but with reluctance. And when love to truth, and the interest of religion, constrain us to show the absurd or dangerous consequences of their mistakes, let us rather underdo than overdo. Let us never hang unnecessary* or false consequences upon their principles: and when we prove that their doctrine necessarily draws absurd and mischievous consequences after it, let us do them the justice to believe that they do not see the necessary connection of such consequences with their principles. And let us candidly hope that they detest those consequences.

---

* I humbly hope that I have followed this part of the direction in my Checks. To the best of my knowledge I have not fixed one consequence upon the principles of my opponents, which does not fairly and necessarily flow from their doctrine. And I have endeavoured to do justice to their piety, by declaring again and again my full persuasion that they abhor such consequences. But whether they have done so by my principles, may be seen in my Genuine Creed, where I show that the absurd and wicked consequences, which my opponents fix upon the doctrines that I maintain, have absolutely nothing to do with it. I do not however say this to justify myself in all things: for I do not doubt, but if I had health and strength to revise my Checks, I should find some things which might have been said in a more guarded, humble, serious, and loving manner.

VII. Let us, as far as we can, have a friendly intercourse with some of the best men of the various denominations of Christians around us. And if we have time for much reading, let us peruse their best writings, to be edified by the devotion which breathes through their works. This will be an effectual mean of breaking the bars of prejudice, contempt, fear, and hard thinking, which want of acquaintance with them puts between them and us. Why are savages frighted at the sight of civilized men? Why do they run away from us as if we were wild beasts? It is because they have no connection with us, are utter strangers to the good will we bear them, and fancy we design to do them mischief. Bigots are religious savages. By keeping to themselves, they contract a shyness toward their fellow Christians: they fancy that their brethren are monsters; they ask, with Nathanael, "Can any good thing come out of Nazareth?" By and by they get into the seats of the Pharisees, and peremptorily say, that "out of Galilee there ariseth no prophet." And it is well if they do not turn in a rage from the precious truths delivered by some of the most favoured servants of God; fondly supposing, with Naaman, that the Jordan of their brethren is not to be compared with the rivers of their own favourite Damascus; and uncharitably concluding, with the pope and Mohammed, that all waters are poisonous except those of their own cistern. The best advice which can be given to these prejudiced people, is that which Philip gave to Nathanael, who fancied that Jesus was not a prophet: "Come and see." I would say to Calvinian bigots, "Come and see" your Arminian brethren; and to Arminian bigots, "Come and see" pious Calvinists; and you will be ashamed to have so long forfeited the blessing annexed to brotherly communion; for "they that fear the Lord, speak often one to another, and the Lord hearkens and hears it, and a book of remembrance is written before him for them. And they shall be mine, saith the Lord of hosts, in that day when I make up my jewels."

VIII. Let our religion influence our hearts as well as our heads. Let us mind the practice as well as the theory of Christianity. The bare knowledge of Christ's doctrine "puffeth up, but charity edifieth." "He that loveth not, knoweth not God, for God is love," and would have us to be loving and "merciful as he is." He receives us notwithstanding our manifold weaknesses and provocations; and he says, by his apostle, "Forgive one another, as God for Christ's sake hath forgiven you; that ye may with one mind, and with one mouth, glorify God." How far from this religion are those, who, instead of receiving one another, keep at the greatest distance from their brethren, and perhaps pronounce damnation against them! The men who rashly condemn their "weak brother to perish," cannot be close followers of our "merciful High Priest," who "died for him," who "is touched with a feeling of our infirmities, and has compassion on them that are ignorant and out of the way. If any man say, I love God, — the love of Christ constraineth me, — and yet hateth his brother," or shuns a reconciliation with his fellow servants, "he is a liar; for he who loveth not his brother, whom he hath seen, how can he love God whom he hath not seen? This commandment have we from Christ, that he who loveth God, love his brother," yea, his enemy also. And love is "pure, peaceable, gentle, easy to be entreated, and full of mercy. It suffereth long, and is kind, it envieth not, is not puffed up, it does not behave itself unseemly, it seeketh not its own, it beareth all things, it endureth all things, it believeth and hopeth all things," and it attempteth many things, that Christians may "be made perfect in one," and may "keep the unity of the Spirit in the bond of peace." Where this love is not, the practice of Christianity is absent. We may have the brain of a Christian, but we want his tongue, his hands, and his heart. We may indeed say many sweet things of Christ; but we spoil them all if we speak bitterly of his members; for he who toucheth them, toucheth the apple of his eye; and he who wounds them, wounds him in the tenderest part. Hence the severity of our Lord's declarations: "Whosoever offendeth one of these little ones, who believe in me, it were better for him that a mill stone were hanged about his neck, and that he were drowned in the depth of the sea. And whosoever shall *uncharitably* say to his brother, Thou fool! shall be in danger of hell fire," as well as a murderer, Matthew 18:6; 5:22. So dreadful is the case of those who make shipwreck of the faith which works by charity, while they contend for real or fancied orthodoxy.

We shall readily set our seals to the justice and propriety of these terrible declarations, if we remember that when Christians offend against the law of kindness, they stab their religion in her very vitals, because Christianity is the religion of love. From first to last, it teaches us love — free, distinguishing, matchless love. The Father so loved the world as to give his only begotten Son that we might not perish. He freely delivered him up to death for us all, and with him he gives us all things; forgiveness, grace, and glory. The Son, who, when he was in the form of God, thought it not robbery to be equal with him, influenced by obedient love to the Father and tender pity toward us, assumed our nature, became a prophet to teach the religion of love, a king to enforce the law of love, a priest and a victim dying for the breaches of the law of love. He lived to keep and enforce the law of love: he wept, prayed, and agonized, to show the force of sympathizing love: he died on the cross to seal with the last drop of his vital blood the plan of redeeming love. He sunk into the grave, and descended into hades, to show the depth of love. He rose again to secure the triumph of love: he ascended into heaven to carry on the schemes of love: from thence he sent, and still sends, upon obedient believers, the spirit of burning; baptizing them with the Holy Ghost, and with the fire of love, which many waters cannot quench; and from thence he shall come again, to send the unloving and contentious to their own place, and to crown loving souls with honour, glory, and immortality. The office of the Holy Ghost answers to the part which the Father and the Son bear in our redemption. When we receive him according to the promise of the Father, we receive him as the Spirit of love: he sheds abroad the love of God in our hearts; he testifies to us the love of Christ; and his fruit, in our hearts and lives, is "love, joy, peace, long suffering, gentleness, goodness, and meekness." This loving spirit is so essential to Christianity, that if you ask St. Paul and St. John an account of their religion, the former answers, The end of Christianity is "charity out of a pure heart, a good conscience, and faith unfeigned:" and therefore if any Christian loveth not the Lord Jesus in his person and in his mystical members, he is accursed. Maranatha, the Lord cometh to cut in sunder that wicked servant, and to appoint him his portion with hypocrites in outer darkness. As for St. John, he thus describes Christianity: — "Beloved, let us love one another: for love is of God: every one that loveth is born of God. We love him because he first loved us. And every one that loveth God who begat *believers*, loveth them also that are begotten of him: and this commandment we have from him, that he who loveth God love his brother also." St. James' testimony to the religion of love will properly close that of St. Paul and St. John. "Hearken, my beloved brethren. If ye fulfil the royal law, Thou shalt love thy neighbour as thyself, ye do well: but if ye have respect to persons," much more if ye bite and devour your brethren, "ye are convinced of the law as transgressors: for whosoever shall keep the whole law [of love] and yet offend in one point, he is guilty of all." He shows himself a bad Christian — a fallen believer. Therefore, "Speak not evil one of another, brethren, nor grudge one against another, lest ye be condemned: behold, the Judge standeth at the door." And Christ the Judge confirms thus the testimony of his apostles, in his awful account of the day of judgment: — Then shall the king say unto them on his right hand, "Come, ye blessed, inherit the kingdom prepared for you, for" ye were kind and loving to me. "The head of every man is Christ," and therefore, "inasmuch as ye have done it [that is, inasmuch as ye have been kind and loving] unto one of the least of these my brethren, ye have done it unto me:" ye have been kind and loving to me: and I will give you "the reward of the inheritance. Then shall he say unto them on the left hand, Depart from me, ye cursed:" for ye were not kind and loving to me: and if they plead "Not guilty" to the charge, he will "answer them, saying, Verily I say unto you, inasmuch as ye did it not unto one of the least of these, ye did it not unto me:" that is, inasmuch as ye were not kind to one of these, ye were not kind and loving to me. And these unloving men "shall go away into everlasting punishment; but the righteous, [that is, the loving and merciful,] into life eternal." How plain is this religion! and how deplorable is it that it should be almost lost in clouds of vain notions, wild opinions, unscriptural systems, empty professions, and noisy contentions! Were professors to embrace this practical Christianity, what a revolution would take place in Christendom! The accuser of the brethren would fall as lightning from heaven, and genuine orthodoxy would combine with humble charity to make the earth a paradise again.

IX. Lastly: if we will attain the full power of godliness, and be peaceable as the Prince of Peace, and merciful as our heavenly Father, let us go on to the perfection and glory of Christianity; let us enter the full dispensation of the Spirit. Till we live in the pentecostal glory of the Church: till we are baptized with the Holy Ghost: till the Spirit of burning and the fire of Divine love have melted us down, and we have been truly cast into the softest mould of the Gospel: till we can say with St. Paul, "We have received the Spirit of love, of power, and of a sound mind;" till then we shall be carnal rather than spiritual believers; we shall divide into sects like the Jews, and at best we shall be like the disciples of John and of Christ before they had received the gift of the Holy Ghost. We shall have an envious spirit: we shall contend about superiority, and be ready to stop those who do good, because they do it not in our way, or because they follow not with us. And supposing we once tasted the first love of the Church, and had really the love of God and our neighbour "shed abroad in our hearts by the Holy Ghost given unto us;" yet if this "love be grown cold," or if we "have left it," by grieving or quenching the Spirit, we are fallen from pentecostal Christianity, and instead of continuing in disinterested fellowship, like the primitive Christians, we shall "seek our own," as the fallen Philippians; or we shall divide into parties like those Corinthians to whom St. Paul wrote: — "Some of you have not the knowledge of the God of love; I speak this to your shame. I cannot speak to you as to spiritual, but as to carnal believers, even as to babes in Christ. For ye are yet carnal: for whereas there is among you envying, and strife, and divisions, are ye not carnal, and walk as the men of the world? Examine yourselves therefore whether ye be in the faith: prove your own selves." Is Christ in you? Have ye the Spirit of power, or have ye obliged him to withdraw? And are ye shorn of your strength, as Samson was, when the Spirit of the Lord was departed from him? Alas! Who can say how many believers are in this deplorable case without suspecting it? The world knows that they are fallen, but they know it not themselves. They make sport for the Philistines by their idle contentions, and they dream that they are the champions of truth. O may they speedily "awake to righteousness," and see their need of "righteousness, peace, and joy in the Holy Ghost!" And may "power from on high" rest again upon them! So shall they break the pillars of the temple of discord, rebuild the temple of peace, and be "continually in it, praising and blessing God," instead of accusing and provoking their brethren.

SECTION VIII.

Farther motives to a speedy reconciliation — An exhortation to it.

I. "ABOVE all things," says St. Peter, "have fervent charity among yourselves." "Little children," says St. John, "love one another." Sweet precepts! but how far are we from regarding them, while we give to bitter zeal, or to indifference, the place allotted to the communion of saints, and to burning love! Had these apostolic injunctions a due effect upon us, how would the fervent charity which victorious faith kindles, set fire to the chaff of our idle contentions, and make us ashamed of having so departed from the Gospel as to give the world to understand (if men may judge of our doctrine by our conduct,) that the Scriptures exhort us to fall out one with another, and to mind charity less than every thing; whereas it enjoins us to mind it "above all things," above all honour, pleasure, and profit, — yea, above all knowledge, orthodoxy, and faith.

II. We are commanded to "glorify God with one heart and one mouth." Our lips should be instruments of praise, ever tuned to celebrate the Prince of Peace, — ever ready to invite all around us to the Gospel feast; the feast of Divine and brotherly love. To neglect this labour of love is bad: but how much worse is it to be as "sounding brass," as a "tinkling cymbal," as an infernal kettle drum, used by the accuser of the brethren, to call professors from the good fight of faith, to the detestable fight of needless or abusive controversy, and perhaps to the bloody work of persecution? Who can describe the injury done to religion by the champions of bigotry? An ingenious writer being one day desired to draw in proper colours the figure of *uncharitableness,* the monster which has so narrowed, disgraced, and murdered Christianity; "I will attempt it," said he "if you will furnish me with a sheet of large paper, and that of the fairest kind, to represent the Christian Church in this world. First, I will pare it round, and reduce it to a very small compass: then with much ink will I stain the whiteness of it, and deform it with many a blot. At the next sitting I will stab it through rudely with an iron pen: and when I put the last hand to complete the likeness: it shall be besmeared with blood." And shall we lend our common enemy iron pens, or tongues sharpened like the murderer's swords, that he may continue to wound the members of Christ, and deform the Christian Church? God forbid! Let as many of us as have turned our pens and tongues into instruments of idle contention, apply them henceforth to the defence of peace and brotherly love.

III. If we refuse to do it, we practically renounce our baptism: for in that solemn ordinance we profess to take God for our common Father, Christ for our common Saviour, and the Spirit for our common Sanctifier. When we receive the Lord's Supper in faith, we solemnly bind this baptismal engagement upon ourselves, and tie faster the knot of brotherly love, by which we are joined to "all those who in every place call upon the name of Jesus Christ, their Lord and ours." Now can any thing be more antichristian and diabolical, than for persons, who constantly communicate, to live in discord, and perhaps to insult one another in a manner contrary to the first rules of heathen civility? O ye, who surround our altars, and there "humbly beseech almighty God continually to inspire the universal Church with the spirit of unity and concord, that all who confess his holy name may live in unity and godly love;" can any thing equal your sacrilegious guilt, if, after such a solemn prayer, you not only refuse to live "in unity and godly love," with your pious Calvinian and Arminian brethren, but also breathe the spirit of discord, and live in variance and ungodly contentions with them, merely because they do not pronounce "Shibboleth" with all the emphasis which our party puts upon some favourite words and phrases? If we continue to offer so excellent a prayer, and to indulge so detestable a temper, are we not fit persons to fight under the banner of Judas? Do we not with a kiss betray the Son of man in his members? Do we not go to the Lord's table to say, "Hail, Master!" and to deliver him for less than thirty pieces of silver, for the poor satisfaction of pleasing the bigots of a party, or for the mischievous pleasure of breaking the balance of the Gospel axioms, and rending the doctrines of grace from those of justice?

IV. "God is love." Let us be like "our Father who is in heaven." Satan is uncharitableness and variance: detest we his likeness, and let not the faithful and true Witness be obliged to say to us one day, "Ye are of your father the devil, whose works ye do," when you keep up divisions. "The devil," says Archbishop Leighton, "being an apostate spirit, revolted and separated from God, doth naturally project and work division." This was his first exploit, and is still his grand design and business in the world. He first divided our first parents from God, and the next we read of in their first child, was enmity against his brother. The tempter wounded truth, in order to destroy love, and therefore he is justly called by our Saviour "a liar, and a murderer from the beginning." He murdered our first parents by lying, and made them murderers by drawing them into his uncharitableness. God forbid that we should any longer do the work of the father of lies and murders! Heaven prevent our committing again two so great evils as those of wounding truth and preventing love! of wounding truth by attacking the Scripture doctrines of free grace and free agency! and of preventing love, by hindering the union of two such large bodies of professors, as the Calvinists and the Arminians! Nor let any lover of peace say, "I will not hinder the reconciliation you speak of;" for it is our bounden duty to farther it by a speedy, constant exertion of all our interest with God, and influence with men: otherwise we shall be found "unprofitable, slothful" servants, and shall be judged according to this declaration of our Lord, "He that gathereth not with me scattereth." For he who, in so noble a cause as that of truth and love, is "neither cold nor hot," pulls down upon his own head the curse denounced against the lukewarm Laodiceans.

Doctrines of Grace and Justice

V. The sin of the want of union with our pious Calvinian or Arminian brethren, is attended with peculiar aggravations. We are not only fellow creatures, but fellow subjects, fellow Christians, fellow Protestants, and fellow sufferers (in reputation at least) for maintaining the capital doctrines of salvation by faith in Christ, and of regeneration by the Spirit of God. How absurd is it for persons who thus share in the reproach, patience, and kingdom of Christ, to imbitter each other's comforts, and add to the load of contempt, which the men of the world cast upon them! Let Pagans, Mohammedans, Jews, Papists, and Deists, do this work. We may reasonably expect it from them. But for such Calvinists and Arminians as the world lumps together under the name of Methodists on account of their peculiar profession of godliness, for such "companions in tribulation," I say, to "bite and devour" each other, is highly unreasonable, and peculiarly scandalous.

VI. The great apostle of modern infidels, Mr. Voltaire, has, it is supposed, caused myriads of men to be ashamed of their baptism, and to renounce the profession of Christianity. His profane witticisms have slain their thousands; but the too cogent argument, which he draws from our divisions, has destroyed its myriads. With what exultation does he sing, —

Des Chretiens divises les infames querelles
Ont, au nom du Seigneur, apporte plus de maux, &c.

"The shameful quarrels of divided Christians have done more mischief under religious pretences, made more bad blood, and shed more human blood, than all the political contentions which have laid waste France and Germany under pretence of maintaining the balance of Europe." And shall we still make good his argument by our ridiculous quarrels? Shall we help him to make the world believe that the Gospel is an apple of discord thrown among men, to make them dispute with an acrimony and an obstinacy which have few precedents among men of the most corrupt and detestable religions in the world? Shall we continue to point the dagger with which that keen author stabs Christianity? Shall we furnish him with new nails to crucify Christ afresh in the sight of all Europe: or shall we continue to clinch those with which he has already done the direful deed? How will he triumph if he hears that the men who distinguish themselves by their zeal for the Gospel in England, maintain an unabated contest about the doctrines of grace and justice — a contest as absurd as that in which the whigs and tories would be involved, if they perpetually debated whether the house of lords or that of commons makes up the British parliament; and whether England or Scotland forms the island of Great Britain! And with what self applause will he apply to us what the apostle says of wicked heathens and apostate Christians: "Because when they knew God, they glorified him not as God" — the sovereign, righteous God of love and justice — "they became vain in their imaginations, and their foolish heart was darkened. Professing themselves wise, they became fools: being filled with envy, debate, malignity, whisperers, backbiters, despiteful, without understanding, without *brotherly* affection, implacable; having a form *of godly ortho*doxy, but denying the power of peaceable charity!

VII. Instead of continuing to give avowed infidels such room to laugh at us and our religion, would it not become us to stop, by a speedy reconciliation, the offence given by our absurd debates? Should we feel less concern for the honour of

Christianity, than Sir Robert Walpole did for the honour of the crown? It is reported that when he stood at the helm of the British empire, he was abused in parliament by some members of the privy council. Soon after, meeting with them in the king's cabinet, he proceeded to the despatch of business with his usual freedom, and with a remarkable degree of courtesy toward his enemies. And being asked how he could do so, he replied, "The king's business requires union. Why should my master's affairs suffer loss by the private quarrels of his servants?" May the time come, when the ministers of the King of peace shall have as much regard for his interest, as that minister showed for the interest of his royal master! Do not circumstances in Church and in state loudly call upon us to unite, in order to make head against the enemy of Christ and our souls? An enemy terrible as the banded powers of earth and hell, headed by the prince of the air, whose name is "Abaddon, Apollyon, Destroyer?"

VIII. Ye are no strangers to the craft and rage of that powerful adversary, O ye pious Calvinists and godly Arminians! For "ye wrestle not with flesh and blood only, but with the principalities and powers" of the kingdom of darkness! Cease then, cease to spend in wrestling one against another, the precious talents of time, strength, and wisdom, with which the Lord has entrusted you, to resist your infernal antagonist. Let it not be said that Herod, a Jew, and Pilate, a heathen, became friends, and united to pursue "the Lamb of God" to death; and that you, fellow Protestants, you, British believers, will not agree to "resist the devil, who goes about as a roaring lion, seeking whom he may devour."

You are astonished when you hear that some obstinate lawyers are so versed in chicanery as to protract for years law suits which might be ended in a few days. Your controversy has already lasted for ages; and the preceding pages show that it might be ended in a few hours: should you then still refuse reasonable terms of accommodation, think, O think of the astonishment of those who will see you protract the needless contention, and entail the curse of discord upon the next generation.

Our Lord bids us "agree quickly with our adversaries;" and will ye for ever dispute with your friends? Joseph said to his brethren, "See that ye fall not out by the way;" and so far as we know, his direction was faithfully observed. Christ says to us, Wear my badge: "By this shall all men know that ye are my disciples, if ye love one another." And will ye still fall out in the way to heaven, and exchange the Christian badge of charity, for the Satanic badge of contention?

Passionate Esau had vowed that he would never be reconciled to his brother. Nevertheless, he relented; and as soon as Jacob was in sight, "he ran to meet him, and embraced him, and fell on his neck and kissed him: and they wept," Genesis 33:4. And shall it be said that Esau, the hairy man, the fierce hunter, the savage who had resolved to imbrue his hands in his own brother's blood, the implacable wretch, whom so many people consider as an absolute reprobate — shall it be said that Esau was sooner softened than you? He was reconciled to his brother who had deprived him of Isaac's blessing by a lie; and they lived in peace ever after. And will ye never be reconciled one to another, and live peaceably with your Calvinian or Arminian brethren, who, far from having deprived you of any blessing, want you to share the blessing of holding with them the doctrines of grace, or those of justice?

The Prince of life "died, that he might gather together in one the children of God, who are scattered abroad," John 11:52. And will ye defeat this important end of his death? He "would gather you as a hen gathers her brood under her wings;" and will ye pursue one another as hawks pursue their prey? Or keep at a distance from each other, as lambs do from serpents? Cannot Christ's blood, "by which you are brought nigh to God," bring you nigh to each other? Does it not "speak better things than the blood of Abel?" kinder things than your mutual complaints? Does it not whisper peace, mercy, gentleness, and joy? "In Christ Jesus neither" rigid Calvinism "availeth any thing, nor" rigid Arminianism, "but faith which worketh by love:" draw near with faith to the Christian altar, which streams with that peace-speaking blood. Behold the bleeding Lamb of God, and become gentle, merciful, and loving! See the antitype of the brazen serpent! He hangs on high and says, "When I am lifted up, I will draw all men unto me:" and in me they shall centre as the solar beams centre in the sun. And will ye reply, "We will not be obedient to thy drawings: we will not be concentrated in thee with our Calvinian or Arminian brethren! Thy Father may sacrifice thee to 'slay the enmity, and so make peace:' and thou mayest lay down thy life to make reconciliation; but reconciled to each other we will not be; for the god of discord draws us asunder, and his infernal drawings we will obey." If you shudder at the thought of speaking such words, why should you so behave, that whoever sees you, may see they are the language of your conduct, — a language which is far more emphatical than that of your lips?

Say then no longer, "Have us excused;" but "come to the banqueting house," — the temple of peace where "the Lord's banner over you will be love," and his mercy "will comfort you on every side." "If there be therefore any consolation in Christ, if any comfort of love, if any fellowship of the Spirit, if any bowels and mercies; fulfil ye the joy" of all who wish Sion's prosperity: "be like minded, having the same love, being of one accord, of one mind, submitting yourselves one to another in the fear of God. He is my record how greatly I long after you all in the bowels of Jesus Christ, in whom there is neither Greek nor Jew, neither bond nor free," neither Calvinist nor Arminian, "but Christ is all in all. My heart is enlarged: for a recompense in the same, be ye also enlarged," and grant me my humble, perhaps my dying request: reject not my plea for peace. If it be not strong, it is earnest: for (considering my bodily weakness) I write it at the hazard of my life. *Animamque in vulnere pono.*

But why should I drop a hint about so insignificant a life, when I can move you to accept of terms of reconciliation by the life and death, by the resurrection and ascension of our Lord Jesus Christ? I recall the frivolous hint; and by the unknown agonies of Him whom you love; "who in the days of his flesh offered up prayers and supplications, with strong crying and tears, unto him who was able to save him from death;" by his second coming; and by our gathering together unto him, I beseech you, "put on, as the [Protestant] elect of God, bowels of mercies, kindness, humbleness of mind, meekness, long suffering; for-bearing one another, and forgiving one another; even as Christ *loved and* forgave you, so also do ye." Instead of absurdly charging one another with heresy, embrace one another, and triumph together in Christ. "Come up out of the wilderness" of idle controversy, "leaning upon *each other* as brethren, holy and beloved:" and with your joint forces attack your common enemies, Pharisaism, Antinomianism, and infidelity. Bless God, ye Arminians, for raising such men as the pious Calvinists, to make a firm stand against Pharisaic delusions, and to maintain with you the doctrines of man's fallen state, and of God's partial grace, which the Pelagians attack with all their might. And ye Calvinists, rejoice, that Heaven has raised you such allies as the godly Arminians, to oppose Manichean delusions, and to contend for the doctrines of holiness and justice, which the Antinomians seem sworn to destroy.

Jerusalem is a city which is at unity in itself. As soon as ye will cordially unite, the Protestant Jerusalem will become a praise in the earth. The moment ye join creeds, hearts, and hands, our reproach is rolled away: the apostasy is ended: the apostolic, pentecostal Church returns from her long captivity in mystical Babylon. The two staves, beauty and bands, become one in the hand of the great Shepherd, who writes upon it "Bible Calvinists reconciled to Bible Arminians:" see Zechariah 11:7, and Ezekiel 37:16, 17. Thus united, how happy are ye among yourselves! How formidable to your enemies! The men of the world are astonished, and say," Who is she that looketh forth as the morning, fair as the moon, clear as the sun, and terrible as an army with banners?" Surely it is a Church formed upon the model of the primitive Church. These people are Christians indeed. See how they "provoke one another to love and to good works!"

Such will be the fruit of your reconciliation, and such the glory of "the Shulamite," the peaceful Church! But, before I am aware, "my *longing* soul makes me like the chariots of Aminadab," to go and admire that truly reformed Church, whose members "are all of one heart and of one soul." O ye pious Calvinists, and godly Arminians, if you desire to see her glory, express your wish in Solomon's prophetic words, "Return, return, O Shulamite: return, return, that we may look upon thee. What will ye see in the Shulamite? As it were the company of two armies:" Song of Solomon 6:10, 12, 13: the combined force of the good men who maintain the doctrines of grace and justice, and who, by their union, will become strong enough to demolish modern Babel, and to batter down Pharisaism and Antinomianism, the two forts by which it is defended. For Pharisaism will never yield, but to the power of Bible Calvinism and the doctrines of grace. Nor can Antinomianism be conquered, without the help of Bible Arminianism and the doctrines of justice. And when Pharisaism and Antinomianism shall be destroyed, the Church will be "sanctified, cleansed, and ready to be presented to Christ, — a glorious Church, not having spot or wrinkle, or any such thing." Then shall we sing with truth, what we sing without propriety: —

> *"Love, like death, has* all *destroy'd,*
> *Render'd all distinctions void:*
> *Names, and sects, and parties fall,*
> *Thou, O Christ, art all in all."**

In the meantime, let us rejoice in hope, and sing with the Christian poet: —

---

* When I hear contending Calvinists and Arminians agree to print and sing this verse, I am tempted to cry to them, "Be at peace among yourselves," or sing at your love-feasts, —

Love has not *our pride destroy'd,*
Render'd our distinctions void;
Names, and sects, and parties rise,
Peace retires, and mounts the skies

Doctrines of Grace and Justice

"Giver of peace and unity,
Send down thy mild, pacific Dove;
We all shall then in one agree,
And breathe the spirit of thy love.

We all shall think and speak the same
Delightful lesson of thy grace;
One undivided Christ proclaim,
And jointly glory in thy praise.

Regard thine own eternal prayer,
And send a peaceful answer down:
To us thy Father's name declare;
Unite and perfect us in one.

So shall the world believe and know,
That God has sent thee from above;
When thou art seen in us below,
And every soul displays thy love."

A REPLY

TO THE

PRINCIPAL ARGUMENTS

BY WHICH

THE CALVINISTS AND THE FATALISTS

SUPPORT THE DOCTRINE OF

ABSOLUTE NECESSITY:

BEING

REMARKS

ON

THE REV. MR. TOPLADY'S "SCHEME OF CHRISTIAN AND PHILOSOPHICAL NECESSITY."

"Beware lest any man spoil you through philosophy and vain deceit," Colossians 2:8.

INTRODUCTION.

MR. VOLTAIRE at the head of the Deists abroad; President Edwards and Mr. Toplady at the head of the Calvinists in America and Great Britain; and Dr. Hartley, seconded by Dr. Priestley and Mr. Hume, at the head of many ingenious philosophers, have of late years joined their literary forces to bind man with what Mr. Toplady calls "*ineluctabilis ordo rerum,*" or "the extensive series of adamantine links," which form the chain of "absolute necessity." An invisible chain this, by which, if their scheme be true, God and nature inevitably bind upon us all our thoughts and actions; so that no good man can absolutely think or do worse — no wicked man can at any time think or do better than he does, each exactly filling up the measure of unavoidable virtue or vice which God, as the first cause, or the predestinating and necessitating author of all things, has allotted to him from all eternity.

Mr. Toplady triumphs in seeing the rapid progress which this doctrine makes, by the help of the above-mentioned authors, who shine with distinguished lustre in the learned world. "Mr. Wesley," says he, "laments that necessity is 'the scheme which is now adopted by not a few of the most sensible men in the nation.' I agree with him as to the fact: but I cannot deplore it as a calamity. The progress which that doctrine has of late years made, and is still making in the kingdom, I consider as a most happy and promising symptom," &c.

I flatter myself that I shall by and by show, upon theological principles, the mischievous absurdity of that spreading doctrine, in an *Answer to Mr. Toplady's Vindication of the Decrees*. But as he has lately published a book entitled, "The scheme of Christian and Philosophical Necessity, asserted in opposition to Mr. J. Wesley's Tract on that Subject;" and as he has advanced in that book some arguments taken from philosophy and Scripture, I shall now take notice of them. To defend truth effectually, error must be entirely demolished. Therefore, without any farther apology, I present the lovers of truth with the following refutation of the grand error which supports the Calvinian and Voltarian gospels.

A REPLY, &C.

SECTION I.

A view of the doctrine of absolute necessity, as it is maintained by Mr. Toplady and his adherents. This doctrine (as well as Manicheism) makes God the author of every sin.

CONTROVERTISTS frequently accuse their opponents of holding detestabl or absurd doctrines, which they never advanced, and which have no necessary connection with their principles. That I may not be guilty of so ungenerous a proceeding, I shall first present the reader with an account of necessity and her pedigree, in Mr. Toplady's own words.

Scheme of Christian and Philosophical Necessity, (pages 13, 14:) "If we distinguish accurately, this seems to have been the order in which the most judicious of the ancients considered the whole matter. First, *God;* then his *will;* then *fate,* or the solemn ratification of his will, by passing and establishing it into an unchangeable decree; then *creation;* then *necessity;* that is, such an indissoluble concatenation of secondary causes and effects as has a native tendency to secure the certainty of all events, as one wave is impelled by another;* then *providence;* that is, the omnipresent, omnivigilant, all-directing [he might have added *all-impelling*] superintendency of Divine wisdom and power, carrying the whole preconcerted scheme into actual execution, by the subservient mediation of second causes, which were created for that end."

This is the full view of the doctrine which the Calvinists and the better sort of fatalists defend. I would only ask a few questions upon it. (1.) If all our actions, and consequently all our *sins,* compose the seventh link of the chain of Calvinism; — if the first link is *God;* the second his *will;* the third his *decree;* the fourth *creation;* the fifth *necessity;* the sixth *providence;* and the seventh *sin;* is it not as easy to trace the pedigree of SIN through providence, necessity, creation, God's decree, and God's will, up to God himself, as it is to trace back the genealogy of the prince of Wales, from George III, by George II, up to George I? And upon this plan is it not clear that SIN is as much the *real offspring of God,* as the prince of Wales is the real offspring of George the First? (2.) If this is the case, does not Calvinism, or if you please, *fatalism* or

---

* Mr. T. puts this clause in Latin: *Velut unda impellitur unda.*

necessitarianism, absolutely make God *the author of sin* by means of his will, his decree, his creation, his necessitation, his impelling providence? And (horrible to think!) does it not unavoidably follow, that the monster SIN is the offspring of God's providence, of God's necessitation, of God's creation, of God's decree, of God's will, of God himself? (3.) If this Manichean doctrine be true, when Christ came to destroy sin, did he not come to destroy the work of God, rather than the work of the devil? And when preachers attack sin, do they not attack God's providence, God's necessitation, God's creation, God's decree, God's will, and God himself? (4.) To do God and his oracles justice, ought we not to give the following Scriptural genealogy of sin? A sinful act is the offspring of a sinful *choice;* a sinful choice is the offspring of *self perversion;* and self perversion *may* or *may not* follow from *free will* put in a *state of probation,* or under a practical law. When you begin at sin, you can never ascend higher than free will; and when you begin at God, you can never descend lower than free will. Thus, (i.) God; (ii.) his will to make free-willing, accountable creatures; (iii.) his putting his will in execution by the actual creation of such creatures; (iv.) legislation on God's part; (v.) voluntary, unnecessitated obedience on the part of those who make a good use of their free will; and (vi.) voluntary, unnecessitated disobedience on the part of those who make a bad use of it. Hence it is evident, that by substituting *necessity* for *free will,* and *absolute decrees* for *righteous legislation,* Mr. Toplady breaks the golden chain which our gracious Creator made, and helps Manes, Augustine, Calvin, Hobbes, Voltaire, Hume, Dr. Hartley, and Dr. Priestley, to hammer out the iron-clay chain by which they hang sin upon God himself. (5.) If all our sins with all their circumstances and aggravations, are only a part of "the whole preconcerted scheme" which "Divine wisdom and power" absolutely and irresistibly "carry into actual execution by the subservient mediation of second causes, which were created for that end;" who can rationally blame sinners for answering *the end* for which they were absolutely created? Who can refuse to exculpate and pity the reprobates, whom *all-impelling* omnipotence carries into sin, and into hell, as irresistibly as a floating cork is carried toward the shore by tossing billows which necessarily impel one another? And who will not be astonished at the erroneous notions which the consistent fatalists have of their God? A God this who necessitates, yea, impels men to sin by his will, his decree, his necessitation, and his providence: then gravely weeps and bleeds over them for sinning. And after having necessitated and impelled the non-elect to disbelieve and despise his blood, will set up a judgment seat to damn them for "necessarily carrying his preconcerted scheme into actual execution," as "second causes which were created for that end!"

"O! but they do it *voluntarily as* well as *necessarily,* and therefore they are accountable and judicable." This Calvinian salvo makes a bad matter worse. For if *all their sins* are necessarily brought about by God's allimpelling decree, their *willing* and bad choice are brought about by the same *preconcerted, irresistible* means; one of the ends of God's necessitation, with respect to the reprobate, being to make them sin with abundantly greater freedom and choice than if they were not necessitated and impelled by God's predestinating, efficacious, irresistible decree. This Mr. Toplady indirectly asserts in the following argument: —

Page 15. "They [man's actions — *man's sins*] may be, at one and the same time, free and necessary too. When Mr. Wesley is very hungry and tired, he is necessarily, and yet freely, disposed to good or rest. His *will* is concerned in sitting down to dinner, or in courting repose, when necessity impels to either. *Necessarily* biassed as he is to those mediums of recruit, he has recourse to them as freely (that is, as voluntarily, and with as much *appetite, choice, desire,* and *relish*) as if *necessity* were quite out of the case; nay, and with abundantly greater freedom and choice than if he was not so necessitated and impelled."

Is not this as much as to say, "As *necessitation,* the daughter of God's decree, impels Mr. Wesley to eat, by giving him an appetite to food: so it formerly impelled Adam, and now it impels all the reprobates to sin, by giving them an appetite to wickedness. And *necessarily biassed as they are* to adultery, robbery, and other crimes, they commit them as freely, i.e. with as much *appetite* and *choice,* as if *necessity* were quite out of the case: nay, and with *abundantly greater* freedom and choice than if they were not so necessitated and impelled." Is not this reviving one of the most impious tenets of the Manichees? Is it not confounding the Lamb of God with the old dragon, and coupling the celestial Dove with the infernal serpent?

If you ask, "Where is the flaw of Mr. Toplady's argumentative illustration?" I answer, It has two capital defects: (1.) That God's will, his decree, and his providence, *impel* Mr. Wesley to eat when he is hungry, is very true; because eating in such a case is, in general, Mr. Wesley's duty; and reminding him of his want of nourishment, by the sensation which we call *hunger,* is a peculiar favour, worthy of the Parent of good to bestow. But the question is, Whether God's will, decree, and providence, *impelled* Adam to choose the forbidden fruit rather than any other, and excited David to go to Uriah's wife, rather than to his own wives? How illogical, how detestable is this conclusion! God necessitates and impels us to do our *duty;* and therefore he necessitates and impels us to do *wickedness!* But, (2.) The greatest absurdity belonging to Mr. Toplady's illustration is, his pretending to overthrow the doctrine of free will by urging the hunger, which God gives to Mr. Wesley, in order to necessitate and impel him to eat, according to the decree of Calvinian necessitation, which is absolutely irresistible. Mr. T. says, (page 13,) "We call that *necessary* which cannot be otherwise than it is." Now Mr. Wesley's eating when he is hungry is by no means *Calvinistically* necessary: for he has a hundred times reversed the decree of his hunger by fasting; and if he were put to the sad alternative of the woman who was to starve or to kill and eat her own child, he both could and would go full against the necessitation of his hunger, and never eat more. Mr. Toplady's illustration, therefore, far from proving that God's necessitation *irresistibly* impels us to commit sin, indirectly demonstrates that God's necessitation does not so much as *absolutely* impel us to do those things which the very laws of our constitution and nature themselves bind upon us, by the strong *necessity* of self preservation. For some people have so far resisted the urgent calls of nature and appetite, as not only to make themselves eunuchs for the kingdom of heaven's sake, but even literally to starve themselves to death.

I once saw a man who played the most amazing tricks with a pack of cards. His skill consisted in so artfully shuffling them, and imperceptibly substituting one for another, that when you thought you had fairly secured the *king of hearts,* you found yourself possessed only of the *knave of clubs.* The defenders of the doctrine of necessity are not less skilful. I shall show, in another tract, with what subtilty Mr. T. uses "permission" for *efficacy,* — no "salvation due," for *eternal torments insured;* "not enriching," for *absolute reprobation;* and "passing by," for *absolutely appointing to remediless sin and everlasting burnings.* Let us now consider the grand, logical substitution which deceives that gentleman, and by which he misleads the admirers of his scheme.

Page 14. "I acquiesce in the old distinction of *necessity* [a distinction adopted by Luther and others] into a necessity of *compulsion,* and a necessity of *infallible certainty.* We say of the earth, for instance, that it circuits the sun by *compulsory necessity.* The *necessity of infallible certainty* is of a very different kind, and only renders the event inevitably future, without any compulsory force on the will of the agent." If Mr. T. had said, "The necessity of *true* prophecy considers an event as *certainly* future, but puts no Calvinian, irresistible bias on the will of the agent;" I would have subscribed to his distinction. But instead of the words *truly certain,* or *certainly future,* which would have perfectly explained what may improperly be called *necessity of true prophecy,* and what should be called *certain futurity;* instead of those words. I say, he artfully substitutes, first, "infallibly certain," and then "inevitably future." The phrase *infallibly certain* may be admitted to pass, if you understand by it *that which does not fail* to happen: but if you take it in a rigid sense, and mean by it that which *cannot absolutely fail* to happen, you get a step out of the way, and you may easily go on shuffling your logical cards, till you have imposed fatalism upon the simple, by making them believe that *certainly* future, *infallibly* future, and *inevitably* future, are three phrases of the same import; whereas the difference between the first and last phrase is as great as the difference between Mr. Wesley's Scriptural doctrine of free will, and Mr. T.'s Manichean doctrine of absolute necessity.

It is the property of error to be inconsistent. Accordingly we find that Mr. T., after having told us, p. 14, that the "necessity of infallible certainty," which renders the event inevitably future, lays "no compulsory force on the will of the agent," tells us, in the very same page, that his Calvinian necessity is "such an indissoluble concatenation of secondary causes, [*created for that end,*] and of effects, as has a native tendency to secure the certainty of events, [i.e. of all volitions, murders, adulteries, and incests,] *sicut unda impellitur unda;*" as one wave impels another; or as the first link of a chain, which you pull, draws the second, the second the third, and so on. Now if all our volitions are *pushed forward* by God through the means of his absolute will, his irresistible decree, his efficacious creation, and his all-conquering necessitation, which is nothing but an adamantine chain of second causes created by Providence in order to produce absolutely all the effects which are produced, and to make them impel each other, "as one wave impels another;" we desire to know how our volitions can be thus *irresistibly impelled* upon us "without any *compulsory* force on our will." I do not see how Mr. T. can get over this contradiction, otherwise than by saying, that although God's necessitation is irresistibly *impulsory,* yet it is not at all *compulsory;* although it absolutely *impels* us to will, yet it does not in the least *compel* us to be willing. But would so frivolous, so absurd a distinction as this, wipe off the foul blot which the scheme of necessity fixes on the Father of lights, when it represents him as the first cause, and the grand contriver of all our sinful volitions?

Mr. T., pp. 133, 134, among other pieces of Manicheism, gives us the following account of that strange religion: — "There are two independent gods, or infinite principles, viz. light and darkness. The first is the author of all good; and the second of all evil. The evil god made sin. The good god and the bad god wage implacable war against each other; and perpetually clog and disconcert one another's schemes and operations. Hence men are *impelled, &c,* to good, or to evil, according as they come under the power of the good deity, or the bad one." Or, to speak Calvinistically, they are necessarily made willing to believe and obey, if they are the elected objects of everlasting love, which is the *good* principle; and they are irresistibly made willing to disbelieve and disobey, if they are the reprobated objects of everlasting wrath, which is the *evil* principle. For free will has no more place in Manicheism than it has in Calvinism. Hence it appears that, setting aside the other peculiarities of each scheme, the grand difference between Calvin and Manes consists in Calvin's making everlasting, electing, necessitating love, and everlasting, reprobating, necessitating wrath, to flow from the *same Divine principle;* whereas Manes more reasonably supposed that they flow from *two contrary principles.* Whoever therefore denies free will, and contends for necessity, embraces, before he is aware, the capital error of the Manichees; and it is well if he do not hold it in a less reasonable manner than Manes himself did. "I believe," adds Mr. Toplady, "it is absolutely impossible to trace quite up to its source the antiquity of that hypothesis which absurdly affirms the existence of two eternal, contrary, independent principles. What led so many wise people, and for so great a series of ages, into such a wretched mistake, were chiefly, I suppose, these two considerations: (1.) That evil, both moral and physical, are *positive* things, and so must have a positive cause. (2.) That a being, perfectly good, could not, from the very nature of his existence, be the cause of such bad things."

Here Mr. Toplady reasons like a judicious divine. The misfortune for his scheme is, that his "two considerations," like two mill stones, grind Calvinism to dust; or, like two cogent arguments, force us to embrace the doctrine of free will, or the error of Manes. Mr. Toplady seems aware of this; and therefore to show that God can, upon the Calvinian plan, absolutely predestinate, and effectually bring about sin, by making men willing to sin in the day of his irresistible power; and that nevertheless he is *not* the author and first cause of sin; to show this, I say, Mr. Toplady asserts, "that evil, whether physical or moral, does not, upon narrow inspection, appear to have *so much of positivity in it, as* it is probable those ancients supposed." Nay, he insinuates that as "sickness is a *privation* of health; so the sinfulness of any human action is said to be a *privation,*" being called ανομια, "illegality;" and he adds, that wonderful as the thing may appear, Dr. Watts, in his Logic, "ventures to treat of sin under the title of *not being.*"* When Mr. Toplady has thus cleared the way, and modestly intimated that sin, being a kind of nonentity, can have no *positive cause,* he proposes the grand question, "whether the great first cause, who is infinitely and merely good, can be either *efficiently* or *deficiently* the author of them?" that is (according to the context) the author of iniquity, injustice, impiety, and vice, as well as the author of the natural evil by which God punishes sin?

Page 139, Mr. Toplady answers this question thus: — "In my opinion, the single word *permission* solves the whole difficulty, as far as it can be solved," &c. And page 141, he says, "We know scarce any of the views which induced uncreated goodness to *ordain* (for, &c, I see no great difference between *permitting* and *ordaining*) the

---

* If the Calvinists, in their unguarded moments, represent sin as a kind of *not being* or *nonentity,* that they may exculpate God for absolutely ordaining it, do they not by this means exculpate the sinner also? If the first cause of sin is excusable, because sin is a *privation,* and has "not so much of positivity in it as the ancients supposed," is not the *second* cause of sin much more excusable on the same account?

introgression, or more properly the *intromission*, of evil." Here Mr. Toplady goes as far as he decently can. Rather than grant that we are endued with free will, and that when God had made angels and men free-willing creatures, in order to judge them according to their own works, he could not, without inconsistency, rob them of free will by *necessitating* them to be either good or wicked; rather, I say, than admit this Scriptural doctrine, which perfectly clears the gracious Judge of all the earth, Mr. Toplady first indirectly and decently extenuates sin, and brings it down to almost nothing, and then he tells us that God *ordained* it. Is not the openness of Manes preferable to this Calvinistic winding? When Mr. Toplady grants that God "ordained" sin, and when he charges "the intromission of evil" upon God, does he not grant all that Manes in this respect contended for? And have not the Manichean necessitarians the advantage over Mr. Toplady, when they assert that a principle, which absolutely ordains, yea, necessitates sin and all the works of darkness, is a *dark* and *evil* principle? Can we doubt of it, if we believe these sayings of Christ? "Out of the [evil] heart proceed evil thoughts, &c. By their works you shall know them. The tree is known by its fruit."

Again: if "sin," or rather the sinfulness of an action, may be properly called a "not being," or a *nonentity, as* Mr. Toplady inconsistently insinuates, page 137, it absurdly follows, that crookedness, or the want of straightness in a line, is a mere *privation* also, or a *not being:* whereas reason and feeling tell us that the crookedness of a crooked line is something every way as positive as the straightness of a straight line. To deny it is as ridiculous as to assert that a circle is a *not being,* because it is not made of straight lines like a square; or that a murder is a species of nonentity, because it is not the legal execution of a condemned malefactor. Nor can Mr. Toplady mend his error by hiding it behind "Dr. Watts' Logic;" for the world knows that Dr. Watts was a Calvinist when he wrote that book; and therefore, judicious as he was, the veil of error prevented him from seeing *then* that part of the truth which I contend for.

Once more: whether sin has a positive cause or not, (for Mr. Toplady insinuates both these doctrines with the inconsistency peculiar to his system,) I beg leave to involve him in a dilemma, which will meet him at the front or back door of his inconsistency. Either sin *is* a real thing, and has a positive cause; or it *is not* a real thing, and has no positive cause. If it IS NOT a real thing, and has no positive cause, why does God positively send the wicked to hell for *a privation* which they have not *positively caused?* And if sin IS a real thing, or a positive moral crookedness of the will of a sinner, and as such *has* a positive cause; can that positive cause be any other than the *self perversion* of free will, or the *impelling decree* of a sin-ordaining God? If the positive cause of sin is the *self perversion* of free will, is it not evident, that so sure as there is sin in the world, the doctrine of free will is true? But if the positive cause of sin is the *impelling decree* of a sin-ordaining, sin-necessitating God; is it not incontestable that the capital doctrine of the Manichees, the doctrine of absolute necessity is true; and that there is in the Godhead an evil principle, (it signifies little whether you call it *matter, darkness, everlasting free wrath,* or *devil,*) which positively ordains and irresistibly causes sin? In a word, is it not clear that the second Gospel axiom is overthrown by the doctrine of necessity; and that the damnation of sinners is of God, and not of themselves?

While Mr. Toplady tries to extricate himself from this dilemma, I shall produce one or two more passages of this book to prove that his scheme makes God the author of sin, according to the most dangerous error of Manes. The heathens imagined that Minerva, the goddess of wisdom, was Jupiter's offspring in the most peculiar manner. Diana was indeed Jupiter's daughter, but Latona, an earthly princess, was her mother: whereas Jupiter was at once the father and mother of Minerva. He begat her himself in the womb of his own brain, and when she was ripe for the birth, his forehead opened after a violent headache, which answered to the pangs of child bearing, and out came the lovely female deity. Mr. Toplady, alluding to this heathen fiction, represents his Diana, *necessity*, as proceeding from God with her immense chain of events, which has among its adamantine links all the follies, heresies, murders, robberies, adulteries, incests, and rebellions, of which men and devils have been, are, or ever shall be guilty. His own words, page 50, are, "Necessity, in general, with all its extensive series of adamantine links in particular, is, in reality, what the poets feigned of Minerva, the issue of Divine wisdom: [he should have said *the issue of the supreme God, by his own wise brain,*] deriving its *whole existence from the free will of God; and its whole effectuosity* from *his* never-ceasing providence." Is not this insinuating, as plainly as decency will allow, that every sin, as a link of the adamantine chain of events, has been hammered in heaven, and that every crime "derives its whole existence from the free will of God?" Take one more instance of the same Manichean doctrine: —

Page 64. Mr. Toplady having said that "he [God] casteth forth his ice like morsels, and causeth his wind to blow," &c, adds, "Neither is *material* nature alone bound fast in fate. All other things, *the human will* itself not excepted, are *not less tightly bound*, i.e. *effectually* influenced and determined." Hence it is evident, that if this Calvinism is true, when sinners send forth volleys of unclean and profane words, Calvin's God has as "tightly bound" them to cast forth Manichean ribaldry, as the God of nature binds the clouds to "cast forth his ice like morsels."

I would not be understood to demonstrate by the preceding quotations, that Mr. Toplady *designs* to make God the author of sin. No: on the contrary, I do him the justice to say, that he does all he can to clear his doctrines of grace from this dreadful imputation. I only produce his own words to show that, notwithstanding all his endeavours, this horrid Manichean consequence unavoidably flows from his *Scheme of Necessity.*

SECTION II.

Mr. Toplady attempts to support his Scheme of Absolute Necessity by philosophy — His philosophical error is overthrown by fourteen arguments — What truth comes nearest to his error.

WE have taken a view of the Scheme of Necessity, and seen how it represents God, directly or indirectly, as the first cause of all sin and damnation. Consider we now how Mr. T. defends this scheme by rational arguments as a philosopher.

Page 22. "The soul is, *in a very extensive degree,* passive as matter is." Here Mr. Toplady, *in some degree,* gives up the point. He is about to prove that the soul is not *self determined;* and that, as our bodily organs are necessarily and irresistibly affected by the objects which strike them; so our souls are necessarily and irresistibly determined by our bodily organs, and by the ideas which those organs necessarily raise in our minds, when they are so affected. Now, to prove this, he should have proved that our souls are *altogether as passive* as our bodies. But, far from proving it, he dares not assert it: for he allows that the soul is passive as matter, only "in a very extensive degree;" and therefore, by his own concession, the argument on which he is going to rest the notion of the absolute passiveness of the soul with respect to self determination, will be at least *in some degree* groundless. But let us consider this mighty argument, and see if Mr. T.'s limitation frees him from the charge of countenancing materialism, "in a very extensive degree."

Page 22. "The senses are *necessarily* impressed by every object from without, and as *necessarily* commove the fibres of the brain; from which nervous commotion, ideas are *necessarily* communicated to, or excited in the soul; and by the judgment, which the soul *necessarily* frames of those ideas, the will is *necessarily* inclined to approve or disapprove, to act or not to act. If so, where is the boasted power of self determination?"

This Mr. Toplady calls "a survey of the soul's *dependence* on the body." Page 27, he enforces the same doctrine in these words: "The human body is *necessarily* encompassed by a multitude of *other* bodies. Which other surrounding bodies, animal, vegetable, &c, so far as we come within their perceivable sphere, *necessarily* impress our nerves with sensations correspondent to the objects themselves. These sensations are *necessarily*, &c, propagated to the soul, which can no more *help* receiving them, and being affected by them, than a tree can resist a stroke of lightning.

"Now, (1.) If all the ideas in the soul derive their existence from sensation; and, (2.) If the soul depend absolutely on the body, for all those sensations; and, (3.) If the body be both primarily and continually dependent on other extrinsic beings, for the very sensations which it [the body] communicates to the soul; the consequence seems to me undeniable, that neither man's mental, nor his outward operations are *self* determined; but, on the contrary, determined by the views with which an infinity of surrounding objects *necessarily*, and almost incessantly impress his intellect."

These arguments bring to my mind St. Paul's caution: "Beware, lest any man spoil you through philosophy, and vain deceit." That Mr. T.'s scheme is founded on a vain philosophy, will, I hope, appear evident to those who weigh the following remarks:—

I. This scheme is contrary to genuine philosophy, which has always represented the soul as able to resist the strongest impressions of the objects that surround the body; and as capable of going against the wind and tide of all the senses. Even Horace, an effeminate disciple of Epicurus, could say, in his sober moments,

Justum et tenacem propositi virum, &c.

"Neither the clamours of a raging mob, nor the frowns of a threatening tyrant; neither furious storms, nor roaring thunders can move a righteous man, who stands firm to his resolution. The wreck of the world might crush his body to atoms, but could not shake his soul with fear." But Mr. T.'s philosophy sinks as much below the poor heathen's, as a man who is perpetually borne down and carried away by every object of sense around him, is inferior to the steady man, whose virtue triumphs over all the objects which strike his senses.

II. This doctrine unmans man. For reason, or a power morally to regulate the appetites which we gratify by means of our senses, is what chiefly distinguishes us from other animals. Now if outward objects *necessarily* bias our senses, if our senses necessarily bias our judgment, and if our judgment necessarily bias our will and practice, what advantage have we over beasts? May we not say of reason, what heated Luther once said of free will; that it is an empty name, a mere nonentity? Thus Mr. Toplady's "Scheme of Philosophical Necessity," by rendering reason useless, saps the very foundation of all moral philosophy, and hardly allows man the low principle of conduct which we call *instinct* in brutes: nay, the very brutes are not so affected by the objects which strike their senses; but they often run away, hungry as they are, from the food which tempts their eye, their nose, and their belly, when they apprehend some danger, though their senses discover none. Beasts frequently act in full opposition to the sight of their eyes; but the wretched scheme, which Mr. T. imposes upon us as *Christian philosophy,* supposes that all men *necessarily* think, judge, and act, not only "according to the sight of their eyes," but according to the impressions made by matter, upon all their senses. How would heathenish fatalists themselves have exploded so carnal a philosophy!

III. As it sets aside reason, so it overthrows conscience, and "the light which enlightens every man that comes into the world." For of what use is conscience? Of what use is the internal light of grace, which enlightens conscience within, if man is necessarily determined from *without;* and if the objects which strike his senses, irresistibly turn his judgment and his will; insomuch that he can no more resist their impression "than a tree can resist the stroke of lightning?"

IV. As this scheme leaves no room for morality, so it robs us of the very essence of God's natural image, which consists chiefly in *self activity* and *self motion.* For, according to Mr. T.'s philosophy, we cannot take one step, no, not in the affairs of common life, without an irresistible, necessitating impulse. Yea, with respect to self activity, he represents us as inferior to our watches: they have their spring of motion *within themselves,* and they can go alone, if they are wound up once in twenty-four hours. But, if we believe Mr. T., our spring of motion is *without us*: nay, we have as many springs of motion as there are objects around us; and these objects necessarily wind up our will from moment to moment. For, by necessarily moving our senses, they necessarily move our understandings; our understanding necessarily moves our will; and our will necessarily moves our tongues, hands, and feet. Thus our will and our body, like the wheels and body of a coach, never move but as they are moved, and cannot help moving when they are acted upon. How different is this mechanical religion from the spiritual religion which the learned and pious Dr. H. More inculcates in these words: — "The first degree of the Divine image was *self motion* or *self activity.* For mere passivity, or to be moved or acted by another, without a man's will, &c, is the condition of such as are either dead or asleep; as to go of a man's self is a symptom of one alive or awake. Men that are dead drunk may be haled, or disposed of where others please." To be irresistibly acted upon is then to be "deprived of that degree of life which is *self activity,* or the doing of things from an inward principle of free agency; and therefore it is to be, so far, in a state of death."

Nor will Mr. T. mend the matter by urging that our understanding and our will are first *necessarily* moved and determined by the objects which surround us. For the motion of a coach drawn by horses, and driven by a coachman, is not the less mechanical, because the smooth axletree, and the oiled wheels, being *first* set in motion, move the whole coach by readily yielding to the impulse of the external mover. Were such wheels as fill of consciousness and willingness as the mystic wheels of Ezekiel's vision; yet, so long as they moved by absolute necessity, or by an *oil of willingness* irresistibly applied to them from without, their motion would not be more commendable than that of a well suspended and oiled wheel, which the touch of your finger moves round its axis. It turns indeed freely and (according to supposition) willingly: but yet, as it wills and moves irresistibly and passively, its moving and willing are merely mechanical. So easy and short is the transition from the scheme of absolute necessity to that of universal mechanism!

V. If Mr. T.'s scheme of necessity be true, all sin may be justly charged upon Providence, who, by the "surrounding objects which necessarily impress our intellect," causes sin as truly, and as irresistibly, as a gunner causes the explosion of a loaded cannon, by the lighted match which he applies to the touch hole. And Eve was unwise when she said, "The serpent beguiled me, and I did eat;" for she might have said, "Lord, I have only followed the appointed law of my nature: for, providentially coming within sight of the tree of knowledge, I perceived that 'the fruit was good for food, and pleasant to the eye.' It *necessarily* impressed my nerves with correspondent sensations; these sensations were necessarily and instantaneously propagated to my soul; and my soul could no more *help* receiving these forcible impressions, and eating in consequence of them, than a tree can resist a stroke of lightning." I should be glad to know with what justice Eve could have been condemned after such a plea, if Mr. T.'s scheme be true? Especially if she had urged, as Mr. T. does, p. 14, that God's necessitation gives birth to "providence;" that is, "to the all-directing superintendency of Divine wisdom and power, carrying the whole preconcerted scheme into actual execution, by the subservient mediation of second causes [such as the fair colour of the fruit, and the eye of Eve] which were created for that end." Can any man say, that if Mr. T. be right, Eve would have "charged God foolishly?"

However, if Eve did not know how to exculpate herself properly, according to the doctrine of Divine necessitation, Mr. Toplady knows how to reduce his Gospel to practice; and therefore, in a humorous manner, he justifies his illiberal treatment of his opponent thus: p. 10, "Mr. Wesley imagines that, upon my own principles, I can be no more than *a clock*. And if so, how can I help *striking?* He himself has several times smarted for coming too near the pendulum." What a sweet and profitable Gospel is this! Who would wonder, if all who love to "strike their fellow servants" should embrace Mr. Toplady's system, as a comfortable "doctrine of grace," by which sin may be humourously palliated, and *striking* sinners completely justified?

VI. It is contrary to Scripture: for, if man be necessarily affected, and irresistibly wrought upon, or led by the forcible impressions of external objects, Paul spake like a heretical free willer when he said, "All things [indifferent] are lawful for me; but I will not be brought under the power of any." How foolish was this saying, if he could "no more help being brought under the irresistible power of the objects which surrounded him, than a tree can help being struck by the lightning?"

VII. It is contrary to common sense: how can God reasonably set life and death, water and fire before us, and bid us choose *eternal life*, and *living water*, if surrounding objects work upon us, as the lightning works upon a tree on which it falls? And when the Lord commands the reprobates to choose virtue, after having bound them over to vice by the adamantine chain of necessitation, does he not insult over their misery, as much as a sheriff would do, who, after having ordered the executioner to bind a man's hands, to fasten his neck to the gallows, and absolutely to drive away the cart from under him, should gravely bid the wretch to choose life and liberty, and bitterly exclaim against him for "neglecting so great" a deliverance?

VIII. It is contrary to the sentiments of all the Churches of Christ, except those of *necessitarian* Rome and Geneva: for they all *reasonably* require us to renounce the pomps of the world, and the alluring, sinful baits of the flesh. But if these pomps and baits work upon us by means of our senses, as necessarily, and determine our will as irresistibly as lightning shivers a tree, can any thing be more absurd than our baptismal engagements? Might we not as well seriously vow never to be struck by the lightning in a storm, as solemnly vow never to be led by, or follow the vanities of the world and the sinful lusts of the flesh?

IX. It represents the proceedings of the day of judgment, as the most unrighteous, cruel, and hypocritical acts, that ever disgraced the tribunal of a tyrant. For if God, by eternal, absolute, and necessitating decrees, places the reprobates in the midst of a current of circumstances, which carries them along as irresistibly as a rapid river wafts a feather; if he encompasses them with tempting objects, which strike their souls with ideas, that cause sin in their hearts and lives, as inevitably as a stroke of lightning raises splinters in the tree which it shatters; and if we *can no more help* being determined by these objects, which God's providence has placed around us on purpose to determine us, than a tree can resist a stroke of lightning; it unavoidably follows, that when God will judicially condemn the wicked, and send them to hell for their sins, he will act with as much justice as the king would do, if he sent to the gallows all his subjects who have had the misfortune of being struck with lightning. Nay, to make the case parallel, we must suppose that the king has the absolute command of the lightning, and had previously struck them with the fiery ball, that he might subsequently condemn them to be hanged for having been struck, according to his absolute decree.

Should the reader, who is not yet initiated into the mystery of the Calvinian decrees, ask, if it be possible that rigid bound willers should fix so horrible a blot upon the character of "the Judge of all the earth?" I answer in the affirmative; and I prove, by the following words of Mr. Toplady, that, if Calvinism be true, the pretended sentence which the Judge shall pass in the great day, will be only a *publication* or *ratification* of the everlasting decrees, by which a Manichean deity absolutely necessitates some men to repent and be saved, and others to sin and be damned. "Christ," says Mr. Toplady, in his *Zanch.* p. 87, "will then properly sit as a Judge; and openly *publish,* and solemnly *ratify* his everlasting decrees, by receiving the elect, &c, into glory; and by passing sentence on the non-elect, [&c,] for their wilful ignorance of Divine things, and their obstinate unbelief," &c. It is true that after the word *non-elect* Mr. T. adds in a parenthesis these words, "not for having done what they could not help." But it is equally true that he had no more right to add this parenthesis, than I have to say that the lightning is at my command: for, throughout his Scheme of Necessity, he attempts to prove that man is not "self determined," but *irresistibly determined by some other being,* viz. by God, who absolutely determines him by "second causes created for that end;" forcible causes these, whose impressions are so strong, that we "can no more help receiving them [and being determined by them] than a tree can resist a stroke of lightning." Beside, if the non-elect are damned "for their obstinate unbelief," as Mr. T. tells us in his quotation; and if it be as impossible for them to believe as to make a world, (an absurd maxim this, which is inculcated by rigid bound willers,) it is evident that the non-elect can no more help their unbelief, than they can help their incapacity to create a world.

X. Mr. Toplady's Scheme of Necessity places *matter* and its impressions far above *spirit* and its influence. If his philosophy be true, every material object around us, by making necessary, irresistible impressions upon our minds, necessarily determines our will, and irresistibly impels our actions. According to this system, therefore, we cannot resist the powerful influence of matter: but, if we believe the Scriptures, we can "resist the Holy Ghost, and do despite to the Spirit of grace." Now, what is this, but to represent *matter,* (which is the God of the materialists, and the *evil* God of the Manichees,) as more active, quick, and powerful than *spirit?* Yea, than the Holy Spirit?

Mr. Toplady may indeed say that the material objects, by which we are absolutely determined, are only God's tools, by which God himself determines us: but, though this salvo may so far reconcile the Scheme of Necessity to itself; it will never reconcile it to such scriptures as these: — "Ye do always resist the Holy Ghost, as your fathers did. I would have gathered you, and ye would not." And, what is still worse, it represents God as working Manichean iniquity by common adulterers and robbers, as forcibly as a miller grinds his corn, by the use he makes of a current of air or a stream of water.

XI. The Scheme of Philosophical Necessity which I attack, supposes that God, to maintain order in the universe, is obliged to necessitate all events, from the wagging of a dog's tail, or the rise of a particle of dust, to the murder of a king, or the rise of an empire. Thus Mr. T. tells us, in his preface to *Zanchius,* p. 4, "Bishop Hopkins did not go a jot too far in asserting," that "not a dust flies on a beaten road, but God raiseth it, conducts its uncertain motion, and, by his particular care, conveys it to the certain place he had *before appointed* for it: nor shall the most fierce and tempestuous wind hurry it any farther." I object to this puerile system: (1.) Because it absurdly multiplies God's decrees; rendering them not only as numerous as the sands on the sea shore, and the particles of dust on beaten roads, but also as countless as all the motions of each grain of sand and particle of dust in all ages. At this rate, a large folio volume could not contain all the decrees of God concerning the least particle of dust; its rises and falls; its stops and hinderances; its situations and modifications; its whirlings to the right, or to the left, &c, &c. And, (2.) Because it represents God as being endued with less wisdom than a prudent king, who can maintain good order in his kingdom without making particular laws or decrees to necessitate every eructation of his drunken soldiers, or every puff of his smoking subjects; and without ordaining every filthy jest which is uttered from the ale bench, appointing every loud invective which disturbs Billingsgate, and predestinating every wry face which the lunatics make in Bedlam

XII. But what I chiefly dislike in this scheme, is its degrading all human souls in such a manner as to make them receive their moral excellence and depravity from the contexture of the brains by which they work, and from the place of the bodies in which they dwell. Insomuch, that all the difference there is between one who thinks loyally, and one who thinks otherwise; between one who believes that Christ is God over all, and one who believes that he is a mere creature, consists only in the make and position of their brains. Supposing, for example, that a gentleman has honourable thoughts of his king and of his Saviour, and is ready, from a principle of loyalty and faith, to defend the dignity of George the Third, and the divinity of Jesus Christ: supposing also, that another gentleman breaks, without ceremony, these two evangelical precepts, "Honour the king, — Let all the angels of God worship him" [Christ;] I ask, Why is their moral and religious conduct so opposite? Is it because the first gentleman's free-willing soul has intrinsically more reverence for the king and for our Lord? Because he keeps his heart more tender by faith and prayer, and his conscience more devoid of prejudice, through a diligent improvement of his talent, or through a more faithful use of his free agency, and a readier submission to the light that enlightens every man? No such thing; if Mr. T.'s scheme be true, the whole difference consists in "mud walls," and external *circumstances.*

Page 33, "The soul of a monthly reviewer, if imprisoned within the same *mud walls* which are tenanted by the soul of Mr. John Wesley, would, similarly *circumstanced,* reason and act, (I verily think,) exactly like the bishop of Moorfields." And, pp. 34, 35, he adds, "I just now hinted the conjecture of some, that a human spirit incarcerated in the brain of a cat, would probably both think and behave as that animal does. But how would the soul of a cat acquit itself if inclosed in the brain of a man? We cannot resolve this question with certainty, any more than the other." Admirable divinity! So Mr. Toplady leaves the orthodox in doubt: (1.) Whether when their souls, and the souls of cats, shall be let out of their respective brains or prisons, the souls of cats will not be equal to the souls of men. (2.) Whether, supposing the soul of a cat had been put in the brain of St. Paul, or of a monthly reviewer, the soul of "puss" would not have made as great an apostle as the soul of Saul of Tarsus; as good a critic as the soul of the most sensible reviewer. And, (3.) Whether, in case the "human spirit" [of Isaiah] "were shut up in the skull of a cat, puss would not, notwithstanding, move prone on all four, purr when stroked, spit when pinched, and birds and mice be her darling objects of pursuit," p. 34. Is not this a pretty large stride, for the first, toward the doctrine of the sameness of the souls of men with the souls of cats and frogs? Wretched Calvinism, new-fangled doctrines of grace, where are you leading your deluded admirers? your principal vindicators? Is it not enough that you have spoiled the fountain of living waters, by turning it into the muddy streams of Zeno's errors? Are ye also going to poison it by the absurdities of Pythagoras' philosophy? What a side stroke is here inadvertently given to these capital doctrines:

God breathed into Adam the breath of life, and he became a living soul," — a soul made "in the image of God," and not in the image of a cat: "the spirit of the beast goeth downward to the earth: but the spirit of man goeth upward: it returns to God who gave it," with all intention to judge and reward it according to its moral works.

But I must do Mr. Toplady justice: he does not yet recommend this doctrine as absolutely certain. However, from his capital doctrine, that human souls have no free will, no inward principle of self determination; and from his avowed opinion, that the soul of one man, placed in the body of another man, "would, similarly circumstanced, reason and act exactly like" the man in whose *mud walls* it is lodged; it evidently follows: (1.) That had the human soul of Christ been placed in the body and circumstances of Nero, it would have been exactly as wicked and atrocious as the soul of that bloody monster was. And, (2.) That if Nero's soul had been placed in Christ's body, and in his trying circumstances, it would have been exactly as virtuous and immaculate as that of the Redeemer: the consequence is undeniable. Thus, the merit of *the man* Christ did not in the least spring from his righteous soul, but from his "mud walls," and from the happiness which his soul had of being lodged in a "brain peculiarly modified." Nor did the demerit of Nero flow from his free agency and self perversion; but only from his "mud walls," and from the infelicity which his necessitated soul had of being lodged in an "ILL-constructed vehicle," and placed on that throne on which Titus soon after deserved to be called *the darling of mankind.* See, O ye engrossers of orthodoxy, to what absurd lengths your aversion to the liberty of the will, and to evangelical worthiness, leads your unwary souls! And yet, if we believe Mr. Toplady, your scheme, which is big with these inevitable consequences, is Christian philosophy, and our doctrine of free will is "philosophy run mad!"

XIII. If our thoughts and actions necessarily flowed from the modifications of our brains, and from the impressions of the objects around us, it would necessarily follow, that as most men, throughout the whole world, see the sun bright, snow white, and scarlet red: or as most men taste aloes bitter, vinegar sour, and honey sweet; so most men would think, speak, and act nearly with the same moral uniformity which is perceivable in their bodily organs, and in the objects which affect those organs: and it would be as impossible to improve in virtue, by a proper exertion of our powers, and by a diligent use of our talents, as it is impossible to improve the whiteness of the snow, or our power to see it white, by a diligent use of our sight. At this rate too, conversion would not be so much a reformation of our spiritual habits as a reformation of our brains.

XIV. But the worst consequences are yet behind: for if God works upon our souls in the same manner in which he works upon matter; if he raises our ideas, volitions, and passions, as necessarily as a strong wind raises the waves of the sea, with their roar, their foam, and their other accidents; in a word, if he works as absolutely and irresistibly upon spirit as he does upon matter; it follows that spirit and matter, being governed upon the same principles, are of the same nature; and that if there be any difference between the soul and the body, it is only such a difference as there is between the tallow which composes a lighted candle, and the flame which arises out of it. The light flame is as really matter as the heavy tallow and the ponderous candlestick; and all are equally passive and subject to the laws of absolute necessity. Again: —

If virtue and vice necessarily depend on the modification of our brains, and the objects which surround us; it follows that the effect will cease with the cause, and that bodily dissolution will consign our virtue or vice to the dust, into which our brains and bodily organs will soon be turned; and that when the souls of the righteous, and the souls of the wicked, shall be removed from their "mud walls," and from the objects which surround those mud walls, they will be (nearly at least) on a level with each other, if they are not on a level with the souls of cats and dogs.

Lest Mr. Toplady's admirers should think that prejudice makes me place his mistakes in too strong a light, I shall close these arguments by the judgment of the monthly reviewers. In their Review for 1775, they give us the following abridged account of Mr. Toplady's *Scheme of Necessity:* —

"The old controversy concerning liberty and necessity has lately been renewed: Mr. Toplady avows himself a strenuous and very positive champion on the side of necessity, and revives those arguments which were long since urged by Spinoza, Hobbes, &c, [two noted infidels, or rather Atheistical materialists.] It is somewhat singular in the history of this dispute, that those who profess themselves the friends of revelation, should so earnestly contend for a system which unbelievers have very generally adopted and maintained. This appears the more strange, when we consider that the present asserters of necessity manifest a very visible tendency to materialism. Fate and universal mechanism seem to be so nearly allied, that they have been usually defended on the same ground, and by the same advocates. Mr. Toplady indeed admits that the two component principles of man, body and soul, 'are not only distinct but essentially different from each other.' But it appears, in the sequel of his reasoning, that he has no high opinion of the nature and powers of the latter, [the soul.] 'An idea,' he observes, 'is that image, form, or conception of any thing which the soul is impressed with from without;' and he expressly denies that the soul has any power of framing new ideas, different from or superior to those which are forced upon it by the bodily senses. 'The soul,' he affirms, 'is, in a very extensive degree, passive as matter itself.' On his scheme, the limitation, with which he guards this assertion, is needless and futile."

While this Monthly Review is before me, I cannot help transcribing from it two other remarkable passages. The one occurs four pages after the preceding quotation. The correspondents of the reviewers give them an account of an absurd and mischievous book, written by some wild Atheistical philosopher abroad, who thinks that all matter is alive, that the earth is a huge animal, and that we feed upon it, as some diminutive insects do upon the back of an ass. "His moral doctrine," say the reviewers, "is of a piece with the rest: the result of his reasoning on this subject is, in his own words, 'Man, in every instant of his duration, is a passive instrument in the hands of necessity.' Then let *us drink and drive care away, drink, and be merry, as* the old song says; which is the practical application." I would not be understood to charge this application upon Mr. Toplady; I only mention it, after the reviewers, as a natural consequence of his system of necessity.

The other passage is taken from the Review of *Dr. Hartley's* Theory of the Human Mind*, published by Dr. Priestley, who pleads as strongly necessity as Mr. Toplady himself.

"Materialism," say the reviewers, "has been, from early ages, considered as one of the chief bulwarks of Atheism. Accordingly, while Epicurus, and Hobbes, and their disciples, have endeavoured to defend it, Theists and Christians have pointed their batteries against it. But we learn from Dr. Priestley that perception, and all the mental powers of man, are the result of such an organical structure as that of the brain. How would Epicurus, how would Collins have triumphed, had they lived to see this point [that the mental powers of man result from such an organical structure as that of the brain] given up to them, even by a Christian divine! Another discovery, very

---

* Mr. Toplady, page 148, intimates to his readers that Dr. Hartley has written an "eminent defence of necessity," and promises himself "a feast of pleasure and instruction" in reading his book.

consonant to the first, is, that the whole man becomes extinct at death. For this concession Atheists will likewise thank him, as it has been one of the chief articles of their creed from the beginning of the world. Let us suppose, with Dr. Priestley, that all the mental powers of Julius Cesar result from the organical structure of his brain. This organical structure is dissolved, and the whole man, Julius Cesar, becomes extinct; the matter of this brain, however, remains, but it is not Julius Cesar; for he (*ex hypothesi*) is wholly extinct."

Having produced a variety of arguments, which, I trust, will altogether have weight enough to sink Mr. Toplady's Scheme of Necessity to the bottom of the sea of error, where a vain philosophy begat it on a monstrous body of corrupted divinity, I shall conclude this section by setting my seal to the truths which border most upon Mr. Toplady's error, and by which he is deceived, according to the old saying, *Decipimur specie recti*, "We embrace falsehood under the deceitful appearance of some truth."

Mr. Toplady is certainly in the right, when he asserts that there is a close connection between our soul and body; and that each has a reciprocal influence on the other. We readily grant that a cheerful mind is conducive to bodily health, and that

> *Corpus onustum*
> *Hesternis vitiis animum quoque prægravat una,*
> *Atque affigit humo divinæ particulam auræ.* — HOR.

"The soul, which dwells in a body oppressed with last night's excess, is clogged with the load which disorders the body." Nor do we deny that, in a thousand cases, our bodies and our circumstances may prevent the full exertion of our spiritual powers, as the lameness of a horse, or its natural sluggishness, added to the badness of the road, may prevent the speed which a good rider could make if he had a better horse and a better road. But to carry this consideration as far as Mr. Toplady does, is as absurd as to suppose that the skill and expedition of a rider depend *entirely* on his beast, and on the goodness of the road. We likewise allow, that sometimes the soul may be as much overpowered by a disordered, dying body, as a rider, who is irresistibly carried away by a mad horse, or lies helpless under the weight of a dying horse. But, in such cases, we do not consider the soul as accountable; as neither delirious persons, nor those who are dying of a paralytic stroke, are answerable for their actions and omissions in such peculiar circumstances.

In all other cases history furnishes us with a variety of examples of men, who, through a faithful use of their talents, have overcome the infelicity of their constitution and circumstances; while others, by a contrary conduct, have perverted the most happy constitution, and the most fortunate circumstances in life. Thus Socrates, by improving his light, mastered an unhappy constitution, which in his youth carried him to violent anger, and an undue gratification of bodily appetites. And thus Solomon, by not improving his light, in his old age made shipwreck of the wisdom, temperance, and piety, that distinguished him in his youth. So Nero outlived the happy dispositions which made him shine in the former part of his life. And Manasses, by "humbling himself before the God of his fathers," overcame in his old age the horrid and abominable propensities which constituted him a monster of iniquity in his youthful days.

Likewise, with respect to the circumstances in which we are placed by Providence, I grant they have a considerable weight in the turn of our affections. Nevertheless, this weight is by no means such as Mr. T. supposes. Diogenes might be as proud in his tub, as Alexander in his magnificent palace. A gown and a band may cover a revengeful clergyman, while a star and garter shine on a benevolent courtier. Cornelius turned to God in the army; and the sons of Eli went after Satan in the temple. Domitian and Marcus Antoninus filled the same throne; where the one astonished the universe by his wickedness, as the other did by his virtue. Abraham and Agathocles were humble in the midst of riches; and too many beggars are proud in the depth of poverty. Some men are content in a sordid cottage; while others murmur in the most splendid palaces. The treasurer of the queen of Ethiopia was (it seems) converted in the vanity of a heathen court; while Judas was perverted in the company of Christ and his fellow apostles. In short, while thousands, like Absalom, have turned out bad, notwithstanding the best instructions; numbers, like the Philippian jailer, have turned out well, maugre the worst education. Such is the power of free grace and free will. To lay therefore so much stress upon external circumstances is to undo by overdoing, and to wiredraw the truth till it is refined into error.

Upon the whole, we have Scripture and experience on our side when we assert that reason, conscience, the "light which [in various degrees] enlightens every man," the general assistance of Divine grace, and the peculiar or providential helps of God our Saviour, are more than sufficient savingly to overrule the infelicity of our bodily constitution, and our circumstances in life, if we are not wilfully and perversely wanting to ourselves; for "of them to whom less is given, less will be required:" and the advantages or disadvantages under which we labour, shall all be taken into the account of our evangelical worthiness or unworthiness, in the day when God shall judge us according to the several editions of his everlasting Gospel, and according to the good or bad use which we make of his talents of nature and grace.

SECTION III.

Remarks upon the manner in which Mr. T. attempts to support his Scheme of Necessity from Scripture — Twelve keys to open the scriptures on which he founds that scheme.

WE have seen how Mr. T. has propped up his system by philosophical arguments; let us now see how he does it by Scriptural proofs. Page 54, he says, "No man can consistently acknowledge the Divine authority of the Scriptures, without — being an *absolute necessitarian.*" To demonstrate this strange proposition, he produces, among many more, the passages which mention the case of Joseph and his brethren, the Lord and Pharaoh, Eli and his sons, Absalom and his father's wives, Shimei and David, Christ and his crucifiers, &c. As I have shown, in other publications, that these scriptures, when taken in connection with the context and the tenor of the Bible, perfectly agree with the doctrines of justice, which are inseparably connected with the doctrine of free will in man, and just wrath in God; I shall not swell this tract by vain repetition, especially as Mr. T. does not support by argument the sense which he fixes on these passages. However, that the public may see what method he follows in trying to vindicate his error from Scripture, I shall present my readers with some keys, by which they will easily open the scriptures which he misapplies, and discover the rotten foundation of Calvinism.

FIRST KEY. Detaching a passage of Scripture from the context, that what God does for particular reasons may appear to be done *absolutely*, and from mere sovereignty, is a polemical stratagem, commonly used by the Calvinists. The first passage which Mr. T. produces draws all its apparent conclusiveness from this artful method: —

Page 56. "*I withheld thee from sinning against me,*" Genesis 20:6. By quoting this detached clause, Mr. T. would insinuate that while God absolutely ordains some men to sin, he absolutely withholds other men from sin. To see that his conclusion is unscriptural, we need only read the whole verse:" God said to him [Abimelech] in a dream, Yea, I know that thou didst this in the INTEGRITY OF THY HEART, for I also withheld thee from sinning against me, therefore I suffered thee not to touch her." Now, who that adverts to the words in capitals, does not see that God's keeping Abimelech from sinning, that is, from marrying Abraham's wife, was a REWARD of Abimelech's INTEGRITY, as well as of Abraham's piety? Therefore, this very text proves, that God rewards upright free will with *restraining grace,* as well as with *glory;* and not that man has no free will, and that he is made willing to work righteousness, or to commit sin, as necessarily as puppets are made to move to the right or to the left by the show man, who absolutely causes and manages their steps. Take another instance of the same stratagem, —

Page 66. "*The Lord of hosts hath sworn, i.e.* hath solemnly and immutably decreed, *saying, Surely as I have thought, so shall it come to pass; and as I have purposed, so shall it stand.*" Here Mr. Toplady breaks off the quotation, and leaves out what follows, "that I will break the Assyrian," that is, the wicked in general, but particularly Sennacherib, the proud, blaspheming king of Assyria, whose immense army was cut off in one night by an angel; "and upon my mountains tread him Under foot," &c. By this means Mr. T. makes his hasty readers believe that God speaks of a Calvinian, absolute decree, founded upon Antinomian grace and free wrath; and not of a judicial, retributive decree, founded upon the humility of the righteous, and the desert of the wicked; though, verse 13, &c, the decree, and its cause, are thus expressly mentioned: — "Thou hast said in thy heart, *I will ascend into heaven, &c, I will be like the Most High, &c.* Yet thou shalt be brought down to hell." When Mr. T. has hidden these keys to the doctrine of justice which we defend, it is easy for him to apply to his doctrine of free wrath the peremptoriness of God's decree, and accordingly he triumphs much in these words: — "This is the purpose which is purposed upon all the earth, &c. For the Lord of hosts hath purposed, and who shall disannul it? And his hand is stretched out, and who shall turn it back?" Isaiah 14:24, &c. "Who shall disannul God's purpose?" (adds Mr. T.) "Why, human free will to be sure! Who shall turn back God's hand? Human self determination can do it with as much ease as our breath can repel the down of a feather!" This argument is full fraught with absurdity. Did we ever assert that when free will has obstinately sinned, it can reverse an absolute decree of punishment? Do we not, on the contrary, maintain the proper exertion of justice in opposition to the Calvinian dreams of absolute election and reprobation, according to which the salvation of some notorious impenitent sinners is now actually finished, and the damnation of some unborn infants is now absolutely secured?

Page 67. By a similar method Mr. T. tries to prove the doctrine of necessitating free wrath, thus: — "I have smitten you with blasting and mildew. I have sent you the pestilence. Your young men have I slain with the sword!" Amos 4:7-10. But he forgets to tell us that this severity is not Calvinistical and diabolical, but righteous and judicially retributive; for the persons thus punished are said, just before, to be wicked men, "who oppress the poor, who crush the needy, who say to their masters, Bring [strong drink] and let us drink," Amos 4:1. Therefore all that can be inferred from these, and a thousand such scriptures, is, that when free agents have obstinately sinned, punishment overtakes them *whether they will or not.* And when the Calvinists ground their Manichean notions of a wrathful, absolute sovereignty in God upon such conclusions, they expose their good sense as much as I should expose my reason, if I said, "I can demonstrate that all robbers are absolutely *necessitated* to go on the highway, because, when they are caught and condemned, they are absolutely necessitated to go to the gallows."

SECOND KEY. Because God can do a thing, and does it on particular occasions, Mr. T. and his adherents infer that he does it always. Thus, to prove that God necessarily turns the hearts of all men, at all times, and in all places, to sin or to righteousness, Mr. T. produces the following text: —

Page 65. "*Even the king's heart is in the hand of the Lord, as the rivers of water: and he turneth it whithersoever he will,* Proverbs 21:1. Odd sort of *self determination* this!" We never denied the supreme power, which God has even over the hearts of proud kings, who generally are the most imperious of men. When he will absolutely turn their will for the accomplishment of some providential design, his wisdom and omnipotence can undoubtedly do it. Thus, by letting the Philistines loose upon Saul's dominions, God turned his heart, and made him change his design of immediately surrounding and destroying David. Thus he turned the heart of Ahasuerus from his purpose of destroying the Jews, by the providential reading of the records, which reminded the king of the obligation he was under to Mordecai. Thus he turned the heart of Pharaoh toward Joseph, by giving Joseph wisdom to explain his prophetic dream. Thus, again, he turned the heart of Nebuchadnezzar from his purpose of destroying Daniel and all the wise men in Babylon, by enabling Daniel to tell and open the king's mysterious vision. And when the king of Assyria was bent upon making war against the Israelites and the Ammonites, and cast lots to know which he should destroy first, Rabbah or Jerusalem, God providentially ordered the lot to fall upon guilty Jerusalem, Isaiah 10:6, 7; Ezekiel 21:21, &c. For, in such cases, "the lot is cast into the lap" without an eye to the Lord, "but the whole disposing thereof is of the Lord," Proverbs 16:33. But these peculiar interpositions of Providence no more prove that God absolutely turns the hearts of all kings, and of *all men* in *all* things, and on *all* occasions, as Mr. T.'s system supposes, than a farrier's drenching now and then a horse, in peculiar circumstances, proves that all horses throughout the world never drink but when they are drenched.

THIRD KEY. The necessitarians confound our inability to do some or all things, with an inability to do any thing. Thus Mr. T. attempts to prove that we can do nothing but what we are *necessitated* to do, and that "Christ himself was an absolute necessitarian," by the following argument: —

Page 71. "*Thou canst not make one hair white or black. Your Father, &c, makes his sun to rise on the evil and on the good, and sendeth rain on the just and the unjust.* Surely, man can neither promote nor hinder the rising of the sun, nor the falling of the rain." But to conclude that all things are *absolutely* necessary, because we cannot alter the colour of our hair, command the clouds, and hasten sun rising, is as absurd as to conclude that a dyer cannot absolutely alter the colour of the silks which he dyes, because he cannot change the colour of his own hair, or eyes. It is as ridiculous as to infer that we cannot move a pebble, because we cannot stir a mountain; that we cannot turn our eyes like men, because we cannot turn our ears like horses; and that we have no immediate command of our thoughts and hands, because we have no immediate command of the clouds and the sun. When Mr. T. imposes such a philosophy upon us, is he not as grossly mistaken as Mons. Voltaire, his companion in necessitarianism, who gives us to understand, that because pear trees can bear no fruit but pears, men can bear no moral fruit but such as they actually produce, and that fate fixes our thoughts in our brains, as necessarily as nature fixes our teeth in our jaw bones? How absurd is a system of philosophy, which a Voltaire and a Toplady are obliged to prop up by such weak arguments as these!

FOURTH KEY. The Calvinists suck Scriptural metaphors, till they imbibe the blood of error instead of "the sincere milk of the word!" And, if I might compare Scripture comparisons to rational animals, I would say, that Mr. T. makes them go *upon all four.* Hence it is that he says, —

Page 58, "*Man is born unto trouble, as the sparks fly upward,* Job 5:7: and I am apt to think, sparks ascend by necessity." By this method of arguing, I can demonstrate that Christ was clothed with feathers; for he says, *I would have gathered you as a hen gathers her brood.* "And I am apt to think" that a hen is covered with feathers. However, I grant to Mr. T. that there is a necessity *of fallen nature:* according to this necessity, man is born to die, and in the meantime he is exposed to the troubles which naturally accompany mortality. But there are a thousand troubles which flow from immorality, and which God puts it in man's power to avoid. To deny this, is to deny the following scriptures: — "He that will love his life, and see good days, let him refrain his tongue from evil. Let him eschew evil, and do good; let him seek peace and ensue 2: 1 Peter 3:10, 11. Whoso keepeth his mouth and his tongue, keepeth his soul from troubles," Proverbs 21:23. It is therefore absurd and unscriptural to suppose, that, because we cannot avoid every trouble in life, all canting gossips are absolutely bound to bring upon *themselves* all the troubles which their slanderous, lying tongues pull down upon their own heads.

FIFTH KEY. If there occur in the Bible a poetical expression, founded upon some common, though erroneous opinion, to which the sacred penmen accommodate their language in condescension to the vulgar, Calvinism fixes upon that expression, and produces it as a demonstration of what she calls ORTHODOXY. Thus Mr. T., p. 57, builds his scheme on the following texts: —

The stars in their courses fought against Sisera, Judges 5:20. It is as absurd to prove fatalism from these words, as it would be to prove that the earth is the fixed centre of our planetary system, by quoting the abovementioned words of our blessed Lord, "Your Father makes his sun to rise on the just." The best philosophers, as well as

Christ, to be understood by the common people, say, agreeably to a false philosophy, *The sun rises,* though they know that it is the earth which turns round on her axis toward the fixed sun. As we say *the crown,* when we mean "the reigning king;" and put *heaven* for "the King of heaven:" so Deborah poetically said in her song, *The stars in their courses,* for "the providential power which keeps the planets in their courses." Herein she, probably, adapted her language to some false notions of astrology, which the Israelites had received from the Egyptians. And all that she meant was that God had peculiarly assisted the Israelites in their battle with Sisera.

SIXTH KEY. As the necessitarians build their doctrine upon poetical expressions, so they do upon *proverbial* sayings. Thus, p. 88, Mr. Toplady endeavours to support the doctrine of absolute necessity, or of the Calvinian decrees, by these words of our Lord: —

"*There shall not a hair of your head perish,* Luke 21:18, i.e. before the appointed time." But this scripture does not prove that God from all eternity made particular decrees, to appoint that men should shave so many times every week, and that such and such a hair of our head or beard should be spared so long, or should be cut off after having grown just so many days. This text is only a proverbial phrase, like that which is sometimes used among us: "I will not give way to error *a hair's breadth.*" As this expression means only, "I will *fully* resist error;" so the other only means, "You shall be *fully* protected." Therefore to build Calvinian necessity upon such a scripture, is to render the pillars of Calvinism as contemptible as the hairs which the barber wipes off his razor, when he shaves my mistaken opponent.

SEVENTH KEY. The word *shall* frequently implies a kind of necessity, and a forcible authority: thus a master says to his arguing servant, "You *shall* do such a thing: I will make you do it, whether you will or not." Mr. Toplady avails himself of this idea, to impose his scheme of necessity upon the ignorant. I say upon *the ignorant,* because he quotes again and again passages, where the word *shall* has absolutely no place in the original. For example: —

Pages 84, 87, 92, he tries to prove that Christ was "an absolute necessitarian," by the following texts: — *I send unto you prophets, &c, and some of them ye* SHALL *kill, and some of them* SHALL *ye scourge. One of you, &c,* SHALL *betray me. Ye all* SHALL *be offended because of me. Other sheep I have which are not of this fold; them also* [from a principle of superior kindness, or of remunerative favour] *I* MUST *bring; and they* SHALL *hear my voice.* I MUST, and they SHALL: what is this but double necessity?" In these, and in many such scriptures, the word *ye shall kill, &c,* in the original is a BARE *future tense.* And for want of such a tense in English, we are obliged to render the words which are in that tense by means of the words *shall* or *will.* These auxiliary words are often used indiscriminately by bur translators, who might as well, in the preceding texts, have rendered the Greek verbs WILL *kill,* WILL *scourge,* WILL *betray,* WILL *be offended,* WILL *hear my voice.* Therefore, to rest Calvinism upon such vague proofs is to rest it upon a defect in the English language, and upon the presumption that the reader is perfectly unacquainted with the original.

EIGHTH KEY. As Mr. T.'s scheme partly rests upon a supposition that his readers are unacquainted with the Greek grammar; so it supposes that they are perfect strangers to ancient geography.

Hence it is that he says, p. 89, "Our Lord knew her [the woman of Samaria] to be one of his elect: and that she might be converted precisely at the very time appointed, he *must needs go through* the territory of *Samaria,* John 4:4." Mr. Whitefield builds his peculiar orthodoxy on the same slender foundations, where he says, "Why *must* Christ *needs* go through Samaria? *Because* there was a woman to be converted there." (See his *Works,* vol. iv, p. 356.) Now the plain reason why our Lord went through Samaria was, that he went from Jerusalem to Galilee; and as Samaria lies exactly between Judea and Galilee, *he must needs go through Samaria,* or go a great many miles out of his way. Absurdity itself, therefore, could hardly have framed a more absurd argument.

NINTH KEY. One of the most common mistakes on which the Calvinists found their doctrine is, confounding *a necessity of consequence* with an *absolute necessity.* A necessity of consequence is the necessary connection which immediate causes have with their effects, immediate effects with their causes, and unavoidable consequences with their premises. Thus, if you run a man through the heart with a sword, by *necessity of* NATURAL *consequence* he must die: and if you are caught, and convicted of having done it like an assassin, by *necessity of* LEGAL *consequence* you must die. Thus again: if I hold that God, from all eternity, absolutely fixed his everlasting wrath upon others, without any respect to their works; by *necessity of* LOGICAL *consequence* I must hold that the former were never children of wrath, and must continue God's pleasant children while they commit the most atrocious crimes; and that the latter were children of wrath while they seminally existed, together with the man Christ, in the loins of sinless Adam, before the fall.

Now these three strong *necessities of consequence* do not amount to one grain of Calvinian, absolute necessity; because, though the abovementioned effects and consequences necessarily follow from their causes and premises, yet those causes and premises are not absolutely necessary. To be more plain: though a man, whom you run through the heart to rob him without opposition, *must* die; and though you *must* suffer as murderer for your crime, yet this double necessity does not prove that you were absolutely necessitated to go on the highway, and to murder the man. Again: though you *must* (indirectly at least) propagate the most detestable errors of Manes, (i.e. the worship of a double-principled Deity,) if you preach a God made up of absolute, everlasting love to some, and of absolute everlasting wrath to others; yet you are not necessitated to do this black work; because you are by no means necessitated to embrace and propagate this black principle of Calvin. Once more: by necessity of consequence, a weak man who drinks to excess is drunk; yet his drunkenness is not Calvinistically necessary; because, though the man cannot help being drunk if he drinks to excess, yet he can help drinking to excess: or, to speak in general terms, though he cannot prevent the effect, *when he has admitted the cause;* yet he can prevent the effect *by not admitting the cause.* However, Mr. Toplady, without adverting to this obvious and important distinction, takes it for granted that his readers will subscribe to his doctrine of absolute necessity, because a variety of scriptures assert such *necessity of consequence* as I have just explained. Take the following instances: —

Page 83. *"How can ye escape the damnation of hell?"* These words of Christ do not prove Calvinian reprobation and absolute necessity; but only that those who *will* obstinately go on in sin, *shall* (by necessity of consequence) infallibly meet with the damnation of hell. Page 91. *"If the Son shall make you free,* [and he shall *make* us free, if we will continue in his word,] *ye shall* [by necessity of consequence] *be free indeed."* Again, p. 92, *"Why do ye not understand my speech? Even because* [while you hug your prejudices] *ye cannot hear my word*" [with the least degree of candour.] This passage does not prove Calvinian necessity; it declares only that while the Jews were biassed by the love of honour, rather than by the love of truth, by *necessity of consequence,* they *could not* candidly hear, and cordially receive Christ's humbling doctrine. Thus he said to them, "How can ye believe, who receive honour one of another?" (*Ibid.*) "*He that is of God heareth God's words; ye therefore hear them not, because ye are not of God.*" Here is no Calvinism, but only a plain declaration, that *by necessity of consequence* no man can serve two masters; no man can gladly receive the truths of God, who gladly receives the lies of Satan. (*Ibid.*) "*Ye believe not, because ye are not of my sheep:*" that is, you eagerly follow the prince of darkness. "The works of your father, the devil, ye will* do;" and therefore, by necessity of consequence, ye cannot do the works of God; ye cannot follow me; ye cannot rank among my sheep. Again: —

Page 93. "I give my sheep eternal life, and they shall never perish, John 10:28; i.e. their salvation is *necessary,* and cannot be hindered." True: it is necessary, but it is only so by *necessity of consequence:* for damnation follows unbelief and disobedience, as punishment does sin; and eternal salvation follows faith and obedience, as rewards follow good works. But this no more proves that God necessitates men to sin or to obey, than hanging a deserter, and rewarding a courageous soldier, prove that the former was absolutely necessitated to desert, and the latter to play the hero. Once more: —

Page 94. "*I will pray the Father, and he shall give you another Comforter, — whom the world* CANNOT *receive*" [as a comforter without a proper preparation.] Now this no more proves that the world cannot *absolutely* receive the Comforter, than my asserting that Mr. Toplady could not take a degree at the university, before he had learned grammar, proves that he was for ever absolutely debarred from that literary honour. If the reader be pleased to advert to this distinction, between *necessity of consequence* and *absolute necessity,* he will be able to steer safe through a thousand Calvinian rocks.

TENTH KEY. The preceding remarks lead us to the detection of another capital mistake of *the orthodox,* so called. They perpetually confound *natural* necessity with what may (improperly speaking) be called *moral* necessity. By natural necessity, infants are born naked, and colts are foaled with a coat on; men have two legs, horses four, and some insects sixteen. And by moral necessity, servants are bound to obey their masters, children their parents, and subjects their king. Now can any thing be more unreasonable than to infer that servants can no more help obeying their masters, than children can help being born with two hands? Is it not absurd thus to confound *natural* and *moral* necessity? This however Mr. T. frequently does; witness the following scriptures, which he produces in defence of *absolute* necessity: —

Page 62, &c. "*He* [the Lord] *made a decree for the rain, and a way for the lightning of the thunder. By the breath of God frost is given,* Job. *He maketh grass to grow. He giveth snow like wool: he scattereth the hoar frost like ashes. Who can stand before his cold? He causes his wind to blow. Fire and hail, snow and vapour, &c, fulfil his word,*" Psalms. From these and the like

---

* Our Lord, when he spake these words, did not use a bare future, ωοιησετε, which Mr. T. would perhaps have triumphantly translated, ye SHALL do; putting the word SHALL in large capitals; but θελετε ωοισειν, a phrase this, which is peculiarly expressive of the obstinate choice of the *free-willing* Jews.

circumstances, Mr. T. infers that all things happen "by a necessity resulting from the will and providence of the supreme First Cause."

That nothing happens independently on that cause, and on the providential laws which God has established, we grant. But this does not prove at all the Calvinian necessity of *all* our actions. Nor does it prove that man, who is made in God's image, cannot, within his narrow sphere, frequently exert his delegated power at his own option, by making and executing *his own decrees*.

If Mr. T. denies it, I appeal to his own experience and candour. Can he not, by a good fire, reverse in his apartment God's decree of frost in winter; and by a candle can he not in his room reverse God's decree of darkness at midnight? Can he not, by icy, cooling draughts, elude the decree of heat in summer? Nay, cannot a gardener, by skilfully distributing heat to vegetables in a hot house, force a pine apple to ripen to perfection in the midst of winter? And by means of a watering pot can he not command an artificial rain to water his drooping plants in the greatest drought of summer? Again: cannot a philosopher, acquainted with the secret laws of nature, imitate, as often as he pleases, most decrees of the God of nature? Can he not form and collect dews, by raising artificial vapours in an alembic? Can he not, when he has a mind, cause diminutive thunder and lightning by means of an electrical machine? Can he not create ice, snow, and hoar frost, by nitrous salts? Can he not produce little earthquakes, by burying in the ground iron filings and sulphur mixed with water? And while he raises a wind by managing a communication of rarified air with condensed air, cannot a smith do it without half the trouble by working his bellows? Once more: cannot a physician do in the little world within you, what a philosopher does without you in the world of nature? By availing himself of some natural law, is it not in general as much in his power, if you submit to his decrees, to raise an artificial blister on your back, as it is in your gardener's to raise a salad in your garden? By skilfully setting the powers of nature at work, can he not cleanse your intestines, as yonder farmer scours his ditches? Can he not, in general, assuage his pains by lenitives, or lull them asleep by opiates? Can he not, through his acquaintance with the means by which God preserves the animal world, often promote the secretion of your fluids, and supply the want of those which are exhausted? Nay, can you not do it yourself by using that cheap medicine, *exercise*, and by taking those agreeable boluses and pleasant draughts which you call *meat and drink?* To say that nature cannot be, in many respects, assisted, and even improved by art, is to say that there are neither houses nor cities in the world; neither shoes on our feet, nor clothes on our back. And to affirm that the works of art are as absolutely necessary as the works of nature, is to confound nature and art, and to advance one of the most monstrous paradoxes that ever disgraced human reason.

ELEVENTH KEY. Confusion reigns in every corner of Babel. Another capital mistake of the necessitarians consists in their confounding *prophetic* certainty with absolute necessity. An illustration will explain my meaning: —

Mr. Toplady discovers a boy who is absolutely bent upon theft. From his knowledge of the force of indulged habits, he foresees and foretels that the boy will one day come to the gallows; and his prediction is fulfilled. The question is, Did Mr. T.'s foresight, or his prophecy, *necessitate* the thievish boy to indulge his wicked habit; and might not that boy have done like many more? Might he not have reformed, and died in his bed? Calvinism answers in the negative; but reason and Scripture agree to declare that a clear foresight, and a bare prophecy, are not of an absolutely necessitating nature; and that, of consequence, it is as absurd to confound *absolute necessity* with *certainty of prophecy,* [if I may use this expression,] as it is to confound the *free* abode of the keepers in Newgate, with the *necessary* abode of the felons who are confined there under bars and locks: in a word, it is as absurd as to confound the necessity of an event with the certainty of it. Your awkward servant has, at various times, broken you a number of china plates: that the plates are broken is certain; but that they were Calvinistically broken, that is, that your servant could *no ways avoid* breaking them *all,* precisely in the manner, place, and instant in which they were broken, is a proposition as absurd as the proof which Mr. T., page 83, draws from the following sentences of the Scriptures, to demonstrate that our Lord was Calvinistically necessitated to lay down his life for us: — "How then shall the Scriptures be fulfilled, that thus it must be? Matthew 26:54. All this was done that the Scriptures of the prophets might be fulfilled," verse 56. To do these passages justice, we should consider three things: —

1. The necessity of fulfilling the Scriptures with respect to our Lord, could never amount to the least degree of absolute, Calvinian necessity; for our Lord was no more obliged to give us the Scriptures in order to fulfil them, than Mr. T. is bound to give me a thousand pounds in order to get my thanks.

2. When we meet with such sayings as these, "This that is written must yet be accomplished in me: the Scripture must be fulfilled," &c, if they relate to Christ, they only indicate a *necessity of resolution,* if I may use this expression. Now, a necessity of resolution is the very reverse of absolute necessity; because a resolution is the offspring of free will, and may be altered by free will; whereas Calvinian necessity never admits of a liberty or power to do a thing otherwise than it is done. *I resolve* to go out this evening, and I *write my resolution;* but this does not imply any absolute necessity: FIRST, because I am at perfect liberty not to make such a resolution; and, SECONDLY, because I am at perfect liberty to break it, and I shall certainly do it, if some sufficient reason detains me at home.

Take a nobler example: God resolved to give Abraham and his seed the land of Canaan "for an everlasting possession;" and the Divine resolution is written, Genesis 17:8, and 48:4. But this does not imply the least degree of Calvinian necessity: for, (1.) Reason dictates that God was no ways obliged to form such a resolution; and, (2.) Experience teaches us, that the obstinacy of the Jews has obliged him to make them "know the breach" of his written resolution, Num. 14:34. Accordingly, they are scattered over all the world, instead of enjoying the promised land "for an everlasting possession."

3. When prophetical sayings refer to the wicked, as in the following texts, *This cometh to pass, that the word might be fulfilled, which is written in the law, They hated me without a cause: the son of perdition is lost; that the Scriptures might be fulfilled. They believe not on him, that the saying of Esaias might be fulfilled, Lord, who has believed our report?* These and the like passages denote only a prophetic necessity, founded upon God's bare foresight of what will be, but might as well (nay, better) have been otherwise. Thus I prophesy that through *logical* necessity I shall (in full opposition to *orthographical* necessity) put a colon, instead of a full point, at the end of the paragraph I am now writing: but this double necessity of *prophecy* and *logic* is so far from absolutely necessitating me, that I have almost a mind to follow the rules of punctuation, and to show, by this mean,

that I am as much at liberty to reverse my *prophetic, logical* decree, as God was to reverse his prophetic, vindictive decree, "Yet forty days and Nineveh shall be destroyed" (:)

However, my decree is accomplished. What was an hour ago a future contingency, is now matter of fact. The preceding period is concluded without a full point as *certainly* as God exists. Should Mr. T. object that I could foresee this *contingent* event, because I had a mind to bring it about: I reply, That this does not invalidate my proof: for, (1.) I foresaw this little event as contingent, and depending on my liberty, and of consequence I could not foresee it as absolutely necessary. (2.) I have a clear foresight of many things, in which I have no hand at all. Thus I foresee that a man, condemned to be hanged for murder, shall certainly be hanged, whether I do the executioner's office or not. Though the murderer might be reprieved; though he might make his escape, or poison himself before the day of execution; yet, from my knowledge of the law, of the king's aversion to murder, of the strength of the prison, and of the particular care taken of condemned criminals, my foreknowledge that the condemned murderer shall be hanged, amounts to a very high degree of certainty. Now, if I, whose foreknowledge, compared to the foreknowledge of God, is no more than a point to the infinity of space; if I, who am so short sighted, can, with such a degree of certainty, foresee an event which is not absolutely necessary; is it not absurd, I had almost said *impious,* to suppose that God's foreknowledge of events, which are not absolutely necessary, may amount to absolute necessity? Cannot God foresee future events without necessitating them, a thousand times more clearly than I can foresee what I am sure I shall not *ordain,* much less *necessitate,* namely, that Mr. T.'s prejudice will hinder him from treating Mr. W. with the respect due to an aged, laborious minister of Christ?

To deny that God's certain knowledge of future events is consistent with our liberty, because we cannot understand *how* God can certainly foresee the variations of our free will; to deny this, I say, is to deny the existence of all the things which we cannot fully comprehend. And at this rate, what is it that we shall not deny? What is it that we perfectly understand? Is there one man in ten thousand that understands how astronomers can certainly foretel the very instant in which an eclipse will begin? But does this ignorance of the vulgar render astronomical calculations less real or certain? And may not God (by the good leave of the necessitarians) surpass all men in his foreknowledge of the actions of free agents, as much as Sir Isaac Newton surpassed all the Hottentots in his foreknowledge of eclipses?

From these remarks it appears, that all the difficulties which the Calvinists have raised, with respect to the consistency of Divine foreknowledge and human free will, arise from two mistakes: the FIRST, of which consists in supposing that the simple, certain knowledge of an event, whether past, present, or future, is necessarily connected with a peculiar influence on that event; and the SECOND consists in measuring God's foreknowledge by our own, and supposing that because we cannot prophesy with absolute certainty, what free-willing creatures will do to-morrow, therefore God cannot do it. A conclusion this, which is as absurd as the following argument: — "We cannot create a grain of sand, nor comprehend how God could create it, and therefore God could neither create a grain of sand, nor comprehend how it was to be created."

I have dwelt so long upon this head, because it is the strong hold of the Calvinists, from which Mr. T. seems to bid defiance to every argument; witness his assertion, p. 80, "Foreknowledge, undarkened by the least shadow of *ignorance,* and superior to all possibility of *mistake,* is a link which draws *invincible necessity* after it." To the preceding arguments, which, I trust, fully prove the contrary, I shall add one more, which is founded on the plain words of Scripture.

So sure as the Bible is true, Mr. T. is mistaken; and God's foreknowledge, far from being connected with "invincible necessity," may exist, not only with respect to an event which is not necessary, but also with respect to an event which is so contingent, that it never comes to pass. Take a proof of it: —

We read, 1 Samuel 23:10-12, that David, while he was in the city of Keilah, heard that Saul designed to come and surprise him there. "Then said David, O *Lord God of Israel, &c, will Saul come down as thy servant has heard?* And the Lord said, HE WILL COME DOWN. Then David said, *Will the men of Keilah deliver me into the hand of Saul?* And the Lord said, THEY WILL DELIVER THEE UP." When David had received this double information he went out of Keilah, and when Saul heard it he did not come to Keilah, neither did the men of Keilah deliver him to Saul. From this remarkable occurrence we learn, (1.) That future, contingent events are clearly seen of God. (2.) That this foresight of God has not the least influence on such events. (3.) That God can foretel such events as contingent. And, (4.) That neither Scripture prophecy, nor Divine foreknowledge, has the least connection with Mr. T.'s scheme of absolute, invincible necessity; since God fore-knew that, if David stayed in Keilah, Saul would come down, and the men of Keilah would deliver David into his hands. But so far were this clear foreknowledge and peremptory prophecy of God from "drawing *invincible necessity* after" them, that Saul did not come to Keilah; neither did the men of Keilah deliver David into his hands. I flatter myself, that if the reader attend to these arguments, he will see that Mr. T.'s doctrine of an absolute connection between the certain foreknowledge of events, and their invincible necessity, is contradicted by experience, reason, and Scripture.

TWELFTH KEY. Because no child can help being born, when the last pang of his mother forces him into the light; and because no man can possibly live when the last pang of death forces his soul into eternity, the necessitarians conclude that our every intermediate action, from our birth to our death, is irresistibly brought about by the iron hand of necessity. But is not their conclusion as absurd as the following argument: "John the Baptist could not speak when he was newly born, nor could he do it when the executioner had cut off his head; absolute necessity hindered him from forming articulate sounds in the moment of his birth, and at the instant of his death; and therefore all the days of his life absolute necessity made him move his tongue when he spake?" Let us see how Mr. T. handles this wonderful argument.

Pages 102, 118. "Birth and death are the era and the period, whose interval constitutes the thread of man's visible, existence on earth. Let us examine whether those important extremes be or be not unalterably fixed by the necessitating providence of God." And by and by we are asked, "if the initial point from whence we start, and the ultimate goal which terminates our race, be Divinely and unchangeably fixed; is it reasonable to suppose that any free will, but the free will of *Deity alone,* may fabricate the intermediate links of the chain?" That is, in plain

English, "Does not God alone fabricate our every action, good or bad, from our cradle to our grave?"

Page 107, &c. Mr. T. produces such scriptures as these, to prove that the free will of *Deity alone* fabricates the link of our birth: — "*He* [Jacob] *said, Am I in God's stead to give* [*a barren woman*] *children? They are my sons, whom God has given me. Thy hands have made me and fashioned me. Thou art he that took me out of the womb. Lo, children are a heritage of the Lord. Thou hast covered me, &c, in my mother's womb. In thy book all my members were written.* God has fixed an exact point of time, for the accomplishment of all his decrees: among which fixed and exact points of time, are *a time to be born, and a time to die.*"

All these passages prove only, (1.) That when a woman is naturally barren, like Rachel or Sarah, an *extraordinary* interposition of God's providence is necessary to render her fruitful. (2.) That the fruitfulness of woman, as that of our fields, is a gift of God. (3.) That children grow in the womb, and come to the birth, according to the peculiar energy of those laws, which God, as the God of nature, has made for the propagation of animals in general, and of man in particular. And, (4.) That as there is *a time to be born,* namely, in general nine months after conception; so there is a *time to die,* which, in the present state of the world, is seventy or eighty years after our nativity, if no peculiar event or circumstance hastens or retards our birth and our death.

That this is the genuine meaning of the scriptures produced by Mr. T., I prove by the following arguments: —

1. God could never Calvinistically appoint the birth of *all* children, without Calvinistically appointing their conception, and every mean conducive thereto: whence it undeniably follows, that (if Calvinism is true) he absolutely appointed, yea, necessitated all the adulteries and whoredoms, with all the criminal intrigues and sinful lusts of the flesh, which are inseparably connected with the birth of base-born children. Now this doctrine makes God the grand author of all those crimes, and represents him as the most inconsistent of all lawgivers; since, by his moral decrees he forbids, and by his Calvinian decrees he enjoins, whoredom and adultery, in order to fabricate the link of the birth of every bastard child.

2. The experience of thousands of virgins shows, that, by keeping themselves single, they may prevent the birth of a multitude of children; and their parents may do it too, for St. Paul says, "He that standeth steadfast in his heart, having no [moral] necessity, [from his daughter's constitution, or his own low circumstances] but hath power over his own will, and hath so decreed in his heart, that he will keep his virgin, doth well."

3. If women have conceived, by their carelessness or cruelty they frequently may so oppose one law of nature to another, as to reverse the decree of nature concerning the maturity of the fruit of the womb: nor can Mr. T. avoid the force of this conclusion otherwise than by saying that God necessitates such cruel mothers to destroy their unborn children, to fulfil the absolute decree which condemns their unhappy embryos never to come to birth.

When Mr. T. has tried to prove that God has Calvinistically appointed the birth of all children, he tries to demonstrate that the manner, moment, and circumstances of every body's death are so absolutely fixed, that no man can possibly live longer or shorter than he does. These are some of his arguments: —

Page 110. "The time drew near that Israel MUST die, Genesis 47. 20." Yes, he must die by *necessity of consequence:* for he was quite worn out; his age, which is mentioned in the preceding verse, being one hundred and forty-seven years. We never dream that old decrepit men are immortal. Again: —

Pages 111, 113. "Is there not an appointed time to man upon earth? In whose hand is the soul of every living thing? Man's days are determined; the number of his months is with thee: thou hast appointed his bounds, which he cannot pass. All the days of my appointed time will I wait till my change come, Job 7:1; 14:5-14. Which of you by taking thought can add one cubit to his term of life? Matthew 6:27." None of these scriptures proves that the free will of *Deity alone* has absolutely fabricated the link of every man's death. They only indicate, (1.) That God has fixed general bounds to the life of vegetables and animals; for as the aloe vegetates a hundred years, so wheat vegetates scarce twelve months: and as men in general lived seven or eight hundred years before the flood; so now "the days of our life are three score years and ten; and if, by reason of strength, they are four score years, yet is their strength then but labour and sorrow, so soon passeth it away, and we are gone," Psalm 90:10. (2.) That as no man lived a thousand years before the flood; so no man lives two hundred years now. And, (3.) That when we are about to die by necessity of consequence, &c, we cannot, without an extraordinary interposition of Providence, suspend the effect of this general decree, "Dust thou art, and unto dust shalt thou return." But to infer from such passages that we cannot in general shorten our days by not taking a proper care of ourselves, or by running headlong into danger, is acting over again the part of the old deceiver, who said, "Cast thyself down, [from the pinnacle of the temple,] for it is written," &c. From such Turkish philosophy, and murderous conclusions, God deliver weak, unwary readers!

Two arguments will, I hope, abundantly prove the falsity of this doctrine: the FIRST is, God does not so fabricate the link of our death, but we may, in general, prolong our days by choosing wisdom, and shorten them by choosing folly. Is not the truth of this proposition immovably founded upon such scriptures as these? "If thou seekest her [wisdom] as silver, then shalt thou understand every good path: length of days is in her hand," while untimely death is in the hand of fool hardiness, Proverbs 2:4, 9; 3:16. "Keep my commandments, for length of days, and long life, and peace shall they add unto thee, Proverbs 3:1, 2. Honour thy father and mother, that thou mayest live long on the earth, Ephesians 6:3. If thou wilt walk in my ways, then will I lengthen thy days, 1 Kings 3:14. Their feet run to evil: they lay wait for their own blood, and lurk privily for their own lives. So are the ways of every one that is greedy of gain; which taketh away the life of the owners thereof, Proverbs 1:16, &c. A sound heart is [in many cases] the life of the flesh; but envy, the rottenness of the bones," Proverbs 14:30. Hence so many persons shorten their days by obstinate grief; for "the sorrow of the world worketh death." What numbers of men put an untimely end to their lives by intemperance, murder, and robbery, and make good that awful saying of David, "Bloody and deceitful men shall not live out half their days," Psalm 55:23. What multitudes verify this doctrine of the wise man, "The fear of the Lord prolongeth days, but the years of the wicked shall be shortened," Proverbs 10:27. Does not the psalmist pray, "O my God, take me not away in the midst of my days?" Psalm 102:24. Does he not say, "As a snail which melteth, so let the wicked pass away like the untimely fruit of a woman?" And was not this the case of the disobedient

Israelites in the wilderness, who committed "the sin unto *bodily* death?" Is not this evident from 1 Corinthians x, "Neither let us commit fornication, as some of them also committed, and fell in one day three and twenty thousand?" &c. Nay, was not this the case of many of the Corinthians themselves? "For this cause [because he that receiveth the Lord's Supper unworthily, eateth and drinketh judgment to himself,] many are weak and sickly among you, and many sleep," [i.e. die,] 1 Corinthians 11:30.

My SECOND argument is taken from reason. If God has absolutely appointed the untimely death of all, who shorten their own days, or the days of others, by intemperance, filthy diseases, adultery, murder, robbery, treason, &c, &c, he has also *absolutely* appointed all the *crimes* by which their days are shortened; and has contrived all the wars and massacres, by which this earth is become a field of blood. I have heard of some Indians who worship a horned grinning idol, with a huge mouth split from ear to ear. But the preaching a God, who has planned and necessitated all the crimes that ever turned the world into an *Aceldama*, and a common sewer of debauchery, is an honour that the Manichees and the *orthodox*, so called, may claim to themselves.

Should Mr. T. answer, that although "the free will of the Deity alone may fabricate" adultery, murder, and *every intermediate link of the chain* of necessity; and that although the generation and death of a child conceived in adultery, and cut off by murder, is "Divinely and unchangeably fixed;" yet God is not at all the author of the adultery and murder; I desire to know how we can cut the Gordian knot, and divide between *adultery* and *the generation or conception* of a child born in adultery; and between the *murder* of such a child, and its *untimely death* caused by the cruelty of its unnatural mother.

From the whole, if I am not mistaken, we may safely conclude, (1.) That the birth and death of all mankind take place according to some providential laws. (2.) That God, in a peculiar manner, interposes in the execution or suspension of these laws, with respect to the *birth* of some men: witness the birth of Isaac, Samuel, John the Baptist, &c. (3.) That he does the same with respect to the untimely *death* of some, and the wonderful preservation of others, as appears by the awful destruction of Ananias, Sapphira, Herod, and by the miraculous preservation of Moses in the Nile, of Daniel in the den of lions, of Jonah in the whale's belly, and of Peter in the prison. (4.) That if neither the first nor the last link of the chain of human life is, in general, fabricated by the *absolute will* of God, it is unreasonable to suppose that "the free will of Deity alone fabricates the intermediate links." (5.) That to carry the doctrine of providence so far as to make God *absolutely* appoint the birth and death of all mankind, with all their circumstances, is to exculpate adulterers and murderers, and to charge God with being the principal contriver, and grand abettor of all the atrocious crimes, and of all the filthy, bloody circumstances which have accompanied the birth and death of countless myriads of men: and therefore, (6.) That the doctrine of the *absolute necessity* of all events, which is commonly called absolute predestination, is to be exploded as unscriptural, irrational, immoral, and big with the most impious consequences. However, Mr. T. seems ready to conclude that the death of every man is absolutely predestinated, because the "fall of a sparrow" is not beneath the notice of our heavenly Father: and that he thinks so, appears from his producing the following texts in defence of absolute necessity: —

Pages 81-87. "Are not two sparrows sold for a farthing? And one of them shall not fall on the ground without your Father, Matthew 10:29. Not one of them, &c, is forgotten before God, Luke 12:6." These, and the like scriptures, do not prove that God made particular decrees from all eternity, concerning the number of times that a sparrow should chirp, the number of seeds that it should eat, and the peculiar time and manner of its death. They prove only that God's providence extends to their preservation; and that they rise into existence or fall according to some law of God's making, the effect of which he can suspend, whenever he pleases. If you shoot a sparrow, it falls indeed according to this natural law of our Father, "that an animal mortally wounded shall fall;" but it by no means follows that you were necessitated thus to wound it. When the Emperor Domitian spent his time in catching and killing flies, those insects *fell* a sacrifice to his childish and cruel sport, according to this general decree of Providence, "In such circumstances a man shall have power to kill a feebler animal." But to suppose that from all eternity God made absolute decrees that Domitian should lock himself up in his apartment, and kill twenty-three flies on such a day, and forty-six the next day — that he should wring off the head of one which was six weeks old, and with a pin impale another which was three months, six hours, and fifteen minutes old; or to imagine that before the foundation of the world, the Almighty decreed that three idle boys should play the truant such an afternoon, in order to seek birds' nests; that they should find a sparrow's nest with five young ones; that they should torment one to death, that they should let another fly away, that they should starve the third, feed the fourth, and give the fifth to a cat, after having put its eyes out, and plucked so many feathers out of its tender wings; to suppose this, I say, is to undo all by overdoing. It is absurd to ascribe to God the cruelty of Nero, and the childishness of Domitian, for fear he should not have all the glory of St. John's love, and Solomon's wisdom. In a word, it is to make "the Father of lights" exactly like *the prince of darkness* — the evil principle of the Manichees, who is the first cause of all iniquity and wo. Who can sufficiently wonder that any good man should be so dreadfully mistaken as to call such a scheme a *Christian* scheme! a doctrine *according to godliness!* a *Gospel!* and the *genuine* Gospel too! And when Mr. T. charges us with Atheism, because we cannot bow to the first cause of all evil, does he not betray as much prejudice as the heathens did, when they called the primitive Christians Atheists, merely because the disciples of Christ bore their testimony against idol gods?

Mr. T. produces many passages of Scripture beside those which I have animadverted upon in this section; but as they are equally misapplied, one or another of the twelve keys with which I have presented the public, will easily rescue all of them from Calvinian bondage.

SECTION IV.

An answer to the capital objections of the necessitarians against the doctrine of liberty.

IF I have broken the unphilosophical and unscriptural pillars on which Mr. T. builds his temple of philosophical and Christian necessity, I have nothing to do now but to answer some plausible objections, by which the necessitarians puzzle those who embrace the doctrine of liberty.

OBJECTION FIRST. And first, they say, that "if God had not secured every link of the chain of events, it would fall to pieces; and the events which God wants *absolutely* to bring about, could not be brought about at all; while those which he designs absolutely to hinder, would take place in full opposition to his decrees."

ANSWER. But we deny these consequences: for, **1.** Nothing that God determines *absolutely* to hinder shall ever come to pass. Thus he has absolutely decreed that the gates of hell shall never totally prevail against or destroy his Church, that is, all true Christians; and therefore, there will always be some true Christians upon earth. It is his absolute will that all who "by patient continuance in well doing seek for glory," shall have *eternal life;* and that all who finally neglect so great salvation shall feel his wrathful indignation; and therefore none shall pluck the former out of the hands of his remunerative mercy, and none shall pluck the latter out of the hands of his vindictive justice.

2. God has ten thousand strings to his providential bow, and ten thousand bridles in his providential hand, to curb and manage free agents, which way soever they please to go: and therefore, to suppose that he has tightly bound all his creatures with cords of absolute necessity, for fear he should not be able to manage them if they had their liberty; to suppose this, I say, is to pour upon Divine Providence the same contempt which a timorous gentleman brings upon himself when he dares not ride a spirited horse any longer than a groom leads him by the bridle, that he may not run away with his unskilful rider.

3. If things had not happened one way, they might have happened another way. Supposing, for example, God had absolutely ordered that Solomon should be David's son by Bathsheba; this event might have taken place without his necessitating David to commit adultery and murder. For Providence might have found out means for marrying Bathsheba to David before she was married to Uriah: or God might have taken Uriah to heaven by a fever, and David could legally have married his widow. Again: if neither Caiaphas nor Pilate had condemned our Lord, he could have made his life an offering for sin, by commanding the clouds to shoot a thousand lightnings upon his devoted head, and to consume him as Elijah's sacrifice was consumed on Mount Carmel.

4. The pious author of Ecclesiasticus says, with great truth, that "God has no need of the sinful man." To suppose that the chain of God's providence would have been absolutely broken if Manasseh or Nero had committed one murder less than they did, is to ascribe to the old murderer and his servants an importance of which Manes himself might have been ashamed. Although God used Nebuchadnezzar, Alexander, and Attila, to scourge guilty nations, and to exercise the patience of his righteous servants, he was by no means obliged to use them. For he might have obtained the same ends by the plague, the famine, or the dreadful ministry of the angel who cut off the first born of the Egyptians, and the numerous army of Sennacherib. I flatter myself that these four answers fully set aside the first objection of the necessitarians: pass we on to another.

OBJECTION SECOND. "If God had not *necessitated* the fall of Adam, and *secured* his sin, Adam might have continued innocent; and then there would have been no need of Christ and of Christianity. Had Adam stood, we should have been without Christ to all eternity: but believers had rather be born in sin, than be Christless: they had rather be sick, than have nothing to do with their heavenly Physician, and with the cordials of his sanctifying Spirit."[*]

ANSWER. It is absurd to insinuate that the Father necessitated Adam to sin, in order to make way for the indwelling of his Word and Spirit in the hearts of believers. For if Adam was made in the image of God; if God is that mysterious, adorable, Supreme Being, whom the Scriptures call *Father, Word, and Holy Ghost;* if the Father gave his Word and light to Adam in paradise, and shed abroad Divine love in his heart by the Holy Ghost given unto him; Adam was full of the Word and Spirit of God by creation. And although the eternal Word was not Adam's Redeemer, yet he was Adam's life and light; for Christ, considered as *the Word of God,* was the wisdom and power of sinless man, just as he is the wisdom and power of holy believers. The reason why man needed not the atoning blood of the Lamb in a state of innocence was because the holy Lamb of God lived in his heart, and, jointly with the Spirit of love, maintained there the mystical kingdom of righteousness, peace, and joy in the Holy Ghost. To suppose, therefore, that if Adam had not sinned he would have had nothing to do with the Word and Spirit of the Father, is as absurd as to fancy that if people did not poison themselves, they would have had nothing to do with health and cheerfulness. And to intimate that God necessarily brought about the sin of Adam, in order to make way for the murder of his incarnate Son, is as impious as to insinuate that our Lord impelled the Jews to despise the day of their visitation, in order to secure the opportunity of weeping over the hardness of their hearts. If God necessitated the mischief, in order to remedy it, the gratitude of the redeemed is partly at an end; and the thanks they owe him are only of the same kind with such as Mr. Toplady would owe me, if I wantonly caused him to break his legs, and then procured him a good surgeon to set them. But what shall we say of the non-redeemed? Those unfortunate creatures whom Mr. Toplady calls "the reprobate?" Are there not countless myriads of these, according to his unscriptural gospel? And what thanks do these owe the evil Manichean God, who absolutely necessitates them to sin, and absolutely debars them from any saving interest in a Redeemer, that he may send them *without fail* to everlasting burnings? How strangely perverted is the rational taste of Mr. T., who calls the doctrine of absolute necessity, which is big with absolute reprobation, absolute wickedness, and absolute damnation, a comfortable doctrine! a doctrine of grace! May we not expect next to hear him cry up midnight gloom as meridian brightness?

But to return: if it was *necessary* that Adam should sin in order to glorify the Father, by making way for the crucifixion of the Lamb of God; is it not also necessary that believers should sin in order to glorify God more abundantly by "crucifying Christ afresh, and putting him again to open shame?" Will they not, by this means, have greater need of their Physician, make a fuller trial of the virtue of his blood, and sing louder in heaven? O, how perilous is a doctrine, which, at every turn, transforms

---

[*] Mr. Toplady dares not produce this objection in all its force: he only hints at it. His own words are, p. 130, "Let me give our free willers a very momentous hint: viz. that the entrance of original *sin* was one of those *essential links, on* which the Messiah's incarnation and crucifixion were suspended."

itself into a doctrine of light, to support the most subtle and pernicious tenet of the Antinomians, "Let us sin that grace may abound!"

Mr. Toplady, who has only hinted at the two preceding objections, triumphs much in that which follows: it shall therefore appear clothed m his own words. In the contents of his book he says, "Methodists, [he gives this name to all who oppose his Scheme of Necessity,] Methodists, more gross Manicheans than Manes himself." The proof occurs, page 144, in the followings words: —

OBJECTION THIRD. "The old Manicheism was a *gentle* impiety, and a slender absurdity, when contrasted with the modern Arminian improvements on that system. For, which is worse? To assert the existence of *two* independent beings, and no more; or, to assert the existence of about *one hundred and fifty millions* of independent beings, all living at one time, and most of them waging successful war on the designs of him that made them? Even confining ourselves to our own world, it will follow that Arminian Manicheism exceeds the paltry oriental quality, at the immense rate of 150,000,000 to two — without reckoning the adult self determiners of past generations."

ANSWER. This argument, cast into. a logical mould, will yield the following syllogism: —

Every being, able to *determine himself* is an *independent being*, and of consequence *a god*.

According to the doctrine of free will, every accountable man is a being able to *determine himself*.

Therefore, according to the doctrine of free will, every accountable man is an independent being, and consequently a god. Hence it follows, that If Manes erred by believing there were two gods, those who espouse the doctrine of free will are more gross Manicheans than Manes himself; since they believe that every man is a god.

Observe Mr. Toplady's consistency! Indeed, when he attacks Mr. W. and Arminianism, no charges (be they ever so contradictory) come amiss to him. In his *Historic Proof,* Arminianism is Atheism; and in his *Scheme of Necessity,* Arminianism is a system which supposes countless myriads of gods! But, letting this pass, I observe that the preceding syllogism is a mere sophism; the first proposition, on which all the others depend, being absolutely false; witness the following appeals to common sense: —

Is a horse *independent* on his master, because he can *determine, himself* to range or lie down in his pasture? Is Mr. Toplady independent on his bishop, because he can determine himself to preach twice next Sunday, or only once, or not at all? Is a captain independent on his general, because he can determine himself lu stand his ground, or to run away in an engagement? Are soldiers independent on their colonel, because they determined themselves to list in such a company? Is a negro slave independent on his master, or is he a little god, because, when he lies down, he can determine himself to do it on the left side, or on the right? Is a highwayman *a god,* because he can determine himself to rob a traveller, or to let him pass without molestation? In a word, are subjects independent on their sovereign, because they can determine themselves to break or to keep the laws of the land?

Every one of the preceding questions pours light upon the absurdity of Mr. Toplady's argument. But that absurdity will appear doubly glaring if you consider three things: (1.) All free agents have received their life and free agency from God, as precious talents, for the good or bad use of which they are accountable to his distributive justice. (2.) All free agents are every moment dependent upon God, for the preservation of their life and free agency; there being no instant in which God may not resume all his temporary talents, by requiring their souls of them. (3.) He has appointed a day in which he will judge the world in righteousness, by Jesus Christ: then shall he publicly convince all moral agents of their dependence on his goodness and justice, by graciously rewarding the righteous, and justly punishing the wicked, according to their works. (4.) In the meantime, he makes them sensible of their dependence, by keeping in his providential hand the "staff of their bread," and the thread of life; saying to the greatest of them, "Ye are gods, [in authority over others,] but ye shall die like men: and after death comes judgment." It is as ridiculous, therefore, to suppose that, upon the scheme of free will, men are *independent* beings, as to assert that prisoners, who are going to the bar to meet their lawgiver and judge, are independent upon his supreme authority, because those who are going to be condemned for robbery or murder, *determined themselves* to rob or murder, without any Antinomian, impulsive decree made by their judge; and because those who are going to be rewarded for their obedience, were not necessitated to obey as a wave is necessitated to roll along, when it is irresistibly impelled by another wave.

However, Mr. Toplady sings the song of victory, as if he had proved that, upon the Arminian scheme of free will, every man is an *independent being*, and *a god*. "Poor Manes!" says he, "with how excellent a grace do Arminians call thee a heretic! And, above all, such Arminians, (whereof Mr. J. Wesley is one,)as agree with thee in believing the attainability of *sinless perfection* here below: or, to use the good old Manichean phrase, who assert that *the evil principle may, be totally separated from man in this present life!*"

The reader will permit me to make a concluding remark upon this triumphant exclamation of Mr. Toplady. I have observed, that Manes believed there are in the Godhead two co-eternal principles: (1.) The absolute sovereignty of free grace, which necessitates men to good. And, (2.) The absolute sovereignty of free wrath, which necessitates them to evil. Nevertheless, Manes was not so mistaken as to suppose that the good principle in his Deity was weaker than the bad principle; and that the latter could never be dislodged by the former from the breast of one single elect person. Manes had faith enough to believe that now is the day of salvation, and that Christ (and not death or a temporary hell) saves good Christians from their sins. Accordingly he asserted that nothing unholy or wicked can dwell with the good-principled God; and that none shall inherit eternal life, but such as so concur with the heavenly light, as to have the works of darkness destroyed in their souls. And therefore he maintained, with St. Paul, that we must be "sanctified throughout," and that our souls must be found at death "blameless and without spot or wrinkle" of sin; and he held, with St. John, that he who is "fully born of God [the good principle] sinneth not, but keepeth himself, and the wicked *principle* toucheth him not," so as to lead him into iniquity. Now, if Mr. Toplady so firmly believes in the evil principle, as to assert, that though believers are ever so willing to have no other Lord but the good-principled God, yet this God can never destroy before death the works of the sin-predestinating God in their hearts; and if, on the other hand, the wicked principle completely destroys all good in all reprobates, even in this life; is it not evident that Mr. Toplady's charge may be justly retorted;* and that, as he ascribes so much more power to the evil principle than to the good, he carries the sovereignty of the evil principle farther than Manes himself did; and is (to use his own expression) a "more gross Manichean than Manes himself?"

OBJECTION FOURTH. "Your scheme of free will labours under a greater difficulty than that with which you clog the Scheme of Necessity; because if it did not represent the sin-necessitating principle as more powerful than the good principle, yet it represents created spirits as stronger than the God who made them: an impotent, disappointed God this, who says, — *I would, and ye would not.*"

ANSWER. **1.** These words were actually spoken by incarnate Omnipotence: nor do they prove that man is stronger than God, but only that when God deals with free agents about those things concerning which he will call them to an account, he does not necessitate their will by an irresistible exertion of his power, (*propter justum Dei judicium,*) "that he may leave room for the display of his justice," as the fathers said: for his perfections, and our probationary circumstances require, that he should maintain the character of Lawgiver and Judge, as well as that of Creator and Sovereign. And, therefore, when we say that free agents are not necessarily determined by God to those actions, for which God is going to punish or reward them, we do not represent free agents as stronger or greater than God. We only place them (*sub justo Dei judicio*) "under God's righteous government," as said the fathers, equally subjected to the *legislative* wisdom, and *executive* power of their omnipotent Lawgiver.

2. Whether free agents are rewarded or punished, saved or damned, God our Saviour will never be disappointed: for, (1.) He will pronounce the sentence; and what he will do himself will not disappoint his expectation. (2.) It is as much God's righteous, eternal design to punish wicked, obstinate free agents, as to reward yielding and obedient free agents. (3.) Every Gospel dispensation yields a savour of life or death. The sword of the Lord is a two-edged sword: if it do not cut down a man's sin, it will cut down his person. And though God, as Creator and Redeemer, does not in the day of salvation Calvinistically desire the death of a sinner; yet, as a holy Lawgiver, a covenant-keeping God, and a righteous Judge, he is determined to "render unto every man according to his deeds: eternal life to them who, by patient continuance in

---

* Page 154, Mr. Toplady produces the following objection: — "'Tis curious to behold Arminians themselves forced to take refuge in the harbour of necessity. It is *necessary,* say they, that man's will should be free: for without freedom, the will were no will at all," [i.e. no free will — no such will as constitutes a man a moral and accountable agent.] "Free agency, themselves being judges, is only a ramification of necessity."

This is playing upon words, and shuffling logical cards in order to delude the simple. I have granted again and again that there is a necessity of nature, a necessity of consequence, a necessity of duty, a necessity of decency, a necessity of convenience, &c, &c, but all these sorts of necessity do no more amount to the Calvinian, absolute necessity of all events, than my granting that the king has a variety of officers about his person by necessity of decency, of office, of custom, &c, implies my granting that he has a certain officer, who *absolutely necessitates* him to move just as he does, insomuch that he cannot turn his eyes, or stir one finger, otherwise than this imaginary officer directs or impels him. This objection of Mr. Toplady is so excessively trifling, that I almost blame myself for taking notice of it, even in a note.

well doing, seek for glory; but indignation and wrath to them who do not obey the truth, but obey unrighteousness:" and God will do this, "in the day when he shall judge the secrets of men according to the Gospel," Romans 2:6-16. Hence it is evident that the bow of Divine justice has two strings, that each string will shoot its peculiar arrow, and although God leaves it to free agents to choose which they will have, the arrow which is winged with remunerative life, or that which carries vindictive death; yet he can never be disappointed: he will most infallibly hit the judicial mark which he has set up: witness the awful declaration which is engraven upon that mark: — "These [obstinate free agents] shall go away into everlasting punishment; but the righteous into life eternal," Matthew 25:46.

Upon the whole, I humbly hope, that whether candid readers consider the inconclusiveness of Mr. T.'s philosophical arguments, the injudicious manner in which he has pressed the Scriptures into the service of absolute necessity, or the weakness of his objections, which he directly or indirectly makes against the doctrine of liberty; they will see that his scheme is as contrary to true philosophy and to well-applied Scripture, as the absolute necessity of adultery and murder is contrary to good morals, and the absolute reprobation of some of our unborn children, and perhaps of our own souls, is contrary to evangelical comfort.

SECTION V.

The doctrine of necessity is the capital error of the Calvinists, and the foundation of the most wretched schemes of philosophy and divinity — How nearly Mr. Toplady agrees with Mr. Hobbes, the apostle of the materialists in England, with respect to the doctrine of necessity — Conclusion.

WE have seen on what *philosophical and Scriptural* proofs Mr. Toplady founds the doctrine of necessity; and, if I am not mistaken, the inconclusiveness of his arguments has been fairly pointed out. I shall now subjoin some remarks, which I hope are not unworthy of the reader's attention.

1. It is not without reason that Mr. T. borrows from false philosophy and misapplied passages of Scripture, whatever seems to countenance his doctrine of necessity; for that doctrine is the very soul of Calvinism; and Calvinism is, in his account, the marrow of the Gospel. If the doctrine of absolute necessity be true, Calvinian election and reprobation are true also: if it be false, Calvinism, so far as we oppose it, is left without either prop or foundation. Take away necessity from the modern doctrines of grace, and you reduce them to the Scripture standard which we follow, and of which Arminius was too much afraid.

2. Those who would see at once the bar which separates us from the Calvinists, need only consider the following questions: — Are *all* those who shall be damned *absolutely necessitated* to continue in sin and perish? And are all those who shall be saved *absolutely necessitated* to work righteousness and be eternally saved? Or, to unite both questions in one, Shall men be judged, that is, shall they be justified or condemned in the last day, as bound agents, according to the unavoidable consequences of Christ's work, or of Adam's work? Or, shall they be justified or condemned, *according to* THEIR OWN *works*, as the Scripture declares? I lay a peculiar stress upon the words *their own*,

because works, which absolute decrees necessitate us to do, are no longer, properly speaking, our own works, but the works of Him who necessitates us to do them.

3. There is but one case in which we can Scripturally admit the Calvinian doctrine of necessity, and that is, the salvation of infants who die before they have committed actual sin. These, we grant, are *necessarily* or Calvinistically saved. But they will not be "judged according to THEIR works," seeing they died before they wrought either iniquity or righteousness. Their salvation will depend only on the irresistible work of Christ, and his Spirit. As they were never called personally to "work out their own salvation;" and as they never personally wrought out their own damnation, they will all be saved by the superabounding grace of God, through the meritorious infancy and death of the holy child Jesus. But it is an abomination to suppose that because God can justly force holiness and salvation upon some infants, he can justly force continued sin and eternal damnation upon myriads of people, by putting them in such circumstances as *absolutely necessitate* them to continue in sin and be damned. I repeat, God may bestow *eternal favours* upon persons whom his decrees necessitate to be righteous. But he can never inflict *eternal punishments* upon persons whom his decrees, according to Mr. Toplady's doctrine, necessitate to be wicked from first to last.

4. The moderate Calvinists say, indeed, that Adam was endued with free will, and that God did not *necessitate* him to sin. But if necessity has nothing to do with the first man's obedience and first transgression, why should it be supposed that it has so much to do with us, as absolutely to beget all our good and bad works? And if it be not unreasonable to say "that God endued one man with a power to determine himself;" why should we be considered as enemies to the Gospel, because we assert that he has made all men in some degree capable of determining themselves; the Scriptures declaring that he treats all adult persons as free agents, or persons endued with the power of self determination?

5. Mr. Toplady and all the rigid Calvinists suppose, indeed, that God's necessitation extended to the commission of Adam's sin; and yet they tell us that God is not the *author,* but only the *permitter* of sin. But they do not consider that their doctrine of absolute necessity leaves no more room for permission, than the absolute decree that a pound shall *always* exactly weigh sixteen ounces, leaves room for a permission of its weighing *sometimes* fifteen ounces and *sometimes* seventeen. Should Mr. Toplady reply that "such a decree, however, leaves room for the permission that a pound shall always exactly weigh sixteen ounces, I reply, that this is playing upon words, it being evident that the word *permission,* in such a case, is artfully put for the plainer word necessity or absolute decree. It is evident, therefore, that although Mr. Toplady aims at being more consistent than the moderate Calvinists, he is in fact as inconsistent as they, if he denies that, upon the scheme of the absolute decrees preached by Calvin, and of the absolute necessity which he himself maintains, God is properly the *contriver and author* of all sin and wickedness.

6. It is dreadful to lay, directly or indirectly, all sin at the door of an omnipotent Being, who is "fearful in holiness, and glorious in praises." Nor is it less dangerous to make poor, deluded Christians swallow down, as Gospel, some of the most dangerous errors that were ever propagated by ancient or modern infidels. We have already seen that the capital error of Manes was the doctrine of necessity. This doctrine was also the grand engine with which Spinosa in Holland, and Hobbes in

England, attempted to overthrow Christianity in the last century. Those two men, who may be called the apostles of modern materialists and Atheists, tried to destroy the Lord's vineyard, by letting loose upon it the very error which Mr. T. recommends to us as the capital doctrine of grace. "Spinosa," says a modern author, "will allow no governor of the universe but necessity." As for Mr. Hobbes, he built his materialism upon the ruins of free will, and the foundation of necessity: hear the above-quoted author giving us an account of the monstrous system of religion known by *Hobbism*: — "Freedom of will it was impossible that Mr. Hobbes should assert to be a property of matter; but he finds a very unexpected way to extricate himself out of the difficulty. The proposition against him stands thus: 'Freedom of will cannot be a property of matter; but there are beings which have freedom of will; therefore there are substances which are not material.' He answers this at once by saying the most strange thing, and the most contradictory to our knowledge of what passes within ourselves, that perhaps was ever advanced, namely, that there is no freedom of will. 'Every effect,' he says, [and this is exactly the doctrine of Mr. Toplady, as the quotations I have produced from his book abundantly prove,] 'Every effect must be owing to some cause, and that cause must produce the effect *necessarily*. Thus, whatever body is moved, is moved by some other body, and that by a third, and so on without end.' In the same manner he [Mr. Hobbes] concludes, 'The will of a *voluntary agent* must be determined by some other external to it, and so on without end: therefore, that the will is not determined by any power of determining itself, inherent in itself; that is, it is not free, nor is there any such thing as freedom of will, but that all is the act of necessity.'" This is part of the account which the author of the *Answer to Lord Bolingbroke's Philosophy* gives us of Mr. Hobbes' detestable scheme of necessity: and it behooves Mr. Toplady and the Calvinists to see if, while they contend for their absolute decrees, and for the doctrine of the absolute necessity and passiveness of all our willings and motions, they do not inadvertently confound matter and spirit, and make way for Hobbes' materialism, as well as for his scheme of necessity.

7. The moment the doctrine of necessity is overthrown, Manicheism, Spinosism, Hobbism, and the spreading religion of Mr. Voltaire, are left without foundation; as well as that part of Calvin's system which we object against. And we beseech Mr. Toplady, and the contenders for Calvinian decrees, to consider, that if we oppose their doctrine, it is not from any prejudice against their persons, much less against God's free grace; but from the same motive which would make us bear our testimony against Manes, Spinosa, Hobbes, and Voltaire, if they would impose their errors upon us as "doctrines of grace." Mr. Wesley and I are ready to testify upon oath that we humbly submit to God's sovereignty, and joyfully glory in the freeness of Gospel grace, which has mercifully distinguished us from countless myriads of our fellow creatures, by gratuitously bestowing upon us numberless favours, of a spiritual and temporal nature, which he has thought proper absolutely to withhold from our fellow creatures. To meet the Calvinists on their own ground, we go so far as to allow there is a *partial, gratuitous election and reprobation*. By this election, Christians are admitted to the enjoyment of privileges far superior to those of the Jews: and, according to this reprobation, myriads of heathens are absolutely cut off from all the prerogatives which accompany God's covenants of peculiar grace. In a word, we grant to the Calvinists every thing they contend for, except the doctrine of absolute necessity: nay,

we even grant the necessary, unavoidable salvation of all that die in their infancy. And our love to peace would make us go farther to meet Mr. Toplady, if we could do it without giving up the justice, mercy, truth, and wisdom of God, together with the truth of the Scriptures, the equity of God's paradisiacal and mediatorial laws, the propriety of the day of judgment, and the reasonableness of the sentences of absolution and condemnation which the righteous Judge will then pronounce. We hope, therefore, that the prejudices of our Calvinian brethren will subside, and that, instead of accounting us inveterate enemies to truth, they will do us the justice to say that we have done our best to hinder them from inadvertently betraying some of the greatest truths of Christianity into the hands of the Manichees, materialists, infidels, and Antinomians of the age. May the Lord hasten the happy day in which we shall no more waste our time in attacking or defending the truths of our holy religion; but bestow every moment in the sweetest exercises of Divine and brotherly love! In the meantime, if we must contend for the faith once delivered to the saints, let us do it with a plainness that may effectually detect error; and with a mildness that may soften our most violent opponents. Lest I should transgress against this rule, I beg leave once more to observe, that though I have made it appear that Mr. Toplady's *Scheme of Necessity* is inseparably connected with the most horrid errors of Manicheism, materialism, and Hobbism, yet I am far from accusing him of *wilfully* countenancing any of those errors. I am persuaded he does it *undesignedly*. The badness of his cause obliges him to collect, from all quarters, every shadow of argument to support his favourite opinion. And I make no doubt but, when he shall candidly review our controversy, it will be his grief to find that, in his hurry, he has contended for a scheme which gives up Christianity into the hands of her greatest enemies, and has poured floods of undeserved contempt upon Mr. Wesley who is one of her best defenders.

AN ANSWER

TO THE

REV. MR. TOPLADY'S

"VINDICATION OF THE DECREES," &C.

BY THE AUTHOR OF THE CHECKS.

"The [*absolute*] predestination of some to LIFE, &c, cannot be maintained without admitting the [*absolute*] reprobation of some others to DEATH, &c; and all who have subscribed the said article [*the seventeenth, in a Calvinian sense*] are bound in honour, conscience, and law to defend [*Calvinian, absolute*] reprobation, were it only to keep the seventeenth article [*taken in a Calvinian sense*] upon its legs." (Revelation Mr. TOPLADY'S *Historic Proof of Calvinism*, p. 574.)

INTRODUCTION.

WHEN the author of *Pietas Oxoniensis* took his temporary leave of me in his *Finishing Stroke,* he recommended to the public the book which I am going to answer. His recommendation runs thus: — "Whosoever will consult the Rev. Mr. Toplady's last publication, entitled, *More Work for Mr. J. Wesley,* [or, *A Vindication of the Decrees,* &c,] will there find a full answer to all those cavils which Papists, Socinians, Pelagians, Arminians, and Perfectionists bring against those doctrines commonly called CALVINIST, as if they tended to promote licentiousness, or to make God cruel, unjust, and unmerciful, and will see every one of their objections retorted upon themselves in a most masterly manner." (*Finishing Stroke,* p. 33.) Soon after Mr. Hill had thus extolled Mr. Toplady's performance, I was informed that many of the Calvinists said that it was an unanswerable defence of their doctrines. This raised in me a desire to judge for myself; and when I had sent for, and read this admired book, I was so far from being of Mr. Hill's sentiment, that I promised my readers to demonstrate, from that very book, the inconclusiveness of the strongest arguments by which Calvinism is supported. Mr. Hill, by unexpectedly entering the lists again, caused me to delay the fulfilling of my promise. But having now completed my answer to his fictitious creed, I hasten to complete also my *Logica Genevensis.*

Did I write a book entitled *Charitas Genevensis,* I might easily show, from Mr. Toplady's performance, that *the "doctrines of grace"* (so called) are closely connected with "the doctrines of free wrath." But if that gentleman, in his controversial heat, has forgotten what he owed to Mr. Wesley and to himself, this is no reason why I should forget the title of my book, which calls me to point out the *bad arguments* of our opponents, and not their *ill humour.* If I absurdly spent my time in passing a censure upon Mr. Toplady's spirit, he would with reason say, as he does in the introduction to his *Historic Proof,* page 35, "After all, what has my pride or my humility to do with the argument in hand? Whether I am haughty or meek is of no more consequence either to that or to the public, than whether I am tall or short." Beside, having again and again, myself, requested our opponents not to withdraw the controversy by personal reflections, but to weigh with candour the arguments which are offered, I should be inexcusable if I did not set them the example. Should it be said that Mr. Wesley's character, which Mr. Toplady has so severely attacked, is at stake, and that I ought purposely to stand up in his defence, I reply, that the personal charges which Mr. Toplady interweaves with his arguments, have been already fully answered* by Mr. Olivers; and that these charges being chiefly founded upon Mr. Toplady's logical mistakes, they will, of their own accord, fall to the ground, as soon as the mistakes on which they rest shall be exposed. If *Logica Genevensis* is disarmed, *Charitas Genevensis* will not be able to keep the field. If *good sense* take the former prisoner, the latter will be obliged to surrender to *good nature*. Should this be the case, how great a blessing will our controversy prove to both parties! The conquerors shall have the glory of *vindicating truth;* and the conquered shall have the profit of retiring from the field with their judgments better informed, and their tempers better regulated! May the God of truth and love grant, that if Mr. Toplady have the honour of producing the best arguments, I (for one) may have the *advantage* of yielding to them! To be conquered by *truth* and *love,* is to prove conqueror over our two greatest enemies, *error* and *sin.*

MADELEY, *Oct.* 1775.

---

* See "A Letter to the Rev. Mr. Toplady," by Mr. Olivers.

AN ANSWER

REV. MR. TOPLADY'S "VINDICATION OF THE DECREES," &C.

SECTION I.

Showing that, upon the Calvinian scheme, it is an indubitable truth that some men shall be saved, do what they will, till the efficacious decree of Calvinian election necessitate them to repent and be saved: and that others shall be damned, do what they can, till the efficacious decree of Calvinian reprobation necessitate them to draw back, and be damned.

THE doctrinal part of the controversy between Mr. Wesley and Mr. Toplady may, in a great degree, be reduced to this question: — If God, from all eternity, absolutely predestinated a fixed number of men, called *the elect*, to eternal life, and absolutely predestinated a fixed number of men, called *the reprobate*, to eternal death, does it not *unavoidably* follow that "the elect shall be saved, *do what they will*," and that "the reprobate shall be damned, *do what they can?*" Mr. Wesley thinks that the consequence is undeniably true: Mr. Toplady says that it is absolutely false, and charges Mr. Wesley with "coining blasphemous propositions," yea, with "hatching blasphemy, and then fathering it on others," pages 7, 8; and, in a note upon the word *blasphemous*, he says, "This epithet is not too strong." To say that any shall be *saved*, do what they will, and others *damned*, do what they can, is, in the first instance, blasphemy against the holiness of God; and, in the second, blasphemy against his goodness: and again, p. 34, after repeating the latter clause of the consequence, viz. "the reprobate shall be damned, *do what they can*," he expresses himself thus: — "One would imagine that none but a reprobate could be capable of advancing a position so execrably shocking. Surely it must have cost even Mr. Wesley much, both of time and pains, to invent the idea, &c. Few men's invention ever sunk deeper into the despicable, launched wider into the horrid, and went farther in the profane. The Satanic guilt of the person who could excogitate, and publish to the world a position like that, baffles all power of description, and is only to be exceeded (if exceedable) by the Satanic shamelessness which dares to lay the black position at the door of other men. Let us examine whether any thing occurring in *Zanchius* could justly furnish this wretched defamer with materials for a deduction so truly infernal." Agreeably to those *spirited* complaints, Mr. Toplady falls his book, not only "More Work for Mr. J. Wesley," but also "A *Vindication of the Decrees and Providence of God, from the* defamations *of a late printed paper, entitled,* 'The Consequence Proved.'" I side with Mr. Wesley for the consequence; guarding it against cavils by a clause, which his love of *brevity* made him think needless. And the *guarded consequence,* which I undertake to defend, runs thus: — From the doctrine of the absolute and unconditional predestination of some men to eternal life, and of all others to eternal death, it necessarily follows, that some men shall be SAVED, *do what they will,* till the absolute and efficacious decree of election actually necessitate them to obey, and be saved; and that all the rest of mankind shall be DAMNED, *do what they can,* till the absolute and efficacious decree of reprobation necessitate them to sin, and be damned.

An illustration will at once show the justness of this consequence to an unprejudiced reader. Fifty fishes sport in a muddy pond, where they have received life. The skilful and almighty Owner of the pond has absolutely decreed that ten of these fishes, properly marked with a shining mark, called *election,* shall absolutely be caught in a certain net, called a *Gospel net,* on a certain day, called *the day of his power;* and that they shall, every one, be cast into a delightful river, where he has engaged himself, by an eternal covenant of particular redemption, to bring them without fail. The same omnipotent Proprietor of the pond has likewise absolutely decreed that all the rest of the fishes, namely, forty, which are properly distinguished by a black mark, called *reprobation,* shall never be caught in the Gospel net; or that if they are entangled in it at any time, they shall always be drawn out of it, and so shall necessarily continue in the muddy pond, till, on a certain day, called *the day of his wrath,* he shall sweep the pond with a certain net, called a *law net,* catch them all, and cast them into a lake of fire and brimstone, where he has engaged himself, by an everlasting covenant of non-redemption, to bring them all without fail, that they may answer the end of their predestination to death, which is to show the goodness of his law net, and to destroy them for having been bred in the muddy pond, and for not having been caught in the Gospel net. The Owner of the pond is wise, as well as powerful. He knows that, absolutely to secure *the end* to which his fishes are absolutely predestinated, he must absolutely secure *the means* which conduced to that end; and therefore, that none may escape their happy or their unfortunate predestination, he keeps night and day his hold of them all, by a strong hook, called *necessity,* and by an invisible line, called *Divine decrees.* By means of this line and hook it happens, that if the fishes, which bear the mark *election,* are ever so loath to come into the Gospel net, or to stay therein, they are always drawn into it in a day of powerful love; and if the fishes which bear the mark of *reprobation,* are, for a time, ever so desirous to wrap themselves in the Gospel net, they are drawn out of it in a day of powerful wrath. For, though the fishes *seem* to swim ever so freely, yet their motions are all *absolutely fixed* by the Owner of the pond, and determined by means of the above-mentioned line and hook. If this is the case, says Mr. Wesley, ten fishes shall, go into the delightful river, let them do what they will, let them plunge in the mud of their pond ever so briskly, or leap toward the lake of fire ever so often, while they have any liberty to plunge or to leap. And all the rest of the fishes, forty in number, shall go into the lake of fire, let them do what they can, let them involve themselves ever so long in the Gospel net, and leap ever so often toward the fine river, before they are absolutely necessitated to go, through the mud of their own pond, into the sulphureous pool. The consequence is undeniable, and I make no doubt that all unprejudiced persons see it as well as myself: as sure as two and two make four, or, if you please, as sure as ten and forty make fifty, so sure ten fishes shall be finally caught in the Gospel net, and forty in the law net.

Should Mr. Toplady say that this is only an illustration, I drop it, and roundly assert that if two men, suppose Solomon and Absalom, are absolutely predestinated to eternal life; while two other men, suppose Mr. Baxter and Mr. Wesley, are absolutely predestinated to eternal death; the two elect shall be saved, *do what they will,* and the two reprobates shall be damned, *do what they can.* That is, let Solomon and Absalom worship the abomination of the Zidonians, and of the Moabites, in ever so public a manner; let them, for years, indulge themselves with heathenish women, collected from all countries; if they have a mind, let them murder their brothers, defile their sisters, and imitate the incestuous Corinthian, who took his own father's wife; yet they can never really endanger their finishedsalvation. The indelible mark of *unconditional election to life* is upon them; and forcible, victorious grace shall, in their last moments, if not before, draw them irresistibly and infallibly from iniquity to repentance. Death shall unavoidably make an end of their indwelling sin; and to heaven they shall unavoidably go. On the other hand, let a Baxter and a Wesley astonish the world by their ministerial labours: let them write, speak, and live in such a manner as to stem the torrent of iniquity, and turn thousands to righteousness: with St. Paul let them take up their cross daily, and preach and pray, not only with tears, but "with the demonstration of the Spirit and with power:" let unwearied patience and matchless diligence carry them with increasing fortitude through all the persecutions, danger, and trials, which they meet with from the men of the world, and from false brethren: let them hold on this wonderful way to their dying day; yet, if the indelible mark of unconditional reprobation to death is upon them, necessitating, victorious wrath shall, in their last moments, if not before, make them *necessarily* turn from righteousness, and *unavoidably* draw back to perdition; so shall they be fitted for the lake of fire, the end to which, if God Calvinistically passed them by, they were absolutely ordained through the predestinated medium of remediless sin and final apostasy.

This is the true state of the case: to spend time in proving it would be offering the judicious reader as great an insult, as if I detained him to prove that the north is opposed to the south. But what does Mr. Toplady say against this consequence, "If Calvinism is true, the reprobates shall be damned, do what they can?" He advances the following warm argument: —

ARGUMENT I. Page 55. "Can Mr. Wesley produce a single instance of any one man, who did all he could to be saved, and yet was lost? If he *can,* let him tell us who that man was, where he lived, when he died, what he did, and how it came to pass he laboured in vain. If he *cannot,* let him either retract his consequences, or continue to be posted for a shameless traducer."

I answer: **1.** To require Mr. Wesley to show a man who did all he could, and yet was lost, is requiring him to prove that Calvinian reprobation is *true:* a thing this, which he can no more do, than he can prove that God is *false.* Mr. Wesley never said that any man was damned after doing his best to be saved: he only says that *if Calvinism is true,* the reprobates shall all be damned, though they should all do their best to be saved, till the *efficacious decree* of their absolute reprobation necessitates them to draw back and be damned.

2. As Mr. Toplady's bold request may impose upon his inattentive readers, I beg leave to point out its absurdity by a short illustration. Mr. Wesley says, *If there is a mountain of gold,* it is heavier than a handful of feathers; and his consequence passes for true in England. But a gentleman who teaches logic in mystic Geneva thinks that it is absolutely false, and that Mr. Wesley's "forehead must be petrified, and quite impervious to a blush," for advancing it. Can Mr. Wesley, says he, show us a mountain of gold, which is really heavier than a handful of feathers? If he can, let him tell us what mountain it is, where it lies, in what latitude, how high it is, and who did ever ascend to the top of it. If he cannot, let him either retract his consequences, or continue to be posted for a shameless traducer.

Equally conclusive is Mr. Toplady's challenge! By such cogent arguments as these, thousands of professors are bound to the chariot wheels of modern orthodoxy, and blindly follow the warm men, who "drive as furiously" over a part of the body of Scripture divinity, as the son of Nimshi did over the body of cursed Jezebel.

SECTION II.

Calvinism upon its legs, or a full view of the arguments by which Mr. Toplady attempts to reconcile Calvinism with God's holiness; — a note upon a letter to an Arminian teacher.

SENSIBLE that Calvinism can never rank among the doctrines of holiness, if "the elect shall be saved, do what they will," and if the "reprobate shall be damned, do what they can;" Mr. Toplady tries to throw off, from *his* doctrines of grace, the deadly weight of Mr. Wesley's consequence. In order to this, he proves that Calvinism insures the holiness of the elect, as the *necessary means* of their predestinated salvation: but he is too judicious to tell us that it insures also the wickedness of the reprobate as the *necessary means* of their predestinated damnation. To make us in love with his orthodoxy, he presents her to our view with one leg, on which she contrives to stand, by artfully leaning upon her faithful maid, *Logica Genevensis.* Her other leg is prudently kept out of sight, so long as the trial about her holiness lasts. This deserves explanation.

The most distinguishing and fundamental doctrines of Calvinism are two; and therefore they may with propriety be called *the legs* of that doctrinal system. The FIRST of these fundamental doctrines is, the personal, unconditional, absolute predestination, or election, of some men to eternal life; and the SECOND is, the personal, unconditional, absolute predestination, or reprobation, of some men to eternal death. Nor can Mr. Toplady find fault with my making his doctrine of grace stand upon her legs, *Calvinian election* and *Calvinian reprobation:* for, supposing that our Church speaks in her seventeenth article of Calvinian, absolute predestination to eternal life, he says himself, in his *Historic Proof,* page 574, "The predestination of some to life, asserted in the seventeenth article, cannot be maintained without admitting the reprobation[*] of some others to death, &c, and all who have subscribed

---

[*] Our opponents are greatly embarrassed about the doctrine of absolute, unconditional reprobation. Though in a happy moment, where candour prevailed over shame, Mr. Toplady stood up so boldly for Calvinian reprobation; the reader, as he goes on, will smile when he sees

the variegated wisdom with which that gentleman disguises, exculpates, or conceals, what he so rationally and so candidly grants here.

The truth is, that as Scriptural election is necessarily attended with an answerable reprobation; so absolute, Calvinian election unavoidably drags after it absolute, Calvinian reprobation: a black reprobation this, which *necessitates* all who are personally written in the book of death to sin on, and to be damned. But some Calvinists are *afraid* to see this doctrine, and well they may, for it is horrible: others are *ashamed* to acknowledge it; and not a few, for want of rational sight, obstinately deny that it is the main pillar of their Gospel; and with the right leg of their system they unmercifully kick the left. Among the persons who are guilty of this absurd conduct, we may rank the author of *A Letter to an Arminian Teacher:* an imperfect copy of which appeared in *the Gospel Magazine* of August, 1775, under the following title: *A Predestinarian's real thoughts of Election and Reprobation, &c.* This writer is so inconsistent as to attempt cutting off the left leg of Calvinism. He, at first, gives us reprobation. "The word *reprobation,"* says he, "is never mentioned in all the Scripture, [no more is the word *predestination,*] nor is the Scriptural word *reprobate* ever mentioned as the continuance of election, or as [its] *opposite."* This is a great mistake, as appears from the two first passages quoted by this author, Jeremiah 6:30, and Romans 1:28, where *reprobate silver* is evidently opposed to *choice silver,* and where a *reprobate mind* is indubitably opposed to *the mind which is after God's own heart —* that is, to the mind which God approves and chooses to crown with evangelical praises and rewards. Our author goes on: —

"There is no immediate connection between election to salvation, and reprobation to damnation." What an argument is this! Did we ever say that there is any *immediate connection* between two things which are as contrary as Christ and Belial? O! but we mean that "they have no necessary dependence on each other." The question is not whether they have a necessary dependence on each other; but whether they have not a necessary opposition to each other; and that they have, is as clear as that light is opposed to darkness. "They proceed from very different causes." True: for election proceeded from free grace, and Calvinian reprobation from free wrath. "The sole cause of election is God's free love, &c. The sole cause of damnation is only sin." Our author wants candour or attention. Had he argued like a candid logician, he would have said, "The sole cause of the reprobation which ends in unavoidable damnation, is only sin:" but if he had fairly argued thus, he would have given up Calvinism, which stands or falls with absolute reprobation; and therefore he thought proper to substitute the word *damnation* for the word reprobation, which the argument absolutely requires. These tricks may pass in Geneva; but in England they appear inconsistent with fair reasoning. It is a common stratagem of the Calvinists to say, "Election depends upon God's love only, but damnation depends upon our sin only;" break the thin shell of this sophism, and you will find this bitter kernel: God's distinguishing love elects some to unavoidable holiness and finished salvation; and his distinguishing wrath reprobates all the rest of mankind to remediless sin and eternal damnation. For the moment the sin of reprobates is necessary, remediless, and insured by the decree of the means, it follows that absolute reprobation to necessary, remediless sin, is the same thing as absolute reprobation to eternal damnation; because such a damnation is the unavoidable consequence of remediless sin.

When the letter writer has absurdly denied Calvinian reprobation, he insinuates, p. 5, that *everlasting torments* and *being unavoidably damned,* are not the necessary consequences of the decree of Calvinian election; "nor," says he, "can they be fairly deduced from the decree of reprobation" So now the secret is out! Our author, after denying reprobation, informs us that there is a Calvinian decree of reprobation. But if there be such a decree, why did he oppose it, p. 2? And if there is no such a decree, why does he mention it, p. 5; where he hints that insured damnation *cannot be fairly deduced from it?* Now, if he, or any Calvinist in the world, can prove that, upon the Calvinian plan, among the thousands of Calvin's reprobates, who are yet in their mothers' wombs, one of them can, any how, avoid finished damnation, I solemnly to the said article are bound in honour, conscience, and law to defend reprobation, were it only to keep the seventeenth article [or rather, the Calvinian sense which Mr. Toplady fixes to that article] *upon its legs.*"

Agreeably to Mr. Toplady's charge, Calvinism shall stand *upon its legs.* He takes care to show the right leg, in order to vindicate God's holiness upon the Calvinian plan; and I shall set forth the left leg, in order to show that the honour of God's holiness is as incompatible with Calvinism, as light with darkness. Mr. Toplady's arguments are produced under No. 1, with the number of the page in his book where he advances them. In the opposite column, under No. 2, the reader will find my answer, which is nothing but Mr. Toplady's own argument, retorted in such a manner as to defend the second Gospel axiom, which Calvinism entirely overthrows. No. 1 displays the unguarded manner in which Mr. Toplady defends the first Gospel axiom, To form No. 2, I only make his arguments stand upon the other leg; and by this simple method, I show the lameness of Calvinism, and the infamy which she pours upon God's holiness and goodness, under fair shows of regard for these adorable attributes.

The right leg of Calvinism, or the Calvinian doctrine of election and necessary holiness.	*The left leg of Calvinism, or the Calvinian doctrine of reprobation and necessary wickedness.*
ARGUMENT II. No. 1. Page 17. "I affirm, with *Scripture,* that they [*the elect*] cannot be *saved* without *sanctification* and *obedience.* Yet is not their *salvation* precarious; for that very decree of *election,*	ANSWER. No. 2. I affirm, with *Calvinism,* that the *reprobates* cannot be *damned* without *wickedness* and *disobedience.* Yet is not their *damnation* precarious; for that very decree *of reprobation,* by which

engage myself before the public, to get my Checks burnt, at Charing Cross, by the common hangman, on any day which Mr. Hill, Mr. Toplady, and Mr. M'Gowan will please to appoint. But if the Calvinists cannot do this, and if the Calvinian decree of reprobation insures the necessary, remediless sin, and the unavoidable, finished damnation of one and all the reprobates of Calvin, born or unborn; Mr. M'Gowan, and Dr. Gill, whom he quotes, insult common sense, when they intimate that insured damnation cannot be fairly deduced from the decree of reprobation. How much less candid are the letter writer and Dr. Gill, than Mr. Toplady and Zanchius, who fairly tell us, p. 75, "The condemnation (that is, the damnation) of the reprobate is *necessary* and *irresistible!*"

The letter writer tells us, p. 6, "What insures holiness, must insure glory; election (that is, Calvinian election) doth so, and glory must follow. This is the right leg of Calvinism; let her stand upon the left leg, and you have this doctrine of grace: what insures remediless sin, must insure damnation; Calvinian reprobation doth so, and damnation must follow. I would as soon bow to Dagon, as to this doctrine of remediless sin and insured wickedness. Ye controversial writers of the Gospel Magazine, if you will confirm Arminian teachers in their attachment to the holy election and righteous reprobation preached by St. Paul, and in their detestation for the Antinomian election and barbarous reprobation, which support your doctrinal peculiarities, only vindicate your election as inconsistently as Mr. M'Gowan, and your reprobation as openly as Mr. Toplady. (See two other notes on the same performance; the one under the Arg. xxxviii, and the other under the Arg. lxvii.)

by which they were nominated and ordained to eternal *life,* ordained their intermediate *renewal* after the image of God, *in righteousness and true holiness.* Nay, that renewal is itself the dawn and beginning of actual *salvation."*

ARG. III. No. 1. Page 17. "The *elect* could no more be *saved* without personal *holiness,* than they could be *saved* without personal existence. And why? Because God's own decree secures the means as well as the end, and accomplishes the end by the means. The same gratuitous predestination which ordained the existence of the *elect* as men, ordained their *purification as saints;* and they were ordained to both, in order to their being finally and completely *saved in Christ* with eternal *glory."*

they were nominated and ordained to eternal *death, ordained* their intermediate *conformity* to the image of *the devil in sin and true wickedness.* Nay, that conformity is itself the dawn and beginning of actual *damnation.*

ANSWER. No. 2. The *reprobates* could no more be *damned* without personal *wickedness,* than they could be *damned* without personal existence. And why? Because God's own decree secures the means as well as the end, and accomplishes the end by the means. The same gratuitous predestination which ordained the existence of the *reprobate* as men, ordained their *pollution as sinners;* and they were ordained to both, in order to their being finally and completely *damned in Adam* with eternal *shame.*

Before I produce the next argument, I think it is proper to observe that "the election of grace," which St. Paul defends, is not, as Calvin supposes an absolute election to eternal life, through *necessitated* holiness: an election this, which, in the very nature of things, drags after it an absolute reprobation to eternal death, through *remediless* sin. But the apostle means a gratuitous election to the privileges of the best covenant of peculiarity, — a most gracious covenant this, which is known under the name of "Christianity, the Gospel of Christ," or simply "the Gospel," by way of eminence. For as, by a partial election of distinguishing favour, the Jews were once chosen to be God's peculiar people, (at which time the Gentiles were reprobated, with respect to Jewish privileges, being left under the *inferior* Gospel dispensation of reprieved Adam and spared Noah,) so, when the Jews provoked God to reject them from being his peculiar people, he elected the Gentiles, to whom he sent "the Gospel of Christ:" he elected them, I say, and called them to believe this precious Gospel, and "to be holy in all manner of conversation, as becomes Christians." But far from absolutely electing those Gentiles to eternal salvation through unavoidable holiness, Calvinistically imposed upon them, he charged them by his messengers to make "their *Christian* calling and election sure, lest they also should be cut off," as the Jews had been, for not "making their *Jewish* calling and election sure." In short, "the election of grace" mentioned in the Scriptures, is a gratuitous election to run the *Christian* race with Paul Peter, and James; rather than the *Jewish* race with Moses, David, and Daniel; or the race of *Gentilism* with Adam, Enoch, and Noah. It is *a gracious* election, which implies no merciless, absolute reprobation of the rest of mankind. And the Calvinists are greatly mistaken when they confound this election with our judicial election to receive the crown of life, a rewarding crown this, the receiving of which depends, (1.) On the *grace* of God in Christ; and, (2.) On the *voluntary obedience* of faith; and will be judicially bestowed according to the impartiality of justice; and not according to the partiality of grace. This will be demonstrated in an

The Works of John Fletcher

Essay *on the Election of Grace and the Election of Justice,* where the reader will see the true meaning of the passages which Mr. Toplady has so plausibly pressed into the service of the following arguments: —

RIGHT LEG.   LEFT LEG.

ARG. IV. No. 1. Page 18. "God the Father hath chosen us in *Christ,* before the foundation of the world, that we should [not *'be saved, do what we will;'* but] 'be holy and without blame before him in love,' Ephesians 1:4. *Election* is always followed by *regeneration,* and regeneration is the source of all good works."

ANSWER. No. 2. God the Father hath reprobated us in *Adam,* before the foundation of the world, that we should [not be *"damned, do what we will,"* but] *be unholy and full of blame before him in malice. Reprobation* is always followed by *apostasy;* and apostasy is the source of all bad works.

ARG. V. No. 1. Page 18. "We [the elect] are his subsequent workmanship, created anew in *Christ Jesus* unto *good works,* which God hath *foreordained,* that we should walk in them. Consequently, it does not follow from the doctrine of absolute predestination that the *'elect* shall be *saved,* do what they will.' On the contrary, they are *chosen* as much to *holiness* as to *heaven;* and are foreordained to walk in *good* works, by virtue of their *election* from eternity, and of their *conversion* in time."

ANSWER. No. 2. We [the reprobates] are his subsequent workmanship, created anew in *Adam* unto *bad works,* which God hath *foreordained,* that we should walk in them. Consequently, it does not follow from the doctrine of absolute predestination that "the *reprobates* shall be damned, do what they will." On the contrary, they are *reprobated* as much to *wickedness* as to *hell;* and are foreordained to walk in bad works, by virtue of their *reprobation* from eternity, and of their *perversion* in time.

ARG. VI. No. 1. Pages 18, 19. "Yet again, God hath from the beginning, [that is, from everlasting, &c,] 'chosen you to salvation, through sanctification of the Spirit, and belief of the truth,' 2 Thessalonians 2:13. All, therefore, who are *chosen* to *salvation,* are no less unalterably destined to *holiness* and *faith* in the meanwhile. And if so, it is giving God himself the lie to say that *'the elect shall be saved, do what they will.'* For the *elect,* like the blessed person who redeemed them, come into the world not to do their own will, but the will of Him that sent them: and this is the will of God concerning them, even their

ANSWER. No. 2. Yet again, God hath from the beginning, [that is, from everlasting,] reprobated you to damnation, through pollution of the Spirit, and disbelief of the truth. All, therefore, who are *reprobated* to *damnation,* are no less unalterably destined to *wickedness* and *unbelief* in the meanwhile. And if so, it is giving God himself the lie to say that "the reprobate shall be damned, do what they will." For the *reprobate,* like the blessed person who *rejected* them, come into the world not to do their own will, but the will of Him that sent them: and this is the will of sanctification. Hence they are expressly said to be *elect unto obedience*. Not indeed chosen *because of* obedience, but chosen *unto* it: for works are not the foundation of *grace,* but streams flowing from it. *Election* does not depend upon *holiness,* but *holiness* depends upon *election.* So far, therefore, is predestination from being subversive of good works, that predestination is the *primary cause* of all the *good* works which have been and shall be wrought from the beginning to the end of time."

God concerning them, even their wickedness. Hence they are expressly said to be *reprobated unto disobedience.* Not indeed reprobated *because of* disobedience, but reprobated *unto* it: for works are not the foundation of wrath, but streams flowing from it. *Reprobation* does not depend upon *wickedness, but wickedness* depends upon *reprobation.* So far, therefore, is predestination from being subversive of bad works, that predestination to death is the *primary cause* of all the *bad* works which have been and shall be wrought from the beginning to the end of time.

Dreadfully crooked as the *left* leg of Mr. Toplady's system is, it perfectly agrees with the *right* leg; that is, with his crooked election, and his bandy predestination. He may deny it as absolutely as prisoners at the bar deny what is laid to their charge: but their denial goes for nothing: the witnesses are called in, and I produce two, who are capital, and to whom I suppose Mr. Toplady will hardly object. The first is Zanchius, and the second is his ingenious translator, who says in his translation, page 50, "He [man] fell in consequence of the Divine decree." (*Observ.* p. 7.) "Whatever comes to pass, comes to pass *by virtue* of this absolute, omnipotent will of God. Whatever things come to pass, come to pass *necessarily.*" (*Ibid.*) "Whatever man does, he does necessarily," page 15. "*All things* turn out according to Divine predestination; not only the works we do outwardly, but even the thoughts we think inwardly," page 7. "The will of God is the primary and supreme cause of *all* things," page 11. "The *sole cause* why some are saved and others perish, proceeds from his *willing* the salvation of the former, and the perdition of the latter," page 15. "We can *only* do what God from eternity willed and foreknew we *should,*" page 7. "No free will of the creature can resist the will of God," page 19. "The purpose or decree of God signifies his everlasting appointment of some men to life, and of others to death: which appointment flows *entirely* from his *own* free and sovereign *will,*" page 57. "If between the elect and the reprobate there was not a great gulf fixed, so that neither *can be otherwise than they are,* then the will of God (which is the *alone cause* why some are chosen and others not) would be rendered of no effect," page 56. "Nor would his word be true with regard to the non-elect, if it was *possible* for them to be saved," page 15. "The condemnation of the reprobate is *necessary* and *irresistible,*" page 25. "God worketh *all* things in *all* men, even *wickedness* in the wicked."

On these propositions, the most unguarded words of which I have produced in Italics, I rest the *left* leg of Calvinism, and taking my leave of the translation of Zanchius, I return to the *Vindication of the Decrees;* and continue to make Mr. Toplady's doctrine of grace stand "on its legs," that is, on absolute reprobation to death, as well as on absolute election to life.

ARG. VII. No. 1. Page 19. "Reason also joins with Scripture in asserting the indispensable necessity of SANCTIFICATION, upon the footing of the most absolute and irrespective election: or, in other words, that the certainty of the end does not supersede, but *insure* the intervention of the means."

ARG. VIII. No. 1. Pages 21, 22. "It was necessary that, as sinners, they [the elect] should not only be *redeemed from* punishment, and entitled to *heaven,* but endued moreover with an internal meetness for that inheritance. This internal meetness for heaven can only be wrought by the *restoring* agency of God the *Holy* Ghost, who *graciously* engaged and took upon himself, in the covenant of *peace,* to *renew* and *sanctify* all the *elect* people of God; saying, 'I will put my law in their minds. *Elect,* &c, through *sanctification* of the Spirit unto *obedience.'* Election, though productive of *good* works, is not founded upon them: on the contrary, they are one of the *glorious ends* to which they are *chosen. Saints* do not bear the *root,* but the root *them. Elect unto obedience.* They who have been *elected,* &c, shall experience the *Holy* Spirit's *sanctification,* in beginning, advancing, and perfecting the work of *grace* in their souls. The elect, &c, are *made to obey* the commandments of God, and to imitate *Christ,* &c. I said, *made to obey.* Here perhaps the *unblushing* Mr. Wesley may ask, 'Are the elect then mere machines?' I answer, No: they are made *willing* in the day of God's power."*

ANSWER. No. 2. Reason also joins with Scripture in asserting the indispensable necessity of WICKEDNESS, upon the footing of the most absolute and irrespective reprobation: or, in other words, that the certainty of the end does not supersede, but *insure* the intervention of the means.

ANSWER. No. 2. It was necessary that, as holy, they [the reprobate] should not only be *appointed* to punishment, and entitled to *hell,* but endued moreover with an internal meetness for that inheritance. This internal meetness for hell, can only be wrought by the *perverting* agency of [the Manichean] god the *unholy* ghost, who *officiously* engaged and took upon himself, in the covenant of wrath, to *pervert* and *defile* all the *reprobate* people of God; saying, "I will put my law in their minds. *Reprobate,* &c, through *pollution* of the spirit unto *disobedience."* Reprobation, though productive of *bad* works, is not founded upon them: on the contrary, they are one of the *inglorious ends* to which they are *reprobated. Sinners* do not bear the *root,* but the root *them. Reprobate unto disobedience.* They who have been *reprobated,* &c, shall experience the *wicked* spirit's *pollution,* in beginning, advancing, and perfecting the work of *sin* in their souls. The reprobates, &c, are *made to disobey* the commandments of God, and to imitate *Satan, &c.* I said, *made to disobey. Here perhaps the blushing Mr. Wesley may ask, "Are the reprobates then mere machines?" I answer, No: they are made willing in the day of God's power.*

---

* Here Mr. Toplady adds, And, I believe, nobody ever yet heard of *a willing machine.* But he is mistaken: for all moral philosophers call machine whatever is fitted for free motions, and yet has no power to begin and determine its own motions. Now willing being the motion of a

ARG. IX. No. 1. Pages 23, 24. "God decreed to bring his *elect* to glory, in a way of *sanctification,* and in *no other* way but that. If so, cries Mr. Wesley, 'they shall be *saved,* whether they *are sanctified or no.'* What, notwithstanding their *sanctification* is itself an essential branch of the decree concerning them? The man may as well affirm that *Abraham* might have been the progenitor of nations, though he had died in infancy, &c. Equally illogical, is Mr. Wesley's impudent slander, that 'the *elect* shall be *saved,* do what they will,' that is, whether they be *holy* or not."

ARG. X. No. 1. Page 20. "Paul's travelling, and Paul's *utterance,* were as certainly and as necessarily included in the decree of the *means* as his *preaching* was determined by the decree of the *end.*"

ARG. XI. No. 1. Pages 28, 29. "Love, when [Calvinistically] predicated of God, signifies his eternal *benevolence;* that is, his everlasting will, purpose, and determination, to *deliver, bless, and save* his [*elect*] people. In order to the eventual accomplishment of that *salvation* in the next world, *grace* is given them in this, to preserve them (and preserve them it does) from doing the *evil* they Otherwise would. This is all the election which Calvinism, &c, contends for; even a predestination to *holiness* and *heaven.*"

ARG. XII. No. 1. Page 33. "Now, if it be the Father's will that *Christ* should lose *none* of his *elect;* if *Christ* himself, in consequence of their covenant donation to him, does actually give unto them eternal *life,* and solemnly avers that they shall never *perish;* if God be so *for* them that none can hinder their *salvation,* &c; if they cannot be *condemned,* and naught shall separate them from the love of

ANSWER. NO. 2. God decreed to bring his *reprobate* to hell in a way of sinning, and in no other way but that. If so, cries Mr. Wesley, "they shall be damned, whether they sin or no." What, notwithstanding their sinning is itself an essential branch of the decree concerning them? 'The man may as well affirm that Paul might have preached the Gospel, viva voce, in fifty different regions, without travelling a step!" page 23. Equally illogical is Mr. Wesley's impudent slander, that "the reprobate shall be damned, do what they will," that is, whether they be wicked or not.*

ANSWER. NO. 2. The rich glutton's gluttony, and his unmercifulness, were as certainly and as necessarily included in the decree of the means as his being tormented in hell was determined by the decree of the end.*

ANSWER. NO. 2. Hate, when Calvinistically predicated of God, signifies his eternal ill will; that is, his everlasting will, purpose, and determination, to enthral, curse, and damn his [reprobated] people. In order to the eventual accomplishment of that damnation in the next world, wickedness is given them in this, to preserve them (and preserve them it does) from doing the good they otherwise would. This is all the reprobation which Calvinism contends for; even a predestination to wickedness and hell.*

ANSWER. NO. 2. Now, if it be the Father's will that Satan should lose none of his reprobate; if Satan himself, in consequence of their covenant donation to him, does actually give unto them eternal death, and solemnly avers that they shall never escape; if God be so against them that none can hinder their damnation, &c; if they cannot be justified, and naught shall separate them from the hate of Christ; it clearly and inevitably follows, that not one of the*

---

spirit, if a spirit cannot *will* but as it is *necessarily made* to will, it is as void of a self-determining principle as a fire engine, and of consequence it is (morally speaking) as a mere machine.

Christ; it clearly and inevitably follows, that not one of the elect can *perish;* but they must all necessarily be *saved.* Which salvation consists as much in the *recovery* of moral rectitude *below, as* in the *enjoyment* of eternal *blessedness above."* *reprobate can escape; but they must all necessarily be damned. Which damnation consists as much in the being stripped of moral rectitude on earth, as in the enduring of eternal torments in hell.*

By such wrested texts, and delusive arguments as these, it is, that Mr. Toplady has vindicated God's holiness upon Calvinian principles. Now as he requests that Calvinism may stand "upon its legs," that is, upon absolute election and absolute reprobation; I appeal to all the unprejudiced world, have I not made the Diana of the Calvinists stand straight? Have I not suffered her to rest upon her left leg, as well as upon the right? If that leg terminates in a horribly cloven foot, is it Mr. Wesley's fault, or mine? Have we formed the doctrinal image, which is set up in mystical Geneva? Is the quotation produced in my motto forged? Is not absolute reprobation one of "the doctrines of grace" (so called) as well as absolute election? May I not show the *full* face of Calvinism, as well as her *side* face? If a man pay me a guinea, have I not a right to suspect that it is false, and to turn it, if he that wants to pass it will never let me see the reverse of it in a clear light? Can Mr. Toplady blame me for holding forth Calvinian reprobation? Can he find fault with me for showing what he says I am "not only bound to show, but to *defend?*" If Calvinism be "the doctrine of grace," which I must engage sinners to espouse, why should I serve her as the soldiers did the thieves on the cross? Why, at least, should I break *one* of her legs? If ever I bring her into the pulpit, she shall come up on *both* "her legs." The chariot of my Diana shall be drawn by the biting serpent, as well as by the silly dove; I will preach Calvinian reprobation, as well as Calvinian election. I will be a man of "conscience and honour."

And now, reader, may I not address thy conscience and reason, and ask, If all the fallen angels had laid their heads together a thousand years to contrive an artful way of "reproaching the living God — the Holy One of Israel," could they have done it more effectually than by getting myriads of Protestants (even all the Calvinists) and myriads of Papists (even all the Dominicans, Jansenists, &c,) to pass the false coin of absolute election and absolute reprobation, with this deceitful, alluring inscription: "Necessary holiness unto the Lord," and this detestable Manichean motto on the reverse: "Necessary wickedness unto the Lord?" And has not Mr. Toplady presumed too much upon thy credulity, in supposing that thou wouldst never have wisdom enough to look at the black reverse of the shining medal by which he wants to bribe thee into Calvinism?

SECTION III.

An answer to some appeals to Scripture and reason, by which Mr.Toplady attempts to support the absoluteness and holiness of the Calvinian decrees.

LET us see if Mr. Toplady is happier in the choice of his Scriptural and rational illustrations, than in that of his arguments. To show that God's decrees respecting man's life and salvation are absolute, or (which is all one) to show that the decree of the *end* necessarily includes the decree of the *means,* he appeals to the case of Hezekiah, thus: —

ARG. XIII. Page 20. "God resolved that Hezekiah should live fifteen years longer than Hezekiah expected, &c. It was as much comprised in God's decree that Hezekiah should eat, drink, and sleep, during those fifteen years, and that he should not jump into the sea, &c, as that fifteen years should be added to his life." From this quotation it is evident that Mr. Toplady would have us believe that *none* of God's decrees are *conditional;* that when God decrees the end, he does it always in such a manner as to insure the means necessary in order to bring about the end; and that Hezekiah is applied to as a proof of this doctrine. Unfortunate appeal! If I had wanted to prove just the contrary, I do not know where I should have found an example more demonstrative of Mr. Toplady's mistake. Witness the following account: "Hezekiah was sick unto death, and Isaiah came to him and said, Thus saith [thus *decrees*] the Lord, Set thy house in order; for thou shalt die, and not live," Isaiah 38:1. Here is an explicit, peremptory decree; a decree where no condition is expressed; a decree which wears a *negative* aspect, "Thou shalt not live," and a *positive* form, "Thou shalt die." The means of executing the decree was already upon Hezekiah: he was "sick unto death." And yet, so far was he from thinking that the decree of the end *absolutely* included that of the means, that he set himself upon praying for life and health; yea, upon doing it as a Jewish perfectionist. "Then Hezekiah turned his face toward the wall, and prayed, *Remember now, O Lord, I beseech thee, how I have walked before thee with a perfect heart,* &c; and Hezekiah wept sore. Then came the word of the Lord to Isaiah, saying, Go, and say to Hezekiah, *Thus saith* [thus *decreeth*] *the Lord, I have heard thy prayer, I have seen thy tears; behold, I will add unto thy days fifteen years,*" verses 2, 5. From this account it is evident that Hezekiah might as easily have reversed the decree about his LIFE, by stabbing or drowning himself, as he reversed the decree about his DEATH, by weeping and praying; and that Mr. Toplady has forgotten himself as much in producing the case of Hezekiah in support of Calvinism, as if he had appealed to our Lord's sermon on the mount in defence of the lawless gospel of the day.

A kind of infatuation attends the wisest men who openly fight the battles of error. In the end, their swords, like that of the champion of the Philistines, do their cause more mischief than service. Mr. Toplady will perhaps afford us another instance of it. After producing Hezekiah to establish the absoluteness of God's decrees, he calls in the first Jewish hero; Joshua is brought to demonstrate that the decree of *the end* always binds upon us an *unavoidable* submission to the decree of *the means;* or, to speak more intelligibly, that God's decrees to bless or to curse, are always absolute, and *necessitate* us to use the means leading to his blessing or his curse.

ARG. XIV. Page 23. "Prior to the taking of Jericho, it was revealed to Joshua that he should certainly be master of the place. Nay, so *peremptory* was the *decree,* and so express the revelation of it, that it was predicted as if it had already taken effect: 'I have given into thy hand Jericho,' &c. This assurance, than which nothing could be more absolute, did not tie up Joshua's hands from action, and make him sit down without using the means, which were no less appointed than the end. On the contrary," &c. Here we are given to understand that Joshua and the Israelites could never cross any of God's gracious *decrees* by neglecting the means of their accomplishment; because they were *necessitated* to use those means. Thus is Joshua pressed into the service of Calvinian *necessity,* and the absoluteness of God's decrees; Joshua, who, of all men in the world, is most unlikely to support the tottering ark of Calvinian necessity. For when he saw in the wilderness the carcasses of several hundred thousand persons, to whom God had promised the good land of Canaan with an oath, and who nevertheless "*entered* not in because of unbelief," he saw several hundred thousand proofs that God's promises are not *absolute,* and that when he deals with rewardable and punishable agents, the decree of the end is not *unconditional,* and does by no means include an irresistible decree which binds upon them the *unavoidable* use of the means.

But, consider the peculiar case of Joshua himself: "The Lord spake unto Joshua, saying, There shall not any man be able to stand before thee all the days of thy life: I will not fail thee, nor forsake thee," Joshua 1:5. Now this peremptory decree of the end, far from necessarily including the means, actually failed by a single flaw in the use of the means. The disobedience of Achan reversed the decree; for he disregarded the means or condition which God had appointed: "Turn not to the right hand or to the left, that thou mayest prosper whithersoever thou goest," Joshua 1:7. Hence it is, that when Achan had "turned to the left," the decree failed, and we find Joshua "prostrate before the ark a whole day *with his* clothes rent, *and* dust upon his head," lamenting the flight of Israel before *Ai,* and wishing that "he had been content, and had dwelt on the other side Jordan." Nor do I see, in God's answer to him, the least hint of Mr. Toplady's doctrine. "Why liest thou upon thy face? Israel hath sinned, and they have also transgressed my covenant: for they have even taken of the accursed thing. Therefore the children of Israel could not stand before their enemies, because they were accursed: neither will I be with you any more, except ye destroy the accursed thing," Joshua 7:1, 13.

Hence it appears that when Mr. Toplady appeals to Joshua in defence of the absoluteness of God's decrees, he displays his skill in the art of logic, as much as if he appealed to the peremptoriness of the famous decree, "Yet forty days, and [ungodly] Nineveh shall be destroyed:" and yet penitent Nineveh was spared. So unscriptural is the assertion, that the decree of the end *insures* the use of the means, when God tries moral agents in the day of salvation, in order to punish or reward them according to their works in the day of judgment!

Mr. Toplady supports these unfortunate appeals to Scripture, by the following appeal to reason: —

ARG. XV. Page 24. "Suppose it were infallibly revealed to an army, or to any single individual, that the former should certainly gain such a battle, and the latter certainly win such a race, would not the army be mad to say, Then we will not fight a stroke? Would not the racer be insane to add, Nor will I move so much as one of my feet, &c? Equally illogical is Mr. Wesley's impudent slander, that *the elect shall be saved, do what they will, &c.* Either he is absolutely unacquainted with the first principles of reasoning, or he offers up the knowledge he has, as a whole burnt sacrifice on the altar of malice, calumny, and falsehood."

This severe censure will appear Calvinistically gratuitous, if we consider that it is entirely founded upon the impropriety of the illustrations produced by Mr. Toplady. If he had exactly represented the case, he would have said, "Suppose it were infallibly revealed to an army that they should certainly gain such a battle; that they could do nothing toward the victory by their own fighting; that the battle was fought, and *absolutely* won for them seventeen hundred years ago; that if they refused to fight to-day, or if they ran away, or were taken prisoners, their triumph would not be less certain; and that putting their bottle to their neighbours' mouths, and defiling their wives, instead of fighting, would only make them sing VICTORY louder, on a certain day called a *day of power*, when Omnipotence would sovereignly exert itself in their behalf, and put all their enemies to flight: suppose again it were revealed to a *racer* that he should certainly win such a race, and receive the prize, whether he ran *to-day* backward or forward; because his winning the race did not at all depend upon *his own* swift running, but upon the swiftness of a great racer, who *yesterday* ran the race for him, and who *absolutely* imputes to him his swift running, even while he gets out of the course to chase an ewe lamb, or visit a Delilah; that the covenant, which, secures him the prize, is unconditionally ordered in all things and sure; that though he may be unwilling to *run* now, yet in a day of irresistible power he shall be made willing to *fly* and receive the prize; and that his former loitering will only set off the greatness of the power which is absolutely engaged to carry him, and all elect racers, quite from Egypt to Canaan in one hour, if they have loitered till the eleventh hour;" suppose, I say, Mr. Toplady had given us such a *just* view of the case, who could charge the soldiers with "madness," and the racer with "being insane," if they agreed to say, "We will neither fight nor run, but take our ease, and indulge ourselves, *till* the day of power come, in which we shall *irresistibly* be made to gain the battle, and to win the race?"

From these *rectified* illustrations it appears, if I am not mistaken, (1.) That, when Mr. Wesley advanced his consequence, he neither "showed himself absolutely unacquainted with the first principles of reasoning," nor "offered up the knowledge he has, as a whole burnt sacrifice on the altar of malice, calumny, and falsehood." And, (2.) That, when Mr. Toplady's appeals to Scripture and reason are made *fairly* to stand "upon their legs," they do his doctrine as little service as his limping arguments.

SECTION IV.

An answer to the arguments by which Mr. Toplady endeavours to reconcile Calvinian reprobation with Divine JUSTICE.

WE have seen how unhappily the translator of *Zanchius* has reconciled his doctrines of grace and absolute election with God's holiness: let us now see if he has been more successful in reconciling his doctrines of wrath and absolute reprobation with Divine justice.

ARG. XVI. Page 35. "Justice consists in rendering to every man his due." Mr. Toplady gives us this narrow definition of justice to make way for this argument: God owes us no blessing, and therefore he may *gratuitously* give us an everlasting curse. He does not owe us heaven, and therefore he may justly appoint that eternal sin and damnation shall be our *unavoidable* portion. But is not a king unjust when he punishes an unavoidable fault with uninterrupted torture, as well as when he refuses to pay his just debts?

ARG. XVII. (*Ibid.*) "God is not a debtor to any man." True, (strictly speaking;) but, (1.) Does not God *owe to himself*, to behave *like himself*, that is, like a *gracious* and *just* Creator toward every man? (2.) When God, by his promise, has engaged himself *judicially* to render to every man "according to his works," is it just in him to necessitate some men to work righteousness, and others to work iniquity, that he may reward the former, and punish the latter, according to arbitrary decrees of absolute election to life, and of absolute reprobation to death? And, (3.) Do not the sacred writers observe, that God has condescended to make himself a debtor to his creatures by his gracious promises? Did Mr. Toplady never read, "He that hath pity upon the poor lendeth to the Lord, and," look, "what he layeth out it shall be paid again?" Proverbs 19:17. When evangelical Paul hath "fought a good fight," does he not look for a crown from the "just Judge," and declare that "God is not unrighteous to forget our labour of love;" and, "if we confess our sins," is not God bound by his justice, as well as by his faithfulness, "to forgive, *and* cleanse us?" 1 John 1:9.

ARG. XVIII. (*Ibid.*) "If it can be proved that he [God] *owes* salvation to every rational being he has made, then, and then only will it follow that God is *unjust* in not paying this debt of salvation to each, &c. What shadow of injustice can be fastened on his conduct for, in some cases, withholding what he does not owe?" This argument is introduced by Mr. Toplady in a variety of dresses. The flaw of it consists in supposing that there can be no medium between eternal salvation, and appointing to eternal damnation; and that, because God may absolutely elect as many of his creatures as he pleases to a crown of glory, he may absolutely reprobate as many as Calvinism pleases to eternal sin and everlasting burnings. The absurdity of this conclusion will be discovered by the reader, if he look at it through the glass of the following illustrations: — Mr. Toplady is not obliged, by any rule of justice, to give Mr. Wesley a hundred pounds, because he owes him no money; and therefore Mr. T. may give Mr. Wesley a hundred gratuitous stripes, without breaking, any rule of justice. The king may, without injustice, gratuitously give a thousand pounds to one man, ten thousand to another, a hundred to a third, and nothing to a fourth; and therefore the king may also, without injustice, gratuitously give a hundred stabs to one man, a thousand to another, and ten thousand to a third; or, he may *necessitate* them to offend, that he may hang and burn them with a *show* of justice.

ARG. XIX. Page 36. "I defy any man to show in what single respect the actual limitation of happiness itself is a lot more just and equitable (in a Being possessed of infinite power) than the decretive limitation of the persons who shall enjoy that happiness." The question is not whether God can justly *limitate the happiness of man;* or the number of the men, whom he will raise to such and such heights of happiness. This we never disputed; on the contrary, we assert with our Lord, that when God gives degrees of happiness, as a benefactor he may "do what he pleases with his own;" he may give *five* talents to *one* man, or to *five thousand* men; and *two* talents to *two* men, or to *two millions* of men. Wherein then does the fallacy of Mr. Toplady's argument consist? In this most irrational and unjust conclusion: God may, *without injustice*, "limit the happiness" of his human creatures, and *the number* of those who shall enjoy such and such a degree of happiness; and therefore he may also, *without injustice*, absolutely reprobate as many of his unborn creatures as he pleases, and decree to protract their infernal torments to all eternity, after having first decreed their necessary fall into sin, and their necessary continuance in sin, as *necessary means,* in order to their *necessary end,* which is *eternal damnation.* Is not this an admirable *Vindication of Calvin's Decrees?* Who does not see that the conclusion has no more to do with the premises than the following argument: — The lord chancellor may, *without injustice,* present Mr. T. to a living of fifty pounds, or to one of two hundred pounds, or he may reprobate Mr. T. from all the crown livings; and therefore the lord chancellor *may, without injustice,* sue Mr. T. for fifty pounds, or two hundred pounds, whenever he pleases. What name shall we give to the logic which deals in such arguments as these?

ARG. XX. Page 37. "He [man] derives his existence from God, and therefore [says Arminianism] God is bound to make his existence happy." I would rather say God is bound both by the rectitude of his nature, and by the promises of his Gospel, not to reprobate any man to remediless sin and eternal misery, till he has actually deserved such a dreadful reprobation, at least by one thought, which he was not absolutely predestinated to think. But Calvinism says that God absolutely reprobated a majority of men before they thought their first thought, or drew their first breath. If Mr. T. had stated the case in this plain manner, all his readers would have seen his doctrine of wrath without veil, and would have shuddered at the sight.

ARG. XXI. (*Ibid.*) "If God owe salvation to all his creatures as *such,* even the workers of iniquity will be saved, or God must cease to be just." I never heard any Arminian say that God owes salvation, that is, heavenly glory, to all his creatures, as such: for then all horses, being God's creatures as well as men, would be taken to heaven. But we maintain that God will never mediately entail necessary, remediless sin upon any of his creatures, that he may infallibly punish them with eternal damnation. And we assert, if God had not graciously designed to replace all mankind in a state of initial salvation from sin and hell, according to the various dispensations of his redeeming grace, he would have punished Adam's personal sin by a personal damnation. Nor would he have suffered him to propagate his fallen race, unless the second Adam had extended the blessings of redemption so far as to save from eternal misery all who die in their infancy, and to put all who live long enough to act as moral agents, in a capacity of avoiding hell by "working out their own eternal salvation" in the day of their temporary salvation; a day this, which inconsistent Calvinists call "the day of grace."

Mr. Toplady, after decrying *our* doctrine of grace, as leading to *gross* iniquity, indirectly owns that the *conditionality* of the promise of eternal salvation guards *our* Gospel against the charge of Antinomianism, — a dreadful charge this, which falls so heavily on Calvinism. Conscious that he cannot defend his lawless, unconditional election to eternal life, and his wrathful, unconditional reprobation to eternal death, without taking the conditionality of eternal salvation out of the way, he attempts to do it by the following dilemma: —

ARG. XXII. Page 38. "Is salvation due to a man that *does not* perform those conditions? If you *say,* Yes; you jump, hand over head, into what you yourself call Antinomianism. If you say that salvation is not due to a man, unless he do fulfil the conditions, it will follow that man's own performances are *meritorious* of salvation, and bring God himself into debt."

We answer, **1.** To show the tares of Calvinism, Mr. Toplady raises an artificial night by confounding the sparing salvation of the Father, the atoning salvation of the Son, the convincing, converting, and perfecting salvation of the Spirit. Yea, he confounds actual salvation from a thousand temporal evils; temporary salvation from death and hell; initial salvation from the guilt and power of sin; present salvation into the blessings of Christianity, Judaism, Heathenism; continued salvation into these blessings; eternal salvation from death and hell; and eternal salvation into glory and heaven: he confounds, I say, *all* these degrees of salvation, which is as absurd as if he confounded all degrees of life, the life of an embryo, of a sucking child, of a school boy, of a youth, of a man, of a departed saint, and of an angel. When he has thus shuffled his cards, and played the dangerous game of confusion, what wonder is it if he wins it, and makes his inattentive readers believe that what can be affirmed with truth of *salvation into heavenly glory,* must be true also when it is affirmed of *salvation from everlasting burnings;* and that because God does not owe heaven and angelical honours to unborn children, he may *justly* reprobate them to *hell* and to Satanical, remediless wickedness as the way to it.

2. Distinguishing what Mr. Toplady confounds, we do not sample to maintain, that though God is not bound to give *existence,* much less heavenly glory, to any creature; yet all his creatures, who never *personally* offended him, have a *right* to expect at his hands *salvation from everlasting fire,* till they have deserved his eternal and absolute reprobation by committing some *personal and avoidable* offence. Hence it is, that all mankind are born in a state of inferior salvation: for they are all born out of eternal fire; and to be out of hell is a considerable *degree of salvation,* unless we are suffered to live *unavoidably* to deserve everlasting burnings, which is the case of all Calvin's imaginary reprobates.

3. Mr. Toplady "throws out a barrel for the amusement of the whale, to keep him in play, and make him lose sight of the ship" — the *fire* ship. For, in order to make us lose sight of absolute reprobation, remediless wickedness, and everlasting fire, which (if Calvinism be true) is the *unavoidable* lot of the greatest part of mankind even in their mother's womb; he throws out this ambiguous expression, "salvation due;" just as if there were no medium between "salvation due," and Calvinian reprobation due! Whereas it is evident that there is the medium of *non-creation,* or that of *destruction in a state of seminal existence!*

4. The flaw of Mr. Toplady's argument will appear in its proper magnitude, if we look at it through the following illustration: — A whole regiment is led to the left by the colonel, whom the general wanted to turn to the right. The colonel, who is *personally* in the fault, is pardoned; and five hundred of the soldiers, who, by the overbearing influence of their colonel's disobedience, were *necessitated* to move to the left, are appointed to be hanged for not going to the right. The general sends to Geneva for a Tertullus, who vindicates the JUSTICE of the execution by the following speech: — "Preferment is not due to obedient soldiers, much less to soldiers who have *necessarily disobeyed* orders; and therefore your gracious general acts consistently with JUSTICE in appointing these five hundred soldiers to be hanged, for, as there is no medium between *not promoting* soldiers, and *hanging* them, he might justly have hanged the whole regiment. He is not bound, by any law, to give any soldier a captain's commission; and therefore he is perfectly just when he sends these military reprobates to the gallows." Some of the auditors clap Tertullus' argument: P.O. cries out, that it is "most masterly;" but a few of the soldiers are not quite convinced, and begin to question whether the holy service of the *mild Saviour of the world* is not preferable to the Antinomian service of the absolute reprobater of countless myriads of unborn infants.

5. The other flaw of Mr. Toplady's dilemma consists in supposing that Gospel worthiness is incompatible with the Gospel; whereas, all the doctrines of justice, which make *one half* of the Gospel, stand or fall with the doctrines of evangelical worthiness. We will shout it on the walls of mystic Geneva: — They that follow Christ shall "walk with him in white? rather than they that follow antichrist; "for they are [more] worthy. Watch and pray always, that you may be counted worthy to escape, and to stand *rewardable* before the Son of man. Whatever ye do, do it heartily, as to the Lord, &c, knowing that of the Lord ye shall receive the reward of the inheritance." For he will say, in the great day of retribution, "Come, ye blessed, inherit the kingdom, &c; for I was hungry, and ye gave me meat, &c. Go, ye cursed, into everlasting fire, &c; for I was hungry, and ye gave me no meat," &c. The doctrine of *Pharisaic* merit we abhor; but the doctrine of *rewardable obedience* we honour, defend, and extol. Believers, let not Mr. Toplady "beguile you of your reward through voluntary humility. If ye live after the flesh ye shall die: but if ye, through the Spirit, mortify the deeds of the body, ye shall live. Whatsoever a man soweth, that shall he also reap. For we shall all appear before the judgment seat of Christ, that every one may receive the things done in the body, according to what he has done, whether it be good or bad." Look to yourselves, that ye lose not the things which ye have wrought. So fight, that you may not be reprobated by remunerative justice. "So run, that you may [judicially] obtain an incorruptible crown. Remember Lot's wife. By patient continuance in well doing seek for glory;" and God, according to his gracious promises, will "render you eternal life: for he is not" untrue to break his evangelical promises, nor "unrighteous to forget your work that proceedeth from love." Your persevering obedience shall be graciously rewarded by "a crown of righteousness, which the Lord, the righteous Judge, shall give you at that day; *and then* great shall be your reward in heaven." For Christ himself hath said, "Be faithful unto death, and I will give thee the crown of life. My sheep follow me, and I will give unto them eternal life" in glory. For I am "the author of eternal salvation to them that obey me." What can be plainer than this Gospel? Shall the absurd cries of popery! merit! &c, make us ashamed of Christ's disciples; of Christ's words, and of Christ himself? God forbid! Let the Scriptures — "let God be true," though Mr. Toplady should be mistaken.

ARG. XXIII. Page 38. "If he [God] be not obliged, in justice, to save mankind, then neither is he unjust in passing by some men; nay, he *might*, had he so pleased, have passed by the whole of mankind, without electing any one individual of the fallen race; and yet have continued holy, *just*, and good."

True: he might have passed them by without fixing any blot upon his justice and goodness, if, by *passing them by*, Mr. T. means "leaving them in the wretched state of *seminal* existence," in which state his vindictive justice found them after Adam's fall. For then an *unknown punishment, seminally endured*, would have borne a just proportion to an *unknown sin, seminally committed*, But if, by *passing some men by*, this gentleman means, as Calvinism does, "absolutely predestinating some men to necessary, remediless sin, and to unavoidable, eternal damnation;" we deny that God might *justly* have passed by the whole of mankind; we deny that he might *justly* have passed by *one* single man, woman, or child. Nay, we affirm that if we conceive Satan, or the evil principle of Manes, as exerting creative power, we could not conceive him worse employed, than in forming an *absolute* reprobate in embryo; that is, "a creature unconditionally and absolutely doomed to remediless wickedness and everlasting fire."

As the simple are frequently imposed upon by an artful substituting of the harmless word, "passing by," for the terrible word, "absolutely reprobating to death," I beg leave to show, by a simile, the vast difference there is between these two phrases: — A king may, without injustice, *pass by* all the beggars in the streets, without giving them any bounty; because, if he does them no good in thus passing them by, he does them no harm. But suppose he called two captains of his guards, and said to the first, If you see me *pass by* little, dirty beggars, without giving them an alms, throw them into the mire; or if their parents have cast them into the mire, keep them there: then let the *second* captain follow with his men, and take all the dirty beggars who have thus been *passed by,* and throw them, for being dirty, into a furnace hotter than that of Nebuchadnezzar: suppose, I say, the king *passed* his little indigent subjects *by* in this manner, would not his decree of *preterition* be a more than diabolical piece of cruelty? I need not inform my judicious readers that the passing by of the king represents Calvinian *passing by,* that is, absolute reprobation to death; that the first captain, who throws little beggars into the dirt, or keeps them there, represents the *decree of the means,* which necessitates the reprobate to sin, or to *continue* in sin; and that the second captain represents the *decree of the end,* which necessitates them to go to everlasting burnings.

ARG. XXIV. Page 39. Mr. Toplady endeavours to reconcile Calvinian reprobation with Divine justice by an appeal "to God's providential dealings with men in the present life." His verbose argument, stript of its Geneva dress, and brought naked to open light, may run thus: — "If God may, without injustice, absolutely place the sons of Adam in circumstances of temporary misery, he may also, Without injustice, reprobate them to eternal torments: but he may justly place the sons of Adam in circumstances of temporary misery; witness his actually doing it: and therefore he may without injustice reprobate them to eternal torments, and to remediless sin, as the way to those torments." The flaw of this argument is in the first proposition, and consists in supposing that because God can justly appoint us to suffer "a light affliction, which [comparatively speaking] is but for a moment, and which [if we are not perversely wanting to ourselves] will work for us a far more exceeding and eternal weight of glory," 2 Corinthians 4:17, he can also justly appoint us to remediless wickedness and eternal damnation. This conclusion is all of a piece with the following argument: — A father may justly punish his disobedient child with a rod, and give his sick child a bitter medicine; and therefore he may justly break all his bones with a forge hammer, and daily drench him with melted lead. To produce such absurd consequences without a mask, is sufficiently to answer them: see farther what is said upon page 42.

ARG. XXV. Page 40. Mr. Toplady is, if possible, still more abundantly mistaken, while, to prove the justice of Calvinian reprobation, he appeals to "the real inequality of providential distributions below." We cannot "pronounce the great Father of all *unjust,* because he does not make all his offspring equally rich, good, and happy," and therefore God may *justly* reprobate some of them to eternal misery; just as if *inferior degrees of goodness and happiness* were the same thing as *remediless wickedness and eternal misery!*

ARG. XXVI. (*Ibid.*) "The devils may be cast down to hell to be everlastingly damned, and be appointed thereto; and it gives no great concern. No hard thoughts against God arise: no charge of cruelty, injustice," &c. Indeed, if Dr. Gill, whom Mr. Toplady quotes, insinuated that God had *absolutely* predestinated myriads of angels to everlasting damnation, through the appointed means of *necessary* sin; and that God had made this appointment thousands of years before most of those angels had any personal existence, it would give us *great concern*, both for the honour of God's justice, and for the angels so cruelly treated by free wrath. But as matters are, the case of devils gives us no great concern, because they fell *knowingly, wilfully, and without necessity*. To the end of the day of their visitation, they personally rejected God's gracious counsel toward them; and, as they obstinately refused to subserve the judicial display of his remunerative bounty, it is highly agreeable to reason and equity, that they should subserve the judicial display of his vindictive justice.

ARG. XXVII. Page 41. "The king of Great Britain has unlimited right of peerage, &c. Will any one be so weak and perverse as to charge him with tyranny and injustice, only because it is not his will, though it is in his power, to make all his subjects noblemen?" This is another barrel thrown out to the whale. This illustration does not touch, but conceal the question. For the similar question is not whether the king is *unjust* in leaving gentlemen and tradesmen among the gentry and commonalty, but whether he could, *without injustice and tyranny*, pretend, that because he has an unlimited right of *peerage*, he has also an unlimited right of (what I beg leave to call) *felonage*, — a Calvinian right, this, of appointing whom he pleases to rob and murder, that he may appoint whom he pleases to a cell in Newgate, and a swing at Tyburn! This is the true state of the case. If Mr. T. had cast a veil over it, it is a sign that he is not destitute of the feeling of justice, and that, if he durst look at his Manichean picture of God's sovereignty without a veil, he would turn from it with the same precipitancy with which he would start back from the abomination of the Moabites, or from the grim idol to which mistaken Israelites sacrificed their children in the valley of Hinnom.

ARG. XXVIII. Page 42. "Misery, though endured but for a year, &c, is, in its own nature, and for the time being, as truly misery, as it would be if protracted ever so long, &c. And God can no more cease to be just for a year, or for a man's lifetime, than he can cease to be just for a century, or for ever. By the same rule that he can, and does, without impeachment of his moral attributes, permit any one being to be miserable for a *moment*, he may permit that being to be miserable for *a much longer time:* and so on, *ad infinitum*," that is, in plain English, *for ever.* The absurdity of this argument may be sufficiently pointed out by a similar plea: — A surgeon may, without injustice, open an imposthume in my breast, and give me pain for an hour, and therefore he may justly scarify me, and flay me alive ten years. A judge may, without impeachment of his justice, order a man to be burnt in the hand for a moment, and therefore his justice will continue unstained, if he order red hot irons to be applied to that man's hands and feet, back and breast, *ad infinitum.* I hope that when Mr. Toplady threw this scrap of Latin over the nakedness of his Diana, his good nature suggested that she is too horrible to be looked at without a veil. But could he not have borrowed the language of mother Church, without borrowing a maxim which might shock any inquisitor, and might have put Bonner himself to a stand?

ARG. XXIX. Page 44. "He [God] permits, and has, for near six thousand years, permitted the reign of *natural* evil. Upon the same principle might he not extend its reign to — a never-ending duration?" *He might,* if a neverending line of moral evil, personally and avoidably brought on by free agents upon themselves, called for a never-ending line of penal misery: and our Lord himself says that *he will:* "These [the wicked, who have *finally* hardened themselves] shall go away into everlasting punishment, where their worm dieth not, and the fire is not quenched," Matthew 25:46; Mark 9:48.

ARG. XXX. (*Ibid.*) "But still the old difficulty, [a difficulty which Arminianism will never solve,] &c, the old difficulty survives. How came moral evil to be *permitted,* when it might as easily have been hindered, by a Being of infinite goodness, power, and wisdom?" Page 39, Mr. T. speaks partly the same language, giving us to understand, as openly as he dares, that God worketh all things in all men, even wickedness in the wicked. His pernicious, though guarded insinuation, runs thus: — "You will find it extremely difficult (may I not say *impossible?*) to point out the difference between *permission* and *design,* in a being possessed (as God most certainly is) of unlimited *wisdom* and unlimited *power.*" Hence we are given to understand, that because God does not absolutely hinder the commission of sin, "it would nonplus all the sagacity of man, should we attempt clearly to show wherein the difference lies" between God's *permitting* sin, and his *designing,* or *decreeing* sin, or (to speak with more candour) between God's placing free agents in a state of probation with a strict charge not to sin, and between his being the author of sin. Is not this a "most masterly" "*Vindication* of the Decrees and Providence of God," supposing you mean by "God" the *sin-begetting* deity worshipped by the Manichees? This Antinomian blow at the root of Divine holiness is dangerous: I shall therefore ward it off by various answers.

1. When God placed man in paradise, far from *permitting* him to sin, he *strictly forbade* him to do it. Is it right then in Mr. Toplady to call God "the permitter of sin," when the Scriptures represent him as the forbidder of it? Nay, is it not very wrong to pour shame upon the holiness of God, and absurdity upon the reason of man, by making a Calvinistic world believe that *forbidding* and *threatening* is one and the same thing with *permitting* and *giving leave;* or, at least, that the difference is so trifling, that "all the sagacity of man will find it extremely difficult, not to say impossible, clearly to point it out?"

2. I pretend to a very little share of "all the sagacity of man;" and yet, without being *nonplused* at all, I hope to show, by the following illustration, that there is a prodigious difference between *not hindering* and *design,* in the case of entering in of sin:—

A general wants to try the faithfulness of his soldiers, that he may reward those who will fight, and punish those who will go over to the enemy; in order to display, before all the army, his love of bravery, his hatred of cowardice, his remunerative goodness, and his impartial justice. To this end, he issues out a proclamation, importing that all the volunteers, who shall gallantly keep the field in such an important engagement, shall be made captains; and that all those who shall go over to the enemy shall be shot. I suppose him endued with infinite wisdom, knowledge, and power. By his omniscience he sees that some *will* desert; by his omnipotence he *could* indeed hinder them from doing it: for he could chain them all to so many posts stuck in the ground around their colours: but his infinite wisdom does not permit him to do it; as it would be a piece of madness in him to defeat by forcible means his design of trying the courage of his soldiers, in order to *reward* and *punish* them according to their *gallant* or *cowardly* behaviour in the field. And therefore, though he is persuaded that many will be shot, he puts his proclamation in force; because, upon the whole, it will best answer his wise designs. However, as he does not *desire*, much less *design*, that any of his soldiers should be shot for desertion, he does what his wisdom permits him to do to prevent their going over to the enemy; and yet, for the above-mentioned reason, he does not *absolutely hinder* them from doing it. Now, in such a case, who does not see that the difference between "not absolutely hindering" and *designing*, is as discernible as the difference between reason and folly; or between wisdom and wickedness? By such dangerous insinuations as that which this illustration exposes, the simple are imperceptibly led to confound Christ and Belial; and to think that there is little difference between the celestial Parent of *good*, and the Manichean Parent of *good* and *evil*: the Janus of the fatalists, who wears two faces, an angel's face and a devil's face; a mongrel, imaginary god this, whose fancied ways are, like his fancied nature, full of duplicity.

3. To the preceding illustration I beg leave to add the following argument:— No unprejudiced person will, I hope, refuse his assent to the truth of this proposition, — A world, wherein there are *rational* free agents, like angels and men; *irrational* free agents, like dogs and horses; *necessary* agents, like plants and trees; and *dead* matter, like stones and clods of earth: such a world, I say, is as much superior in perfection to a world where there are only necessary agents and dead matter, as a place inhabited by learned men and curious beasts, contains more wonders than one which is only stocked with fine flowers and curious stones. If this be granted, it necessarily follows that *this* world was very perfect, calculated to display his infinite power and manifold wisdom. Now, in the very nature of things, *rational* free agents, being capable of knowing their Creator, owe to him gratitude and obedience, and to one another assistance and love; and therefore they are "under a law," which (as free agents) they may keep or break as they please.

"But could not God necessitate free agents to keep the law they are under?"

Yes, says Calvinism, for he is endued with infinite power: but Scripture, good sense, and matter of fact say, No: because, although God is endued with infinite power, he is also endued with infinite wisdom. And it would be as absurd to *create* free agents in order to *necessitate* them, as to *do* a thing in order to *undo* it. Beside, (I repeat it,) God's distributive justice could never be displayed, nor would free obedience be paid by rationals, and crowned by the Rewarder and "Judge of all the earth," unless rationals *were free-willing* creatures, and therefore, the moment you absolutely necessitate them, you destroy them as free agents, and you rob God of two of his most glorious titles, that of Rewarder, and that of Judge. Thus we account for the origin of evil in a Scriptural and rational manner, without the help of fatalism, Manicheism, or Calvinism. Mr. Toplady replies: —

ARG. XXXI. Pages 44, 45. "O, but God himself is a *free agent*, though his will is *necessarily*, unchangeably, and singly determined to good, and to *good only*. So are the elect angels. So are the glorious souls of saints departed, &c, and so might Adam have been, had God pleased to have so created him."

This is the grand objection of President Edwards, which I have answered in the *Scripture Scales,* page 196. I shall, however, make here a few remarks upon it. (1.) If "God worketh all things, &c, even wickedness in the wicked," as the consistent Predestinarians directly or indirectly tell us, it is absurd in them to plead that he is *singly* determined to good, and to *good only:* for every body knows that the God of Manes is full of *duplicity;* having an *evil* principle, Which absolutely predestinates and causes all the wickedness, and a *good* principle, which absolutely predestinates and causes all the virtue in the world. As for the God of Christians, he is not so necessitated to do that which is good, but he might, *if he would,* do the most astonishing act of injustice and barbarity: for he might, *if he would,* absolutely doom myriads of unborn infants to remediless wickedness and everlasting fire, before they have deserved this dreadful doom, so much as by the awkward motion of their little finger. Nor need I tell Mr. Toplady this, who believes that God has actually done so.

2. God is not in a state of probation under a superior being, who calls himself the rewarder, and who says, "Vengeance is mine, and I will repay:" nor shall he ever be tried by one who will judicially "render to *him* according to what he hath done, whether it be good or bad."

3. If faithful angels are unchangeably fixed in virtue, and unfaithful angels in vice, the fixedness of their nature is the consequence of the *good* or *bad* use which they have made of their *liberty;* and therefore their confirmation in *good,* or in *evil,* flows from a *judicial* election or reprobation, which displays the distributive justice of their Judge, Rewarder, and Avenger.

4. Nothing can be more absurd than to couple absolute necessity with moral free agency. Angels and glorified souls are necessitated to serve God and love one another, as a good man is necessitated not to murder the king, and not to blow his own brains out. Such a *necessity* is far from being *absolute:* for, if a good man would, he might gradually overcome his reluctance to the greatest crimes. Thus David, who was no doubt as chaste and loving once as Joseph, overcame his strong aversion to adultery and murder.

Should it be said, What! *Can glorified saints and angels fall away?* I reply, They *will* never fall away, because they are called off the stage of probation, stand far above the reach of temptation, and have "henceforth crowns of righteousness laid up for them, which the Lord, the righteous Judge, shall give them at that day." In the meantime, "they rest from their [probatory] labours, and their works follow them." But still, in the nature of things, they are as *able* to disobey, as Joseph was to commit adultery, had he set his heart upon it: for if they had no capacity of *disobeying,* they would have no capacity of *obeying,* in the *moral* sense of the word: their obedience would be as *necessary,* and as far from *morality, as* the passive obedience of a leaden ball, which you drop, with an absurd command to tend toward the centre. If I am not mistaken, these answers fully set aside Mr. T.'s argument taken from the *necessary goodness* of God, angels, and glorified saints.

ARG. XXXII. Page 45. "God *is,* and *cannot but be* inviolably *just,* amidst all the sufferings of fallen angels and fallen men, involuntary beings as they are. And he will continue to be just in all they are yet to suffer." That "God is, and will be just," in all that fallen angels and men have suffered, and may yet suffer, is most true, because they are *voluntary* beings (Mr. Toplady says, "involuntary beings") and free agents (Mr. Toplady would say, *necessary* agents) who *personally* deserve what they suffer; or who, if they suffer without personal offence, as infants do, have in Christ a rich cordial, and an efficacious remedy, which will cause their *temporary* sufferings to answer *to all eternity* the most admirable ends for themselves, if they do not reject God's gracious, castigatory, probatory, or purificatory counsels toward them, when they come to *act* as free agents. But that "God is and will be just," in absolutely ordaining "involuntary beings" to sin and be damned, is what has not yet been proved by one argument which can bear the light. However, Mr. Toplady, with the confidence which suits his peculiar logic, concludes this part of his subject by the following triumphal exclamation: —

ARG. XXXIII. (*Ibid.*) "And if so, what becomes of the objection to God's decree of preterition, [a soft word for *absolute reprobation to remediless sin and eternal death,*] drawn from the article of injustice?"

Why, it stands in full force, notwithstanding all the arguments which have yet been produced. Nay, the way to show that an objection is *unanswerable*, is to answer it as Mr. Toplady has done; that is, by producing arguments which equally shock reason and conscience, and which are crowned with this new paradox: — "Fallen angels, and fallen men are *involuntary* beings." So that the last subterfuge of moderate Calvinists is now given up. For when they try to vindicate God's justice, with respect to the damnation of their imaginary reprobates, they say that the poor creatures are damned as *voluntary* agents. But Mr. Toplady informs us that they are damned as "involuntary beings," that is, as excusable beings; and might I not add, as *sinless* beings? For (evangelically speaking) is it possible that an "involuntary being" should be *sinful?* Why is the murderer's sword *sinless?* Why is the candle by which an incendiary fires your house an *innocent* flame? Is it not because they are "involuntary beings," or mere tools used by other beings? A cart accidentally falls upon you, and you involuntarily fall upon a child, who is killed upon the spot. The father of the child wants you hanged as a murderer: but the judge pronounces you perfectly guiltless. Why? Truly because you were, in that case, an "involuntary being" as well as the cart. When, therefore, Mr. Toplady asserts that we "are involuntary beings," and insinuates that God is *just* in absolutely predestinating us to sin necessarily, and to be damned eternally, he proves *absurdum per absurdius — injustum per injustius — crudele per crudelius.* In a word, he gives a finishing stroke to God's justice; and his pretended "*Vindication*" of that tremendous attribute proves, it I may use his own expression, a public, though (I am persuaded) an undesigned, "defamation" of it.

SECTION V.

An answer to the arguments by which Mr. Toplady endeavours to reconcile Calvinian REPROBATION *with Divine* MERCY.

IF it is impossible to reconcile Calvinian reprobation with Divine JUSTICE, how much more with Divine MERCY! This is however the difficult task which Mr. T. sets about next. Consider we his arguments: —

ARG. XXXIV. Page 45. "As God's forbearing to *create* more worlds than he has, is no impeachment of his omnipotence: so his forbearing to *save* as many as he might, is no impeachment of his infinite mercy." The capital flaw of this argument consists in substituting still the phrase "not saving," for the phrase "*absolutely* reprobating to remediless sin and everlasting burnings." The difference between these phrases, which Mr. Toplady uses as equivalent, is prodigious. Nobody ever supposed that God is *unmerciful* because he does not take stones into heaven, or because he does not save every pebble from its opacity, by making it transparent and glorious as a diamond: for pebbles suffer nothing by being "passed by," and not saved into adamantine glory. But if God made every pebble an organized, living body, capable of the keenest sensations; and if he appointed that most of these "involuntary [sensible] beings" should be absolutely opaque, and should be cast into a lime kiln, there to endure everlasting burnings, for not having the transparency which he decreed they should never have; would it not be impossible to reconcile his conduct to the lowest idea we can form even of Bonner's *mercy?*

Having thus pointed out the sandy foundation of Mr. Toplady's argument, I shall expose its absurdity by a similar way of arguing. I am to prove that the king may, without impeachment of his mercy, put the greatest part of his soldiers in such trying circumstances as shall *necessitate* them to desert and to be shot for desertion. To do this, I learn logic of Mr. T. and say," As the king's forbearing to create more lords than he has, is no impeachment of his unlimited right of peerage; so his forbearing to raise as many soldiers as he might, is no impeachment of his mercy." So far the argument is conclusive. But if by *not raising* soldiers I *artfully* mean *absolutely appointing* and *necessitating* them to desert and be shot, I vindicate the king's mercy as logically as Mr. T. vindicates the *mercy* of Manes' God.

ARG. XXXV. Page 46. "If therefore the decree of [Calvinian] reprobation be exploded, on account of its imaginary incompatibility with Divine *mercy, we* must, upon the same principle, charge God with want of goodness in almost every part of his relative conduct." If this dark argument be brought to the light, it will read thus:— "God is *infinitely good* in himself, though he *limits* the exercise of his goodness in not forming so many beings as he *might,* and in not making them all so glorious as he *could;* and therefore he is *infinitely merciful,* though he *absolutely appoints* millions of unborn creatures to remediless sin and everlasting fire." But what has the conclusion to do with the premise? What would Mr. T. think of me, if I presented the public with the following sophism? "Nobody can reasonably charge the king with want of goodness for not enriching and ennobling every body; and therefore nobody can reasonably charge him with want of mercy for decreeing that so many of his new-born subjects shall necessarily be trained up in absolute rebellion, that he may legally throw them into a fiery furnace, for necessarily fulfilling his absolute decree concerning their rebellion." Nevertheless, this absurd argument contains just as much truth and mercy, as that of Mr. Toplady.

ARG. XXXVI. (*Ibid.*) "There is no way of solidly, &c, justifying the ways of God with men, but upon this grand *datum*, That the exercise of his own infinite mercy is regulated by the voluntary determination of his own most wise and sovereign pleasure. Allow but this rational, Scriptural, &c,proposition, and every cavil, grounded on the chimerical unmercifulness of non-election ceases even to be plausible." The defect of this argument consists also in covering the *left leg* of Calvinism, and in supposing that Calvinian non-election is a bare *non-exertion of a peculiar mercy* displayed toward some; whereas it is a positive act of barbarity. We readily grant that God is *infinitely merciful,* though his infinite wisdom, truth, and justice do not suffer him to show the same mercy to ALL, which he does to SOME. But it is absurd to suppose, that because he is not bound to "show mercy" to all those who have *personally and unnecessarily* offended him (or indeed to any one of them,) he may show injustice and cruelty to unborn creatures, who never *personally* offended him so much as by one wandering thought, and he may absolutely doom myriads of them to sin without remedy, and to be damned without fail.

ARG. XXXVII. Page 48. After all his pleas, to show that God can, without impeachment of his holiness, justice, and mercy, absolutely appoint his unborn creatures to remediless wickedness and everlasting torments, Mr. Toplady relents, and seems a little ashamed of Calvinian reprobation. He tells us that "reprobation is, for the most part, something purely negative," and "has, so far as God is concerned, more in it of negation than positivity." But Mr. Toplady knows that the unavoidable END of absolute reprobation is DAMNATION, and that the *means* conducive to this fearful end is unavoidable *wickedness;* and he has already told us, p. 17, that "God's own decree secures the means as well as the end, and accomplishes the end by the means." Now *securing* and *accomplishing* a thing, is something *altogether positive.* Hence it is, that, p. 83, Mr. T. calls the decrees by which the reprobates sin, not only *permissive* but "*effective;*" and tells us, p. 77, that "God efficaciously permitted horrible wickedness." And herein he exactly follows Calvin, who, in his comment on Romans 9:18, says, "INDURANI *verbum, quum Deo in Scripturis tribuitur, non solum,* PERMISSIONEM *(ut volunt diluti quidam moderatores sed) Divinæ quoque* IRÆ ACTIONEM *significat.*" "The word HARDEN when it is attributed to God in Scripture, means not only PERMISSION, (as some washy, compromising divines would have it,) but it signifies also THE ACTION of Divine wrath.'

Beside, something negative amounts, in a thousand cases, to something positive. A general, for example, denies gunpowder to some of his soldiers, to whom he owes a grudge; he hangs them for *not firing,* and then exculpates himself by saying, "My not giving them powder was *a thing purely negative.* I did nothing to them to hinder them from firing: on the contrary, I bid them fire away." This is exactly the case with the Manichean God and his imaginary reprobates. He bids them repent or perish, believe or be damned, do good works or depart into everlasting fire. And yet, all the while, he keeps from them every dram of true grace, Whereby they might savingly repent, believe, and obey. Is it not surprising that so many of our Gospel ministers should call preaching such a doctrine, *preaching the Gospel* and *exalting Christ?* But Mr. Toplady replies: —

ARG. XXXVIII. Page 48. "If I am acquainted with an indigent neighbour, and have it in my power to enrich him, but do it not, am I the author of that man's poverty, only for resolving to permit him, and for actually permitting* him to *continue* poor? Am I blamable for his poverty, because I do not give him the utmost I am able? Similar is the case now in debate. Ever since the fall of Adam, mankind are by nature spiritually poor."

Mr. T. is greatly mistaken, when he says, "Similar is the case now in debate." To show that it is entirely *dissimilar,* we need only make his partial illustration stand fairly "upon its legs." If you know that your neighbour, who is an industrious tenant of yours, must work or break; and if, in order to make him *break,* according to your decree of the end, you make a decree of the means — an *efficacious* decree that his cattle shall die, that his plough shall be stolen, that he shall fall sick, and that nobody shall help him; I boldly say, You are "the author of that man's poverty:" and if, when you have reduced him to sordid want, and have, by this means, clothed his numerous family with filthy rags, you make another *efficacious, absolute* decree, that a majority of

---

* Not unlike this argument is that of the letter writer, on whom I have already bestowed a note, sec. 2.

"Divine justice," says he, pp. 4, 5, could not condemn, till the law was broken." True; but Calvinian free wrath reprobated *from all eternity,* and consequently before the law was either broken or given. "Therefore condemnation did not take place before a law was given and broken." This author trifles; for if Calvinian reprobation took place before the creation of Adam, and if it *necessarily* draws after it the uninterrupted breach of the law, and the condemnation consequent upon that breach, Calvinian reprobation differs no more from everlasting damnation, than *condemning* and *necessitating* a man to commit murder, that he may infallibly be hanged, differs from *condemning* him to be hanged. But "suppose that out of twenty found guilty, his majesty King George should pardon ten, he is not the cause of the other ten being executed. It was his clemency that pardoned any: it was their breaking the laws of the kingdom that condemned them, and not his majesty." Indeed, it was his majesty who condemned them, if, in order to do it without fail, he made, (1.) Efficacious and irresistible decrees of the *means,* that they should necessarily and unavoidably be guilty of robbery; and, (2.) Efficacious and irresistible decrees of the *end,* that they should unavoidably be condemned for their crimes, and inevitable guilt. The chain by which the God of Manes and Calvin drags poor reprobates to hell, has three capital links; the first is *absolute, unconditional reprobation:* the second is *necessary, remediless sin:* and the third is *insured, eternal damnation.* Now although the middle link intervenes between the first and the last link, it is only a necessary connection between them: for, says Mr. Toplady, p. 17, "God's own decree *secures* the means as well as the end, and *accomplishes* the end by the means" That is, (when this doctrine is applied to the present case,) the first link, which is Calvinian reprobation, draws the middle, diabolical link, which is remediless wickedness, as well as the last link, which is infernal and finished damnation. Thus Calvin's God *accomplishes* damnation by means of sin; or, if you please, he draws the third link by means of the second. Who can consider this and not wonder at the prejudice of the letter writer, who boldly affirms that, upon the Calvinian scheme, God is no more the author and cause of the damnation of the reprobates, than the king is the cause of the condemnation of the criminals whom he does not pardon! For my part, the more I consider Calvinism, the more I see that the decree of absolute reprobation, which is inseparable from the decree of absolute election, represents God as the sure author of *sin* in order to represent him as the sure author of *damnation.* The horrible mystery of absolute reprobation, necessary sin, and insured damnation, is not less essential to Calvinism, than the glorious mystery of Father, Son, and Holy Ghost, is essential to Christianity; and yet Calvinism is *the Gospel! The doctrines of grace!*

his children shall never have a good garment, and that at whatsoever time the constable shall find them with the only ragged coat which their bankrupt father could afford to give them, they shall all be sent to the house of correction, and severely whipt there, merely for not having on a certain coat, which you took care they should never have; and for wearing the filthy rags, which you decreed they should *necessarily* wear, you show yourself as *merciless* to the poor man's children, as you showed yourself *ill natured* to the poor man himself. To prove that this is a just state of the case, if the doctrine of absolute predestination be true, I refer the reader to section ii, where he will find Calvinism "on its legs."

Upon the whole, if I mistake not, it is evident that the arguments by which Mr. Toplady endeavours to reconcile Calvinian reprobation with Divine MERCY, are as inconclusive as those by which he tries to reconcile it with Divine JUSTICE; both sorts of arguments drawing all their plausibility from the skill with which *Logica Genevensis* tucks up the *left leg* of Calvinism, or covers it with deceitful buskins, which are called by a variety of delusive names, such as *"passing by, not electing, not owing salvation, limiting the display of goodness, not extending mercy infinitely, not enriching,"* &c, just as if all these phrases together conveyed one just idea of Calvinian reprobation, which is an *absolute, unconditional dooming* of myriads of unborn creatures to live and die in *necessary, remediless wickedness,* and then to "depart into everlasting fire," merely because Adam, according to Divine predestination, necessarily sinned; obediently fulfilling God's absolute, irreversible, and efficacious *decree of the means (sin:)* an Antinomian decree this, by which, if Calvinism be true, God *secured* and *accomplished the decree of the end,* that is, the remediless sin and eternal damnation of the reprobate: for, says Mr. T., p. 17, "God's own decree secures the means as well as the end, and accomplishes the end by the means."

And now, candid reader, say if Mr. T. did not act with a degree of partiality, when he called his book *"A Vindication* of God's Decrees, &c, from the *defamations* of Mr. Wesley;" and if he could not, with greater propriety, have called it, "An Unscriptural and Illogical Vindication of *the Horrible Decree,* from the Scriptural and rational exceptions made against it by Mr. Wesley."

SECTION VI.

A view of the SCRIPTURE PROOFS by which Mr. T. attempts to demonstrate the truth of Calvinian reprobation.

THAT the Old and New Testament hold forth a PARTIAL REPROBATION *of distinguishing grace,* and an IMPARTIAL REPROBATION *of retributive justice,* is a capital truth of the Gospel. One of the leading errors of the Calvinists consists in confounding these two reprobations, and the elections which they draw after them. By the impetuous blast of prejudice, and the fire of a heated imagination, modern Aarons melt the *partial* election of grace, and the *impartial* election of justice; and, casting them in the mould of confusion, they make their one partial election of unscriptural, necessitating, Antinomian FREE GRACE, to which they are obliged to oppose their one partial reprobation of necessitating, Manichean FREE WRATH. Now, as the Scriptures frequently speak of the harmless reprobation of grace, and of the awful reprobation of justice, it would be surprising, indeed, if out of so large a book as the Bible, *Logica Genevensis* could not extract a few passages which, by being wrested from the context, and misapplied according to art, *seem to* favour Calvinian reprobation. Such passages are produced in the following pages: —

ARG. XXXIX. Page 19. After transcribing Romans 9:20-28, Mr. Toplady says, "Now are these the words of Scripture, or are they not? If not, prove the forgery. If they be, you cannot fight against *reprobation* without fighting against God." Far from fighting against *Scripture* reprobation, we maintain, as St. Paul does in Romans ix, (1.) That God has an absolute right *gratuitously* to call whom he pleases to either of his two grand covenants of peculiarity, (Judaism and Christianity,) and *gratuitously* to *reprobate* whom he will from the blessings peculiar to these covenants; leaving as many nations and individuals as he thinks fit, under the general blessings of the gracious covenants which he made with reprieved Adam, and with spared Noah. (2.) We assert that God has an indubitable right *judicially to reprobate* obstinate unbelievers under all the dispensations of his grace, and to appoint that (as stubborn unbelievers) they shall be "vessels of wrath fitted for destruction" by their own unbelief, and not by God's free wrath. This is all the reprobation which St. Paul contends for in Romans 9. (See *Scales*, sec. xi, where Mr. T.'s objection is answered at large.) Therefore, with one hand we defend Scripture reprobation, and with the other we attack Calvinian reprobation; maintaining that the Scripture reprobation of grace, and of justice, are as different from Calvinian, damning reprobation, as appointing a soldier to continue a soldier, and to be a captain, or a willful deserter to be shot, is different from appointing a soldier necessarily to desert, that he may be unavoidably shot for desertion.

Having thus vindicated the *godly* reprobation maintained by St. Paul from the misapprehensions of Mr. Toplady, we point at all the passages which we have produced in the Scripture Scales, in defence of the doctrines of justice, the CONDITIONALITY of the reward of the inheritance, and the FREEDOM of the will; and, retorting Mr. T.'s argument, we say, "Now, are these the words of Scripture, or are they not? If not, prove the forgery. If they be, you cannot fight against [the *conditional*] reprobation [which we defend,] without fighting against God." You cannot fight for Calvinian reprobation without fighting for free wrath and the evil-principled Deity worshipped by the Manichees.

ARG. XL. Page 51. Mr. T. supports absolute reprobation by quoting 1 Samuel 2:25: "They [the sons of Eli] hearkened not to the voice of their father, because the Lord would slay them," 1 Samuel 2:25. Here we are given to understand, that by the decree of *the means*, the Lord secured the disobedience of these wicked men, in order to accomplish his decree of *the end*, that is, their absolute destruction.

To this truly Calvinian insinuation we answer, (1.) The sons of Eli, who had turned the tabernacle into a house of ill fame, and a den of thieves, had *personally* deserved a *judicial* reprobation; God therefore could *justly* give them up to a reprobate mind, in consequence of their personal, avoidable, repeated, and aggravated crimes. (2.) The word "killing" does not here necessarily imply eternal damnation. The Lord killed, by a lion, the man of God from Judah, for having stopped in Bethel: he killed Nadab and Abihu for offering strange fire: he killed the child of David and Bathsheba: he killed many of the Corinthians, for their irreverent partaking of the

Lord's Supper: but the "sin unto [bodily] death" is not the sin unto *eternal* death. For St. Paul informs us that the body is sometimes "given up to Satan for the destruction of the flesh, that the spirit may be saved in the day of the Lord," 1 Corinthians 5:5. (3.) The Hebrew particle כִּי, which is rendered in our translation "because," means also "therefore:" and so our translators themselves have rendered it after St. Paul, and the Septuagint, Psalm 116:10, "I believed, כִּי, and *therefore* will I speak:" see 2 Corinthians 4:13. If they had done their part as well in translating the verse quoted by Mr. Toplady, the doctrines of free wrath would have gone propless; and we should have had these edifying words: "They [the sons of Eli] hearkened not to the voice of their father; and THEREFORE the Lord would slay them." Thus the *voluntary sin* of free agents would be represented as the cause of their deserved reprobation; and not their *undeserved* reprobation as the cause of their *necessary sin*. (See sec. 2.)

ARG. XLI. Page 51. Mr. T. tries to prove absolute reprobation by quoting these words of our Lord: "Thou Capernaum, which art exalted to heaven, shalt be brought down to hell; for if the mighty works which have been done in thee had been done in Sodom, it would [or *might*] have remained unto this day."

This passage, if I am not mistaken, is nothing but a strong expostulation and reproof, admirably calculated to shame the unbelief and alarm the fears of the Capernaites. Suppose I had an enemy, whose obstinate hatred had resisted for years the constant tokens of my love; and suppose I said to him, "Your obduracy is astonishing; if I had shown to the fiercest tiger the kindness which I have shown you, I could have melted the savage beast into love;" would it be right, from such a figurative supposition, to conclude that I *absolutely* believed I could have tamed the fiercest tiger?

But this passage, taken in a literal sense, far from proving the absolute reprobation of Sodom, demonstrates that Sodom was never reprobated in the Calvinian sense of the word: for if it had been *absolutely* reprobated from all eternity, no works done in her by Christ and his apostles could have overcome her unbelief. But our Lord observes that her strong unbelief could have been overcome by the extraordinary means of faith, which could not conquer the unbelief of Capernaum. Mr. T. goes on: —

ARG. XLII. (*Ibid.*) "But though God knew the citizens of Sodom would [or *might*] have reformed their conduct, had his providence made use of effectual [Mr. T. should say of *every effectual*] means to that end; still these effectual [Mr. T. should say, *all* these *extraordinary* and *peculiar*] means were not vouchsafed." True because, according to the election of grace, God uses *more* means and *more powerful* means to convert some cities than he does to convert others: witness the case of Nineveh, compared with that of Jericho. This is strongly maintained in my *Essay on the Partial Reprobation of Distinguishing Grace*, where this very passage is produced. But still we affirm two things: (1.) God always uses means sufficient to demonstrate that his goodness, patience, and mercy, are over all his works, (though in different degrees,) and to testify that he is unwilling that sinners should die, unless they have first obstinately, and without necessity, refused to "work out their own *eternal* salvation" with the talent of *temporary* salvation, which is given to all, for the sake of Him whose "saving grace has appeared to all men," and who "enlightens [in various degrees] every man that comes into the world." (2.) As the men of Sodom were not absolutely lost, though they had but *one* talent of means, no more were the men of Capernaum absolutely saved, though God favoured them with so many *more* talents of means than he did the men of Sodom. Hence it appears that Mr. T. has run upon the point of his own sword; the passage which he appeals to proving that God does not work so *irresistibly* upon either Jews or Gentiles as to secure his absolute approbation of some, and his absolute reprobation of others.

ARG. XLIII. Page 52. Mr. T., to prop up Calvinian reprobation, quotes these words of Christ: "Fill ye up the measure of your fathers," Matthew xxiii, 32, and he takes care to produce the words, "Fill ye up," in capitals; as if he would give us to understand that Christ is extremely busy in getting reprobates to sin and be damned. For my part, as I believe that Christ never preached up sin and wickedness, I am persuaded that this expression is nothing but a strong, *ironical reproof* of sin, like that in the Revelation, "Let him that is unjust, be unjust still;' or that in the Gospel, "Sleep on now and take your rest;" or that in the book of Ecclesiastes, "Rejoice, O young man, in thy youth, and walk in the ways of thy heart, &c, but know," &c. I shudder when I consider "doctrines of grace," so called, which support themselves by representing Christ as a preacher of wickedness. Calvinism may be compared to that insect which feeds on putrefying carcasses, lights only upon real or apparent sores, and delights chiefly in the smell of *corruption.* If there be a fault in our translation, Calvinism will pass over a hundred plain passages well translated, and will eagerly light upon the error. Thus, pp. 53 and 57, Mr. Toplady quotes, "being disobedient, whereunto they were appointed," 1 Peter 2:8. He had rather take it for granted that the God of Manes absolutely predestinates some people *to be disobedient,* than do the holy God the justice to admit this godly sense, which the original bears, "Being disobedient, whereunto they have set, or disposed themselves." (See the proofs, *Scales,* pages 78, 104.)

ARG. XLIV. Page 52. Mr. T., still pleading for the "horrible decree" of Calvinian reprobation, says, "St. Matthew, if possible, expresses it still more strongly: 'It is given unto you to know the mysteries of the kingdom of heaven; but to them it is not given,' Matthew 13:11." I answer: (1.) If by "the mysteries of the kingdom of heaven," you understand *the mysteries of Christianity,* it is absurd to say that all who are not blessed with the knowledge of these mysteries are Calvinistically reprobated. This I demonstrate by verses 16, 17, and by the parallel place in St. Luke: "All things are delivered to me of my Father; and no man knoweth who the Son is, but the Father; and who the Father is, but the Son, and he to whom the Son will reveal him. [That is, the mystery of a relative personality of Father and Son in the Godhead has not been expressly revealed to others, as I choose to reveal it to you, my Christian friends:] and [to show that this was his meaning] he turned him unto his disciples, and said, *privately,* Blessed are the eyes which see the things which ye see: for I tell you that many prophets [such as Samuel, Isaiah, Daniel, &c,] and kings [such as David, Solomon, Josiah, Hezekiah, &c, St. Matthew adds, 'and righteous men,' such as Noah, Abraham, &c,] have desired to see the things which ye see, and have not seen them; and to hear the things which ye hear, and have not heard them," Luke 10:22-24; Matthew 13:17. Is not Mr. T. excessively fond of reprobating people to death, if he supposes that because "it was not given to *those* prophets, kings, *and* righteous men, to know the mysteries of the" Christian dispensation, they were all absolutely doomed to continue in sin, and be damned?

But, (2.) Should it be asserted, that by "the mysteries of the kingdom," we are to understand here *every degree of saving light,* then the reprobation mentioned in Matthew 13:11, is not the *partial* reprobation of grace, but the *impartial* reprobation of justice: and, in this case, to appeal to this verse in support of a chimerical reprobation of free wrath, argues great inattention to the context; for the *very next* verse fixes the reason of the reprobation of the Jews, who heard the Gospel of Christ without being benefited by it: a reason this, which saps the foundation of absolute reprobation. "But unto them it is not given:" for they are Calvinistically reprobated! No: "Unto them it is not given: for, whosoever hath, to him shall be given, and he shall have more abundance: but whosoever hath not, [to purpose] from him shall be taken away, even that he hath," Matthew 13:12. This anti-Calvinian sense is strongly confirmed by our Lord's words two verses below: "To them it is not given, &c, for this people's heart is waxed gross: [NOTE: it is *waxed gross,* therefore it was not *so gross* at first as it is now:] and their ears are dull of hearing, and their eyes they have closed; lest at any time they should see with their eyes, and hear with their ears, and should understand with their heart, and should be converted, and I should heal them," Matthew 13:15. To produce, therefore, Matthew 13:11, as a capital proof of Calvinian reprobation, is as daring an imposition upon the credulity of the simple, as to produce Exodus xx, in defence of adultery and murder. However, such arguments will not only be swallowed down in Geneva as tolerable, but the author of P.O. will cry them up as *"most masterly."*

ARG. XLV. Page 53. Mr. T. concludes his Scripture proofs of Calvinian reprobation by these words: "Now I leave it to the decision of any unprejudiced, capable man upon earth, whether it be not evident, from these passages, &c, that *God hath determined to leave some men to perish in their sins and to be justly punished for them?* In affirming which, I only give the scripture as I found it." That the scriptures produced by Mr. T. prove this, is true; we maintain it as well as he: and if he will impose no other reprobation upon us, we are ready to shake hands with him. Nor needs he call his book, "More Work for Mr. Wesley," but, *A Reconciliation with Mr. Wesley:* for, when we speak of the reprobation of JUSTICE, we assert that "God hath determined to leave some men, [namely, the wise and prudent in their own eyes, the proud and disobedient, who do despite to the Spirit of grace to the end of their day of salvation] to perish in their sins, and to be justly punished for them." But, according to Mr. T.'s system, the men "left to perish in their sins," are not the men whom the scriptures which he has quoted describe; but poor creatures absolutely sentenced to necessary, remediless sin, and to unavoidable, eternal damnation, long before they had an existence in their mother's womb. And, in this case, we affirm that their endless torments can never be *just:* and, of consequence, that the Calvinian reprobation of unborn men, which Mr. T. has tried to dress up in Scripture phrases, is as contrary to the Scripture reprobation of stubborn offenders, as Herod's ordering the *barbarous* destruction of the holy innocents, is different from his ordering the *righteous* execution of bloody murderers.

SECTION VII.

An answer to the arguments by which Mr. T. tries to reconcile Calvinism with the doctrine of a future judgment, and ABSOLUTE necessity with MORAL agency.

THEY who indirectly set aside the day of judgment, do the cause of religion as much mischief as they who indirectly set aside the immortality of the soul. Mr. Wesley asserts that the Calvinists are the men. His words are: "On the principle of absolute predestination, there can be no future judgment. It requires more pains than all the men upon earth, than all the devils in hell will ever be able to take, to reconcile the doctrine of [Calvinian] reprobation, with the doctrine of a judgment day." Mr. T. answers: —

ARG. XLVI. Page 82. "The consequence is false; for absolute predestination is the very thing that renders the future judgment certain: 'God hath APPOINTED a day in which he will judge the world in righteousness by the man whom he hath ORDAINED.'" If Mr. T. had put the words "in righteousness" in capitals, instead of the words "appointed" and "ordained," (which he fondly hopes will convey the idea of the Calvinian decrees,) he would have touched the knot of the difficulty: for the question is not, whether there *will be* a day of judgment; but whether, on the principle of absolute predestination, there *can be* a day of judgment, consistently with Divine equity, justice, wisdom, and sincerity: and that there *can,* Mr. T. attempts to prove by the following reasoning: —

ARG. XLVII. Page 83. "The most flagrant sinners sin *voluntarily,* notwithstanding the *inevitable* accomplishment of God's effective and permissive decrees. Now they who sin voluntarily are *accountable:* and accountable sinners are *judicable:* and if judicable, they are *punishable.*"

Mr. T. has told us, p. 45, that "*fallen* men are involuntary beings;" and in this page he tells us that they sin voluntarily. Now we, who never learned Mr. T.'s logic, cannot understand how "*involuntary beings*" can sin *voluntarily.* But, letting this contradiction pass, and granting that sinners offend voluntarily, I ask, Is their *will* at liberty to choose otherwise than it does, or is it not? If you say it is at liberty to choose otherwise than it does, you renounce necessitating predestination, and you will allow the doctrine of free will, which is the bulwark of the second Gospel axiom, and the Scripture engine which batters down Calvinian reprobation; and, upon this Scriptural plan, it is most certain that God *can* "judge the world in righteousness," that is, in a manner which reflects praise upon his essential justice and wisdom. But if you insinuate that the will of sinners is absolutely bound by "the efficacious purposes of Heaven," and by the "effective decrees" of Him who "worketh all things in all men, and even wickedness in the wicked;" if you say that God's decree concerning every man is *irreversible,* whether it be a decree of absolute election to life, or of absolute reprobation to death, "because God's own decree secures the means as well as the end, and accomplishes the end by the means;" (p. 17;) or, which comes to the same thing, if you assert that the reprobate always sin *necessarily,* having no power, no liberty to *will* righteousness, you answer like a consistent Calvinist, and pour your shame, folly, and unrighteousness upon the tribunal where Christ will judge the world in righteousness.

Doctrines of Grace and Justice

A just illustration will convince the unprejudiced reader, that this is really the case. By the king's "efficacious permission," a certain strong man, called Adam, binds the hands of a thousand children behind their backs with a chain of brass, and a strong lock, of which the king himself keeps the key. When the children are thus chained, the king commands them all, *upon pain of death,* to put their hands upon their breasts, and promises ample rewards to those who will do it. Now, as the king is absolute, he *passes by* seven hundred of the bound children, and as he passes them by he hangs about their necks *a black stone,* with this inscription, "Unconditional reprobation to death:" but being merciful too, he graciously fixes his love upon the rest of the children, just three hundred in number, and he ordains them to finished salvation by hanging about their necks *a white stone,* with this inscription, "Unconditional election to life." And, that they may not miss their reward by non-performance of the abovementioned condition, he gives the key of the locks to another strong man, named Christ, who, in a day of irresistible power, looses the hands of the three hundred elect children, and chains them upon their breasts, as strongly as they were before chained behind their backs. When all the elect are properly bound, agreeably to orders, the king proceeds to judge the children according to their works, that is, according to their having put their hands behind their backs, or upon their breasts. In the meantime a question arises in the court: Can the king judge the children concerning the position of their hands, without rendering himself ridiculous? Can he *wisely reward* the elect favourites with life according to their works, when he has absolutely done the rewardable work for them by the stronger man? And can he *justly punish* the reprobate with eternal death, for not putting their hands upon their breasts, when the strong man has, according to a royal decree, absolutely bound them behind their backs? "Yes, he can;" says a counsellor, who has learned logic in mystic Geneva; "for the children have *hands,* notwithstanding the inevitable accomplishment of the king's effective and permissive decrees: now children who have hands, and do not place them as they are bid, are *accountable,* and accountable children are *judicable;* and if judicable, they are *punishable.*" This argument would be excellent, if the counsellor did not speak of *hands which are absolutely tied.* But it is not barely the having hands, but the having *hands free,* which makes us accountable for not placing them properly.

Apply this plain observation to the case in hand, and you will see, (1.) That it is not barely the having a *will,* but the having *free will,* which constitutes us accountable, judicable, and punishable. (2.) That, of consequence, Mr. Toplady's grand argument is as inconclusive as that of the counsellor. (3.) That both arguments are as contrary to good sense, as the state of hands *at liberty* is contrary to the state of hands *absolutely tied;* as contrary to reason, as *free will* is contrary to a *will absolutely bound.* And, (4.) That, of consequence, the doctrine of the day of judgment is as incompatible with Calvinian predestination, as sense with nonsense, and Christ with Belial.

However, if Mr. T. cannot carry his point by reason, he will do it by Scripture; and therefore he raises such an argument as this: — We often read in the Bible that there will be a day of judgment; we often meet also in the Bible with the words "must" and "necessity;" and, therefore, according to the Bible, the doctrine of a day of judgment is consistent with the doctrine of the absolute necessity of human actions: just as if, in a thousand cases, a *decree* of necessity, or a *must,* were not as different from *absolute* necessity, as the *want* of an apartment in the king's palace is different from the *absolute want* of a room in any house in the kingdom. The absurdity of this argument will be better under. stood by considering the passages which Mr. T. produces, to prove that when men do good or evil, God's absolute decree of predestination necessitates them to do it.

ARG. XLVIII. Page 60. "*It must needs be that offences come. There must be heresies among you. Such things* [*wars, &c,*] *must needs be.*" When Mr. T. builds Calvinian necessity upon these scriptures, he is as much mistaken as if he fancied that Mr. Wesley and I were fatalists, because we say, "Considering the course and wickedness of the world, it *cannot but be* Christendom will be distracted by heresies, lawsuits, wars, and murders: for so long as men *will* follow worldly maxims, rather than evangelical precepts, such things must come to pass." Again: — Would not the reader think that I trifled, if I attempted to prove absolute necessity from such Scriptural expressions as these: "Seven days ye must eat unleavened bread. New wine must be put into new bottles. He must needs go through Samaria. I have bought a piece of ground, and I must needs go and see it. How can I sin against God? I have married a wife, and therefore I cannot come. The multitude must needs come together [to mob Paul,] (Acts 21:22.) A bishop must be blameless. Ye must needs be subject [to rulers] not only for wrath, but also for conscience' sake?"

Once more: who does not see that there is what the poverty of language obliges me to call, (1.) A necessity of *duty:* "I must pay my debts: I must preach next Sunday." (2.) A necessity of *civility:* "I must pay such a visit." (3.) A necessity of *circumstance:* "in going from Jerusalem to Galilee, 'I must needs pass through Samaria,' because the high way lies directly through Samaria." (4.) A necessity of *convenience:* "I am tired with writing, I must leave off." (5.) A necessity of *decency:* "I must not go naked." (6.) A necessity of *prudence:* "I must look before I leap, &c." Now, *all* these sorts of necessity, and a hundred more of the like stamp, do not amount to one single grain of Calvinian, absolute, insuperable necessity. However, a rigid Predestinarian (such is the force of prejudice!) sees his imaginary necessity in almost every *must;* just as a jealous man sees adultery in almost every look which his virtuous wife casts upon the man whom he fancies to be his rival.

ARG. XLIX. Page 61. "Absolute necessity, then, is perfectly consistent with willingness and freedom in good agency, no less than in bad. For it is a true maxim, *Ubi voluntas, ibi libertas;*" that is, *where there is a will, there is liberty.* This maxim, which has led many good men into Calvinism, I have already exposed. (See *Scales,* page 186.) To what is there advanced, I add the following remark: — As there may be *liberty,* where there is not a *will,* so there may be a will, where there is not *liberty.* The first idle school boy whom you meet will convince you of it. I ask him, "When you are at school, and have a will, or (as you call it) a *mind* to go and play, have you liberty, or freedom to do it?" He answers, "No." Here is then *a will without liberty.* I ask him again: "When you are at school, where you have freedom or liberty to ply your book, have you a will to do it?" He honestly answers, "No, again. Here is then *liberty without a will.* How false therefore is this proposition, that "where there is a will there is liberty!" Did judicious Calvinists consider this, they would no more say, "If all men were redeemed, they *would* all come out of the dungeon of sin." For there may be a freedom to come out consequent upon redemption, where there is no will exercised. "O, but God makes us willing in the day of his power." True: in the day of salvation he restores to us the faculty of choosing moral good with some degree of ease; and, from time to time, he *peculiarly helps* us to make acts of willingness. But to suppose that he absolutely *wills* for us, is as absurd as to say, that when, after a quinsy, his gracious providence restores us a degree of liberty to swallow, he necessitates us to eat and drink, or actually swallows *for us.*

ARG. L. Page 61. In his refusal to dismiss the Israelites, &c, "he [Pharaoh] could *will* no otherwise than he did, Exodus 7:3, 4." Is not this a mistake? When Pharaoh considered, did he not alter his mind? Did he not say to Moses, "Be gone, and bless me also?" If Omnipotence had absolutely hardened him, could he have complied at last? Do the unchangeable decrees change as the will of Pharaoh changed?

ARG. LI. Pages 61, 62. "So when Saul went home to Gibeah, it is said, 'There went with him a band of men, whose hearts God had touched.' In like manner, God is said to have 'stirred up the spirit of Cyrus. Then rose up, &c, the Levites, with all them whose spirit God had raised up.' Will any man say that these did not will *freely,* only because they willed necessarily?"

1. I (for one) say, that while they willed necessarily, (in the Calvinian sense of the word "necessary,") they *could not* will freely in the *moral* sense of the word *free.* Mr. Toplady is not morally free to will, so long as he is absolutely bound to will one thing, any more than a man is free to look to the left, who is absolutely bound to look to the right, let the object he looks at engage his heart and eye ever so pleasingly. God's Spirit prevents, accompanies, and follows us in every good thing: all our good works are "begun, continued, and ended in him;" but they are not *necessary,* in the Calvinian sense of the word. In *moral* cases, God does not absolutely necessitate us, though he may do it in *prophetic* and *political* cases. Thus, he necessitated Balaam, when he blessed Israel by the mouth of that covetous prophet; and thus he necessitated Balaam's ass, when the dumb animal reproved his rider's madness. But then, whatever we do under such *necessitating impulses,* will not be rewarded as our own work, any more than Balaam's good prophecy, and his ass' good reproof, were rewarded as their own works.

2. From the above-mentioned passages, Mr. Toplady would make us believe, that upon the whole, the touches of God's grace act *necessarily* like charms: but what says the stream of the Scriptures? God "touched the hearts" of all the Israelites, and stirred them up to faith: but the effect of that touch was so far from being absolutely forcible, that their hearts soon "started aside like a broken bow;" and, after having been "saved in Egypt *through* faith, *they* perished in the wilderness *through* unbelief." "God gave King Saul a new heart;" and yet Saul cast away the heavenly gift. "God gave Solomon a wise and understanding heart;" and yet Solomon, in his old age, "made himself a foolish heart, darkened" by the love of heathenish women. God stirred up the heart of Peter to confess Christ, and to walk upon the sea; and yet, by and by, Peter sunk, cursed, swore, and denied his Lord. Awful demonstrations these, that, where Divine grace works most powerfully, when its first grand impulse is over, there is an end of the overbearing power; and the soul, returning to its free agency, chooses *without necessity* the good which constitutes her rewardable; or the evil which constitutes her punishable. Of this Mr. Toplady himself produces a remarkable instance, 2 Corinthians 8:16, 17, "Thanks be to God," says the apostle, "who put the same earnest care into the heart of Titus for you; *of his own accord* he went unto you."

If a gentleman, who delights to be in houses of ill fame, more than in the house of God, sees, in a circle of ladies, one whom he suspects of being immodest, he singles her out as one that may suit his purpose: and to her he makes his bold addresses. I am sorry to observe that this is exactly the case with Calvinism unmasked. We find, in the Scriptures, a few places where God's suffering some men to do a lesser evil, in order to prevent, or to punish a greater evil, is expressed in a strong, figurative manner, which *seems* to ascribe sin to him, just as, in other places, jealousy, repentance, wrath, and fury, together with hands, feet, ears, and a nose, are figuratively attributed to him. Now as popish idolatry screens herself behind *these* metaphors, so Calvinian Antinomianism perpetually singles out *those* metaphorical expressions which *seem* to make God the author of sin. Accordingly, —

ARG. LII. Page 61, &c. Mr. Toplady produces these words of Joseph: "It was not you that sent me hither, but God;" these words of David: "The Lord said to him, [Shimei,] Curse David;" these words of the sacred historian: "God had appointed to defeat the good counsel of Ahithophel, to the intent that the Lord might bring evil upon Absalom;" and these words of the prophet: "Howbeit, he [the Assyrian king, turned loose upon Israel to avenge God's righteous quarrel with that hypocritical people] meaneth not so, neither does his heart think so: but it is in his heart to destroy;" these words in the Revelation: "God hath put it into their hearts [the hearts of the kings who shall hate the mystic harlot and destroy her, and burn her with fire] to fulfil his will, and to agree, and to give their kingdom to the beast, till the words of God shall be fulfilled;" and the words of Peter: "They [the accomplishers of the crucifixion of Christ] were gathered together to do whatsoever God's hand, and God's counsel had predestinated to be done," &c.

With respect to the last text, if it be rightly* translated, it is explained by these words of Peter, Acts 2:23: "Christ was delivered by the determinate counsel and foreknowledge of God:" by his gracious "counsel," that Christ should lay down his life as a ransom for all; and by his clear "foreknowledge" of the disposition of the Jews to take that precious life away. This passage then, and all those which Mr. T. has produced, or may yet produce, only prove: —

(1.) That God foresees the evil which is in the hearts of the wicked, and their future steps in peculiar circumstances, with ten thousand times more clearness and

---

* With Episcopius, and some other learned critics, I doubt it is not. Why should it not be read thus? Acts 4:26-28, "The rulers were gathered together against the Lord and against his Christ. For of a truth against thy holy child Jesus, whom thou hast anointed, (both Herod and Pontius Pilate, with the Gentiles, and the people of Israel, were gathered together,) for to do whatsoever thy hand and thy counsel determined before to be done." By putting the clause "Both Herod," &c, in a parenthesis, you have this evangelical sense which gives no handle to the pleaders for sin: "Both Herod and Pilate, &c, were gathered together against thy holy child Jesus, whom thou hast anointed to do whatsoever thy hand and counsel determined before to be done." I prefer this reading to the common one, for the following reasons: (1.) It is perfectly, agreeable to the Greek; and the peculiar construction of the sentence is expressive of the peculiar earnestness with which the apostles prayed. (2.) It is attended with no Manichean inconveniency. (3.) It is *more* agreeable to the context: for if the sanhedrim, was "gathered by God's direction and decree," in order to threaten the apostles, with what propriety could they say, verse 29, "Now, Lord, behold their threatenings?" And, (4.) It is strongly supported by verse 30, where Peter (after having observed, verses 27, 28, according to our reading, that God had anointed his holy child Jesus to do all the miracles which he did on earth) prays, that now Christ is gone to heaven, the effects of this powerful anointing may continue, and "signs and wonders may *still* be done by the name of his holy child Jesus."

certainty, than a good huntsmen foresees all the windings, doublings, and shifts of a hunted fox; and that be overrules their wicked counsels to the execution of his own wise and holy designs, as a good rider overrules the mad prancings of a vicious horse, to the display of his perfect skill in horsemanship, and to the treading down of the enemy in a day of battle. (2.) That God "catches the wise in their own craftiness," and that, to punish the wicked, he permits their wicked counsels to be defeated, and their best-concerted schemes to prove abortive. (3.) That he frequently tries the faith, and exercises the patience of good men, by letting loose the wicked upon them, as in the case of Job and of Christ. (4.) That he often punishes the wickedness of one man by letting loose upon him the wickedness of another; and that he frequently avenges himself of one wicked nation by letting loose upon it the wickedness of another nation. Thus he let Absalom and Shimei loose upon David. Thus a parable spoken by the Prophet Micaiah informs us that God, after having let a lying spirit loose upon Zedekiah, the false prophet, let Zedekiah loose upon wicked Ahab. Thus the Lord let loose the Philistines upon disobedient Israel, and the Romans upon the obdurate Jews, and their accursed city; using those wicked heathen as his vindictive scourge, just as he used swarms of frogs and locusts when he punished rebellious Egypt with his plagues. (5.) That he sometimes let a wicked man loose upon himself, as in the case of Ahithophel, Nabal, and Judas, who became their own executioners. (6.) That, when wicked men are going to commit atrocious wickedness, he sometimes inclines their hearts so to relent, that they commit a *less* crime than they intended. For instance: when Joseph's brethren were going to starve him to death, by providential circumstances God inclined their hearts to *spare his life*: thus instead of destroying him, they only sold him into Egypt. (7.) With respect to Revelation 17:17, the context, and the full stream of the Scripture require that it should be understood thus: — "*As* God, by providential circumstances, which seemed to favour their worldly views, suffered wicked kings to agree, and give their kingdom unto the beast, to help the beast to execute God's judgments upon corrupted Churches and wicked states; so he will peculiarly let those kings loose upon the whore, and they shall agree to hate her, and shall make her desolate and naked."

Upon the whole, it is contrary to all the rules of criticism, decency, and piety, to take advantage of the dark construction of a sentence, or to avail one's self of a parable, a hyperbole, a bold metaphor, or an unguarded saying of a good man, interwoven with the thread, of Scripture history, in order to make appear, (so far as Calvinism can,) that "God worketh all things in all men, even wickedness in the wicked." Such a method of wresting the oracles of God, to make them speak the language of Belial and Moloch, is as ungenerous, as our inferring from these words, "I do not condemn thee," that Christ does not condemn adulterers, that Christianity encourages adultery, and that this single sentence, taken in a filthy, Antinomian sense, outweighs all the sermon upon the mount, as well as the holy meaning of the context: for these words being spoken to an adulteress, whom the magistrates had not condemned to die, and whom the Pharisees wanted Christ to "condemn to be stoned according to the law of Moses;" it is evident that our Lord's words, when taken in connection with the context, carry this edifying meaning: — "I am come to act the part of a Saviour, and not that of a magistrate: if the magistrates have not 'condemned thee to be stoned,' neither do I condemn thee to that dreadful kind of death; avail thyself of thy undeserved reprieve: 'Go and' repent, and evidence the sincerity of thy repentance by 'sinning no more.'" Hence I conclude that all the texts quoted by the fatalists prove that God *necessitates* men to sin by his decrees, just as John 8:11, proves that Christ *countenances* the filthy sin of adultery.

ARG. LIII. Page 64. Mr. T. thinks to demonstrate that the doctrine of the absolute necessity of all our actions, and consequently of all our sins is true, by producing "St. Paul's case as a preacher. 'Though I preach the Gospel I have nothing to glory of; for necessity is laid upon me, yea, wo is me if I preach not the Gospel,' 1 Corinthians 9:16. Yet he preached the Gospel *freely*, &c; *necessity*, therefore, and *freedom*, are very good friends, notwithstanding all the efforts of Arminianism to set them at variance." The apostle evidently speaks here of a necessity of precept on God's part, and of *duty* on his own part: and such a necessity, being perfectly consistent with the alternative of obedience or of disobedience, is also perfectly consistent with freedom and with a day of judgment: and Mr. T. trifles when he speaks of "all the efforts of Arminianism, to set such a necessity at variance with freedom;" for it is the distinguishing glory of our doctrine to maintain both the freedom of the will, and the indispensable necessity of cordial obedience. But, in the name of candour and common sense, I ask, What has a necessity of *precept and duty* to do with *Calvinian* necessity, which, in the day of God's power, absolutely necessitates the *elect* to obey and the *reprobate* to disobey; entirely debarring the *former* from the alternative of disobedience, and the *latter* from the alternative of obedience? That the apostle, in the text before us, does not mean a Calvinian, absolute necessity, is evident from the last clause of the verse, where he mentions the *possibility* of his disobeying, and the punishment that awaited him in case of disobedience: "Wo is me," says he, "if I preach not the Gospel." A necessity of *precept* was laid on Jonah to preach the Gospel to the Ninevites; but THIS necessity was so far from Calvinistically binding him to preach, that, (like Demas and the clergy, who fleece a flock which they do not feed,) he ran away from his appointed work, and incurred the "wo" mentioned by the apostle. Therefore, St. Paul's words, candidly taken together, far from establishing absolute necessity, which admits of no alternative, are evidently subversive of this dangerous error, which exculpates the sinner, and makes God the author of sin.

Hence Mr. Wesley says, with great truth, that if the doctrines of absolute predestination and Calvinian necessity are true, there can be *no sin;* seeing "it cannot be a sin in a spark to rise, or in a stone to fall." And therefore "the reprobate [tending to evil by the irresistible power of Divine predestination, as unavoidably as stones tend to the centre, by the irresistible force of natural gravitation] can have no sin at all." This is a just observation, taken from the absurdity of an absolute necessity, originally brought on by God's absolute and irresistible decrees. Let us see how Mr. T. shows his wit on this occasion.

ARG. LIV. Pages 71, 72. "The reprobate can have no sin at all. Indeed? They are quite sinless, are they? As perfect as Mr. Wesley himself? O excellent reprobation! &c. What then must the *elect* be? &c. Beside: if reprobates be sinless — nay, immutably perfect, so that they can have *no sin at all,* will it not follow that Mr. Wesley's own perfectionists are reprobates? For surely if reprobates may be sinless, the sinless may be reprobates. Did not Mr. John's malice outrun his *craft*, when he advanced an objection, &c, so easily retortible?"

This illogical, not to say *illiberal* answer, is of a piece with the challenge, which the reader may see illustrated, at the end of sec. i, by my remarks upon a consequence as just as that of Mr. Wesley: for it is as evident that if the reprobate are "involuntary beings;" beings absolutely necessitated by efficacious, irresistible predestination to act as they do; they are as really sinless, as a mountain of gold is really heavier than a handful of feathers. And Mr. Wesley may believe that both consequences are just, without believing either that "the wicked are sinless," or that "there is a mountain of gold." On what a slender foundation does *Logica Genevensis* rest her charges of *craft* and *malice!* And yet this foundation is as solid as that on which she raises her doctrines of unscriptural grace and free wrath. But Mr. T. advances other arguments: —

ARG. LV. Pages 69, 70. "The holy Baptist, without any ceremony or scruple, compared some of his unregenerate hearers to stones; saying, 'God is able even of these stones to raise up children to Abraham, &c. Ye therefore, as lively stones, are built up a spiritual house, &c. They [the elect] shall be mine, saith the Lord of hosts— in the day when I make up my jewels:' now, unless I am vehemently mistaken, *jewels* are but another name for *precious stones*." Hence the reader is given to understand that when Mr. Wesley opposes the doctrine of absolute necessity, by saying, that "it cannot be a sin in a stone to fall," he turns "the Bible's own artillery against itself, and gives us too much room to fear, that it is as natural to him to pervert, as it is for a stone to sink."

By such arguments as these, I could prove transubstantiation: for Christ said of a bit of bread, "This is my body." Nay, I could prove any other absurdity: I could prove that Christ could not "think," and that his disciples could not "walk:" for he says, "I am the vine, and ye are the branches;" and a vine can no more think, than branches can walk. I could prove that he was a "hen," and the Jews "chickens:" for he says that he "would have gathered them, as a hen gathers her chickens under her wings." Nay, I could prove that Christ had no more hand in our redemption, than we are supposed by Calvinists to have in our conversion; that his "poor free will," (to use Mr. Toplady's expressions, page 70, with respect to us,) "had no employ," that he was "absolutely passive, and that [redemption] is as totally the operation of [the Father] as the severing of stones from their native quarry, and the erecting them into an elegant building, are the effects of human agency." If the astonished reader ask, How I can prove a proposition so subversive of the gratitude which we owe to Christ for our redemption? I reply, By the very same argument by which Mr. T. proves that we are "absolutely passive" in the work of conversion, and that "conversion is totally the operation of God:" that is, by producing passages where Christ is metaphorically called a "stone;" and of these there are not a few. "Thus saith the Lord God, Behold, I lay in Zion a stone, a tried stone, a precious corner stone, a sure foundation, Isaiah 28:16. Whosoever shall fall on this stone, shall be broken; but on whomsoever it shall fall, it will grind him to powder, Matthew 21:34. The stone which the builders rejected is become the head of the corner, Acts 4:11. To whom coming as to a living stone," &c, 1 Peter 2:4. If to these texts we add those in which he is compared to a "foundation," to a "rock," and to "jewels," or precious "stones," I could demonstrate, (in the Calvinian way,) that Christ was once as "absolutely passive" in the work of our redemption as a stone. When I consider such arguments as these, I cannot help wondering at the gross impositions of Pagan, popish, and Calvinian doctors. I find myself again in the midst of Ovid's Metamorphoses. Jupiter, if we believe the poet, turned Niobe into a rock. The tempter wanted Christ to turn a "stone" into "bread." *Logica Romana* turns "bread" into Christ. But *Logica Genevensis* carries the bell; for she can, even without the hocus pocus of a massing priest, turn Christ into a stone. Mr. Toplady, far from recanting his argument *a lapide*, confirms it by the following: —

ARG. LVI. Page 71. "A stone has the advantage of you: man's rebellious heart is, by nature, and so far as spiritual things are concerned, *more* intractable and unyielding than a stone itself. I may take up a stone, and throw it this way or that, and it obeys the impulse of my arm. Whereas, in the sinner's heart, there is every species of hatred and opposition to God: nor can any thing, but omnipotent power, slay its enmity."

I am glad Mr. T. vouchsafes, in this place, to grant that "omnipotent power can slay the enmity." I hope he will remember this concession, and no more turn from the Prince of life, and preach up the monster death, as the slayer of the enmity. But to come to the argument: would Mr. T. think me in earnest, if I attempted to prove that a stone "had [once] the advantage" of him, with respect to getting learning, and that there was more omnipotence required to make him a scholar, than to make the stone he stands upon fit to take a degree in the university? However, I shall attempt to do it: displaying my skill in orthodox logic, I personate the school master, who taught Mr. Toplady grammar, and probably found him once at play, when he should have been at his book, and I say, "Indeed, master, a stone has the advantage of you. A boy's playful heart is by nature, so far as grammar is concerned, *more* intractable and unyielding than a stone itself." [Now for the proof!] "I may take up a stone, and throw it this way or that, and it instantly, and without the least degree of resistance, obeys the impulse of my arm: whereas *you* resist my orders; you run away from your book; or you look off from it. In your playful heart there is every species of hatred and opposition to your accidence; and therefore *more* power is required to make you a scholar, than to make that stone a grammarian." Mr. Toplady's "voluntary humility" claps this argument as excellent; but his good sense hisses it as absurd, and says with St. Paul, "When I was a child, I spake as a child: but when I became a man, I put away childish things."

ARG. LVII. Page 71. Ah, but "God's gracious promise to renew his people runs in this remarkable style: — *I will take away the stony heart out of your flesh.*" And does this prove Calvinian bound will, any more than these gracious commands to renew our own hearts prove Pelagian free will? "Circumcise the foreskin of your heart, and be no more stiff necked. Make you a new heart and a new spirit. Turn yourselves, and live ye." Who does not see that the evangelical union of such passages gives birth to the Scripture doctrine of *assisted* free will, which stands at an equal distance from Calvinian necessity, and from Pelagian, self-sufficient exertion?

ARG. LVIII. Page 73. But God "worketh ALL things according to the counsel of his own will, Ephesians 1:11." By putting the word "all" in very large capitals, Mr. T. seems willing to insinuate that God's decree *causes* all things; and, of consequence, that God absolutely works the good actions of the righteous, and the bad deeds of the wicked. Whereas the apostle means only, that *all the things which God works,* he works them "according to the counsel of his own" most wise, gracious, and righteous "will." But the things which God works are, in many cases, as different from the things which *we* work, as light is different from darkness. This passage, therefore, does not prove Calvinian necessity: for, when God made man "according to the counsel of his own will," he made him a free agent, and "set before him life and death;" bidding him choose life. Now, to include Adam's eating of the forbidden fruit, and choosing death, among "the things which God worketh," is to turn Manichee with a witness: it is to confound Christ and Belial; the acts of God, and the deeds of sinners. It is to suppose (horrible to think!) that God will send the reprobates to hell for his own deeds; or, if you please, for what he has wrought absolutely in them, and by them, "according to the counsel of his own *necessitating* will." This dreadful doctrine is that capital part of Calvinism which is called absolute predestination to death. If Mr. T. denies that it is the second pillar of his doctrine of grace, he may turn to section ii, where he will find his peculiar gospel "upon its legs."

I hope I need say no more upon this head, to convince the unprejudiced reader that Mr. T.'s arguments in favour of Calvinian necessity are frivolous, and that Mr. Wesley advances a glaring truth when he asserts that, on the principle of absolute predestination, there can be no future judgment, (upon any known principle of wisdom, equity, and justice,) and that it requires more pains than all rational creatures will be ever able to take, to reconcile the doctrine of (Calvinian) reprobation, with the doctrine of a judgment day.

SECTION VIII.

An answer to the argument taken from God's PRESCIENCE, *whereby Mr. Toplady tries to prove that the* VERY CRUELTY *which Mr. Wesley charges on Calvinism, is really chargeable on the doctrine of general grace.*

MR. Toplady is a spirited writer. He not only tries to reconcile Calvinian reprobation with Divine mercy, but he attempts to retort upon us the charge of holding a *cruel* doctrine.

ARG. LIX. Page 47. "But what if, after all, that very *cruelty* which Mr. Wesley pretends to charge on Calvinism, be found really chargeable on Arminianism? I pledge myself to *prove* this before I conclude this tract." And, accordingly, pp. 86, 87, Mr. Toplady, after observing in his way that, according to Mr. Wesley's doctrine, God offers his grace to many who "put it from them," and gives it to many who "receive it in vain," and who, on this account are condemned; Mr. Toplady, I say, sums up his argument in these words: — "If God knows that the offered grace will be rejected, it would be mercy to forbear the offer. Prove the contrary if you are able."

I have answered this objection at large, *Scripture Scales,* section 6. However, I shall say something upon it here. (1.) God's perfections shine in such a manner as not to eclipse one another. Wisdom, justice, mercy, and truth, are the adorable and well-proportioned features of God's *moral* face, if I may venture upon that expression. Now, if, in order to magnify his mercy, I thrust out his wisdom and justice, as I should do if I held a lawless, Calvinian election; or if, in order to magnify his justice, I thrust out his mercy and wisdom, as I should do if I consistently held Calvinian reprobation; should I not disfigure God's *moral* face, as much as I should spoil Mr. Toplady's *natural* face, if I swelled his eyes or cheeks to such a degree as to leave absolutely no room for his other features? The Calvinists forget, that as human beauty does not consist in the monstrous bigness of one or two features, but in the harmonious and symmetrical proportion of *all;* so Divine glory does not consist in displaying a mercy and a justice, which would absolutely swallow up each other, together with wisdom, holiness, and truth. This would, however, be the case, if God, after having wisely decreed to make free agents, in order to display his holiness, justice, and truth, by "judging them according to their works," *necessitated* them to be good or wicked, by decrees of absolute predestination to life and heaven, or of absolute reprobation to hell and damnation.

2. Do but allow that God made rational creatures in order to rule them as rational, namely, by laws adapted to their nature; do but admit this truth, I say, which stands or falls with the Bible, and it necessarily follows that such creatures were made with an eye to "a day of judgment:" and the moment this is granted, Mr. Toplady's argument vanishes into smoke. For, supposing that God had displayed *more mercy* toward those who die in their sins, by forbearing to give them grace, and to offer them more grace; or, in other words, supposing that God had shown the wicked more mercy, by showing them *no mercy at all,* (which, by the by, is a contradiction in terms,) yet such a *merciless* mercy (if I may use the expression) would have blackened his wisdom, overthrown his truth, and destroyed his justice. What a poor figure, for instance, would his justice have made among his other attributes, if he had said that he would judicially cast his unprofitable servants into outer darkness, for burying a talent which they never had, or for not receiving a Saviour who was always kept from them? And what rationals would not have wondered at a Governor who, after having made moral agents in order to rule them according to their free nature, and to judge them "in righteousness according to their works," should nevertheless show himself, (i.) so *inconsistent* as to rule them by efficacious decrees, which should absolutely necessitate some of them to work iniquity, and others to work righteousness. (ii.) So *unjust* as to judge them according to the works which his own binding decrees had necessitated them to do. And, (iii.) So *cruel* and unwise as to punish them with eternal death, according to a sentence of absolute reprobation to death, or of absolute election to life, which he passed beforehand, *without any respect to their works,* thousands of years before most of them were born? By what art could so strange a conduct have been reconciled with the titles of Lawgiver, and "Judge of all the earth," which God assumes; or with his repeated declarations that justice and equity are the basis of his throne, and that, in point of judgment, his ways are perfectly equal?

If Mr. T. should try to vindicate so strange a proceeding, by saying that God could justly reprobate to eternal death myriads of unborn infants *for the sin of Adam;* would he not make a bad matter worse, since, upon the plan of the absolute predestination of all events, Adam's sin was *necessarily* brought about by the decree of the means, which decree, if Calvinism be true, God made in order to *secure* and *accomplish* the two grand decrees of the end, namely, the eternal decree of finished damnation by Adam, and the eternal decree of finished salvation by Christ?

The absurdity of Mr. Toplady's argument may be placed in a clearer light by an illustration: — The king, to display his royal benevolence, equity, and justice; to maintain good order in his army, and excite his troopers to military diligence, promises to give a reward to all the men of a regiment of light horse who shall ride so many miles without dismounting to plunder: and he engages himself to punish severely those who shall be guilty of that offence. He foresees, indeed, that many will slight his offered rewards, and incur his threatened punishment: nevertheless, for the above-mentioned reasons, he proceeds. Some men are promoted, and others are punished. A Calvinist highly blames the king's conduct. He says that his majesty would have shown himself *more gracious,* and would have asserted his sovereignty much better, if he had refused horses to the plunderers, and had punished them for lighting off horses *which they never had:* and that, on the other hand, it became his free grace to tie the rewardable dragoons fast to their saddles, and by this means to *necessitate* them to keep on horseback, and deserve the promised reward. Would not such a conduct have marked his majesty's reputation with the stamp of disingenuity, cruelty, and folly? And yet, astonishing! because we do not approve of *such a judicial* distribution of the rewards of eternal life, and the punishments of eternal death, Mr. Toplady fixes the charge of CRUELTY upon the Gospel which we preach! He goes on:—

ARG. LX. Page 85. "According to Mr. Wesley's own fundamental principle of universal grace, grace itself, or the saving influence of the Holy Spirit on the hearts of men, *does* and *must* become the ministration of eternal death to thousands and millions." Page 89: "Level therefore your tragical exclamations, about *unmercifulness,* at your own scheme, which truly and properly deserves them."

The flaw of this argument consists in the words "does and must," which Mr. T. puts in Italics. (1.) In the word "does;" it is a great mistake to say that, upon Mr. W.'s principles, grace itself *does* become the ministration of eternal death to any soul. It is not for *grace,* but for the *abuse* or *neglect* of grace and its saving light, that men are condemned. "This is the condemnation," says Christ himself, "that light [the light of grace] is come into the world, and men love darkness rather than light." And St. Paul adds, that the "grace of God, which bringeth salvation, hath [in different degrees] appeared to all men," John 3:19; Titus 2:11. There is no medium between condemning men for not using a talent of grace which *they had,* or for not using a talent of grace which *they* NEVER *had.* The former sentiment, which is perfectly agreeable to reason, Scripture, and conscience, is that of Mr. Wesley; the latter sentiment, which contradicts one half of the Bible, shocks reason, and demolishes the doctrines of justice, is that of Mr. Toplady. (2.) When this gentleman says that God's grace, upon Mr. Wesley's principles, *must* become the ministration of death to millions, he advances as groundless a proposition as I would do if I said that the grace of creation, the grace of preservation, and the grace of a preached Gospel, absolutely destroy millions; because millions, by wilfully abusing their created and preserved powers, or by neglecting so great salvation as the Gospel brings, pull down upon themselves an unnecessary, and therefore a *just* destruction. (3.) We oppose the doctrine of absolute necessity, or the Calvinian *must,* as being inseparable from Manicheism: and we assert that there is no *needs must* in the eternal death of any man, because Christ imparts a degree of temporary salvation to all, with power to obey, and a promise to bestow eternal salvation upon all that *will* obey. How ungenerous is it then to charge upon us the very doctrine which we detest, when it has no necessary connection with any of our principles! How irrational to say, that if our doctrine of grace be true, God's grace must become the ministration of death to millions! Ten men have a mortal disorder: a physician prepares a sovereign remedy for them all: five take it properly, and recover; and five, who will not follow his prescriptions, die of their disorder. Now, who but a prejudiced person would infer from thence that the physician's sovereign remedy is "become the ministration of death" to the patients who die, because they would not take it? Is it right thus to confound a *remedy* with the *obstinate neglect* of it? A man wilfully starves himself to death with good food before him. I say that his *wilfulness* is the cause of his death: "No," replies a decretist, "it is the *good food* which you desire him to take." This absurd conclusion is all of a piece with that of Mr. Toplady.

ARG. LXI. Page 89. "The Arminian system represents the Father of mercies as offering grace to them, who, he *knows*, will only add sin to sin, and make themselves twofold more the children of hell by refusing it." Indeed, it is not the Arminian system only that says this: (1.) All the Calvinists who allow that God gave angelic grace to angels, though he knew that many of them would fall from that grace, and would fall deeper than if they had fallen from a less exalted station. (2.) Jesus Christ who gave Judas the grace of apostleship, and represents God as giving a pound to his servants who squander it, as well as to those who use it properly. And, (3.) Mr. Toplady himself, who (notwithstanding his pretended horror for so Scriptural a doctrine) dares not deny that God gave the grace of creation to those who shall perish. Now the grace of creation implies spotless holiness; and if God could once graciously give spotless holiness to Judas in the loins of Adam, why could he not graciously restore to that apostle a degree of free agency to good, that he might be judged according to "his own works," and not according to Calvinian decrees of "finished wickedness" and "finished damnation" in Adam? But, (4.) What is still more surprising, Mr. T. himself, p. 51, quotes these words, which so abundantly decide the question: "Thou, Capernaum, which art exalted unto heaven [by the peculiar favours and Gospel privileges bestowed upon thee] shalt be brought down to hell: for if the mighty works which have been done in thee had been done in Sodom, it would have remained unto this day," Matthew 11:23. Now, I ask, Why were these "mighty works" done in Capernaum? Was it out of *love* — to bring Capernaum to repentance? Or, was it out of *wrath* — that it might be "more tolerable in the day of judgment for Sodom than Capernaum?" There is no medium: Mr. Toplady must recant this part of the Bible, and of his book; or he must answer one of these two questions in the affirmative. If he say (as we do) that these "*mighty* works," which might have converted Tyre, Sidon, and Sodom, were primarily wrought to bring Capernaum to repentance, he gives up Calvinism, which stands or falls with the doctrine of *necessitating means* used in order to bring about a *necessary end*. If he say (as Calvinism does) that these mighty works were *primarily* wrought to sink Capernaum into hell — into a deeper hell than Sodom, because the end always shows what the means were used for; he runs upon the point of his own objection; he pulls upon *his* doctrines of grace the very unmercifulness which he charges upon *ours;* and he shows, to every unprejudiced reader, that the difficulty arising from the prescience of God, with which the Calvinists think to demolish the doctrine of general grace, falls upon Calvinism with a double weight. Mr. Toplady is sensible that God could never have appeared good and just, unless the wicked had been absolutely inexcusable; and that they could never have been inexcusable if God had condemned them for burying a talent of grace which they never had: and therefore Mr. T. tries to overthrow this easy solution of the difficulty by saying, —

ARG. LXII. Page 88. "Be it so," that the wicked *are made inexcusable* by a day of grace and temporary salvation, "yet, surely, God can never be thought knowingly to render a man *more* inexcusable, by taking such measures as will certainly load him with accumulated condemnation, out of *mere love* to that man?" We grant it; and therefore we assert that it is not out of "mere love" that God puts us in a gracious state of probation, or temporary salvation; but out of wisdom, truth, and distributive justice, as well as out of mercy and love. If God, therefore, were endued with no other perfection than that of merciful love, we would give up the doctrine of judicial reprobation; for a God devoid of distributive justice could and would save all sinners in the Calvinian way, that is, with a salvation perfectly finished, without any of their works. But then he would neither *judge* them, nor bestow eternal salvation upon them by way of *reward* for their works, as the Scriptures say he will.

O! how much more reasonable and Scriptural is it to allow the doctrine of free grace, and free will, established in the *Scripture Scales;* and to maintain the reprobation of justice — an avoidable reprobation this, which is perpetually asserted in the Gospel, and will leave the wicked entirely inexcusable, and God perfectly righteous: how much better is it, I say, to hold *such* a reprobation, than to admit Calvinian reprobation, which renders the wicked excusable and pitiable, as being condemned for doing what Omnipotence necessitated them to do; a reprobation this, which stigmatizes Christ as a shuffler, for offering to all a salvation from which most are absolutely debarred; a cruel reprobation, which represents the Father of mercies as an unjust sovereign, who takes such measures as will *unavoidably* load myriads of unborn men with accumulated condemnation, out of free wrath to their unformed souls!

Should Mr. Toplady say, "That according to the Gospel which we preach, the wicked shall certainly be damned; and therefore the difference between us is but trifling after all; seeing the Calvinists assert that some men, namely, those who are *eternally* reprobated by Divine sovereignty, shall *certainly* and *unavoidably* be damned; and the anti-Calvinists say that some men, namely, those who are *finally* reprobated by Divine justice, shall be *certainly* though *avoidably* damned:" I reply, that, frivolous as the difference between these two doctrines may appear to those who judge according to the APPEARANCE of words, it is as capital as the difference between *avoidable* ruin and *unavoidable* destruction; between justice and injustice; between *initial* election and *finished* reprobation; between saying that GOD is the *first cause* of the damnation of the wicked, and asserting that THEY are the *first cause* of their own damnation. In a word, it is as great as the difference between the north and the south; between a Gospel made up of Antinomian free grace and barbarian free wrath, and a Gospel made up of Scriptural free grace, and impartial, retributive justice.

Upon the whole, from the preceding answers it is evident, if I am not mistaken, that, though the grand Calvinian objection, taken from God's foreknowledge, may, at first sight, puzzle the simple; yet it can bear neither the light of Scripture, nor that of reason; and it recoils upon Calvinism, with all the force with which it is supposed to attack "the saving grace which has appeared to all men."

SECTION IX.

An answer to the charges of robbing the trinity, and encouraging Deism, which charges Mr. T. brings against the doctrine of the anti-Calvinists.

MR. T. thinks his cause so good, that he supposes himself able, not only to stand on the defensive, but also to attack the Gospel which we preach. From his *Babel,* therefore, (his strong tower of *confusion,*) he makes a bold sally, and charges us thus:—

ARG. LXIII. Page 91. "Arminianism robs the Father of his sovereignty." This is a mistake: Arminianism dares not attribute to him the grim sovereignty of a Nero; but if it does not humbly allow him *all* the sovereignty which Scripture and reason ascribe to him, so far it is wrong, and so far we oppose Pelagian Arminianism as well as Manichean Calvinism. It "robs the Father of his decrees." This is a mistake: it reverences all *his righteous,* Scriptural decrees; though it shudders at the thought of imputing to him unscriptural, Calvinian decrees, more wicked and absurd than the decrees of Nebuchadnezzar and Darius. It "robs the Father of his providence." Another mistake! Our doctrine only refuses to make God the author of sin, and to lead men to the Pagan error of fatalism, or to the Manichean error of a two-principled God, who absolutely works all things in all men, as a showman works all things in his puppets; fixing his necessary virtue on the good, and necessary wickedness on the wicked, to the subversion of all the Divine perfections, and to the entire overthrow of the second Gospel axiom, of Christ's tribunal, and of the wisdom and justice which the Scriptures ascribe to God, as "Judge of the whole earth."

ARG. LXIV. (*Ibid.*) "It [Arminianism] robs the Son of his efficacy as a Saviour." Another mistake! It only dares not pour upon him the shame of being the absolute reprobater of myriads of unborn creatures, whose nature he assumed with a gracious design to be absolutely their *temporary* Saviour; promising to prove their *eternal* Saviour upon Gospel terms: and, accordingly, he *saves all* mankind with a *temporary* salvation; and *those who obey him* with an *eternal* salvation. The EFFICACY of his blood is then complete, so far as he absolutely designed it should be.

ARG. LXV. (*Ibid.*) "It [Arminianism] robs the Spirit of his efficacy as a Sanctifier." By no means; for it maintains that the Spirit, which is the grace and light of Christ, "enlightens every man that comes into the world," and leads the worst of men to some temporary good, or at least restrains them from the commission of a thousand crimes. So far the Spirit's grace is efficacious in *all;* and, if it is not completely and eternally efficacious in those who "harden their hearts, *and* by their *wilful* hardness treasure up unto themselves wrath against the day of wrath," it is because "the day of wrath," for which the wicked were* *secondarily* made, is to be "the day of the righteous

---

* All angels and men were PRIMARILY made to enjoy an "accepted time," and a temporary "day of salvation." Those angels and men, who know and improve their day of salvation, were SECONDARILY made for the day of remunerative love, and for a kingdom "prepared for them from the beginning of the world." But those angels and men, who do not know and improve their day of salvation, were SECONDARILY made for "the day of *retributive* wrath," and for the "fire prepared for the devil and his angels."

judgment of God who will render to every man according to his deeds," Romans 2:5, 6: and not the day of the *unrighteous* judgment of Calvin, who (doctrinally) renders to every man according to a finished salvation in Christ, productive of necessary goodness; and according to a finished damnation in Adam, productive of remediless wickedness, and all its dreadful consequences.

ARG. LXVI. Page 92. Mr. Toplady produces a long quotation from Mr. Sloss, which, being divested of the verbose dress in which error generally appears, amounts to this plain abridged argument: "If the doctrine of Calvinian election be false, because all mankind are not the objects of that election, and because all men have an equal right to the Divine favour, it follows that infidels are right when they say that the Jewish and the Christian revelations are false: for all mankind are not *elected* to the favour of having the Old and New Testament; and therefore Arminianism encourages infidelity."

This argument is good to convince Pelagian levellers that God is *partial* in the distribution of his talents, and that he indulges Jews and Christians with a holy, *peculiar* election and calling, of which those who never heard of the Bible are utterly deprived. I have myself made this remark in the *Essay* on the *gratuitous* election, and *partial* reprobation which St. Paul frequently preaches: but the argument does not affect *our* anti-Calvinian Gospel. For, 1. WE do not say that the Calvinian election is false, because it supposes that God is peculiarly gracious to some men; (for this we strongly assert, as well as the Calvinists;) but because it supposes that God is so PECULIARLY gracious to some men, as to be ABSOLUTELY MERCILESS and unjust to all the rest of mankind.

2. That very revelation, which Mr. Sloss thinks we betray to the Deists, informs us, that though all men are not indulged with the peculiar blessings of Judaism and Christianity, yet they are all *chosen* and *called* to be righteous, at least, according to the covenants made with fallen Adam and spared Noah. Hence St. Peter says, that, "in every nation, he that feareth God, and worketh righteousness [according to his light, though it should be only the lowest degree of that light, which enlightens every man that cometh into the world] is accepted of him:" and St. Paul speaks of some "Gentiles, who, *though they* have not the law *of Moses or* the law *of Christ,* do by nature [in its state of initial restoration through the seed of life given to fallen Adam in the promise] the things contained in the law, and are a law unto themselves; showing the work of the law, written in their hearts." Therefore, though there is a gratuitous election, which draws after it a gratuitous reprobation from the blessings peculiar to Judaism and Christianity; there is no Calvinian election, which draws after it a gratuitous reprobation from all saving grace, and *necessarily* involves the greatest part of mankind in unavoidable damnation. Hence, if I mistake not, it appears that when Mr. Sloss charges us with "having contributed to the prevailing Deism of the present time, by furnishing the adversaries of Divine revelation with arguments against Christianity," he (as well as Mr. Toplady) gratuitously imputes to our doctrine, what really belongs to Calvinism. For there is a perfect agreement between the absolute necessity of events, which is asserted by Calvinian bound willers; and that which is maintained by Deistical fatalists: and it is well known that the horrors of the absolute reprobation which the Calvinists fancy they see in Romans ix, have tempted many moralists, who read that chapter with the reprobating glosses of Calvin and his followers, to bid adieu to revelation; it being impossible that a scheme of doctrine,

which represents God as the absolute reprobater of myriads of unborn infants, should have *the Parent of good,* and the *God of love* for its author.

SECTION X.

An answer to the arguments by which Mr. Toplady attempts to retort the charge of Antinomianism, and to show that Calvinism is more conducive to holiness than the opposite doctrine.

MR. HILL asserts that Mr. T. "retorts all our objections upon us in a most masterly manner." Let us see how he retorts the objection which we make to absolute predestination — a doctrine this, by which necessary holiness is imposed upon the elect, and necessary wickedness upon the reprobates. How the fixing unavoidable holiness upon a minority, and unavoidable wickedness upon a majority of mankind, is reconcilable with the glory of Divine holiness, Mr. Toplady informs us in the following argument: —

ARG. LXVII. Pages 93, 94. Calvinian* "election insures holiness to a very great part of mankind: whereas precarious grace, deriving all its efficacy from the caprice of free will, could not insure holiness to any one individual of the whole species." Had Mr. T. stated the case properly, he would have said, Calvinian election, which insures necessary holiness to a minority of mankind; and Calvinian reprobation, which insures necessary wickedness to a majority of mankind, promote human sanctity more than *the partial election of grace,* which formerly afforded the Jews, and now affords the Christians abundant helps to be peculiarly holy under their dispensations of peculiar grace: yea, more than *the impartial election of justice,* which, under all the dispensations of Divine grace, "chooses the man that is godly" to rewards of grace and glory: and more than *the reprobation of justice,* which is extended to none but such as bury their talent of grace by willful unbelief and voluntary disobedience.

If Mr. T. had thus stated the case, according to his real sentiments and ours, every candid reader would have seen that our doctrines of grace are far more conducive to human sanctity than those of Calvin (1.) Because Calvinism insures *human sanctity* to none of the elect: for a sanctity which is as necessary to a creature, as motion is to a moved puppet, is not the sanctity of a free agent; and, of consequence, it is not human sanctity. (2.) Because Calvinism insures *remediless wickedness* to all the reprobate, and remediless wickedness can never be "human sanctity."

---

* The author of *A Letter to an Arminian Teacher,* (a letter this which I have quoted in a preceding note,) advances the same argument in these words, p. 5: "The doctrine of eternal [he means *Calvinian*] election," *for we believe the right, godly, eternal election maintained in the Scriptures,* "concludes God more merciful than the Arminian doctrine of supposed universal redemption, because that doctrine which absolutely ascertains the regeneration, effectually calling, the sanctification, &c, as well as the eternal salvation of an innumerable company, &c, Revelation 7:9, must represent God more merciful than the Arminian scheme, which cannot ascertain the eternal salvation of one man now living," &c. As it is possible to kill two birds with one stone, I hope that my answer to Mr. Toplady will satisfy Mr. M'Gowan.

Doctrines of Grace and Justice

With respect to what Mr. T. says, that our doctrines of grace do "not insure holiness to any one individual of the whole species;" if by *insured holiness*, he means a certain salvation without any work of faith and labour of love, he is greatly mistaken: for our Gospel absolutely insures such a salvation, and of consequence infant holiness, to that numerous part of mankind who die in their infancy. Nay, it absolutely insures a seed of redeeming, sanctifying grace to *all mankind*, so long as the day of grace or initial salvation lasts; for we maintain, as well as St. Paul, that "the free gift is come upon all men to justification of life," Romans 5:18; and we assert, as well as our Lord, that "of such [of infants] is the kingdom of heaven," and therefore some capacity to enjoy it, which capacity we believe to be inseparably connected with a seed of holiness. Add to this, that our Gospel, as well as Calvinism, insures eternal salvation to all the adult who are "faithful unto death." According to our doctrine, "these sheep shall never perish:" to these elect of justice, who "make their election *of grace* sure" by obedience, Christ "gives eternal life" in the fullest sense of the word: and "none shall pluck them out of his hand." If Mr. T. had placed our Gospel in this true light, his objection would have appeared as just as the rhodomontade of Goliah, when he was going to despatch David.

ARG. LXVIII. Page 94. Mr. T. tries to make up the Antinomian gap, by doing that which borders upon giving up Calvinism. "No man (says he) according to our system, has a right to look upon himself as elected, till sanctifying grace has *converted* him to faith and good works."

This flimsy salvo has quieted the fears of many godly Calvinists, when the Antinomianism of their system stared them in the face. To show the absurdity of this evasion, I need only ask, Has not every man *a right* to believe truth? If I am absolutely elected to eternal life, while I commit adultery and murder, while I defile my father's wife, and deny my Saviour with oaths and curses; why may not I believe it? Is there one sentence of Scripture which commands me to believe a lie, or forbids me to believe the truth? "O, but you have *no right* to believe yourself elected, *till* sanctifying grace has converted you to faith and good works." Then it follows, that, as an adult sinner, I am not elected to the reward of the inheritance, or to eternal life in glory, *till* I believe and do good works: or it follows that I have *no right* to believe the truth. If Mr. T. affirm that I have no right to believe the truth, he makes himself ridiculous before all the world: and if he say that I am not absolutely elected *till I am converted to faith and good works*, it follows that every time I am *perverted from faith and good works*, I forfeit my election of justice. Thus, under the guidance of Mr. T. himself, I escape the fatal rock of Calvinian election, and find myself in the safe harbour of old, practical Christianity: "Ye know that no whoremonger, nor unclean person, nor covetous man, hath any inheritance in the kingdom of Christ and of God: let no man deceive you with vain words." For if I have no right to believe myself an heir of God, and a joint heir with Christ, while I turn whoremonger; it is evident that whoredom deprives me of my right; much more adultery and murder. Hence it appears that Mr. T. cannot prop up the Calvinian ark, but by flatly contradicting St. Paul, which is a piece of impiety; and by asserting that elect whoremongers have no right to believe the truth while they commit whoredom, which is a glaring absurdity.

ARG. LXIX. Page 95. After having made up the Antinomian gap, by giving up either Calvinian election, or the incontestable right which every man has to believe the truth, Mr. Toplady tries to retort the charge of Antinomianism upon *our* doctrines of grace; and he does it by producing one "Thomson, who, when he was in a fit of intemperance, if any one reminded him of the wrath of God, threatened against such courses, would answer, *I am a child of the devil to-day; but I have free will; and tomorrow I will make myself a child of God.*"

To this I answer: (1.) The man spoke like a person "in a fit of intemperance," and there is no reasoning with such, any more than with mad men. But Dr. Crisp, when he was sober, and in the pulpit too, could say, "A believer may be assured of pardon as soon as he commits any sin, even adultery and murder. Sins are but scare-crows and bug-bears to frighten ignorant children, but men of understanding see they are counterfeit things:" and indeed it must be so, if, as Mr. Toplady tells us, *Whatever is, is right,* and necessarily flows from the predestinating will of Him who does all things well.

2. This Thomson (as appears by his speech) was a rigid free willer; one who discarded the first Gospel axiom, and the doctrine of free grace; and therefore his error does not affect our Gospel. Nay, we oppose such free willers as much as we do the rigid bound willers who discard the second Gospel axiom, and the necessity of sincere obedience in order to our judicial justification, and eternal salvation.

3. If Thomson had been sober and reasonable, Mr. Wesley might easily have made up the pretended Antinomian gap of Arminianism five different ways: (1.) By showing, him, that although free will *may reject* a good motion, yet it *cannot raise* one without free grace; and therefore, to say, "To-morrow I will make myself a child of God," is as absurd in a man, as it would be in a woman, to say, "To-morrow I will conceive alone." It is as impious as to say, "To-morrow I will absolutely command God, and he shall obey me." (2.) By showing him his imminent danger, and the horror of his present state, which he himself acknowledged when he said, "I am a child of the devil to-day." (3.) By arguing the uncertain length of the day of salvation. Grace gives us no room to depend upon *to-morrow;* its constant language being, "Now is the accepted time." (4.) By pressing the hardening nature of presumptuous sin. And, (5.) By displaying the terrors of just wrath, which frequently says, "Take the talent from him. Because ye refused, I will be avenged. I give thee up to thy own heart's lusts, to a reprobate mind. Thou fool! this night shall thy soul be required of thee."

These are five rational and Scriptural ways of making up the supposed Antinomian gap of our Gospel. But if Mr. Thomson had been a Calvinist, and had said, like Mr. Fulsome, "I have had a call, and my election is safe: as my good works can add nothing to my finished salvation, so my bad works can take nothing from it. Satan may pound me, if he pleases; but Jesus must replevy me. Let me wander where I will from God, Christ must fetch me back again. The covenant is unconditionally ordered in all things and sure. All things work for good to the elect." "And if all things," says Mr, Hill, "then their very sins and corruptions are included in the royal promise." "Whoredom and drunkenness may hurt another, but they cannot hurt me. God will overrule sin for my good, and his glory. Whatsoever is, is right: for God worketh all things in all men, even wickedness in the wicked, and how much more in his elect, who are his chosen instruments!" If Mr. Thomson, I say, had been a Calvinist, and had thus stood his ground in the Antinomian gap, which Calvin, Dr. Crisp, Mr. Fulsome, Mr. Hill, and Mr. Toplady have made; who could reasonably have beaten him off? Do not all his conclusions flow from the doctrine of absolute election and finished salvation, as unavoidably as four is the result of two and two?

ARG. LXX. Page 97. Mr. Toplady attempts again to stop up the Antinomian gap, which fatalism and Calvinian predestination make in practical religion. Calling to his assistance Zeno, the founder of the stoics, or rigid Predestinarians among the heathens, he says, "Zeno one day thrashed his servant for pilfering. The fellow, knowing his master was a fatalist, thought to bring himself off by alleging that he was *destined to steal,* and therefore ought not to be beat for it. 'You are destined to steal, are you?' answered the philosopher; 'then you are no less *destined to be thrashed* for it:' and laid on some hearty blows extraordinary." I do not wonder that Mr. Hill, in his *Finishing Stroke,* calls Mr. Toplady's arguments "most masterly;" for this argument of Zeno is yet more masterly than his own: "I shall not take the least notice of him, any more than, if I were travelling on the road, I would stop to lash, or even to order my footman to lash every little impertinent quadruped in a village, that should come out and bark at me." Mr. Toplady, in the advertisement placed at the head of his pamphlet, represents some of us as "unworthy of even being pilloried in a preface, or flogged at a pamphlet's tail:" we are now arrived at the tail of his pamphlet, in the body of which he has thought Mr. Wesley so highly worthy of his rod, as to "flog" him with the gratuity, absoluteness, mercy, and justice, which are peculiar to the reprobation defended through the whole performance. If seriousness did not become us, when we vindicate the injured attributes of "the Judge of all the earth," I might be tempted to ask, with a smile, Has Mr. Toplady so worn out his rod in making "more work for Mr. Wesley," that he is now obliged to borrow Zeno's stick to finish the execution "at the pamphlet's tail?" For my part, as I have no idea of rivetting orthodoxy upon my readers with a stick, and of solving the rational objections of my opponents by "laying on some hearty blows," and so "thrashing" them into conviction, or into silence, I own that *Logica Zenonis and Logica Genevensis* being of a piece, either of them can easily beat me out of the field. Arguments *a lapide* are laughable; but I flee before arguments *a baculo.* However, in my retreat, I will venture to present Mr. Toplady with the following queries:—

If Zeno, in vindicating fatalism, could say to a thief, that he was absolutely predestinated to steal, and to be thrashed for stealing; is it not more than Mr. Toplady can say in vindication of Calvinism? For, upon his scheme, may not a man be absolutely predestinated not only to steal, but also to escape thrashing, and to obtain salvation by stealing? Mr. Toplady is Mr. Hill's second: and Mr. Hill, in his fourth letter, (where he shows the happy effects of sin,) tells the public and me, "Onesimus robbed Philemon his master; and fleeing from justice, was brought under Paul's preaching, and converted." Thus Zeno's predestination failed, and with it Zeno's argument: for robbery led not Onesimus to thrashing, but to conversion and glory, if we believe Mr. Hill. And if Mr. Fulsome is an elect person, why might he not be guilty of as fortunate a robbery? Why might not a similar decree "secure and accomplish the [same evangelical] end by the [same Antinomian] means?" Mr. Toplady may prevail over us by borrowing Zeno's cane, and the whip of Mr. Hill's lashing footman; but his pen will never demonstrate, (1.) That Calvinism does not rationally lead all her admirers to the deepest mire of *speculative* Antinomianism. And, (2.) That when they are there, nothing can keep them from weltering in the dirt of *practical* Antinomianism, but a happy inconsistence between their actions and their principles.

SECTION XI.

A caution against the tenet, WHATEVER IS, IS RIGHT: an Antinomian tenet this, which Mr. T. calls "a first principle of the Bible" — An answer to his challenge about finding a middle way between the Calvinian doctrine of providence, and the Atheistical doctrine of chance.

WHATEVER the true God works, is undoubtedly right. But if the Deity absolutely works all things in all men, good and bad, it evidently follows, (1.) That the two-principled Deity preached by Manes is the true God. (2.) That the bad principle of this double Deity works wickedness in the wicked, as necessarily as the good principle works righteousness in the righteous. And, (3.) That the original of wickedness being Divine, wickedness is as right as the Deity from whom it flows. Upon this horrid, Manichean scheme, who can wonder at Mr. Toplady saying: —

ARG. LXXI. Page 96. "This is a first principle of the Bible, and of sound reason, that *whatever is, is right*, or will answer some great end, &c, in its relation to the whole." Error is never more dangerous than when it looks a little like truth. But when it is imposed upon the simple as "a first principle of the Bible and of sound reason," it makes dreadful work. How conclusively will a rigid Predestinarian reason if he says, "*Whatever is, is right;* and therefore sin is right. Again: it is wrong to hinder what is right: sin is right, and therefore it is wrong to hinder sin. Once more: we ought to do what is right; and therefore we ought to commit sin." Now, in opposition to Mr. Toplady's first principle, I assert, as a "first principle of reason," that though it was right in God not absolutely to hinder sin, yet *sin is always wrong.* "O! but God permitted it, and will get himself glory by displaying his vindictive justice in punishing it: for 'the ministration of condemnation is glorious.'" This argument has deluded many a pious Calvinist. To overthrow it, I need only observe that "righteousness exceeds *condemnation* in glory!"

In what respect is sin right? Can it be right in respect of God, if it brings him less glory than righteousness? Can it be right in respect of man, if it brings temporal misery upon ALL, and eternal misery upon SOME? Can it be right in respect of the Adamic law, the law of Moses, or the law of Christ? Certainly no: for sin is equally the transgression of all these laws. "O! but it is right with respect to the evangelical promise." By no means: for the evangelical promise, vulgarly called the Gospel, testifies of Christ, the destroyer of sin, and offers us a remedy against sin. Now, if sin were right, the Gospel which remedies it, and Christ who destroys it, would be wrong. I conclude, then, that if sin be right, neither with respect of God, nor with respect of man; neither with regard to the law, nor with regard to the Gospel; it is right in no shape, it is wrong in every point of view. "But why did God permit it?" Indeed, he never properly permitted it, unless Mr. Toplady, who does not scruple to call God "the permitter of evil," can prove, that *to forbid,* in the most solemn manner, and under the severest penalty, is the same thing as to *permit.*

Should you say, Why did not God *absolutely hinder* sin? I still answer, (1.) Because his wisdom saw that a world where free agents and necessary agents are mixed, is better (all things considered) than a world stocked with nothing but its necessary agents, i.e. creatures absolutely hindered from sinning. (2.) Because his distributive justice could be displayed no other way, than by the creation of accountable free agents, made with an eye to a day of judgment. (3.) Because it would be as absurd to necessitate free agents, as to bid free agents *be,* that they might *not be free agents;* as foolish as to form *accountable* creatures, that they might *not be accountable.* And, (4.) Because when God saw that the free agency of his creatures would introduce sin, he determined to overrule it, or remedy it in such a manner as would, upon the whole, render this world, with all the *voluntary* evil, and *voluntary* good in it, better than a world of *necessary* agents, where nothing but *necessary* good would have been displayed: an inferior sort of good, this, which would no more have admitted of the exercise of God's political wisdom and distributive justice, than the excellence of stones and fine flowers admits of laws, rewards, and punishments.

Should the reader ask how far we may safely go to meet the truth which borders most on Mr. Toplady's false principle, *Whatever is, is right?* I answer, (1.) We may grant, nay, we ought to assert, that God will get himself glory every way. Evangelical grace, and just wrath, minister to his praise, though not equally: and therefore God willeth not primarily the death of his creatures. Punishment is his strange work; and he delights more in the exercise of his remunerative goodness, than in the exercise of his vindictive justice. (2.) Hence it appears that the wrath of man, and the rage of the devil, will turn to God's praise: but it is only to his inferior praise. For though the blessed will sing loud hallelujahs to Divine justice, when vengeance shall overtake the ungodly; and though the consciences of the ungodly will give God glory, and testify that he is holy in all his works, and righteous in all his vindictive ways; yet this glory will be only the glory of the ministration of condemnation: a dispensation this, which is inferior to the dispensation of righteous mercy. Hence it appears that those who die in their sins would have brought more glory to God by choosing righteousness and life, than they do by choosing death in the errors of their ways. But still, this inferior praise, arising from the condemnation and punishment of ungodly free agents — this inferior praise, I say, mixed with the *superior* praise arising from the justification and rewards of godly free agents, will far exceed the praise which might have accrued to God from the unavoidable obedience and absurd rewards of necessitated agents, of angels and men absolutely bound to obey by a necessitating grace like that which rigid bound willers preach; were we even to suppose that this forcible grace had Calvinistically caught ALL rational creatures in a net of finished salvation, and had drawn them all to heaven, as irresistibly as "Simon Peter drew the net to land full of great fishes, a hundred and fifty and three." For before the Lawgiver and Judge of all the earth, the unnecessitated, voluntary goodness of *one angel,* or *one man,* is more excellent than the necessary goodness of a *world of creatures* as unavoidably and passively virtuous, as a diamond is unavoidably and passively bright.

ARG. LXXII. Page 96. With respect to the second part of Mr. Toplady's doctrine, that *whatever is, is right,* because "it will answer some great end, &c, in its relation to the whole," it is nothing but logical paint put on a false principle to cover its deformity:

for error can imitate Jezebel, who laid natural paint on her withered face to fill up her hideous wrinkles, and impose upon the spectators. I may perhaps prove it by an illustration. I want to demonstrate that cheating, extortion, litigiousness, breaking the peace, robberies, and murders, are all right, and I do it by asserting "that they answer some great ends in their relation to the whole; for they employ the parliament in making laws to prevent, end, or punish them; they afford business to all the judges, magistrates, lawyers, sheriffs, constables, jailers, turnkeys, thief catchers, and executioners in the kingdom: and when robbers and murderers are hanged, they reflect praise upon the government which extirpates them; they strike terror into the wicked; and their untimely, dreadful end, sets off the happiness of a virtuous course of life, and the bliss which crowns the death of the righteous. Beside, many murderers and robbers have been brought to Christ for pardon and salvation, like the dying thief, who, by his robbery, had the good luck to meet Christ on the cross: so that his own gallows, as well as our Lord's cross, proved the tree of life to that happy felon." The mischievous absurdity of these pleas for the excellence of wickedness, puts me in mind of the arguments by which a greedy publican of my parish once exculpated himself, when I reproved him for encouraging tippling and drunkenness. "The more ale we sell," said he, "the greater is the king's revenue. If it were not for *us,* the king could not live; nor could he pay the fleet and army; and if we had neither fleet nor army, we should soon fall into the hands of the French." So "great are the ends" which tippling "answers in its relation to the whole" British empire, if we may believe a tapster, who pleads for drunkenness as plausibly as some good, mistaken men do for all manner of wickedness.

From the whole, if I am not mistaken, we may safely conclude, that though all God's works are right, yet sin, the work of fallen angels and fallen men, is never right; and that though the universe, with all its sinfulness, is better than a sinless world necessitated to be sinless by the destruction of free agents; yet, as there is so much sin in the world, through the wrong use which free agents make of their powers, Mr. T. advances an unscriptural and irrational maxim, when he says that *whatever is, is right;* and he imposes upon us an Antinomian paradox, when he asserts that this dangerous maxim "is a first principle of the Bible, and of sound reason." I repeat it: it was right in God to create free agents, to put them under a practicable law, and to determine to punish them according to their works, if they wantonly broke that law; but it could never be right in free agents to break it, unless God had bound them to do it, by making Calvinian decrees necessarily productive of sin and wickedness. And supposing God had forbid free agents to sin by his law, and had *necessitated* (which is more than to *enjoin*) them to sin by Calvinian decrees; we desire Mr. T. to show how it could have been right in God to forbid sin by law, to necessitate men to sin by a decree, and to send them into eternal fire for not keeping a law which he had necessitated them to break.

The reasonableness of this doctrine brings to my remembrance the boldness of Mr. T.'s challenge about the Calvinian doctrine of providence — a doctrine this, which asserts that God absolutely necessitates some men to sin and be damned. (See sec. 2.)

ARG. LXXIII. Page 73. "Upon the plan of Mr. Wesley's consequence, the wretch was not a fool, but wise, who said in his heart, *There is no God.* I defy the Pelagian to strike out a middle way between providence and chance," that is, between chance and the Calvinian notions of a providence, which absolutely predestinates sin, and *necessitates* men and devils to commit it, &c. "Why did the heathens themselves justly deem Epicurus an Atheist? Not because he denied the being of a God, (for he asserted that,) but because he denied the agency of God's universal providence."

From this quotation it is evident, (1.) That Mr. T. indirectly charges us with holding an Epicurean, Atheistical doctrine about providence, because we abhor the doctrine of a predestination, which represents God as the author of sin. And, (2.) That he defies or challenges us to point out a middle way between the Atheistical doctrine of chance, and the Calvinian doctrine of providence. This challenge is too important to be disregarded: an answer to this will conclude the argumentative part of this tract.

There are two opposite errors with respect to providence. The FIRST is that of the Epicurean philosophers, who thought that God does not at all concern himself about our sins, but leaves us to go on as we please, and as chance directs. The SECOND is that of the rigid Predestinarians, who imagine that God absolutely predestinates sin, and necessarily brings it about to accomplish his absolute decrees of eternally saving some men through Christ, and of eternally damning all the rest of mankind through Adam. Of these two erroneous sentiments, the latter appears to us the worse; seeing it is better to represent God as doing *nothing,* than to represent him as doing *wickedness.* The truth lies between these two opinions; God's providence is *peculiarly concerned about sin,* but it does by no means *necessarily bring it about.* By this reasonable doctrine we answer Mr. T.'s challenge, and strike out the middle way between hi error, and that of Epicurus.

If you ask how far God's providence is concerned about sin, we reply, that it is concerned about it four ways. *First,* In MORALLY hindering the *internal* commission of it before it is committed. *Secondly,* In PROVIDENTIALLY hindering (at times) the *external* commission of it when it has been intentionally committed. *Thirdly,* In making, bounding, and overruling it, while it is committed. And, *Fourthly,* In bringing about means of properly pardoning, or exemplarily punishing it, after it has been committed. Dwell we a moment upon each of these particulars.

1. Before sin is committed, Divine providence is engaged in *morally* hindering the internal commission of it. In order to this, God does two things: *first,* he forbids sin by natural, verbal, or written laws. And, *secondly,* he keeps up our powers of body and soul; enduing us with liberty, whereby we may abstain, like moral agents, from the commission of sin; furnishing us beside with a variety of motives and helps to resist every temptation to sin: a great variety this, which includes all God's threatening and promises; all his exhortations and warnings; all the checks of our consciences, and the strivings of the Holy Spirit; all the counsels of good men and the exemplary punishments of the wicked, together with the tears and blood of Christ, and the other peculiar means of grace, which God has appointed to keep Christians from sin, and to strengthen them in the performance of their duty.

2. When sin is committed in the intention, God frequently prevents the *outward* commission, or the *full* completion of it, by peculiar interpositions of his providence. Thus he hindered the men of Sodom from injuring Lot, by striking them with blindness: he hindered Pharaoh from enslaving the Israelites, by drowning him in the Red Sea: he hindered Balaam from cursing Israel, by putting a bridle in his mouth: he hindered Jeroboam from hurting the prophet who came out of Judah, by drying up

his royal hand, when he stretched it forth, saying, "Lay hold on him:" he hindered Herod from destroying the holy child Jesus, by warning Joseph to flee into Egypt, &c, &c. The Scriptures, and the history of the world, are full of accounts of the ordinary and extraordinary interpositions of Divine Providence, respecting the detection of intended mischief, and the preservation of persons and states whom the wicked determined to destroy: and, to go no farther than England, the providential discovery of the gunpowder plot is as remarkable an instance as any, that God keeps a watchful eye upon the counsels of men, and confounds their devices whenever he pleases.

3. During the commission of sin, God's providence is engaged in marking it, in setting bounds to it, or in overruling it in a manner quite contrary to the expectation of sinners. When Joseph's brethren contrived the getting money by selling him into Egypt, God contrived the preservation of Jacob's household. Thus, when Haman contrived a gallows to hang Mordecai thereon, the Lord so overruled this cruel design, that Haman was hung on that very gallows. Thus, when Satan wanted to destroy Job, God set bounds to his rage, and bid the fierce accuser spare the good man's life. That envious fiend did his worst to make the patient saint curse God to his face; but the Lord so overruled his malice, that it worked for good to Job: for when Job's patience had had its perfect work, all his misfortunes ended in double prosperity, and all his tempestuous *tossings* raised him to a higher degree of perfection: for "the Lord knows how to deliver the godly out of temptation, and to reserve the unjust to the day of judgment," 2 Peter 2:9. Thus, again, to preserve the seed of the righteous, God formerly kept one hundred prophets, and seven thousand true Israelites, from the cruelty of Jezebel; and, for the sake of the sincere Christians in Judea, he shortened the great tribulation spoken of, Matthew 24:22. When the ungodly are most busy in sinning, God's providence is most employed in counterworking their sin, in putting bounds to their desperate designs, and in making "a way for the godly to escape out of temptation, that they may be able to bear it: for the rod of the ungodly cometh not [with its full force] into the lot of the righteous, lest the righteous put forth their hand unto iniquity," through such powerful and lasting temptations, as would make it impossible for them to stand firm in the way of duty, Psalm 125:3.

4. When sin is actually committed, the providence of God, in conjunction with his mercy and justice, is employed, either in using means to bring sinners to repentance, confession, and pardon, or in inflicting upon them such punishments as seem most proper to Divine wisdom. To be convinced of it, read the history of man's redemption by Jesus Christ. Mark the various steps by which Providence brings the guilty to conviction, the penitent to pardon, the finally impenitent to destruction, and all to some degree of punishment. By what an amazing train of providential dispensations were Joseph's brethren, for instance, brought to remember, lament, and smart for their cruel behaviour to him! And how did God, by various afflictions, bring his rebellious people to consider their ways, and to humble themselves before him in the land of their captivity! What anamazing work had Divine Providence in checking and punishing the sin of Pharoah in Egypt; that of the Israelites in the wilderness; that of David and his house in Jerusalem; and that of Nebuchadnezzar and Belshazzar in Babylon!

Evangelically and providentially opening the way for the return of sinners, and repaying obdurate offenders to their face, make one half of God's work, as he is the gracious and righteous Governor of men. We cannot doubt it, if we take notice of the innumerable means by which conversions and punishments are brought about. To touch only upon *punishments:* some extend to the sea, others to the land: some spread over particular districts, others over whole kingdoms: some affect a whole family, and others a whole community: some affect the soul, and others the body: some only fall upon one limb, or one of the senses, others upon the whole animal frame, and all the senses: some affect our well being, others our being itself: some are confined to this world, and others extend to a future state: some are of a temporal, and others of an eternal nature. Now, since Providence, in subserviency to Divine justice, manages all these punishments, and their innumerable consequences, how mistaken is Mr. T. when he insinuates that our doctrine supposes God to be an idle spectator while sin is committed!

5. With respect to the gracious tempers of the righteous, we believe that they all flow, (though without Calvinian necessity,) from "the free gift which is come upon all men, and from the light which enlightens every man that cometh into the world." And as to their good works, we are so far from excluding Divine grace and providence, in order to exalt absolute free will, that we assert, Not one good work would ever be begun, continued, or ended, if Divine grace within us, and Divine Providence without us, did not animate our souls, support our bodies, help our infirmities, and (to use the language of our Church) "prevent, accompany, and follow us" through the whole. And yet, in *all* moral, and in *many* natural actions, we are as free from the laws of Calvinian necessity, as from those of the great mogul.

6. With regard to the families and kingdoms of this world, we assert that God's providence either baffles, controls, or sets bounds to the bad designs of the wicked; while it has the principal hand in succeeding the good designs of the righteous as often as they have any success: "for, except the Lord keep the city," as well as the watchman, "the watchman waketh but in vain." And with respect to the course of nature, we believe that it is ordered by his unerring counsel. With a view to maintain order in the universe, his providential wisdom made admirable laws of attraction, repulsion, generation, fermentation, vegetation, and dissolution. And his providential power and watchfulness are, though without either labour or anxiety, continually engaged in conducting all things according to those laws; except, when on proper occasions, he suspends the influence of his own natural decrees; and then fire may cease to burn; iron to sink in water; and hungry lions to devour their helpless prey. Nay, at the beck of Omnipotence, a widow's cruise of oil, and barrel of meal, shall be filled without the help of the olive tree, and the formality of a growing harvest; a dry rod shall suddenly blossom, and a green fig tree shall instantly be dried up; garments in daily use shall not wear out in forty years; a prophet shall live forty days without food; the liquid waves shall afford a solid walk to a believing apostle; a fish shall bring back the piece of money which it had swallowed; and water shall be turned into wine without the gradual process of vegetation.

If Mr. T. do us the justice to weigh these six observations upon the prodigious work, which God's providence carries on in the moral, spiritual, and natural world, according to our doctrine; we hope he will no more intimate that we Atheistically deny, or heretically defame that Divine attribute.

To conclude: we exactly steer our course between rigid free willers, who suppose they are independent on God's providence; and rigid bound willers, who fancy they do nothing but what fate or God's providence absolutely binds them to do. We equally detest the error of Epicurus, and that of Mr. Toplady. The former taught that God took no notice of sin, the latter says that God, by *efficacious permissions and irresistible decrees*, absolutely necessitates men to commit it. But we maintain that although God never absolutely necessitated his creatures to sin, yet his providence is remarkably employed about sin, in all the above-described ways. And if Mr. Toplady will call us *defamers* of Divine Providence, and *Atheists*, because we dare not represent God directly or indirectly as the author of sin; we rejoice in so honourable a reproach, and humbly trust that this, as well as all manner of similar evil, is rashly said of us for righteousness' sake.

SECTION XII.

Some encouragements for those who, from a principle of conscience, bear their testimony against the Antinomian doctrine of Calvinian election, and the barbarous doctrine of Calvinian reprobation.

I HUMBLY hope that I have, in the preceding pages, contended for the truth of the Gospel, and the honour of God's perfections. My conscience bears me witness, that I have endeavoured to do it with the sincerity of a candid inquirer after truth; and I have not, *knowingly*, leaped over one material difficulty, which Mr. T. has thrown in the way of the laborious divine, whose evangelical principles I vindicate. And now, judicious reader, as I have done my part as a detecter of the falacies by which the modern doctrines of grace are "kept upon their legs," let me prevail upon thee to do thy part as a judge, and to say if the right leg of Calvinism (i.e. the lawless election of an unscriptural grace) so draws thy admiration as to make thee overlook the deformity of the left leg, i.e. the absurd, unholy, sin-insuring, hell-procuring, merciless, and unjust reprobation which Mr. T. has attempted to vindicate. Shall thy reason, thy conscience, thy Bible — and (what is more than this) shall all the perfections of thy God, and the veracity of thy Saviour, be sacrificed on the altar of a reprobation which none of the prophets, apostles, and early fathers ever heard of? A barbarous reprobation, which heated Augustine drew from the horrible error of Manichean necessity, and clothed with some Scripture expressions detached from the context, and wrested from their original meaning? A Pharisaic reprobation which the Church of Rome took from him, and which some of our reformers unhappily brought from that corrupted society into the Protestant Churches? In a word, a reprobation which disgraces Christianity, when that holy religion is considered as a system of evangelical doctrine, as much as our most enormous crimes disgrace it, when it is considered as a system of pure morality? Shall such a system of reprobation, I say, find a place in thy creed? yea, among thy *"doctrines of grace!"* God forbid!

Dii meliora piis! erroremque hostibus illum! I hope better things of thy candour, good sense, and piety. If prejudice, human authority, and voluntary humility, seduce many good men into a profound reverence for that stupendous dogma, be not carried away by their number, or biassed by their shouts. Remember that all Israel, and good

Aaron at their head, danced once round the golden calf; that deluded Solomon was seen bowing at the shrine of Ashtaroth, the abomination of the Sidonians; that all our godly forefathers worshipped a consecrated wafer four hundred years ago; that "all the world wandered after the beast;" and that God's chosen people "went whoring after their own inventions, and once sacrificed their sons and their daughters to devils" upon the altar of Moloch. Consider this, I say, and take courage: be not afraid to "be pilloried in a preface, flogged at a pamphlet's tail," and treated as a knave, a felon, or a blasphemer, through the whole of the next Vindication of the deified Decrees,* which are commonly called *Calvinism*. This may be thy lot, if thou shouldst dare to bear thy plain testimony against the Antinomian idol of the day.

Nor say that thou art not in Italy or Portugal; but in a Protestant land, a land of liberty — in England: for thou mightest meet with more mercy from *reprobating* priests in popish Naples than in orthodox Geneva. Being some years ago in the former of those cities, among the fine buildings which I viewed, one peculiarly drew my attention. It was a towering monument, several stories high, erected by the Jesuits in honour of the Virgin Mary, whose image stood on the top of the elegant structure. But what surprised me most was an Italian inscription engraven upon a stone of the monument, to this purpose: "Pope Benedict the XIVth grants a plenary indulgence to all those who shall honour this holy image; with privilege to deliver one soul out of purgatory every time they shall pay their respects to this immaculate mother." While I copied this inscription in my pocket book, and dropped to my fellow traveller an innocent irony about the absurdity of this popish decree, two or three priests passed by; they smelt out our heresy, looked displeased, but did not insult us. Mr. Wesley took, some years ago, a similar liberty with a literary monument, erected in mystic Geneva, to the honour of absolute reprobation. He smiled at the severity of Calvinian bigotry; and not without reason, since popish bigotry kindly sends a soul out of purgatory if you reverence the black image which is pompously called *the immaculate mother of God*: whereas Calvinian bigotry indirectly sends to hell all those who shall not bow to the doctrinal image which she calls *Divine sovereignty*, upon as good grounds as some ancient devotees called the appetite of Bel [Baal] and the dragon *Divine voracity*. He Mr. Wesley] added to his smile the publication of an ironical reproof. A gentleman who serves at the altar of absolute reprobation caught him in the fact, and said something about "transmitting the criminal to Virginia or Maryland,† if not to Tyburn." But free wrath yielded to free grace. Calvinian mercy rejoiced over orthodox judgment. Mr. Wesley is spared. The vindicator "of the doctrines of grace," after "rapping his knuckles," "pillorying him in a preface," and "flogging" him again and again in two pamphlets, and in a huge book, with a tenderness peculiar to the *house of mercy*, where popish reprobation checks Protestant heresy; the vindicator of Protestant reprobation, I say, has let the gray-headed heretic go with this gentle and civil reprimand, p. 10:— "Had I publicly distorted and defamed the decrees of God; [should it not be, *Had I fairly held out to public view the absurdity of the imaginary decrees preached by Calvin?*] had I, moreover, advanced so many miles beyond boldness, as to

---

* Mr. T. calls them *the decrees of God*, and it is an axiom among the Calvinists that "God's decrees are God himself."

† See Mr. Toplady's Letter to Mr. Wesley, p. 6.

lay those distortions and defamations at the door of another; [should it not be, Had I, moreover, ironically asserted that monstrous consequences necessarily flow from monstrous premises?] bold as I am affirmed to be, I could never have looked up afterward. I should have thought every miscreant I met an honester man than myself. But Mr. John seems a perfect stranger to these feelings. His *Murus aheneus* [his brassy hardness] has been too long transferred from his conscience to his forehead. On the whole, &c, I had rather let the ancient offender pass unchastised, than soil my hands in the operation." As Mr. Wesley is so kindly dismissed by Mr. Toplady, I must also dismiss thee, gentle reader, and leave thee to decide which is most likely to convert thee to Calvinian reprobation, *Urbanitas* or *Logica Genevensis;* the courtesy of our opponents, or their arguments.

In the meantime, if thou desire to know how near Calvinian election comes to the truth, and what is the reprobation which the Scriptures maintain, I refer thee to *An Essay on the partial election of Grace, and on the impartial election of Justice. — A double essay* this, that unfolds the difficulties in which prejudiced divines and system makers have for these fourteen hundred years involved the fundamental doctrine of election; and which, I flatter myself, will check party spirit, reconcile judicious Protestants to one another, and give some useful hints to more respectable divines, who, in happier days, will exert themselves in the, total extirpation of the errors which disgrace modern Christianity.

THE

LAST CHECK TO ANTINOMIANISM.

A POLEMICAL ESSAY

ON THE

TWIN DOCTRINES OF CHRISTIAN IMPERFECTION

AND

A DEATH PURGATORY.

Be ye perfect. Every one that is perfect shall be as his Master. If thou wilt be perfect,
go and sell that thou hast, and give to the poor. — *Jesus Christ.*

If any man teach otherwise, and consent not to wholesome words, even the words of
our Lord Jesus Christ, and the doctrine which is according to godliness, he is
proud. — *St. Paul.*

Let no man deceive you, &c. For this purpose the Son of God was manifested, that
he might destroy the works of the devil. Herein is our love made perfect, that we
may have boldness in the day of judgment; because as he [the vine] is, so are we
[the branches] in this world, — *St. John.*

PREFACE TO THE LAST CHECK.

Why the following tract is called "The Last Check to Antinomianism," and "A Polemical Essay" — Mr. Hill's creed for perfectionists — A short account of the manner in which souls are purged from the remains of sin, according to the doctrine of the heathens, the Romanists, and Calvinists — The purgatory recommended by the Church of England, and vindicated in this book, is Christ's blood, and a soul-purifying faith.

I CALL the following essay *The Last Check to Antinomianism*, because it properly continues and closes the preceding Checks. When a late fellow of Clare Hall, Cambridge, attacked the doctrine of sincere obedience, which I defend in the Checks, he said, with great truth, "*Sincere* obedience, as a condition, will lead you unavoidably up to *perfect* obedience." What he urged as an argument against our views of the Gospel, is one of the reasons by which we defend them, and perhaps the strongest of all: for our doctrine leads us as naturally to holiness and perfect obedience, as that of our opponent does to sin and imperfections. If the streams of Mr. Hill's doctrine never stop, till they have carried men into a sea of *indwelling sin,* where he leaves them to struggle with waves of immorality, or with billows of corruption, all the days of their life; it is evident that our doctrine, which is the very reverse of his, must take us to a sea of *indwelling holiness,* where we calmly outride all the storms which Satan raised to destroy Job's perfection; and where all our pursuing corruptions are as much destroyed as the Egyptians were in the Red Sea.

Truth, like Moses' rod, is all of a piece; and so is the serpent, which truth devours. Look at the tail of the error which we attack, and you will see the venomous mortal sting of *indwelling sin.* Consider the but-end of the rod, with which we defend ourselves against that smooth, yet biting error, and you will find the pearl of great price, the invaluable diamond of Christian perfection. In the very nature of things, therefore, our long controversial warfare must end in a close engagement for the preservation of the *sting,* or for the recovery of the *jewel.* If our adversaries can save indwelling sin, the deadly sting, Antinomianism has won the day: but if we can rescue Christian perfection, the precious jewel, then will perfect Christianity again dare to show herself, without being attacked as a dangerous monster; or scoffed at as the base offspring of self ignorance and Pharisaic pride. This remark on the Antinomianism of our opponents is founded upon the following arguments:—

1. All those who represent Christian believers as lawless, *first,* by denying that Christ's law is a rule of judgment, which absolutely requires our own personal

obedience; *secondly*, by representing this law as a mere rule of life; and, *thirdly*, by insinuating that this rule of life is, after all, absolutely impracticable; that a personal fulfilment of it is not expected from any believer; that there never was a Christian who lived one day without breaking it; and that believers shall be eternally saved, merely because Christ kept it for them: all those, I say, who hold this Solifidian doctrine concerning Christ's law, are Christian Antinomians with a witness; that is, they are *lawless Christians* in principle, if not in practice. Now, all those who attack the doctrine of constant obedience, and Christian perfection, which we maintain, are under this threefold error concerning Christ's law; and therefore they are all Antinomians, that is, Christless, lawless in principle, though many of them, we are persuaded, are not so in practice; the fear of God causing in them a happy inconsistency, between their *legal* conduct, and their *lawless* tenets.

2. If those who plead for the breaking of Christ's law, by the necessary indwelling of a revengeful thought, only for one week, or for one day, are bare-faced Antinomians; what shall we say of the men who, on various pretences, plead for the necessary indwelling of all manner of corruption, during the term of life? Can it be said, with any propriety, that these men are free from the plague of Antinomianism?

3. And lastly, when the reader comes to section xvi, wherein I produce and answer the arguments by which the ministers of the imperfect gospel defend the continuance of indwelling sin in all believers till death, he will find that their strongest reasons for this continuance are the very same which the most lawless apostates, and the most dating renegadoes daily produce, when they plead for their continuing in drunkenness, lying, fornication, and adultery: and if these immoral gospellers deserve the name of *gross Antinomians,* why should not the moral men, who hold their loose principles, and publicly recommend them as "doctrines of grace," deserve the name of *refined Antinomians?* May not a silk weaver, who softly works a piece of taffeta, be as justly called a weaver, as the man who weaves the coarsest sackcloth?

Through the force of these observations, after weighing my subject in the balances of meditation and prayer for some months, I am come to these alarming conclusions: (1.) There is no medium between pleading for the continuance of indwelling sin, and pleading for the continuance of heart Antinomianism. And, (2.) All who attack the doctrine of an evangelically sinless perfection, deserve, when they do it, (which I would hope is not often,) the name of *advocates for sin,* better than the name of Gospel ministers and preachers of righteousness. I am conscious that this twofold conclusion wounds, in the tenderest part, several of my dear, mistaken brethren in the ministry, whom, on various accounts, I highly honour in the Lord. Nevertheless, I am obliged in conscience to publish it, lest any of my readers, or any of those whom they may warn, should be misled into Antinomianism, through the mistakes of those popular preachers: for the interests of truth, the honour of Christ's holy religion, and the welfare of precious souls are, and ought to be to me, and to every Christian, far dearer that the credit of some good, injudicious men, who inadvertently undermine the cause of godliness; thinking to do God service by stretching forth a Solifidian hand to uphold the ark of Gospel truth. Thus much for the reasons which have engaged me to call this essay *The Last Check to Antinomianism*.

If the reader desire to know why I call it also *A Polemical Essay,* he is informed, that Richard Hill, Esq., (at the end of a pamphlet entitled, "Three Letters written to the Rev. J. Fletcher, Vicar of Madeley,") has published "A Creed for Arminians and Perfectionists." The ten first articles of this creed, Which respect the Arminians, I have already answered in *The Fictitious and Genuine Creed;* and the following sheets contain my reply to the last article, which entirely refers to the perfectionists.

That gentleman introduces the whole of his fictitious creed by these lines:— "The following confession of faith, however shocking, not to say blasphemous, it may appear to the humble Christian, must inevitably be adopted, if not in express words, yet in substance, by every Arminian and perfectionist whatsoever; though the last article of it chiefly concerns such as are ordained ministers of the Church of England." The last article, which is the Creed I answer here, runs thus: —

"Though I have solemnly subscribed to the thirty-nine articles of the Church of England, and have affirmed that I believe them from my heart, yet I think our reformers were profoundly ignorant of true Christianity, when they declared, in the ninth article, that 'the infection of nature does remain in them which are regenerate;' and in the fifteenth that 'all we the rest (Christ only excepted) although baptized and born again in Christ, yet offend in many things, and if we say we have no sin, we deceive ourselves, and the truth is not in us.' This I totally deny, because it cuts up, root and branch, my favourite doctrine of perfection: and therefore let Peter, Paul, James, and John, say what they will, and let the reformers and martyrs join their syren song, their eyes were at best but half opened, (for want of a little Foundry eye salve,) therefore I cannot look upon them as adult believers in Jesus Christ.

"J. F."

"J. W."

"W. S."

These initial letters probably stand for John Fletcher, John Wesley, and Walter Sellon. As Mr. Hill seems to level his witty creed at me first, I shall first make my observations upon it. The van, without the main body and the rear, may perhaps make a proper stand against that gentleman's mistake: a dangerous mistake this, which is inseparably connected with the doctrine of a purgatory little better than that of the Papists; it being evident that if we cannot be purged from the remains of sin in this life, we must be purged from them in death, or after death; or we must be banished from God's presence; for reason and Scripture jointly depose that "nothing unholy or unclean shall enter into the heavenly Jerusalem."

If we understand by *purgatory,* the manner in which souls, still polluted with the remains of sin, are, or may be *purged* from these remains, that they may see a holy God, and dwell with him for ever; the question, *Which is the true purgatory?* is by no means frivolous: for it is the grand inquiry, *How shall I be eternally saved?* proposed in different expressions.

There are four opinions concerning *purgatory,* or the *purgation* of souls from the remains of sin. The wildest is that of the heathens, who supposed "that the souls, who depart this life with some moral filth cleaving to them, are purified by being hanged out to sharp, cutting winds; by being plunged into a deep, impetuous whirlpool; or being thrown into a refining fire in some Tartarean region;" witness these lines of Virgil: —

> Alioe panduntur inanes
> Suspensoe ad ventos: aliis sub gurgite vasto
> Infectum eluitur scelus, aut exuritur igni.

The second opinion is that of the Romanists, who teach that such souls are completely sanctified by the virtue of Christ's blood, and the sharp operation of a penal, temporary fire in the suburbs of hell. The third opinion is that of the Calvinists, who think that the stroke of death must absolutely be joined with Christ's blood and Spirit, and with our faith, to cleanse the thoughts of our hearts, and to kill the inbred man of sin.

The last sentiment is that of the Church of England, which teaches that there is no other purgatory but "Christ's blood," — "steadfast, perfect faith;" and "the inspiration of God's Holy Spirit, cleansing the thoughts of our hearts, that we may perfectly love him, and worthily magnify his holy name." "The only purgatory, wherein we must trust to be saved," says she, "is the death and blood of Christ, which, if we apprehend with a true and steadfast faith, [called soon after 'a perfect faith,'] it purgeth and cleanseth us from all our sins. 'The blood of Christ,' says St. John, 'hath cleansed us from all sin.' 'The blood of Christ,' says St. Paul, 'hath purged our consciences from dead works to serve the living God,' &c. This then is the purgatory wherein all Christian men put their trust and confidence." (*Homily on Prayer,* part 3.)

Nor is this doctrine of purgatory peculiar to the Church of England; for the unprejudiced Puritans themselves maintained it in the last century. Mr. R. Alleine, in his excellent treatise on *Godly Fear*, printed in London, 1674, says, page 161, "The Lord Christ is sometimes resembled to a refining fire, &c. 'He is a refiner's fire, and he shall sit as a refiner and purifier of silver.' He shall purify, 'he shall save his people from their sins,' yet so as by fire. God has his purgatory as well as his hell; though not according to that popish dream, a purgatory after this life." And I beg leave to add, — though not according to that Calvinian dream, a purgatory when we leave this life,— a purgatory in the article of death.

The Scriptural doctrine of purgatory is vindicated, and the newfangled doctrine of a death purgatory is exploded in the following pages: wherein I endeavour both to defend "the glorious liberty of the children of God," and to attack the false liberty of those "who, while they promise liberty to others in Christ, are themselves [doctrinally at least] the servants of corruption;" pleading hard for the indwelling of sin in our hearts so long as we live; and thinking it almost "blasphemous" to assert that Christ's blood, fully applied by the Spirit, through a steadfast faith, can radically "cleanse us from all sin," without the least assistance from the arrows or sweats of death.

Reader, I plead for the most precious liberty in the world, heart liberty; for liberty from the most galling of all yokes, the yoke of heart corruption. Let not thy prejudices turn a deaf ear to the important plea. If thou candidly, believingly, and practically receive "the truth as it is in Jesus, it shall make thee free, and thou shalt be free indeed." Then, instead of shouting, "Indwelling sin and death purgatory," thou wilt fulfil the law of liberty; shouting, "Christ and Christian liberty for ever!" In the meantime, when thou makest intercession for thy well wishers, remember the author of this essay, and pray that he may plead on his knees against the remains of sin, far more earnestly than he does in these sheets against Mr. Hill's mistakes.

THE

LAST CHECK TO ANTINOMIANISM.

SECTION I.

The best way of opposing the doctrines of Christian imperfection and a death purgatory, is to place the doctrine of Christian perfection in a proper light — Christian perfection is the maturity of a believer's grace under the Gospel of Christ — It is absurd to suppose that this perfection is sinless, if it be measured by our Creator's law of paradisiacal innocence and obedience — Established believers fulfil our Redeemer's evangelical law of liberty — While they fulfil it, they do not transgress it, that is, (evangelically speaking,) they do not sin.

MOST of the controversies, which arise between men who fear God, spring from the hurry with which some of them find fault with what they have not yet examined, and speak evil of what they do not understand. Why does Mr. Hill, at the head of the Calvinists, attack the doctrine of Christian perfection which we contend for? Is it because he and they are sworn enemies to righteousness, and zealous protectors of iniquity? Not at all. The grand reason, next to their Calvinian prejudice, is their inattention to the question, and to the arguments by which our sentiments are supported. Notwithstanding the manner in which that gentleman has treated me and my friends in his controversial heats, I still entertain so good an opinion of him as to think that if he understood our doctrine, he would no more pour contempt upon it, than upon the oracles of God. I shall, therefore, endeavour to rectify his ideas of the glorious Christian liberty which we press after. If producing light is the best method of opposing darkness, setting the doctrine of Christian perfection in a proper point of view will be the best means of opposing the doctrines of Christian imperfection, and of a death purgatory. Begin we then by taking a view of our Jerusalem and her perfection: and when we shall have "marked her bulwarks," and cleared the ground between her towers and Mr. Hill's battery, we shall march up to it, and see whether his arguments have the solidity of brass, or only the showy appearance of wooden artillery, painted and mounted like brazen ordnance.

CHRISTIAN PERFECTION! Why should the harmless phrase offend us? *Perfection!* Why should that lovely word frighten us? Is it not common and plain? Did not Cicero speak intelligibly when he called *accomplished* philosophers PERFECTOS *philosophos,* and an EXCELLENT orator PERFECTUM *oratorem?* Did Ovid expose his reputation when he said that "Chiron* *perfected* Achilles in music," or "taught him to play on the lute to *perfection?*" And does Mr. Hill think it wrong to observe that fruit *grown to maturity* is in its perfection? We, whom that gentleman calls perfectionists, use

---

* Phillyrides puerum cithara *perfecit* Achillem.

the word* *perfection* exactly in the same sense; giving that name to the maturity of grace peculiar to established believers under their respective dispensations; and if this be an error, we are led into it by the sacred writers, who use the word *perfection* as well as we.

The word *predestinate* occurs but four times in all the Scriptures, and the word *predestination* not once; and yet Mr. Hill would justly exclaim against us, if we showed our wit by calling for "a little *Foundry* [or *Tabernacle*] eye salve," to help us to see the word *predestination* once in all the Bible. Not so the word *perfection:* it occurs, with all its derivatives, as frequently as most words in the Scriptures, and not seldom in the very same sense in which we take it. Nevertheless, we do not lay an undue stress upon the expression; and if we thought that our condescension would answer any good end, we would entirely give up that harmless and significant word. But, if it is expedient to retain the *unscriptural* word *trinity,* because it is a kind of watchword by which we frequently discover the secret opposers of the mysterious distinction of Father, Son, and Holy Ghost in the Divine unity, how much more proper is it not to renounce the *Scriptural* word *perfection,* by which the dispirited spies, who bring an evil report upon the good land of holiness, are often detected? Add to this that the following declaration of our Lord does not permit us to renounce either the word or the thing:— "Whosoever shall be ashamed of me, and of my words, in this sinful generation, of him also shall the Son of man be ashamed, when he cometh in the glory of his Father." Now the words of my motto, "Be ye perfect," &c, being Christ's own words, we dare no more be ashamed of them, than we dare desire him to be ashamed of us in the great day. Thus much for the word *perfection.*

Again: we give the name of "Christian perfection" to that maturity of grace and holiness which established adult believers attain to under the Christian dispensation: and thus we distinguish that maturity of grace, both from the ripeness of *grace,* which belongs to the dispensation of *the Jews below us;* and from the ripeness of *glory,* which belongs to *departed saints above us.* Hence it appears, that by "Christian perfection" we mean nothing but the cluster and maturity of the graces which compose the Christian character in the Church militant.

In other words, Christian perfection is a spiritual constellation made up of these gracious stars, perfect repentance, perfect faith, perfect humility, perfect meekness, perfect self denial, perfect resignation, perfect hope, perfect charity for our *visible* enemies, as well as for our *earthly* relations; and, above all, perfect love for our *invisible* God, through the explicit knowledge of our Mediator Jesus Christ. And as this last

---

* The word *perfection* comes from the Latin *perficio,* to *perfect,* to *finish,* to *accomplish;* it exactly answers to the words םמת, and τελειοω, generally used in the Old and New Testament. Nor can their derivatives be more literally and exactly rendered, than by *perfect* and *perfection.* If our translators render sometimes the word םת by *upright* and *sincere,* or by *sincerity* and *integrity,* it is because they know that these expressions, like the original word, admit of a great latitude. Thus Columel calls wood that has no rotten part, and is perfectly sound, *lignum sincerum;* and Horace says that a sweet cask, which has no bad smell of any sort, is *vas sincerum.* Thus also Cicero calls purity of diction, which is perfectly free from faults against grammar, *integritas sermonis:* Plautus says that a pure, undefiled virgin is *filia integra.* And our translators call the perfectly pure milk of God's word, *the sincere milk of the word,* 1 Peter 2:2. If, therefore, the words *sincerity* and *integrity* are taken in their full latitude, they convey the fullest meaning of תמה , and τελειοτή, that is, perfection.

star is always accompanied by all the others, as Jupiter is by his satellites, we frequently use, as St. John, the phrase "perfect love," instead of the word *perfection;* understanding by it the pure love of God shed abroad in the hearts of established believers by the Holy Ghost, which is abundantly given them under the fulness of the Christian dispensation.

Should Mr. Hill ask if the Christian perfection which we contend for, is a *sinless* perfection, we reply, Sin is the transgression of a Divine law, and man may be considered either as being under the *anti-evangelical, Christless, remediless law of our Creator;* or, as being under *the evangelical, mediatorial, remedying law of our Redeemer:* and the question must be answered according to the nature of these two laws.

With respect to the FIRST, that is, the Adamic, Christless law of innocence and paradisiacal perfection, we utterly renounce the doctrine of sinless perfection, for three reasons: (1.) We are conceived and born in a state of sinful degeneracy, whereby *that* law is already virtually broken. (2.) Our mental and bodily powers are so enfeebled, that we cannot help actually breaking *that* law in numberless instances, even after our full conversion. And, (3.) When once we have broken *that* law, it considers us as transgressors for ever: nor can it any more pronounce us *sinless,* than the rigorous law which condemns a man to be hanged for murder, can absolve a murderer, let his repentance and faith be ever so perfect. Therefore, I repeat it, with respect to the Christless law of paradisiacal obedience, we entirely disclaim *sinless* perfection; and, improperly speaking, we say with Luther, "In every good work the just man sinneth;" that is, he more or less transgresses the law of paradisiacal innocence, by not thinking so deeply, not speaking so gracefully, not acting so properly, not obeying so vigorously, as he would do if he were still endued with original perfection, and paradisiacal powers. Nor do we, *in the same sense,* scruple to say with Bishop Latimer, "He [Christ] saved us, not that we should be without sin; that no sin should be left in our hearts: no; he saved us not so. For *all manner of imperfections* remain in us, yea, in the best of us: so that, if God should enter into judgment with us, [according to the Christless law given to Adam before the fall,] we should be damned. For there neither is nor was any man born into this world, who could say, I am clean from sin, [I fulfil the Adamic law of innocence,] except Jesus Christ:" and in that sense we have all reason to pray with David, "Cleanse thou me from my secret faults;" for "if thou wilt mark what is done amiss, Lord, who may abide it?" If thou wilt judge us according to the law of paradisiacal perfection, "what man living shall be justified in thy sight?" But Christ has so completely fulfilled our Creator's paradisiacal law of innocence, which allows neither of repentance nor of renewed obedience, that we shall not be judged by *that* law, but by a law adapted to our present state and circumstances, a milder law, called "the law of Christ," i.e. the Mediator's law, which is, like himself, "full of *evangelical* grace and truth."

To the many arguments which I have advanced in the Checks in defence of *this* law, I shall add one more, taken from Hebrews 7:12: — "The priesthood being changed, there is made of necessity a change also of the law." From these words I conclude, that if the law under which the Jews were, was of necessity changed when God substituted the priesthood of Christ for that of Aaron, much more was the Adamic law of paradisiacal innocence of necessity changed, when God gave to Adam by promise "the Bruiser of the serpent's head, the High Priest after the order of Melchisedec." For if a change in the external priesthood of necessity implied a change of the Mosaic law, how much more did the institution of the priesthood itself necessarily imply a change of the Adamic law, which was given without any mediating priest!

If Mr. Hill, therefore, will do our doctrine justice, we entreat him to consider that "we are not without law to God," nor yet under a Christless law with Adam; but "under a law to Christ," that is, under the law of our royal Priest, the evangelical "law of liberty:" a more gracious law this, which allows a sincere repentance, and is fulfilled by loving faith. Now as we shall be "judged by this law of liberty," we maintain not only that it *may,* but also that it *must* be kept; and that it is actually kept by established Christians, according to the last and fullest edition of it, which is that of the New Testament. Nor do we think it "shocking," to hear an adult believer say, "The law of the Spirit of life in Christ Jesus hath made me free from the law of sin and death. For what the law [of innocence, or the letter of the Mosaic law] could not do, in that it was weak through the flesh, God, sending his own Son, condemned sin in the flesh, that the righteousness of the law might be [evangelically] fulfilled in us who walk not after the flesh, but after the Spirit," Romans 8:2, &c.

Reason and Scripture seem to us to confirm this doctrine: for we think it is far less absurd to say that the king and parliament make laws which no Englishman can possibly keep; than to suppose that Christ and his apostles have given us precepts which no Christian is able to observe: and St. James assures us the evangelical law of Christ and liberty is that by which we shall stand or fall in judgment: "So speak ye, and so do," says he, "as they that shall be judged by the law of liberty," James 2:12. We find the Christian edition of that law, in all parts of the New Testament, but especially in our Lord's sermon on the mount, and in St. Paul's description of charity. We are persuaded, with St. John and St. Paul, that as "sin is the transgression," so penitential, pure "love is the fulfilling of *that evangelical* law;" and therefore do not scruple to say with the apostle, "that he who loveth another hath fulfilled it; and that there is no occasion of stumbling, i.e. no sin in him;" *fulfilling the law* of Christ, and *sinning,* (in the evangelical sense of the word,) being as diametrically opposite to each other as *obeying and disobeying,* working righteousness and working iniquity.

We do not doubt but, as a reasonable, loving father never requires of his child, who is only ten years old, the work of one who is thirty years of age; so our heavenly Father never expects of us, in our debilitated state, the obedience of immortal Adam in paradise, or the uninterrupted worship of sleepless angels in heaven. We are persuaded, therefore, that, for Christ's sake, he is pleased with an humble obedience to our present light; and a loving exertion of our present powers; accepting our Gospel services "according to what we have, and not according to what we have not." Nor dare we call that loving exertion of our present power, sin, lest by doing so we should contradict the Scriptures, confound sin and obedience, and remove all the landmarks which divide the devil's common from the Lord's vineyard. And if at any time we have exaggerated the difficulty of keeping Christ's law, we acknowledge our error, and confess that, by this mean, we have Calvinistically traduced the equity of our gracious God, and inadvertently encouraged the Antinomian delusions.

To conclude. We believe, that although adult, established believers, or perfect Christians, may admit of many involuntary mistakes, errors, and faults; and of many involuntary improprieties of speech and behaviour; yet so long as their will is bent upon doing God's will; so long as they walk not after the flesh, but after the Spirit; so long as they fulfil the law of liberty by pure love, they do not *sin* according to the Gospel: because (evangelically speaking) "sin is the transgression, and love is the fulfilling of that law." Far then from thinking that there is the least absurdity in saying daily, "Vouchsafe to keep me this day without sin," we doubt not but in the believers, who "walk in the light as Christ is in the light," that deep petition is answered, — the righteousness of the law, which they are under, is fulfilled; and, of consequence, an evangelically *sinless* perfection is daily experienced. I say *evangelically sinless*, because, without the word *evangelically*, the phrase "sinless perfection" gives an occasion of caviling to those who seek it, as Mr. Wesley intimates in the following quotation, which is taken from his "Plain Account of Christian Perfection," p. 60:— "To explain myself a little farther on this head: (1.) Not only sin, *properly* so called, that is, a *voluntary* transgression of a known law; but sin, *improperly* so called, that is, an *involuntary* transgression of a Divine law, known or unknown, needs the atoning blood. (2.) I believe there is no such perfection in this life as excludes these *involuntary* transgressions which I apprehend to be naturally consequent on the ignorance and mistakes inseparable from mortality. (3.) Therefore *sinless perfection* is a phrase I never use, lest I should seem to contradict myself. (4.). I believe a person filled with the love of God is still liable to these involuntary transgressions. (5.) Such transgressions you may call *sins* if you please: I do not, for the reasons above mentioned."

SECTION II.

Pious Calvinists have had, at times, nearly the same views of Christian perfection as we have — They dissent from us chiefly because they confound the anti-evangelical law of innocence, and the evangelical law of liberty; Adamic and Christian perfection; and because they do not consider that Christian perfection, falling infinitely short of God's absolute perfection, admits of a daily growth.

IF it were necessary, we could support the doctrine of Christian perfection stated in the preceding pages, by almost numberless quotations from the most judicious and pious Calvinists, the sentiments of two or three of them may edify the reader, and give him a specimen of the candour with which they have written upon the subject, when a springtide of evangelical truth raised them above the shallows of their system.

"If love be sincere," says pious Mr. Henry, "it is accepted as the fulfilling of the law. Surely we serve a good Master, that has summed up all our duty in one word, and that a short word, and a sweet word, *love*, the beauty and harmony of the universe. Loving and being loved is all the pleasure, joy, and happiness of an intelligent being. God is love; and love is his image upon the soul. Where it is, the soul is well moulded, and the heart fitted for every good work." (*Henry's Exposition on Romans* 13:10.) Again: "It is well for us that, by virtue of the covenant of grace, upon the score of Christ's righteousness, *sincerity* is accepted as our Gospel perfection." (*Henry on Genesis* 6:2.) See the note on the word *perfection*, sec. 1.

Pious Bishop Hopkins is exactly of the same mind. "Consider," says he, "for your encouragement, that this is not so much the absolute and legal perfection of the work, as the [evangelical] perfection of the worker, that is, the perfection of the heart, which is looked at and rewarded by God. There is a twofold perfection, the perfection of the work, and that of the workman. The perfection of the work is, when the work does so exactly and strictly answer the holy law of God, that there is no irregularity in it. The perfection of the workman is nothing but inward sincerity and uprightness of the heart toward God, which may be where there are many imperfections and defects intermingled. If God accepted and rewarded no work, but what is absolutely perfect in respect of the law; this would take off the wheels of all endeavours, for our obedience falls far short of legal perfection in this life; [the Adamic law making no allowance for the weakness of fallen man.] But we do not stand upon such terms as these with our God. It is not so much what our works are, as what our heart is, that God looks at and will reward. Yet know, also, that if our hearts are perfect and sincere, we shall endeavour, to the utmost of our power, that our works may be perfect, according to the strictness of the law."

Archbishop Leighton pleads also for the perfection we maintain, and by Calvinistically supposing that perseverance is necessary to Christian perfection, he extols it above Adam's paradisiacal perfection. Take his own words abridged:— "By obedience, sanctification is here intimated: it signifies both habitual and actual obedience, renovation of the heart, and conformity to the Divine will: the mind is illuminated by the Holy Ghost to know and believe the Divine will; yea, this faith is the great and chief part of this obedience, Romans 1:8. The truth of the doctrine is impressed upon the mind, hence flows out pleasant obedience and full [he does not say *of sin,* but] of love: hence all the affections, and the whole body with its members, learn to give a willing obedience, and submit to God; whereas before they resisted him, being under the standard of Satan. This obedience, though imperfect, [when it is measured by the Christless law of paradisiacal innocence] yet has a certain, if I may so say, *imperfect perfection.* [It is not *legally* but *evangelically* perfect.] It is universal [or *perfect*] three manner of ways. (1.) In the subject: it is not in the tongue alone, or in the hand, &c, but has its root in the heart. (2.) In the object: it embraces the whole law, &c. It accounts no command little, which is from God, because he is great and highly esteemed; no command hard, though contrary to the flesh, because all things are easy to love; there is the same authority in all, as St. James Divinely argues. And this authority is the golden chain to all the commandments, [of the law of liberty preached by St. James,] which, if broken in any link, falls to pieces. (3.) In the duration: the whole man is subjected to the whole law, and that constantly. That this threefold perfection of obedience is not a picture drawn by fancy, is evident in David, Psalm 119." (*Archbishop Leighton's Com. on St. Peter,* p. 15.)

That learned prelate, as a *pious man,* could not but be a perfectionist; though, as *a Calvinist,* he frequently spoke the language of the imperfectionists. Take one more quotation, where he grants all that we contend for: — "To be subject to him [God] is truer happiness than to command the whole world. Pure love reckons thus, though no farther reward were to follow; obedience to God (the perfection of his creature, and its very happiness) carries its full recompense in its own bosom. Yea, love delights most in the hardest services, &c. It is love to him, indeed, to love the labour of love, and the service of it; and that not so much because it leads to rest, and ends in it, but because it is service to him Whom we love: yea, that labour is in itself a rest, it is so natural and sweet to a soul that loves. As the revolution of the heavens, which is a motion in rest, and rest in motion, changes not place, though running still; so the motion of love is truly heavenly, and circular still in God; beginning in him, and ending in him; and so not ending, but moving still without weariness, &c. According as the love is, so is the soul: it is made like to, yea, it is made one with that which it loves, &c. By the love of God it is made Divine, is one with him, &c. Now though fallen from this, we are invited to it; though degenerated and accursed in sinful nature, yet we are renewed in Christ, and this commandment is renewed in him, and a new way of fulfilling it [even the way of faith in our Redeemer] is pointed out." (*Select Works of Archbishop Leighton*, p. 461.) Where has Mr. Wesley ever exceeded this high description of Christian perfection?

I grant that this pious prelate frequently confounds our celestial perfection of glory with our progressive perfection of grace, and on that account supposes that the latter is not attainable in this life: but even then he exhorts us to quit ourselves like sincere perfectionists. "Though men," says he, "fall short of their aim, yet it is good to aim high. They shall shoot so much the higher, but not full so high as they aim. Thus we ought to be setting the state of perfection in our eye, resolving* not to rest content below that, and to come as near as we can, even before we come at it, Philippians 3:11, 12. This is to act as one that has such a hope, such a state in view, and is still advancing toward it." (*Ibid.* p. 184.) The mistake of the archbishop will be particularly pointed out where I shall show the true meaning of Philippians 3:11, the passage behind which he screens the remains of his Calvinian prejudices.

By the preceding quotations, and by two more from the Rev. Messrs. Whitefield and Romaine, which the reader will find at the end of sec. ix, it appears that pious Calvinists come *at times* very near the doctrine of Christian perfection; and if they do not constantly enforce it, it is, we apprehend, chiefly for the following reasons: —

1. They generally confound the *Christless law of innocence* with the *evangelical law of Christ;* and because the former cannot be fulfilled by believers, they conclude that pure obedience to the latter is impracticable.

2. They confound *peccability* with *sin;* the power of sinning with the actual use of that power. And so long as they suppose that a bare natural capacity to sin, is either original sin, or an evil propensity, we do not wonder at their believing that original sin, or evil propensities, must remain in our hearts till death removes us from this tempting world. But on what argument do they found this notion? Did not God create angels and man peccable? Or, in other terms, did he not endue them with a power to sin, or not to sin, to disobey, or obey, as they pleased? Did not the event show that they had this tremendous power? But would it not be "blasphemous" to assert that God created them full of original sin and evil propensities? If an adult

---

* I think I have said in one of the Checks that Archbishop Leighton doubted whether those who do not sincerely aspire after perfection, have saving grace: that doubt (if I now remember right) is Mr. Alleine's, though this quotation from the archbishop shows that he was not far from Alleine's sentiment, if he was not in it. Pious Dr. Doddridge is explicit on this head: — "To allow yourself," said he, "deliberately to sit down satisfied with any imperfect attainments in religion, and to look upon a more confirmed and improved state of it as what you do not desire, nay, as what you secretly resolve that you will not pursue, is one of the most fatal signs we can well imagine, that you are an entire stranger to the first principles of it." (*Doddridge's Rise and Progress,* chap. 20.)

believer yields to temptation, and falls into sin as our first parents did, is it a proof that he never was cleansed from inbred sin? If sinning necessarily demonstrates that the heart was always teeming with depravity, will it not follow that Adam and Eve were tainted with sin *before* their will began to decline from original righteousness? Is it not, however, indubitable, from the nature of God, from Scripture, and from sad experience, that after having been created in God's *sinless* image and holy likeness, our first parents, as well as some angels, were "drawn away of their own *selfconceited* lust," and became evil by the power of their own free agency? Is it reasonable to think that the most holy Christians, so long as the day of their visitation and probation lasts in this tempting wilderness, are in that respect above Adam in paradise, and above angels in heaven? And may we not conclude that as Satan and Adam insensibly fell into sin, the one from the height of his celestial perfection, and the other from the summit of his paradisiacal excellence, without any previous bias inclining him to corruption; so may those believers, whose hearts have been completely purified by faith, gradually depart from the faith, and fall so low as to "account the blood of the covenant, wherewith they were sanctified, an unholy thing?"

3. The prejudices of our opponents are increased by their confounding Adamic[*] and Christian perfection; two perfections, these, which are as distinct as the garden of Eden and the Christian Church. Adamic perfection came from God our Creator in paradise, before any trial of Adam's faithful obedience: and Christian perfection comes from God our Redeemer and Sanctifier in the Christian Church, after a severe trial of the obedience of faith. Adamic perfection might be lost by doing despite to the preserving love of God our Creator; and Christian perfection may be lost by doing despite to the redeeming love of God our Saviour. Adamic perfection extended to the whole man: his body was perfectly sound in all its parts, and his soul in all its powers. But Christian perfection extends chiefly to the will, which is the capital, moral power of the soul; leaving the understanding ignorant of ten thousand things, and the body "dead because of sin."

4. Another capital mistake lies at the root of the opposition which our Calvinian brethren make against Christian perfection. They imagine that, upon our principles, the grace of an adult Christian is like the body of an adult man, which can grow no more. But this consequence flows from their fancy, and not from our doctrine. We

---

[*] Between Adamic and Christian perfection we place the gracious *innocence* of little children. They are not only full of peccability like Adam, but debilitated in all their animal and rational faculties, and, of consequence, fit to become an easy prey to temptation, through the weakness of their reason, and the corruption of their concupiscible and irascible powers. Nevertheless, till they begin personally to prefer moral evil to moral good, we may consider them as evangelically or graciously innocent. I say *graciously innocent,* because, if we consider them in the seed of fallen Adam, we find them naturally "children of wrath," and under the curse: but if we consider them "in the seed of the woman," which was promised to Adam and to his posterity, we find them graciously placed in a state of redemption and evangelical salvation. For "the free gift which is come upon all men to justification," belongs first to them, Christ having sanctified infancy first. And therefore we do not scruple to say, after our Lord, "Of such is the kingdom of heaven." Now the kingdom of heaven is not of sinners as *sinners,* but of little children, *as being innocent* through the free gift; or of adults, *as being penitent,* that is, turned from their sins to Christ.

exhort the strongest believers to "grow up to Christ in all things;" asserting that there is no holiness and no happiness in heaven, (much less upon earth,) which does not admit of a growth; except the holiness and happiness of God himself; because, in the very nature of things, a being absolutely perfect, and in every sense infinite, can never have any thing added to him. But infinite additions may be made to beings every way finite, such as glorified saints and holy angels are.

Hence it appears that the comparison which we make between the ripeness of a fruit, and the maturity of a believer's grace, cannot be carried into an exact parallel. For a perfect Christian grows far more than a feeble believer, whose growth is still obstructed by the shady thorns of sin, and by the draining suckers of iniquity. Beside, a fruit which is come to its perfection) instead of growing, falls and decays: whereas a "babe in Christ" is called to grow till he becomes a perfect Christian; a perfect Christian, till he becomes a disembodied spirit; a disembodied spirit, till he reaches the perfection of a saint glorified in body and soul; and such a saint, till he has fathomed the infinite depths of Divine perfection, that is, to all eternity. For if we go on from faith to faith, and are spiritually "changed from glory to glory," by beholding God "darkly through a glass" on earth; much more shall we experience improving changes, when we shall "see him as he is," and behold him face to face in various, numberless, and still brighter discoveries of himself in heaven. If Mr. Hill did but consider this, he would no more suppose that Christian perfection is the Pharisaic rickets which put a stop to the growth of believers, and turn them into "temporary monsters." Again: —

Does a well-meant mistake defile the conscience? You inadvertently encourage idleness and drunkenness, by kindly relieving an idle, drunken beggar, who imposes upon your charity by plausible lies: is this loving error a sin? A blundering apothecary sends you arsenic for alum; you use it as alum, and poison your child; but are you a murderer, if you give the fatal dose in love? Suppose the tempter had secretly mixed some of the forbidden fruit with other fruits that Eve had lawfully gathered for use; would she have *sinned* if she had inadvertently eaten of it, and given a share to her husband? After humbly confessing and deploring her undesigned error, her *secret* fault, her *accidental* offence, her *involuntary* trespass, would she not have been as innocent as ever? I go farther still, and ask, May not a man who holds many *right* opinions, be a perfect lover of the world? And by a parity of reason, may not a man who holds many wrong opinions, be a perfect lover of God? Have not some Calvinists died with their hearts overflowing with perfect love, and their heads full of the notion that God set his everlasting, absolute hatred upon myriads of men before the foundation of the world? Nay, is it not even possible that a man, whose heart is renewed in love, should, through mistaken humility, or through weakness of understanding, oppose the name of *Christian perfection*, when he desires, and perhaps enjoys *the thing?*

Once more Does not St. Paul's rule hold in spirituals as well as in temporals? "It is accepted according to what a man hath, and not according to what he hath not." Does our Lord actually require more of believers than they can actually do through his grace? And when they do it to the best of their power, does he not see some perfection in their works, insignificant as those works may be? "Remove this immense heap of stones," says an indulgent father to his children, "and be diligent according to your strength." While the eldest, a strong man, removes rocks, the youngest, a little child, is as cheerfully busy as any of the rest in carrying sands and pebbles. Now, may not his *childlike* obedience be as excellent in its degree, and, of consequence, as acceptable to his parent, as the *manly* obedience of his eldest brother? Nay, though he does next to nothing, may not his endeavours, if they are more cordial, excite a smile of *superior* approbation of his loving father, who looks at the disposition of the heart more than at the appearance of the work? Had the believers of Sardis cordially laid out *all* their talents, would our Lord have complained that he did not "find their works perfect before God?" Revelation 3:2. And was it not according to this rule of perfection that Christ testified the poor widow, who had given but *two mites*, had nevertheless cast more into the treasury than all the rich, "though they had cast in much;" because, our Lord himself being Judge, she had "given all that she had?" Now could she give, or did God require more than her *all?* And when she thus heartily gave her all, did she not do (evangelically speaking) a perfect work, according to her dispensation and circumstances? We flatter ourselves that if these Scriptural observations and rational queries do not remove Mr. Hill's prejudice, they will at least make way for a more candid perusal of the following pages.

SECTION III.

Several objections raised against our doctrine are solved merely by considering the nature of Christian perfection — It is absurd to say that all our Christian perfection is in the person of Christ.

I REPEAT it, if our pious opponents decry the doctrine of Christian perfection, it is chiefly through misapprehension; it being as natural for pious men to recommend exalted piety, as for covetous persons to extol great riches. And this misapprehension frequently springs from their inattention to the nature of Christian perfection. To prove it, I need only oppose our definition of Christian perfection to the OBJECTIONS which are most commonly raised against our doctrine.

I. "Your doctrine of perfection leads to pride." Impossible! if Christian perfection is "perfect humility."

II. "It exalts believers; but it is only to the state of the vain-glorious Pharisee." Impossible! If our perfection is "perfect humility," it makes us sink deeper into the state of the humble, justified publican.

III. "It fills men with the conceit of their own excellence, and makes them say to a weak brother, *Stand by, I am holier than thou.*" Impossible again! We do not preach Pharisaic, but Christian perfection, which consists in "perfect poverty of spirit," and in that "perfect charity which vaunteth not itself, honours all men, and bears with the infirmities of the weak!"

IV. "It sets repentance aside." Impossible! for it is "perfect repentance."

V. "It will make us slight Christ." More and more improbable! How can "perfect faith" in Christ make us slight Christ? Could it be more absurd to say that the perfect love of God will make us despise God?

VI. "It will supersede the use of mortification and watchfulness; for, if sin be dead, what need have we to mortify it and to watch against it?"

This objection has some plausibility; I shall therefore answer it in various ways: (1.) If Adam, in his state of paradisiacal perfection, needed perfect watchfulness and perfect mortification, how much more do we need them who find "the tree of the knowledge of good and evil" planted, not only in the midst of our gardens, but in the midst of our houses, markets, and churches? (2.) When we are delivered from sin, are we delivered from peccability and temptation? When the inward man of sin is dead, is the devil dead? Is the corruption that is in the world destroyed? And have we not still our five senses and our appetite, "to keep with all diligence," as well as our "hearts," that the tempter may not enter into us, or that we may not enter into his temptations? Lastly: Jesus Christ, as son of Mary, was a perfect man: but how was he kept so to the end? Was it not by "keeping his mouth with a bridle, while the ungodly were in his sight," and by guarding all his senses with a perfect assiduity, that the wicked one might not touch them to his hurt? And if Christ our head kept his human perfection only through watchfulness, and constant self denial; is it not absurd to suppose that his perfect members can keep their perfection without treading in his steps?

VII. Another objection probably stands in Mr. Hill's way: it runs thus:— "Your doctrine of perfection makes it needless for perfect Christians to say the Lord's prayer: for if God vouchsafes to 'keep us this day without sin,' we shall have no need to pray at night, that God would 'forgive us our trespasses, as we forgive them that trespass against us.'"

We answer: (1.) Though a perfect Christian does not trespass voluntarily, and break the law of love, yet he daily breaks the law of Adamic perfection through the imperfection of his bodily and mental powers: and he has frequently a deeper sense of these involuntary trespasses than many weak believers have of their voluntary breaches of the moral law. (2.) Although a perfect Christian has a witness, that his sins are now forgiven, in the court of his conscience, yet he "knows the terrors of the Lord:" he hastens to meet the awful day of God: he waits for the appearance of our Lord Jesus Christ, in the character of a righteous Judge: he keeps an eye to the awful tribunal, before which he must soon "be justified or condemned by his words:" he is conscious that his final justification is not yet come; and therefore he would think himself a monster of stupidity and pride, if, with an eye to his absolution in the great day, he scrupled saying to the end of his life, "Forgive us our trespasses." (3.) He is surrounded with sinners, who daily "trespass against him," and whom he is daily bound to "forgive;" and his praying that he may be forgiven now, and in the great day, "as he forgives others," reminds him that he may forfeit his pardon, and binds him more and more to the performance of the important duty of forgiving his enemies. And, (4.) His charity is so ardent that it melts him, as it were, into the common mass of mankind. Bowing himself, therefore, under all the enormous load of all the wilful trespasses which his fellow mortals, and particularly his relatives and his brethren, daily commit against God, he says, with a fervour that imperfect Christians seldom feel, *Forgive us our trespasses, &c;* "we are heartily sorry for our misdoings, [my own and those of my fellow sinners;] the remembrance of them is grievous unto us; the burthen of them is intolerable." Nor do we doubt but, when the spirit of mourning leads a numerous assembly of supplicants into the vale of humiliation, the person who puts the shoulder of faith most readily to the common burden of sin, and heaves most powerfully in order to roll the enormous load into the Redeemer's grave, is the most perfect penitent — the most exact observer of the apostolical precept, "Bear ye one another's burdens, and so fulfil the law of Christ;" and, of consequence, we do not scruple to say that such person is *the most perfect Christian* in the whole assembly.

If Mr. Hill consider these answers, we doubt not but he will confess that his opposition to Christian perfection chiefly springs from his inattention to our definition of it, which I once more sum up in these comprehensive lines of Mr. Wesley: —

> O let me gain perfection's height!
> O let me into nothing fall!
> (As less than nothing in thy sight,)
> And feel that Christ is all in all!

VIII. Our opponents produce another plausible objection, which runs thus: — "it is plain from your account of Christian perfection that adult believers are *free from sin*. their hearts being purified by perfect faith, and filled with perfect love. Now sin is that which humbles us, and drives us to Christ; and therefore, if we were free from indwelling sin, we should lose a most powerful incentive to humility, which is the greatest ornament of a true Christian."

We answer, Sin never humbled any soul. Who has more sin than Satan? And who is prouder? Did sin make our first parents humble? If it did not, how do our brethren suppose that its nature is altered for the better? Who was humbler than Christ? But was he indebted to sin for his humility? Do we not see daily that the more sinful men are, the prouder they are also? Did Mr. Hill never observe that the holier a believer is, the humbler he shows himself? And what is holiness but the *reverse of sin?* If sin be necessary to make us humble and keep us near Christ, does it not follow that glorified saints, whom all acknowledge to be sinless, are all proud despisers of Christ? If humility is obedience, and if sin is disobedience, is it not as absurd to say that sin will make us *humble, i.e. obedient,* as it is to affirm that rebellion will make us *loyal,* and adultery *chaste?* See we not sin enough, when we look ten or twenty years back, to humble us to the dust for ever, if sin can do it? Need we plead for any more of it in our hearts and lives? If the sins of our youth do not humble us, are the sins of our old age likely to do it? If we contend for the life of the man of sin that he may subdue our pride, do we not take a large stride after those who say, *Let us sin that grace may abound.* Let us continue full of indwelling sin that humility may increase! What is, after all, the evangelical method of getting humility? Is it not to look at Christ in the manger, in Gethsemane, or on the cross; to consider him when he washes his disciples' feet; and obediently to listen to him when he says, "Learn of me to be meek and lowly in heart?" Where does the Gospel plead the cause of the Barabbas, and the thieves within? Where does it say that they may indeed be nailed to the cross, and have "their legs broken," but their life must be left whole within them, lest we should be proud of their death? Lastly: what is indwelling sin but indwelling pride? At least, is not inbred pride one of the chief ingredients of indwelling sin? And how can pride be productive of humility? Can a serpent beget a dove? And will not men gather grapes from thorns, sooner than humility of heart from haughtiness of spirit?

IX. The strange mistake which I detect would not be so prevalent among our prejudiced brethren, if they were not deceived by the plausibility of the following argument: — "When believers are humbled *for* a thing, they are humbled by it: but believers are humbled *for* sin; and therefore they are humbled *by* sin."

The flaw of this argument is in the first proposition. We readily grant that penitents are humbled *for* sin; or, in other terms, that they humbly repent of sin; but we deny that they are humbled *by* sin. To show the absurdity of the whole argument, I need only produce a sophism exactly parallel: "When people are blooded for a thing, they are blooded *by* it: but people are sometimes blooded *for* a cold; and therefore people are sometimes blooded *by* a cold."

X. "We do not assert that all perfection is imaginary. Our meaning is, that all Christian perfection is *in Christ;* and that we are perfect in his person, and not in our own."

ANSWER. If you mean by our being *perfect only in Christ,* that we can attain to Christian perfection no other way, than by being perfectly grafted in him, the true vine; and by deriving, like vigorous branches, the perfect sap of his perfect righteousness, to enable us to bring forth fruit unto perfection, we are entirely agreed: for we perpetually assert that nothing but "Christ in us the hope of glory," nothing but "Christ dwelling in our hearts by faith," or, which is all one, nothing but "the law of the Spirit of life in Christ Jesus, can make us free from the law of sin, and perfect us in love."

But as we never advanced that Christian perfection is attainable any other way than by a faith that "roots and grounds us" in Christ, we doubt some mystery of iniquity lies hid under these equivocal phrases: "All our perfection is in Christ's person: we are perfect in him and not in ourselves."

Should those who use them insinuate by such language that we need not, cannot be perfect, by an inherent personal conformity to God's holiness, because Christ is thus perfect for us; or should they mean that we are perfect in him, just as country freeholders, entirely strangers to state affairs, are perfect politicians in the knights of the shire who represent them in parliament; as the sick in a hospital are perfectly. healthy in the physician that gives them his attendance; as the blind man enjoyed perfect sight in Christ, when he saw walking men like moving trees; as the filthy leper was perfectly clean in the Lord, before he had felt the power of Christ's gracious words, "I will, be thou clean;" or, as hungry Lazarus was perfectly fed in the person of the rich man, at whose gate he lay starving; should this, I say, be their meaning, we are in conscience bound to oppose it, for the reasons contained in the following queries: —

1. If believers are perfect, because Christ is perfect for them, why does the apostle exhort them to "go on to perfection?"

2. If all our perfection be inherent in Christ, is it not strange that St. Paul should exhort us to "perfect holiness in the fear of God, by cleansing ourselves from all filthiness of the flesh and spirit?" Did not Christ perfect his own holiness? And will his personal sanctity be imperfect, till we have cleansed ourselves from all defilement?

3. If Christ be perfect for us, why does St. James say, "Let patience have her perfect work," that ye may be perfect? Is Christ's perfection suspended upon the perfect work of our patience?

4. Upon the scheme which I oppose, what does St. Peter mean, when he says, "After ye have suffered awhile, the Lord make you perfect?" What has our suffering awhile to do with Christ's perfection? Was not Christ "made perfect through *his own* sufferings?"

5. If believers were perfect in Christ's person, they would all be equally perfect. But is this the case? Does not St. John talk of some who are perfected, and of others who "are not yet made perfect in love?" Beside, the apostle exhorts us to be perfect, not in Antinomian notions, but "in all the will of God, and in every good work;" and common sense dictates, that there is some difference between our good works and the person of Christ.

6. Does not our Lord himself show that his personal righteousness will by no means be accepted instead of our personal perfection, where he says, "Every branch in me that beareth not fruit, [or whose fruit never grows to any perfection, see Luke 8:14,] my Father taketh away," far from imputing to it his perfect fruitfulness?

7. In the nature of things can Christ's perfection supply the want of that perfection which he calls us to? Is there not a more essential difference between Christ's perfection and that of a believer, than there is between the perfection of a rose and that of the grass of the field? between the perfection of a soaring eagle, and that of a creeping insect? If our Lord is the head of the Church, and we are the members, is it not absurd to suppose that his perfection becomes us in every respect? Were I allowed to carry on a Scriptural metaphor, I would ask, Is not the perfection of the head very different from that of the hand? And do we not take advantage of the credulity of the simple, when we make them believe that an impenitent adulterer and murderer is perfect in Christ; or, if you please, that a crooked leg and cloven foot are perfectly handsome, if they do but somehow belong to a beautiful face?

8. Let us illustrate this a little more. Does not the Redeemer's personal perfection consist in his being GOD and MAN in one person; in his being *eternally begotten* by the Father as the "Son of God;" and *unbegotten* in time by a father, as "the son of man;" in his having "given his life a ransom for all;" in his having "taken it up again; and his standing in the midst of the throne, able to save to the uttermost all that come unto God through him?" Consider this, candid believer, and say if any man or angel can decently hope that such an incommunicable perfection can ever fall to his share.

9. As the Redeemer's personal perfection cannot suit the redeemed, no more can the personal perfection of the redeemed be found in the Redeemer. A believer's perfection consists in such a degree of faith as works by perfect love. And does not this high degree of faith chiefly imply uninterrupted self diffidence, self denial, self despair? A heartfelt, ceaseless recourse to the blood, merits, and righteousness of Christ? And a grateful love to him, "because he first loved us," and fervent charity toward all mankind "for his sake?" Three things, these, which, in the very nature of things, either cannot be in the Saviour at all, or cannot possibly be in him in the same manner in which they must be in believers.

10. Is not the doctrine of our being perfect in Christ's person big with mischief? Does it not open a refuge of lies to the loosest ranters in the land? Are there none who say, We are perfect in Christ's person? In him we have perfect chastity and honesty, perfect temperance and meekness; and we should be guilty of Pharisaic insolence if we patched his perfection with the filthy rags of our personal holiness?

And has not this doctrine a direct tendency to set godliness aside, and to countenance gross Antinomianism?

Lastly. When our Lord preached the doctrine of perfection, did he not do it in such a manner as to demonstrate that our perfection must be personal? Did he ever say, "*If thou wilt be perfect,* only believe that I am perfect for thee?" On the contrary, did he not declare, "If thou wilt be perfect, sell what thou hast; [part with all that stands in thy way;] and follow me" in the way of perfection? And again: "Do good to them that hate you, that ye may be the children of your Father who is in heaven; for he sendeth rain upon the just and the unjust, &c. Be ye therefore perfect, even as your Father who is in heaven is perfect?" Who can read these words and not see that the perfection which Christ preached, is a perfection of holy dispositions, productive of holy actions in all his followers? And that, of consequence, it is a personal perfection, as much *inherent* in us, and yet as much *derived* from him, and *dependent* upon him, as the perfection of our bodily health? The chief difference consisting in this, that the perfection of our health comes to us from God in Christ, as the God of NATURE; whereas our Christian perfection comes to us from God in Christ, as the God of GRACE.

SECTION IV.

Mr. Hill's first argument against Christian perfection is taken from the ninth and fifteenth articles of the Church of England — These articles, properly understood, are not contrary to that doctrine — That our Church holds it, is proved by thirteen arguments — She opposes Pharisaic, but not Christian perfection — Eight reasons are produced to show that it is absurd to embrace the doctrine of a death purgatory because our reformers and martyrs, in following after the perfection of humility, have used some unguarded expressions, which seem to bear hard upon the doctrine of Christian perfection.

IN the preceding sections I have laid the axe at the root of some prejudices, and cut up a variety of objections. The controversial field is cleared. The engagement may begin: nay, it is already begun; for Mr. Hill, in his *Creed for Perfectionists,* and Mr. Toplady, in his *Caveat against unsound Doctrines,* have brought up, and fired at our doctrine, two pieces of ecclesiastical artillery; — the ninth and fifteenth articles of our Church: and they conclude that the contents of these doctrinal cannons absolutely demolish the perfection we contend for. The report of their wrong-pointed ordnance, and the noise they make about our subscriptions are loud; but that we need not be afraid of the shot, will, I hope, appear from the following observations: —

The design of the fifteenth article of our Church is pointed out by the title, "Of Christ alone without Sin." From this title we conclude that the scope and design of the article is not to secure to Christ the honour of being *alone cleansed from sin;* because such an honour would be a reproach to his *original* and *uninterrupted* purity, which placed him far above the need of *cleansing.* Nor does the article drop the least hint about the impossibility of our being "cleansed from sin" before we go into the purgatory of the Calvinists: I mean the chambers of death. What our Church intends, is to distinguish Christ from all mankind, and especially from the Virgin Mary, whom the Papists assert to have been always totally free from original and actual sin. Our Church does this by maintaining, (1.) That Christ was born without the least taint of original sin, and never committed any actual transgression (2.) That all other men, the Virgin Mary and the most holy believers not excepted, are the very reverse of Christ in both these respects; all being conceived in original sin, and offending in many things, even after baptism,* and with all the helps which we have under the Christian dispensation to keep us "without sin" from day to day. And, therefore, (3.) That "if we say we have no sin;" if we pretend, like some Pelagians, that we have no *original sin;* or if we intimate, like some Pharisees, that "we never did any harm in all our lives," that is, that we have no *actual sin, "we* deceive ourselves, and the truth is not in us;" there being absolutely no adult person without sin in those respects, except our Lord Jesus Christ.

That this is the genuine sense of the article appears, (1.) By the absurdity which follows from the contrary sentiment. For if these words, "Christ alone without Sin," are to be taken in an absolute and unlimited sense; if the word *alone* entirely excludes all mankind, *at all times;* if it is levelled at our *being cleansed* from sin, as well as at our *having been always free* from original and actual pollution; if this is the case, I say, it is evident that not only fathers in Christ, but also Enoch and Elijah, St. John and St. Paul, are to this day tainted with sin, and must to all eternity continue so, lest Mr. Hill's opinion of *Christ alone without sin* should not be true.

2. Our sentiment is confirmed by the article itself, part of which runs thus: — "Christ, in the truth of our nature, was made like unto us in all things, sin only excepted, from which he was clearly void, both in his flesh and in his spirit. He came to be a Lamb without spot; and sin, as St. John says, was not in him. But all we the rest, although baptized and born again in Christ, [i.e. although we have from our infancy all the helps that the Christian dispensation affords men to keep them without sin,] yet we offend in many things, [after our baptism,] and if we say, [as the abovementioned Pelagians and Pharisees,] that we have no [original or actual] sin, [i.e. that we are like Christ, in either of these respects; our conception, infancy, childhood, youth, and age, being all taken into the account,] we deceive ourselves, and the truth is not in us."

Having thus opened the plain, rational, and Scriptural sense in which we subscribe to our fifteenth article, it remains to make a remark upon the ninth.

Some bigoted Pelagians deny original sin, or the Adamic infection of our nature; and some bigoted Papists suppose that this infection is entirely done away in baptism: in opposition to both these, our Church prudently requires our subscription to her ninth article, which asserts, (1.) That "the fault and corruption of our nature" is a melancholy reality: and, (2.) That this "fault, corruption, or infection doth remain in them who are regenerated;" that is, in them who are "baptized, or made children of

---

* The Rev. Mr. Toplady, in his Historic Proof, p. 235, informs us that a popish archbishop of St. Andrews condemned Patrick Hamilton to death, for holding among other doctrines, "That children incontinent after baptism are sinners," or, which is all one, that baptism does not absolutely take away original sin. This anecdote is important, and shows that our Church levels at a popish error the words of her articles, which Mr. Hill and Mr. Toplady suppose to be levelled at Christian perfection.

God," according to the Christian dispensation. For every person who has attentively read our liturgy, knows that these expressions, *baptized, regenerated,* and *made a member of Christ, and a child of God,* are synonymous in the language of our Church. Now, because we have acknowledged, by our subscription to our ninth article, that "the infection of our nature" is not done away in baptism, but "does remain in them which are regenerate," or baptized, Mr. Hill thinks himself authorized to impose upon us the yoke of indwelling sin for life; supposing that we cannot be fair subscribers to that article, unless we renounce the glorious liberty of God's children, and embrace the Antinomian gospel, which is summed up in these unguarded words of Luther, quoted by Bogatsky in his *Golden Treasury:** "The sins of a Christian are for his good, and if he had no sin, he would not be so well off; neither would prayer flow so well," Can any thing be either more unscriptural or absurd? What unprejudiced person does not see we may, with the greatest consistency, maintain that baptism does not remove the Adamic infection of sin, and that nevertheless this infection may be removed before death?

Nevertheless, we are willing to make Mr. Hill all the concessions we can, consistently with a good conscience. If by "the infection of nature, he understand the natural ignorance which has *infected* our understanding; the natural forgetfulness which has *affected* our memory; the inbred debility of all our mental powers, and the poisonous seeds of mortality which *infect* all men from head to foot, and hinder the strongest believers from serving God with all the fervour they would be capable of, were they not fallen from paradisiacal perfection, under the curse of a body sentenced to die, and "dead because of sin:" if Mr. Hill, I say, understand this by the "infection of nature," we believe that such an infection, with all the natural, innocent appetites of the flesh, remains, not only in those whom the Scriptures call "babes in Christ," but also in "fathers;" there being no adult believer that may not say, as well as Christ, Adam, or St. Paul, "I thirst. I am hungry. I want a help-meet for me. I know but in part. I see darkly through a glass. I groan, being burdened. He that marrieth sinneth not. It is better to marry than to burn," &c.

But if Mr. Hill, by "the infection of nature," mean the *sinful* lusts of the flesh, such as drunkenness, gluttony, whoredom, &c; or, if he understand unloving, diabolical tempers, such as envy, pride, stubbornness, malice, sinful anger, ungodly jealousy, unbelief, fretfulness, impatience, hypocrisy, revenge, or any moral opposition to the will of God: if Mr. Hill, I say, understand this by "the infection of nature;" and if he suppose that these evils must radically and necessarily remain in the hearts of all believers (fathers in Christ not excepted) till death comes to "cleanse the thoughts of their hearts" by the inspiration of his ill-smelling breath, we must take the liberty of dissenting from him; and we produce the following arguments to prove that, whatever Mr. Hill may insinuate to the contrary, the Church of England is not against the doctrine of evangelical perfection which we vindicate.

I. Our Church can never be so inconsistent as to level her articles against what she ardently prays for in her liturgy: but she ardently prays for Christian perfection, or for perfect love in this life. Therefore she is not against Christian perfection. The second proposition of this argument can alone be disputed, and I support it by the

---

* See the edition printed in London in 1773, p. 328.

---

well-known collect in the communion service, "Cleanse the thoughts of our hearts by the inspiration of thy Holy Spirit, that we may perfectly love thee, and worthily magnify thy holy name, through Jesus Christ our Lord." Here we see, (1.) The nature of Christian perfection; it is *perfect love.* (2.) The seat of this perfect love, *a heart cleansed from its own thoughts.* (3.) The blessed effect of it, *a worthy magnifying of God's holy name.* (4.) Its author, *God,* of whom the blessing is asked. (5.) The immediate mean of it, *the inspiration of his Holy Spirit.* And, lastly, the gracious procurer of it, *our Lord Jesus Christ.*

II. This vein of godly desire after Christian perfection runs through her daily service. In her confession she prays: "Restore thou them that are penitent, according to thy promises, &c, that hereafter we may live a godly righteous, and sober life, to the glory of thy holy name." Now, godliness, righteousness, and sobriety, being the sum of our duty toward God, our neighbour, and ourselves, are also the sum of Christian perfection. Nor does our Church absolve any but such as desire "that the rest of their lives may be pure and holy, so that at the last they may come to God's eternal joy;" plainly intimating that we may get a pure heart; and lead a pure and holy life, without going into a death purgatory; and those who do not attain to purity of heart and life, that is, to perfection, are in danger of missing God's eternal joy.

III. Hence it is that she is not ashamed to pray daily for sinless purity in the *Te Deum:* — "Vouchsafe, O Lord, to keep us this day *without sin,*" that is, *sinless;* for, I suppose, that the title of our fifteenth article, "Of Christ alone without Sin," means, *Of Christ alone sinless from his conception to his last gasp.* This deep petition is perfectly agreeable to the collects for the ninth, seventeenth, eighteenth, and nineteenth Sundays after Trinity: "Grant to us the Spirit *to think* and *do always* such things as be rightful, that we may be enabled to *live according to thy will,*" *i.e.* to live without sin. "We pray thee, that thy grace may *always* prevent and follow us, and make us to be continually given to *all good works,*" &c. "Grant thy people grace to withstand the temptations of the world, the flesh, and the devil, and with *pure hearts and minds* to follow thee." "Mercifully grant that thy Holy Spirit may *in all things* direct and rule our hearts." Again: "May it please thee, that by the wholesome medicines of the doctrine delivered by him, [Luke, the evangelist and physician of the soul,] *all the diseases of our souls* may be healed," &c. (*St. Luke's Day.*) "Mortify and kill in us all vices, [and among them envy, selfishness, and pride,] and so strengthen us by thy grace, that by the innocency of our lives, and constancy of our faith unto death, we may glorify thy holy name," &c. (*The Innocents' Day.*) "Grant us the help of thy grace, that *in keeping thy commandments* we may please thee both in *will and deed.*" (*First Sunday after Trinity.*) "Direct, sanctify, and govern both our hearts and bodies, in the ways of thy laws, and in the works of thy commandments, that we may be preserved [in these ways and works] in body and soul." "Prevent us in all our doings, &c, and farther us with thy continual help; that in all our works, begun, continued, and ended in thee, we may glorify thy holy name." (*Communion Service.*) Once more: "Grant that in *all* our sufferings here on earth, &c, we may steadfastly look up to heaven, and by faith behold the glory that shall be revealed; and being *filled with the Holy Ghost,* may learn to bless our persecutors by the example of thy first martyr," &c. (*St. Stephen's Day.*) It is worth our notice. that *blessing our persecutors and murderers* is the last beatitude, the highest instance of Christian perfection, and the most difficult of all the duties, which, if we may believe our Lord, constitute us perfect in our sphere, "as our heavenly Father is perfect:" see Matthew 5:11, 44, 45, 48.

IV. Perfect love, i.e. Christian perfection, instantaneously springs from perfect faith: and as our Church would have all her members perfect in love, she requires them to pray thus for perfect faith, which must be obtained in this life or never: "Grant us so perfectly, and without all doubt, to believe in thy Son Jesus Christ, that our faith in thy sight may never be reproved." (*St. Thomas' Day.*)

V. Our Lord teaches us to ask for the highest degree of Christian perfection, where he commands us "when we pray to say, &c, *Thy kingdom come; thy will be done on earth as it is in heaven.*" And our Church, by introducing this deep prayer in all her services, shows how greatly Mr. Hill is mistaken, when he supposes that she looks upon our doctrine of Christian perfection as "shocking."

Should this gentleman object that although our Church bids us pray for Christian perfection in the above-cited collects, and in our Lord's prayer, yet she does not intimate that these deep prayers may be answered in this life: I oppose to that argument not only the word *on earth*, which she so frequently mentions in the Lord's prayer, but also her own words: "Everlasting God, who art more ready to hear than we to pray, and art wont to give more than we desire, &c, pour down upon us the *abundance* of thy mercy," &c. (*Twelfth Sunday after Trinity.*) Mr. Hill must therefore excuse us, if we side with our praying Church, and are not ashamed to say, with St. Paul, "Glory be to him that is able to do exceeding abundantly above all that we can ask or think, according to the power that worketh in us," Ephesians 3:20.

VI. That our Church cannot reasonably be against Christian perfection, I farther prove thus: what the Church of England recommends as the end of baptism, can never be contrary to her doctrine: but she recommends a "death unto sin," or Christian perfection, as the end of baptism; therefore she cannot be against Christian perfection. The second proposition, which alone is disputable, I prove by these words of her catechism: "What is the inward or spiritual grace in baptism? A death unto sin, and new birth unto righteousness." Hence she prays at the grave, "We beseech thee to raise us from the death of sin to the life of righteousness, that when we shall depart this life, we may rest in him," [Christ.] Now, that a *death to sin* is the end of baptism, and that this end is never fully answered till this death has fully taken place, is evident by the following extract from our baptismal office: "Grant that the old Adam in this person may be so buried that the new may be raised up in him." "Grant that *all carnal affections* [and consequently all the carnal mind and all inbred sin] *may die in him,* and that all things belonging to the Spirit may live and grow in him." "Grant that the person now to be baptized may receive *the fulness of thy grace.* Grant that he being dead to sin, and living to righteousness, and being buried with Christ in his death, may crucify the old man, and *utterly abolish the whole body of sin."* How can we maintain, with our Church, that we to *crucify, mortify,* (i.e. kill,) *and utterly abolish the whole body of sin;* so as to be dead to sin, and to have the old Adam buried in this life; and yet hold, with Mr. Hill, that this "whole body of sin," which we are utterly to abolish, is to remain wholly and *utterly unabolished* till death come to abolish it?

VII. Our Church is not against that end of the Lord's Supper which she constantly inculcates: but that end of the Lord's Supper which she constantly inculcates is Christian perfection: therefore our Church is not against Christian perfection. The second proposition, which alone needs proof, is founded upon these deep words of our Communion Service: — "Grant us to eat the flesh of thy dear Son Jesus Christ, and to drink his blood, that our sinful bodies may be *made clean* by his body, and our *souls washed* through his precious blood, and that we may evermore *dwell in him and he in us.*" These words express the height of Christian perfection, nor has the Lord's Supper had its full end upon us till that prayer is answered.

VIII. Our Church is not against what she considers the end of Christ's nativity, and of his being presented in the temple: but what she considers as that end, is Christian perfection: therefore she is not against Christian perfection. The second proposition of this argument is founded, (1.) Upon *the proper preface to Christmas day* in the Communion Service: — "Christ, &c, was made very man, &c, without spot of sin, to *make us clean from all sin.*" And, (2.) Upon these words of the collect for the presentation of Christ in the temple: — "We humbly beseech thee, that as thy only begotten Son was presented in the temple in substance of our flesh, so we may be presented unto thee with *pure and clean hearts.*"

IX. The same argument holds good with respect to our Lord's circumcision, his keeping of the passover with unleavened bread, his ascending into heaven, and his sending the Comforter from thence. That, according to our Church, the end of these events is our Christian perfection, appears by the following extracts from her collects:— "Grant us the true circumcision of the Spirit, that our *hearts and all our members being mortified* from all worldly and carnal lusts, we may *in all things obey,*" &c. (*The Circumcision of Christ.*) "Grant us so to put away the leaven of malice and wickedness, that we may alway serve thee in *pureness* of living and truth." (*First Sunday after Easter.*) "Grant, &c, that we may also *in heart and mind* thither [to heaven] ascend, and with him [Christ] *continually dwell,*" &c. (*Ascension Day.*) "Grant us, by the same Spirit, to have a right judgment in all things, and *evermore* to rejoice in his *holy comfort.*" (*Whitsuntide.*)

X. Our Church cannot reasonably oppose what she ardently wishes to all her communicants, and what she earnestly asks for and strongly recommends to all her members: but she thus wishes, asks, and recommends *deliverance from all sin, and perfect charity,* that is, Christian perfection: and therefore she cannot be against Christian perfection. The second proposition is founded, (1.) Upon these words of the absolution which she gives to all communicants: — "Almighty God, &c, pardon and *deliver you from all your sins, confirm and strengthen you in all goodness.*" (2.) Upon her collect for Quinquagesima Sunday: — "Send thy Holy Ghost, and pour into our hearts that most excellent gift of charity, *the very bond of peace and of all virtues.*" (St. Paul calls it "the bond of perfection.") And, (3.)Upon the definition which she gives us of charity, in her homilies: — "Charity," says she, "is to love God with all our heart, all our soul, and all our power and strength. *With all our heart;* that is to say, that our heart, mind, and study be set to believe his word, and to love him *above all things* that we love best in heaven or in earth. *With all our soul;* that is to say, that our *chief* joy and delight be set upon him, and our *whole life* given to his service. *With all our power;* that is to say, that, with our hands and feet, with our eyes and ears, our mouths and tongues, and with *all our parts and powers, both of body and soul,* we should be given to the keeping of his commandments. This is the principal part of charity, but it is not the whole; for charity is also to love every man, good and evil, friend and foe, whatsoever cause be given to the contrary." (*Hom. on Charity.*) "Of charity [St. John] says, He that doth keep God's word and commandment, in 'him is truly the perfect love of God,' &c. And St. John wrote not this as a subtle saying, &c, but as a most certain and necessary truth." (*Homily of Faith*, part 2.) "Thus it is declared unto you what true charity or *Christian love* is, &c, which love, whosoever keepeth, not only toward God, whom he is bound to love above all things, but also toward his neighbour, as well friend as foe, *it shall surely keep him from all offence of God, and just offence of man.*" (*Homily on Charity*, part 2.) Again: "Every man persuadeth himself to be in charity; but let him examine his own heart, his life and conversation, and he shall truly discern whether he be in perfect charity or not. For he that followeth not his own will, but giveth himself earnestly to God, to do all his will and commandment, he may be sure that he loveth God above all things, or else surely he loveth him not, whatsoever he pretend." (*Homily on Charity.*) Once more: perfect "patience careth not what, nor how much it suffereth, nor of whom it suffereth, whether of friend or foe, but studieth to suffer innocently. Yea, he in whom perfect charity is, careth so little to revenge, that he rather studieth to do good for evil, according to the most perfect example of Christ upon the cross. Such charity and love as Christ showed in his passion, should we bear one to another, if we will be his true servants. If we love but them that love us, what great thing do we do? We must be perfect in our charity, even as our Father in heaven is perfect." (*Homily for Good Friday.*)

XI. That state which our Church wants all her priests to bring their flocks to is not a "shocking" or chimerical state: but she wants all her priests to bring all their flocks to "perfectness in Christ," that is, to Christian perfection: and therefore the state of Christian perfection is neither shocking nor chimerical. The minor, which alone is contestable, rests upon this awful part of the charge which all her bishops give to her priests: — "See that you never cease your labour, care, and diligence, until you have done all that lieth in you to bring all such as shall be committed to your charge unto that agreement of faith, and that *ripeness and perfectness of age in Christ,* that there be no place left among you for *error* in religion, or *viciousness in* life." (*Ordin. Office.*)

XII. Nor is our Church less strict with the laity than with the clergy; for she receives none into her congregation but such as profess a determination of coming up to Christian perfection. Accordingly, all her members have solemnly promised and vowed by their sponsors at their baptism, and in their own persons when they were confirmed by the bishop: (1.) "To renounce the devil and all his works, the pomps and vanities of this wicked world, without reserve, and all the sinful lusts of the flesh. (2.) To believe all the articles of the Christian faith. And, (3.) To keep God's holy will and commandments, and walk in the same all the days of their life." And is not this vowing to "perfect holiness in the fear of God?" Does the first part of this sacred engagement leave any room for a moment's agreement with the devil, the world, or the flesh? Does the second make the least allowance for one doubt with respect to any one article of the Christian faith? Or the third for one wilful breach of God's commandments? Again: are not these commandments thus summed up in our Church catechism: — "I learn in them my duty toward God, which is to love him with all my heart; and my duty toward my neighbour, which is to love him as myself?" Is not this perfect love, or Christian perfection? And have we not "vowed to walk in the same all the days of our life?" As many Churchmen, therefore, as make conscience of keeping their baptismal vow, must not only "go on, *but attain* unto perfection:" and if there have been no perfect Christians in our Church, all her members have died in the actual breach of the awful promise which they made in their baptism: a supposition too shocking either to make or allow.

If you ask, Where are those perfect Churchmen or Christians? I answer, that if *the perfect love that keeps the commandments* is not attainable, our baptismal vow is absurd and detestable; for it is both irrational, and very wicked, to vow things absolutely impossible. But this is not all: upon that supposition the Bible, which makes such frequent mention of *the perfect* and of *perfection,* is not better than a popish legend; for that book ought to rank among religious romances, which recommends imaginary things as if they were indubitable realities. So sure then as the Bible is true, there *are,* or *may be* perfect Christians; but

> Virtutem incolumem odimus,
> Sublatam ex oculis quærimus, invidi.

"While we honour dead saints, we call those who are alive enthusiasts, hypocrites, or heretics." It is not proper, therefore, to expose them to the darts of envy and malice. And suppose living witnesses of perfect love were produced, what would be the consequence? Their testimony would be excepted against by those who disbelieve the doctrine of Christian perfection, just as the testimony of the believers, who enjoy the sense of their justification, is rejected by those who do not believe that a clear experience of the peace and pardoning love of God is attainable in this life. If the original, direct perfection of Christ himself was horribly blackened by his bigoted opposers, how could the derived, reflected perfection of his members escape the same treatment from men, whose hearts are tinctured with a degree of the same bigotry?

Add to this, that in order to harden unbelievers, "the accuser of the brethren" perpetually obtrudes upon the Church, not only false witnesses of pardoning grace, but also vain pretenders to perfect love: for he knows that by putting off as many counterfeits as he possibly can, he will give the enemies of the truth room to say that there is in the Church no gold purified seven times, — no coin truly stamped with the king's image, *perfect* love; and bearing the royal inscription, "Holiness unto the Lord."*

Therefore, instead of saying that this or the other eminent believer has attained Christian perfection, we rest the cause upon the experience of St. John, and of those with whom that apostle could say, "There is no occasion of stumbling in him that loveth. Herein is our love made perfect, that we may have boldness in the day of judgment, because [with respect to holiness] as He is [in his human nature] so are we in this world — pure, undefiled; and filled with perfect love; with this difference nevertheless, that he is in the kingdom of glory, and we in the kingdom of grace; he has a glorified, and we a corruptible body; he has the original perfection of a tree, and we the derived perfection of branches growing upon it. Or, to use another

---

* Among the professors, who have lately set up as witnesses of perfect love, I am not a little surprised to find Mr. Hill himself. This gentleman, who has treated Mr. Wesley with such severity, for standing up in defence of perfect love, or Christian perfection, most solemnly ranks himself among the perfect lovers of their neighbours, yea, of their adversaries! Hear him make his astonishing profession before the world, at the end of his pamphlet called, *The Admonisher Admonished.* "I most solemnly declare," says he, "that I am in perfect charity with Dr. Adams, as well as with you, sir, my unknown antagonist." I never yet heard a perfectionist make so solemn and so public a profession of perfect love.

comparison, he shines with the communicative perfection of a pure, bright, unextinguishable fire; and we with a borrowed, and yet inherent perfection of a coal entirely lighted. The burning mineral was black, cold, and filthy, before it was impregnated with the perfection of the fire; it continues bright, hot, and pure, only so long as it remains in the fire that kindled it: for if it fall from it by any accident, the shining perfection which it had acquired gradually vanishes, and it becomes a filthy cinder, the black emblem of an apostate. So true is that saying of our Lord, "Without me [or rather *separate from me*] ye can do nothing;" ye can neither get, nor keep light or heat, knowledge or love. But when we live not, and Christ liveth in us; when our life is hid with Christ in God, when we dwell in God, and God dwells in us; then it is that our love is made perfect, and that, loving one another even as Christ hath loved us, as he is loving, "so are we in this world," 1 John 4:17.

Such was the avowed experience of fathers in Christ in the apostolic times, and such it undoubtedly is also in our days. Nor can I persuade myself that our Church trifles with her children when she describes the perfect Christian thus, in our Homily for Good Friday: — "He in whom perfect charity is, careth so little to revenge, that he rather studieth to do good for evil, according to the most perfect example of Christ upon the cross."

XII. If Mr. Hill reply, that our Church speaks there of a mere nonentity; and that we can never have a grain of perfect charity in this life, because the old leaven of *indwelling sin* will always corrupt the sweetness of our tempers before God; I answer his objection by producing my last proof, that our Church holds the very doctrine for which we are called perfectionists. Hear her pressing perfect love and purity, (1.) Upon all her communicants: — "Have a lively and steadfast faith in Christ, &c, and be in perfect charity with all men." (*Com. Office.*) And, (2.) Upon all her feeble children: — "Though your power be weak," says she to them, "yet Christ is risen again to strengthen you in your battle: his Holy Spirit shall help your infirmities. In trust of his mercy take you in hand to purge the leaven of sin, that corrupteth and soureth the sweetness of our life before God; that ye may be as new and fresh dough, void of all sour leaven of wickedness; so shall ye show yourselves to be sweet bread to God, that he may have his delight in you." (*Hom. on the Resur.*)

All the preceding arguments support our sense of the ninth and fifteenth articles; and if Mr. Hill urge that our Church contradicts herself, and sometimes pleads for Christian imperfection and a death purgatory; we reply, that, supposing the charge were well grounded, yet we ought rather to follow her, when she soberly follows Scripture, than when she hastily follows inconsistent Augustine. But we would rather hope that when she speaks of human depravity in a manner which *seems* to bear hard upon the preceding quotations, it is either when she speaks of human depravity *in general,* or when she inculcates the perfection of humility; or when she opposes the feigned perfection of those whom she ironically calls "proud, just, perfect, and holy Pharisees." (*Hom. on the Misery of Man.*) From these and the like words, therefore, we have as much reason to conclude that she renounces true Christian holiness, as to infer that she decries true Christian perfection. Beside, the delusion of those Pharisees, who have missed a perfection of evangelical righteousness and humility, and have attained a perfection of self righteousness and pride, is so horrible and so diametrically opposite to the spirit of Christianity, that our reformers deserve to be excused, if they have sometimes opposed that error in an unguarded manner;

especially as they have so clearly and so frequently asserted the glorious liberty of God's children.

I shall close this vindication of the Church of England with some remarks upon her "martyrs," whom Mr. Hill produces also in his creed, to keep the doctrine of Christian imperfection in countenance.

1. If any of our martyrs, speaking of his converted, renewed, and sanctified state, said, "I am all sin," or words to that purpose, he spoke the words of unguarded humility, rather than the words of evangelical soberness: for a man may have grace and zeal enough to burn for one truth, without having time and prudence enough properly to investigate and state *every* truth.

2. In our state of weakness, the very *perfection of humility* may betray an injudicious martyr into the use of expressions which seem to clash with the glorious liberty of God's children; just as an excessive love for our friends may betray us into an injudicious and teasing officiousness.

3. When a martyr considers himself in his fallen state in Adam, or in his former state of disobedience, he may say, "I am all sin," in the very same sense *in* which St. Paul said, "I am the chief of sinners." But allow him time to explain himself, and he will soon give you to understand that he "rejoices in the testimony of a good conscience, purged from dead works to serve the living God;" and that, far from harbouring any sin in himself, he is determined to "strive against sin *in others*, resisting unto blood." And is not such a disposition as this one of the highest steps in the ladder of Christian perfection?

4. Hence it appears that the unguarded expressions of our martyrs were levelled at Pharisaic pride, or at absolute perfection, and not at Christian perfection. Like some pious Calvinists in our days, they embraced Christian perfection in *deed*, while, through misapprehension, they disclaimed it in *word*. And therefore their speeches against the glorious liberty of God's children, show only that Christian perfection is a perfection of *humility and love*, and not a perfection of *wisdom and knowledge*.

5. If it can be proved that any of those who rank among our martyrs died full of indwelling sin, I will not scruple to say that he died *a bigot* and not *a martyr;* for to die full of *indwelling sin* is to die full of secret obstinacy and uncharitableness; and St. Paul declares that were an apostle himself to "give his body to be burned" in such a disposition, "it would profit him nothing."

6. As many brave Englishmen have laid down their lives in the field of battle, to defend their country against the French, without being properly acquainted with the liberties and boundaries of the British empire; so many Protestants have laid down their lives in Smithfield, to defend their religion against the Papists, without being acquainted with all the landmarks which divide the land of spiritual Israel from that of the Philistines, and perfect Christianity from *Antinomian dotages*.

7. The Jews can produce their martyrs as well as the Protestants. The Maccabees, for example, died entirely satisfied with the Mosaic covenant, and strangers to the transcendent glory of the Christian dispensation. But is this a sufficient reason for preferring Judaism to Christianity? Yes, if Mr. Hill be in the right, when he decries the doctrine of perfect faith and perfect love, and imposes upon us the doctrine of a death purgatory, because some good men formerly died without having clear views of the doctrine of Christian perfection; though, like men who eat honey in the dark, they tasted its sweetness, and delightfully experienced its power.

8. To conclude: I am persuaded that were all our reformers and martyrs alive, none of them would object to this argument, which sums up the doctrine of the Church of England with respect to purgatory: "If death cleanseth us from indwelling sin, it is not Christ's blood applied by the Spirit through faith. But the only purgatory wherein we [Christian men] trust to be saved, is the death and blood of Christ, which, if we apprehend it with a true and steadfast faith, purgeth and cleanseth us from all our sins. 'The blood of Christ,' says St. John, 'hath cleansed us from all sin.'" (*Homily on Prayer*, part 3.) Therefore, the doctrine, that "death, &c, cleanseth us from all indwelling sin," or the doctrine of a death purgatory, is as contrary to the doctrine of our Church as to that of St. John.

SECTION V.

Mr. Hill intimates that the apostles were imperfectionists — St. Peter and St. James, far from pleading for a death purgatory, stand up for Christian perfection.

WHEN Mr. Hill has so unadvisedly brought the Church of England against us, it is not surprising to see him press four apostles, "Peter, Paul, James, and John," into the field to "cut up," (as he calls it,) "root and branch, my favourite doctrine of perfection." Never were these holy men set upon a more unholy piece of work. Methinks I hear them say, Let Mr. Hill rank us with the Gibeonites: let him make us "hewers of wood" to the congregation for ever: but let him not set us upon *cutting up, root and branch,* the lovely and fruitful tree of *Christian perfection.* Happily for that rare tree, Mr. Hill only produces the *names* of the apostolic woodmen, while we produce their *axe,* and show that they lay it at the root of Antinomianism; a deadly tree this, which is, to our favourite tree, what the fatal tree in paradise was to the tree of life. Mr. Hill appeals first to Peter; let then Peter first answer for himself.

1. Where does that apostle plead for Christian imperfection, and a death purgatory? Is it where he says, "As He who has called you is holy: so be ye HOLY IN ALL manner of conversation. Seeing you have purified your souls, &c, love one another with a PURE HEART FERVENTLY. Christ left us an example, that ye should follow his steps; who did no sin — who bare our sins, that we, being DEAD TO SIN, should live to righteousness: forasmuch then as Christ hath suffered for us in the flesh, arm yourselves with the same mind; for he that hath suffered in the flesh, hath ceased from sin. The God of all grace, &c, after that ye have suffered awhile, make you PERFECT." Had Peter been against our doctrine, is it probable that he would thus have excited believers to attain perfection; wishing it them, as we wish our flocks "the peace of God which passes all understanding?"

If that apostle pleads not for the necessary indwelling of sin in his first epistle, doth he do it in the second? Is it where he says, that "exceeding great and precious promises are given us, that by these we might be *partakers of the Divine nature,* having escaped the pollution that is in the world through lust?" Is there indwelling sin in the Divine nature? And can those people, whose hearts are still full of sin and indwelling corruption, be said to "have escaped the pollution that is in the world through lust?"

Might not a man, whose lungs are still full of dangerous ulcers, be said with as much propriety to have escaped the misery that is in the world through consumptions? Is it where St. Peter describes Christian perfection, and exhorts believers to attain it, or to rise higher in it, by adding with "all diligence to faith virtue, to virtue knowledge, temperance, patience, godliness, brotherly kindness, and charity," the key of the arch, and the bond of perfection? Is it where he states the difference between fallen believers, weak believers, and perfect Christians; hinting that the first "LACK these things," i.e. Christian graces; that "these things ARE in" the second: and that they "ABOUND" in the third? Or is it where he bids "us be diligent that we may be found of God in peace, *without spot and blameless*?" For my part I do not see here the shadow of a plea for the *root* of every evil in the hearts of believers till they die, any more than for the *fruit* of adultery, murder, and incest in their lives till they go hence.

But what principally strikes us in Mr. Hill's appeal to St. Peter is, that although Peter was naturally led by his subject to speak of the *necessary* indwelling of sin in our hearts during the term of life, if that doctrine had been true, yet he does not so much as drop one hint about it. The design of his first epistle was, undoubtedly, to confirm believers, under the fiery trials which their faith meets with. "You are kept," says he, "by the power of God, through [obedient] faith unto salvation wherein ye greatly rejoice, though now for a season (if need be) ye are in heaviness, through manifold temptations." What a fair opportunity had Peter to say here, without an *if need be*, "You MUST be in heaviness, not only through manifold temptations, but also through the remaining corruptions of your hearts: the Canaanites and wild beasts must still dwell in the land, to be goads in your sides, and thorns in your eyes, or you would grow proud and careless; your heart leprosy must cleave to you, as Gehazi's leprosy cleaved to him. Death radically cured him and nothing but death can radically cure you. Till then, your heads must remain full of *imputed righteousness*, and your hearts full of *indwelling sin*." But, happily for the honour of Christianity, this Antinomian, this impure gospel has not the least countenance from St. Peter and he cuts up the very roots of it where he says, "Who shall harm you, if you be followers of that which is good? Commit the keeping of your souls unto God in well doing. [The very reverse of sinning.] You are his daughters, [the daughters of him to whom God said, *Walk before me, and be thou perfect*,] so long as ye DO WELL, and are not AFRAID with any amazement," that is, so long as your conduct and tempers become the Gospel. And every body knows that a man's tempers are always as his heart; and that, if his heart be "full of evil," his tempers cannot be "full of goodness," Romans 15:14.

II. If St. Peter, the first of Mr. Hill's witnesses, does not say one word to countenance Antinomianism, and to recommend Christian imperfection; let us see if St. James pleads for Baal in the hearts, any more than for Baal in the *lives* of perfect believers. Turn to his epistle. O ye that thirst after holiness! To your comfort you will find, that in the first chapter he shows himself a bold asserter of Christian perfection. "Let patience," says he, "have her PERFECT WORK, that ye may be *perfect and entire, wanting nothing*." He speaks the same language in other places: "Whoso looketh into the perfect law of liberty, and CONTINUETH THEREIN, he, being a doer of the work, shall be blessed in his deed." And again: "If any man offend not in word, the same is *a perfect man*." Nor is it difficult to demonstrate from his second chapter, that established believers, or perfect Christians, "keep the royal, perfect law of liberty;" and that those who "break it in one point are" in a deplorable case.

Doctrines of Grace and Justice

If Mr. Wesley had written an epistle to Antinomian believers, to make them go on to Christian perfection, could he have expressed himself in a stronger manner than St. James does in the following passages? — "Grudge not one against another, brethren, lest ye be condemned, [or damned,] James 5:9. Speak not evil one of another, brethren. He that judgeth his brother, judgeth the law. But if thou judge the law, thou art not a doer of the law, but a judge. There is one Lawgiver, who is able to save and to destroy" [those believers who keep or break his royal law,] James 4:11, 12. Again: "If ye FULFIL THE ROYAL LAW, according to the Scripture, *Thou shalt love thy neighbour as thyself,* ye DO WELL: but [if ye do not fulfil it] if ye have respect to persons, *ye commit sin.* For whosoever shall keep the whole law, and yet offend [i.e. commit sin] in one point, he is guilty of all, &c. So speak ye, and so do, as they that shall be judged by the law of liberty," James 2:8, &c.

What follows demonstrates that fallen believers, if they do not repent and rise to the state of Christian perfection, will be condemned for *one sin.* St. James properly instances in the sin of uncharitableness, because it is directly contrary to our Lord's new commandment of loving one another as he has loved us, and because charity is the fulfilling of "the royal law, and the bond of perfection." "Can faith save him" [the uncharitable believer?] says St. James. "If a brother or sister be naked and destitute of daily food, and one of you [believers] say, *Be ye warmed and filled,* notwithstanding ye give them not those things which are needful to the body, what doth it profit? Even so, faith, if it hath not works, [and of consequence, the fallen believer, if he has sin unrepented of,] is dead." Such a one "is of the devil, for he committeth sin, and sin is the transgression of the law of liberty, by which he shall be judged, yea, by which he shall have judgment without mercy, that has (thus) showed no mercy;" whether he sinned negatively by not relieving his poor brother in deed, though he gave him good words; or whether he did it positively, by "having respect to persons, or by grudging against his brother:" compare James 2:13, &c, with 1 John 3:4, &c, to the end of both chapters, which are two strong batteries raised on purpose to defend the doctrine of Christian perfection, and to demolish the doctrine of Christian imperfection, which is all one with Antinomianism.

Should it be objected, that, "at this rate, no Christian believer is safe, till he has obtained Christian perfection:" we reply, that all Christian believers are safe, who either *stand in it, or press after it.* And if they do neither, we are ready to prove that they rank among fallen believers, and are in as imminent danger of being "spued out of Christ's mouth," as the Laodiceans were. Let Mr. Hill candidly read the Epistle to the Hebrews, the Second Epistle of St. Peter, and the First of St. John, and let him doubt of it if he can.

Should Mr. Hill object that "St. James himself says, *In many things we offend all;* and that this one saying abundantly proves that he was a strong imperfectionist;" I beg leave to involve my honoured opponent in the following dilemma:— Are the offences, of which St. James speaks, *involuntary?* Or are they *voluntary?* If Mr. Hill says, "They are involuntary, I answer, Then they are not proper breaches of "the law of liberty," which St. James preaches; because that law curses us for no *involuntary* offences; and therefore such offences, (like St. Paul's reproving of the high priest more sharply than he would have done, had he known what high dignity his unjust judge was invested with,) such offences, I say, are not *sins* according to the royal and evangelical law of our Melchisedec: and therefore they do not prove that all believers remain full of indwelling sin till death. If Mr. Hill reply, that "the many offences, of which St. James speaks, are *voluntary* offences, and therefore real breaches of the law of liberty;" I answer, that this *genuine* sense of the words, taken in connection with the context, confirms our doctrine of Christian perfection, and our opposition to Antinomianism; and I prove it thus:—

The text and context run thus:— "My brethren, be not many masters; [i.e. lord it not over one another;] knowing that we [who do so] shall receive the greater condemnation" if we do not learn humility. "I say *we*, because I would not have you think that God our Judge is a respecter of persons, and will spare an apostle, who breaks the law of liberty and does not repent, any more than he would spare you. For if I represented God as a partial Judge, Judas' greater condemnation would prove me mistaken. And I insist the more upon this awful doctrine, because 'in many things we offend all,' especially *in word*, till we are made perfect in love, that 'love which is the fulfilling of the law,' and enables us to 'keep our tongue as it were with a bridle' all the day long." If Mr. Hill ask, by what means I can show that this is really St. James' meaning; I reply, By that plain rule of divinity and criticism, which bids us take the beginning of a verse in connection with the end. And if we do this here, we find the doctrine of Christian perfection in this very text, thus: — "We shall receive the greater damnation" if we do not repent and cease to "be many masters; for in many things we *from time to time* offend all," especially by our words, till we are perfected in love. "If any man offend not in word, the same is, *what each of us should be,* a perfect man, and able also to bridle his whole body," James 3:1, 2. So certain, therefore, as there are men able to bridle their tongue, and their whole bodies, there are men perfect in the body, perfect before death, according to the doctrine contained in this controverted passage of St. James.

"But St. James says also, *The spirit that dwelleth in us lusteth to envy,* James 4:5."

I reply, 1. It is usual for modest teachers to rank themselves with the persons, of whom they say something disagreeable: and this they do to take away the harshness of their doctrine, and to make way for the severity of their charges. Thus Peter writes: "The time past of our life may suffice us to have wrought the will of the Gentiles, when we walked in lasciviousness, lusts, excess of wine, revellings, banquetings, and abominable idolatries;" though it is evident that Peter, a poor, industrious, godly Jew, never "walked in abominable idolatries, working the will of the Gentiles." Now the same delicacy of charity, which made St. Peter rank himself with heathens, who walked in drunkenness, whoredom, and gross idolatry, makes St. James rank himself with the carnal Christians, who are possessed by an envious spirit.

2. Nay, St. James himself, using the same figure of speech, says, "The tongue is an unruly evil, full of deadly poison, &c; therewith curse we men, who are made after the similitude of God." But would it be reasonable to infer from these words that his tongue was still "full of deadly poison," and that he therewith continued to curse his neighbour? Therefore all that is implied in his words about envy, is that, till we are made perfect in the "charity which envieth not, and is not puffed up, the spirit that is in us lusteth to envy" and pride. And that we, who have not yet attained Christian perfection, need not be always envious and proud, is evident from the very next words, "But he giveth more grace, wherefore he says, *God resisteth the proud,* envious man, *but giveth grace to the humble:* resist the devil and he will flee from you: purify your hearts, ye double minded: be afflicted, and mourn, and weep: let your laughter be turned into mourning, and your joy into heaviness." So severe was St. James to those *adulterers and adulteresses,* those genteel believers, who stopped short of Christian perfection, loved the world, and envied one another! Therefore, to press him into the service of Solifidianism, is as rash an attempt as to call his epistle *an epistle of straw,* worthy of being committed to the flames: and (if the preceding remarks are just) Mr. Hill is as much mistaken, when he appeals to St. James, as when he quotes St. Peter, in defence of Christian imperfection.

SECTION VI.

St. Paul preached Christian perfection, and professed to have attained it — A view of the different sorts of perfection which belong to the different dispensations of grace and glory — The holy child Jesus' imperfection in knowledge and suffering, and his growing in wisdom and stature, and in favour with God and man, were entirely consistent with his perfection of humble love.

ST. PAUL'S name appears upon Mr. Hill's list of witnesses against Christian perfection; but it is without the apostle's consent: for Peter and James did not plead more strenuously for the glorious liberty of God's children, than St. Paul. Nay, he professed to have attained it, and addressed fathers in Christ as persons that were partakers of it together with himself. "We speak wisdom," says he, "among them that are perfect," 1 Corinthians 2:6. "Let us, as many as be perfect, be thus minded," Philippians 3:15.

Nor did St. Paul fancy that Christian perfection was to be confined to the apostolic order: for he wanted all believers to be like him in this respect. Hence it is, that he exhorted the Corinthians "to perfect holiness in the fear of God, 2 Corinthians 7:1; to be perfect, 2 Corinthians 13:11; to be perfectly joined together in the same mind," 1 Corinthians 1:10; and showed them the perfect, or "more excellent way," 1 Corinthians 13. He told the Ephesians, that "God gave pastors for the perfecting of the saints, till all come in the unity of the faith, — unto a perfect man, unto the measure of the stature of the fulness of Christ," Ephesians 4:12, 13. He "taught every man, &c, that he might present every man perfect in Christ Jesus," Colossians 1:28. He wanted the Colossians fully to "put on charity, which is the bond of perfection, that they might stand perfect and complete in all the will of God," Colossians 3:14; 4:12. He would have "the man of God to be perfect, thoroughly furnished to every good work," 2 Timothy 3:27. He exhorted his converts, "whether they did eat, drink, or do any thing else, to do all to the glory of God, and in the name of the Lord Jesus; rejoicing evermore, praying without ceasing, and in every thing giving thanks;" that is, he exhorted them to walk according to the of Christian perfection. He blamed the Hebrews for being still such "as have need of milk, and not of strong meat;" observing that "strong meat, εστι τελειων, *belongeth to them that are perfect,* even to them who by reason of use, [or experience,] have their [spiritual] senses exercised to discern both good and evil," Hebrews 5:12, &c. He begins the next chapter by exhorting them to "go on to perfection;" intimating that if they do not, they may insensibly fall away, "put the Son of God to open shame, and not be renewed again to repentance." And he concludes the whole epistle by a pathetic wish that "the God of peace would make them perfect in every good work to do his will." Hence it appears that it would not be less unreasonable to set St. Paul upon "crucifying Christ afresh," than to make him attack Christ's well-known doctrine, "Be ye [morally] perfect, [according to your narrow capacity and bounded power,] even as your heavenly Father is [morally] perfect" [in his infinite nature, and boundless Godhead,] Matthew 5:48.

Mr. Hill will probably attempt to set all these scriptures aside, by saying that nothing can be more absurd than to represent Paul as a perfectionist, because he says himself, "Not as though I had already attained, or were already perfect," Philippians 3:12. But some remarks upon the different sorts of perfection, and upon the peculiar perfection which the apostle said he had not yet attained, will easily solve this difficulty.

Mr. Hill is too well acquainted with divinity, not to know that absolute perfection belongs to God alone; and that Christ himself, with respect to his humanity, fell and still falls short of infinite perfection. Omniscience, and a wisdom admitting of no growth, are essential to absolute perfection: but the man Christ was not omniscient; for *he did not know the day of judgment:* nor was his wisdom infinite; for *he grew in wisdom.* Nay, his happiness is not yet absolute; for it daily increases as he sees his seed, and is more and more satisfied. God alone is supremely perfect: all beings are imperfect, when they are compared to him; and though all his works were perfect in their places, yet, as he gave them different degrees of perfection, they which have inferior degrees of goodness, may be said to be imperfect in comparison of them which are endued with superior degrees of excellence. Thus archangels are perfect as archangels, but imperfect in comparison of Jesus Christ. Angels are perfect as angels, but imperfect in comparison of archangels. Enoch, Elijah, and the saints who arose with our Lord, are perfect as glorified saints; and, in comparison of them, the departed "spirits of just men made perfect" continue in a state of imperfection: for the risen saints are glorified in body and soul; but the mouldered bodies of departed saints, not having yet felt "the power of Christ's resurrection," are still under the power of corruption. Imperfect as St. Paul and St. John are now, in comparison of Enoch, Elijah, and the twenty-four elders so often mentioned by St. John; yet they are far more perfect than when they were pressed down by a corruptible body, under which they "groaned, being burdened:" for the disembodied spirits of "just men made perfect" are more perfect than the most perfect Christians, who are yet in a "body dead because of sin." And, as among rich men, some are richer than others; or among tall men, some are taller than others; so among perfect Christians, some are more perfect than others.

According to the gradation which belongs to all the works of God; and according to the doctrine of the dispensations of Divine grace; the least perfect of all perfect Christians, is more perfect than the most perfect Jew; yea, than John the Baptist, whose dispensation linked together Judaism and Christianity. Or, to speak the language of our Lord, "He that is least in the [Christian] kingdom of God, is greater than John;" though John himself was "the greatest born of a woman" under any preceding dispensation. By the same rule, he that is perfect under the Jewish dispensation, is more perfect than he that is only perfect according to the dispensation of the Gentiles.

Doctrines of Grace and Justice

The standard of these different perfections is fixed in the Scriptures. "To fear God and work righteousness," that is, to do to others as we would be done to, from the principle of the fear of God, is the standard of a Gentile's perfection. The standard of a Jew's perfection, with respect to morality, may be seen in Deuteronomy 27:14-26, and in Psalm 15. And, with respect to devotion, it is fixed in Psalm 119. The whole of this perfection is thus summed up by Micah: — "O Israel, what does the Lord thy God require of thee, but to do justice, to love mercy, and to walk humbly with thy God?"

The perfection of infant Christianity, which is called, in the Scriptures, "the baptism of John," is thus described by John and by Christ: — "He that hath two coats, let him impart to him that hath none, &c. If thou wilt be perfect, sell what thou hast, give to the poor, and follow me. If any man come to me and hate not [i.e. is not willing for my sake to leave] his father and mother, his wife and children, yea, and his own life also, he cannot be my disciple. And whosoever does not bear his cross and come after me, cannot be my disciple."

With respect to adult perfect Christianity, which is consequent upon the baptism of the Holy Ghost, administered by Christ himself, its perfection is described in the sermon on the mount; in 1 Corinthians xiii; and in all those parts of the epistles where the apostles exhort believers to walk agreeabl to "the glorious liberty of God's children,"

The perfection of disembodied spirits is thus described by *a voice from heaven:* — "Blessed are the dead who die in the Lord: even so, saith the Spirit, for they rest from their labours, [not *from their sins;* this they did before death,] and their works follow them." And the complete perfection of glorified saints is thus described by St. John and St. Paul: — "They shall live and reign with Christ in a city wherein there is no temple, for the Lord God Almighty and the Lamb are the temple of it, and the city hath no need of the sun to shine in it, for the glory of God enlightens it, and the Lamb is the light thereof. And there shall be no curse: but the throne of God and of the Lamb shall be in it, and his servants shall serve him, and they shall see his face; and his name shall be on their foreheads, and they shall reign for ever and ever" in glorified bodies. For "this corruptible *body* shall put on incorruption, and this mortal shall put on immortality. It is sown in dishonour, it is raised in glory; it is sown in weakness, it is raised in power: it is sown a natural body, it is raised a spiritual body: as is the heavenly Adam, such are they also that are heavenly: and as we have borne the image of the earthly, we shall also bear the image of the heavenly: for flesh and blood cannot inherit the kingdom of God:" but the spiritual, i.e. the glorified body shall inherit the heavenly Canaan.

Persons, whose orthodoxy consists in obstinately refusing to peep over the wall of prejudice, will probably say that these observations upon the different sorts and degrees of perfection are "novel chimeras," and that I multiply perfections, as I do justifications, "inventing them by the dozen." To this I answer, that we advance nothing but what, we hope, recommends itself to the candour of those who have a regard for reason and revelation.

1. REASON tells us that all God's works are perfect in their places; and that, some having a higher place than others upon the scale of beings, they are of consequence more perfect. If Mr. Hill will not believe it, we appeal to his banker, and ask, if there is not an essential difference between the metallic perfection of brass, that of silver, and that of gold? We appeal to his jeweller, and ask if the perfection of an agate is not inferior to that of an emerald — the perfection of a ruby to that of a diamond; and if some diamonds cannot be said to be more perfect than others? We appeal to his gardener, and ask if a blackberry is not inferior to a strawberry, a strawberry to a nectarine, and a nectarine to a pineapple: and if, nevertheless, those various fruits have not each their perfection? Nay, we will venture to ask his under gardener, if the perfection of the fruit does not imply the perfection of the blossom; if the perfection of the blossom does not presuppose that of the bud; and if a bud, whose perfection is destroyed by the frost in March, is likely to produce perfect blossoms in May, and perfect fruit in October?

Should the fear of becoming a perfectionist make Mr. Hill refuse his assent to these obvious truths, we will address him as a *master of arts,* a gentleman who is versed in natural philosophy, as well as in Calvinism. Is it absurd to say that some just men rise progressively from the perfection of a lower, to the perfection of a higher dispensation in the spiritual world? Do we not see a similar promotion, even among the basest classes of animals in the natural world? Consider that beautiful insect, which exults to display its crown, and expand its wings in the sun. Will you not say that it is a *perfect butterfly?* Nevertheless, three weeks ago it was a *perfect aurelia,* quietly sleeping in its silken tomb. Some months before, it was a *perfect silkworm,* busily preparing itself for another state of existence, by spinning and weaving its shroud. And had you seen it a year ago, you would have seen nothing but a *perfect egg.* Thus, in one year, it has experienced three grand changes, which may be called metamorphoses, births, or conversions. Each change was perfect in its kind: and, nevertheless, the last is as far superior to the first, as a beautiful, flying butterfly exceeds a black, crawling worm; and such a worm, the invisible seed of life, that lies dormant in the diminutive egg of an insect.

2. SCRIPTURE and experience do not support our doctrine of the difference of perfections, less than reason and philosophy. We read, Genesis 6:9, that "Noah was a just man, and perfect in his generation." We read also, Job 1:1, "There was a man in the land of Uz, whose name was Job, and that man was PERFECT." Now, whatever the perfection of Noah and Job consisted in, it is evident that it was not Jewish perfection" for the perfection of Judaism requires the sacrament of circumcision; and Mr. Hill will hardly say that men were circumcised in the land of Uz, and before the flood. Hence I conclude that Noah and Job had attained the perfection of Gentilism, and not that of Judaism.

Again: "Mark the perfect man" says David, "for his end is peace." No doubt he spake this of the perfect Jew; and such were, I think, Moses, Samuel, and Daniel: if Mr. Hill will not allow it, I produce Simeon or Anna, or Zacharias and Elizabeth, "who were both righteous before God, walking in all the commandments and ordinances of God blameless," Luke 1:16. Now these excellent Jews were not perfect according to the dispensation of John the Baptist; for water baptism was not less essential to a perfect disciple of John, than circumcision was to a perfect disciple of Moses, and they, or some of them, probably died long before John opened his dispensation by "preaching the baptism of repentance."

Once more: John the Baptist was undoubtedly perfect according to his own dispensation; his penitential severity, his great reputation for holiness, and the high encomium which our Lord passed upon him, naturally lead us to conclude it. But that he was not a perfect Christian is evident from the following considerations: (1.) Our Lord said, that "the least in the *Christian* kingdom of God should be greater than John." (2.) John himself confessed the imperfection of his baptism, or dispensation, in comparison of the perfection of Christ's baptism and spiritual dispensation: "I have need to be baptized of thee," said he to Christ, "and comest thou to me?" And to his disciples he said, "I indeed baptize you with water, but he [the Lamb of God] shall baptize you with the Holy Ghost and with fire." (3.) John was beheaded before Christ was crucified; and the outpouring of the Spirit, the baptism of the Holy Ghost, did not begin till after Christ's ascension; the apostle St. John having particularly mentioned that "the Holy Ghost was not yet given," or that a full dispensation of the Spirit was not yet opened, "because Jesus was not yet glorified," John 7:39: an important observation this, which is confirmed by Christ's own words to his disciples, John 16:7, "I tell you the truth; it is expedient for you that I go away; for if I go not away, the Comforter will not come unto you: [the full dispensation of the Holy Ghost shall not be opened:] but if I depart, I will send him to you." Agreeably to this, "he commanded them that they should not depart from Jerusalem, but wait for the promise of the Father, [i.e. the promised Spirit,] *which*, says he, *ye have heard of me; for John truly baptized with water, but ye shall be baptized with the Holy Ghost not many days hence.*" And when they had been thus baptized, they began to preach the full baptism of Christ, which has two branches, the baptism of water, and the baptism of the Spirit, or of celestial fire. Therefore, when the penitent Jews asked, "Men and brethren, what shall we do?" Peter answered, "Be baptized every one of you in the name of Jesus Christ, and ye shall receive the gift of the Holy Ghost; for the promise of it is unto you, and unto your children, and to all that are afar off; even as many as the Lord our God shall call" to the perfection of the Christian dispensation: "and we are witnesses of these things; and so is also the Holy Ghost, whom God [since the day of pentecost] hath given to them that obey him," i.e. to obedient believers: compare Acts 2:38, and 5:32, with John 7:38.

From the preceding reasons, we conclude that the case of John the Baptist was as singular as that of Moses. Moses knew Joshua, and pointed him out as the man who was to lead the Israelites into the land of promise: but Moses died before Joshua opened the way. Thus Moses saw the good land: he was not far from the typical kingdom of God; but he did not enter into it. In like manner the Baptist knew Christ, and pointed him out as the wonderful person who was to introduce believers into the spiritual kingdom of God. But John was beheaded before Christ glorified opened his peculiar kingdom. Thus John saw the kingdom of heaven: he was not far from it. But yet he did not enter into it. He died a "just man, made perfect" according to his own incomplete dispensation, but not according to the dispensation of Christ and his Spirit. This was the Baptist's grief, not his guilt: for he earnestly desired to be baptized of Christ with the Holy Ghost; but the Holy Ghost was not yet given in the Christian measure. The gift of the Spirit was rather distilled as a dew, than poured out as a shower; "because Jesus was not yet glorified:" but now, that he is ascended up on high to receive that unspeakable gift for men in its fulness; now that the promise of the Father is fulfilled to all who plead it aright; we are culpable if we rest satisfied with the inferior manifestations of the Spirit which belong to the baptism of John or to infant Christianity: and we act in an unchristian-like manner if we ridicule the kingdom of the Holy Ghost, and speak evil of perfect Christianity.

To return: a perfect Gentile sees God in his works and providences; but wanting a more particular manifestation of his existence and goodness, he sighs, *O where shall I find him?* A perfect Jew ardently expects his coming as Messiah and Emmanuel, or *God with us;* and he groans, *O that thou wouldst rend the heavens and come* down! A perfect disciple of John believes that the Messiah is come in the flesh, and prays, *O Lamb of God, that takest away the sins of the world, restore the kingdom to a waiting Israelite: baptize me with the Holy Ghost: fill me with the Spirit!* And perfect Christians can witness from blessed experience that He who was "manifest in the flesh," is come in the Spirit's power to establish within them his gracious "kingdom of righteousness, peace, and joy in the Holy Ghost."

In this blessed kingdom St. Paul lived, when he said, "Let us, as many as are perfect, be thus minded." Nevertheless, though he was not only a perfect Christian, but also able to "preach wisdom among them that were perfect," he justly acknowledges himself imperfect in knowledge, in comparison of perfectly glorified saints. "We know but in part," says he, "but when that which is perfect is come, then that which is in part shall be done away. For now we see through a glass darkly," but when we shall drop these dark veils of flesh and blood, and be clothed with celestial, incorruptible bodies, we shall be capable of beholding God, "we shall see him face to face," 1 Corinthians 13:9, &c. "For though we are now the sons of God, it does not yet appear what we shall be: but we know, that when he shall appear, we shall be like him, for we shall see him as he is," 1 John 3:2.

It is of *this final* perfecting of the saints in the day of the resurrection that the apostle writes to the Hebrews, where he says, "These, having all obtained a good report through faith, received not the promise," which relates to the full perfection of the just: "God having provided some better things for us [Christians] that they [the Jewish saints] without us should not be made perfect, [that is, that we should all be perfected in glory together.] For we shall all be changed in a moment, in the twinkling of an eye, at the last trump, (for the trumpet shall sound, and the dead shall be raised incorruptible,) and we [who shall have died, or shall then be found living in a state of initial perfection] shall be changed," Hebrews 11:39; 1 Corinthians 15:51.

Nor does it follow from hence that all glorified saints shall be equally perfect. I cannot but embrace here the reasonable sentiment of Dr. Watts: — "The worship of heaven," says that judicious divine, "and the joy that attends it, may be exceedingly different in degrees, according to the different capacities of spirits; and yet all may be perfect, and free from sinful defects. Does not the sparrow praise its Maker upon the ridge of a cottage, chirping in its native perfection? And yet the lark advances, in her flight and song, as far above the sparrow as the clouds are above the housetop. Surely superior joys and glories must belong to superior powers and services. The word *perfection* does not always imply *equality*. If all the souls in heaven be of one mould, and make, and inclination; yet there may be different sizes of capacity even in the same genus, and a different degree of preparation for the same delights; therefore should all the spirits of the just be uniform in their natures and pleasures, and all perfect; yet one spirit may possess more happiness and glory than another, because it is more capacious of intellectual blessings, and better prepared for them. So when vessels of various size are thrown into the same ocean, there will be a great difference in the quantity of the liquid which they receive; though all may be full to the brim, and all made of the richest metal." (*Watts on the Happiness of Separate Spirits.*)

Doctrines of Grace and Justice

Having thus proved both by reason and Scripture that there are various sorts and degrees of perfection; and that a man may be perfect according to the dispensation of Divine *grace* he is under upon earth, though he be not yet perfect according to the dispensation of Divine *glory,* which will take place when our mortal bodies shall know the power of Christ's resurrection: having proved this, I say, nothing is easier than to reconcile St. Paul with himself, when he speaks in the same chapter of his *being perfect,* and of his *not being yet perfect.* For when he says, "Let us, as many as are perfect, be thus minded," he speaks of Christian perfection, that is, of the maturity of grace and holiness, which men still burdened with corruptible flesh and blood arrive at under the *full* dispensation of the Gospel of Christ. But when he says, "Not as though I had already attained, or were already perfect," &c, he speaks of his perfection as a candidate for a *crown of martyrdom* on earth, and for a *crown of glory* in heaven. Just as if he said, "Though I am dead to sin, and perfected in love; though *I live not, but Christ liveth in me;* yet I am not satisfied with my present perfection: I want to be perfected like Christ. *Ought not Christ to have suffered these things, and* [then] *to enter into his glory?* Luke 24:26. I want, in short, to be perfected *in suffering,* as well as *in love.* I cannot, I will not rest, till I end my race of pain and shame, *and know the fellowship of Christ's sufferings* on the ignominious tree. I am filled with a noble ambition of dying a martyr for him; being persuaded that this perfection of sufferings will ripen me for my heavenly perfection — the perfection to which I shall be raised at the resurrection of the just."

That this was the apostle's meaning, when he denied his "being already made perfect," will, I hope, appear indubitable to those who consider the context. The words which immediately precede St. Paul's observation that "he had not yet attained," express a pathetic wish of sharing both in Christ's *exaltation,* by a glorious resurrection, and in his *humiliation,* by perfect sufferings. "That I may know him," as he says, "and the power of his resurrection, and the fellowship of his sufferings; being made conformable unto his [painful, ignominious] death, if by any means I may attain to the resurrection of the dead," which is the full perfection of the human nature; and secure a part in the first resurrection of the just, in which martyrs will be peculiarly interested: witness this plain scripture, "I saw the souls of them that were beheaded for the witness of Jesus, and for the word of God, &c, and they lived and reigned with Christ a thousand years: but the rest of the dead lived not again until the thousand years were finished. This is the first resurrection. Blessed and holy is he that has part in the first resurrection," Revelation 20:4, &c.

But I repeat it, although St. Paul disclaimed his having yet attained a perfection of *shame* and *glory,* he nevertheless professed his having attained a perfection of Christian faith working by love. This is evident from the words that follow the controverted text: — "This one thing I do, &c, I press toward the mark, for the prize of the high calling of God in Christ Jesus [which is my complete glorification in heaven.] Let us, therefore, as many as are perfect [in faith and love] be thus minded." Let us press after our perfection of *suffering* here, and of *glory* hereafter: a bodily perfection this, which the apostle describes thus at the end of the chapter: — "We look for the Saviour, the Lord Jesus Christ, who shall change our vile body, according to the working whereby he is able to subdue all things unto himself," Philippians 3:21. Hence it appears, if we are not strangely mistaken, that it is not less absurd to oppose our doctrine of Christian perfection from Philippians 3, than to oppose the divinity of Christ from the first chapter of St. John's Gospel.

I shall conclude these remarks upon the various sorts of perfection by an observation which may help Mr. Hill to understand how St. Paul could be perfect in *love*, when he professed that he was not perfect either in *glory, knowledge, or sufferings*.

Had not our Lord been *perfect in love* from a child, he would have broken the two great commandments on which hang all the law and the prophets. But "in him was no sin:" therefore he was *perfect in love*, though his love admitted of an increase, as well as his wisdom and knowledge; just as a perfect bud admits of a perfect growth into a perfect blossom, and such a blossom into a perfect fruit. Hence it is that our Lord's perfect love grew, "he increased in favour with God and man:" an additional degree of approbation being due to him from all rationals, upon every display of his growing perfection, Luke 1:52. But though our Lord was always, perfect in *love*, yet it is certain that he was not always perfect in *sufferings*, much less in *glory:* for he was not perfected in sufferings till after he had expired between the two thieves; nor was he perfected in glory before he took his place at the right hand of God. This is evidently the apostle's doctrine where he says, "It became Him by whom are all things, to make the Captain of our salvation perfect through sufferings," Hebrews 2:10. And again, chap. 5:8, "Though he was a son, yet learned he obedience by the things which he suffered: and being made perfect [in sufferings and in glory] he became the author of eternal salvation to all them that obey him." Mr. Hill must then allow that St. Paul's IMPERFECTION, with respect to *sufferings and glory*, was no obstacle to the PERFECTION of his *love:* or he must assert that Christ was sinfully imperfect in love so long as he continued imperfect in sufferings and glory; a supposition this which is too horrible to be admitted by a merely nominal Christians much more by Mr. Hill.

SECTION VII.

St. Paul was not carnal, and sold under sin — The true meaning of Galatians 5:17, and of Romans 7:14, &c, is openedconsistently with the context, the design of the Epistles to the Galatians and to the Romans, and the privileges of Christians, and the doctrine of perfection.

IT is easier to raise dust than to answer an argument. I expect, therefore, that our opponents, instead of solidly answering the contents of the preceding section, will assert that St. Paul was an avowed enemy to deliverance from evil tempers before death, and of consequence a strong opposer of the doctrine of Christian perfection. And to support their assertion they will probably quote the following text:— "The flesh lusteth against the Spirit, and the Spirit againt the flesh, so that ye cannot do the things that ye would," Galatians 5:17. For they conclude from these words, that, so long as we dwell in bodies of corruptible flesh, we cannot help breaking the law of liberty (at least from time to time) by sinful, internal lusts. As this objection passes among them for unanswerable, it may not be amiss to give it a fourfold answer:—

1. St. Paul wrote these words to the carnal, fallen Galatians. To them he said, "So that ye cannot do the things that ye would:" and there was a good reason why "they could not do" what they had a weak desire to do. They were bewitched by the flesh, and by carnal teachers, who led them from the power of the Spirit to the weakness of the letter; yea, to the letter of Judaism too. But did he not speak of himself to the Philippians in a very different strain? Did he not declare, "I can do all things through Christ, who strengtheneth me?" And cannot every believer, who steadily walks in the Spirit, say the same thing? Who does not see the flaw of this argument? The "disobedient, fallen, bewitched" believers of Galatia, of whom St. Paul stood in doubt, could not but fulfil the lusts of the flesh when they were led by the flesh: "neither hot nor cold," like the Laodiceans, they could neither be perfect Christians nor perfect worldlings, because they fully sided neither with the Spirit nor with the flesh: or, to use the apostle's words, "they could not do the things that they would," through the opposition which the flesh made against the Spirit, and the Spirit against the flesh; neither of these principles being yet fully victorious in their halting, distracted hearts: therefore this must be also the miserable case of all obedient, faithful, established believers through all ages all the world over What has this Antinomian conclusion to do with the Scriptural premises? When I assert that those who have put out their knees cannot run a race swiftly, do I so much as intimate that no man can be a swift racer?

2. It is as unscriptural to judge of the power and liberty of established believers by the power and liberty of the Galatians, as it is unreasonable to judge of the liberty of a free nation by the servitude of a half-enslaved people; or of the strength of a vigorous child by the weakness of a halfformed embryo. I found this remark, (1.) Upon Galatians 5:1, where the apostle indirectly reproves his Judaizing, wrangling converts, for being fallen from "the liberty wherewith Christ hath made us free, and for being entangled again with the yoke of bondage." And, (2.) Upon Galatians 4:19, "My little children, of whom I travail in birth again, until Christ be formed in you." The dawn of day is not more different from the meridian light, than the imperfect state described in this verse is different from the perfect state described in the following lines, which are descriptive of the adult Christian: — "I am crucified with Christ: nevertheless, I live, yet not I, but Christ liveth in me; and the life which I now live in the flesh, I live by the faith of the Son of God," Galatians 2:20.

3. The sense which is commonly fixed upon the texts produced by our opponents is entirely overturned by the context: read the preceding verse and you will find a glorious, though a conditional promise of the liberty which we plead for: "This I say, walk in the Spirit, and ye shall not fulfil the [sinful] lusts of the flesh;" that is, far from harbouring either outward or inward sin, ye shall, with myself, and as many as are perfect, steadily keep your body under, and be in every thing spiritually minded, which "is life and peace."

4. We should properly distinguish between the *lawful* and the *sinful* lusts or desires of the flesh. To desire to eat, to drink, to sleep, to marry, to rest, to shun pain, at proper times and in a proper manner, is no sin; such lusts or desires are not contrary to the law of liberty. Our Lord himself properly indulged most of these harmless propensities of the flesh, without ceasing to be the immaculate Lamb of God. Hence it is that our Church requires us in our baptism to renounce only "the sinful lusts of the flesh;" giving us a tacit leave lawfully to indulge its lawful appetites. I should be glad, for example, to recruit my strength by one hour's sleep; or by an ounce of food; as well as by a good night's rest, or a good meal. But the flesh harmlessly lusteth against the Spirit: so that in these, and in a thousand such instances, "I cannot do the things that I would." But do I commit sin when I use my body according to its nature? Nay, if I were as strongly solicited unlawfully to indulge the lawful appetites of my flesh, as Christ was to turn stones into bread when he felt keen hunger in the wilderness, would not such a temptation increase the glory of my victory, rather than the number of my sins? Is it right in our opponents to avail themselves of the vague, unfixed meaning of the words *flesh* and *lust,* to make the simple believe that, so long as we have human *flesh* about us, and *bodily appetites* within us, our hearts must necessarily remain pregnant with sinful lusts, and we shall "have innumerable lusts (as says an imperfectionist whom I shall soon mention) swarming about our hearts?" Does not this doctrine put a worm at the root of Christian liberty, while it nourishes Antinomian freedom; a freedom to sin, even to adultery and murder, without ceasing to be sinless and perfect in Christ?

5. Two lines after St. Paul's supposed plea for the necessary continuance of indwelling sin in believers, the apostle begins a long enumeration of the "works of the flesh, of the which," says he, "I tell you before, as I have also told you in time past, that they who do such things, [or admit in their hearts such lusts as *hatred, variance, strife, or envyings,*] shall not inherit the kingdom of God "' whereas, "they that are Christ's [they that *are led by the Spirit of God,* for in St. Paul's account *only such are Christ's,* that is, properly belong to Christ's spiritual dispensation, Romans 8:9, 14,] have crucified the flesh with its affections and lusts," Galatians 5:24. Now these spiritual believers "can do all things through Christ:" and accordingly the apostle observes that, far from bearing the fruit of the flesh, they bear the fruit of the Spirit, which is love, joy, peace, long suffering, gentleness, goodness, faithfulness, meekness, temperance, — the whole cluster of inherent graces which makes up Christian perfection; and then he observes that "the law is not against such, [because they fulfil it:] for all the law is fulfilled in one word, even in this, Thou shalt love thy neighbour as thyself," Galatians 5:14-23.

6. The sense which the imperfectionists give to Galatians 5:17, is not only flatly contrary to the rest of the chapter, but to the end and design of all the epistle. What the apostle has chiefly in view through the whole, is to reprove the Galatians for their carnality in following Judaizing teachers, and in bearing the fruits of the flesh, *envy, variance,* &c, insomuch that they were ready to bite and devour one another. Now, if when he had sharply reproved them as persons *who ended in the flesh, after having begun in the Spirit,* he had written Galatians 5:17, in the sense of our opponents, he would fairly have excused these bewitched men, absolutely defeated his reproof, and absurdly furnished them with an excellent plea to continue in their bad course of life. For if they could not "fulfil the law of Christ," but must remain carnal, and sold under indwelling sin, had they not a right to answer the apostle thus:— "If neither we whom thou callest *bewitched Galatians,* nor any spiritual believer, can possibly do the things we should and would do, because the flesh sinfully and unavoidably lusteth against the Spirit; why dost thou blame us for our carnality? Why dost thou take us to task rather than other believers? Are we not all bound by adamantine chains of carnal necessity to break the law of Christ so long as we are in the body? Art thou not the very man who givest us to understand that we *cannot do what we* should and *would do,* because *the flesh,* which we cannot possibly part with before death, *lusteth against the Spirit?* And is not absolute necessity the best excuse in the world?"

7. Should Mr. Hill ask, What is then the genuine meaning of Galatians 5:17? We reply, that when we consider that verse in the light of the context, we do not doubt but the sense of it is fairly expressed in the following lines: — "The flesh and the Spirit are two contrary principles. 'They that are in, or walk after the flesh, cannot please God.' And ye are undoubtedly in the flesh, and walk after the flesh, while 'ye bite and devour one another. This I say then, Walk in the Spirit: be led by the Spirit, and ye shall not fulfil the lust of the flesh, as ye now do: for the flesh lusteth against the Spirit,' and prevails in all carnal people; 'and the Spirit lusteth against the flesh,' and prevails in all spiritual people; 'and these two,' far from nesting together, as Antinomian teachers make you believe, 'are contrary to each other.' They are irreconcilable enemies: 'so that' as obedient, spiritual believers while they are led by the Spirit, 'cannot do what they would do if they were led by the flesh; ye bewitched, carnal, disobedient Galatians, who are led by the flesh, cannot do what ye would do' if ye were led by the Spirit, and what ye still have some desire to do, so far as ye have not yet absolutely quenched the Spirit. Would ye then return to your liberty? Return to your duty: change your guide: forsake the carnal mind: let 'Christ be formed in you: be led by the Spirit: so shall ye fulfil the law of Christ;' and it shall no more condemn you, than the law of Moses binds you. 'For if ye be led by the Spirit, ye are not under *the curse of* the law:' ye are equally free from the bondage of the Mosaic law, and from the condemnation of the law of Christ," Galatians 5:16-18.

8. Should Mr. Hill say "that by *the flesh* he understands not only *the body,* but also *the natural desires, appetites, and aversions,* which are necessarily excited in the soul, in consequence of its intimate union with the body; and that the body of sin must needs live and die with the body which our spirit inhabits; because, so long as we continue in the body, we are unavoidably tried by a variety of situations, passions, inclinations, aversions, and infirmities which burden us, hinder us from doing and suffering all we could wish to do and to suffer, and occasion our doing or feeling what we should be glad in some respects not to do or feel:"

I answer, It is excessively wrong to conclude that all these burdens, infirmities, appetites, passions, and aversions, are those *sinful* workings of our corrupt nature which are sometimes called *the flesh.* You cannot continue a whole day in deep prostration of body and soul, nor perhaps one hour upon your knees. Your stomach involuntarily rises at the sight of some food which some persons esteem delicious: your strength fails in outward works: your spirits are exhausted; you faint or sleep, when others are active and toil: you need the spiritual and bodily cordials which others can administer: perhaps also you are afflicted with disagreeable sensations in the outward man, through the natural, necessary play of the various springs which belong to flesh and blood: your just grief vents itself in tears: your zeal for God is attended with a proper anger at sin: nay, misapplying what the apostle says of the carnal man under the law, you may declare with great truth, The extensive good I would, I do not; and the accidental evil I would not, that I do; I would convert every sinner, relieve every distressed object, and daily visit every sick bed in the kingdom, but I cannot do it. I would never try the patience of my friends, never stir up the envy of my rivals, never excite the malice of my enemies; but I cannot help doing this undesigned evil, as often as I strongly exert myself in the discharge of my duty.

If you say, "All these things, or most of them, are quite inconsistent with the perfection you contend for," I ask, Upon this footing was not our Lord himself imperfect? Did his bodily strength never fail in agonizing prayer, or intense labour? Did his animal spirits always move with the same sprightliness? Do we not read of his sleeping in the ship, when his disciples wrestled with a tempestuous sea? Did he not fulfil the precept, "Be ye angry and sin not?" Had he not the troublesome sensation of grief at Lazarus' grave; of hunger in the wilderness; of weariness at Jacob's well; and of thirst upon the cross? If he was "made in the likeness of sinful flesh, and tempted in all things as we are;" is it not highly probable that he was not an utter stranger to the other natural appetites, and uneasy sensations which are incident to flesh, and blood? Is it a sin to feel them? Is it not rather a virtue totally to deny them, or not to gratify them out of the line of duty, or not to indulge them in an excessive manner in that line? Again: did not his holy flesh testify a natural innocent abhorrence to suffering? Did not his sacred body faint in the garden? Were not his spirits so depressed, that he stood in need of the strengthening assistance of an angel? Did he do all the good he would? To suppose that he wished not the conversion of his friends and brethren, is to suppose him totally devoid of natural affection; but were they all converted? Did you never read, "Neither did his brethren believe in him: and his friends went out to lay hold on him; for they said, He is beside himself?" To conclude: did he not accidentally stir up the evil he would not, when he gave occasion to the *envy* of the Pharisees; the *scorn* of Herod; the *fears* of Pilate; the *rage* of the Jewish mob? And when he prayed that the bitter "cup might pass from him, if it were possible;" did he not manifest a resigned desire to escape pain and shame? If every such desire be indwelling sin, or the flesh "sinfully lusting against the Spirit," did he not go through the sinful conflict as well as those whom we call perfect men in Christ? And, consequently, did he not fall at once from mediatorial, Adamic, and Christian perfection; indwelling sin being equally inconsistent with all these kinds of perfection? What true believer does not shudder at the bare supposition? And if our *sinless* Lord felt the *weakness* of the flesh harmlessly lusting against the *willingness* of the spirit, according to his own doctrine, "The spirit indeed is willing, but the flesh is weak," is it not evident that the conflict we speak of, (if the spirit maintains its superior, victorious lusting against the flesh, and by that means steadily keeps the flesh in its proper place,) is it not evident, I say, that this conflict is no more inconsistent with Christian perfection, than suffering, agonizing, fainting, crying, and dying, which were the lot of our *sinless, perfect* Saviour, to the last?

If I am not greatly mistaken, the preceding remarks prove, (1.) That when our opponents pretend to demonstrate the necessary indwelling of sin in all believers, from Galatians 5:17, they wretchedly tear that text from the context, to make it speak a language which St. Paul abhors. (2.) That this text, fairly taken together with the context, and the design of the whole epistle, is a proof that obedient, spiritual believers, can do what the "bewitched Galatians" could not do; that is, they can "crucify the flesh with all its affections and lusts," and walk as perfect Christians who utterly destroy the whole body of sin, and "fulfil the law of Christ." And, (3.) That to produce Galatians v, against the doctrine of Christian perfection, is full as absurd as to quote the sermon upon the mount in defence of Antinomian delusions. I have dwelt so long upon this head, because I have before me* "An Essay on Galatians

---

* The arguments by which the doctrine of *the necessary indwelling of sin in all believers till death* is supported in that essay, will be considered in section 14.

5:17," lately published by an ingenious divine, who takes it for granted that the apostle contends, in this verse, for *the necessary indwelling of sin.*

Mr. Hill will probably say, "That he does not rest the doctrine of Christian imperfection so much upon the experience of the fallen Galatians, as upon that of St. Paul himself, who, in Romans vii, frankly acknowledges that he was still a wretched, carnal man, sold under sin, and serving with the flesh the law of sin. Whence it follows that it is high presumption in modern believers to aspire at more perfection, and a greater freedom from sin upon earth, than had been attained by St. Paul, who was 'not a whit behind the very chiefest apostles, but laboured more abundantly than they all.'" To this common objection I answer:—

1. The perfection we preach is nothing but perfect repentance, perfect faith, and perfect love, productive of the gracious tempers which St. Paul himself describes, 1 Corinthians 13. We see those blessed tempers shining through his epistles, discourses, and conduct; and I have proved in the preceding section that he himself professed Christian perfection. This objection, therefore, appears to us an ungenerous attempt to make St. Paul grossly contradict himself. For what can be more ungenerous than to take advantage of a figurative mode of expression, to blast a good man's character, and to traduce him as a slave of his fleshly lusts, a drudge to carnality, a wretch sold under sin? What would Mr. Hill think of me, if, under the plausible pretence of magnifying God's grace to the chief of sinners, and of proving that there is no deliverance from sin in this life, I made the following speech? —

"The more we grow in grace, the more clearly we see our sins; and the more willingly we acknowledge them to God and men. This is abundantly verified by the confessions that the most holy men have made of their wickedness. Paul himself, holy Paul, is not ashamed to humble himself for the sins which he committed, even after his conversion. 'I robbed other Churches,' says he, 'taking wages to do you service,' 2 Corinthians 11:8. Hence it appears that the apostle had agreed to serve some Churches for a proper salary: but, being 'carnal, and sold under sin,' he broke his word; he fleeced, but refused to feed the flocks; and robbing the Churches, he went to the Corinthians, perhaps to see what he could get of them also in the end; for 'the heart is deceitful above all things, and desperately wicked,' Jeremiah 17:9. Nay, partial as he was to those Corinthians, for whom he turned Church robber, he showed that his love to them was not sinless and free from rage; for once he threatened to come to them 'with a rod;' and he gave one of them to 'Satan for the destruction of the flesh.' With great propriety, therefore, did holy Paul say to the last, 'I am the chief of sinners.' And now, when the chief of the apostles thus abases himself before God, and publicly testifies, both by his words and works, that there is *no deliverance from sin, no perfection in this life;* who can help being frightened at the Pharisaic pride of the men who dare inculcate the doctrine of sinless perfection?"

I question if Mr. Hill himself, upon reading this ungenerous and absurd, though in one sense Scriptural plea for St. Paul's imperfection, would not be as much out of conceit with my fictitious explanation of 2 Corinthians 11, as I am with his Calvinistic exposition of Romans 7. Nor do I think it more criminal to represent the apostle as a Church robber, than to traduce him as a "wretched, carnal man, sold under sin;" another Ahab, that is, a man who did "evil in the sight of the Lord, above all that were before him."

2. St. Paul no more professes himself actually a carnal man in Romans 7:7, than he professes himself actually a liar in Romans 3:7, where he says, "But if the truth of God has more abounded through my lie, why am I judged as a sinner?" He no more professes himself a man *actually sold under sin,* than St. James and his fellow believers profess themselves a generation of vipers, and actual cursers of men, when the one wrote and the others read, "The tongue can no man tame: it is full of deadly poison; therewith curse we men." When St. Paul reproves the partiality of some of the Corinthians to this or that preacher, he introduces Apollos and himself; though it seems that his reproof was chiefly intended for other preachers, who fomented a party spirit in the corrupted Church of Corinth. And then he says, "These things, brethren, I have in a figure transferred to myself and to Apollos, for your sakes; that ye might learn in us not to think of men above that which is written," 1 Corinthians 4:6. By the same figure he says of himself, what he might have said of any other man, or of all mankind: "Though I speak with the tongues of men and of angels, and have not charity, I am become as sounding brass." Thrice in three verses he speaks of *his not having charity:* and suppose he had done it three hundred times, this would no more have proved that he was really *uncharitable,* than his saying, Romans 7, "I am sold under sin," proves that he "served the law of sin with his body," as a slave is forced to serve the master who bought him.

3. It frequently happens, also, that by a figure of rhetoric, which is called *hypotyposis,* writers relate things past, or things to come, in the present tense, that their narration may be more lively, and may make a stronger impression. Thus, Genesis 6:17, we read, "Behold I, even I, do bring [i.e. I will bring one hundred and twenty years hence] a flood upon the earth to destroy all flesh." Thus also, 2 Samuel 22:1, 35, 48, "When the Lord had delivered David out of the hands of all his enemies, and given him peace in all his borders, he spake the words of this song. He teacheth [i.e. he taught] my hands to war, so that a bow of steel is [i.e. was] broken by mine arms: it is God that avengeth [i.e. that hath avenged] me, and that bringeth [i.e. has brought] me forth from mine enemies." A thousand such expressions, or this figure continued through a thousand verses, would never prove, before unprejudiced persons, that King Saul was alive, and that David was not yet delivered for good out of his bloody hands. Now, if St. Paul, by a similar figure, which he carries throughout part of a chapter, relates his past experience in the present tense: if the Christian apostle, to humble himself, and to make his description more lively, and the opposition between the bondage of sin and Christian liberty more striking; if the apostle, I say, with such a design as this, appears upon the stage of instruction in his old Jewish dress, a dress this, in which he could serve God day and night, and yet, like another Ahab, breathe threatenings and slaughter against God's children, and if in this dress he says, "I am carnal, sold under sin," &c, is it not ridiculous to measure his growth as an apostle of Christ by the standard of his stature when he was a Jewish bigot, a fiery zealot, full of good meanings and bad performances?

4. To take a scripture out of the context, is often like taking the stone that binds an arch out of its place: you know not what to make of it. Nay, you may put it to a use quite contrary to that for which it was intended. This our opponents do, when they so take Romans 7, out of its connection with Romans 6, and Romans 8, as to make it mean the very reverse of what the apostle designed. St. Paul, in Romans fifth and sixth, and in the beginning of the seventh chapter, describes "the glorious liberty of the children of God" under the Christian dispensation. And as a skilful painter puts shades in his pictures to heighten the effect of the lights; so the judicious apostle introduces, in the latter part of Romans 7, a lively description of the domineering power of sin, and of the intolerable burden of guilt: a burden this, which he had so severely felt, when the convincing Spirit charged sin home upon his conscience after he had broken his good resolutions; but especially during the three days of his blindness and fasting at Damascus. Then he groaned, "O wretched man that I am," &c, hanging night and day between despair and hope, between unbelief and faith, between bondage and freedom, till God brought him into Christian liberty by the ministry of Ananias; of this liberty the apostle gives us a farther and fuller account in Romans 8. Therefore the description of the man who groans under the galling yoke of sin, is brought in merely by contrast, to set off the amazing difference there is between the bondage of sin and the liberty of Gospel holiness: just as the generals, who entered Rome in triumph, used to make a show of the prince whom they had conquered. On such occasions the conqueror rode in a triumphal chariot crowned with laurel, while the captive king followed him on foot, loaded with chains, and making, next to the conqueror, the most striking part of the show. Now, if in a Roman triumph, some of the spectators had taken the *chained king on foot* for the *victorious general in the chariot,* because the one immediately followed the other, they would have been guilty of a mistake not unlike that of our opponents, who take the carnal Jew, "sold under sin," and groaning as he goes along, for the Christian believer, who "walks in the Spirit," exults in the liberty of God's children, and always triumphs in Christ.

5. To see the propriety of the preceding observation, we need only take notice of the contrariety there is between the bondage of *the carnal penitent,* described Romans 7:14, &c, and the liberty of *the spiritual man,* described in the beginning of that very chapter. The one says, "Who shall deliver me? Sin revives: it works in him all manner of concupiscence, yea, it works death in him: he is carnal, sold under sin," forced by his bad habits to what he is ashamed of, and kept from doing what he sees his duty. "In him, that is, in his flesh, dwells no good thing: sin dwelleth in him. How to perform that which is good he finds not." Though he has a desire to be better, yet still he "does not do good, he does evil; evil is present with him." His "inward man," his reason and conscience approve, yea, delight in God's law," i.e. in that which is right; but still he does it not; his good resolutions are no sooner made than they are broken: for "another law in his members wars against the law of his mind," that is, his carnal appetites oppose the dictates of his conscience, and "bring him into captivity to the law of sin;" so that, like a poor chained slave, he has just liberty enough to rattle his chains, and to say, "O wretched man that I am, who shall deliver me from the body of this death," from this complete assemblage of corruption, misery, and death! Is it not ridiculous to conclude, that because his groaning slave has now and then a hope of deliverance, and at times "thanks God through Jesus Christ" for that hope; he is actually a partaker of the liberty, which is thus described in the beginning of the chapter? "Ye are become dead to the law [the Mosaic dispensation] that ye should be married to Him, who is raised from the dead, that [instead of omitting to do good, and doing evil] we should bring forth fruit unto God. For when we were in the flesh, [in the state of the carnal man sold under sin, a sure proof this that the apostle was no more in that state] the motions of sin which were by the law [abstracted from the Gospel promise] did work in our members to bring forth fruit unto death. But now we are delivered from the [curse of the moral, as well as from the bondage of the Mosaic] law, that being dead wherein we were held; that we should serve God in newness of spirit, and not in the oldness of the letter," Romans 7:4, 5, 6. Immediately after this glorious profession of liberty, the apostle, in his own person, by way of contrast, describes to the end of the chapter the poor, lame, sinful obedience of those who serve God in the oldness of the letter: so that nothing can be more unreasonable than to take this description for a description of the obedience of those who "serve God in the newness of the Spirit." We have, therefore, in Romans 7:4, 5, 6, a strong rampart against the mistake which our opponents build on the rest of the chapter.

6. This mistake will appear still more astonishing, if we read Romans 6, where the apostle particularly describes the liberty of those who "serve God in newness of the spirit," according to the glorious privileges of the new covenant. Is darkness more contrary to light than the preceding description of the carnal Jew is to the following description of the spiritual Christian? "How shall we that are dead to sin live any longer therein? Our old man is crucified with Christ, that the body of sin might be destroyed, that henceforth we might not serve sin. [Note: the carnal Jew, though against his conscience, still *serves the law of sin,* Romans 7:25.] Now he that is dead is freed from sin. Reckon ye yourselves also to be dead indeed unto sin. Yield yourselves unto God as those that are alive from the dead. [Note: the carnal Jew says, "Sin revived and I died," Romans 7:9, but the spiritual Christian is alive from the dead.] Sin shall not have dominion over you [now you are spiritual: you need not say, *I do the evil that I hate, and the evil I would not, that I do:*] for you are not under the law [under the weak dispensation of Moses;] but under grace [under the powerful, gracious dispensation of Christ.] God be thanked that [whereas] ye were the servants of sin, when you carnally served God in the oldness of the letter, ye have obeyed from the heart the form of doctrine which was delivered you; [that is, ye have heartily embraced the doctrine of Christ, who gives rest to all that come to him travailing and heavy laden.] Being then made free from sin, ye became the servants of righteousness: for when ye were the servants of sin, ye were free from righteousness. — But now being — carnal, sold under sin, [*ye serve the law of sin?* No: just the reverse:] but now being made free from sin, and become the servants of God, ye have your fruit unto holiness, and the end everlasting life," Romans 6:2-22. Is it possible to reconcile this description of Christian liberty with the preceding description of Jewish bondage? Can a man at the same time exult in the one, and groan under the other? When our opponents assert it, do they not confound the Mosaic and the Christian dispensations; the workings of the spirit of bondage, and the workings of the Spirit of adoption? And yet, astonishing! they charge us with confounding LAW and GOSPEL!

7. We shall see their mistake in a still more glaring light if we pass to Romans 8, and consider the description which St. Paul continues to give us of the glorious liberty of those who have done with "the oldness of the [Jewish] letter, and serve God in newness of the Spirit." The poor Jew carnally sticking in the letter, is condemned for all he does, if his conscience be awake. "But there is now no condemnation to them which are in Christ Jesus, [who are come up to the privileges of the Christian dispensation,] who walk not after the flesh, but after the Spirit. For the law of the Spirit of life in Christ Jesus [the power of the quickening Spirit given me, and my fellow believers, under the spiritual and perfect dispensation of Christ Jesus] hath made me free from the law of sin and death. For what the law [the letter of the Mosaic dispensation] could not do, in that it was weak through the flesh, God, sending his own Son, condemned sin in the flesh; that the righteousness of the law," the spiritual obedience, which the moral law of Moses, adopted by Christ, requires, "might be fulfilled in us, who walk not after the flesh, but after the Spirit. For [so far from professing that [am *carnal and sold under sin,* I declare that] to be carnally minded is death: [well may then the carnal Jew groan, *Who shall deliver me from the body of this death!*] But to be spiritually minded is life and peace! So then, they that are in the flesh, [i.e. carnal, sold under sin,] cannot please God. But ye are not in the flesh, but in the Spirit, if so be that the Spirit of God dwell in you. Now if any man have not the Spirit of Christ, he is none of his:" he is, at best, a disciple of Moses, a poor, carnal Jew, and remains still a stranger to the glorious privileges of the Christian dispensation. "But if Christ be in you, the body is dead, [weak, and full of the seeds of death,] because of [original] sin; but the spirit is life, [strong and full of immortality,] because of [implanted and living] righteousness. For ye have not received the spirit of bondage again to fear, [like the poor, carnal man, who through fear and anguish groans out, *O wretched man that I am!*] But ye have received the Spirit of adoption, whereby we [who walk in newness of the Spirit, and please God — we, who have the Spirit of Christ,] cry, *Abba, Father!* the Spirit itself bearing witness with our spirits that we are the children of God; and if children, then heirs; heirs of God," whom we please, "and joint heirs with Christ," through whom we please God, Romans 8:1-17.

This glorious liberty, which God's children enjoy in their souls, under the perfection of the Christian dispensation, will one day extend to their bodies, which are dead [i.e. infirm and condemned to die] "because of [original] sin." And with respect to the body only it is that the apostle says, Romans 8:23, "We ourselves, also, who have the first fruits of the Spirit, groan within ourselves, waiting for the adoption" of our outward man, "that is, the redemption of our body: for," with respect to the body, whose imperfection is so great a clog to the soul, "we are saved by hope." In the meantime, "we know that all things work together for good to them that love God. Who shall separate us," that love God, and walk not after the flesh, but after the Spirit, "from the love of Christ? Shall tribulation or distress," &c, do it? "Nay, in all these things," much more in respect of sin and carnal mindedness, "we are more than conquerors, through him that loved us," Romans 8:23-37.

And that this abundant victory extends to the destruction of the carnal mind, we prove by these words of the context, "To be carnally minded is death; but to be spiritually minded is life and peace; because the carnal mind is enmity against God; for it is not subject to the law of God, neither indeed can be. So then they that are in the flesh," they that are carnally minded, "cannot please God. But ye are not in the flesh," ye are not carnally minded, "if so be that the Spirit of God dwell in you. For where the Spirit of the Lord is," and dwells as a Spirit of adoption, "there is *constant* liberty: now if any man have not that Spirit," or if he hath it only as a Spirit of bondage, to make him groan, *O wretched man!* he may indeed be a servant of God in the land of his spiritual captivity, but "he is none of Christ's" freemen: he may serve God "in the oldness of the letter," as a Jew; but he does not "serve him in newness of the Spirit," as a Christian. For, I repeat it, "where the Spirit of Christ is," and dwells according to the fulness of the Christian dispensation, "there is a liberty, a glorious liberty," which is the very reverse of the bondage that Mr. Hill pleads for during the term of life: see Romans 8:14-21.

Whether therefore we consider Romans 7, Romans 6, or Romans 8, it appears indubitable, that the sense which our opponents fix upon Romans 7:14, &c, is entirely contrary to the apostle's meaning, to the context, and to the design of the whole epistle, which is to extol the privilege of those who are Christ's, above the privileges of those who are Noah's or Moses'; or, if you please, to extol the privileges of spiritual Christians, who serve God "in newness of the Spirit," above the privileges of carnal heathens and Jews, who serve him only "in the oldness of the letter."

SECTION VIII.

An answer to the arguments by which St. Paul's supposed carnality is generally defended.

IF the sense which our opponents give to Romans 7:14, be true, the doctrine of Christian perfection is a dream, and our utmost attainment on earth is St. Paul's apostolic *carnality,* and involuntary *servitude to the law of sin;* with a hopeful prospect of deliverance in a death purgatory. It is therefore of the utmost importance to establish our exposition of that verse, by answering the arguments which are supposed to favour the Antinomian meaning rashly fixed upon that portion of Scripture.

ARG. I. "If St. Paul was not *carnal and sold under sin* when he wrote to the Romans, why does he say, 'I am carnal?' Could he not have said, I was carnal once, but now *the law of the Spirit of life in Christ Jesus has set me free from the law of sin and death?* Can you give a good reason why, in Romans 7:14, the phrase, *I am carnal,* must mean, *I was carnal?* Is it right thus to substitute the past time for the present?"

ANSWER. We have already shown that this figurative way of speaking is not uncommon in the Scriptures. We grant, however, that we ought not to depart from the literal sense of any phrase, without good reasons. Several such, I trust, have already been produced, to show the necessity of taking St. Paul's words, "I am carnal," in the sense stated in the preceding section. I shall offer one more remark upon this head, which, if I mistake not, might alone convince the unprejudiced.

The states of all souls may in general be reduced to three: (1.) That of *unawakened* sinners, who quietly sleep in the chains of their sins, and dream of self righteousness and heaven. (2.) That of *awakened,* uneasy, reluctant sinners, who try in vain to break the galling chains of their sins. And, (3.) That of *delivered* sinners, or victorious believers, who enjoy the liberty of God's children. This last state is described in Romans 7:4, 6. The rest of that chapter is judiciously brought in, to show how the *unawakened* sinner is roused out of his carnal state, and how the *awakened* sinner is driven to Christ for liberty by the lashing and binding commandment. The apostle shows this by observing, ver. 7, &c, how the law makes a *sinner* (or if you please made *him*) pass from the unawakened to the awakened state: "I had not known sin," says he, "but by the law," &c. When he had described his unawakened state without the law, and began to describe his awakened state under the law, nothing was more natural than to change the time or tense. But having already used the past tense in the description of the first or the unawakened state; and having said, "Without the law sin was dead: I was alive without the law once: sin revived and I died," &c, he could no more use that tense, when he began to describe the second, or the awakened state; I mean the state in which he found himself when the commandment had roused his sleepy conscience, and slain his Pharisaic hopes. He was therefore obliged to use another tense; and none, in that case, was fitter than the present; just as if he had said, "When the commandment slew the conceited Pharisee in me; when I died to my selfrighteous hopes; I did not die without a groan. Nor did I pass into the life of God without severe pangs: no; I straggled with earnestness, I complained with bitterness, and the language of my oppressed heart was, *I am carnal, sold under sin,*" &c, to the end of the chapter.* It is, therefore, with the utmost rhetorical propriety that the apostle says, *I am,* and not, *I was carnal, &c.* But rhetorical propriety is not theological exactness. David may say as a poet, "God was wroth: there went up a smoke out of his nostrils, and fire out of his mouth devoured: coals were kindled by it." But it would be ridiculous to take these expressions in a literal sense. Nor is it much less absurd to assert that St. Paul's words, "I am carnal, sold under sin," are to be understood of Christian and apostolic liberty.

ARG. II. "St. Paul says to the Corinthians, 'I write not to you as to spiritual men, but as to carnal, even to babes in Christ.' Now if the Corinthians could be at once *holy* and yet *carnal;* why could not St. Paul be at the same time an eminent, apostolic *saint,* and *a carnal, wretched man, sold under sin?*"

ANSWER. (1.) The Corinthians were by no means established believers in general, for the apostle concludes his last epistle to them by bidding them "examine themselves whether they were in the faith." (2.) If St. Paul proved carnal still, and was to continue so till death, with all the body of Christian believers, why did he upbraid the Corinthians with their unavoidable carnality? Why did he wonder at it, and say, "Ye are yet carnal, for whereas there is among you envyings and strife, &c, are ye not carnal?" Might not these carnal Corinthians have justly replied, *Carnal physician, heal thyself?* (3.) In the language of the apostle, *to be carnal, to be carnally minded, to walk after the flesh, not to walk after the Spirit,* and *to be in the flesh,* are phrases of the same import. This is evident from Romans 7:14; 8:1-9; and he says, directly or indirectly, that to those who are in that state, "there is condemnation; that they cannot please God; and that they are in a state of death; because, to be carnal, or carnally minded, is death," Romans 8:1, 6, 8. Now if he was *carnal* himself, does it not follow that he "could not please God," and that he was in a state of "condemnation and death?" But how does

---

* Some time after I had written this, looking into "Dr. Doddridge's Lectures on Divinity," p. 451, I was agreeably surprised to find that what that judicious and moderate Calvinist presents as the most plausible sense of Romans 7:14, is exactly the sense which I defend in these pages. Take his own words: — "St. Paul at first represents a man as ignorant of the law, and then insensible of sin; but afterward being acquainted with it, and then thrown into a kind of despair, by the sentence of death which it denounces, on account of sins he is now conscious of having committed; he then farther shows that even where there is so good a disposition as to 'delight in the law,' yet the motives are too weak to maintain that uniform tenor of obedience, which a good man greatly desires, and which the Gospel by its superior motives and grace does in fact produce."

this agree with the profession which he immediately makes of being "led by the Spirit, of walking in the Spirit, and of being made free from the law of sin and death, by the Spirit of life in Christ Jesus?" (4.) We do not deny that the remains of the carnal mind still cleave to imperfect Christians; and that, when the expression *carnal* is softened and qualified, it may, in a low sense, be applied to such professors as those Corinthians were, to whom St. Paul said, "I could not speak to you as to spiritual." But could not the apostle be yet *spoken to as a spiritual man?* And does he not allow that, even in the corrupted Churches of Corinth and Galatia, there were some truly spiritual men — some adult, perfect Christians? See 1 Corinthians 14:37, and Galatians 6:1. (5.) When the apostle calls the divided Corinthians *carnal,* he immediately softens the expression by adding, "babes in Christ." If therefore the word *carnal is* applied to St. Paul in this sense, it must follow that the apostle was but "a babe in Christ," and if he was but a babe, is it not as absurd to judge of the growth of adult Christians by his growth, as to measure the stature of a man by that of an infant? (6.) And, lastly: the man described in Romans 7:14, is not only called *carnal* without any softening, qualifying phrase; but the word *carnal is* immediately heightened by an uncommon expression, "sold under sin," which is descriptive of the strongest "bondage of corruption." Thus reason, Scripture, and criticism agree to set this argument aside.

ARG. III. "The carnal man, whose cause we plead, says, Romans 7:20, 'If I do that I would not, it is no more I that do it, but sin which dwelleth in me,' that is, in my unrenewed part: and therefore he might be an eminent, apostolic saint in his *renewed part;* and a carnal, wretched man, sold under sin, in his *unrenewed part.*"

ANSWER. **1.** The apostle, speaking there as a *carnal,* and yet *awakened* man, who has light enough to see his sinful habits, but not faith and resolution enough to overcome them; his meaning is evidently this: — *If I,* as a carnal man, *do what I,* as an awakened man, *would not; it is no more I that do it,* that is, I do not do it according to my *awakened* conscience, for my conscience rises against my conduct: *but it is sin that dwelleth in me;* it is the tyrant sin, that has full possession of me, and minds the dictates of my conscience no more than an inexorable task master minds the cries of an oppressed slave.

2. If the pure love of God was shed abroad in St. Paul's heart and constrained him, he dwelt, in love, and of consequence in God. For St. John says, "He that dwelleth in love, dwelleth in God, and God in him. He that is in you, is greater than he that is in the world." Now if God dwelt in Paul by his loving Spirit, it becomes our objectors to show that *an indwelling God* and *indwelling sin* are one and the same thing; or that the apostle had strangely altered his doctrine when he asked, with indignation, "What concord has Christ with Belial?" For if indwelling sin, the Belial within, was necessary to nestle with Christ in St. Paul's heart, and in the hearts of all believers, should not the apostle have rather cried out with admiration, "See how great is the concord between Christ and Belial! They are inseparable! They always live in the same heart together: and nothing ever parted them, but what parts man and wife, that is, *death.*"

3. If *a reluctance to serve the law of sin* be a proof that we are holy as Paul was holy, is there not joy in heaven over the apostolic holiness of most robbers and murderers in the kingdom? Can they not sooner or later say, "*With my mind,* or conscience, *I serve the law of God; but with my flesh the law of sin. How to perform what is good, I find not. I would be* honest and loving, if I could be so without denying myself; *but I find a law, that when I would do good, evil is present with me?*"

For can any thing be stronger upon this head than the words of the inhuman princess, who, being at the point of committing murder, cried out, "My mind, [that is, my reason or conscience,] leads me to one thing, but my new, impetuous passion carries me to another, against my will. I see, I approve what is right, but I do what is criminal."[*]

ARG. IV. "The man whose experience is described in Romans 7, is said 'to delight in the law of God after the inward man, and to serve the law of God with the mind;' therefore he was partaker of apostolic holiness."

ANSWER. Does he not also say, "With the flesh I serve the law of sin?" And did not Medea say as much in her way before she imbrued her hands in innocent blood? What else could She mean when she cried out, "I see and approve with my mind what is right, though I do what is criminal?" Did not the Pharisees for a time "rejoice in the burning and shining light" of John the Baptist? And does not an evangelist inform us that Herod himself heard that man of God (ηοεως) "with delight," and "did many things" too? Mark 6:20. But is this a proof that either Medea, the Pharisees, or Herod had attained apostolic holiness?

ARG. V. "The person who describes his unavailing struggles under the power of sin, cries out at last, *Who shall deliver me,* &c, and immediately expresses a hope of future deliverance, *thanking God for it, through Jesus Christ our Lord,* Romans 7:24, 25. Does not this show that *the carnal man sold under sin* was a *Christian believer,* and, of consequence, Paul himself?"

ANSWER. This shows only that the man sold under sin, and groaning for evangelical liberty, is supported under his unhappy circumstances by a hope of deliverance; and that when the law, like a severe school master, has almost brought him to Jesus Christ; when he is come to the borders of Canaan, and "is not far from the kingdom of God and the city of refuge," he begins to look and long earnestly for Christ; and has at times comfortable hopes of deliverance through him. He has a faith that desires liberty, but not a faith that obtains it. He has a degree of the "faith to be healed," which is mentioned Acts 19:9; but he has not yet the actually healing, prevailing faith, which St. John calls the victory, and which is accompanied with an *internal witness* that "Christ is formed in our hearts." It is absurd to confound the carnal man who struggles into Christ and liberty, saying, "Who shall deliver me," &c, with the spiritual man who is come to Christ, stands in his redeeming power, and witnesses that "the law of the Spirit of life in Christ Jesus has made him free from the law of sin and death." The one may say, in his hopeful moments, "I thank God, *I shall have* the victory, through Jesus Christ:" but the other can say, "I have it now. *Thanks be to God, who giveth us the victory though Jesus Christ our Lord,*" 1 Corinthians 15:67. The one wishes for, and the other enjoys liberty: the one has ineffectual desires, and the other has victorious habits. Such is the contrast between the carnal penitent described in Romans 7:14, and the obedient believer described in Romans 8. "There is a great difference," says the Rev. Mr. Whitefield, "between good desires and good habits.

---

[*] Sed trahit invitam nova vis, aliudque cupido, Mens aliud suadet. Video meliora, proboque, Deteriota sequor. — OVID.

Many have the one who never attain the other." Many come up to the experience of a carnal penitent, who never attain the experience of an obedient believer. "Many have good desires to subdue sin, and yet, resting in those good desires, sin has always had the dominion over them;" *with the flesh they have always served the law of sin.* "A person sick of a fever may desire to be in health, but that desire is not health itself." (*Whitefield's Works,* vol. iv, page 7.) If the Calvinists would do justice to this important distinction, they would soon drop the argument which I answer, and the yoke of carnality which they try to fix upon St. Paul's neck.

ARG. VI. "You plead hard for the apostle's spirituality; but his own plain confession shows that he was really carnal, and sold under sin. Does he not say to the Corinthians, that 'there was given him a thorn in the flesh, a messenger of Satan to buffet him, lest he should be exalted above measure, by the abundance of the revelations which had been vouchsafed him?' 2 Corinthians 12:7. Now what could this 'thorn in the flesh' be, but *a sinful lust?* And what 'this messenger of Satan,' but *pride or immoderate anger?* Thrice he besought the Lord that these plagues might depart from him; but God would not hear him. Indwelling sin was to keep him humble; and if St. Paul stood in need of that remedy, how much more we?"

ANSWER. 1. Indwelling anger keeps us angry and not meek: indwelling pride keeps us proud, and not humble. The streams answer to the fountain. It is absurd to suppose that a salt spring will send forth fresh water.

2. You entirely mistake the apostle's meaning. While you try to make him a modest imperfectionist, you inadvertently represent him as an impudent Antinomian: for, speaking of his "thorn in the flesh," and of the "buffeting of Satan's messenger," he calls them his *infirmities,* and says, "Most gladly therefore will I glory in my infirmities." Now, if his infirmities were *pride, a wrathful disposition, and a filthy lust,* did he not act the part of a filthy Antinomian, when he said that "he gloried in them?" Would not even Paul's carnal man have blushed to speak thus! Far from glorying in his pride, wrath, or indwelling lust, did he not groan, "O wretched man that I am?"

3. The apostle, still speaking of his thorn in the flesh, and of Satan buffeting him by proxy, and still calling these trials *his infirmities,* explains himself farther in these words: — "Therefore I take pleasure in infirmities, in reproaches, in persecutions, &c, for Christ's sake; for when I am weak, then am I strong. Christ's strength is made perfect in my weakness." Those infirmities, that thorn in the flesh, that buffeting of Satan, cannot, then, be indwelling sin, or any outbreaking of it; for the devil himself could do no more than to take pleasure in his wickedness: and in Romans vii, the carnal penitent himself delights "in the law of God after the inward man," instead of taking pleasure in his indwelling sin.

4. The infirmities in which St. Paul glories and takes pleasure were such as had been given him to keep him humble after his revelations. "There was given to me a thorn in the flesh," &c, 2 Corinthians 12:7. Those infirmities and that thorn were not then indwelling sin, for indwelling sin was not given him after his visions, seeing it stuck fast in him long before he went to Damascus. It is absurd therefore to suppose that God gave him the thorn of indwelling sin afterward, or indeed that he gave it him at all.

5. If Mr. Hill wants to know what we understand by St. Paul's *thorn in the flesh,* and by *the messenger of Satan* that buffeted him; we reply, that we understand his bodily infirmities — the great weakness, and the violent headache with which Tertullian and

St. Chrysostom inform us the apostle was afflicted. The same God, who said to Satan concerning Job, "Behold he is in thine hand to touch his bone and his flesh, but save his life;" the same God, who permitted that adversary to "bind a daughter of Abraham with a spirit of *bodily* infirmity for eighteen years;" the same gracious God, I say, permitted Satan to afflict St. Paul's body with uncommon pains; and, at times, it seems, with preternatural weakness, which made his appearance and delivery contemptible in the eyes of his adversaries. That this is not a conjecture, grounded upon uncertain tradition, is evident from the apostle's own words two pages before. "His letters, say they, [that buffeted me in the name of Satan] are weighty and powerful; but his bodily presence is weak, and his speech contemptible," 2 Corinthians 10:10. And soon after, describing these emissaries of the devil, he says, "Such are false apostles, deceitful workers, transforming themselves into the apostles of Christ, [to oppose me, and to prejudice you against my ministry:] and no marvel; for Satan himself [who sets them on] is transformed into an angel of light," 2 Corinthians 11:13. But if the *thorn in the flesh* be all one with the *buffering messenger of Satan*, St. Paul's meaning is evidently this:— "God, who suffered the Canaanites to be scourges in the sides of the Israelites, and thorns in their eyes, Joshua 23:13, has suffered Satan to bruise my heel, while I bruise his head: and that, adversary afflicts me thus, by his thorns and pricking briers, that is, by false apostles, who buffet me through malicious misrepresentations which render me vile in your sight." This sense is strongly countenanced by these words of Ezekiel: — "They shall know that I am the Lord, and there shall be no more a pricking brier to the house of Israel, nor any grieving thorn of all that are round about them that despised them," Ezekiel 28:24.

Both these senses agree with reason and godliness, with the text and the context. Satan immediately pierced the apostle's body with preternatural pain; and, by the malice of false brethren, the opposition of false apostles within the Church, and the fierceness of cruel persecutors without, he immediately endeavoured to cast down or destroy the zealous apostle. But Paul walked in the perfect way, and we may well say of him, what was said of Job on a similar occasion, "In all this, Paul sinned not," as appears from his own words in this very epistle: "I am exceedingly joyful in all our tribulation. Our flesh had no rest, but we were troubled on every side: without *the Church* were fightings, within were fears:" we had furious opposition from the heathens *without;* and *within,* we feared lest our brethren should be discouraged by the number and violence of our adversaries: "nevertheless God, who comforteth those that are cast down, comforted us. We are troubled on every side, yet not distressed; we are perplexed, but not in despair; persecuted, but not forsaken; cast down, but not destroyed; always bearing about in the body the dying of the Lord Jesus. For which cause we faint not; but though our outward man perish" through the thorns in our flesh, and the buffetings of Satan, "yet the inward man is renewed day by day;" it grows stronger and stronger in the Lord. When I see St. Paul bear up with such undaunted fortitude, under the bruising hand of Satan's messengers, and the pungent operation of the "thorns in his flesh," methinks I see the general of the Christians waiving the standard of Christian perfection, and crying, "Be ye followers of me." Be wholly spiritual. "Take unto you the whole armour of God, that ye may be able to withstand in the evil day, and having done all, to stand," and to witness with me, that "in all these things we are more than conquerors through him that loved us."

ARG. VII. "You extol the apostle too much. He certainly was a carnal man still; for St. Luke informs us, that the contention [παροξυσμος] was so sharp between Barnabas and him, that they departed asunder one from the other, Acts 15:39. Now charity [ou paroxunetai] is not provoked, or does not contend. Strife or contention is one of the fruits of the flesh, and if St. Paul bore that fruit, I do not see why you should scruple to call him a carnal, wretched man, sold under sin."

ANSWER. 1. Every contention is not sinful. The apostle says himself, "Contend for the faith. Be angry and sin not. It is good to be zealously affected always in a good thing." Jesus Christ did not break the law of love, when he looked round with anger upon the Pharisees, "being grieved for the hardness of their hearts." Nor does Moses charge sin upon God, where he says, "The Lord rooted them out of their land in anger, and in wrath, and in great indignation." If St. Paul had contended in an uncharitable manner, I would directly grant that in that hour he fell from Christian perfection; for we assert, that as a carnal professor may occasionally cross Jordan, take a turn into the good land, and come back into the wilderness, as the spies did in the days, of Joshua; so a spiritual man, who lives in Canaan, may occasionally draw back, and take a turn in the wilderness, especially before he is "strengthened, established, and settled" under his heavenly vine, in the good land that flows with spiritual milk and honey. But this was not the apostle's case. There is not the least intimation given of his sinning in the affair. Barnabas, says the historian, determined to take with them his own nephew, John Mark; but Paul thought not good to do it, because, when they had tried him before, he went not with them to the work, but departed from them from Pamphylia, Acts 15:38. Now by every rule of reason and Scripture, Paul was in the right: for we are to try the spirits, and lovingly to beware of men, especially of such men as have already made us smart by their cowardly fickleness, as John Mark had done, when he had left the itinerant apostles in the midst of their dangers.

With respect to the word (παραξοσμ--)*contention* or *provoking*, it is used in a good, as well as in a bad sense. Thus, Hebrews 10:24, we read of (παραξοσμον αγαπης) *a contention* or *a provoking unto love and good works.* And therefore, granting that a grain of partiality to his nephew made Barnabas stretch too much that fine saying, "Charity hopeth all things;" yet, from the circumstances of Barnabas' parting with St. Paul, we have not the least proof that St. Paul stained at all his Christian perfection in the affair.

If the reader will properly weigh these answers to the arguments, by which our opponents try to stain the character of St. Paul as a spiritual man, he will see, I hope, that the apostle is as much misrepresented by Mr. Hill's doctrine, as Christian perfection is by his fictitious creed.

SECTION IX.

St. Paul, instead of owning himself a "carnal man," still "sold under sin," presents us with a striking picture of the perfect Christian, by occasionally describing his own spirituality and heavenly mindedness and therefore his genuine experiences are so many proofs that Christian perfection is attainable, and has actually been attained in this life — What St. Augustine and the Rev. Mr. Whitefield once thought of Romans 7 — And how near this last divine, and the Rev. Mr. Romaine, sometimes come to the doctrine of Christian perfection.

MR. HILL'S mistake, with respect to St. Paul's supposed carnality, is so much the more astonishing, as the apostle's professed spirituality not only clears him, but demonstrates the truth of our doctrine. Having therefore rescued his character from under the feet of those who tread his honour in the dust, and sell his person under sin at an Antinomian market, I shall retort the argument of our opponents; and appealing to St. Paul's genuine and undoubted experiences, when he taught wisdom "among the perfect," I shall present the reader with a picture of the perfect Christian, drawn at full length. Nor need I inform Mr. Hill that the misrepresented apostle sits for his own picture before the glass of evangelical sincerity; and that, turning spiritual self painter, with the pencil of a good conscience, and with colours mixed by the Spirit of truth, the draws this admirable portrait from the life —

"Be followers of me. This one thing I do; leaving the things that are behind, I press toward the mark for the prize of the heavenly calling [a crown of glory.] Charity is the bond of perfection. Love is the fulfilling of the law. If I have not charity, I am nothing." And what charity or love St. Paul had, appears from Christ's words and from his own. "Greater [i.e. more perfect] love hath no man than this," says our Lord, "that he lay down his life for his friends." Now, this very love Paul had for Christ, for souls, yea, for the souls of his fiercest adversaries, the Jews. Hear him:— "The love of Christ constraineth us. For me to live is Christ, and to die is gain. I long to depart and to be with Christ. I count not my life dear unto myself, that I may finish my course with joy. I am ready not to be bound only, but to die also for the name of the Lord Jesus. If I be offered upon the sacrifice and service of your faith, I joy and rejoice with you all." And in the next chapter but one to that in which the apostle is supposed to profess himself actually "sold under sin," he professes perfect love to his sworn enemies; even that love by which "the righteousness of the law is fulfilled in them who walk after the Spirit." Hear him:— "I say the truth in Christ, I lie not; my conscience also bearing me witness in the Holy Ghost, that I, &c, could wish that myself were accursed, i.e. made a curse (απο Χριστου) *after the example of Christ*, for my kinsmen according to the flesh;" meaning his inexorable, bloody persecutors, the Jews.

Nor was this love of St. Paul like a land flood: it constantly flowed like a river. This living water sprang up constantly in his soul: witness these words:— "Remember, that, by the space of three years, I ceased not to warn every one night and day with tears. Of many I have told you often, and now tell you even weeping, that they mind earthly things: for our conversation is in heaven. Our rejoicing is this, the testimony of our conscience, that in simplicity and godly sincerity, not with fleshly wisdom, but by the grace of God, we have had our conversation in the world. I know nothing [i.e. no evil] by [or of] myself. We can do nothing against the truth, but for the truth. Whether we are beside [i.e. carried out beyond] ourselves, it is to God: or whether we be sober, [i.e. calm,] it is for your cause: [i.e. the love of God and man is the only source of all my tempers.] Giving no offence in any thing, but in all things approving ourselves as the ministers of God, in much patience, by pureness, by kindness, by love unfeigned; being filled with comfort, and exceedingly joyful in all our tribulation. I will gladly spend and be spent for you; though the more abundantly I love you, the less I be loved: [a rare instance this, of the most perfect love!] We speak before God in Christ, we do all things, dearly beloved, for your edifying. I am crucified with Christ: nevertheless I live, yet not I, [see here the destruction of sinful self!] but Christ liveth in me; and the life I now live in the flesh, I live by the faith of the Son of God. As always, so now also Christ shall be magnified in my body, whether it be by life or by death: we worship God in the spirit, and rejoice in Christ Jesus, and have no confidence in the flesh. Mark them who walk so, as ye have us for an example. I have learned, in whatsoever state I am, therewith to be content; every where and in all things I am instructed, both to abound and to suffer need: I can do all things through Christ who strengtheneth me. Teaching every man in all wisdom, that I may present every man perfect in Christ Jesus; whereunto also I labour, striving according to his working which worketh in me mightily."

This description of the perfect Christian, and of St. Paul, is so exceedingly glorious, and it appears to me such a refutation of the Calvinian mistake which I oppose, that I cannot deny myself the pleasure, and my readers the edification of seeing the misrepresented apostle give his own lovely picture a few more finishing strokes: — "We speak not as pleasing men," says he, "but as pleasing God, who trieth our hearts. For neither at any time used we flattering words, &c, God is witness; nor of men sought we glory, neither of you, nor yet of others. But we were gentle among you, even as a nurse cherisheth her children. Being affectionately desirous of you, we were willing to have imparted to you, not the Gospel of God only, but also our own souls; labouring night and day, because we would not be chargeable to any of you. Ye are witnesses, and God also, how holily, and justly, and unblamably we behaved ourselves among you. The Lord make you abound in love one toward another, and toward all men, even as we do toward you. Thou hast fully known my manner of life, purpose, faith; long suffering, charity, patience: I have kept the faith: henceforth there is laid up for me a crown of righteousness, which the Lord, the righteous Judge, shall give in that day."

When I read this wonderful experience of St. Paul, written by himself, and see his doctrine of Christian perfection so gloriously exemplified in his own tempers and conduct, I am surprised that good men should still confound *Saul the Jew* with PAUL THE CHRISTIAN: and should take the son of "the earthly Jerusalem, which is in bondage with her children," for the son of "the Jerusalem from above, which is free, and is the mother of us all, who stand in the liberty wherewith Christ hath made us free." But, upon second thoughts, I wonder no more: for if those who engross to themselves the title of *Catholics,* can believe that Christ took his own body into his own fingers, broke it through the middle, when he took bread, broke it, and said, "This is my body which is broken for you;" why cannot those who monopolize the name of *orthodox* among us, believe also that St. Paul spoke with a figure when he said, "'I am carnal, and sold under sin, and brought into captivity to the law of sin which is in my members. Brethren, I beseech you be as I am: those things which ye have heard and seen in me, do, and the God of peace shall be with you.' Now you have heard and seen, 'that the evil which I would not, that I do; and that with my flesh I serve the law of sin.' In short, you have heard and seen that 'I am carnal and sold under sin.'"

I am not at all surprised that carnal and injudicious professors should contend for this contradictory doctrine, this flesh-pleasing standard of Calvinian inconsistency and Christian imperfection. But that good, and in other respects judicious men, should so zealously contend for it, appears to me astonishing. They can never design to confound carnal bondage with evangelical liberty, and St. Paul's Christian experience with that of Medea, and "Mr. Fulsome," in order to countenance gross Antinomianism: nor can they take any pleasure in misrepresenting the holy apostle. Why do they then patronize so great a mistake? I answer still, By the same reason which makes pious Papists believe that consecrated bread is the real flesh of Christ. Their priests and the pope say so: some figurative expressions of our Lord seem to countenance their saying. We Protestants, whom the Papists call *carnal reasoners* and *heretics,* are of a different sentiment: and should they believe as we do, their humility and orthodoxy would be in danger. Apply this to the present case. Calvinian divines and St. Augustine affirm that St. Paul humbly spoke his present experience when he said, *I am carnal, &c.* We, who are called "Arminians and perfectionists," think the contrary; and our pious opponents suppose that if they thought as we do, they should lose their humility and orthodoxy. Their error therefore springs chiefly from mistaken fears, and not from wilful opposition to truth.

Nor is St. Augustine fully for our opponents: we have our part in the bishop of Hippo as well as they. If he was for them when his controversy with Pelagius had heated him; he was for us when he yet stood upon the Scriptural line of moderation. Then he fairly owned that the man whom the apostle personates in Romans vii, is *homo sub lege positus ante gratiam;* "a man under the [condemning, irritating] power of the law, who is yet a stranger to the liberty and power of Christ's Gospel." Therefore, if Mr. Hill claim St. Augustine, the prejudiced controvertist, we claim St. Augustine, the unprejudiced father of the Church; or rather, setting aside his dubious authority, we continue our appeal to unprejudiced reason and plain Scripture.

What I say of St. Augustine may be said of the Rev. Mr. Whitefield. Before he had embraced St. Augustine's mistakes, which are known among us by the name of "Calvinism," he believed, as well as that father, that the disconsolate man who groans, *Who shall deliver me?* is not a *possessor* but a *seeker* of Christian liberty. To prove it, I need only transcribe the latter part of his sermon, entitled, The Marks of the New Birth:—

"Thirdly," says he, "I address myself to those who are under the drawings of the Father, and are *going through the Spirit of bondage;* but, not finding the marks [of the new birth] before mentioned, are ever crying out, [as the carnal penitent, Romans 7,] *Who shall deliver us from the body of this death?* Despair not: for, notwithstanding your present trouble, it may be the Divine pleasure to give you the kingdom." Hence it appears that Mr. Whitefield did not look upon such mourners as *Christian believers;* but only as persons who might become such if they earnestly sought. He therefore most judiciously exhorts them to seek till they find. "The grace of God, through Jesus Christ," adds he, "is able to deliver you, and give you what you want; even *you* may receive the Spirit of adoption, the promise of the Father. All things are possible with him; persevere, therefore, in seeking, and determine to find no rest in your spirit, till you know and feel that you are thus born again from above, and God's Spirit witnesses with your spirits that you are the children of God."

What immediately follows is a demonstration that, at that time, Mr. Whitefield was no enemy to Christian perfection, and thought that some had actually attained it; or else nothing would have been more trifling than his concluding address to perfect Christians. Take his own words, and remember that when he preached them, by the ardour of his zeal, and the devotedness of his heart, he showed himself a young man in Christ, able to trample under foot the most alluring baits of the flesh and of the world.

"Fourthly and lastly," says he, "I address myself to those who have received the Holy Ghost in all its sanctifying graces, and are almost ripe for glory. Hail, happy saints! For your heaven is begun upon earth. You have already received the first fruits of the Spirit, and are patiently waiting till that blessed change come, when your harvest shall be complete. I see and admire you, though, alas, at* so great a distance from you. Your life, I know, is hid with Christ in God. You have comforts, you have meat to eat, which a sinful, carnal world knows nothing of. Christ's yoke is now become easy to you, and his burden light: you have passed through the pangs of the new birth, and now rejoice that Christ Jesus is formed in your hearts. You know what it is to dwell in Christ, and Christ in you. Like Jacob's ladder, although your bodies are on earth, yet your souls and hearts are in heaven; and by your faith and constant recollection, *like the blessed angels, you do always behold the face of your Father, which is in heaven. I need not then exhort you to press forward, &c.* Rather I will exhort you in patience to possess your souls: yet a little while, and Jesus Christ will deliver you from the burden of the flesh, and an abundant entrance shall be administered unto you into the eternal joy, &c, of his heavenly kingdom." I have met with few descriptions of the perfect Christian that please me better. I make but one objection to it: Mr. Whitefield thought that the believers who "by constant recollection, like the blessed angels, always behold the face of their Father," are so advanced in grace, that they "need not to be exhorted to press forward." This is carrying the doctrine of perfection higher than Mr. Wesley ever did. For my part, were I to preach to a congregation of such "happy saints," I would not scruple taking this text: "So run that ye may [eternally] obtain:" nor would I forget to set before them the example of the perfect apostle, who said, "This one thing I do, leaving the things that are behind, and reaching forth, I press toward the mark," &c. Had I been in Mr. Whitefield's case, I own I would either have refused to join the imperfectionists, or I would have recanted my address to perfect Christians.

---

* At that time Mr. Whitefield was in orders, and had "received the Spirit of adoption." As a proof of it, I appeal, (1.) To the account of his conversion at Oxford, before he was ordained; and, (2.) To these his own words: "I can say, to the honour of rich, free, distinguishing grace, that I received the Spirit of adoption before I had conversed with one man, or read a single book on the doctrine of free justification by the imputed righteousness of Jesus Christ." That is, before he had any opportunity of being drawn from the simplicity of the Scripture Gospel, into the Calvinian refinements. (See his Works, vol. iv, page 45.) Now, those Christians, who leave babes and young men in Christ "at so great a distance from them," are the very persons whom we call "fathers in Christ," "perfect Christians."

Doctrines of Grace and Justice

So strong is the Scriptural tide in favour of our doctrine, that it sometimes carried away the Rev. Mr. Romaine himself. Nor can I confirm the wavering reader in his belief of the possibility of obtaining the glorious liberty which we contend for, better than by transcribing a fine exhortation of that great minister, to what we call Christian perfection, and what he calls *the walk of faith:*—

"The new covenant runs thus: — 'I will put,' says God, 'my law in their inward parts, and write it in their hearts,' &c. The Lord here engages to take away the stony heart, and to give a heart of flesh, upon which he will write the ten commandments, &c. The love of God will open the contracted heart, enlarge the selfish, warm the cold, and bring liberality out of the covetous. When the Holy Spirit teaches brotherly love, he overcomes all opposition to it, &c. He writes upon their hearts the two great commandments, 'on which hang all the law and the prophets. The love of God,' says the apostle to the Romans, 'is shed abroad in their hearts by the Holy Ghost;' and to the Thessalonians, 'Ye yourselves are taught of God to love one another.' Thus he engages the soul to the holy law, and inclines the inner man to love obedience. It ceases to be a yoke and a burden. How easy is it to do what one loves! If you dearly love any person, what a pleasure it is to serve him! What will not love put you upon doing or suffering to oblige him! Let love rule in the heart to God and to man, his law will then become delightful, and obedience to it will be pleasantness. The soul will run; yea, inspired by love, it will mount up with wings as eagles, in the way of God's commandments. Happy are the people that are in such a case." Now, such a case is what we call, *the state of Christian perfection;* to the obtaining of which, Mr. Romaine excites his own soul by the following excellent exhortation:—

"This is the very tenor of the covenant of grace, which the almighty Spirit has undertaken to fulfil, [if we mix faith with the promises, as Mr. Romaine himself will soon intimate,] and he cannot fail in his office. It is his crown and glory to make good his covenant engagements. O trust him then, and put honour upon his faithfulness, [that is, if I mistake not, make good your own covenant engagements.] He has promised to guide thee with his counsel, and to strengthen thee with his might, &c. What is within thee, or without thee, to oppose thy walking in love with him, he will incline thee to resist, and he will enable thee to overcome. O what mayest thou not expect from such a Divine Friend, who is to abide with thee on purpose to keep thine heart right with God! [Query: when the heart is kept full of indwelling sin, is it kept right with God?] What cannot he do? What will he not do for thee? Such as is the love of the Father and of the Son, such is the love of the Holy Ghost: the same free, perfect, everlasting love. Read his promises of it. Meditate on them. Pray to him for increasing faith to mix with them; that he [not sin] dwelling in the temple of thy heart, thou mayest have fellowship there with the Father and with the Son. Whatever in thee is pardoned through the Son's atonement, pray the Holy Spirit to subdue, that it may not interrupt communion with thy God. And whatever grace is to be received out of the fulness of Jesus, in order to keep up and promote that communion, entreat the Holy Spirit to give it thee with growing strength. But pray in faith, nothing wavering. So shall the love of God rule in thy heart. And then thou shalt be like the sun, when it goeth forth in its might, shining clearer and clearer to the perfect day. O may thy course be like his, as free, as regular, and as communicative of good, that thy daily petition may be answered, and that the will of thy Father may be done on earth, as it is in heaven." (*Walk of Faith,* vol. i, page 227, &c.)

I do not produce this excellent quotation to insinuate that the Rev. Mr. Romaine is a perfectionist, but only to edify the reader, and to show that the good, mistaken men, who are most prejudiced against our doctrine, see it sometimes so true, and so excellent, that, forgetting their pleas for indwelling sin, they intimate that our daily petition may be answered; and that the "will of our Father may be done on earth as it is in heaven;" an expression this, which includes the height and depth of all Christian perfection.

SECTION X.

St. John is for Christian perfection, and not for a death purgatory — 1 John 1:8, &c, is explained agreeably to St. John's design, the context, and the vein of holy doctrine which runs through the rest of the epistle.

THE Scriptures declare that "we are built upon the foundation of the apostles, Jesus Christ himself being the chief corner stone:" and St. Paul being deservedly considered as the chief of the apostles, and of consequence as the chief stone of the *foundation* on which, next to the corner stone, our holy religion is built, who can wonder at the pains which our opponents take to represent this important part of our foundation as *carnal, wretched, and sold under sin?* Does not every body see that such a foundation becomes the Antinomian structure which is raised upon it? And is it not incumbent upon the opposers of Antinomianism to uncover that wretched foundation by removing the heaps of dirt in which St. Paul's spirituality is daily buried; and by this means to rescue the holy apostle, whom our adversaries endeavour to "sell under sin," as a *carnal wretch?* This rescue has been attempted in the four last sections. If I have succeeded in this charitable attempt, I may proceed to vindicate the holiness of St. John, who is the last apostle that Mr. Hill calls to the help of *indwelling sin, Christian imperfection, and a death purgatory.*

Before I show how the loving apostle is pressed into a service which is so contrary to his experience, and to his doctrine of perfect love, I shall make a preliminary remark. To take a passage of Scripture out from the context, and to make it speak a language contrary to the obvious design of the sacred writer, is the way to butcher the body of Scriptural divinity. This conduct injures truth, as much as the Galatians would have injured themselves, if they had literally "pulled their eyes out, and given them to St. Paul:" an edifying passage, thus displaced, may become as loathsome to a moral mind, as a good eye, torn out of its bleeding orb in a good face, is odious to a tender heart.

Among the passages which have been thus treated, none has suffered more violence than this:— "If we say that we have no sin, we deceive ourselves, and the truth is not in us," 1 John 1:8. "That's enough for me," says a hasty imperfectionist: "St. John clearly pleads for the *indwelling of sin* in us during the term of life; and he is so set against those who profess deliverance from sin, and Christian perfection in this life, that he does not scruple to represent them as *liars* and *self deceivers.*"

Doctrines of Grace and Justice

Our opponents suppose that this argument is unanswerable. But to convince them that they are mistaken, we need only prove that the sense which they so confidently give to the words of St. John is contrary, (1.) To his design. (2.) To the context. And, (3.) To the pure and strict doctrine which he enforces in the rest of the epistle.

I. With respect to St. John's *design,* it evidently was to confirm believers who were in danger of being deceived by Antinomian and anti-christian seducers. When he wrote this epistle, the Church began to be corrupted by men, who, under pretence of knowing the mysteries of the Gospel better than the apostles, imposed upon the simple Jewish fables, heathenish dreams, or vain, philosophic speculations; insinuating that their doctrinal peculiarities were the very marrow of the Gospel. Many such arose at the time of the reformation, who introduced stoical dreams into Protestantism, and whom Bishop Latimer and others steadily opposed under the name of "Gospellers."

The doctrines of all these Gospellers centred in making Christ, indirectly at least, the minister of sin; and in representing the preachers of *practical, self-denying* Christianity, as persons unacquainted with Christian liberty. It does not indeed appear that the Gnostics, or *knowing ones,* (for so the ancient Gospellers were called,) carried matters so far as openly to say that believers might be God's dear children in the very commission of adultery and murder, or while they worshipped Milcom and Ashtaroth: but it is certain that they could already reconcile the verbal denial of Christ, fornication and idolatrous feasting, with true faith; directly or indirectly "teaching and seducing *Christ's* servants to commit fornication, and to eat things sacrificed to idols," Revelation 2:20. At these Antinomians, St. Peter, St. James, and St. Jude, levelled their epistles. St. Paul strongly cautioned Timothy, Titus, and the Ephesians against them: see Ephesians 4:14; 5:6. And St. John wrote his first epistle to warn the believers who had not yet been seduced into their error: a dreadful, though pleasing error this, which, by degrees, led some to deny Christ's law, and then his very name; hence the triumph of the spirit of antichrist. Now, as these men insinuated that believers might *be righteous* without *doing righteousness;* and as they supposed that *Christ's righteousness,* or our own k*nowledge and faith,* would supply the want of internal sanctification and external obedience; St. John maintains against them the necessity of that practical godliness which consists in not "committing sin," and in "walking as Christ walked:" nay, he asserts that Christ's blood, through the faith which is our victory, purifies "from all sin, and cleanses from all unrighteousness." To make him, therefore, plead for the necessary continuance of indwelling sin, till we go into a death purgatory, is evidently to make him defeat his own design.

II. To be more convinced of it, we need only read the controverted text in connection with the CONTEXT; illustrating both by some notes in brackets. St. John opens his commission thus, FirstJohn 1:5, 6, 7: — "This is the message which we have received of him [Christ] and declare unto you, that God is light, [bright, transcendent purity,] and in him is no darkness [no impurity] at all. If we [believers] say that we have fellowship with him, [that we are united to him by an actually living faith,] and walk in darkness, [in impurity or sin,] we lie, and do not the truth. But if we walk in the light as he is in the light, [if we live up to our Christian light and do righteousness,] we have fellowship one with another, and the blood of Jesus Christ his Son cleanseth us from all sin. For let no man deceive you: he that does righteousness is righteous, even as he, *Christ,* is righteous; and in him is no sin," 1 John 3:5, 7. So far we see no plea, either for sin, or for the Calvinian purgatory.

Should Mr. Hill reply, that "when St. John says, 'The blood of Christ cleanseth us from all sin,' the apostle does not mean *all indwelling sin;* because this is a sin from which death alone can cleanse us:" we demand a proof, and in the meantime we answer, that St. John, in the above-quoted passages, says, that "he who does righteousness," in the full sense of the word, "is righteous, as Christ is righteous;" observing that "in him [Christ] is no sin." So certain, then, as there is no indwelling sin in Christ, there is no indwelling sin in a believer *who does righteousness* in the full sense of the word; for he is made "perfect in love," and is "cleansed from all sin." Nor was St. John himself ashamed to profess this glorious liberty; for he said," Our love is made perfect, that we may have boldness in the day of judgment; because as he [Christ] is [perfect in love, and of consequence without sin,] so are we in this world," 1 John 4:17. And the whole context shows that the beloved apostle spake these great words of a likeness to Christ with respect to the perfect love which "fulfils the law, abolishes tormenting fear, and enables the believer to stand with boldness in the day of judgment," as being forgiven, and "conformed to the image of God's Son."

If Mr. Hill urge that "the blood of Christ, powerfully applied by the Spirit, cleanses us indeed from the *guilt,* but not from the *filthiness* of sin; blood having a reference to justification and *pardon,* but not to sanctification and *holiness:*" we reply, that this argument is not only contrary to the preceding answer, but to the text, the context, and other plain scriptures. (1.) To *the text,* where our being cleansed from all sin is evidently suspended on our humble and faithful walk: "If we walk in the light as he is in the light, the blood of Christ cleanses us," &c. Now every novice in Gospel grace knows that true Protestants do not suspend a sinner's justification on his "walking in the light as God is in the light." (2.) It is contrary to *the context;* for in the next verse but one, where St. John evidently distinguishes *forgiveness* and *holiness,* he peculiarly applies the word *cleansing* to the latter of these blessings: "He is faithful to forgive us our sin," by taking away our guilt; "and to cleanse us from all unrighteousness," by taking away all the filth of indwelling sin. And, (3.) It is contrary to *other places of Scripture,* where Christ's blood is represented as having a reference to purification, as well as to forgiveness. God himself says, "Wash ye; make you clean; put away the evil of your doings; cease to do evil; learn to do well." The washing and cleansing here spoken of, have undoubtedly a reference to the removal of the *filth,* as well as the *guilt* of sin. Accordingly we read that all those who "stand before the throne, have *both* washed their robes, and made them white in the blood of the Lamb;" that is, they are justified by, and sanctified with his blood. Hence our Church prays "that we may so eat the flesh of Christ, and drink his blood, that our sinful bodies may be made clean by his body, and our souls washed [i.e. made clean also] through his most precious blood." To rob Christ's blood of its sanctifying power, and to confine its efficacy to the atonement, is therefore an Antinomian mistake, by which our opponents greatly injure the Saviour, whom they pretend to exalt.

Should Mr. Hill assert, that "when St. John says, *If we walk in the light, &c, the blood of Christ cleanses us from all sin,* the loving apostle's meaning is not that the blood of Christ *radically* cleanses us, but only that it *begets and carries on* a cleansing from all sin, which cleansing will be completed in a death purgatory:" we answer: (1.) This assertion leaves Mr. Hill's doctrine open to all the abovementioned difficulties. (2.) It overthrows the doctrine of the Protestants, who have always maintained that nothing is absolutely necessary to eternal salvation, and, of consequence, to our perfect cleansing, but an obedient, steadfast faith, apprehending the full virtue of Christ's purifying blood, according to Acts 15:9, "God giving them the Holy Ghost, put no difference between them and us, purifying their hearts by faith," — not by death. (3.) It is contrary to matter of fact: Enoch and Elijah having been translated to heaven, and therefore having been perfectly purified even in body, without going into the Calvinian purgatory. But, (4.) What displeases us most in the evasive argument which I answer, is, that it puts the greatest contempt on Christ's blood, and puts the greatest cheat on weak believers, who sincerely wait to be now "made perfect in love," that they may now worthily magnify God's holy name.

An illustration will prove it. I suppose that Christ is now in England, doing as many wonderful cures as he formerly did in Judea. My benevolent opponent runs to the Salop infirmary, and tells all the patients there that the great Physician, the Son of God, has once more visited the earth; and he again "heals all manner of sickness and diseases among the people, and cleanses" from the most inveterate leprosy by a touch or a word. All the patients believe Mr. Hill; some hop to this wonderful Saviour, and others are carried to his footstool. They touch and retouch him; he strokes them round again and again: but not one of them is cured. The wounds of some, indeed, are skinned over for a time; but it soon appears that they still fester at the bottom, and that a painful core remains unextracted in every sore. The poor creatures complain to Mr. Hill, "Did you not, sir, assure us upon your honour, as a Christian gentleman, that Christ heals all manner of diseases, and cleanses from all kinds of leprosies?" "True," says Mr. Hill; "but you must know that these words do not mean that he *radically cures* any disease, or *cleanses* from any leprosy: they only signify that he *begins* to cure every disease, and *continues* to cleanse from *all* leprosies; but notwithstanding all his cures, *begun* and *continued,* nobody is cured before death. So, my friends, you must bear your festering sores as well as you can, till death comes radically to cleanse and cure you from them all." Instead of crying, "Sweet grace! Rich grace!" and of clapping Mr. Hill for his evangelical message, the disappointed patients desire him to take them back to the infirmary, saying, "We have there a chance for a cure before death; but your great Physician pronounces us incurable, unless death comes to the help of his art: and we think that any surgeon could do as much, if he did not do more." (See sec. xii, argument 20.)

If Mr. Hill say that I beat the air, and that the text which he quotes in his "Creed for Perfectionists," to show that it is impossible to be cleansed from all sin before death, is not 1 John 1:7, but the next verse; I reply, that if St. John assert in the seventh verse that "Christ's blood," powerfully applied by the Spirit of faith, "cleanses us from all sin," that inspired writer cannot be so exceedingly inconsistent as to contradict himself in the very next verse.

Should the reader ask, "What then can be St. John's meaning in that verse, where he declares that 'if we say that we have no sin, we deceive ourselves, and the truth is not in us?' How can these words possibly agree with the doctrine of a perfect cleansing from all sin?"

We answer, that St. John having given his first stroke to the Antinomian believers of his day, strikes, by the by, a blow at Pharisaic professors. There were in St. John's time, as there are in our own, numbers of men who had never been properly convinced of sin, and who boasted, as Paul once did, that touching the righteousness of the law, they were blameless; they served God; they did their duty; they gave alms; they never did any body any harm; they thanked God that they were not as other men; but especially that they were not like those mourners in Sion, who were no doubt very wicked, since they made so much ado about God's mercy, and a powerful application of the Redeemer's all-cleansing blood. How proper then was it for St. John to inform his readers that these *whole-hearted* Christians, these *perfect* Pharisees, were no better than *liars* and *self deceivers;* and that true Christian righteousness is always attended by a genuine conviction of our *native* depravity, and by an humble acknowledgment of our *actual* transgressions.

This being premised, it appears that the text so dear to us, and so mistaken by our opponents, has this fair, Scriptural meaning:— "If we [followers of Him who came not to call the righteous, but sinners to repentance] say, We have no sin [no *native* depravity from our first parents, and no *actual* sin, at least no such sin as deserves God's wrath; fancying we need not secure a particular application of Christ's atoning and purifying blood] we deceive ourselves, and the truth [of repentance and faith] is not in us."

That the words are levelled at the monstrous error of self-conceited, and self-perfected Pharisees, and not at "the glorious liberty of the children of God," appears to us indubitable from the following reasons: (1.) The immediately preceding verse strongly asserts this liberty. (2.) The verse immediately following secures it also, and cuts down the doctrine of our opponents; the apostle's meaning being evidently this:— "Though I write to you, that 'if we say' we are originally free from sin, and never did any harm, 'we deceive ourselves;' yet, mistake me not: I no not mean to continue under the guilt, or in the moral infection of any sin, original or actual. For if we penitently and believingly confess both, 'he is faithful and just to forgive us our sins, and to cleanse us from all unrighteousness,' whether it be native or self contracted, internal or external. Therefore, if we have attained the glorious liberty of God's children, we need not, through voluntary humility, say that we do nothing but sin. It will be sufficient, when we are 'cleansed from all unrighteousness,' still to be deeply humbled for our present infirmities, and for our past sins; confessing both with godly sorrow and filial shame. For if we should say, 'We have not sinned, [note: St. John does not write, *If we should say,* WE DO NOT SIN,] we make him a liar, and the truth is not in us;' common sense dictating that if 'we have not sinned,' we speak an untruth when we profess that Christ has *forgiven our sins*." This appears to us the true meaning of 1 John 1:8, when it is fairly considered in the light of the context.

III. We humbly hope that Mr. Hill himself will be of our sentiment if he compare the verse in debate with the pure and strict doctrine which St. John enforces throughout his epistle. In the second chapter he says, "We know that we know him, if we keep his commandments, &c. Whoso KEEPETH HIS WORD, in him verily is the love of God PERFECTED. He that abideth in him ought himself also so to walk, even as he walked, &c. He that loveth his brother abideth in the light [where the blood of Christ cleanseth from all sin] and there is none occasion of stumbling in him."

The same doctrine runs also through the next chapter: "Every one that hath this hope in him, PURIFIETH HIMSELF AS HE (Christ) IS PURE. Whosoever committeth sin transgresseth also the law, &c, and ye know that he was manifested to take away our sins, [i.e. to destroy them root and branch;] and in him is no sin. Whosoever abideth in him sinneth not: whosoever sinneth, does not [properly] see him, neither know him; he that does righteousness is righteous, even as he [Christ] is righteous. He that committeth sin, [i.e. as appears by the context, he that transgresseth the law,] is of the devil; for the devil sinneth from the beginning: for this purpose was the Son of God manifested, that he might destroy the works of the devil. Whosoever is born of God [whosoever is made partaker of God's holiness, according to the perfection of the Christian dispensation] doth not commit sin, [i.e. does not transgress the law;] for his seed," the ingrafted word, made quick and powerful by the indwelling Spirit, "remaineth in him, and [morally speaking] he cannot sin because he is [thus] born of God. For if ye know that he is righteous, ye know that every one that doth righteousness is born of him;" and that he that doth not righteousness, — he "that committeth sin," or transgresseth the law, — is, so far, of the devil, for "the devil" transgresseth the law, i.e. "sinneth from the beginning. In this the children of God are manifest, and the children of the devil.* Whosoever does not righteousness, [i.e. whosoever sinneth, taking the word in its evangelical meaning,] is not of God," 1 John 3:3- 11; 2:29.

If Mr. Hill cry out, "Shocking! Who are those men that do not sin?" I reply, All those whom St. John speaks of, a few verses below: "Beloved, if our heart condemn us; [and it will condemn us if we sin, but God much more, for] God is greater than our hearts, &c. Beloved, if our hearts condemn us not; we have confidence toward God, &c, because we keep his commandments, and do those things that are pleasing in his sight," 1 John 3:20, &c. Now, we apprehend, all the sophistry in the world will never prove that, evangelically speaking, "keeping God's commandments," and "doing what pleases him," is *sinning.* Therefore, when St. John professed to keep God's commandments, and to do what is pleasing in his sight, he professed what our opponents call sinless perfection, and what we call Christian perfection.

Mr. Hill is so very unhappy in his choice of St. John, to close the number of his apostolic witnesses for Christian imperfection, that, were it not for a few clauses of his first epistle, the anti-Solifidian severity of that apostle might drive all imperfect Christians to despair. And what is most remarkable, those few encouraging clauses are all conditional: "If any man sin," for there is no necessity that he should; or rather, (according to the most literal sense of the word αμαρτη, which being in the Aorist has generally the force of a past tense,) "If any man HAVE SINNED: if he have not sinned unto death: if we confess our sins: if that which ye have heard shall remain in you: if ye walk in the light:" then do we evangelically enjoy the benefit of our Advocate's intercession. Add to this, that the first of those clauses is prefaced by these words, "My little children, these things I write unto you, THAT YE SIN NOT;" and all together are guarded by these dreadful declarations:— "He that says, *I know*

---

* This doctrine of St. John is perfectly agreeable to that of our Lord, who said that "Judas had a devil," because he gave place to the love of money; and who called Peter himself "Satan," when he "savoured the things of men," in opposition to "the things of God."

him, and keepeth not his commandments, is a liar. If any man love the world, the love of the Father is not in him. If any man say, I love God, and loveth not his brother, [note: he that loveth another hath fulfilled the law,] he is a liar. There is a sin unto death, I do not say that he shall pray for it. Let no man deceive you; he that does righteousness is righteous. He that committeth sin [or transgresseth the law] is of the devil." To represent St. John, therefore, as an enemy to the doctrine of Christian perfection, does not appear to us less absurd than to represent Satan as a friend to complete holiness.

SECTION XI.

Why the privileges of believers under the Gospel of Christ cannot be justly measured by the experience of believers under the law of Moses — A review of the passages upon which the enemies of Christian perfection found their hopes that Solomon, Isaiah, and Job, were strong imperfectionists.

IF Mr. Hill had quoted Solomon, instead of St. John; and Jewish, instead of Christian saints, he might have attacked the glorious Christian liberty of God's children with more success: for "the heir, as long as he is a child, [in Jewish nonage,] differeth nothing from a servant, but is under tutors [and school masters] until the time appointed by the father. Even so we, when we were children, were in bondage: but when the fulness of the time was come, God sent his Son, made of a woman, made under the law, that we might receive the adoption of sons, and stand in the [peculiar] liberty, wherewith Christ has made us [Christians] free," Galatians 3:1; 4:1. But this very passage, which shows that Jews are, comparatively speaking, in bondage, shows also that the Christian dispensation and its high privileges cannot be measured by the inferior privileges of the Jewish dispensation, under which Solomon lived: for the "law made nothing perfect," in the Christian sense of the word. And "what the law could not do, God, sending his only Son, condemned sin in the flesh, that the righteousness of the law might be fulfilled in us [Christian believers] who walk after the Spirit;" being endued with that large measure of it, which began to be poured out on believers on the day of pentecost: for that measure of the Spirit was not given before, "because Jesus was not yet glorified," John 7:39. But after "he had ascended on high, and had obtained the gift of the indwelling Comforter" for believers; they received, says St. Peter, "the end of their faith, even the *Christian* salvation of their souls:" a salvation which St. Paul justly calls *so great salvation,* when he compares it with Jewish privileges, Hebrews 2:3. "Of which [Christian] salvation," proceeds St. Peter, "the prophets have inquired, who prophesied of the grace that should come unto you [Christians,] searching what, or what manner of time, the Spirit of Christ which was in them [according to their dispensation] did signify, when it testified beforehand the sufferings of Christ, and the glory [the glorious dispensation] that should follow [his return to heaven, and accompany the outpouring of the Spirit.] Unto whom [the Jewish prophets] it was revealed, that not unto themselves, but unto us [Christians] they did minister the things which are now preached unto you, with the Holy Ghost sent down from heaven," 1 Peter 1:9, &c. And, among those things, the Scriptures reckon the coming of the spiritual kingdom of Christ, with power into the hearts of believers, and the baptism of fire, or the perfect love, which "burns up the chaff" of sin, "thoroughly purges God's floor," and makes the hearts of perfect believers "a habitation of God through the Spirit, and not a nest for indwelling sin." As this doctrine may appear new to Mr. Hill, I beg leave to confirm it by the testimony of two as eminent divines as England has lately produced. The one is Mr. Baxter, who, in his comment upon these words, "A testament is of force after men are dead," &c, Hebrews 9:17, very justly observes, that "his (Christ's) covenant has the nature of a testament, which supposeth the death of the testator, and is not of efficacy till then, to give full right of what he bequeatheth. Note: that the eminent, evangelical kingdom of the Mediator, in its last, full edition, called *the kingdom of Christ* and *of heaven,* distinct from the obscure state of promise before Christ's incarnation, began at Christ's resurrection, ascension, and sending of the eminent gift of the Holy Ghost, and was but as an embryo before." My other witness is the Rev. Mr. Whitefield, who proposes and answers the following question: "Why was not the Holy Ghost given till Jesus Christ was glorified? Because till then he was himself on the earth, and had not taken on him the kingly office, nor pleaded the merits of his death before his heavenly Father, by which he purchased that invaluable blessing for us." (See his *Works,* vol. iv, p. 362.) Hence I conclude, that as the full measure of the Spirit, which perfects Christian believers, was not given before our Lord's ascension, it is as absurd to judge of Christian perfection by the experiences of those who died before that remarkable event, as to measure the powers of a sucking child by those of an embryo.

This might suffice to unnerve all the arguments which our opponents produce from the Old Testament against Christian perfection. However, we are willing to consider a moment those passages by which they plead for the necessary indwelling of sin, in all Christian believers, and defend the walls of the Jericho within, that accursed city of refuge for spiritual Canaanites and Diabolonians.

I. 1 Kings 8:46, &c. Solomon prays and says, "If they [the Jews] sin against thee (for there is no man* that sinneth not) and thou be angry with them, and deliver them to the enemy, so that they carry them away captive — yet, if they bethink themselves and repent, and make supplication unto thee, and return unto thee with all their heart, and with all their soul, then hear thou their prayer." No unprejudiced person, who, in reading this passage, takes the parenthesis ("for there is no man that sinneth not") in connection with the context, can, I think, help seeing that the Rev. Mr. Toplady, who, if I remember right, quotes this text against us, mistakes Solomon, as much as Mr. Hill does St. John. The meaning is evidently, *there is no man who is not liable to sin;* and that a man actually sins, when he actually departs from God. Now, *peccability,* or a *liableness to sin,* is not indwelling sin; for angels, Adam and Eve, were all liable to sin, in their sinless state. And that there are some men who do not actually sin is indubitable, (1.)From the hypothetical phrase in the context, "if any man sin," which shows that

---

* If Mr. Hill consult the original, he will find that the word translated *sinneth,* is in the future tense, which is often used for an indefinite tense in the potential mood, because the Hebrews have no such mood or tense. Therefore our translators would only have done justice to the original, as well as to the context, if they had rendered the whole clause, "There is no man that may not sin; instead of "There is no man that sinneth not."

their sinning is not unavoidable. (2.) From God's anger against those that sin, which is immediately mentioned. Hence it appears, that so certain as God is not angry with all his people, some of them do not sin in the sense of the wise man. And, (3.) From Solomon's intimating that these very men who have sinned, or have actually departed from God, may "bethink themselves, repent and turn to God with all their heart, and with all their soul," that is, may attain the perfection of their dispensation; the two poles not being more opposed to each other than *sinning* is to *repenting;* and *departing from God,* to *returning to him with all our heart and with all our soul.* Take therefore the whole passage together, and you have a demonstration that "where sin hath abounded, there grace may much more abound." And what is this but a demonstration that our doctrine is not chimerical? For if Jews (Solomon himself being judge) instead of sinning and departing from God, can "repent, and turn to him with all their heart," how much more Christians, whose privileges are so much greater!

II. "But Solomon says also, There is not a just man upon earth, that does good and sinneth not," Ecclesiastes 7:20.

(1.) We are not sure that Solomon. says it: for he may introduce here the very same man who, four verses before, says, "Be not righteous overmuch," &c, and Mr. Toplady may mistake the interlocutor's meaning in one text, as Dr. Trap had done in the other. But, (2.)Supposing Solomon speaks, may not he in general assert what St. Paul does, Romans 3:23? "All have sinned, and come short of the glory of God," the just not excepted: is not this the very sense which Canne, Calvinist as he was, gives to the wise man's words, when he refers the reader to this assertion of the apostle? And did we ever speak against this true doctrine? (3.) If you take the original word *to sin,* in the lowest sense which it bears' if it mean in Ecclesiastes 7:20, what it does in Judges 20:16, namely, *to miss a mark,* we shall not differ; for we maintain, that, according to the standard of paradisiacal perfection, "there is not a just man upon earth, that does good and misses not" the mark of that perfection, i.e. that does not lessen the good he does, by some involuntary, and therefore (evangelically speaking) sinless defect. (4.) It is bold to pretend to overthrow the glorious liberty of God's children, which is asserted in a hundred plain passages of the New Testament, by producing so vague a text as Ecclesiastes 7:20. And to measure the spiritual attainments of all believers, in all ages, by this obscure standard, appears to us as ridiculous as to affirm, that of a thousand believing men, nine hundred and ninety-nine are indubitably villains; and that of a thousand Christian women, there is not one but is a strumpet; because Solomon says a few lines below, "One man among a thousand have I found; but a woman among all those have I not found," Ecclesiastes 7:28.

III. If it be objected that "Solomon asks, 'Who can say, *I have made my heart clean, I am pure from my sin?*' Proverbs 20:9:" we answer: —

1. Does not Solomon's father ask, "Who shall dwell in thy holy hill?" Does a question of that nature always imply an absurdity, or an impossibility? Might not Solomon's query be evangelically answered thus? "The man in whom thy father David's prayer is answered, *Create in me a clean heart, O God:* the man who has regarded St. James' direction to the primitive Solifidians, *Cleanse your hearts, ye double minded:* the man who has obeyed God's awful command, *O Jerusalem, wash thy heart from iniquity, that thou mayest be saved:* or the man who is interested in the sixth beatitude, *Blessed are* *the pure in heart, for they shall see God:* that man, I say, can testify to the honour of the *blood which cleanseth from all sin, that he has made his heart clean."*

2. However, if Solomon, as is most probable, reproves in this passage the conceit of a perfect, boasting Pharisee, the answer is obvious: no man of that stamp can say with any truth, "I have made my heart clean;" for the law of faith excludes all proud boasting, and if we say, with the temper of the Pharisee, "that we have no sin, we deceive ourselves, and the truth is not in us;" for we have pride, and Pharisaic pride too, which, in the sight of God, is perhaps the greatest of all sins. If our opponents take the wise man's question in either of the preceding Scriptural senses, they will find that it perfectly agrees with the doctrine of Jewish and Christian perfection.

IV. Solomon's pretended testimony against Christian perfection is frequently backed by two of Isaiah's sayings, considered apart from the context, one of which respects the "filthiness of our righteousness;" and the other the *uncleanness of our lips.* I have already proved, (vol. i, Fourth Check, letter viii,) that the righteousness which Isaiah compares *to filthy rags,* and St. Paul to *dung,* is only the anti-evangelical, Pharisaic righteousness of unhumbled professors: a righteousness this, which may be called "the righteousness of impenitent pride," rather than "the righteousness of humble faith;" therefore the excellence of the righteousness of faith cannot, with any propriety, be struck at by that passage.

V. "But Isaiah, undoubtedly speaking of himself, says, *Wo is me, for I am undone, because I am a man of unclean lips,* Isaiah 6:5." True: but give yourself the trouble to read the two following verses, and you will hear him declare that the power of God's Spirit applying the blood of sprinkling (which power was represented by "a live coal taken from off the altar,") touched his lips; so that "his iniquity was taken away and his sin purged." This passage, therefore, when it is considered with the context, instead of disproving the doctrine of Christian perfection, strongly proves the doctrine of Jewish perfection.

If Isaiah is discharged from the service into which he is so unwarrantably pressed, our opponents will bring Job, whom the Lord himself pronounces *perfect* according to his dispensation, notwithstanding the hard thoughts which his friends entertained of him.

VI. Perfect Job is absurdly set upon demolishing Christian perfection, because he says, "If I justify myself, mine own mouth shall condemn me; if I say, [in a self-justifying spirit] *I am perfect,* it shall also prove me perverse," Job 9:20. But, (1.) What does Job assert here more than Solomon does in the word, to which Canne on this text judiciously refers his readers: "Let another man praise thee, and not thine own mouth; a stranger, and not thine own lips." Though even this rule is not without exception; witness the circumstance which drove St. Paul to what he calls a confidence of boasting. (2.) That professing the perfection of our dispensation in a self-abasing and Christ-exalting spirit is not a proof of perverseness, is evident from the profession which humble Paul made of his being one of the perfect Christians of his time, Philippians 3:15, and from St. John's declaration, that his "love was made perfect," John 4:17. For when we have "the witnessing Spirit, whereby we know the things which are freely given to us of God, we may, nay, at proper times we should acknowledge his gifts, to his glory, though not our own. (3.) If God himself had pronounced Job *perfect,* according to his dispensation, Job's modest fear of pronouncing himself so, does not at all overthrow the Divine testimony; such a timorousness only shows that the more we are advanced in grace, the more we are averse to whatever has the appearance of ostentation; and the more deeply we feel what Job felt, when he said, "Behold, I am vile; what shall I answer thee? I will put my hand upon my mouth," Job 40:4.

VII. "But Job himself, far from mentioning his perfection, says, *Now mine eye seeth thee, I abhor myself, and repent in dust and ashes,* Job 42:6." And does this disprove our doctrine? Do we not assert that our perfection admits of a continual growth; and that perfect repentance, and perfect humility, are essential parts of it? These words of Job, therefore, far from overthrowing our doctrine, prove that the patient man's perfection grew; and that from the top of the perfection of Gentilism, he saw the day of Christian perfection, and had a taste of what Mr. Wesley prays for, when he sings,—

> O let me gain perfection's height,
> O let me into nothing fall, &c.

> Confound, o'erpower me with thy grace;
> I would be by myself abhorr'd;
> All might, all majesty, all praise,
> All glory be to Christ my Lord!

VIII. With respect to the words, "The stars are not pure — the heavens are not clean in his sight: his angels he charged with folly," Job 15:15; 5:18, we must consider them as a proof that absolute perfection belongs to God alone; a truth this, which we inculcate as well as our opponents. Beside, if such passages overthrow the doctrine of perfection, they would principally overthrow the doctrine of angelical perfection, which Mr. Hill holds as well as we. To conclude: —

IX. When Job asks, "What is man that he should be clean? How can he be clean that is born of a woman? Who can bring a clean thing out of an unclean?" And when he answers, "Not one;" he means not one who falls short of infinite power. If he excluded Emmanuel, *God with us,* I would directly point at him who said, "I will, be thou clean; and at the believers who declare, "We can do all things through Christ that strengtheneth us," and accordingly "cleanse themselves from all filthiness of the flesh and spirit, that they may be found of him without spot and blameless." Yea, I would point at the poor leper, who has faith enough to say, *Lord, if thou wilt, thou canst make me clean.* They tell me that my leprosy must cleave to me till death batter down this tenement of clay; but faith speaks a different language: only say the word, *Be thou clean,* and I shall be cleansed: *purge me with hyssop: sprinkle clean water upon me, and I shall be clean from all my filthiness.*

If these remarks be just, does it not appear that it is as absurd to stab Christian perfection through the sides of Job, Isaiah, and Solomon, as to set Peter, Paul, James, and John, upon "cutting it up, root and branch?"

SECTION XII.

Containing a variety of arguments, to prove the absurdity of the twin doctrines of Christian imperfection and a death purgatory.

I HAVE hitherto stood chiefly upon the defensive, by showing that Mr. Hill has no ground for insinuating that our Church, and Peter, Paul, James, and John, are defenders of the twin doctrines of Christian imperfection and a death purgatory: I shall now attack these doctrines by a variety of arguments, which, I hope, will recommend themselves to the candid reader's conscience and reason.

If I wanted to encounter Mr. Hill with a broken reed, and not with the weapons of a Protestant, REASON and SCRIPTURE, I would retort here the grand argument by which he attempts to cut down our doctrines of *free agency* and *cordial obedience:* — "The generality of the carnal clergy are for you, therefore your doctrines are false." If this argument be good, is not that which follows better still? "The generality of bad men are for your doctrine of Christian imperfection; therefore that doctrine is false: for if it were true, wicked people would not so readily embrace it." But as I see no solidity in that argument, by which I could disprove the very *being of a God,* (for the generality of wicked men believe there is a Supreme Being,) I discard it, and begin with one, which I hope is not unworthy the reader's attention.

I. Does not St. Paul insinuate that no soul goes to heaven without perfection, where he calls the blessed souls that wait for a happy resurrection, πνευματα δικαιων τετελειωμενων, "the spirits of just men made perfect," and not τετελειωμενα πνευματα δικαιων, *the perfected spirits of just men?* Hebrews 12:23. Does not this mode of expression denote a perfection which they attained while they were men, and before they commenced *separate spirits;* that is, *before death?* Can any one go to a holy and just God, without first being made just and holy? Does not the apostle say, that "the unrighteous, *or unjust,* shall not inherit the kingdom of God?" and that "without holiness no man shall see the Lord?" Must not this holiness, of whatsoever degree it is, be free from every mixture of unrighteousness? If a man have at death the least degree of any unrighteousness and defiling mixture in his soul, must he not go to some purgatory, or to hell? Can he go to heaven, if "nothing that defileth shall enter the New Jerusalem?" And if at death his righteous disposition is free from every unrighteous and immoral mixture, is he not "a just man perfected on earth," according to the dispensation he is under?

II. If Christ takes away the *outward* pollution of believers, while he absolutely leaves their hearts full of indwelling sin in this life, why did he find fault with the Pharisees for cleansing the "outside of the cup and platter, while they left the inside full of all corruption?" If God says, "My son, give me thy heart;" if he requires "truth in the inward parts;" and complains that the "Jews drew near to him with their lips, when their hearts were far from him;" is it not strange he should be willing that the hearts of his most peculiar people, the hearts of Christians, should necessarily remain unclean during the term of life? Beside, is there any other Gospel way of fully cleansing the lips and hands, but by thoroughly cleansing the heart? And is not a cleansing so far *Pharisaical* as it is *heartless?* Once more: if Christ has assured us that "blessed are the pure in heart," and that "if the Son shall make us free, we shall be free indeed," does it not behoove our opponents to prove that a believer has a *pure heart*, who is full of indwelling corruption; and that a man is *free indeed*, who is still sold under inbred sin?

III. When our Lord has bound the indwelling "man of sin, the strong man armed, can he not cast him out?" When he "cast out devils, and unclean spirits with a word," did he call death to his assistance? Did he not radically perform the wonderful cure, to show his readiness and ability radically to cure those whose hearts are possessed by indwelling iniquity, that cursed sin, whose name is LEGION? When the legion of expelled fiends "entered into the swine," the poor brutes were delivered from their infernal guests by being "choked in the sea." Death therefore cured them, not Christ. And can we have no cure but that of the swine? No deliverance from indwelling sin, but in the arms of death. If this is the case, go, drown your plaguing corruptions in the first pond which you will meet with, O ye poor mourners, who are more weary of your life, because of indwelling sin, than Rebecca was because of the daughters of Heth.

IV. How does the notion of sin *necessarily* dwelling in the hearts of the most advanced Christians agree with the full tenor of the new covenant, which runs thus? "I will put my laws in their minds, and write them in their hearts. The law of the Spirit of life in Christ Jesus shall make them free from the law of sin and death." If the law of perfect love to God and man be fully put into the heart of a believer, according to the full tenor of Christ's Gospel, what room remains for the hellish statutes of Satan? Does not the Lord cleanse the believer's heart, as he writes the law of love there? And when that law is wholly written by the Spirit, "the finger of God," which applies the all-cleansing blood, is not the heart wholly cleansed? When God completely gives "the heart of flesh," does he not completely take away "the heart of stone?" Is not the heart of stone the very rock in which the serpent, *indwelling sin*, lurks? And will God take away that cursed rock, and spare the venomous viper that breeds in its clefts?

V. Cannot the "little leaven of sincerity and truth leaven the whole" heart? But can this be done without "purging out entirely the old leaven of malice and wickedness?" May not a father in Christ be as "free from sin," as one who is totally given up to a reprobate mind is "free from righteousness?" Is not the glorious liberty of God's children the very reverse of the total and constant slavery to sin, in which the strongest sons of Belial live and die? If a full admittance of Satan's temptation could radically destroy original righteousness in the hearts of our first parents, why cannot a full admittance of Christ's Gospel radically destroy original unrighteousness in the hearts of believers? Does not the Gospel promise us that "where sin has abounded, grace shall much more abound?" And did not sin so abound once as entirely to sweep away inward holiness before death? But how does grace abound much more than sin, if it never can entirely sweep away inward sin without the help of death?

VI. Is there not a present, *cleansing power*, as well as a present, *atoning efficacy*, in the Redeemer's blood? Have we not already taken notice that the same passage of Scripture which informs us that "if we confess our sins, he is faithful and just to forgive us our sins," declares also, that, upon the same gracious terms, "he is faithful and just to cleanse us from all unrighteousness?" Now, if the faithful and just God is ready to forgive *today* a poor mourner who sincerely confesses his guilt; and if it would be doing Divine faithfulness and justice great dishonour to say that God will not forgive a weeping penitent before the article of death; is it doing those Divine perfections honour to assert that God will not cleanse *before death* a believer, who humbly confesses and deeply laments the remains of sin? Why should not God display his faithfulness and justice in cleansing us now from inbred sin, as well as in forgiving us now our actual iniquities, if we now comply with the gracious terms, to the performance of which this double blessing is annexed in the Gospel charter?

VII. If our opponents allow that faith and love may be made perfect two or three minutes before death, they give up the point. Death is no longer absolutely necessary to the destruction of unbelief and sin: for if the "evil heart of unbelief departing from the living God" may be taken away, and the completely "honest and good heart" given two or three minutes before death, we desire to know why this change may not take place two or three hours, two or three weeks, two or three years before that awful moment?

VIII. It is, I think, allowed on all sides that "we are saved," that is, sanctified as well as justified, "by faith." Now, that particular height of sanctification, that full "circumcision of the heart," which centrally purifies the soul, springs from a peculiar degree of saving faith, and from a particular operation of the "Spirit of burning:" a quick operation this, which is compared to a baptism of fire, and proves sometimes so sharp and searching, that it is as much as a healthy, strong man can do to bear up under it. It seems, therefore, absurd to suppose that God's infinite wisdom has tied this powerful operation to the article of death, that is, to a time when people, through delirium or excessive weakness, are frequently unable to think, or to bear the feeble operation of a little wine and water.

IX. When our Lord says, "Make the tree good and its fruit good: a good man out of the good treasure of his heart bringeth forth good things," does he suppose that the hearts of his faithful people must always remain fraught with indwelling sin? Is indwelling sin a *good treasure?* Or does Christ any where plead for the necessary indwelling of a *bad treasure* in a good man? When "the spouse is all glorious within; when her eye is single, and her whole body full of light," — how can she still be full of darkness, and inbred iniquity? And when St. Paul observes that established Christians are "full of goodness," Romans 15:14, who can think he means that they are *full of heart corruption,* and (what is worse still) that they must continue so to their dying day?

X. If Christian perfection be nothing but the *depth* of evangelical repentance, the *full* assurance of faith, and the *pure* love of God and man, shed abroad in a *faithful* believer's heart by the Holy Ghost given unto him, to cleanse him, and to keep him clean "from all the filthiness of the flesh and spirit," and to enable him to "fulfil the law of Christ," according to the talents he is entrusted with, and the circumstances in which he is placed in this world: if this, I say, is Christian perfection, nothing can be more absurd than to put off the attaining of it till we die and go to heaven. This is evident from the descriptions of it which we find in the New Testament. The first is in our Lord's account of the beatitudes. For how can holy *mourning* be perfected in heaven, where there will be nothing but perfect joy? Will not the loving disposition of *peace makers* ripen too late for the Church, if it ripen only in heaven, where there will be no peace breakers; or *in the article of death,* when people lose their senses, and are utterly disabled from acting a reconciler's part? Ye that are "persecuted for righteousness' sake," will ye stay till ye are among the blessed, to "rejoice in tribulation?" Will the blessed "revile you, and say all manner of evil of you falsely," to give you an opportunity of being "exceeding glad," when you are counted worthy to suffer for Christ's name? And ye, doubleminded Christians, will ye tarry for the "blessedness of the pure in heart," till ye come to heaven? Have you forgot that heaven is no purgatory, but a glorious reward for those who "are pure in heart?" for those who have "purified themselves even as God is pure?"

XI. From the beatitudes our Lord passes to precepts descriptive of Christian perfection reduced to practice. "If thy brother hath aught against thee, go thy way, and be reconciled to him. Agree quickly with thine adversary. Resist not evil. Turn thy left cheek to him that smites thee on the right. Give alms so as not to let thy left hand know what thy right hand does. Fast evangelically. Lay not up treasures upon earth. Take no [anxious] thoughts what ye shall eat. Bless them that curse you. Do good to them that hate you, that ye may be the children of your Father, who is in heaven; for he maketh the sun to shine on the just and on the unjust. Be ye perfect as your Father who is in heaven is perfect." What attentive reader does not see that none of these branches of a Christian's practical profession can grow in the article of death; and that to suppose they can flourish in heaven, is to suppose that Christ says, "Be thus and thus perfect, when it will be impossible for you to be thus and thus perfect? *Love your enemies,* when all will be your friends: *do good to them that hate you,* when all will flame with love toward you? *Turn your cheek to the smiters,* when the cold hand of death will disable you to move a finger; or when God shall have fixed 'a great gulf' between the smiters and you?"

XII. The same observation holds with respect to that important branch of Christian perfection which we call *perfect self denial.* "If thine eye offend thee," says our Lord, "pluck it out. If thy right hand offend thee, cut it off," &c. Now can any thing be more absurd than to put off the perfect performance of these severe duties till we die, and totally lose our power over our eyes and hands? Or, till we arrive at heaven, where nothing that offendeth can possibly be admitted?

XIII. St. Luke gives us, in the Acts of the Apostles, a sketch of the perfection of Christians living in community. "The multitude of them that believed," says he, "were of one heart and one soul. They continued steadfastly in the apostle's doctrine, and in prayer. They had all things common: parting their possessions to all, as every man had need; neither said any of them that aught of the things which he possessed was his own: and continuing daily in the temple, and breaking bread from house to house, they ate their meat with gladness, and singleness of heart, praisingGod!" When I read this description of the practical perfection of a Christian Church, I am tempted to smile at the mistake of our opponents, and to ask them, if we can "eat our meat with gladness" in the article of death, or "sell our possessions" for the relief of our brethren upon earth, when we are gone to heaven?

XIV. Consider we some of St. Paul's exhortations for the display of the perfection which we contend for, and we shall see in a still stronger light the absurdity that I point out. He says to the Romans, "Present your bodies a living sacrifice; and be not conformed to this present world, that ye may prove what is that perfect will of God. Having different gifts," use them all for God; "exhorting with diligence, giving with simplicity, showing mercy with cheerfulness, not slothful in business, fervent in spirit, serving the Lord, communicating to the necessities of the saints, given to hospitality, weeping with them that weep, being of the same mind, condescending to men of low estate, providing things honest in the sight of all men, heaping coals of fire [coals of burning love and melting kindness] on the head of your enemy, by giving him meat, if he be hungry; or drink, if he be thirsty; overcoming *thus* evil with good." Again: exhorting the Corinthians to Christian perfection, he says, "Brethren, the time is short. I would have you without carefulness. It remaineth that those who have wiles, be as though they had none; they that weep, as if they wept not; they that rejoice, as ifthey rejoiced not; they that buy, as if they possessed not; and they that use this world, as not abusing it," &c. Once more: stirring up the Philippians to the perfection of humble love, he writes, "Fulfil ye my joy, that ye think the same thing, have the same love; being of one soul, of one mind. Do nothing through vain glory, but in lowliness of mind esteem each the others better than themselves. Look not every one on his own things, but every one also on the things of others. Let this mind be in you, which was also in Christ Jesus, who humbled himself, and became obedient unto death." Now all these descriptions of the practical part of Christian perfection, in the very nature of things, cannot be confined to the article of death, much less to our arrival at heaven. For when we are dying, or dead, we cannot "present our bodies a living sacrifice;" we cannot "use this world as not abusing it;" nor can we "look at the things of others" as well as at our own.

XV. The same thing maybe said of St. Paul's fine description of Christian perfection under the name of charity. "Charity suffereth long;" but at death all our sufferings are cut short. "Charity is not provoked: it thinketh no evil: it covereth all things: it rejoiceth not in iniquity: it hopeth all things, believeth all things, endureth all things," &c. The bare reading of this description shows that it does not respect the article of death, when we cease to endure any thing; much less does it respect heaven, where we shall have absolutely nothing to endure.

XVI. If a pefect fulfilling of our relative duties be a most important part of Christian perfection, how ungenerous, how foolish is it to promise the simple that they shall be perfect Christians at *death,* or *in heaven?* Does not this assertion include all the following absurdities? Ye shall perfectly love your husbands and wives in the article of death, when you shall not be able to distinguish your husbands and wives from other men and women: or in heaven, where "ye shall be like the angels of God," and have neither husbands nor wives. Ye shall assist your parents, and instruct your children with perfect tenderness, when ye shall be past instructing or assisting them at all; when they shall be in heaven or in hell; past needing, or past admitting your assistance or instructions. Ye shall inspect your servants in perfect love, or serve your master with perfect faithfulness, when the relations of *master* and *servant* will exist no more. Ye shall perfectly bear with the infirmities of your weak brethren, when ye shall leave all your weak brethren behind, and go where all your brethren will be free from every degree of trying weakness. Ye shall entertain strangers, attend the sick, and visit the prisoners, with perfect love, when ye shall give up the ghost, or when ye shall be in paradise, where these duties have no more place than lazar houses, sick beds, prisons, &c.

XVII. Death, far from introducing imperfect Christians into the state of Christian perfection, will take them out of the very possibility of ever attaining it. This will appear indubitable, if we remember that Christian perfection consists in perfect repentance, perfect faith, perfect hope, perfect love of an invisible God, perfect charity for visible enemies, perfect patience in pain, and perfect resignation under losses; in a constant bridling of our bodily appetites, in an assiduous keeping of our senses, in a cheerful taking up of our cross, in a resolute "following of Christ without the camp," and in a deliberate choice to "suffer affliction with the people of God, rather than to enjoy the pleasures of sin for a season." Now so certain as there can be no perfect repentance in the grave; no Christian *faith* where all is *sight;* no perfect *hope* where all is *enjoyment;* no perfect love of an invisible God, or of visible enemies, where God is visible, and enemies are invisible; no bearing pain with perfect patience when pain is no more; and suffering affliction with the people of God, where no shadow of affliction lights upon the people of God, &c. So certain, I say, as death incapacitates us for all these Christian duties, it incapacitates us also for every branch of Christian perfection. Mr. Hill might then as well persuade the simple that they shall become perfect surgeons and perfect midwives, perfect masons and perfect gardeners in the grave, or beyond it, as persuade them that they shall become perfect penitents and perfect believers in the article of death, or in the New Jerusalem.

XVIII. From the preceding argument it follows, that the graces of repentance, faith, hope, and Christian charity, or love for an invisible God, for trying friends, and for visible enemies, must be perfected *here* or *never*. If Mr. Hill grant that these graces are, or may be perfected here, he allows all that we contend for. And if he assert that they shall never be perfected, because there is "no perfection here," and because the perfection of repentance, &c, can have no more place in heaven than sinning and mourning, I ask, What becomes then of the scriptures which Mr. Hill is so ready to produce when he defends Calvinian perseverance? "As for God, his work is perfect: being confident of this very thing, that he who hath begun a good work in you (who have always obeyed, Philippians 2:12) will perform, or επιτελεσι will perfect it," if you continue to obey. "The Lord will perfect that which concerneth me. Praying exceedingly that we as workers together with God might perfect that which is lacking in your faith. Looking unto Jesus, the author, and (τελειωτην) the perfecter of our faith; for he is faithful that promised." How can the Lord be faithful, and yet never perfect the repentance and faith of his obedient people? Will he sow such a blessed seed as that of faith, hope, and love to our enemies, and never let a grain of it either miscarry or bring forth fruit to perfection? Is not this a flat contradiction? How can a pregnant woman *never miscarry,* and yet *never bring forth the fruit* of her womb to any perfection? Such, however, is the inconsistency which Mr. Hill obtrudes upon us as Gospel. If his doctrine of Calvinian perseverance be true, no believer can miscarry; no grain of true faith can fail of producing fruit to perfection: and if his doctrine of Christian perfection be true, no believer can be perfect; no grain of faith, repentance, hope, and love for our husbands and wives, can possibly grow to perfection. How different is this doctrine from that of our Lord, who, in the parable of the sower, represents all those who do not "bear fruit unto perfection," as miscarrying professors!

XIX. If impatience were that bodily disorder which is commonly called the heart burn; if obstinacy were a crick in the neck; pride an imposthume in the breast; raging anger a fit of the toothache; vanity the dropsy; disobedience a bodily lameness; uncharitableness the rheumatism, and despair a broken bone; there would be some sense in the doctrine of Christian imperfection, and reason could subscribe to Mr. Hill's creed: for it is certain that death effectually cures the heart burn, a crick in the neck, the toothache, &c. But what real affinity have *moral* disorders with *bodily* death? And why do our opponents think we maintain a "shocking" doctrine, when we assert that death has no more power to cure our pride, than old age to remove our covetous*ness?* Nay, do we not see that the most decrepit old age does not cure men even of the grossest lusts of the carnal mind? When old drunkards and fornicators are as unable to indulge their sensual appetites as if they actually ranked among corpses, do they not betray the same inclinations which they showed when the strong tide of their youthful blood joined with the rapid stream of their vicious habit? Is not this a demonstration that no decay of the body, — no, not that complete decay which we call *death,* has any necessary tendency to alter our moral habits? And do not the ancients set their seal to this observation? Does not Solomon *say,* that "*in* the place where the tree faileth, there it shall be?" And has Mr. Hill forgotten those remarkable lines of Virgil? —

> Quæ cura nitentes
> Pascere equos, eadem sequitur tellure repostos?

"Disembodied souls have, in the world of spirits, the very same dispositions and propensities which they had when they dwelt in the body."

XX. If God hath appointed death to make an end of heart pollution, and to be our complete saviour from sin, our opponents might screen their doctrine of a death purgatory behind God's appointment; it being certain that God, who can command iron to swim, and fire to cool, could also command the filthy hands of death to cleanse the thoughts of our hearts. But we do not read in our Bible, either that God ever gave to indwelling sin a lease of any believer's heart for life; or that he ever appointed the king of terrors to deliver us from the deadly seeds of iniquity. And although the Old Testament contains an account of many carnal ordinances adapted to the carnal disposition of the Jews, we do not remember to have read there, "DEATH shall circumcise thy heart, that thou mayest love the Lord thy God with all thy heart, Death shall sprinkle clean water upon you, and ye shall be clean: from all your filthiness death will cleanse you. Death will put my Spirit within you, and cause you to walk in my statutes, and (when you are dead) ye shall keep my judgments and do them." And if death was never so far honoured under the Mosaic dispensation, we ask where he has been invested with higher privileges under the Gospel of Christ? Is it where St. Paul says that "Christ hath abolished death, and hath brought life and immortality to light through the Gospel?" It appears to us that it is a high degree of rashness in the Calvinists, and in the Romanists, to appoint the pangs of death, and the sorrows of hell, to do the most difficult, and, of consequence, the most glorious work of Christ's Spirit, which is powerfully to "redeem us from all iniquity, and to purify unto himself a peculiar people, [not full of all inbred unrighteousness, but 'dead to sin, free from sin, pure in heart,' and] zealous of good works." And we shall think ourselves far more guilty of impertinence, if we nominate either death or hell to do the office of the final purifier of our hearts, than if we ordered a sexton to do the office of the prime minister, or an executioner to act as the king's physician. With respect to salvation from the root, as well as from the branches of sin, we will therefore "know nothing," as absolutely necessary, "but Jesus Christ and him crucified," risen again, ascended on high, that he might send the Holy Ghost to perfect us in love, through "a faith that purifies the heart, and through a hope which, if any man hath, he will purify himself, even as God is pure."

XXI. To conclude: if Christian perfection implies the perfect use of "the whole armour of God," what can be more absurd than the thought that we shall be made perfect Christians in heaven or at death? How will Mr. Hill prove that we shall perfectly use the helmet of hope, perfectly wield the shield of faith, and perfectly quench the fiery darts of the devil in heaven, where faith, hope, and the devil's darts shall never enter? Or, how will he demonstrate that a soldier shall perfectly go through his exercise in the article of death, that is, in the very moment he leaves the army, and for ever puts off the harness?

Mr. Baxter wrote, in the last century, a vindication of holiness, which he calls, "A Saint, or a Brute." The title is bold; but all that can be said to defend iniquity cannot make me think it too strong, so many are the arguments by which the Scriptures recommend a holy life. And I own to thee, reader, that when I consider all that can be said in defence of Christian perfection, and all the absurdities which clog the doctrine of Christian imperfection, I am inclined to imitate Mr. Baxter's positiveness, and to call this essay, *A Perfect Christian in this World, or a Perfect Dupe in the next.*

SECTION XIII.

Containing a variety of arguments to prove the mischievousness of the doctrines of Christian imperfection.

THE arguments of the preceding section are produced to show the ABSURDITY of Mr. Hill's doctrine of Christian imperfection; those which follow are intended to prove the MISCHIEVOUSNESS of that modish tenet.

I. It strikes at the doctrine of *salvation by faith.* "By grace are ye saved through faith," not only from the guilt and outward acts of sin, but also from its root and secret buds. "Not of* works," says the apostle, "lest any man should [Pharisaically] boast;" and may we not add, Not of DEATH, lest he that had the power of death, that is, the devil, should [absurdly] boast? Does not what strikes at the doctrine of faith, and abridges the salvation which we obtain by it, equally strike at Christ's power and glory? Is it not the business of faith to receive Christ's saving word, to apprehend the power of his sanctifying Spirit, and to inherit all the great promises by which he saves

---

* Here, and in some other places, St. Paul by "works" means only the deeds of a Christless, anti-mediatorial law, and the obedience paid to the Jewish covenant, which is frequently called "the law," in opposition to the Christian covenant, which is commonly called "the Gospel," that is, the Gospel of Christ, because Christ's Gospel is the most excellent of all the Gospel dispensations. The apostle, therefore, by the expression, "not of works," does by no means exclude from "final" salvation, the law of faith, and the works done in obedience to that law: for, in the preceding verse, he secures the obedience of faith when he says, "Ye are saved, [that is, made partakers of the blessing of the Christian dispensation,] by grace through faith." Here then the word "by grace" secures the first Gospel axiom, and the word "through faith" secures the second.

his penitent, believing people from their sins? Is it not evident that if no believers can be saved from indwelling sin through faith, we must correct the apostle's doctrine, and say, "By grace are ye saved *from the remains of sin,* through death?" And can unprejudiced Protestants admit so Christ-debasing, death-exalting a tenet, without giving a dangerous blow to the genuine doctrines of the reformation?

II. It dishonours Christ as *a Prophet:* for, as such, he came to teach us to be now "meek and lowly in heart:" but the imperfect gospel of the day teaches that we must necessarily continue passionate and proud in heart till death; for pride and immoderate anger are, I apprehend, two main branches of indwelling sin. Again: my motto demonstrates that he publicly taught the multitudes the doctrine of perfection, and Mr. Hill insinuates that this doctrine is "shocking," not to say "blasphemous."

III. It disgraces Christ as *the Captain of our salvation:* for St. Paul says, that our Captain furnishes us with "weapons mighty through God to the pulling down of Satan's strong holds, and to the bringing of every thought into captivity to the obedience of Christ." But our opponents represent the devil's strong hold as absolutely inpregnable. No weapons of our warfare can pull down Apollyon's throne. Inbred sin shall maintain its place in man's heart till death strike the victorious blow. Christ may indeed fight against the Jericho within, as "Joab fought against Rabbah of the children of Ammon:" but then he must send for death, as Joab sent for David, saying, "I have fought against Rabbah, and have taken the city of waters: now, therefore, gather the rest of the people together, encamp against the city, and take it, lest I take the city, and it be called after my name," 2 Samuel 12:27, 28.

IV. It pours contempt upon him as *the Surety of the new covenant,* in which God has engaged himself to deliver obedient believers "from their enemies, that they may serve him without [tormenting] fear, all the days of their lives." For how does he execute his office in this respect, if he never sees that such believers be delivered from their most oppressive and inveterate enemy, indwelling, sin? Or if that deliverance take place only at death, how can they, in consequence of their death freedom, "serve God without fear all the days of their lives?"

V. It affronts Christ as a *King,* when it represents the believer's heart, which is Christ's spiritual throne, as being necessarily full of indwelling sin, — a spiritual rebel, who, notwithstanding the joint efforts of Christ and the believer, maintains his power against them both during the term of life. Again: does not a good king deliver his loyal subjects from oppression, and avenge them of a tyrannical adversary, when they cry to him in their distress? But does our Lord show himself such a king, if he never avenge them, nor turn the usurper, the murderer, sin, out of their breasts? Once more: if our deliverance from sin depend upon the stroke of death, and not upon a stroke of Christ's grace, might we not call upon *the king of terrors,* as well as upon *the King of saints,* for deliverance from the remains of sin? But where is the difference between saying "O death, help us!" and crying, "O Baal, save us?"

VI. It injures Christ as *a Restorer* of pure, spiritual worship in God's spiritual temple, the heart of man. For it indirectly represents him as a Pharisaic Saviour, who made much ado about driving, with a whip, harmless sheep and oxen out of his Father's material temple; but who gives full leave to Satan, not only to bring sheep and doves into the believer's heart, but also to harbour and breed there during the term of life, the swelling toad, pride; and the hissing viper, envy; to say nothing of the greedy dog, avarice, and the filthy swine, impurity; under pretence of "exercising the patience, and engaging the industry" of the worshippers, if we may believe the Calvin of the day. (See the argument against Christian perfection at the end of this section.)

VII. It insults Christ as *a Priest*; for our Melchisedec shed his all-cleansing blood upon the cross, and now pours his all-availing prayer before the throne; asking, that, upon evangelical terms, we may now be "cleansed from all unrighteousness, and perfected in one." But if we assert that believers, let them be ever so faithful, can never be thus cleansed and perfected in one till death comes to the Saviour's assistance, do we not place our Lord's cleansing blood, and powerful intercession, and of consequence his priesthood, in an unscriptural and contemptible light?

Should Mr. Hill attempt to retort this argument by saying, "*that* it is our doctrine, not his, which derogates from the honour of Christ's priesthood, because we should no longer need our High Priest's blood, if we were cleansed from all sin." I reply: —

(1.) Perfect Christians need as much the virtue of Christ's blood, to prevent the guilt and pollution of sin from returning, as imperfect Christians want it to drive that guilt and pollution away. It is not enough that the blood of the true paschal Lamb has been sprinkled upon our souls to keep off the destroyer; it must still remain there to hinder his coming back "with seven other spirits more wicked than himself." (2.) Mr. Hill is in the dark; he calls for a light; and when it is brought, he observes, The darkness of the room is now totally removed. "Is it so, sir?" replies his footman; "then you need these candles no more; if they have totally removed the darkness of your apartment, you have no more need of them." Mr. Hill smiles at the absurdity of his servant's argument; and yet it is well if he does not admire the wisdom of my opponent's objection. (3.) The hearts of perfect Christians are cleansed, and kept clean by faith; and Christian perfection means the perfection of Christian faith, whose property it is to endear Christ and his blood more and more; nothing then can be less reasonable than to say that, upon our principles, perfect believers have done with the atoning blood. (4.) Such believers continually "overcome the accuser of the brethren through the blood of the Lamb; there is no moment, therefore, in which they can spare it: they are feeble believers who can yet dispense with its constant application; and hence it is that they continue feeble. None make so much use of Christ's blood as perfect Christians. Once it was only their medicine, which they took now and then, when a fit of fear, or a pang of guilt, obliged them to it; but now it is the Divine preservative, which keeps off the infection of sin. Now it is the reviving cordial, which they take to prevent their "growing weary, or faint in their minds." Now it is their daily drink; now it is what they sprinkle their every thought, word, and work with. In a word, it is that blood which constantly speaks before God and in their consciences "better things than the blood of Abel," and actually procures for them all the blessings which they enjoy or expect. To say, therefore, that the doctrine of Christian perfection supersedes the need of Christ's blood, is not less absurd than to assert that the perfection of navigation renders the great deep a useless reservoir of water. Lastly: are not the saints before the throne perfectly sinless? And who are more ready than they to extol the blood and sing the song of the Lamb: "To him that loved us, and washed us from our sins in his blood, be glory," &c? If an angel preached to them the modern Gospel, and desired them to plead for the remains of sin, lest they should lose their peculiar value for the atoning blood; would not they all suspect him to be an angel of darkness, transforming himself into an angel of light? And shall we be the dupes of the tempter, who deceives good men, that they may deceive us by a similar argument?

VIII. It discredits Christ as *the Fulfiller* of the Father's promise, and as *the Sender* of the indwelling, abiding Comforter, in order that our joy may be full. For the Spirit never takes his constant abode as a Comforter in a heart full of indwelling sin. If he visit such a heart with his consolations, it is only "as a guest that tarrieth but a day." When he enters a soul fraught with inbred corruption, he rather acts as a Reprover than as a Comforter; throwing down the tables of the spiritual money changers; hindering the vessels, which are not holiness unto the Lord, from being carried through God's spiritual temple, and expelling, according to the degree of our faith, whatsoever would make God's house "a den of thieves."

But, instead of this, Mr. Hill's doctrine considers the heart of a believer as a "den of lions;" and represents Christ's Spirit, not as the destroyer, but as the keeper of the wild beasts, and evil tempers which dwell therein. This I conclude from these words of the Rev. Mr. Toplady: — "They," indwelling sin and unholy tempers, "do not quite expire, till the renewed soul is taken up from earth to heaven. In the meantime these heated remains of depravity will, too often, like prisoners in a dungeon, crawl toward the window, though in chains, and show themselves through the grate. Nay, I do not know whether the strivings of inherent corruption for mastery be not, frequently, more violent in a regenerate person, than even in one who is dead in trespasses; as wild beasts are sometimes the more rampant and furious for being wounded." (See *Caveat against Unsound Doctrines*, p. 65.) When I read this Gospel, I cannot but throw in a Caveat against Mr. Toplady's Caveat. For if his be not unsound, every body must allow it to be uncomfortable and unsafe. Who would not think it dreadfully dangerous to dwell with one wild beast that cannot be killed, unless we are first killed ourselves? But how much more dangerous is it to be condemned to dwell for life with a number of them which are not only immortal, so long as we are alive, but "are sometimes the more rampant and furious for being wounded!" The Saviour preached by Mr. Toplady only wounds the Egyptian dragon, the inward Pharaoh, and makes him rage, but our Jesus drowns him in the sea of his own blood, barely by stretching out the rod of his power, when we stretch out to him our arms of faith. Mr. Hill's Redeemer only takes Agag prisoner, as double-minded Saul did; but our Redeemer "hews him in pieces" as upright Samuel. The Christ of the Calvinists says, "Confine the enemy; though he may possibly be fiercer than before." But ours "thrusts out the enemy before us, and says, Destroy," Deuteronomy 33:27. O, ye preachers of finished salvation, we leave it to your candour to decide which of these doctrines brings most glory to the saving name of Jesus.

IX. The doctrine of our *necessary* continuance in indwelling sin to our last moments, makes us naturally overlook or despise the "exceeding great and precious promises given unto us, that by these we might be partakers of the Divine nature," that is, of God's perfect holiness, "having escaped the corruption that is in the world through lust," 2 Peter 1:4; and thus it naturally defeats the full effect of evangelical truths and ministerial labours; an effect this, which is thus described by St. Paul; "teaching every man in all wisdom, that we may present every man perfect in Christ Jesus," that is, perfect according to the richest dispensation of Divine grace, which is, "the Gospel of Christ Jesus," Colossians 1:28. Again: "The Scripture is profitable for instruction in righteousness, that the man of God may be perfect, thoroughly furnished to all good works," 2 Timothy 3:16. Now we apprehend that the perfection which thoroughly furnishes believers unto all good works, is a perfection productive of all the "good works" evangelically as well as providentially "prepared that we should walk in them" before death: because, (whatever Mr. Hill may insinuate to the contrary in England, and father Walsh at Paris,) the Scriptures say, "Whatsoever thy hand findeth to do, do it with thy might; for there is no work nor device" in death, that is, "in the grave whither thou goest." For as the tree falls, so it lies: if it falls full of rottenness with a brood of vipers, and a never-dying worm in its hollow centre; it will continue in that very condition; and wo to the man who trusts that the pangs of death will kill the worm, or that a purgative fire will spare the rotten wood and consume the vipers!

X. It defeats in part the end of the Gospel precepts, to the fulfilling of which Gospel promises are but means. "All the law, the prophets," and the apostolic writings, "hang on these two commandments: — *Thou shalt love the Lord thy God with all thy heart*, and thy neighbour as thyself," through penitential faith in the light of thy dispensation; that is, in two words, thou shalt be *evangelically perfect*. Now, if we believe that it is absolutely impossible to be thus perfect by keeping these two blessed commandments in faith, we cannot but believe also that God, who requires us to keep them, is defective in *wisdom, equity, and goodness*, by requiring us to do what is absolutely impossible; and we represent our Church as a wicked step mother who betrays her children into the wanton commission of perjury, by requiring of every one of them, in the sacrament of baptism, a most solemn vow, by which they bind themselves, in the presence of God and of the congregation, that "they will keep God's holy will and commandments," that is, that they will keep God's evangelical law, "and walk in the same all the days of their life."

XI. It has a necessary tendency to unnerve our deepest prayers. How can we pray in faith that God would help us to "do his will on earth as it is done in heaven," or that he would "cleanse the thoughts of our hearts, that we may perfectly love him and worthily magnify his holy name:" how can we, I say, ask this in faith, if we disbelieve the very possibility of having these petitions answered? And what poor encouragement has Epaphras, upon the scheme which we oppose, "always to labour fervently for the Colossians in prayer, that they might stand perfect and complete in the will of God;" or St. Paul to wish that "the very God of peace would sanctify the Thessalonians wholly, and that their whole spirit, and soul, and body might be preserved blameless," if these requests could not be granted
before death, and were unavoidably to be granted to them and to all
believers in the article thereof?

XII. It soothes lukewarm, unholy professors, and encourages them to sit quietly under the vine of Sodom, and under their own barren fig tree: I mean under the baneful influence of their unbelief and indwelling sin; nothing being more pleasing to the carnal mind than this syren song: — "It is absolutely impossible that the thoughts of your hearts should be cleansed in this life. God himself does not expect that you should be purified from all iniquity on this side the grave. It is proper that sin should dwell in your hearts by unbelief, to endear Christ to you, and so to *work together for your good*." The preachers of mere morality insinuate that God does not forgive sins before death. This dangerous, uncomfortable doctrine damps the faith of penitents, who think it absurd to expect *before death* what they are taught they can only receive *at death*.

And as it is with the pardon of sins, so it is also with "cleansing from all unrighteousness." The preachers of Christian imperfection tell their hearers that nobody can be cleansed from heart sin *before death*. This new doctrine makes them secretly trust in a death purgatory, and hinders them from pleading in faith the promises of full sanctification before death stares them in the face; while others, like spared Agag, madly venture upon the spear of the king of terrors with their hearts full of indwelling sin. The dead tell no tales now; but it will be well if, in the day of resurrection, those who plead for the *necessary* indwelling of sin during the term of life, do not meet in the great day with some deluded souls, who will give them no thanks for betraying them, to their last moments, into the hands of indwelling sin, by insinuating that there can be no deliverance from our evil tempers before we are ready to exchange a death bed for a coffin.

XIII. It greatly discourages willing Israelites, and weakens the hands of the faithful spies who want to lead feeble believers on, and to take by force the kingdom which consists in righteousness, peace, and joy in the Holy Ghost; nothing being more proper to damp their ardour than such a speech as this: — "You may strive against your corruptions and evil tempers as long as you please: but you shall never get rid of them; the Jericho within is impregnable: it is fenced up to heaven, and garrisoned by the tall, invincible, immortal sons of Anak: so strong are these adversaries, that the twelve apostles, with the help of Christ and the Holy Ghost, could never turn one of them out of his post. Nay, they so buffeted and overpowered St. Paul, the most zealous of the apostles, that they fairly took him prisoner, 'sold him under sin,' and made him groan to the last, 'O wretched, carnal man that I am, who shall deliver me from the law of *my inbred corruptions,* which brings me into captivity to the law of sin: I thank God through *death*. So then with the flesh,' you must, as well as St. Paul, 'serve the law of sin' till you die. Nor need you fret at these tidings; for they are the pure Gospel of Christ, the genuine doctrines of free grace and Christian liberty. In Christ you are free, but in yourselves you must continue to serve the law of sin: and indeed why should you not do it, since *the sins of a Christian are for his good;* and *even the dung of a sheep of Christ is of some use,* nay, of the most excellent use, if we believe Mr. Hill; for the most grievous falls — falls into repeated acts of adultery and deliberate murder, serve to make us know our place, to drive us nearer to Christ, and to make us sing louder the praises of restoring grace." Beside, that gentleman represents those who preach deliverance from indwelling sin before we go into a death purgatory, as "men of a Pharisaic cast; blind men, who never saw their own hearts; proud men, who oppose the righteousness of God; vain men, who aspire at robbing Christ of the glory of being *alone without sin:* in short, men who hold doctrines which are shocking, not to say blasphemous."

How would this speech damp our desires after salvation from indwelling sin! How would it make us hug the cursed chains of our inbred corruptions, if the cloven foot of the imperfect, unchaste Diana, which it holds out to public view without Gospel sandals, were not sufficient to shock us back from this impure gospel to the pure Gospel of Jesus Christ! And yet (if I am not mistaken) this dangerous speech only unfolds the scope of Mr. Hill's "Creed for Perfectionists."

XIV. To conclude. The modish doctrine of Christian imperfection and death purgatory is so contrived, that carnal men will always prefer the purgatory of the Calvinists to that of the Papists. For the Papists prescribe I know not how many cups of Divine wrath and dire vengeance, which are to be drunk by the souls of the believers who die half purged, or *threeparts* cleansed. These *half*-damned, or a *quarter*-damned creatures, must go through a severe discipline, and fiery salvation, in the very suburbs of hell, before they can be perfectly purified. But our opponents have found out a way to deliver half-hearted believers out of all fear in this respect. Such believers need not "utterly abolish the body of sin" in this world. The inbred man of sin not only *may*, but he *shall* live as long as we do. You will possibly ask, "What is to become of this sinful guest? Shall he take us to hell, or shall we take him to heaven? If he cannot die in this world, will Christ destroy him in the next?" No: here Christ is almost left out of the question, by those who pretend to be determined to "know nothing but Christ and him crucified." Our indwelling adversary is not destroyed by the brightness of the Redeemer's spiritual appearing, but by the gloom of the appearance of death. Thus they have found another Jesus; another Saviour from sin. The king of terrors comes to the assistance of Jesus' sanctifying grace, and instantaneously delivers the carnal believer from indwelling pride, unbelief, covetousness, peevishness, uncharitableness, love of the world, and inordinate affection. Thus the clammy sweats, brought on by the greedy monster, kill, it seems, the tree of sin, of which the blood of Christ could only kill the buds! The dying sinner's breath does the capital work of the Spirit of holiness! And by the most astonishing of all miracles, the faint, infectious, last gasp of a sinful believer blows away, in the twinkling of an eye, the great mountain of inward corruption, which all the means of grace, all the faith, prayers, and sacraments of twenty, perhaps of forty years, with all the love in the heart of our Zerubbabel, all the blood in his veins, all the power in his hands, and all the faithfulness in his breast, were never able to remove! If this doctrine be true, how greatly was St. Paul mistaken when he said, "The sting of death is sin, &c. Thanks be to God, who giveth us the victory through Christ our Lord!" — Should he not have said, *Death is the cure of sin*, instead of saying, "Sin is the sting of death?" And should not his praises flow thus: "Thanks be to God, who giveth us the victory through DEATH, our great and only deliverer from our greatest and fiercest enemy, *indwelling sin?*"

SECTION XIV.

An answer to the arguments by which the imperfectionists support the doctrine of the necessary indwelling of sin in all believers till they go into the death purgatory.

THE pleasing effect of the light in a picture, is considerably heightened by the bold opposition of strong shades: if the preceding arguments are the lights by which we hope agreeably to strike the mental eyes of the reader, who candidly considers the doctrine of Christian perfection, it will not be improper to heighten those lights by the amazing contrast of the arguments which our opponents advance in defence of indwelling sin and Christian imperfection. These arguments appear to us shades — bold, logical shades: but the bolder they are, the more they will set off the lustre of the truth which we recommend; for, if "all things work for good to them that love

God," why should not all the errors of others work for good to them that love the truth? I am abundantly furnished with the erroneous shades I want, by three of the most approved authors, who support the ark of the imperfect gospel — the Rev. Mr. Toplady, author of the "Historic Proof of Calvinism;" the Rev. Mr. Martin, author of several tracts which are esteemed by the Calvinists; and the Rev. Mr. Henry, famous for his voluminous Exposition of the Bible.

The first of these authors, in his "Caveat against Unsound Doctrine," intimates that there never were on earth but three persons possessed of the sinless perfection which we contend for; *Adam, Eve,* and *Jesus Christ:* a bold intimation this, which, like the Babel I attack, has its foundation in confusion, — in the confusion of three perfections which are entirely different; the paradisiacal sinless perfection of our first parents; the mediatorial, sinless perfection of Jesus Christ; and the Christian, evangelically sinless perfection of St. John. This intimation is supported by some passages from Solomon, which have been already considered in section xi, and by the following argument: —

ARGUMENT I. "A person of the amplest fortune cannot help the harbouring of snakes, toads, &c, on his lands; but they will breed, and nestle, and crawl about his estate, whether he will or no. All he can do is, to pursue and kill them, whenever they make their appearance. Yet, let him be ever so vigilant and diligent, there will always be a succession of those creatures, to *exercise his patience and engage his industry.* So it is with the true believer, in respect to indwelling sin." (*Caveat against Unsound Doctrines,* page 54.) To this we answer: —

1. From the clause which I produce in Italics in this argument, one would think that *patience and industry* cannot be properly *exercised* without indwelling sin; if so, does it not follow that our Lord's patience and industry always wanted proper exercise, because he was always perfectly free from indwelling sin? We are of a different sentiment with respect to our Lord's Christian virtues; and we apprehend that the patience and industry of the most perfect believer will always, without the opposition of indwelling sin, find *full* exercise in doing and suffering the whole will of God; in keeping the body under; in striving against the sin of others; in testifying, by word and deed, that the works of the world are evil; in resisting the numberless temptations of him, who "goes about as a roaring lion, seeking whom he may devour;" and in preparing to conflict with the king of terrors.

2. Why should not assiduous vigilance clear an estate of *snakes,* as one of our kings cleared Great Britain of *wolves?* Did he not attempt and accomplish what appeared impossible to less resolute minds? Mr. Toplady is too well acquainted with the classics not to know what the heathens themselves have said of *industry* and *love;*—

Omnia vincit amor. Labor improbus omnia vincit:

if "love and incessant labour overcome the greatest difficulties," what cannot a diligent believer do, who is animated by the love of God, and feels that he "can do all things through Christ who strengthens him?"

3. But the capital flaw of Mr. Toplady's argument consists in so considering *the weakness of free will,* as entirely to leave God and the sanctifying power of his Spirit out of the question. That gentleman forgets, that, "for this purpose the Son of God was manifested, that he might destroy the works of the devil." Nor does he consider, that a worm, assisted by Omnipotence itself, is capable of the greatest achievements. Of this we have an illustrious instance in Moses, with respect to the removal of the lice, the frogs, and the locusts. "Moses entreated the Lord, and the Lord turned a mighty, strong west wind, which took away the locusts, and cast them into the Red Sea; there remained not one locust in all the coasts of Egypt," Exodus 10:19. If Mr. Toplady had not forgot the mighty God, with whom Moses and believers have to do, he would never have supposed that the comparison holds good between CHRIST "cleansing the thoughts and hearts of *a praying believer* by the inspiration of his Holy Spirit," and a MAN, who can by no means destroy the snakes and toads that breed, nestle, and crawl about his estate.

4. The reverend author of the "Caveat" sinks in this argument even below the doctrine of heathen moralists. For, suppose the extirpation of a vicious habit were considered, would not a heathen be inexcusable, if he overlooked the succour and inspiration of the Almighty? And what shall we say of a Gospel minister, who, writing upon the destruction of sin, entirely overlooks what at other times he calls *the sovereign, matchless, all-conquering, irresistible* power of Divine grace, which (if we believe him) is absolutely to do all *in* us and *for* us; who insinuates, that the toad pride, and the viper envy, must continue to nestle and crawl in our breasts for want of ability to destroy them; and who concludes that the extirpation of sin is impossible, because we cannot bring it about by our own strength? Just as if the power of God, which "helps our infirmities," did not deserve a thought! Who does not see, that when a divine argues in this manner, he puts his bushel upon the light of Christ's victorious grace, hides this sinkilling and heart-cleansing light, and then absurdly concludes that the darkness of sin *must necessarily* remain in all believers? Thus, if I mistake not, it appears, that Mr. Toplady's argument, in favour of the death purgatory, is contrary to history, experience, and Gentilism; and how much more to Christianity, and to the honour of Him who "to the uttermost saves his believing people from their" heart toads and bosom vipers, when they go to him for this great salvation!

The next author who shall furnish me with logical shades, is the ingenious and Rev. Mr. Martin, who has just published a plea for the necessary indwelling of sin in all believers. He calls it, "The Christian's peculiar Conflict, an essay on Galatians 5:17:" and from it I extract the arguments which follow: —

ARG. II. (15, &c.) "O ye vain boasters of inherent perfection, say, where is the man among you to be found, who always *doth the things that he would?* If there be one who has this pre-eminence among his brethren, why should his name be concealed? Is he a preacher? and dare he assert he has, at all times, that discovery of the truth to his own soul he could wish, &c. Is he a private Christian? and will he venture to declare that in every character he sustains, &c, he continually acts not only the conscientious part, but in every respect fulfils the desire of his mind? What! does he hesitate? Is he afraid to attest this in the presence of a heart-searching God? How deceitful then is his confidence! &c. Strange infatuation! If he cannot at all times do the things, the good things that he would, can he suppose his best desires are more extensive than that law which is exceeding broad? &c. If he can be so vain as to suppose this, there is more hope of a fool than of him who is so wise in his own conceit. If he disowns the inference, and yet maintain his premises, that he is perfect, i.e. without sin, has ceased to commit iniquity, what is the conclusion? I am obliged to conclude that perfection and imperfection, things as contrary to each other as light and darkness, are with such a deluded person considered as one and the same thing."

This argument, stript of its rhetorical ornaments, and put into a plain logical dress, runs thus: —

"When Christians do not do all the good things which they *desire* to do, they sin, or break God's law, which is purer and broader than their desires: but the best ministers, and the best private Christian, do not do all the good things which they *desire* to do: and therefore the best ministers, and the best private Christians *sin,* and their sinless perfection is an empty boast." We may bring the argument into a still narrower compass, thus: "All deficiencies are sinful, and therefore inconsistent with every kind of perfection." Now this proposition, which is the basis of the whole argument, has error for its foundation. Granting that deficiencies are inconsistent with the absolute will of God, and with the perfection of his boundless power, I affirm four things, each of which, if I mistake not, overturns our objector's argument:—

1. The separate "spirits of just men made perfect" are *perfectly sinless;* nevertheless, they "do not do all *the good that they would,*" for they have not yet prevailed to get the blood of God's martyrs avenged: a display of justice this, which they ardently *wish* for. And I prove it by these words of St. John: — "I saw under the altar the souls of them that were slain for the word of God, and they cried with a loud voice, saying, *How long, O Lord, holy and true, dost thou not judge, and avenge our blood on them that dwell on the earth!*" Revelation 6:9. Had they done what they *wished, i.e.* actually prevailed with God, their prayer would have been immediately turned into praises, and persecutors would long ago have been rooted out from the earth.

2. For want of *infinite* wisdom, does not perfect love in *finite* creatures frequently desire to do more for its object than it can? When "Michael fought with the dragon," is it not highly probable that he lovingly desired to hinder his cruel adversary from doing any farther mischief? But did not his performance fall short of his pious, *resigned* desire? May not this be said also of the guardian care of the angels, who minister to the heirs of salvation? Do these loving spirits afford us all the help, or procure us all the bliss, which their tender compassion prompts them to *wish* us? If not, is it not absurd to suppose that, barely on this account, they are *sinfully* imperfect? Nay, would it not be a high degree of rashness and injustice to insinuate that they are transgressors of God's spiritual law; and that his commandment, which is broader than their *desires,* is broken by their not doing us all the good which they desire to do us, and which they would actually do us, if a wise Providence had not set bounds to their commission? Does not this unscriptural, Calvinian legality put the stamp of sinfulness upon all angels and archangels, merely to keep in countenance the Antinomian doctrine of the necessary sinfulness of all believers?

3. If we consider our Lord himself as *a man,* did he do all the good he would while he was upon earth? Did he preach as successfully as his perfect love made him desire to do? If he had all the success he desired in his ministry, why did he "look round upon his hearers with anger, being grieved for the hardness of their hearts?" Why did he weep and complain, "How often would I have gathered you, &c, and ye would not?" Were even his private instructions so much blessed to his own disciples as he could have *wished?* If they were, what meant these strange expostulations, "How is it that ye have no faith? Faithless generation, how long shall I be with you? Hast thou been so long time with me, Philip, and yet hast thou not known me? Will ye also go away?"

Nay, had not Christ his *innocent infirmities* too? Did he not shudder at the prospect of the cup of trembling? Needed he not the "strengthening *support* of an angel in the garden of Gethsemane?" Did he not "offer up prayers, with strong cryings and tears, unto Him that was able to save him from death? Was he not heard in that he feared?" Hebrews 5:7. Did he not innocently cry out upon the cross, "My God! my God! why hast thou forsaken me?" And does not the apostle observe, that "we have not a High Priest who cannot be touched with the feeling of our infirmities; but [one who] was in all points tempted as we are, yet without sin?" Hebrews 4:15. When our opponents, therefore, confound *sin* with natural, *innocent infirmities,* or with our not doing all the good we would, do they not inadvertently fix a blot upon the immaculate character of Him who could say, "Which of you convinceth me of sin?"

4. My pious opponent wishes, no doubt, to praise God as perfectly as an *angel;* while an angel probably desires to do it as completely as an *archangel;* but in the nature of things this cannot be. Thousands of God's moral vessels, which are perfect in their place and degree, and as such adorn God's universal temple, fall short of each other's perfection without being sinfully imperfect on that account. When deficiencies are natural, and not moral, if we call them sin, in many cases we charge God with *the creation of sin.* Nor is it any more sin in a *man* not to magnify God so vigorously as an angel, or in an *angel* not to serve his Creator so perfectly as an archangel, than it is a sin in a good *soldier* not to do the king such excellent service as an experienced *captain,* or a consummate general. In the moral world, as well as in the natural, "one star may differ from another star in glory," without the least disparagement to its peculiar perfection. The injudicious refinements of Calvinism make a confused jumble of God's works, as they do of God's truth, and of the various perfections which belong to the various classes of his children: but a wise dispenser of the word will do by those various truths and perfections as Joseph did by his brothers: "He placed them the first born according to his birthright, [or superiority,] and the youngest according to his youth" [or inferiority.]

5. We are not ashamed to assert that perfection in one respect, and imperfection in another respect, may consistently meet in the same subject; or that men and things may be *perfect* in one sense and *imperfect* in another. If our opponents ridicule us for it, we will present them with an ocular, and by no means "metaphysical" demonstration of their mistake. Two perfect grains, the one of barley, and the other of wheat, lie before us. I say with the perfectionists that the grain of barley is *perfect* in its kind, but *imperfect,* or inferior in excellence, when it is compared to the grain of wheat. But Mr. Martin, at the head of the imperfectionists, thinks me deluded, and placing himself in his judgment seat, gravely says, "I am obliged to conclude that perfection and imperfection, things as contrary to each other as light and darkness, are with such a deluded person considered as one and the same." "Some are so unaccountably absurd and ridiculous." Reader, thou art judge and jury: pronounce which of the two deserves best this imputation of "unaccountable absurdity," — the author of *this Essay,* or that of the "Essay on Galatians 5:17.

6. With respect to this gentleman's triumphant question, "Where is the (perfect) man? Why should his name be concealed?" I hope it has already been satisfactorily answered in sec. iv, arg. 12. To what is advanced there, I add here the following remark: — Inveterate prejudice is blind. If it believe not reason, Moses, the prophets, and the apostles, "neither would it be persuaded though one rose from the dead." And were we to point out a person as perfect as Jesus of Nazareth, and to say, "Behold the man!" I should not wonder if the prepossessed professors cried out, as some ancient engrossers of orthodoxy did, "He is a deceiver of the people, teaching perfection throughout all Jewry." And if they did not say, "He is the friend of publicans and sinners, away with him!" it is not improbable they would say, "He is a friend of the Pharisees and Arminians, why do you hear him? Would ye also be his disciples?" It is in vain to hope that prejudice expired with those who scoffed at perfection incarnate, and spit in the face of Jesus Christ, "thinking to do God *and the Messiah.* service." Man is man in London, as well as in Jerusalem. Our author goes on:—

ARG. III. Page 18. "It is not more essential to those who are partakers of the grace of God in truth, to desire this, [the destruction of sin,] than it is for every creature, as such, to desire an exemption from pain and shame." Then follows a dangerous insinuation, that we must say by the cup of *indwelling sin,* as our Saviour did by the cup of *pain and shame:* "The cup that my Father giveth me, shall I not drink of it?"

ANSWER. Never was a cup of subtle poison more artfully mixed! And that the reader may not suspect any mischief, the author borrows the very cup which our heavenly Father presented to Christ in the garden of Gethsemane; a cup of *pain and shame.* Reader, examine this cup, before thou drink it. Death is in it. Pour out the new wine, which makes the poison it contains palatable, and at the bottom thou wilt find this mortal sediment: — "It is as absurd absolutely to desire deliverance from sin in this life, as absolutely to desire deliverance from pain and shame." To discover the falsehood of this proposition we need only weigh the following remarks:— (1.) Man mixed for himself the *moral* cup of sin, and God, to punish him, mixed the *natural* cup of pain and shame. (2.) It is excessively wrong so to confound *moral* and *natural* evil, as to say that, because we cannot with any propriety absolutely pray for deliverance from *all natural* evil in this life, we ought not absolutely to ask and expect deliverance from *all moral* evil before death. (3.) When the imperfectionists confound the moral cup of sin, with the natural cup of shame and pain, they are as grossly mistaken, as if they confounded poison, and counter-poison; sin, and its punishment; the murderer's revengeful heart, and the gallows on which he is hanged. (4.) Shame and pain, when they are appointed for a trial of faith, and endured for righteousness' sake, compose the last and greatest of all the beatitudes; a beatitude this, of which our Lord drank so deeply, when, "for the joy that was set before him, he endured the pain, and despised the shame of the cross," Hebrews 12:2. But where was *indwelling sin* ever ranked among the ingredients which compose the beatitudes, that our opponents should thus confound it with pain and shame? (5.) When they insinuate that we must bear with sin as patiently as with pain and shame, the *moral* cup of indwelling iniquity as readily as the *natural* cup of outward affliction, do they not grossly confound "the cup of devils" with "the cup of the Lord," and make the simple believe that because we must patiently drink the latter *with Christ,* we must also patiently drink the former *with Belial?* The Captain of our salvation bids us "rejoice and be exceeding glad," when we patiently suffer pain and shame for righteousness' sake; therefore absolutely to deprecate all pain and shame would be to pray against our "exceeding great joy;" yea, against "our reigning with Christ:" for, only "if we suffer, shall we also reign with him." But where does Christ bid us "rejoice and be exceeding glad" when we are full of indwelling sin? Or where does he promise that if we harbor indwelling sin, "we shall also reign with him?" Christians, awake! We pour out this rank poison before you, that you may advert to its offensive smell. While rash Solifidians gather it up, as if it were the honey of Canaan; boldly trample it under foot, and be ye more and more persuaded that *righteousness Calvinistically imputed,* and *indwelling sin,* are the two arms in which the Delilah of the imperfectionists clasps her deluded admirers.

Page 31. Our ingenious author proposes an important question: — "If the grace of God," says he, "be so abundant as the Scriptures represent it, (and the Scripture cannot be broken,) why are believers permitted to struggle so long for that victory they cannot yet obtain?" that victory which death is to bring them? "Whence is it that they, who pant for purity, should not immediately obtain a request so desirable?" For our author lays it down as an undoubted truth, that "flesh and spirit mutually lust, desire, and strive to obtain a complete conquest, but at present, [i.e. in this life,] neither can prevail." (p. 26.)

This important question we answer thus: — Imperfect Christians do not attain perfect purity of heart, (1.) Because they do not see the need of it; because they still hug some accursed thing, or because the burden of indwelling sin is not yet become intolerable to them. They make shift to bear it yet, as they do the toothache, when they are still loath to have a rotten tooth pulled out. (2.) If they are truly willing to be made clean, they do not yet believe that the Lord both can and will make them clean; or that "now is the day of this salvation." And, as faith inherits the promises of God, it is no wonder if their unbelief miss this portion of their inheritance. (3.) If they have some faith in the promises that the Lord can and will "circumcise their hearts, that they may love him with all their hearts;" yet it is not that kind or degree of faith which makes them completely willing to sell all, to deny themselves, faithfully to use their *inferior* talent, and to continue instant in prayer for this very blessing. In short, "they have not, because they ask not," which is the case of the Laodicean imperfectionists; or "because they ask amiss," which is the case of the imperfect perfectionists. (4.) Frequently also they will receive God's blessing in their own preconceived method, and not in God's appointed way. Hence God suspends the operation of his sanctifying Spirit, till they humbly confess their obstinacy and false wisdom, as well as their unbelief, and want of perfect love. Thus we clear our sanctifier, and take the shame of our impurity to ourselves. Not so our opponents. They exculpate themselves, and insinuate that God has appointed the *necessary* continuance of indwelling sin in us for life, that the conflict which we maintain with that enemy may answer excellent ends. Their arguments, collected in the abovequoted "Essay," are produced and answered in the following pages: —

ARG. IV. Page 37, &c. "By this warfare the Lord manifests and magnifies himself to his people; and, if I am not mistaken, &c, the continuance of it is a mean by which believers have such views of the perfections and glory of God, as it does not seem to us probable they could here obtain without it." Then our author instances in God's "unchanging love toward the elect," and in his "sovereign grace, that reigns through righteousness to the salvation of the guilty." He next observes that "those believers who are most conscious of this internal conflict; most sensible of the power and prevalency of indwelling sin. are most thankful that the endearing declarations of

God's distinguishing love are true." And, pp. 39, 40, we are distinctly told that the doctrine of the necessary continuance of indwelling sin magnifies "the power and patience of God; the *power* of God to support us under this conflict, and his *patience* in bearing with our manifold weakness and ingratitude." For, great as the burden of our ingratitude is, "yet he fainteth not, neither is he weary."

This is an extract of our author's argument, which, like a snake, works its way through verbose windings, where I have not leisure to follow it. Crush this snake, and out will come this less viper: "The longer sin continues in us, the more God's sovereign love, grace, power, and patience, by which he saves guilty, weak, and ungrateful sinners, is manifested unto us." Or, if you please, "The longer we continue in sin, or the longer sin continues in us, the more is grace manifested and magnified." Or, if you will speak as the apostolic controvertist, "Let us *continue in sin that grace may abound.*" A notion this, which is the very soul of Antinomianism unmasked.

To fill the pious reader with a just detestation of this doctrine, I need only unfold it thus: if the continuance of indwelling sin magnifies God's sovereign grace and patience, in saving ungrateful sinners; the continuance of outward sin will do this much more: for the greater our outward sins are, the greater will God's patience appear in bearing with us, and his grace in forgiving us; seeing "he fainteth not, neither is he weary." Thus we are come almost to the top of Antinomianism: and, to reach the highest step of the fatal ladder, we need only declare, as the author of the five letters has done, that "a grievous fall [into sin, such as adultery, robbery, murder, and incest,] will make us sing louder to the praise of restoring grace throughout all the ages of eternity." (See the fourth of those letters.) Now, if "a grievous fall" will infallibly have that happy effect, it follows that ten such fails will multiply ten times the display of God's power and patience. What a boundless field opens here, to run an Antinomian race, and to enlarge our wickedness as hell! What a ladder is here lent us to descend to the depth of the abomination of desolation, in order to reach the loudest notes of praise in heaven! If this Solifidian Gospel be not one of "the depths of Satan," and the greatest too, I am not capable of discerning midnight gloom from noon-day brightness.

ARG. V. Page 4. "To save the guilty in such a manner as, &c, effectually to humble them who are saved, displays the manifold wisdom of God. Does it not seem necessary, to attain that great end, to make believers experimentally 'know what an evil and bitter thing' sin is, &c? If so, when can the objects of salvation see this with becoming shame and sorrow? Not while they are 'in the gall of bitterness,' &c. For, in that state, 'so abominable is man, that he drinketh in iniquity like water.' On the other hand, this cannot be after they are brought to glory: for then all the painful and shameful memorials of sin will be finally removed. It must be while flesh and spirit dwell in the same man."

Granted; but what has this argument to do with the question? Did we ever deny that, as long as we live, we must repent, or be deeply conscious "what an evil and bitter thing" sin is? The question is, whether indwelling sin is the cause or source of true repentance, or an incentive to it; and whether God has appointed that this should remain in our hearts till death, lest we should forget "what an evil and bitter thing sin is," or lest we should not remember it "with becoming shame and sorrow?" The absurdity of this plea has already been exposed in sec. 3, obj. 8, 9. And, to the arguments there advanced, I now add those which follow: (1.) Does not experience convince imperfect believers, that the more fretfulness, self will, and obstinacy they have in their hearts, the less they do repent? How absurd is it then to suppose that the remains of these evil dispositions will help them to feel "becoming shame and sorrow" for sin! (2.) Do not our opponents tell their hearers that we get more *becoming shame and sorrow* by looking one moment "at Him whom we have pierced," than by poring upon our corruptions for an hour? If so, why will they plead for indwelling sin, that "becoming shame and sorrow" may abound? And why do they pretend that they exalt Christ more than we, who maintain that our most becoming shame and deepest sorrow flow from his ignominy and sufferings, and not from our indwelling sin, and conflicting corruptions? Did not Job "abhor himself and repent in dust and ashes," when he saw his redeeming God by faith, much more than when he just kept his head above the bitter waters of impatience and murmuring? (3.) The pleaders for the continuance of indwelling sin tell us, "that as the sight and attacks of a living and roaring lion will make us dread lions more than all the descriptions and pictures which represent their destructive fierceness; so the feeling the onsets of indwelling sin will make us abhor sin more than all the descriptions of its odious nature, and the accounts of its fearful consequences: because a burnt child naturally dreads the fire." To this we answer: — A burnt child, who pleads for the keeping of a burning coal upon his breast to make him dread the fire, has hitherto been burned to little purpose. Who had ever less to do with indwelling sin, and its cursed attacks, than the holy Jesus, and faithful angels? And yet, who is more filled with a perfect abhorrence of all iniquity? On the other hand, who has been more distracted, and longer torn by indwelling sin, than the devil? And who, nevertheless, is better reconciled to it? Or, who is more plagued by the continual rendings and bitings of the lions and vipers within, than those passionate, revengeful people, who say, with all the positiveness of Jonah and Absalom, "I do well to be angry, and revenge is sweet?" Experience, therefore, demonstrates the inconclusiveness of this argument. (4.) If the penitent thief properly learned, in a few hours, "what an evil and bitter thing *external and internal* sin is," is it not absurd to suppose that he must have continued forty years full of indwelling sin to learn that lesson, if God had added forty years to his life? Would this delay have been to the honour of his Divine Teacher? Lastly: when Christ cast seven devils out of Mary Magdalene, did he leave one or two devils behind, to teach her "becoming shame and sorrow" for sin? And was it these two remaining "Diabolonians" that made her dissolve in tears at Christ's feet; or the grateful, penitential love which she felt for her gracious deliverer? Is it not astonishing that Gospel ministers should so far forget themselves and their Saviour as to teach, as openly as for decency they dare, that we must fetch our tears of godly sorrow from the infernal lake, and rekindle the candle of repentance at the fire of hell! And that the fanning breath of the Spirit, and the golden, hallowed snuffers of the sanctuary cannot make that candle burn continually clear, unless we use, to the end of our life, the black finger of Satan, indwelling sin; and Adam's accursed extinguisher, original corruption!

ARG. VI. Our author's next argument, in favour of the *necessary* indwelling of sin during life, is more decent, and consequently more dangerous. The cloven feet of error delicately wear the sandals of truth: but, with a little attention, we shall soon see that they are only borrowed or stolen. The argument, abridged from page 44, and rendered more perspicuous, may run thus: — "If we have frequently been slothful, and have not at all times exerted our abilities to the uttermost, why may not God in wisdom rebuke us for it, and make us sensible of that evil, by not permitting us to effect what at other times we Seem determined, if possible, to accomplish? [that is, *by not permitting us* utterly to abolish the whole body of sin.] If Samson abuse his strength, it is fit he should have cause severely to repent of his folly, by being deprived of it for a season, and becoming as weak as other men." Here we are left to infer, that as Samson through his unfaithfulness became "as weak as other men" for a season; so all believers, on account of their unfaithfulness, must be weakened by indwelling sin, during the term of life.

To this we answer, (1.) That although believers frequently give place to sloth and unfaithfulness, yet they are no more *necessitated* to do it, than Samson was to daily with Delilah. (2.) If the constant indwelling of sin be a just punishment for not making a proper use of the talent of grace which God gives us, it evidently follows that *our unfaithfulness,* and not *a necessity appointed by God,* is the very worm which destroys our evangelically sinless perfection: and the moment our opponents grant this, they allow all that we contend for; unless they should be able to prove that God necessitates us to be unfaithful, in order to punish us infallibly with indwelling sin for life.

As for Samson, he is most unfortunately brought in to support the doctrine of the *necessary* indwelling of that weakening sin, which we call "inbred corruption:" and he might be most happily produced to encourage those unfaithful believers, who, like him, have not made a proper use of their strength in time past. For he outlived his penal weakness, and recovered the strength of a perfect Nazarite before death; witness his last achievement, which exceeded all his former exploits. For it would be highly absurd to suppose that he got in a death purgatory the amazing strength by which he pulled down the pillars that supported the large building where the Philistines feasted. Nor need I the strength of a logical Samson to break the argumentative reeds which support the temple of error, in which the imperfectionists make sport, to their hurt, with the doctrine of that Christian Samson, who said, "I can do all things through Christ that strengtheneth me."

ARG. VII. Page 47, &c. We are indirectly told, (for pious men cannot utter gross Antinomianism without the mask of circumlocution,) that indwelling sin must continue in us, that "grace [may] not only be exercised, but distinguished from all that has only the appearance of it. But — how is the true grace of God to be here distinguished from that which is but the semblance of it? By its effects — a clear and spiritual discovery of the depravity, deceit, and desperate wickedness of our own hearts." And then we are given to understand that lest we should not be deeply convinced of that "desperate wickedness," the *continuance* of indwelling sin is absolutely necessary. This argument runs into the fifth, which I have already answered. It is another indirect plea for the continuance of outward adultery and murder, as well as for the continuance of indwelling sin; it being certain that outward adultery, &c, "will convince us of the desperate wickedness of our hearts," still more powerfully than heart adultery, &c. To what hard shifts are good men put, when they fight for the continuance of the bud, or root of any sin! Their every stroke for sin is a stab at the very vitals of godliness.

ARG. VIII. Page 48. "The continuance of indwelling sin," which is (with great modesty in the ingenious author, and therefore with great danger to the unwary reader) called "this warfare," is supported by the following reason: — "It is often an *occasion* to discover the *strength* of grace received, as well as the truth of it." This argument is all of a piece with the preceding, and puts me in mind of a speech, which a shameless young debauchee made once to me: — "I kept (said he) drinking and dosing in such a tavern, without ever going to bed, ever being sober one hour for twenty-three days. I never had so remarkable an *occasion* to discover the *strength* of my body, and the excellence of my constitution." However, in a few months, while he continued in the conclusion to discover his strength, a mortal disorder seized upon him, and by removing him into eternity, taught me that if Fulsome, the professor, speaks the truth, when he says, *Once in grace always in grace,* Nabal, the sot, was mistaken, when he hinted, *Once in health always in health.* To make the imperfectionists ashamed of this argument, I hope I need only observe, (1.) That nothing ever showed more the strength of grace than the conflicts which the man Christ Jesus went through, though he never conflicted a moment with indwelling sin. (2.) That the strength and excellence of a remedy is much better discovered by the removal of the disorder which it is designed to cure, than by the conflicts which the poor patient has with pain, till death comes to terminate his misery. And, (3.) That the argument I refute, indirectly represents Christ as a physician, who keeps his patients upon the rack to render himself more necessary to them, and to show the strength of the anodyne mixture, by which he gives them, now and then, a little ease under their continued, racking pain!

Our author adds, p. 49, "If those who bear the heaviest burdens are sometimes esteemed the strongest men, they who are thus engaged in this warfare [I wish he would speak quite out, and say, *They who bear the heaviest burden of indwelling sin,*] have that evidence of the strength of grace, &c, which is peculiar to themselves." A great mistake this: for if we may believe Ovid, when Medea murdered her own child, under a severe conflict with indwelling sin, she "had that fatal evidence of" what is here preposterously called *the strength of grace;* but what I beg leave to call *the obstinacy of free will. Sed trahit invitam nova vis, &c.* "Passion," said she, "hurries away my unwilling, reluctant mind." Judas, it seems, was not an utter stranger to this conflict, (any more than to the burden of guilt,) when he hurried out of it into a death purgatory. Nor do I blame him for having chosen strangling rather than life, if death can terminate the misery which accompanies indwelling sin, and do more in that respect for fallen believers than Christ himself ever did. But supposing that "the saving grace of God, which has appeared to all men," never appeared to Medea and Judas; supposing these two sinful souls never conflicted with indwelling sin; it will, however, follow from our author's insinuation, that, in case David had defiled half a dozen married women, and killed their husbands, to enjoy them without a rival, we should esteem him six times stronger in grace, if he had not fainted under his sixfold burden, like Judas; because "in this [Antinomian] warfare, those who bear the heaviest burdens are esteemed the strongest" believers; and because "they have that testimony of their love to Christ which is peculiar to themselves." If Satan were to transform himself into an angel of light, could he preach a more dangerous and immoral gospel to an Antinomian and perverse generation?

ARG. IX. Our author's last argument in favour of the *necessary* continuance of sin in us, occurs page 51, and runs thus: — "I will only add, that by this warfare the Lord weans his people from the present evil world, and makes them long for the land of promise, as the land of rest, &c. I know some will say, This is impossible; and be ready to ask, *Are we then debtors to the flesh?* [A very proper question! which the author answers thus:] By no means, &c. In our flesh dwells no good thing, &c. Nevertheless — he [God] can and does make the presence of evil so irksome to the believer, that it makes him ardently long for complete deliverance from it." That is, in plain English, he keeps his patients so long upon the rack of their indwelling sin, that at last they are forced to long for death, the great cleanser from heart iniquity. This argument would have been complete if it had been supported by these two passages: — "I do well to be angry even unto death." "In those days men, [plagued by the locusts which ascend out of the bottomless pit,] shall desire to die, and death shall flee from them." To show its absurdity I need only make two or three remarks upon it: —

1. Mark the inconsistency of our opponents. When they hear us press *obedient* faith upon a fallen or wavering believer, by mentioning to him the *terrors* of the Lord, the *fear* of losing the Divine favour, and the *danger* of being even "spued out of Christ's mouth, and condemned without mercy" if he show no mercy; they say that enforcing the love of Christ on a disobedient believer, will abundantly answer all the good ends which we propose by thus preaching Christ's law: but, when they plead for the continuance of sin, they forget their own doctrine, and tell us that indwelling sin is necessary to keep us in the way of duty, namely, in ardent longing for heaven. They blame us for making use of Christ's law, to spur believers: and yet they, (see to what astonishing height their partiality is grown!) *they* do not blush to preach openly the *law of sin* to believers; insisting that its working in their members is necessary to "make them long for the land of promise, as for the land of rest, and for the speedy possession of that great good which God has laid up for them." (p. 52.) We are heretics for preaching the law of Christ, the law of liberty; they who preach the law of sin, the law of bondage, are orthodox, and engross to themselves the glorious title of Gospel ministers!

2. How absurd is it to prop up the throne of indwelling sin in the hearts of believers, that its tyrannical law may make them long for heaven! Did not Christ long for heaven without indwelling sin? Do not the holiest believers, who are most free from indwelling sin, long most for the beatific vision? And do we not see that fallen believers, who are most filled with indwelling sin, are most apt to be lovers of sin and the world, "more than lovers of God" and heaven? Are they not the very people, who, unmindful of Lot's wife, stay in the plain, instead of escaping for their life, and fleeing to the celestial mount of God without ever looking behind them?

3. Is not indwelling sin a clog, rather than a spur, to the heavenly racers? If sin be of such service to us, to make us run the career of holy longing after heavenly rest, why does the apostle exhort us to "set aside every weight and the sin which does so easily beset us?" If we want a spur to make us mend our pace, need we keep the spur, indwelling sin? Is it not more likely to spur us to hell than to heaven? If we have thousands of sinless spurs, what need have we of keeping that to drive us to heaven, which drove Adam behind the trees of the garden, not to say out of his native paradise?

If you ask, What are the *sinless* spurs of believers? We reply, all the toils, infirmities, and pains of our weary, decaying, mortal bodies: all the troubles, disappointments, and sorrows, which arise as naturally out of our present circumstances, as sparks do out of the fire: a share of the dreadful temptations which harassed Christ in the wilderness: and frequent tastes of the bitter cup which made him sweat blood in the garden, and cry out on Calvary. Hear one, to whom our opponents absurdly give the spur of indwelling sin, as if he had not spurring enough without it: "I fill up that which is behind of the afflictions of Christ in my flesh," Colossians 1:24. And surely indwelling sin was never one of Christ's afflictions. Again: "Who shall separate us from the love of Christ? Shall it be tribulation, or distress, or persecution, or famine, or nakedness, or peril, or sword? As it is written, *For thy sake we are killed all the day long; we are accounted as sheep for the slaughter.*" Once more: some were "tortured, not accepting deliverance; and others had trials of cruel mockings, and scourgings; yea, moreover, of bonds and imprisonments. They were stoned, they were sawn asunder, were tempted, were slain with the sword; they wandered about in sheep skins, and goat skins, being destitute, afflicted, tormented; they wandered in deserts and in mountains, and in dens and caves of the earth."

I grant that all true believers have not these thorns in the flesh, and feel not the spurs which made Elijah flee for his life before incensed Jezebel, and "request that he might die under the juniper tree;" but, at the best of times, they have, or should have David's affliction, "My eyes run down with water because men keep not thy law:" they have, or should have Jeremiah's grief, "O that my head were waters, and mine eyes a fountain of tears, that I might weep, day and night, for the desolation of Jerusalem, or for the slain of the daughter of God's people!" They have, or should have the sorrow of just Lot, who was vexed "from day to day with the filthy conversation of the wicked among whom he dwelt." To suppose, therefore, that in this vale of tears, tribulation, and sin, we need keep the sting of indwelling sin, because we must "strive against the sin" which is in the world to the end, even *unto blood,* if we are called to secure the crown of martyrdom; or, because it "is the will of God, that through much tribulation we should enter the kingdom;" (p. 46;) and because we should long for heaven: to suppose, I say, that we must keep the sting, indwelling sin, on these accounts, is as absurd as to suppose that all the keepers and nurses in bedlam must be mad, and must continue to be plagued with personal lunacy, lest they should not "strive against" madness to the end; lest they should not come out of great disturbances when they remove from their dreary habitation; and lest, while they continue there, they should not see mad people enough to make them long for the conversation of reasonable persons.

ARG. X. Page 52. Our author closes his shrewd plea for the death purgatory by proposing a very material objection: "If any exclaim and say, *These sentiments have a tendency to reconcile believers to sin*; I must say; The flesh might as soon be reconciled to the spirit, as the spirit to the flesh; or sin to grace, as grace to sin. It is often said, *That nature will be nature.* And why may not this be applied to the Divine nature, of which believers are said to be partakers?" Hence our author insinuates that the Divine nature of believers is "immutable;" and that, because "to will is present with them," when they sin they still retain God's holiness, as "lions and eagles, however confined or caressed, retain their ferocity and brutal appetites."

I am glad to see that this pious author has still the cause of holiness at heart, and desires to stop up the Antinomian gap. I am persuaded that he *intends* to do God service by pleading for the continuance of indwelling sin. If he ask for the reprieve of that robber and murderer, it is merely because Antinomianism has deceived him, as formerly Pharisaism deceived the Jews, who cried, "Release unto us Barabbas." If he saw that *Christ in us* must be crucified afresh, in case the *robber in us* is not put to death; I doubt not he would be as sorry for his publication, as the devout Jews were for their antichristian request, when they "were pricked to the heart" on the day of pentecost. But, alas! if a good intention excuse bad performances, it does not stop their mischief. The very desire which our author evidences to secure godliness, is so unfortunately expressed, that it gives her as fatal a blow as the tempter did, when he said to our first parents, "Ye shall not surely die." For, when that gentleman intimates to fallen believers, Ye are possessed of the Divine nature; and, be your works what they will, if to will be "in some degree present," (p. 54,) ye are as much possessed of God's holy image, as a lion is possessed of a lion's fierce nature. What is this, but to preach the very gospel which the serpent preached in paradise; with this difference, that the serpent said, "Ye shall not die: ye shall be as gods." But the imperfectionists say, Your salvation is finished: *ye* have already the "immutable nature" of God: ye *are already as gods?* Adam believed the tempter, and lost his holy nature. The imperfectionists believe our author: O! may none of them remain "immutable" in the sinful imperfection which he so earnestly contends for!

XI. A Caveat. Having said so much upon our author's mistakes, I should be inexcusable if I did not drop a caution about the veil with which they are covered. His book goes into the world under the harmless title of "The Christian's peculiar Conflict;" whereas it should be called, *A plea for the propriety and usefulness of the continuance of indwelling sin in all Christians.* This plain, artless title would have made true Christians stand upon their guard; but now they take up *without suspicion* the cup mixed by the author: and it is well if some have not already drank it to the dregs *without fear.*

An illustration will give the reader an idea of the wisdom with which the title of this essay is contrived. I write a treatise full upon the advantage of a standing rebellion in the kingdom, and urge a variety of plausible arguments to show the great good that will arise from an inveterate opposition to the government. "If a spirit of rebellion ceases in any subject, the king's patience, mercy, love, and power will not be so fully displayed, nor will the loyalty of his good subjects be so well distinguished and proved: rebellion, and the burdens that attend it, will make us long for peace: guilty, ungrateful rebels will love the king and admire his mercy the more when they are forgiven after their manifold rebellions. And therefore [to use the unguarded words of our author, page 53,] *it becomes us seriously to consider how far this great end* [of a spirit of rebellion continually dwelling in every Briton's breast] is *understood, approved, and answered.*" I show my manuscript to a friend, who says, Your essay will alarm every well wisher to the constitution of the realm. But I remove his objection by saying, I will not call it "An essay on the propriety and usefulness of a spirit of rebellion constantly harboured in the breast of every one of his majesty's subjects:" but I will call it, *The loyal subject's peculiar conflict, an essay on* 1 Samuel 12:19; and this plausible title will modestly make way for my boldest arguments. Pleas for the continuance of rebellion and indwelling sin may properly enough be introduced by such a stratagem.

SECTION XV.

Mr. Hill objects, that the doctrine of Christian perfection is popish; and the author shows that it is truly evangelical, and stands inseparably connected with the cordial obedience required by the mediatorial law of Moses and Christ, insomuch that there is absolutely no medium between the doctrine of an evangelically sinless perfection and lawless Antinomianism — This section contains a recapitulation of the Scripture proofs of the doctrine maintained in these sheets; and therefore the careful perusal of it is humbly recommended to the reader.

HAVING taken my leave of the ingenious author of *The Christian's peculiar Conflict*, I return to Mr. Hill, who by this time meets me with his "Review" in his hand, and, with that theological sling, casts at our doctrine a stone which has indeed frighted thousands of weak souls, but has never done any execution among the judicious. Your doctrine, says he, "is a popish doctrine;" and he might have added, with as much reason, that it is *a Pelagian doctrine too:* for, bold as Pelagius and some popes have been in coining new doctrines, they never came to such a pitch of boldness as to say that they were the authors of the doctrine of evangelical obedience, and of those commandments which bind us to love God, — our covenant God, with all our hearts, and our neighbours as ourselves: precious Gospel commandments these, upon which the doctrine of perfection securely rests!

What pope was ever silly enough to pretend that he wrote the book of Deuteronomy, where we find this sweet, evangelical law, "Hear, O Israel: thou shalt love the Lord thy God with all thine heart, and with all thy soul, and with all thy might. And these words which I command thee this day, shall be in thy heart," [*to do them*, I suppose, and not to ridicule them under the names of *perfection* and *popery?*] Deuteronomy 6:5, 6. Now, by what argument will Mr. Hill prove that the pope is the inventor of this blessed doctrine?

Should that gentleman reply, that when God gave his ancient people this gracious law of perfection, he did not give it with an intention that they should *personally* keep it as an evangelical law; but only with an intention to drive them to the promised Messiah, who was to keep it for them, and to give eternal indulgences to all the believers who break it; we demand a proof: and till Mr. Hill produce it, we show his mistake by the following arguments: — **1.** Although the Jewish dispensation revealed a "gracious God, abundant in goodness, mercy, and truth, forgiving iniquity, transgression, and sin," to returning sinners, who penitentially laid hold on his Jewish covenant; yet, if I remember right, it never promised to accept of an obedience performed by another. Hence it is that God never commanded that Jewish females should be circumcised, but confined his ordinance to the males, who alone could personally obey it. We frequently read of vicarious *sufferings* in the Jewish Gospel, but not of vicarious *obedience* and vicarious *love*. For although the obedience of godly parents engaged God to bestow many blessings upon their children, yet the children were to obey for themselves, or to be cut off in the end. The Jews were undone by a conceit of the contrary doctrine, and by wild notions about the obedience of Abraham, and the holiness of the temple, which they fancied was imputed to them in the Calvinian way: and a similar mistake, it is to be feared, still undoes multitudes of Christians, who fatally mistake the nature of Christian obedience, absurdly put on

Doctrines of Grace and Justice

robes of self-imputed righteousness, and rashly bespatter the roses of personal and evangelically perfect obedience, which God requires of every one of us.

2. The mistake I oppose would never have been made by our opponents, if they had not used themselves to tear the evangelically legal part of the Scriptures from the context, in order to give it a sense contrary to that of the sacred writers; it being certain, that, when you have torn a man's tongue out of his mouth; you may afterward force it down his throat, and leave it there with the root against his teeth, and the tip toward his stomach. To show that the precept of perfect love, which I have quoted from Deuteronomy vi, is treated in this manner as often as our opponents insinuate God did not intend that Jewish believers should personally observe it as a term of final acceptance, but only that they should be driven thereby to the Mediator, who should perfectly love God for them: to show, I say, the absurdity, of this notion, we need only do Moses the justice to hear him out. Let any unprejudiced person read the whole chapter, and he will, I am persuaded, side against the Calvinian imputation of a Jewish perfection to Jewish believers. Moses begins by saying, "Now these are the commandments, which the Lord your God [yours, through an evangelical covenant] commanded to teach you, that ye might do them, [and not that your Mediator might do them for you,] Deuteronomy 6:1. Two verses after, he adds, "Hear, O Israel, and observe and do, [not, *Hear, O Israel, and another shall observe and do for thee,*] that it may be well with thee." Then comes our capital doctrine and precept of perfect love, which, a few verses below, Moses continues to enforce thus: "Ye shall not tempt the Lord your [covenant] God. You shall diligently keep the [evangelical] commands of the Lord your [covenant] God; and his [Gospel] testimonies, which he has commanded thee. And thou shalt do that which is right and good in the sight of the Lord thy God, that it may be well with thee. And when thy son asketh thee, saying, *What do mean these statutes,* [of perfect love, &c,] then thou shalt say unto thy son, *We were Pharaoh's bondmen in Egypt, and the Lord brought us out.*" And, lest Antinomian hands should draw the golden nail of this perfect obedience for want of proper clenching, this precious chapter, which our Church has properly selected for a Sunday lesson, ends with these words, which must raise a blush on the face, or strike conviction into the breast, of all who trample under foot the robes of our own evangelical perfection: "And the Lord commanded us to do all these statutes, that he might preserve us alive: and it shall be our righteousness [our Gospel perfection] if we observe to do all these commandments, before the Lord our [covenant] God, as he has commanded us," Deuteronomy 6:1-25.

If our opponents say that this is a transcript of Adam's anti-mediatorial law of paradisiacal perfection; and not a copy of Moses' mediatorial law of Jewish perfection: or if they assert, that Moses Calvinistically hints that the Jews were to keep this law by proxy, they may say that light is darkness. And if they grant that Moses was no Antinomian shuffler; but really meant what he spoke and wrote, it unavoidably follows, (1.) That God really required of every Jew an evangelical and personal perfection of love, according to the degree of light and power imparted under the Jewish dispensation. (2.) That this evangelical, Jewish perfection of love was attainable by every sincere Jew; because, whatever God requires of us in a covenant of grace, he graciously engages himself to help us to perform, if we believingly and obediently embrace his promised assistance. And, (3.) That if an evangelical perfection of love was attainable under the Jewish Gospel, (for "the

Gospel was preached to the Jews as well as to us," although not so clearly, Hebrews 4:2,) it is absurd to deny that the Gospel of Christ requires less perfection, or makes less provision, that Christians may attain what their dispensation calls them to.

If Mr. Hill thinks that this inference is not just, I refer him to our Lord's declaration: "Think not that I am come to destroy the law and the prophets: I am not come to destroy, but to fulfil:" first, by perfectly obeying myself the two great moral precepts of Moses and the prophets: and, *next*, by teaching and helping all my faithful disciples to do the same, Matthew 5:17. Should that gentleman object to the latter part of this little comment, because it leaves no room for the Calvinian imputation of Christ's mediatorial perfection to fallen believers, who sleep in impenitency, under the guilt of adultery, covered by murder: we reply, that this part of our exposition, far from being forced, is highly agreeable to the text, when it is taken in connection with the scope of our Lord's sermon and with the context. For,

(1.) All Christ's sermons, and especially that upon the mount, inculcate the doctrine of personal perfection, and not the doctrine of imputed perfection. (2.) The very chapter out of which this text is taken, ends with these words: "Be ye perfect, even as your Father which is in heaven is perfect." And Mr. Hill, prejudiced as he is against our doctrine, is too candid to assert that our Lord meant, "Be ye therefore perfect as your heavenly Father is perfect: now, he is perfect only by the Calvinian imputation of my righteousness: it is merely by imputation that he makes his sun to rise on the evil and on the good. And he sendeth only a Calvinistically imputed rain upon the just and upon the unjust. Be ye therefore perfect only by the imputation of my perfect righteousness."

Mr. Hill's mistake has not only no countenance from the distant part of the context, but it is flatly contrary to the words which immediately follow the controverted text. "For verily I say unto you, [that, far from being come to destroy the law and the prophets, that is, the spirituality and strictness of the moral part of the Jewish Gospel,] till heaven and earth pass, one jot or one tittle shall in no wise pass from the law [which Pharisaic glosses have unnerved] till all be fulfilled." And lest you should think that I speak of your fulfilling this law by proxy and imputation, I add, "Whosoever shall break one of these commandments, [which I am going to enforce upon you, as my own mediatorial law; though hitherto you have considered them only as Moses' mediatorial law;] whosoever, I say, shall break one of these least commandments, and [by precept and example] teach men so, he shall be called the least in the kingdom of heaven; [if he have any place among my people in my spiritual kingdom, it shall be only among my carnal babes, who are the least of my subjects.] But whosoever shall do and teach them, [the commandments whose spirituality I am going to assert,] the same shall be called great in the kingdom of heaven," [he shall be an adult, perfect Christian in the kingdom of my grace here; and he shall receive a proportionable crown of righteousness in the kingdom of my glory hereafter,] Matthew 5:18, 19.

If I am not mistaken, it evidently follows from these plain words of Christ, (1.) That he taught a personal perfection, and an evangelically sinless perfection too. (2.) That this perfection consists in not breaking, by wilful commission, the least of the commandments which our Lord rescued both from the false glosses of Antinomian Pharisees, who rested on the imputed righteousness of Abraham, saying, "We have Abraham for our father: we are the children of Abraham: we are perfect in Abraham:

all our perfection is in Abraham:" and from the no less false glosses of those absurdly legal Pharisees, who paid the tithe of anise, mint, and cummin, with the greatest scrupulosity, while they secretly neglected mercy, truth, and the love of God. And, (3.) That the perfection which Christ enforced upon his disciples, was not merely of the negative kind, but of the positive also; since it consisted both in *doing* and *teaching* the least, as well as the greatest of God's commandments.

If you ask what are the *greatest* of these commandments, which Christ says his disciples must "do and teach," if they will be great or perfect in his kingdom and dispensation, St. Matthew answers, "One of the Pharisees, who was a lawyer, asked him a question, saying, Master, which is the great commandment in the law, [the name then given to the Jewish Gospel which Moses preached;] Jesus said unto him, *Thou shalt love the Lord thy God with all thy heart, and with all thy soul, and with all thy mind:* that is the first and great commandment. And the second is like unto it [in nature and importance:] *Thou shalt love thy neighbour as thyself.* On these two commandments hang all the law and the prophets," Matthew 22:35. That is, whatever Moses and the other prophets taught and promised, hangs on the nail of perfect love. All came from, all tended to perfect love under the Jewish dispensation: nor is my dispensation less holy and gracious. On the contrary, "What the law could not do," in a manner sufficiently perfect for my dispensation, (for Jewish perfection is not the highest perfection at which man may arrive on earth,) "God sending me into the world for *the atonement and destruction of* sin, has *hereby abundantly* condemned sin in the flesh, that the righteousness of the mediatorial law," which enjoins perfect love, "might be *abundantly* fulfilled in *the hearts of* them that walk after the Spirit" of my Gospel: a brighter Gospel this, which transmits more direct and warmer beams from the Sun of righteousness, and can raise the exquisitely delicious fruit of perfect love to a greater perfection than the Gospel which Moses preached. (Compare Romans 8:3, with Hebrews 4:2. See also an account of the superiority of Christ's Gospel in the Scripture Scales, sec. 6.)

Agreeably to this doctrine of perfection, our Lord said to the rich young man, "If thou wilt enter into life, keep the commandments; if thou wilt be perfect, follow me" in the way of my commandments. "Love God with all thy heart, and thy neighbour as thyself; for blessed are they that do his commandments, that they may enter through the gates into the city, and have right to the tree of life which is in the street of that city, on either side of the pure river of the water of life. This do and thou shalt live" eternally in heaven. "Bring forth fruit unto perfection," according to the talents of grace and power which thou art entrusted with, and thou shalt "inherit eternal life; thou shalt receive the reward of the inheritance; thou shalt receive the crown of life, which the Lord has promised to them that love him," with the love which keepeth the commandments, and fulfilleth the royal law. Compare Matthew 19:17; Luke 10:28; Revelation 22:2, 14; James 1:12, and Luke 8:14.

On these, and the above-mentioned scriptures, we rest the truth and importance of the doctrine of perfection. Jewish perfection *principally* stands or falls with Deuteronomy 6, and Matthew 22; and Christian perfection with Matthew 5, and 19, to which you may add the joint testimony of St. Paul and St. James. The former, whom our opponents absurdly make the captain of their imperfection, says to the Judaizing Galatians, "Bear ye one another's burdens, [a rare instance of perfect love!] and so fulfil the [mediatorial] law of Christ," Galatians 6:2. Nor let Mr. Hill say that the apostle means we should fulfil it by proxy; for St. Paul adds, in the next verse but one, "Let every man prove his own work, and then [with respect to that work] he shall have rejoicing in himself alone, and not in another, for [with regard to personal, evangelical obedience] every man shall bear his own burden:" a proverbial expression, which answers to this Gospel axiom, *Every man shall be judged according to his own works.*

St. Paul urges the same evangelical and lawful doctrine upon the Romans:—"Love one another; for he that loveth another, hath fulfilled the law. For this, *Thou shalt not commit adultery. Thou shalt not covet;* and if there be any other commandment, it is briefly comprehended in this saying, namely, *Thou shalt love thy neighbour as thyself.* Love is the fulfilling of the law," Romans 13:8, &c. And that St. Paul spake this of the mediatorial law of liberty and Christian perfection, and not of the Christless law of innocence and paradisiacal perfection, is evident from his calling it "the law of Christ," that is, *our Redeemer's law,* in opposition to *our Creator's law,* which was given without an atoning sacrifice and a mediating priest, and therefore made no allowance for infirmities, and admitted neither of repentance nor of renovated obedience. Beside, St. Paul was not such a novice as not to know that the Galatians and the Romans, who had all sinned, as he observes, Romans 3:23, could never be exhorted by any man in his senses, to fulfil the paradisiacal law of innocence, by now loving one another. He therefore indubitably spake of the gracious law of our gentle Melchisedec; the law of Him who said, "A new commandment I give unto you, that ye love one another; as I have loved you, that ye also love one another," John 13:34. A precious commandment this, which our Lord calls *new,* not because the Jewish mediator had not given it to the Israelites, but because the Christian Mediator enforced it by *new* motives, gave *new,* unparalleled instances of obedience to it, annexed *new* rewards to the keeping of it, and required it to be fulfilled with a *new* perfection. And that Christians shall be eternally saved or damned, according to their keeping or breaking this mediatorial law of Christian perfection, this "law of Christ, this royal law of Jesus, the King of the Jews," we prove by Matthew 18:35; 7:26; 25:45; and Luke 6:46, &c.

If Mr. Hill's prejudices are not removed by what St. Paul says in Romans 13, concerning our fulfilling the Gospel law of perfection, we entreat him to ponder the glorious testimony which the apostle, in Romans 2, bears to this law, which he does not scruple to call "his Gospel." With regard to this gracious rule of judgment, says he, "There is no respect of persons with God. For as many as have sinned without a [Mediator's written] law, shall also perish with a [Mediator's written] law. And as many as have sinned in [or under a Mediator's written] law, shall be judged by the [Mediator's written] law. For not the hearers of the [Mediator's] law are just before God, but the doers of the [Mediator's] law shall be justified. [Nor are the heathens totally destitute of this law:] for when the Gentiles, which have not the [Mediator's written] law, do by nature, [by natural conscience, which is the echo of the Mediator's voice, and the reflection of *the light which enlightens every man that cometh into the world,*] when the Gentiles, I say, do [by these means] the things contained in the law, they, having not the law, are a law unto themselves; their conscience also beating witness; and their thoughts [in consequence of the witness borne] accusing, or else excusing one another; in the day when God shall judge the secrets of men by Jesus Christ, according to my Gospel," [that is, according to the Gospel law which I preach,] Romans 2:11, &c. For, while some "lay up treasures in heaven, others treasure up to themselves wrath against the day of wrath and of the righteous judgment of God, who will render to every man according to his deeds: to them who, by patient continuance in well doing, [or in keeping the Mediator's law according to their dispensation,] seek for glory [he will render] eternal life, [like a righteous Judge, and gracious Rewarder of them that diligently seek him.] But unto them that do not obey the truth, but obey unrighteousness, [he will render] indignation and wrath," [in just proportion to the more or less bright discoveries of the truth, which shall have been made to them,] Romans 2:5, &c. "For that servant, who knew his Lord's will, [by a written law, delivered through the hands of a Mediator,] and prepared not himself, [that he might have boldness in the day of judgment,] neither did according to his will, shall be beaten with many stripes [in the hell of unbelieving Jews and disobedient Christians.] But he that knew not, [his Master's will, by an outwardly written law,] and did [break the law of nature, disobey the voice of his conscience, and] commit things worthy of stripes, shall be beaten with few stripes. For unto whomsoever much is given, of him shall be much required," Luke 12:47, 48. An indubitable proof this, that as something is required of all, something, even a talent of grace, a measure of the spiritual light which enlightens every man, is given to all to improve with, and bring forth fruit to perfection; some thirty fold, some sixty fold, and others a hundred fold, according to their respective dispensations.

From these quotations it appears to us indubitable, that the Gospel of St. Paul, and, of consequence, the Gospel of Christ, is not a wanton, lawless Gospel; but a holy, lawful Gospel, in which evangelical promises are properly guarded by evangelical rules of judgment; and the doctrines of grace, wisely connected with the doctrines of justice. If this be a glaring truth, what a dangerous game do many good men play, when they emasculate St. Paul's Gospel, and with Antinomian rashness cut off, and cast away that morally legal part of it, which distinguishes it both from the ceremonial gospel which the Galatians foolishly embraced, and from the lawless gospel which Solifidian gospellers contend for under the perverted name of "free grace!" And how seriously should we all consider these awful words of St. Paul! — "There are some that trouble you, and would pervert the Gospel of Christ; but though we, or an angel from heaven, preach any other Gospel unto you [whether it be a more severe, Judaizing gospel, or a less strict, Solifidianizing gospel] than that which we, have preached unto you, [which stands at an equal distance from burthensome, Jewish ceremonies, and from lawless, Solifidian tenets,] let him be accursed," Galatians 1:7, 8.

This recapitulation of the principal Scripture proofs of our doctrine would be exceedingly deficient, if I did not once more remind the reader of the glorious testimony which St. James bears to the law of liberty:-"If ye [believers, says he] fulfil the royal law, according to the scripture, *Thou shalt love thy neighbour as thyself,* ye do well, [ye quit yourselves like perfect Christians.] But if ye have [uncharitably] respect to persons, ye commit sin, and are convinced of the law as transgressors, [that is, ye are condemned by the Mediator's law, under which ye are.] For whosoever shall keep the whole law, [of the Mediator,] and yet [uncharitably] offend in one point, he is guilty of all, &c. So speak ye, therefore, and so do, as people that shall be judged by the law of liberty [the Mediator's law.] For he [the imperfect, uncharitable, fallen believer] shall have judgment without mercy that hath showed no [charity or] mercy," James 2:8.

We rest our doctrine of Jewish and Christian perfection on these consentaneous testimonies of St. James and St. Paul; of Moses, the great lawgiver of the Jews, and of Christ, the great Lawgiver of the Christians: the doctrine of perfection, or of perfectly cordial obedience, being inseparably connected with the mediatorial laws of Moses and of Christ. The moment you destroy these laws, by turning them into "rules of life," through the personal observance of which no believer shall ever be justified or condemned, you destroy the ground of Jewish and Christian perfection, and you impose upon us the lawless, unscriptural tenet of an obedience *performed by proxy,* and of an *imputed perfection,* which will do us as little good in life, death, and judgment, as imputed health, opposed to inherent health, will do to a poor, sickly, dying criminal. Thus, after leading my reader round a large circle of proofs, I return to the very point whence I started: (see the beginning of the preface:) and I conclude that a gospel without a mediatorial law, without an evangelical law, without the conditional promise of a crown of heavenly glory to the obedient, and without the conditional threatening of infernal stripes to the disobedient; — I conclude, I say, that such a gospel will always lead us to the centre of Antinomianism; to the Diana and Hecate of the Calvinists; to lawless free grace and everlasting free wrath; or, if you please, finished salvation and finished damnation. On the other hand, the moment you admit what the Jewish and Christian Gospel covenants are so express about, I mean *an evangelical law,* or a *practicable rule of judgment, as well as of conduct,* eternal salvation and eternal damnation become conditional: they are suspended upon the evangelical perfection or imperfection of our obedience; and the Rev. Mr. Berridge hits on the head of the golden nail, on which "hang all the law and the prophets," all the four Gospels and the epistles, when he says, "Sincere obedience, *as a condition,* will lead you unavoidably up to a perfect obedience."

And now, reader, choose which thou wilt follow, Mr. Hill's lawless Antinomian Gospel, or St. Paul's and St. James' Gospel, including the evangelical law of Christian liberty and perfection, by which law thou shalt be conditionally justified or condemned, "when God shall judge the secrets of men by Jesus Christ, according to the Gospel," Romans 2:16. If thou choose imputed righteousness and imputed perfection without any condition, it will "unavoidably" lead thee down into a death purgatory, through the chamber of indwelling sin, if thou art an *elect person,* in the Calvinian sense of the word; or to eternal damnation through the chambers of necessary sin, if thou art one of those whom our opponents call *reprobates.* But if thou cordially choose the sincere, voluntary, evangelical obedience of faith, which we preach both as a condition and as a privilege, it will (Mr. Hill's second being judge) "unavoidably lead thee up to perfect obedience." There is absolutely no medium between these two Gospels. Thou must either be a Crispian, lawless imperfectionist, or an evangelical, lawful perfectionist; unless thou choose to be a Gallio — one who cares for none of these things. Thou must wrap thyself up in unscriptural notions of imputed righteousness, imputed holiness, and imputed obedience, which make up the ideal garment of Calvinistically imputed perfection; or thou must perfectly "wash in the blood of the Lamb thy robes" of inherent, though derived righteousness, holiness, and obedience, which (when they are thus washed) are the rich wedding garment of evangelical perfection.

SECTION XVI.

The author shows that the distinction between sins, and (evangelically speaking) innocent infirmities, is truly Scriptural, and that judicious Calvinists and the Church of England hold it — He draws the line between sins and innocent infirmities — A view of the extremes into which rigid, Pelagian perfectionists, and rigid, Calvinian imperfectionists, have run east and west, from the Gospel line of an evangelical perfection — An answer to Mr. Henry's grand argument for the continuance of indwelling sin — Conclusion of the argumentative part of this essay.

WE have proved, in the preceding section, that the doctrine of an evangelically sinless perfection is truly Scriptural, being inseparably connected with the greatest and most excellent precepts of the Old and New Testament, and with the most evangelical and awful sanctions of Moses and Jesus Christ. This might suffice to show that our doctrine of perfection cannot be called popish or Pelagian, with any more candour than the doctrine of the trinity can be branded with those epithets, because Pelagius and the pope embrace it. If, in order to be good Protestants, we were obliged to renounce all that the Jews, Turks, and infidels hold; we should renounce the Old Testament, because the Jews revere it; we should renounce the unity of God, because the Mohammedans contend for it; nay, we should renounce common humanity, because all infidels approve of it. I beg leave, however, to dwell a moment longer upon Mr. Hill's objection, that the pope holds our doctrine.

When this gentleman was at Rome, he may remember that his Cicerone showed him, in the ancient Church of *St. Paul without the gate,* (if I remember the name,) the picture of all the popes from St. Peter, Linus, Cletus, and Clement, down to the pope who then filled what is called "St. Peter's chair." According to this view of papacy, Mr. Hill is certainly in the right; for if he turn back to sec. v, he will see that Peter, the first pope, so called, was a complete perfectionist, and if Clemens, or St. Clement, Paul's fellow labourer, was really the fourth pope, it is certain that he also held our doctrine as well as Peter and Christ; for he wrote to the Corinthians, "By love were all the elect of God *made perfect.* Those who were *mad perfect in love* are in the region of the just, and shall appear in glory. Happy then are we if we fulfil the commandments of God in the unity of love. Following the commandments of God *they sin not.*" (*St. Clem. Ep. To the Corinthians*) This glorious testimony, which St. Clement bears to the doctrine of perfection, might be supported by many correspondent quotations from the other fathers. But as this would too much swell this essay, I shall only produce one, which is so much the more remarkable, as it is taken from St. Jerome's third Dialogue against Pelagius, the rigid, overdoing perfectist: *Hoc et nos dicimus, posse hominem non peccare, si velit, pro tempore, pro loco, pro imbecillitate corporea, quamdiu intentus est animus, quamdiu chorda nullo vitio laxatur in cithara.* That is, "We [who oppose Pelagius' notion about Adamic perfection] maintain also that, considering our time, place, and bodily weakness, we can avoid sin if we will, as long as our mind is bent upon it, and the string of our harp [i.e. of our Christian resolution] is not slackened by any wilful fault.

When I read these blessed testimonies in favour of the truth which we vindicate, my pleased mind flies to Rome, and I am ready to say, Hail! Ye holy popes and fathers, ye perfect servants of my perfect Lord! I am ambitious to share with you the names of "Arminian, Pelagian, Papist, temporary monster, and Atheist in masquerade." I publish to the world my steady resolution to follow you, and any of your successors, who have done and taught Christ's commandments. And I enter my protest against the mistakes of the ministers who teach that Christ's law is impracticable, that sin must dwell in our hearts as long as we live, and that we must continue to break the Lord's precepts in our inward parts unto death.

I shall close my answer to this argument of Mr. Hill by a quotation from Mr. Wesley's *Remarks upon the Review.* — "It [our doctrine of Christian perfection] has been condemned by the pope and his whole conclave, even in this present century. In the famous bull *Unigenitus,* they utterly condemn the uninterrupted act [of faith and love which some men talked of, of continually rejoicing, praying, and giving thanks] as dreadful heresy." If we have Peter and Clement on our side, we are willing to let Mr. Hill screen his doctrine behind the pope who issued out the bull *Unigenitus,* and, if he pleases, behind the present pope too.

However, says Mr. Hill, "The distinction between *sins* and *innocent infirmities* is derived from the Romish Church."

Answer. **1.** We rejoice if the Church of Rome was never so unreasonable and so deluded by Antinomian popes as to confound an involuntary, wandering thought, an undesigned mistake, and a lamented fit of drowsiness at prayer, with adultery, murder, and incest; in order to represent Christ's mediatorial law as absolutely impracticable, and to insinuate that fallen believers, who actually commit the above-mentioned *crimes,* are God's dear children, as well as the obedient believers, who labour under the above-described *infirmities.*

2. We apprehend that Mr. Hill and the divines who have espoused Dr. Crisp's errors, are some of the last persons in the world by whom we may with decency be charged to hold "licentious" doctrines. And we are truly sorry that any Protestants should make it their business to corrupt that part of the Gospel which, if we believe Mr. Hill, the pope himself has modestly spared.

3. Mr. Hill might, with much more propriety, have objected that our distinction is derived from the Jewish Church; for "the old rogue," as some Solifidians have rashly called Moses, evidently made a distinction between sin and infirmities; he punished a daring Sabbath breaker and an audacious rebel with death, with present death, with the most terrible kind of death. The language of his burning zeal seemed to be that of David, "Be not merciful to them that offend of malicious wickedness," Psalm 59:5. But upon such as accidentally contracted some involuntary pollution, he inflicted no other punishment than that of a separation from the congregation till evening. If Mr. Hill consider the difference of these two punishments, he must either give place to perverseness, or confess that wilful sins and involuntary infirmities were not Calvinistically confounded by the mediator of the old covenant; and that Moses himself made a rational and evangelical distinction between "the spot of God's children," and that "of the perverse and crooked generation," Deuteronomy 32:4.

4. That Christ, the equitable and gracious Mediator of the new covenant, was not less merciful than stern Moses, with respect to the distinction we contend for, appears to us evident from his making a wide difference between the almost involuntary drowsiness of the eleven disciples in Gethsemane, and the malicious watchfulness of the traitor Judas. Concerning the offence of the former, he said, "The spirit indeed is willing, but the flesh is weak;" and with respect to the crime of the latter, he declared, "It would be good for that man if he had never been born."

5. David and Paul exactly followed herein the doctrine of Moses and Christ. The psalmist says, "Keep back thy servant also from presumptuous sins: let them not have the dominion over me; then shall I be upright, [or rather, as the word literally means in the original, *I shall be perfect,*] and innocent from the great transgression," Psalm 19:13. Hence it is evident that some transgressions are incompatible with the perfection which David prayed for; and that some errors, or some secret [unnoticed, involuntary] faults, are not.

6. This, we apprehend, is evident from his own words: "Blessed is the man unto whom the Lord imputeth not sin, and in whose spirit there is no guile," though there may be some improprieties in his words and actions, Psalm 32:2. David's meaning may be illustrated by the well-known case of Nathanael. Philip said unto him, "We have found him of whom Moses wrote in the law: [a clear proof this, by the by, that the law frequently means the *Jewish Gospel,* which testifies of *Christ to come:*] it is Jesus of Nazareth. And Nathanael said unto him, Can any good thing come out of Nazareth?" Here was an *involuntary* fault, an *improper* quoting of a proverbial expression: and, nevertheless, as he quoted it with a good intention, and to make way for a commendable inquiry into the report which he heard, his error was consistent with that degree of perfection which implies "innocence from the great [wilful] transgression." This I prove, (1.)By his conduct: "Philip saith unto him, *Come and see;*" and he instantly went, without betraying the least degree of the self-conceited *stiffness,* surly pride, and morose resistance, which always accompany the unloving prejudice by which the law of Christ is broken. And, (2.) By our Lord's testimony: — "Jesus saw Nathanael coming to him, and saith of him, *Behold an Israelite indeed, in whom there is no guile!*" Our Lord's word for *guile,* in the original, is δολος, the very word, which being also Connected with a negative, forms the epithet αδολος, whereby St. Peter denotes the *unadulterated purity* of God's word, which he compares to *sincere* or *perfectly pure milk,* 1 Peter 2:2. Hence I conclude that, Christ himself being witness, (evangelically speaking,) there was no more indwelling insincerity in Nathanael than there is in the pure word of God; and that this is the happy case of all those who fully deserve the glorious title of "Israelite indeed," which our Lord publicly bestowed upon Nathanael. To return: —

7. If to make a distinction between sins and infirmities constitutes a man half a Papist, it is evident that St. Paul was not less tinctured with popery (so called) than David, Moses, and Jesus Christ: for he writes to Timothy, "Them that sin rebuke before all, that others may also fear," 1 Timothy 5:20. And yet he writes to the Romans, "We that are strong should bear with the infirmities of the weak," Romans 15:1. Here are two plain commands; the first, not to bear with sins; and the second to bear with infirmities: a demonstration this, that there is an essential difference between sins and infirmities, and that this difference is discoverable to others, and much more to ourselves. Nay, in most cases, it is so discernible to those who have their spiritual senses properly disposed, that they can as easily distinguish between sins (properly so called) and infirmities, as a wise judge can distinguish between accidental death and wilful murder; or between unknowingly passing a false guinea with a kind intention to relieve the poor, and treasonably coining it with a roguish design to defraud the public. The difference between the sun and the moon is not more striking in the natural world, than the difference between sins and infirmities in the moral world. Nevertheless, blind prejudice will probably confound them still, to darken counsel, and to raise a cloud of logical dust, that Antinomianism (the Diana of the imperfectionists) may make her escape, and save indwelling sin, which is the claw of the hellish lion, the tooth of the old dragon, the fishing hook of Satan, and the deadly sting of the king of terrors.

8. Judicious Calvinists have seen the propriety of the distinction, for which we are represented as unsound Protestants. Of many whom I could mention, I shall only quote one, who for his piety, wisdom, and moderation, is an honour to Calvinism, — I mean the Rev. Mr. Newton, minister of Olney. In his *Letters on Religious Subjects,* p. 199, he makes this ingenuous confession: — "The experience of past years has taught me [and I hope that, some day or other, it will also teach our other opponents] to distinguish between ignorance and disobedience. The Lord is gracious to the weakness of his people; *many involuntary mistakes* will not interrupt their communion with him. He pities their infirmity, and teaches them to do better. But if they dispute his *known will,* and act *against the dictates of conscience,* they will surely suffer for it. Wilful sin sadly perplexes and retards our progress." Here is, if I mistake not, a clear distinction made, by a true Protestant, between disobedience or wilful sin, and weakness, involuntary mistakes, or infirmity.

9. If Mr. Hill will not regard Mr. Newton's authority, I beg he would show some respect for the authority of our Church, and the import of his own prayers. If there be absolutely no difference between wilful sins, involuntary negligences, and unavoidable ignorances; why does our Church distinguish them, when she directs us to pray in the liturgy, "that it may please God to forgive us all our sins, negligences, and ignorances?' If these three words have but one meaning, should not Mr. Hill leave out the two last as ridiculous tautology? Or, at least, to remove from our Church the suspicion of popery, should he not pray every Sunday that God would *forgive us all our sins, sins, and sins!*

From the nine preceding remarks, and the quotations made therein, it appears, if I mistake not, that our important distinction between wilful sin and infirmities, or involuntary offences, recommends itself to reason and conscience: that it is supported by the law of Moses, and the Gospel of Christ; by the Psalms of David, and the epistles of St. Paul; by the writings of judicious Calvinists, and the liturgy of our Church; and therefore it is as absurd to call it a popish distinction, because the Papists are not injudicious enough to reject it, as it is absurd to call the doctrine of Christ's divinity "a doctrine of devils," because devils acknowledged him to be the Son of God, and their omnipotent Controller.

Should Mr. Hill reply, that if this distinction cannot properly be called popish, it deserves to be called "Antinomian," and "licentious;" because it countenances all the men who give to their *grossest sins* the soft names of "innocent infirmities;" we can answer: (1.) It has been proved that Moses and Jesus Christ held this distinction; and therefore to call it *Antinomian* and *licentious,* is to call not only Christ, the holy one of God, but even "legal" Moses, an Antinomian, and an advocate for licentiousness. See what these Calvinian refinements come to! (2.) The men who abuse the doctrine of the distinction between sins and infirmities, abuse as much the doctrine of God's mercy, and the important distinction between *working days* and *the Lord's day:* but is this a proof that the doctrines of God's mercy, and the distinction between the Lord's day and other days, are "licentious tenets, against which all that wish well to the interest of Protestantism should protest in a body?"

If Mr. Hill try to embarrass us by saying, "Where will you draw the line between wilful sins and [evangelically speaking] innocent infirmities?" We reply, without the least degree of embarrassment, Where Moses and the prophets have drawn it in the Old Testament; where Christ and the apostles have drawn it in the New; and where we draw it after them in these pages. And, retorting the question to show its frivolousness, we ask, Where will Mr. Hill draw the line between the free, evangelical observing of the Lord's day, and the superstitious, pharisaic keeping of the Sabbath; or between weak, saving faith, and wilful unbelief? Nay, upon his principles, where will he draw it even between a good and a bad work; if all our good works are really dung, dross, and filthy rags?

However, as the question is important, I shall give it a more particular answer. An infirmity is a breach of Adam's law of paradisiacal perfection, which our covenant God does not require of us now: and (evangelically speaking) a sin for Christians is a breach of Christ's evangelical law of Christian perfection; a perfection this, which God requires of all Christian believers. An infirmity (considering it with the error which it occasions) is consistent with pure love to God and man: but a sin is inconsistent with that love. An infirmity is free from guile; and has its root in our *animal* frame: but a sin is attended with guile, and has its root in our *moral* frame, springing either from the habitual corruption of our hearts, or from the momentary perversion of our tempers. An infirmity unavoidably results from our unhappy circumstances, and from the necessary infelicities of our present state: but a sin flows from the avoidable and perverse choice of our own will. All infirmity has its foundation in an involuntary want of power: and a sin in a wilful abuse of the present light and power we have. The one arises from involuntary ignorance and weakness, and is always attended with a good meaning; a meaning unmixed with any bad design, or wicked prejudice: but the other has its source in voluntary perverseness and presumption, and is always attended with a meaning altogether bad; or, at best, with a good meaning, founded on wicked prejudices. If to this line the candid reader add the line which we have drawn (section vi) between the perfection of a Gentile, that of a Jew, and that of a Christian, he will not easily mistake in passing a judgment between the wilful sins, which are inconsistent with an evangelically sinless perfection, and the innocent infirmities which are consistent with such a perfection.

Confounding what God has divided, and *dividing* what the God of truth has joined, are the two capital stratagems of the god of error. The first he has chiefly used to eclipse or darken the doctrine of Christian perfection. By means of his instruments he has perpetually confounded the Christless law of perfect innocence, given to Adam before the fall; and the mediatorial, evangelical law of penitential faith, under which our first parents were put, when God promised them the seed of the woman, the mild Lawgiver, the Prince of Peace, the gentle King of the Jews; who "breaks not the bruised reed, nor quenches the smoking flax," but compassionately tempers the doctrines of justice by the doctrines of grace; and instead of the law of innocence, which he has kept and made honourable for us, has substituted his own evangelical law of repentance, faith, and Gospel obedience, which law is actually kept, according to one or another of its various editions, by all "just men, made perfect;" that is, by all the wise virgins, who are ready for the midnight cry, and the marriage of the Lamb.

Hence it appears that Pelagius and Augustine were both right in some things, and wrong in a capital point. Pelagius, the father of the rigid perfectionists and rigid free willers, asserted that Christ's law could be kept, and that the keeping of that law was all the perfection which that law requires. So far was Pelagius right; having reason, conscience, and Scripture on his side. But he was grossly mistaken if he confounded Christ's mediatorial law with the law of paradisiacal perfection. This was his capital error, which led him to deny original sin, and to extol human powers so excessively as to intimate that by a faithful and diligent use of them, man may be as innocent, and as perfect as Adam was before the fall.

On the other hand, Augustine, the father of the rigid imperfectionists and rigid bound willers, maintained that our natural powers, being greatly weakened and depraved by the fall, we cannot, by all the helps which the Gospel affords, keep the law of innocence; that is, always think, speak, and act, with that exactness and propriety which became immortal man, when God pronounced him *very good* in paradise: he asserted that every impropriety of thought, language, or behaviour, is a breach of the law of perfection, under which God placed innocent man in the garden of Eden; and he proved that every breach of this law is sin: and that of consequence there can be no Adamic, paradisiacal perfection in this life. So far Augustine was very right: so far reason and Scripture support his doctrine: and so far the Church is obliged to him for having made a stand against Pelagius. But he was very much mistaken when he abolished the essential difference which there is between our Creator's law of strict justice, and our Redeemer's mediatorial law of justice, tempered with grace and mercy. Hence he concluded that there is absolutely no keeping the law, and consequently no performing any perfect obedience in this life; and that we must sin as long as we continue in the body. Thus, while Pelagius made adult Christians as *perfectly sinless* as Adam was in paradise, Augustine made them so *completely sinful* as to make it necessary for every one of them to go into a death purgatory, crying, "There is a law in my members, which brings me into captivity to the law of sin. Sin dwelleth in me. With my flesh I serve the law of sin. I am carnal, sold under sin. O wretched man that I am, who shall deliver me?"

The Scripture doctrine, which we vindicate, stands at an equal distance from these extremes of Pelagius and Augustine. It rejects, with Augustine, the Adamic perfection which Pelagius absurdly pleaded for; and it explodes, with Pelagius, the necessary continuance of indwelling sin and carnal bondage, which Augustine no less absurdly maintained. Thus adult believers are still sinners, still imperfect according to the righteous law of paradisiacal innocence and perfection: and yet they are really saints, and perfect according to the gracious law of evangelical justification and perfection: a law this, which considers as upright and perfect, all the godly heathens, Jews, and Christians, who are "without guile" in their respective folds, or under their various dispensations. Thus by still vindicating the various editions of Christ's mediatorial law, which has been at times almost buried under heaps of Pharisaic and Antinomian mistakes, we still defend practical religion. And, as in the Scripture Scales, by proving the evangelical marriage of free grace and free will, we have reconciled Zelotes and Honestus with respect to faith and works; so in this essay, by proving the evangelical union of the doctrines of grace and justice in the *mild* and *righteous* law of our Redeemer, we reconcile Augustine and Pelagius, and force them to give up reason and Scripture, or to renounce the monstrous errors which keep them asunder: I mean the deep, Antinomian errors of Augustine with respect to indwelling sin and a death purgatory; and the high-flown, Pharisaic errors of Pelagius, with regard to Adamic perfection, and a complete freedom from original degeneracy.

The method we have used to bring about this reconciliation is quite plain and uniform. We have kept our Scripture Scales even, and used every weight of the sanctuary without prejudice; especially those weights which the moralists throw aside as Calvinistic and Antinomian; and those which the Solifidians cast away as Mosaic and legal. Thus, by evenly balancing the two Gospel axioms, we have reunited the doctrines of grace and of justice, which heated Augustine and heated Pelagius have separated; and we have distinguished our Redeemer's *evangelical* law, from our Creator's paradisiacal law; two distinct laws these, which our illustrious antagonists have confounded; and we flatter ourselves that, by this artless mean, another step is taken toward bringing the two partial gospels of the day to the old standard of the one complete Gospel of Jesus Christ.

I have done unfolding our reconciling plan: but the disciples of Augustine, rallied by Calvin, have not done attacking it. I hope that I have answered the objections of Mr. Hill, Mr. Toplady, and Mr. Martin, against the evangelical perfection which we defend; but another noted divine of their persuasion comes up to their assistance. It is the Rev. Mr. Matthew Henry, who has deservedly got a great name among the Calvinists, by his valuable "Exposition of the Bible," in five folio volumes. This huge piece of ordnance carries a heavy ball, which threatens the very heart of our sinless Gospel. It is too late to attempt an abrupt and silent flight. Let then Mr. Henry fire away. If our doctrine of an evangelically sinless perfection is founded upon a rock, it will stand; the ponderous ball, which seems likely to demolish it, will rebound against the doctrine of indwelling sin; and the standard of Christian liberty which we waive, will be more respected than ever.

"Corruption," saith that illustrious commentator, "is left remaining in the hearts of good Christians, that they may learn war, may keep on the whole armour of God, and stand continually upon their guard." "Thus corruption is driven out of the hearts of believers *by little and little.* The work of sanctification is carried on gradually: but that judgment will at length be brought forth into a complete victory:" namely, when death shall come to the assistance of the atoning blood, and of the Spirit's power. That this is Mr. Henry's doctrine, is evident from his comment on Galatians 5:17: "In a renewed man, where there is something of a good principle, there is a struggle between, &c, *the remainders of sin,* and *the beginnings of grace;* and this, Christians must expect, will be their exercise *as long as they continue in this world;*" or, to speak more intelligibly, *till they go into the death purgatory.*

Not to mention here again, Galatians 5:17, &c, Mr. Henry builds this uncomfortable doctrine upon the following text: "The Lord thy God will put out those nations before thee by little and little; thou mayest not consume them at once, lest the beasts of the field increase upon thee," Deuteronomy 7:22. And he gives us to understand that "pride and security, and other sins," are "the enemies more dangerous than the beasts of the field, that would be apt to increase" upon us, if God delivered us from indwelling sin, i.e. from the remains of *pride* and *carnal security,* and *other sins.* This exposition is backed by an appeal to the following text: — "Now these are the nations which the Lord left to prove Israel by them — to know whether they [the Israelites] would hearken to the commandments of the Lord," Judges 3:1, 4. (See Mr. Henry's exposition on these passages.)

To this we answer: — **1.** That it is absurd to build the mighty doctrine of a death purgatory upon a historical allusion. If such allusions were proofs, we could easily multiply our arguments. We could say, that sin is to be *utterly destroyed,* because Moses says, "The Lord delivered into our hands Og and all his people, and we smote him until none was left unto him remaining," Deuteronomy 3:3. Because "Joshua smote Horam, king of Gezer, and his people, until he had left him none remaining, Deuteronomy 3:33. Because Saul was commanded "utterly to destroy the sinners, the Amalekites," and lost his crown for sparing their king: because, when God "overthrew Pharaoh and all his host, there remained not so much as one of them," Exodus 14:28. Because, when God rained fire upon Sodom and Gomorrah, "he overthrew all their [wicked] inhabitants;" and because Moses says, "I took your sin, the calf which ye had made, and burnt it with fire, and stamped it, and ground it very small, even until it was as small as dust, and cast the dust thereof into the brook," Deuteronomy 9:21. But we should blush to build the doctrine of Christian perfection upon so absurd and slender a foundation. And yet such a foundation would be far more solid, than that on which Mr. Henry builds the doctrine of Christian imperfection, and of the *necessary* indwelling of sin in the most holy believers; for,

2. Before God permitted the Canaanites to remain in the land, he had said, "When ye are passed over Jordan, then ye shall drive out *all* the inhabitants of the land before you, and destroy *all* their pictures; for I have given you the land to possess it. But if ye will not drive out the inhabitants of the land before you, then it shall come to pass, that those which ye let remain of them shall be pricks in your eyes, and thorns in your sides, and shall vex you in the land wherein you dwell. And moreover I shall do unto *you,* as I thought to do unto *them,*" Numbers 33:51, &c. Hence it appears, that the sparing of the Canaanites was a punishment inflicted upon the Israelites, as well as a favour shown to the Canaanites, some of whom, like Rahab and the Gibeonites, probably turned to the Lord, and as "God's creatures," enjoyed his saving mercy in the land of promise. But isindwelling sin one of "God's creatures," that God should show it any favour, and should refuse his assistance to the faithful believers, who are determined to give it no quarter? Can indwelling sin be converted to God, as the indwelling Canaanites might, and as some of them undoubtedly were?

3. But the capital flaws of Mr. Henry's argument are, I apprehend, two suppositions, the absurdity of which is glaring: — "Corruption," says he, "is left remaining in the hearts of good Christians, that they may learn war, may keep on the whole armour of God, and stand continually upon their guard." Just as if Christ had not "learned war, kept on the breastplate of *righteousness,* and stood continually upon his guard," without the help of indwelling sin! Just as if the world, the devil, the weakness of the flesh, and death, our last enemy, with which our Lord so severely conflicted, were not adversaries powerful enough to prove us, to engage us to learn war, and to make us "keep on *and use* the whole armour of God" to the end of our life! The other absurd supposition is, that "pride, and security, and other sins," which are supposed to be typified by "the wild beasts" mentioned in Deuteronomy 7:22, *will increase upon us by the destruction of indwelling sin.* But is it not as ridiculous to suppose this, as to say, Pride will increase upon us by *the destruction of pride;* and carnal security will gather strength by *the extirpation of carnal security*, and by the implanting of *constant watchfulness*, which is a branch of the Christian perfection which we contend for?

4. With respect to the inference which Mr. Henry draws from these words, "Thou mayest not consume them at once: the Lord will put them out before thee by little and little;" is it not highly absurd also? Does he give us the shadow of an argument to prove that this verse was spoken of our indwelling corruptions; and suppose it was, would this prove that the doctrine of a death purgatory is true? You say to a greedy person You must eat your dinner "by little and little," you cannot swallow it down at one gulp. A farmer teaches his son to plough, and says, We cannot plough this field *at once*, but we may plough it "by little and little," i.e. by making one furrow after another, till we end the last furrow. Hence I draw the following inferences: — We eat our meals, and plough our fields, "by little and little;" and therefore no dinner can be eaten, and no field ploughed before death. A surgeon says, "that the healing of a wound is carried on gradually:" hence his prejudiced mate runs away with the notion that no wound can be healed so long as a patient is alive. Who does not see the flaw of these conclusions?

5. But the greatest absurdity, I apprehend, is yet behind. Not to observe that we do not remember to have read any command in our Bibles *not to consume sin at once;* or any declaration that God will put it out only "by little and little;" we ask, What length of time do you suppose God means? You make him say that he will make an end of our indwelling sin "by little and little;" do you think he means four days, four years, or fourscore years? If you say that God cannot or will not wholly cleanse the thoughts of our hearts under fourscore years, you send all who die under that age into hell, or into some purgatory where they must wait till the eighty years of their conflict with indwelling sin are ended. If you say that God can or will do it in four days, but not under, you absurdly suppose that the penitent thief remained at least three days in paradise full of indwelling sin; seeing his sanctification was to be "carried on gradually" in the space of four days at least. If you are obliged to grant that when the words "by little and little" are applied to the destruction of indwelling sin, they may mean four hours, (the time which the penitent thief probably lived after his conversion,) as well as four days; do you not begin to be ashamed of your system? And if you reply, that death alone fully extirpates indwelling sin, does not this favourite tenet of yours overturn Mr. Henry's doctrine about the necessity of the slow, "gradual," destruction of indwelling sin? May not a sinner believe in a moment, when God helps him to believe? And may not a believer (whom you suppose *necessarily* full of indwelling sin as long as he is in this world) die in a moment? If you answer in the negative, you deny the sudden death of John the Baptist, St. James, and St. Paul, who had their heads cut off in a moment: in a word, you deny that any believer can die suddenly. If you reply in the affirmative, you give up the point, and grant that indwelling sin may be instantaneously destroyed. And now, what becomes of Mr. Henry's argument, which supposes that sanctification can never be complete *without a long, gradual process;* and that the extirpation of sin cannot take place but "by little and little?"

I have set before thee, reader, the lights and shades of our doctrine: I have produced our arguments, and those of our opponents; and now, say, which of them bear the stamp of imperfection? If thou pronounce that *urim and thummim,* light and perfection, belong to the arguments of Mr. Hill, Mr. Toplady, Mr. Martin, and Mr.

Henry, I must lay by my pen, and deplore the infelicity of our having a reason, which unsays in my breast what it says in thine. But if thou find, after mature deliberation, that our arguments are "light in the Lord," as being more agreeable to the dictates of unprejudiced reason, than those of our antagonists, more conformable to the plain declarations of the sacred writers, fitter to encourage believers in the way of holiness, more suitable to the nature of undefiled religion, and better adapted to the display of the Redeemer's glory; I shall enjoy the double pleasure of *embracing the truth,* and of embracing her *together with thee.* In the meantime, closing here the argumentative part of this essay, I just beg the continuance of thy favourable attention, while I *practically* address perfect Pharisees, prejudiced imperfectionists, imperfect believers, and perfect Christians.

SECTION XVII.

An address to perfect Christian Pharisees.

I ADDRESS you first, ye perfect Christian Pharisees, because ye are most ready to profess Christian perfection, though, alas! ye stand at the greatest distance from perfect humility, the grace which is most essential to the perfect Christian's character; and because the enemies of our doctrine make use of you first, when they endeavour to root it up from the earth.

That ye may know whom I mean by *perfect Christian Pharisees,* give me leave to show you your own picture, in the glass of a plain description. Ye have, *professedly,* entered into the fold where Christ's sheep, which are perfected in love, rest all at each other's feet, and at the feet of the Lamb of God. But how have ye entered? By "Christ the door," or at the door of presumption? Not by Christ the door: for Christ is meekness and lowliness manifested in the flesh; but ye are still ungentle and fond of praise. When he pours out his soul as a Divine Prophet, he says, "Learn of me, for I am meek and lowly in heart; take my yoke upon you, and ye shall find rest unto your souls." But ye overlook this humble door. Your proud, gigantic minds are above stooping low enough to follow Him, who "made himself of no reputation" that he might raise us to heavenly honours; and who, to pour just contempt upon human pride, had his first night's lodging in a stable, and spent his last night partly on the cold ground, in a storm of Divine wrath, and partly in an ignominious confinement, exposed to the greatest indignities, which Jews and Gentiles could pour upon him. He rested his infant head upon hay, his dying head upon thorns. A manger was his cradle, and a cross his death bed. Thirty years he travelled from the sordid stable to the accursed tree, unnoticed by his own peculiar people. In the brightest of his days, poor fishermen, some Galilean women, and a company of shouting children, formed all his retinue. Shepherds were his first attendants, and malefactors his last companions.

His first beatitude was, "Blessed are *the poor in spirit;*" and the last, "Blessed are ye, when men shall revile you, and persecute you, and say all manner of evil against you falsely, for my sake." His first doctrine was, "Repent:" nor was the last unlike to it: "If I have washed your feet, ye ought also to wash one another's feet, for I have given you an example that ye should do as I have done to you. He that will be first among you, let him be the least of all." Now, far from practising with godly sincerity this last lesson of our humble Lord, you do not so much as truly relish the first. Ye do not delight in, nay, ye abhor penitential poverty of spirit. Your humility is not cordial, and wrought into your nature by grace; but complimental, and woven into your carriage by art. Ye are humble in looks, in gestures, in voice, in dress, in behaviour; so far as external humility helps you to secure the reputation of perfect Christians, at which ye aspire from a motive of Pharisaic ambition: but ye continue strangers to the childlike simplicity, and unaffected lowliness of Christ's perfect disciples. Ye are the very reverse of those "Israelites in whom there is no guile," Ye resemble the artful Gibeonites, who, for a time, imposed upon Joshua's artless simplicity. Your feigned profession of special grace deceives those of God's children, who have more of the simplicity of the dove than of the serpent's wisdom. Ye choose the lowest place, but ye do not love it. If ye cheerfully take it, it is not among your equals, but among your inferiors: because you think that such a condescending step may raise the credit of your humility, without endangering your superiority. If ye stoop, and go down, it is not because ye see yourselves unworthy of the seat of honour; but because ye hope that people will by and by say to you, Come up higher. Your Pharisaic cunning rams at wearing at once the coronet of genuine humility, and the crown of self-exalting pride. Ye love to be esteemed of men for your goodness and devotion: ye want to be admired for your exactness, zeal, and gracious attainments. The pride of the Jewish Pharisees was coarse in comparison of yours. They wore the rough garment, and you wear the silks of spiritual vanity; and even when ye dye them in the blood of the Lamb, which you extol in word, it is to draw the confidence of humble Christians by your Christian appearance and language, more than to follow the propensity of a new nature, which loves to be clothed with humility, and feels itself in its own centre when it rests in deep poverty of spirit, and sees that God is "all in all."

One of the greatest ends of Christ's coming into the world, was to empty us of ourselves, and to fill us with humble love; but ye are still full of yourselves and void of Christ, that is, void of humility incarnate. Ye still aim at some wrong mark; whether it be self glory, self interest, self pleasure, self party, or self applause. In a word, one selfish scheme or another, contrary to the pure love of God and of your neighbour, secretly destroys the root of your profession, and may be compared to the unseen worm that ate the root of Jonah's gourd. Ye have a narrow, contracted spirit: ye do not gladly sacrifice your private satisfaction, your interest, your reputation, your prejudices, to the general interest of truth and love, and to the public good of the whole body of Christ. Ye are in secret bondage to men, places, and things. Ye do not heartily entertain the wisdom from above, which is pure, gentle, easy to be entreated, and full of mercy. Nay, ye are above conviction: gross sinners yield to truth before you. Like Jehu, ye are zealous, and ye pretend that it is for the Lord of hosts: but alas! it is for your opinions, your party, your honour. In a word, ye do not walk in constant, solemn expectation of death and judgment; your will is not broken; your carnal confidence is yet alive; the heavenly dove does not sit in your breast: self, wrapt up in the cloak of humility, is still set up in your hearts, and in secret you serve that cursed idol more than God. Satan, transformed into an angel of light, has artfully led you to the profession of Christian perfection through a circle of external performances, through glorious forms of doctrine in the letter, and through a fair show of zeal for complete holiness: the Lord, to punish your formality, has in part given you up to your delusion; and now ye as much believe yourselves perfect Christians, as the Pharisees, in our Lord's day, believed themselves perfect Jews.

Mr. Wesley, in his *Plain Account of Christian Perfection,* has borne his faithful testimony against such witnesses of perfect love as ye are. If ye despise this address, regard his remarks: "Others," says he, "who think they have the direct witness of their being renewed in love, are nevertheless manifestly wanting in the fruit. Some are undoubtedly wanting in *long suffering,* Christian resignation. They do not see the hand of God in whatever occurs, and cheerfully embrace it. They do not 'in every thing give thanks, and rejoice evermore.' They are not happy; at least, not always happy. For sometimes they complain. They say, 'This is hard!' Some are wanting in *gentleness.* They 'resist evil,' instead of turning the other cheek. They do not receive reproach with gentleness: no, nor even reproof. Nay, they are not able to bear contradiction without the appearance, at least, of resentment. If they are reproved, or contradicted, though mildly, they do not take it well. They behave with more distance and reserve than they did before, &c. Some are wanting in *goodness.* They are not kind, mild, sweet, amiable, soft, and loving at all times, in their spirit, in their words, in their look, in their air, in the whole tenor of their behaviour; not kind to all, high and low, rich and poor, without respect of person; particularly to them that are out of the way, to opposers, and to those of their own household. They do not long, study, endeavour, by every means, to make all about them happy. Some are wanting in *fidelity,* a nice regard to truth, simplicity, and godly sincerity. Their love is hardly 'without dissimulation:' something like guile is found in their mouth. To avoid roughness, they lean to the other extreme. They are smooth to an excess, so as scarce to avoid a degree of fawning. Some are wanting in *meekness,* quietness of spirit, composure, evenness of temper. They are up and down, sometimes high, sometimes low; their mind is not well balanced. Their affections are either not in due proportion; they have too much of the one, too little of the other; or they are not duly mixt and tempered together so as to counterpoise each other. Hence there is often a jar. Their soul is out of tune, and cannot make the true harmony. Some are wanting in *temperance.* They do not steadily use that kind and degree of food which they know, or might know, would most conduce to the health, strength, and vigour of the body. Or they are not temperate in sleep: they do not rigorously adhere to what is best for body and mind. They use neither fasting nor abstinence," &c.

I have described your delusion: but who can describe its fatal consequences? Who can tell the mischief it has done, and continues to do? The few sincere perfectionists, and the multitude of captious imperfectionists, have equally found you out. The former are grieved for you; and the latter triumph through you.

When the sincere perfectionists consider the inconsistency of your profession, they are ready to give up their faith in Christ's all-cleansing blood, and their hope of getting a clean heart in this life. They are tempted to follow the multitude of professors, who sit down in self-imputed righteousness, or in Solifidian notions of an ideal perfection in Christ. And it is well if some of them have not already yielded to the temptation, and begun to fight against the hopes which they once entertained of loving God with all their hearts. It is well if some, through you, have not been led to say, "I once sweetly enjoyed the thought of doing the will of God on earth, as it is done in heaven. Once I hopefully prayed God would 'so cleanse my heart, that I might perfectly love and worthily magnify his holy name' in this world. But now I have renounced my hopes, and I equally abhor the doctrine of evangelical perfection, and that of evangelical worthiness. When I was a young convert, I believed that Christ could really make an end of all moral pollution, cast out the man of sin, and cleanse us from the sins of the heart as well as from outward iniquity in this life; but I soon met with unhumbled, self-willed people, who, boldly standing up for this glorious liberty, made me question the truth of the doctrine. Nay, in process of time, I found that some of those who most confidently professed to have attained this salvation, were farther from the gentleness, simplicity, catholic spirit, and unfeigned humility of Christ, than many believers, who had never considered the doctrine of Christian perfection. These offences striking in with the disappointment which I myself met with, in feebly seeking the pearl of perfect love, made me conclude that it can no more be found than the philosopher's stone, and that they are all either fools or knaves, who set believers upon seeking it. And now I every where decry the doctrine of perfection as a dangerous delusion. I set people against it wherever I go; and my zeal in this respect has been attended with the greatest success. I have damped the hopes of many perfectionists! And I have proselyted several to the doctrine of Christian imperfection. With them I now quietly wait to be purified from indwelling sin in the article of death, and to be made perfect in another world."

This is, I fear, the language of many hearts, although it is not openly spoken by many lips. Thus are you, O ye perfect Pharisees, the great instruments by which the tempter tears away the shield of those unsettled Israelites, who look more at your inconsistencies than they do at the beauty of holiness, the promise of God, the blood of Christ, and the power of the Spirit.

But this is not all; as ye destroy the budding faith of sincere perfectionists, so ye strengthen the unbelief of the Solifidians. Through you their prejudices are grown up into a fixed detestation of Christian perfection. Ye have hardened them in their error, and furnished them with plausible arguments to destroy the truth which ye contend for. Did ye never hear their triumphs! "Ha! ha! So would we have it! These are some of the people who stand up for sinless perfection! They are all alike. Did not I tell you that you would find them out to be no better than temporary monsters? What monstrous pride! What touchiness, obstinacy, bigotry, and stoicism characterizes them! How do they strain at gnats and swallow camels! I had rather be an open drunkard than a perfectionist. Publicans and harlots shall enter into the kingdom of heaven before them." These are the cutting speeches to which your glaring inconsistency, and the severe prejudices of our opponents, give birth. Is it not deplorable that your tempers should thus drive men to abhor the doctrine which your lips recommend?

And what do you get by thus dispiriting the real friends of Christian perfection, and by furnishing its sworn enemies with such sharp weapons against it? Think ye that the mischief ye do shall not recoil upon yourselves? Is not Christ the same yesterday, to-day, and for ever? If he detested the perfect Pharisaism of unhumbled Jews, will he admire the perfect self-righteousness of aspiring Christians? If he formerly "resisted the proud, and gave grace to the humble," what reason have ye to hope that he will submit to your spiritual pride, and reward your religious ostentation with a crown of glory? Ye perhaps cry out against Antinomianism, and I commend you for it: but are ye not deeply tainted with the worst sort of Antinomianism — that which starches, stiffens, and swells the soul? Ye justly bear your testimony against those who render the law of Christ of none effect to believers, by degrading it into a rule which they stripped of the punitive and remunerative sanctions with which it stands armed in the sacred records. But are ye not doubly guilty, who maintain that this law is still in force as a law, and nevertheless refuse to pay it sincere, internal obedience? For when ye break the first commandment of Christ's evangelical law, by practically discarding penitential "poverty of spirit;" and when ye transgress the last, by abhorring the lowest place, by disdaining to "wash each other's feet," and by refusing to "prefer others in honour before yourselves;" are ye not guilty of breaking all the law by breaking it in one point, — in the capital point of humble love, which runs through all the parts of the law, as vital blood does through all the parts of the body? O how much more dangerous is the case of an unhumbled man, who stiffly walks in robes of self-made perfection, than that of an humble man who through prejudice, and the force of example, meekly walks in robes of self-imputed righteousness!

Behold, thou callest thyself *a perfect Christian,* and restest in the evangelical law of Christ, which is commonly called the Gospel: thou makest thy boast of God, and knowest his will, and approvest the things that are more excellent, even the way of Christian perfection, being instructed out of the Gospel; and art confident that "thou thyself art a guide of the blind, a light of them who are in darkness, an instructer of the foolish, and a teacher of babes," or imperfect believers; having the form of knowledge and of the truth in the Gospel. Thou therefore who teachest another, teachest thou not thyself? Thou that preachest, another should not break the law of Christ, through breaking it dishonourest thou God? For the name of God is blasphemed through you among those who seek an occasion to blaspheme it, Romans 2:17, &c. And think ye that ye shall escape the righteous judgment of God? Has Christ no woes but for the Jewish Pharisees? O be no longer mistaken. Before ye are punished by being here given up to a reprobate mind, and by being hereafter cast into the hell of hypocrites, the outer darkness where there will be more weeping, wailing, and gnashing of teeth than in any other hell! Before ye are overtaken by the awful hour of death, and the dreadful day of judgment, practically learn that Christian perfection is the mind which was in Christ, especially his humble, meek, quiet mind; his gentle, free, loving spirit. Aim at it by sinking into deep self abhorrence; and not by using, as ye have hitherto done, the empty talk and profession of Christian perfection as a step to reach the top of spiritual pride.

Mistake me not: I do not blame you for holding the doctrine of Christian perfection, but for wilfully missing the only way that leads to it; I mean the humble, meek, and loving Jesus, who says, "I am the way, and the door: by me if any man enter in, he shall be saved into so great salvation. He that entereth not by this door into this sheep fold, but climbeth up some other way, [and especially he that climbeth by the way of Pharisaic formality,] the same is a thief and a robber:" he robs Christ of his glory, and pretends to what he has no more right to than a thief has to your property. Would ye then be right? Do not cast away the doctrine of an evangelically sinless holiness; but contend more for it with your heart than with your lips. With all your soul press after such a perfection as Christ, St. Paul, and St. John taught and exemplified; a perfection of meekness and humble love. Earnestly believe all the woes which the Gospel denounces against selfrighteous Pharisees, and all the blessings which it promises to perfect penitents. Drink less into the letter, and more into the Spirit of Christ, till, like a fountain of living water, it spring up to everlasting life in your heart. Ye have climbed to the Pharisaic perfection of Saul of Tarsus, when, "touching the righteousness of the law, he was blameless." Would ye now attain the evangelical perfection which he was possessed of, when he said, "Let us, as many as are perfect, be thus minded?" Only follow him through the regeneration: fall to the dust before God; rise conscious of the blindness of your heart, meekly deplore it with penitential shame; and if you follow the directions laid down in the third address, I doubt not but, dangerous as your case is at present, you will be, like St. Paul, as eminent for Christian perfection, as you have hitherto been for Pharisaic formality.

SECTION XVIII.

An address to prejudiced imperfectionists.

I FEAR that, next to the persons whom I have just addressed, ye injure the cause of holiness, O ye believers, who have been deluded into doctrinal Antinomianism, by the bad arguments which are answered in the preceding pages. Permit me therefore to address you next: nor suffer prejudice to make you throw away this expostulation, before you have granted it a fair perusal.

Ye directly or indirectly plead for the necessary continuance of indwelling sin in your own hearts, and in the hearts of all true Christians. But may I be so bold as to ask, Who gave you leave so to do? And when were ye commissioned to propagate this unholy gospel? Was it at your baptism, when ye were ranked among Christ's soldiers, and received a Christian name, in token that ye would "keep God's holy will and commandments all the days of your life?" And that you would "not be ashamed to fight manfully against *the world, the flesh, and the devil,* unto your life's end?" Are not these three enemies strong enough sufficiently to exercise your patience, and to try your warlike skill to the last? Did your sponsors promise for you that you would quarter a fourth enemy, called indwelling sin, in your very breast, lest ye should not have enemies enough to fight against? On the contrary, were ye not exhorted "utterly to abolish the whole body of sin?" If so, is it not strange that ye should spend part of your precious time in pleading, under various pretexts, for the preservation of heart sin, a sin this, which gives life, warmth, and vigour to the whole body of sin? And is it not deplorable that, instead of conscientiously fulfilling your baptismal engagements, ye should attack those who desire to fulfil them by seeking to have "the whole body of sin" utterly abolished?

But ye are, perhaps, ministers of the Established Church: and, in this case, I ask, When did the bishop send you upon this strange warfare? Was it at your confirmation, in which he bound upon you your solemn obligations to "keep God's holy will and commandments" so as utterly "to abolish the whole body of sin?" Is it probable that he commissioned you to pull down what he confirmed, and to demolish the perfection which he made you vow to attain, and to "walk in all the days of your life?" If the bishop gave you no such commission at your confirmation, did he do it at your ordination, when he said, "Receive authority to preach the word of God?" Is there no difference between "the word of God," which cuts up all sin, root and branch, and *the word of Satan,* which asserts the propriety of the continuance of heart sin during the term of life? If not, did the bishop do it when he exhorted and charged you "never to cease your labour, care, and diligence, till you have done all that lieth in you, to bring all such as are committed to your charge to that agreement of faith, and that perfectness of age in Christ, that there shall be no place left among you for error in religion or viciousness in life," that is, I apprehend, till the truth of the Gospel and the love of the Spirit have perfectly purified the minds, and renewed the hearts of all your hearers?

How can ye, in all your confessions and sacramental offices, renounce sin, the accursed thing which God abhors, and which obedient believers detest; and yet plead for its life, its strength, its constant energy, so long as we are in this world? We could better bear with you, if ye appropriated a hand or a foot, an eye or an ear to sin, during the term of life; but who can bear your pleas for the necessary continuance of sin *in the heart? Is* it not enough that this murderer of Christ, and of all mankind, rambles about the walls of the city? Will ye still insinuate that he must have the citade to the last, and keep it garrisoned with filthy lusts, base affections, bad tempers, or "diabolonians," who, like prisoners, show themselves at the grate: and" like snakes, toads, and wild beasts, are the fiercer for being confined?" Who has taught you thus to represent Christ as the keeper, and not the destroyer of our corruptions? If believers be truly willing to get rid of sin, but cannot, because Christ has bolted their hearts with an adamantine decree, which prevents sin from being turned out: if he have irrevocably given leave to indwelling sin, to quarter for life in ever), Christian's heart, as the king of France, in the last century, gave leave to his dragoons to quarter for some months in the houses of the poor, oppressed Protestants, who does not see that Christ may be called *the protector of indwelling sin,* rather than its *enemy?*

Ye absurdly complain that the doctrine of Christian perfection does not exalt our Saviour, because it represents him as radically saving his obedient people from their indwelling sin in this life. But are ye not guilty of the very error which ye charge upon us, when ye insinuate that he cannot or will not say to our inbred sins," Those mine enemies which will not that I should reign over them, bring hither and slay them before me?" If a common judge has power to pass sentence of death upon all the robbers and murderers who are properly prosecuted; and if they are hanged and destroyed in a few days, weeks, or months, in consequence of his sentence, how strangely do ye reflect upon Christ, and revive the Agag within us, when ye insinuate that he, the Judge of all, who was "manifested for this very purpose, that he might destroy the works of the devil," so far forgets his errand, that he never destroys indwelling sin in one of his willing people, so long as they are in this world, although that sin is the capital and most mischievous "work of the devil?"

Your doctrine of the necessary continuance of indwelling sin in all faithful believers traduces not only the Son of man, but also the adorable trinity. The Father gives his only begotten Son, his Isaac, to be crucified, that the ram, sin, may be offered up and slain. But you insinuate that the life of that cursed ram is secured by a decree, which allots At the heart of all believers for a safe retreat, and a warm stable, so long as we are in this world. You represent the Son as an almighty Saviour, who offers to "make us free" from sin; and yet appoints that the galling yoke of indwelling sin shall remain tied to, and bound upon our very hearts for life. Ye describe the Holy Ghost as a Sanctifier, who applies Christ's all-cleansing blood to the believer's heart; filling it with the oil of holiness and gladness: and yet ye suppose that our hearts must necessarily remain "desperately wicked," and full of indwelling sin! Is it right to pour contempt upon Christianity, by charging such inconsistencies upon Father, Son, and Holy Ghost?

It can hardly be expected that those, who thus misrepresent their God, should do their neighbour justice. Hence the liberty which ye take to fix a blot upon the most holy characters. What have the prophets and apostles done to you that ye should represent them, not only as *men who had hearts partly evil to the last,* but also as *advocates for the necessary indwelling of sin in all believers till death?* And why do ye so eagerly take your advantage of holy Paul in particular, and catch at a figurative mode of speech, to insinuate that he was "a carnal wretch, sold under sin," even when he expected "a crown of righteousness at the hand of his righteous Judge," for having "finished his course with the just men made perfect?" Nay, what have we done to you, that ye should endeavour to take from us the greatest comfort we have in fighting against the remains of sin? Why will ye deprive us of the pleasing and purifying hope of taking the Jericho which we encompass, and killing the Goliath whom we attack? And what has indwelling sin done for you, that ye should still plead for the propriety of its continuance in our hearts? Is it not the root of all outward sin, and the spring of all the streams of iniquity, which carry desolation through every part of the globe? If ye hate the fruit, why do ye so eagerly contend for the necessary continuance of the root? And if ye favour godliness, (for many of you undoubtedly do,) why do you put such a conclusive argument as this into the mouths of the wicked: "These good men contend for the propriety of indwelling sin, that grace may abound: and why should we not plead for the propriety of outward sin for the same important reason? Does not God approve of an honest heart, which scorns to cloak the inward iniquity with outward demureness?"

Mr. Hill has lately published an ingenious dialogue, called, *A Lash to Enthusiasm,* in which, (p. 26,) he uses an argument againt pleading for lukewarmness, which, with very little variation, may be retorted against his plea for indwelling sin: — "Suffer me," says he, "to put the sentiments of such persons [as plead for the middle way of lukewarmness] into the form of a prayer, which we may suppose would run in some such expressions as the following: 'O Lord, thy word requires that I should love thee with all my heart, with all my mind, with all my soul, and with all my strength; that I should renounce the world, [and indwelling sin,] and should present myself as a holy, reasonable, and lively sacrifice unto thee: but, Lord, these are such over-righteous extremes [and such heights of sinless perfection] as I cannot away with; and therefore grant that thy love, and a moderate share of the love of the world, [or of indwelling sin,] may both reign [or at least continue] in my heart at once. I ask it for Jesus Christ's sake, Amen.'" Mr. Hill justly adds, "Now, dear madam, if you are shocked at such a petition, consider that it is the exact language of your own heart while you can plead for what you call *the middle way of religion.*" And I beg leave to take up his own argument, and to add, with equal propriety, "Now, dear sirs, if you are shocked at such a petition, consider that it is the exact language of your own heart while ye can plead for what ye call *indwelling sin,* or *the remains of sin."*

Nor can I see what ye get by such a conduct. The excruciating thorn of indwelling sin sticks in your hearts; we assert that Christ can and will extract it, if ye plead his promise of "sanctifying you wholly in soul, body, and spirit." But ye say, "This cannot be; the thorn must stay in till death extract it; and the leprosy shall cleave to the walls till the house is demolished." Just as if Christ, by radically cleansing the lepers in the days of his flesh, had not given repeated proofs of the absurdity of your argument! Just as if part of the Gospel were not, "The lepers are cleansed," and, "if the Son make you free, ye shall be free indeed!"

If ye get nothing in pleading for Christian imperfection, permit me to tell you what you lose by it, and what ye might get by steadily going on to perfection.

1. If ye earnestly tamed at Christian perfection, ye would have a bright testimony in your own souls that you are sincere, and that ye walk agreeably to your baptismal engagements. I have already observed, that some of the most pious Calvinists doubt if those who do not pursue Christian perfection are Christians at all. Hence it follows, that the more earnestly you pursue it, the stronger will be your confidence that you are upright Christians; and when ye shall be perfected in love, ye shall have that evidence of your sincerity which will perfectly "cast out *servile* fear, which hath torment," and nourish the filial fear which has safety and delight. It is hard to conceive how we can constantly enjoy the full assurance of faith, out of the state of Christian perfection. For so long as a Christian inwardly breaks Christ's evangelical law, he is justly condemned in his own conscience. If his heart do not condemn him for it, it is merely because he is asleep in the lap of Antinomianism. On the other hand, says St. John, "If our heart condemn us, God is greater than our heart, and knoweth all things" that make for our condemnation. But if we "love in deed and in truth," which none but the perfect do at all times, "hereby we know that we are of the truth, and shall assure our hearts before him," 1 John 3:19, 20.

2. The perfect Christian, who has left all to follow Christ, is peculiarly near and dear to God. He is, if I may use the expression, one of God's favourites; and his prayers are remarkably answered. This will appear to you indubitable, if ye can receive the testimony of those who are perfected in obedient love. "Behold," say they, "whatsoever we ask, we receive of him; because we keep his commandments, and do those things which are pleasing in his sight;" that is, because we are perfected in obedient love, 1 John 3:22. This peculiar blessing ye lose by despising Christian perfection. Nay, so great is the union which subsists between God and the perfect members of his Son, that it is compared to *dwelling in God,* and having God *dwelling in us,* in such a manner that the Father, the Son, and the Comforter, are said *to make their abode with us.* "At that day [when ye shall be perfected in one] ye shall know that I am in my Father, and you in me, and I in you. If a man love me, he will keep my words; and my Father will love him; and we will come to him, and make our abode with him," John 14:20, 23. Again: "He that keepeth God's commandments dwelleth in God, and God in him," 1 John 3:24. "Ye are my [dearest] friends, if ye do whatsoever I command you," [i.e. if ye attain the perfection of your dispensation,] John 15:14. Once more: — "Keep my commandments; and I will pray the Father, and he shall give you another Comforter, that he may abide with you for ever," John 14:15, 16. From these scriptures it appears that, under every dispensation, the perfect, or they who keep the commandments, have unspeakable advantages, from which the lovers of imperfection debar themselves.

3. Ye bring far less glory to God in the state of indwelling sin than ye would do if ye were perfected in love; for perfect Christians (other things being equal) glorify God more than those who remain full of inbred iniquity. Hence it is, that in the very chapter where our Lord so strongly presses Christian perfection upon his disciples, he says, "Let your light so shine before men, that they may see your good works, and glorify your Father who is in heaven," Matthew 5:16. For, "Herein is my Father glorified, that ye bear much fruit," John 15:8. It is true that the fruit of the perfect is not always relished by men, who judge only according to appearances; but God, who judges righteous judgment, finds it rich and precious; and therefore the two mites which the poor widow gave with a cheerful and perfect heart, were more precious in his account, and brought him more glory, than all the money which the imperfect worshippers cast into the treasury, though some of them cast in much. Hence also our Lord commanded that the work of perfect love which Mary wrought when she anointed his feet for burial, "should be told for a memorial of her, wherever this [the Christian] Gospel should be preached in the whole world." Such is the honour which the Lord puts upon the branches in him that bear fruit to perfection!

4. The perfect Christian (other things being equal) is a more useful member of society than the imperfect. Never will ye be such humble men, such good parents, such dutiful children, such loving brothers, such loyal subjects, such kind neighbours, such indulgent husbands, and such faithful friends, as when ye shall have obtained the perfect sincerity of obedience. Ye will then, in your degree, have the simplicity of the gentle dove, the patience of the laborious ox, the courage of the magnanimous lion, and the wisdom of the wary serpent, without any of its poison. In your little sphere of action ye will abound in "the work of faith, the patience of hope, and the labour of love," far more than ye did before: for a field properly weeded, and cleared from briers, is naturally more fruitful than one which is shaded by spreading brambles, or filled with indwelling roots of noxious weeds; it being a capital mistake of the spiritual husbandmen who till the Lord's field in mystical Geneva, to suppose that the plant of humility thrives best when the roots of indwelling sin are twisted round its root.

5. None but "just men made perfect are meet to be made partakers of the inheritance among the saints in light;" an inheritance this, which no man is fit for, till he has "purified himself from the filthiness of the flesh and spirit." If modern divines, therefore, assure you that a believer, full of indwelling sin, has a full title to heaven, believe them not: for the Holy Ghost has said, that the believer who "breaks the law *of liberty* in one point, is guilty of all," and that no defilement shall enter into heaven: and our Lord himself has assured us, that "the pure in heart shall see God," and that they who are ready for that sight, "went in with the bridegroom to the marriage feast of the Lamb." And who is ready? Undoubtedly the believer whose lamp is trimmed and burning. But is a spiritual lamp trimmed, when its flame is darkened by the black fungus of indwelling sin? Again: who shall be saved into glory, but the man whose "heart was washed from iniquity?" But is that heart *washed,* which continues full of indwelling corruption? Wo, therefore, be to the heathens, Jews, and Christians, who trifle away "the accepted time," and die without being in a state of heathen, Jewish, or Christian perfection! They have no chance of going to heaven, but through the purgatory preached by the heathens, the Papists, and the Calvinists. And should the notions of these purgatories be groundless, it unavoidably follows, that unpurged or imperfect souls must, at death, rank with the unready souls whom our Lord calls "foolish virgins," and against whom the door of heaven will be shut. How awful is this consideration, my dear brethren! How should it make us stretch every nerve till we have attained the perfection of our dispensation! I would not encourage tormenting fears in an unscriptural manner; but I should rejoice if all who call Jesus LORD, would mind his solemn declarations, "I say unto you my friends, Be not afraid of them that kill the body, &c; but I will forewarn you whom you shall fear: fear Him, who after he hath killed, hath power to cast into hell: yea, I say unto you, fear him," who will burn in the fire of wrath those who harbour the indwelling man of sin, lest he should be utterly consumed by the fire of love.

Should ye cry out against this doctrine, and ask if all imperfect Christians are in *a damnable state?* We reply, that so long as a Christian believer sincerely presses after Christian perfection, he is safe; because he is in the way of duty: and were he to die at midnight, before midnight God would certainly bring him to Christian perfection, or bring Christian perfection to him; for we "are confident of this very thing, that He who hath begun a good work in them, will perform it until the day of Jesus Christ, because they work out their salvation with fear and trembling." But if a believer fall, loiter, and rest upon former experiences; depending upon a self-made, Pharisaical perfection, our chief message to him is that of St. Paul, "Awake, thou that sleepest! Awake to righteousness, and sin not, for thou hast not the *heart-purifying* knowledge of God, which is eternal life. Arise from the dead;" call for oil; "and Christ will give thee light." Otherwise thou shalt share the dreadful fate of the lukewarm Laodiceans, and of the foolish virgins, "whose lamps went out," instead of "shining more and more to the perfect day."

6. This is not all: as ye will be fit for judgment, and a glorious heaven, when ye shall be perfected in love; so you will actually enjoy a gracious heaven in your own souls. You will possess "within you the kingdom of God," which consists in settled "righteousness, peace, and joy in the Holy Ghost." But so long as ye neglect Christian perfection, and continue sold under indwelling sin, ye not only risk the loss of the heaven of heavens, but ye lose a little heaven upon earth; for perfect Christians are so full of peace and love, that they "triumph in Christ, with joy unspeakable, and full of glory, and rejoice in tribulation with a patience which has its perfect work." Yea, they "count it all joy when they fall into divers trials;" and such is their deadness to the world, that they "are exceeding glad when men say all manner of evil of them falsely for Christ's sake." How desirable is such a state! And who, but the blessed above, can enjoy a happiness superior to him who can say, "I am ready to be offered up. The sting of death is sin, and the strength of sin is the law; but, O death, where is thy sting?" *Not in my heart,* since "the righteousness of the law is fulfilled in us, who walk not after the flesh, but after the Spirit." *Not in my mind,* "for to be spiritually minded is life and peace." Now this peculiar happiness ye lose, so long as ye continue imperfect Christians.

7. But supposing a Christian, who dies in a state of Christian imperfection, can escape damnation, and make shift to get to heaven; it is certain that he cannot go into the glorious mansion of perfect Christians, nor shine among the stars of the first magnitude. The wish of my soul is, that, if God's wisdom has so ordered it, imperfect

Christians may one day rank among perfect Jews, or perfect heathens. But even upon this supposition, what will they do with their indwelling sin? For a perfect Gentile, and a perfect Jew, are "without guile" according to their light, as well as a perfect Christian. Lean not then to the doctrine of the continuance of indwelling sin till death. A doctrine this, on which a Socrates, or a Melchisedec, would be afraid to mention his heathen perfection, and eternal salvation. On the contrary, by Christian perfection ye may rise to the brightest crowns of righteousness, and "shine like the sun in the kingdom of your Father." O for a noble ambition to obtain one of the first seats in glory! O for a constant, evangelical striving to have the most "abundant entrance ministered unto you into the kingdom of God!" O for a throne among these peculiarly redeemed saints, who "sing the new song, which none can learn" but themselves. It is not Christ's to give those exalted thrones out of mere distinguishing grace: no, they may be forfeited; for they shall be given to those for whom they are prepared; and they are prepared for them who, evangelically speaking, are *worthy*: "They shall walk with me in white, for they are worthy," says Christ: and they shall "sit at my right hand, and at my left in my kingdom," who shall be worthy of that honour: "For them that honour me;" says the Lord, "I will honour. Behold I come quickly: my reward is with me, and I will render to every man according to his works." And what reward, think ye, will Christ give you, O my dear, mistaken brethren, if he find you still passing jests upon the doctrine of Christian perfection, which he so strongly recommends? Still pleading for the continuance of indwelling sin, which he so greatly abhors?

8. Your whole system of indwelling sin and imputed perfection stands upon two of the most dangerous and false maxims which were ever advanced. The first, which begets Antinomian presumption, runs thus: "Sin cannot destroy us either in this world or in the world to come." And the second, which is productive of Antinomian despair, is, "Sin cannot be destroyed in this world." O how hard is it for those who worship where these siren songs pass for sweet songs of Zion, not to be drawn into one of these fatal conclusions! "What need is there of attacking sin with so much eagerness, since, even in the name of the Lord, I cannot destroy it? And why should I resist it with so much watchfulness, since my eternal life and salvation are absolutely secured, and the most poisonous cup of iniquity cannot destroy me, though I should drink of it every day for months or years?" If ye fondly think that ye can neither go backward into a sinful, cursed Egypt, nor yet go forward into a sinless, holy Canaan; how natural will it be for you to say, "Soul, take thine ease," and rest awhile in this wilderness on the pillow of self-imputed perfection? O! how many are surprised by the midnight cry in this Laodicean rest! What numbers meet death with a Solifidian "Lord! Lord!" in their mouths, and with indwelling sin in their hearts! And how inexpressible will be our horror, if we perceive our want of holiness and Christian perfection, only when it will be too late to attain them! To conclude: —

9. Indwelling sin is not only "the sting of death," but *the very hell of hells*, if I may use the expression: for a sinless saint in a local hell would dwell in a holy, loving God; and, of consequence, in a spiritual heaven: like Shadrach in Nebuchadnezzar's fiery furnace, he might have devouting flames curling about him; but, within him, he would still have the flame of Divine love, and the joy of a good conscience. But so much of *indwelling sin* as we carry about us, so much of *indwelling hell*; so much of the sting which pierces the damned; so much of the spiritual fire which will burn up the wicked; so much of the never-dying worm which will prey upon them; so much of the dreadful instrument which will rack them; so much of Satan's image which will frighten them; so much of the characteristic by which, the devil's children shall be distinguished from the children of God; so much of the black mark whereby the goats shall be separated from the sheep. To plead therefore for the continuance of indwelling sin, is no better than to plead for keeping in your hearts one of the sharpest stings of death, and one of the hottest coals in hell-fire. On the other hand, to attain Christian perfection is to have the last feature of Belial's image erased from your loving souls, the last bit of the sting of death extracted from your composed breasts, and the last spark of hell-fire extinguished in your peaceful bosoms. It is to enter into the spiritual rest which remains on earth for the people of God; a delightful rest this, where your soul will enjoy a calm in the midst of outward storm; and where your spirit will no longer be tossed by the billows of swelling pride, dissatisfied avarice, pining envy, disappointed hopes, fruitless cares, dubious anxiety, turbulent anger, fretting impatience, and racking unbelief. It is to enjoy that even state of mind in which all things will work together for your good. There your love will bear its excellent fruits during the sharpest winter of affliction, as well as in the finest summer of prosperity. There you will be more and more settled in peaceful humility. There you will continually grow in a holy familiarity with the Friend of penitent sinners, and your prospect of eternal felicity will brighten every day.*

Innumerable are the advantages which established, perfect Christians have over carnal, unsettled believers, who continue sold under indwelling sin. And will ye despise those blessings to your dying day, O ye prejudiced imperfectionists? Will ye secure to yourselves the contrary curses? Nay, will ye entail them upon the generations which are yet unborn, by continuing to print, preach, or argue for the continuance of indwelling sin, the capital wo belonging to the devil and his angels? God forbid! We hope better things from you; not doubting but the error of several of you lies chiefly in your judgment, and springs from a misunderstanding of the question, rather than from a malicious opposition to that "holiness, without which no man shall see the Lord." With pleasure we remember and follow St. Jude's loving direction: "Of some [the simple hearted, who are seduced into Antinomianism] have compassion, making a difference; and others [the bigots and obstinate seducers, who wilfully shut their eyes against the truth] save with fear, hating even the garment spotted by the flesh:" although they will not be ashamed to plead for the continuance of a defiling fountain of carnality in the very hearts of all God's people. We are fully persuaded, my dear brethren, that we should wrong you, if we did not acknowledge that many of you have a sincere desire to be saved by Christ into all purity of heart and life; and with regard to such imperfectionists, our chief complaint is, that their desire is "not according to knowledge."

---

* If the arguments and expostulations contained in these sheets be rational and Scriptural, is not Mr. Wesley in the right when he says, that "all preachers should make a point of preaching perfection to believers, constantly, strongly, and explicitly:" and that "all believers should mind this one thing, and continually agonize for it?" And do not all the ministers, who preach against Christian perfection, preach against the perfection of Christianity, oppose holiness, resist the sanctifying truth as it is in Jesus, recommend an unscriptural purgatory, plead for sin, instead of striving against it, and delude imperfect Christians into Laodicean ease?

If others of you, of a different stamp, should laugh at these pages, and (still producing banter instead of argument) should continue to say, "Where are your perfect Christians? Show us but one and we will believe your doctrine of perfection;" I shall just put them in mind of St. Peter's awful prophecy: "Know this first, that there shall come in the last days scoffers walking after their own [indwelling] lusts, and saying, *Where is the promise of his* spiritual *coming* [to make an end of sin, thoroughly to purge his floor, and to burn the chaff with unquenchable fire?] *For since the fathers fell asleep, all things continue as they were from the beginning:*" all believers are still carnal and sold under sin as well as father Paul. And if such mockers continue to display their prejudice by such taunts, I shall take the liberty to show them their own picture, by pointing at those prejudiced professors of old, who said concerning the most perfect of all the perfect, "What sign showest thou, that we may receive thy doctrine? Come down from the cross, and we will believe." O the folly and danger of such scoffs! "Blessed is he that sitteth not in the seat of the scornful," and maketh much of them "that fear the Lord." Yea, he is blessed next to them "that are undefiled in the way, who walk in the law of the Lord, keep his testimonies, and seek him with their whole heart," Psalm 119:1, 2.

Should ye ask, "To what purpose do you make all this ado about Christian perfection? Do those who maintain this doctrine live more holy and useful lives than other believers?" I answer: —

1. Every thing being equal, they undoubtedly do, if they hold not the truth in unrighteousness; for the best principles, when they are cordially embraced, will always produce the best practices. But alas! too many merely contend for Christian perfection in a speculative, systematical manner. They recommend it to others with their lips, as a point of doctrine which makes a part of their religious system; instead of following after it with their hearts, as a blessing which they must attain, if they will not be found as unprepared for judgment as the foolish virgins. These perfectionists are, so far, hypocrites; nor should their fatal inconsistency make us to despise the truth which they contend for, any more than the conduct of thousands, who contend for the truth of the Scriptures, while they live in full opposition to the Scriptures, ought to make us despise the Bible.

2. On the other hand, some gracious persons, (like the pious and *inconsistent Antinomians,* whom I have described in the preceding Checks,) speak against Christian perfection with their lips, but cannot help following hard after it with their hearts; and while they do so, they sometimes attain the thing, although they continue to quarrel with the name. These perfect imperfectionists undoubtedly adorn the Gospel of Christ far more than the imperfect, hypocritical perfectionists whom I have just described; and God, who looks at the simplicity of the heart more than at the consistency of the judgment, pities their mistakes and accepts their works.

But, (3.)Some there are, who both maintain doctrinally and practically the necessity of a perfect devotedness of ourselves to God. They hold the truth, and they hold it in wisdom and righteousness; their tempers and conduct enforce it, as well as their words and profession. And, on this account, they have a great advantage over the two preceding classes of professors. Reason and revelation jointly crown the orthodoxy and faithfulness of these *perfect perfectionists,* who neither strengthen the hands of the wicked, nor excite the wonder of the judicious, by absurdly pleading for indwelling sin with their lips, while they strive to work righteousness with their hands and hearts. If ye candidly weigh this threefold distinction, I doubt not but ye will blame the irrational inconsistency of holy imperfectionists, condemn the immoral inconsistency of unholy perfectionists, and agree with me, that the most excellent Christian is a consistent, holy perfectionist.

And now, my dear, mistaken brethren, take in good part these plain solutions, expostulations, and reproofs; and give glory to God, by believing that he can and will yet save you to the uttermost from your evil tempers, if ye humbly come to him by Christ. Day and night ask of him the new heart, which "keeps the commandments;" and when ye shall have received it, if you keep it with all diligence, sin shall no more pollute it, than it polluted our Lord's soul, when he said, "If ye keep my commandments, ye shall abide in my love; even as I have kept my Father's commandments, and abide in his love." Burn, in the meantime, the unhallowed pens, and bridle the rash tongues, with which ye have pleaded for the continuance of sin till death. Honour us with the right hand of fellowship; and like reconciled brethren let us at every opportunity lovingly fall upon our knees together, to implore the help of Him, who "can do far exceeding abundantly above all that we ask or think." Nor let us give him any rest, till he has perfected all our souls in "the charity which rejoiceth in the truth" without prejudice, in the obedience which keeps the commandments without reserve, and in the perseverance which finds that "in keeping of them there is great reward."

Nothing but such a conduct as this can remove the stumbling blocks, which the contentions ye breed have laid in the way of a Deistical world. When the men, whom your mistakes have hardened, shall see that you listen to Scripture and reason, who knows but their prejudices may subside, and some of them may yet say, "See the good which arises from friendly controversy! See how these Christians desire to be perfected in one! They now understand one another. Babylonish confusion is at an end; evangelical truth prevails; and love, the most delicious fruit of truth, visibly grows to Christian perfection." God grant that, through the concurrence of your candour, this may soon be the language of all those whom the bigotry of professors has confirmed in their prejudices against Christianity.

Should this plain address so far influence you, my dear brethren, as to abate the force of your aversion to the doctrine of pure love, or to stagger your unaccountable faith in a death purgatory; and should you seriously ask which is the way to Christian perfection, I entreat you to pass on to the next section, where, I hope, you will find a Scriptural answer to some important questions, which, I trust, a few of you are by this time ready to propose.

SECTION XIX.

An address to imperfect believers, who cordially embrace the doctrine of Christian perfection.

YOUR regard for Scripture and reason, and your desire to answer the ends of God's predestination, "by being conformed to the image of his Son," have happily kept or reclaimed you from the Antinomianism exposed in these sheets.

Doctrines of Grace and Justice

Ye see the absolute necessity of personally "fulfilling the law of Christ;" your bosom glows with desire to "perfect holiness in the fear of God;" and, far from blushing to be called perfectionists, ye openly assert that *a perfect faith*, productive of *perfect love* to God and man, is the pearl of great price, for which you are determined to sell all, and which (next to Christ) you will seek early and late, as the one thing needful for your spiritual and eternal welfare. Some directions, therefore, about the manner of seeking this pearl, cannot but be acceptable to you, if they are Scriptural and rational; and such, I humbly trust, are those which follow: —

1. First, if ye would attain an evangelically sinless perfection, let your full assent to the truth of that deep doctrine firmly stand upon the evangelical foundation of a precept and a promise. A precept without a promise would not sufficiently animate you; nor would a promise without a precept properly bind you; but a Divine precept and a Divine promise form an unshaken foundation. Let then your faith deliberately rest her right foot upon these precepts: —

"Hear, O Israel — thou shalt love the Lord thy God with all thy heart, and with all thy soul, and with all thy might, Deuteronomy 6:5. Thou shalt not hate thy neighbour in thy heart. Thou shalt in any wise rebuke thy neighbour, and not suffer sin upon him. Thou shalt not avenge, nor bear any grudge against the children of thy people: but thou shalt love thy neighbour as thyself. I am the Lord. Ye shall keep my statutes, Leviticus 19:17, 18. And now, Israel, what does the Lord thy God require of thee, but to fear the Lord thy God, to walk in his ways, and to love him, and to serve the Lord thy God with all thy heart, and with all thy soul, to keep the commandments of the Lord God, and his statutes, which I command thee this day for thy good, &c? Circumcise therefore the foreskin of your heart, and be no more stiff necked, Deuteronomy 10:12, &c. Serve God with a perfect heart, and a willing mind: for the Lord searcheth all hearts, and understandeth the imaginations of the thoughts," 1 Chronicles 28:9.

Should unbelief suggest that these are only Old Testament injunctions, trample upon the false suggestion, and rest the same foot of your faith upon the following New Testament precepts: — "Think not that I am come to destroy the law, or the prophets. I say unto you, Love your enemies; bless them that curse you; do good to them that hate you, &c, that ye may be the children of your Father who is in heaven, &c. For it ye love them which love you, what reward have ye? Do not even the publicans the same? Be ye therefore perfect, even as your Father which is in heaven is perfect, Matthew 5:17, 44, &c. If thou wilt enter into life, keep the commandments, Matthew 19:17. Bear ye one another's burdens, and so fulfil the law of Christ, Galatians 6:2. This is my commandment, that ye love one another as I have loved you, John 15:12. He that loveth another hath fulfilled the law: for this, Thou shalt not commit adultery, &c. Thou shalt not covet, and if there be any other commandment, it is briefly comprehended in this saying, *Thou shalt love thy neighbour as thyself*. Love worketh no ill, &c, therefore, love is the fulfilling of the law, Romans 13:8, 10. This commandment we have from him, that he who loves God, love his brother also, 1 John 4:21. If ye fulfil the royal law, *Thou shalt love thy neighbour as thyself*, ye do well. But if ye have respect to persons, ye commit sin, and are convinced of the law as transgressors, James 2:8, 9. Circumcision is nothing, uncircumcision is nothing [comparatively speaking;] but [under Christ] the keeping of the commandments of God [is the one thing needful,] 1 Corinthians 7:19. For the end of the commandment is charity, out of a pure heart, and of a good conscience, and of faith unfeigned, 1 Timothy 1:5. Though I have all faith, &c, and have not charity, I am nothing, 1 Corinthians 13:2. Whosoever shall keep the whole law [of liberty] and yet offend in one point [in uncharitable respect of persons] he is guilty of all, &c. So speak ye, and so do, as they that shall be judged by the law of liberty," [which requires perfect love, and therefore makes no allowance for the least degree of uncharitableness,] James 2:10, 12.

When the right foot of your faith stands on these evangelical precepts and proclamations, lest she should stagger for want of a promise every way adequate to such weighty commandments, let her place her left foot upon the following promises, which are extracted from the Old Testament: "The Lord thy God will circumcise thine heart, and the heart of thy seed, to love the Lord thy God with all thine heart, Deuteronomy 30:6. I will give them a heart to know me, that I am the Lord, and they shall be my people, and I will be their God, [in a new and peculiar manner,] for they shall return unto me with their whole heart. This shall be the covenant that I will make with the house of Israel. After those days, saith the Lord, I will put my law in their inward parts, and write it in their hearts, and will be their God, and they shall be my people, Jeremiah 24:7; 31:33. Then will I sprinkle clean water upon you, and ye shall be clean: from all your filthiness and from all your idols will I cleanse you: a new heart also will I give you, and a new spirit will I put within you: and I will take away the heart of stone out of your flesh, and I will give you a heart of flesh. And I will put my Spirit within you, and cause you to walk in my statutes, and ye shall keep my judgments and do them," Ezekiel 36:25-27.

And let nobody suppose that the promises of *the circumcision* of the heart, *the cleansing, the clean water,* and *the Spirit,* which are mentioned in these scriptures, and by which the hearts of believers are to be made new, and God's law is to be so written therein, that they shall "keep his judgments and do them;" let none, I say, suppose that these glorious promises belong only to the Jews; for their full accomplishment peculiarly refers to the Christian dispensation. Beside, if *sprinklings of the Spirit* were sufficient, under the Jewish dispensation, to raise the plant of Jewish perfection in Jewish believers, how much more will the revelation of "the horn of our salvation," and the *outpourings of the Spirit,* raise the plant of Christian perfection in faithful, Christian believers!

And that this revelation of Christ in the Spirit as well as in the flesh, these effusions of the water of life, these baptisms of fire which burn up the chaff of sin, thoroughly purge God's spiritual floor, save us from all our uncleanness, and deliver us from all our enemies; that these blessings, I say, are peculiarly promised to Christians, is demonstrable by the following cloud of New Testament declarations and promises: —

"Blessed be the Lord God of Israel, — for he hath raised up a horn of salvation for us, — as he spake by the mouth of his holy prophets, — that we, being delivered out of the hands of our enemies, might serve him without [unbelieving] fear, [that is, with perfect love,] in holiness and righteousness before him all the days of our life, Luke 1:68, 75. Blessed are the poor in spirit, who thirst after righteousness, for they shall be filled, Matthew 5:3, 6. If thou knewest the gift of God, &c, thou wouldest have asked of him, and he would have given thee living water: and the water that I shall give him, shall be in him a well of water springing up to everlasting life, John

4:10, 14. Jesus stood and cried, saying, *If any man thirst, let him come to me and drink. He that believeth on me,* [when I shall have ascended up on high to receive gifts for men,] out *of his belly shall flow rivers of living water,* [to cleanse his soul, and keep it clean.] But this he spake of the Spirit, which they that believe on him should receive; for the Holy Ghost was not yet given, [in such a manner as to raise the plant of Christian perfection,] because Jesus was not yet glorified," [and his spiritual dispensation was not yet fully opened,] John 7:37, &c. Mr. Wesley, in his *Plain Account of Christian Perfection,* has published some excellent queries, and proposed them to those who deny perfection to be attainable in this life. They are close to the point, and therefore the two first attack the imperfectionists from the very ground on which I want you to stand. They run thus: "(1.) Has there not been a larger measure of the Holy Spirit given under the Gospel than under the Jewish dispensation? If not, in what sense was *the Spirit not given before Christ was glorified?* John 7:39. (2.) Was that *glory which followed the sufferings of Christ,* 1 Peter 1:11, an external glory, or an internal, viz. the glory of holiness?" Always rest the doctrine of Christian perfection on this Scriptural foundation, and it will stand as firm as revelation itself.

It is allowed on all sides that the dispensation of John the Baptist exceeded that of the other prophets, because it immediately introduced the Gospel of Christ, and because John was not only appointed to "preach the baptism of repentance," but also clearly to point out the very person of Christ, and to give knowledge of salvation to God's people by the remission of sins, Luke 1:77; and nevertheless, John only promised the blessing of the Spirit, which Christ bestowed when he had received gifts for men. "I indeed," said John, "baptize you with water unto repentance; but he that cometh after me is mightier than I, — he shall baptize you with the Holy Ghost and with fire," Matthew 3:44. Such is the importance of this promise, that it is particularly recorded not only by the three other evangelists, see Mark 1:8; Luke 3:16; and John 1:26, but also by our Lord himself, who said just before his ascension, "John truly baptized with water, but ye shall be baptized with the Holy Ghost not many days hence," Acts 1:5.

So capital is this promise of the Spirit's stronger influences to raise the rare plant of Christian perfection, that when our Lord speaks of this promise, he emphatically calls it, *The promise of the Father;* because it shines among the other promises of the Gospel of Christ, as the moon does among the stars. Thus, Acts 1:4, "Wait," says he, "for the promise of the Father, which ye have heard of me." And again, Luke 24:49, "Behold I send the promise of my Father upon you." Agreeably to this, St. Peter says, "Jesus being by the right hand of God exalted, and having received of the Father the promise of the Holy Ghost, he hath shed forth this:" he has begun abundantly to fulfil "that which was spoken by the Prophet Joel: And it shall come to pass in the last days, saith God, that I will pour out [bestow a more abundant measure] of my Spirit upon all flesh. Therefore repent and be baptized [i.e. make an open profession of your faith] in the name of the Lord Jesus, for the remission of sins; and ye shall receive the gift of the Holy Ghost; for the promise is unto you and to your children, and to as many as the Lord our God shall call" to enjoy the full blessings of the Christian dispensation, Acts 2:17, 33, 38. This promise, when it is received in its fulness, is undoubtedly the greatest of all the "exceeding great and precious promises, which are given to us, that by them you might be partakers of the Divine nature," [that is, of pure love and unmixed holiness,] 2 Peter 1:4. Have therefore a peculiar eye to it, and to these deep words of our Lord: "I will ask the Father, and he shall give you another Comforter, that he may abide with you for ever, even the Spirit of truth [and power] whom the world knows not, &c, but ye know him, for he remaineth with you, and shall be in you. At that day ye shall know that I am in my Father, and you in me, and I in you: for if any man [i.e. any believer] love me, he will keep my words, and my Father will love him, and we will come to him, and make our abode with him," John 14:15, 23: "Which," says Mr. Wesley, in his note on the place, "implies such a large manifestation of the Divine presence and love, that the former, in justification, is as nothing in comparison of it." Agreeably to this the same judicious divine expresses himself thus in another of his publications. "These virtues [meekness, humility, and true resignation to God] are the only *wedding garment;* they are the *lamps and vessels* well furnished with oil. There is nothing that will do instead of them: they must have their full and perfect work in you, or the soul can never be delivered from its fallen, wrathful state. There is no possibility of salvation but in this. And when the Lamb of God has brought forth his own meekness, &c, in our souls, then are our lamps trimmed, and our virgin hearts made ready for the marriage feast. This marriage feast signifies the entrance into the highest state of union that can be between God and the soul in this life. This birthday of the Spirit of love in our souls, whenever we attain it, will feast our souls with such peace and joy in God, as will blot out the remembrance of every thing that we called peace or joy before."

To make you believe this important promise with more ardour, consider that our Lord spent some of his last moments in sealing it with his powerful intercession. After having prayed the Father to sanctify his disciples through the truth, firmly embraced by their faith, and powerfully applied by his Spirit, he adds, "Neither pray I for these alone, but for them who will believe on me through their word." And what is it that our Lord asks for these believers? Truly, what St. Paul asked for the imperfect believers at Corinth, "even their perfection," 2 Corinthians 13:9. A state of soul this, which Christ describes thus: — "That they all may be one, as thou Father art in me, and I in thee, that they may be made one in us, &c, that they may be one as we are one: I in them, and thou in me, that they may be perfected in one, and that the world may know that thou hast loved them as thou hast loved me," John 17:17, 23. Our Lord could not pray in vain: it is not to be supposed that the Scriptures are silent with respect to the effect of this solemn prayer, an answer to which was to give the world an *idea* of the New Jerusalem coming down from heaven, a *specimen* of the power which introduces believers into the state of Christian perfection; and therefore we read that on the day of pentecost the kingdom of Satan was powerfully shaken, and the kingdom of God, "righteousness, peace, and joy in the Holy Ghost," began to come with a new power: then were thousands wonderfully converted, and clearly justified; then was the kingdom of heaven taken by force; and the love of Christ and of the brethren began to burn the chaff of selfishness and sin with a force which the world had never seen before: see Acts 2:42, &c. Some time after, another glorious baptism, or capital outpouring of the Spirit, carried the disciples of Christ farther into the kingdom of grace which perfects believers in one. And therefore we find that the account which St. Luke gives us of them after this second, capital manifestation of the Holy Spirit, in a great degree answers to our Lord's prayer for their perfection. He had asked "that they all might be one, and that they might be one as the Father and he are one, and that they might be perfected in one," John 17:17, &c. And now a fuller answer is given to his deep request. Take it in the words of an inspired historian: — "And when they had prayed, the place was shaken where they were assembled together, and they were [once more] filled with the Holy Ghost, and they spake the word with [still greater] boldness; and the multitude of them that believed were of one heart, and of one soul; neither said any of them, that aught of the things which he possessed were his own; but they had all things common, &c, and great grace was upon them all!" Acts 4:31-33. Who does not see in this account a *specimen* of that grace which our Lord had asked for believers, when he had prayed that his disciples, and those who would believe on him through their word, might be "perfected in one?"

It may be asked here, whether "the multitude of them that believed," in those happy days, were all perfect in love? I answer, that if pure love had cast out all selfishness, and sinful fear from their hearts, they were undoubtedly "made perfect in love:" but as God does not usually remove the plague of indwelling sin till it has been discovered and lamented; and as we find, in the two next chapters, an account of the *guile* of Ananias and his wife, and of the *partiality* or selfish *murmuring* of some believers, it seems that those chiefly, who before were strong in the grace of their dispensation, arose *then* into sinless fathers; and that the first love of other believers, through the peculiar blessing of Christ upon his infant Church, was so bright and powerful for a time, that *little children* had, or seemed to have, the strength of *young men,* and young men the grace of *fathers.* And, in this case, the account which St. Luke gives of the primitive believers ought to be taken with some restriction. Thus, while many of them were perfect in love, many might have the imperfection of their love only covered over by a land flood of peace and joy in believing. And, in this case, what is said of their being "all of one heart and mind, and of their having all things common," &c, may only mean that the harmony of love had not yet been broken, and that none had yet betrayed any of the uncharitableness for which Christians in after ages became so conspicuous. With respect to the "great grace which was upon them all," this does not *necessarily* mean that they were all equally strong in grace; for great unity and happiness may rest upon a whole family where the difference between *a father, a young man,* and *a child,* continues to subsist. However, it is not improbable that God, to open the dispensation of the Spirit, in a manner which might fix the attention of all ages upon its importance and glory, permitted the whole body of believers to take an extraordinary turn together into the Canaan of perfect love, and to show the world the admirable fruit which grows there, as the spies sent by Joshua took a turn into the good land of promise before they were settled in it, and brought from thence the bunch of grapes which astonished and spirited up the Israelites, who had not yet crossed Jordan.

Upon the whole, it is, I think, undeniable, from the four first chapters of the Acts, that a peculiar power of the Spirit is bestowed upon believers under the Gospel of Christ; that this power, through faith on our part, can operate the most sudden and surprising change in our souls; and that when our faith shall fully embrace the promise of full sanctification, or of a complete "circumcision of the heart in the Spirit," the Holy Ghost, who kindled so much love on the day of pentecost, that all the primitive believers loved or seemed to love each other perfectly, will not fail to help us to love one another without sinful self seeking; and as soon as we do so, "God dwelleth in us, and his love is perfected in us," 1 John 4:12; John 14:23.

Should you ask, how many baptisms, or effusions of the sanctifying Spirit are necessary to cleanse a believer from all sin, and to kindle his soul into perfect love; I reply, that the effect of a sanctifying truth depending upon the ardour of the faith with which that truth is embraced, and upon the power of the Spirit with which it is applied, I should betray a want of modesty if I brought the operations of the Holy Ghost, and the energy of faith, under a rule which is not expressly laid down in the Scriptures. If you ask your physician how many doses of physic you must take before all the crudities of your stomach can be carried off, and your appetite perfectly restored; he would probably answer you, that this depends upon the nature of those crudities, the strength of the medicine, and the manner in which your constitution will allow it to operate; and that in general you must repeat the dose, as you can bear, till the remedy has fully answered the desired end. I return a similar answer: if one powerful baptism of the Spirit "seal you unto the day of redemption, and cleanse you from all [moral] filthiness," so much the better. If two or more be necessary, the Lord can repeat them: "His arm is not shortened, that it cannot save;" nor is his promise of the Spirit stinted: he says, in general, "Whosoever will, let him come and take of the water of life freely. If you, being evil, know how togive good gifts unto your children, how much more will your heavenly Father [who is goodness itself] give his Holy [sanctifying] Spirit to them that ask him!" I may, however, venture to say, in general, that before we can rank among perfect Christians, we must receive so much of the truth and Spirit of Christ by faith, as to have the pure love of God and man shed abroad in our hearts by the Holy Ghost given unto us, and to be filled with the meek and lowly mind which was in Christ. And if one outpouring of the Spirit, one bright manifestation of the sanctifying truth, so empties us of self, as to fill us with the mind of Christ, and with pure love, we are undoubtedly Christians in the full sense of the word. From the ground of my soul I therefore subscribe to the answer which a great divine makes to the following objection: —

"But some who are newly justified, do come up to this [Christian perfection:] what then will you say to these?" Mr. Wesley says with great propriety: "If they really do, I will say, they are sanctified, saved from sin *in that moment;* and that they never need lose what God has given, or feel sin any more. But certainly this is an exempt case. It is otherwise with the generality of those that are justified. They feel in themselves, more or less, pride, anger, self will, and a heart bent to backsliding. And till they have *gradually* mortified these, they are not fully renewed in love. God usually gives a considerable time for men to receive light, to grow in grace, to do and to suffer his will before they are either justified or sanctified. But he does not invariably adhere to this. Sometimes he 'cuts short his work.' He does the work of many years in a few weeks; perhaps in a week, a day, an hour. He justifies, or sanctifies both those who have done or suffered nothing, and who have not had time for a gradual growth either in light or grace. And may he not 'do what he will with his own? Is thine eye evil, because he is good?' It need not therefore be proved by forty texts of Scripture, either that most men are perfected in love *at last,* or that there is a gradual work of God in the soul; and that, generally speaking, it is *a long time,* even many years, before sin is destroyed. All this we know. But we know, likewise, that God may, with man's good leave, 'cut short his work,' in whatever degree he pleases, and do the usual work of many years in a moment. He does so in a great many instances. And yet there is a gradual work both before and after that moment. So that one may affirm, the work is *gradual;* another, it is *instantaneous,* without any manner of contradiction." (*Plain Account,* page 115, &c.) Page 155, the same eminent Divine explains himself more fully thus: "It [Christian perfection] is constantly preceded and followed by a *gradual* work. But is it in itself *instantaneous* or not? In examining this, let us go on step by step. An instantaneous change has been wrought in some believers. None can deny this. Since that change, they enjoy perfect love. They feel this, and this alone. They rejoice evermore, pray without ceasing, in every thing give thanks. Now this is all that I mean by *perfection.* Therefore these are witnesses of the perfection which I preach. 'But in some this change was not instantaneous.' They did not perceive the instant when it was wrought; it is often difficult to perceive the instant when a man dies. Yet there is an instant in which life ceases. And if ever sin ceases, there must be a last moment of its existence, and a first moment of our deliverance from it. 'But if they have this love now, they will lose it.' They may; but they need not. And whether they do or no, they have it now; they now experience what we teach. They now are *all love.* They now rejoice, pray, and praise without ceasing. 'However, sin is only suspended in them; it is not destroyed.' Call it which you please. They are all love to-day; and they take no thought for the morrow." To return: —

2. When you firmly assent to the truth of the precepts and promises, on which the doctrine of Christian perfection is founded; when you understand the meaning of these scriptures, "Sanctify them through thy truth, thy word is truth. I will send the Comforter, [the Spirit of truth and holiness,] unto you; God hath chosen you to [eternal] salvation through sanctification of the Spirit and belief of the truth:" when you see that the way to Christian perfection is by the word of the Gospel of Christ, by faith, and by the Spirit of God; in the next place, get tolerably clear ideas of this perfection. This is absolutely necessary. If you will hit a mark, you must know where it is. Some people aim at Christian perfection; but mistaking it for angelical perfection, they shoot above the mark, miss it, and then peevishly give up their hopes. Others place the mark as much too low; hence it is that you hear them profess to have attained Christian perfection, when they have not so much as attained the mental serenity of a philosopher, or the candour of a good-natured, conscientious heathen. In the preceding pages, if I am not mistaken, the mark is fixed according to the rules of Scriptural moderation. It is not placed so high, as to make you despair of hitting it, if you do your best in an evangelical manner; nor yet so low, as to allow you to presume that you can reach it, without exerting all your abilities to the uttermost, in due subordination to the efficacy of Jesus' blood, and the Spirit's sanctifying influences.

3. Should you ask, "Which is the way to Christian perfection? Shall we go on to it by internal stillness, agreeably to this direction of Moses and David? 'The Lord will fight for you, and ye shall hold your peace; stand still and see the salvation of God. Be still and know that I am God. Stand in awe and sin not; commune with your own heart upon your bed, and be still.' Or shall we press after it by an internal wrestling, according to these commands of Christ? 'Strive to enter in at the strait gate: the kingdom of heaven suffereth violence, and the violent take it by force.'" &c.

According to the evangelical balance of the doctrines of free grace and free will, I answer, that the way to perfection is by the due combination of prevenient, assisting free grace; and of submissive, assisted free will. Antinomian stillness, therefore, which says that free grace must do all, is not the way. Pharisaic activity, which will do most, if not all, is not the way. Join these two partial systems, allowing free grace the lead and high pre-eminence which it so justly claims, and you have the balance of the two Gospel axioms. You do justice to the doctrines of mercy and justice, of free grace and free will, of Divine faithfulness in keeping the covenant of grace, and of human faithfulness in laying hold on that covenant, and keeping within its bounds: in short, you have the Scripture method of waiting upon God, which Mr. Wesley describes thus: —

> Restless, resign'd, for God I wait,
> For God my vehement soul stands still.

To understand these lines, consider that faith, like the Virgin Mary, is alternately *a receiver* and *a bestower*: first, it passively receives the impregnation of Divine grace, saying, "Behold the handmaid of the Lord: let it be done to me according to thy word;" and then it actively brings forth its heavenly fruit with earnest labour. "God worketh in you to will and to do," says St. Paul: here he describes the passive office of faith, which submits to, and acquiesces in every dispensation and operation. "Therefore work out your salvation with fear and trembling," and, of consequence, with haste, diligence, ardour, and faithfulness: here the apostle describes the active office of that mother grace, which carefully lays out the talent she has already received. Would you then wait aright for Christian perfection? Impartially admit the Gospel axioms, and faithfully reduce them to practice. In order to this, let them meet in your hearts, as the two legs of a pair of compasses meet in the rivet, which makes them one compounded instrument. Let your faith in the doctrine of free grace and Christ's righteousness fix your mind upon God as you fix one of the legs of your compasses immovably in the centre of the circle which you are about to draw: so shall you "stand still," according to the first text produced in the question, and then let your faith in the doctrine of free will, and evangelical obedience, make you steadily run the circle of duty round that firm centre: so shall you imitate the other leg of the compasses, which evenly moves around the centre, and traces the circumference of a perfect circle. By this activity, subordinate to grace, you will "take the kingdom of heaven by force." When your heart quietly rests in God by faith, as it steadily acts the part of *a passive receiver*, it resembles the leg of the compasses which rests in the centre of the circle; and then the poet's expressions, "restless — resigned," describe its fixedness in God. But when your heart swiftly moves toward God by faith, as it acts the part of *a diligent worker*, when your ardent soul follows after God as a thirsty deer does after the water brooks, it may be compared to the leg of the compasses which traces the circumference of the circle; and then these words of the poet, "restless and vehement," properly belong to it. To go on steadily to perfection, you must therefore endeavour steadily to believe, according to the doctrine of the first Gospel axiom; and (as there is opportunity) diligently to work, according to the doctrine of the second; and the moment your faith is steadily fixed in God as in your centre, and your obedience swiftly moves in the circle of duty from the rest and power which you find in that centre you have attained, you are made perfect in the faith which works by love. Your humble faith saves you from Pharisaism, your obedient love from Antinomianism, and both, in due subordination to Christ, constitute you a just man made perfect according to your dispensation.

4. Another question has also puzzled many sincere perfectionists; and the solution of it may remove a considerable hinderance out of your way: — "Is Christian perfection," say they, "to be *instantaneously* brought down to us, or are we *gradually* to grow up to it? Shall we be made perfect in love by a habit of holiness suddenly infused into us, or by acts of feeble faith and feeble love so frequently reported as to become strong, habitual, and evangelically natural to us, according to the well-known maxim, *A strong habit is a second nature?*"

Both ways are good; and instances of some believers *gradually* perfected, and of others [comparatively speaking] *instantaneously* fixed in perfect love, might probably be produced, if we were acquainted with the experiences of all those who have died in a state of evangelical perfection. It may be with the root of sin, as it is with its fruit: some souls parley many years before they can be persuaded to give up all their outward sins, and others part with them, as it were, instantaneously. You may compare the former to those besieged towns which make a long resistance, or to those mothers who go through a tedious and lingering labour: and the latter resemble those fortresses which are surprised and carried by storm; or those women who are delivered almost as soon as labour comes upon them. Travellers inform us that vegetation is so quick and powerful in some warm climates, that the seeds of some vegetables yield a salad in less than twenty-four hours. Should a northern philosopher say, "Impossible!" and should an English gardener exclaim against such *mushroom salad*, they would only expose their prejudices, as do those who decry instantaneous justification, or mock at the possibility of the instantaneous destruction of indwelling sin.

For where is the absurdity of this doctrine? If the light of a candle brought into a dark room can instantly expel the darkness; and if, upon opening your shutters at noon, your gloomy apartment can instantaneously be filled with meridian light; why may not the instantaneous rending of the veil of unbelief, or the sudden and full opening of your faith, instantly fill your soul with the light of truth, and the fire of love; supposing the Sun of righteousness arise upon you with powerful healing in his wings? May not the Sanctifier descend upon your waiting soul, as quickly as the Spirit descended upon your Lord at his baptism? Did it not descend "as a dove," that is, with the soft motion of a dove, which swiftly shoots down, and instantly lights? A good man said once, with truth, "A mote is little, when it is compared with the sun; but I am far less before God." Alluding to this comparison, I ask, If the sun could instantly kindle a mote; nay, if a burning glass can in a moment calcine a bone, and turn a stone to lime; and if the dim flame of a candle can in the twinkling of an eye destroy the flying insect which comes within its sphere, how unscriptural and irrational is it to suppose that, when God fully baptizes a soul with his sanctifying Spirit and with the celestial fire of his love, he cannot in an instant destroy the man of sin, burn up the chaff of corruption, melt the heart of stone into a heart of flesh, and kindle the believing soul into pure, seraphic love!

An appeal to parallel cases may throw some light upon the question which I answer. If you were sick, and asked of God the perfect recovery of your health, how would you look for it? Would you expect to have your strength restored to you at *once,* without any external means, as the lepers who were instantly cleansed; and as the paralytic, who at our Lord's word took up the bed upon which he lay, and carried it away upon his shoulders? Or by using some external means of a slower operation, as the "ten lepers" did, who were more "gradually cleansed as they went to show themselves to the priests?" Or as King Hezekiah, whose gradual, but equally sure recovery, was owing to God's blessing upon the poultice of figs prescribed by Isaiah? Again: if you were blind, and besought the Lord to give you perfect human sight, how should you wait for it? As Bartimeus, whose eyes were opened in an instant? Or as the man who received his sight by degrees? At first he saw nothing; by and by he confusedly discovered the objects before him, but at last he saw all things clearly. Would ye not earnestly wait for an answer to your prayers now, leaving to Divine wisdom the particular manner of your recovery? And why should ye not go and do likewise with respect to the dreadful disorder which we call *indwelling sin?*

If our hearts be purified by faith, as the Scriptures expressly testify if the faith which peculiarly purifies the hearts of Christians be a faith in "the promise of the Father," which promise was made by the Son and directly points at a peculiar effusion of the Holy Ghost, the purifier of spirits; if we may believe in a moment; and if God may, in a moment, seal our sanctifying faith by sending us a fulness of his sanctifying Spirit: if this, I say, be the case, does it not follow, that to deny the possibility of the instantaneous destruction of sin, is to deny, contrary to Scripture and matter of fact, that we can make an instantaneous act of faith in the sanctifying promise of the Father, and in the all-cleansing blood of the Son, and that God can seal that act by the instantaneous operation of his Spirit? which St. Paul calls the *"circumcision* of the heart in [or by] the Spirit," according to the Lord's ancient promise, "I will circumcise thy heart, to love the Lord thy God with all thy heart." Where is the absurdity of believing that "the God of all grace" can give an answer to the poet's rational and evangelical request?

> Open my faith's interior eye;
> Display thy glory from above:
> And sinful self shall sink and die,
> Lost in astonishment and love.

If a momentary display of Christ's-bodily glory could, in an instant, turn Saul, the blaspheming, bloody persecutor, into Paul, the praying, gentle apostle; if a sudden sight of Christ's hands could in a moment root up from Thomas' heart that detestable resolution, "I will not believe," and produce that deep confession of faith, "My Lord and my God!" what cannot the display of Christ's spiritual glory operate in a believing soul, to which he manifests himself "according to that power whereby he is able to subdue all things to himself?" Again: if Christ's body could in an instant become so glorious on the mount, that his very garments partook of the sudden irradiation, became not only free from every spot, but also "white as the light, shining exceeding white as snow; so as no fuller on the earth could whiten them;" and if our bodies "shall be changed, if this corruptible shall put on incorruption, and if this mortal shall put on immortality, in a moment, in the twinkling of an eye, at the last trump;" why may not our believing souls, when they fully submit to God's terms, be fully changed— fully turned from the power of Satan unto God? When the Holy Ghost says, "Now is the day of salvation," does he exclude salvation from heart iniquity? If Christ now deserves fully the *name* of JESUS, "because he *fully* saves his believing people from their sins;" and if now the Gospel trumpet sounds, and sinners arise from the dead, why should we not, upon the performance of the condition, be changed in a moment from indwelling sin to indwelling holiness? Why should we not pass, in the twinkling of an eye, or in a short time, from indwelling death, to indwelling life?

This is not all. If you deny the possibility of a quick destruction of indwelling sin, you send to hell, or to some unscriptural purgatory, not only the dying thief, but also all those martyrs who suddenly embraced the Christian faith, and were instantly put to death by bloody persecutors, for confessing the faith which they had just embraced. And if you allow that God may "cut his work short in righteousness" in such case, why not in other cases? Why not, especially when a believer confesses his indwelling sin, ardently prays Christ would, and sincerely believes that Christ can, "now cleanse him from all unrighteousness?"

Nobody is so apt to laugh at the instantaneous destruction of sin as the Calvinists, and yet (such is the inconsistency which characterizes some men!) their doctrine of purgatory is built upon it. For, if you credit them, all dying believers have a nature which is still morally corrupted, and a heart which is yet desperately wicked. These believers, still full of indwelling sin, instantaneously breathe out their last, and, without any peculiar act of faith, without any peculiar outpouring of the sanctifying Spirit, corruption is instantaneously gone. The indwelling "man of sin" has passed through the Geneva purgatory, he is entirely consumed! And behold! the souls which would not hear of the instantaneous act of a sanctifying faith, which receives the indwelling Spirit of holiness — the souls which pleaded hard for the continuance of indwelling sin, are now completely sinless; and, in the twinkling of an eye, they appear in the third heaven among the spirits of just Christians made perfect in love! Such is the doctrine of our opponents: and yet they think it incredible that God should do for us, while we pray in faith, what they suppose death will do for them, when they lie in his cold arms, perhaps delirious or senseless!

On the other hand, to deny that imperfect believers may and do gradually grow in grace, and of course that the remains of their sins may, and do gradually decay, is as absurd as to deny that God waters the earth by daily dews, as well as by thunder showers: it is as ridiculous as to assert that nobody is carried off by lingering disorders, but that all men die suddenly or a few hours after they are taken ill.

I use these comparisons about death, to throw some light upon the question which I solve, and not to insinuate that the decay and destruction of sin run parallel with the decay and dissolution of the body, and that of course sin must end with our bodily life. Were I to admit this unscriptural tenet, I should build again what I have all along endeavoured to destroy, and, as I love consistency, I should promise eternal salvation to all unbelievers; for unbelievers, I presume, will die, i.e. will go into the Geneva purgatory, as well as believers. Nor do I see why death should not be able to destroy the *van* and the *main body* of sin's forces, if it can so readily cut the *rear* (the remains of sin) in pieces.

From the preceding observations it appears, that believers generally go on to Christian perfection, as the disciples went to the other side of the sea of Galilee. They toiled some time very hard, and with little success. But after they had "rowed about twenty-five; or thirty furlongs, they saw Jesus walking on the sea. He said to them, *It is I, be not afraid:* then they willingly received him into the ship, and immediately the ship was at the land whither they went." Just so, we toil till our faith discovers Christ in the promise, and welcomes him into our hearts; and such is the effect of his presence, that immediately we arrive at the land of perfection. Or, to use another illustration, God says to believers, "Go to the Canaan of perfect love: arise, why do ye tarry? Wash away the remains of sin, calling, i.e. believing, on the name of the Lord." And if they submit to the obedience of faith, he deals with them as he did with the Evangelist Philip, to whom he had said, "Arise and go toward the south." For when they "arise and run," as Philip did, "the Spirit of the Lord takes" them, as he did the evangelist; and they are found in the New Jerusalem, as "Philip was found at Azotus." They "dwell in God, [or in perfect love,] and God [or perfect love] dwells in them."

Hence it follows, that the most evangelical method of following after the perfection to which we are immediately called, is that of seeking it *now*, by endeavouring *fully* to lay hold on the promise of that perfection through faith, just as if our repeated acts of obedience could never help us forward. But, in the meantime, we should do the works of faith, and repeat our internal and external acts of obedience with as much earnestness and faithfulness, according to our present power, as if we were sure to enter into rest merely by a diligent use of our talents, and a faithful exertion of the powers which Divine grace has bestowed upon us. If we do not attend to the first of these directions, we shall seek to be sanctified by works like the Pharisees; and if we disregard the second, we shall fall into Solifidian sloth with the Antinomians.

This double direction is founded upon the connection of the two Gospel axioms. If the second axiom, which implies the doctrine of free will, were false, I would only say, "Be still, or rather do nothing; free grace alone will do all in you and for you." But as this axiom is as true as the first, I must add, "Strive in humble subordination to free grace: for Christ saith, 'To him that hath' initiating grace to purpose, 'more grace shall be given, and he shall have abundance:' his faithful and equitable Benefactor will give him the reward of perfecting grace."

5. Beware therefore of unscriptural refinements. Set out for the Canaan of perfect love with a firm resolution to labour for the rest which remains on earth for the people of God. Some good, mistaken men, wise above what is written, and fond of striking out paths which were unknown to the apostles, — new paths marked out by voluntary humility, and leading to Antinomianism: some people of that stamp, I say, have made it their business, from the days of heated Augustine, to decry making resolutions. They represent this practice as a branch of what they are pleased to call *legality*. They insinuate that it is utterly inconsistent with the knowledge of our inconstancy and weakness: in a word, they frighten us from the first step to Christian perfection; from an humble evangelical determination to run till we reach the prize, or, if you please, to go down till we come to the lowest place. It may not be amiss to point out the ground of their mistake. Once they broke the balance of the Gospel axioms by leaning too much toward free will, and by not laying their first and principal stress upon free grace. God, to bring them to the evangelical mean, refused his blessing to their unevangelical willing and running; hence it is that their self-righteous resolutions started aside like a broken bow. When they found out their mistake, instead of coming back to the line of moderation, they fled to the other extreme. Casting all their weights into the scale of free grace, they absurdly formed a resolution never to form a resolution; and, determining not to throw one determination into the scale of free will, they began to draw all the believers they met with into the ditch of a slothful quietism and Laodicean stillness.

You will never steadily go on to perfection, unless you get over this mistake. Let the imperfectionists laugh at you for making humble resolutions; but go on "steadfastly purposing to lead a new life," as says our Church; and in order to this, "steadfastly purpose" to get *a new heart* in the full sense of the word: for so long as your heart continues partly *unrenewed*, your life will be partly *unholy*. And, therefore, St. James justly observes that "if any man, offend not in word, he is a perfect man," he loves God with all his heart, his heart is fully renewed; it being impossible that a heart, still tainted in part with vanity and guile, should always dictate the words of sincerity and love. Your good resolutions need not fail: nor will they fail, if, under a due sense of the fickleness and helplessness of your unassisted free will, you properly depend upon God's faithfulness and *assistance*. However, should they fail, as they probably will do more than once, be not discouraged, but repent, search out the cause, and, in the strength of free grace, let your assisted free will renew your evangelical purpose, till the Lord seals it with his mighty *fiat*, and says, "Let it be done to thee according to thy resolving faith." It is much better to be laughed at as "poor creatures, who know nothing of themselves," than to be deluded as foolish virgins, who fondly imagine that their vessels are full of imputed oil. Take therefore the sword of the Spirit, and boldly cut this dangerous snare in pieces. Conscious of your impotence, and yet laying out your talent of free will, say with the prodigal son, "I will arise and go to my father:" say with David, "I will love thee, O Lord my God: I will behold thy face in righteousness: I am purposed that my mouth shall not transgress: I will keep it, as it were, with a bridle: I have said that I would keep thy word: the proud," and they who are humble in an unscriptural way, "have had me exceedingly in derision, but I will keep thy precepts with my whole heart. I have sworn, and I will perform it, that I will keep thy righteous judgments:" say with St. Paul, "I am determined not to know any thing save Jesus, and him crucified." And with Jacob, "I will not let thee go, unless thou bless me!" And, to sum up all good resolutions in one, if you are a member of the Church of England, say, "I have engaged to renounce all the vanities of this wicked world, all the sinful lusts of the flesh, and all the works of the devil: to believe all the articles of the Christian faith; and to keep God's commandments all the days of my life;" that is, I have most solemnly resolved to be a perfect Christian. And this resolution I have publicly sealed by receiving the two sacraments upon it: baptism, after my parents and sponsors had laid me under this blessed vow: and the Lord's Supper, after I had personally ratified, in the bishop's presence, what they had done. Nor do I only think that I am bound to keep this vow; but "by God's grace so I will; and I heartily thank our heavenly Father, that he has called me to this state of salvation [and Christian perfection;] and I pray unto him to give me his grace, that I may not only attain it, but also continue in the same unto my life's end." (*Church Catechism.*)

"Much diligence," says Kempis, "is necessary to him that will profit much. If he who firmly purposeth, often faileth, what shall he do who seldom or feebly purposeth any thing?" But, I say it again and again, do not lean upon your free will and good purposes, so as to encroach upon the glorious pre-eminence of free grace. Let the first Gospel axiom stand invariably in its honourable place. Lay your principal stress upon Divine mercy, and say with the good man, whom I have just quoted, "Help me, O Lord God, in thy holy service, and grant that I may now this day begin perfectly."

In following this method, ye will do the two Gospel axioms justice: ye will so depend upon God's free grace as not to fall into Pharisaic running: and ye will so exert your own free will as not to slide into Antinomian sloth. Your course lies exactly between these rocks. To pass these perilous straits, your resolving heart must acquire a heavenly polarity. Through the spiritually magnetic touch of Christ, the corner stone, your soul must learn to point toward faith and works, or, if you please, toward a due submission to free grace, and a due exertion of free will, as the opposite ends of the needle of a compass point toward the north and the south.

6. From this direction flows the following advice. Resolve to be perfect in yourselves, but not *of* yourselves: the Antinomians boast that they are perfect only in their heavenly representative. Christ was filled with perfect humility and love: they are perfect in his person: they need not a perfection of humble love in themselves. To avoid their error, be perfect in yourselves and not in another: let your perfection of humility and love be inherent; let it dwell in you. Let it fill your own heart and influence your own life: so shall you avoid the delusions of the virgins, who give you to understand that the oil of their perfection is all contained in the sacred vessel which formerly hung on the cross, and therefore their salvation is finished, they have oil enough in that rich vessel; manna enough and to spare in that golden pot. Christ's heart was perfect, and therefore theirs may safely remain imperfect, yea, full of indwelling sin, till death, the messenger of the bridegroom, come to cleanse them, and fill them with perfect love at the midnight cry! Delusive hope! Can any thing be more absurd than for a sapless, dry branch to fancy that it has sap and moisture enough in the vine which it cumbers? or for an impenitent adulterer to boast that "in the Lord he has" chastity and righteousness? Where did Christ ever say, "Have salt in another?" Does he not say, "Take heed, that ye be not deceived! Have salt in yourselves?" Mark 9:50. Does he not impute the destruction of stony ground hearers to their "not having root in themselves?" Matthew 13:21. If it was the patient man's comfort, that "the root of the matter was found in him," is it not deplorable to hear modern believers say, without any explanatory clause, that they have nothing but sin in themselves? But is it enough to have "*the root* in ourselves?" Must we not also have *the fruit,* — yea, "be filled with the fruits of righteousness?" Philippians 1:11. Is it not St. Peter's doctrine, where he says, "If these things be in you, and abound, ye shall neither be barren nor unfruitful in the knowledge of Christ?" 2 Peter 1:8. And is it not that of David, where he prays, "Create in me a clean heart," &c? Away, then, with all Antinomian refinements! And if, with St. Paul, you will have salvation and rejoicing in yourselves, and not in another, make sure of holiness and perfection "in yourselves, and not in another."

But while you endeavour to avoid the snare of the Antinomians, do not run into that of the Pharisees; who will have their perfection *of themselves;* and therefore, by their own unevangelical efforts, self-concerted willings, and self-prescribed runnings, endeavour to "raise sparks of their own kindling, and to warm themselves" by their own painted fires and fruitless agitations. Feel your impotence. Own that "no man has quickened [and perfected] his own soul." Be contented to invite, receive, and welcome the light of life: but never attempt to form or to engross it. It is your duty to wait for the morning light, and to rejoice when it visits you: but if you grow so self conceited as to say, "I will create a sun: *let there be light*:" or if, when the light visits your eyes you say, "I will bear a stock of light: I will so fill my eyes with light to-day, that to-morrow I shall be almost able to do my work without the sun, or at least without a constant dependence upon its beams;" would ye not betray a species of self-deifying idolatry and Satanical pride? If our Lord himself, as "Son of man," would not have one grain of human goodness himself; if he said, "Why callest thou me *good*? There is none good [*self good*, or *good of himself*] but God:" who can wonder enough at those proud Christians who claim some self-originated goodness; boasting of what they have received, as if they had not received it: or using what they have received without an humble sense of their constant dependence upon their heavenly Benefactor. To avoid this horrid delusion of the Pharisees, learn to see, to feel, and to acknowledge, that of the Father, through the Son, and by the Holy Ghost, are all your urim and thummim, *your lights and perfections* and while the Lord says, "From me is thy fruit found," Hoses xiv, bow at his footstool, and gratefully reply, "Of thy fulness have all we received, and grace for grace," John 1:16. For thou art "the Father of lights, from whom cometh every good and perfect gift," James 1:17 Of thee, and through thee, and to thee are all things: to thee, therefore be the glory for ever. *Amen*," Romans 11:36.

7. You will have this humble and thankful disposition if you let your repentance cast deeper roots. For if Christian perfection implies a forsaking all inward, as well as outward sin; and if true repentance is a grace *whereby we forsake sin*, it follows, that, to attain Christian perfection, we must so follow our Lord's evangelical precept, "Repent for the kingdom of heaven is at hand," as to leave no sin, no bosom sin, no indwelling sin *unrepented of, and*, of consequence, *unforsaken*. He, whose heart is still full of indwelling sin, has no more truly repented of indwelling sin, than the man whose mouth is still defiled with filthy talking and jesting has truly repented of his ribaldry. The deeper our sorrow for, and detestation of indwelling sin is, the more penitently do we confess the plague of our hearts; and when we properly confess it, we inherit the blessing promised in these words: "If we confess our sins, he is faithful and just to forgive us our sins, and to cleanse us from all unrighteousness."

To promote this deep repentance, consider how many spiritual evils still haunt your breast. Look into the inward "chamber of imagery," where assuming self love, surrounded by a multitude of vain thoughts, foolish desires, and wild imaginations, keeps her court. Grieve that your heart, which should be all flesh, is yet partly stone; and that your soul, which should be only a temple for the Holy Ghost, is yet so frequently turned into a den of thieves, a hole for the cockatrice, a nest for a brood of spiritual vipers, — for the remains of envy, jealousy, fretfulness, anger, pride, impatience, peevishness, formality, sloth, prejudice, bigotry, carnal confidence, evil shame, self righteousness, tormenting fears, uncharitable suspicions, idolatrous love, and I know not how many of the evils which form the retinue of hypocrisy and unbelief. Through grace detect these evils by a close attention to what passes in your own heart at all times, but especially in an hour of temptation By frequent and deep confession, drag out all these abominations: these sins, which would not have Christ to reign alone over you, bring before him: place them in the light of his countenance; and (if you do it in faith) that light and the warmth of his love will kill them, as the light and heat of the sun kill the worms which the plough turns up to the open air in a dry summer's day.

Nor plead that you can do nothing: for, by the help of Christ, who is always ready to assist the helpless, ye can solemnly say upon your knees what ye have probably said in an airy manner to your professing friends. If ye ever acknowledged to them that your heart is deceitful, prone to leave undone what ye ought to do, and ready to do what ye ought to leave undone; ye can undoubtedly make the same confession to God. Complain to him who can help you, as ye have done to those who cannot. Lament, as you are able, the darkness of your mind, the stubbornness of your will, the dulness or exorbitancy of your affections, and importunately entreat the God of all grace to "renew a right spirit within you. If ye sorrow after this godly sort, what carefulness will be wrought in you! what indignation! what fear! what vehement desire! what zeal! yea, what revenge!" Ye will then sing in faith, what the mperfectionists sing in unbelief: —

> O how I hate those lusts of mine,
>   That crucified my God:
> Those sins that pierced and nail'd his flesh
>   Fast to the fatal wood!

> Yes, my Redeemer, they shall die,
>   My heart hath so decreed;
> Nor will I spare those guilty things
>   That made my Saviour bleed.

> While with a melting, broken heart,
>   My murder'd Lord I view,
> I'll raise revenge against my sins,
>   And slay the murderers too.

8. Closely connected with this deep repentance is the practice of a judicious, universal self denial. "If thou wilt be perfect," says our Lord, "deny thyself, take up thy cross daily, and follow me. He that loveth father or mother [much more he that loveth praise, pleasure, or money] more than me, is not worthy of me." nay, "Whosoever will save his life shall lose it; and whosoever will lose it for my sake, shall find it." Many desire to live and reign with Christ, but few choose to suffer and die with him. However, as the way of the cross leads to heaven, it undoubtedly leads to Christian perfection. To avoid the cross, therefore, or to decline drinking the cup of vinegar and gall, which God permits your friends or foes to mix for you, is to throw away the aloes which Divine wisdom puts to the breasts of the mother of harlots, to wean you from her and her witchcrafts: it is to refuse a medicine which is kindly prepared to restore your health and appetite: in a word, it is to renounce the Physician who "heals all our infirmities," when we take his bitter draughts, submit to have our imposthumes opened by his sharp lancet, and yield to have our proud flesh wasted away by his painful caustics. Our Lord "was made a perfect *Saviour* through sufferings," and we may be made perfect Christians in the same manner. We may be called to suffer, till all that which we have brought out of spiritual Egypt is consumed in a howling wilderness, in a dismal Gethsemane, or on a shameful Calvary. Should this lot be reserved for us, let us not imitate our Lord's imperfect disciples, who "forsook him and fled," but let us stand the fiery trial, till all our fetters are melted, and our dross is purged away Fire is of a purgative nature: it separates the dross from the gold; and the fiercer it is the more quick and powerful is its operation. "He that is left in Zion, and he that remaineth in Jerusalem, shall be called holy, &c, when the Lord shall have washed away the filth of the daughters of Zion, and shall have purged the blood of Jerusalem by the spirit of judgment and by the spirit of burning," Isaiah 4:4. "I will bring the third part through the fire, saith the Lord, and will refine them as silver is refined, and will try them as gold is tried; they shall call on my name, and I will hear them: I will say, It is my people; and they shall say, The Lord is my God," Zechariah 3:9. Therefore, if the Lord should suffer the best men in his camp, or the strongest men in Satan's army, to cast you into a furnace of fiery temptations, come not out of it till you are called. "Let patience have its perfect work:" meekly keep your trying station till your heart is disengaged from all that is earthly, and till the sense of God's preserving power kindles in you such a faith in his omnipotent love as few experimentally know but they who have seen themselves, like the mysterious bush in Horeb, burning and yet unconsumed; or they who can say with St. Paul, "We are killed all the day long — dying, and behold we live!"

"Temptations," says Kempis, "are often very profitable to men, though they be troublesome and grievous: for in them a man is humbled, purified, and instructed. All the saints have passed through and profited by many tribulations: and they that could not bear temptations, became reprobates and fell away." "My son," adds the author of Ecclesiasticus, (chap. 2:1,) "if thou come to serve the Lord" in the perfect beauty of holiness, "prepare thy soul for temptation. Set thy heart aright; constantly endure; and make not haste in the time of trouble. Whatever is brought upon thee take cheerfully; and be patient when thou art changed to a low estate: for gold is tried and purified in the fire, and acceptable men in the furnace of adversity." And therefore, says St. James, "Blessed is the man that endureth temptation; for, when he is tried, [if he stands the fiery trial,] he shall receive the crown of life, which the Lord has promised to them that love him" [with the love which endureth all things, that is, with perfect love,] James 1:12. Patiently endure, then, when God "for a season (if need be) suffers you to be in heaviness through manifold temptations." By this mean, "the trial of your faith, being much more precious than that of gold which perisheth, though it be tried in the fire, will be found unto praise, and honour, and glory, at the appearing of Jesus Christ," 1 Peter 1:7.

9. Deep repentance is good, Gospel self denial is excellent, and a degree of patient resignation in trials is of unspeakable use to attain the perfection of love; but as "faith *immediately* works by love," it is of far more immediate use to purify the soul. Hence it is that Christ, the prophets, and the apostles, so strongly insist upon faith; assuring us that, "if we will not believe, we shall not be established;" that, "if we will believe, we shall see the glory of God; we shall be saved; and rivers of living water shall flow from our inmost souls; and that our hearts are purified by faith; and that we are saved by grace through faith." They tell us that "Christ gave himself for the Church, that he might sanctify and cleanse it — by the word; that he might present it to himself a glorious Church, not having spot, or wrinkle, or any such thing; but that it should be holy and without blemish." Now, if believers are not to be "cleansed and made without blemish" by the word, (which testifies of the all-atoning blood, and the love of the Spirit,) it is evident that they are to be sanctified by faith; for faith, or believing, has as necessary a reference to the word, as eating has to food. For the same reason the apostle observes that "they who believe enter into rest; that a promise being given us to enter in, we should take care not to fall short of it" through unbelief; that we ought to take warning by the Israelites, who "could not enter" into the land of promise "through unbelief;" that we are "filled with all joy and peace in believing;" and that "Christ is able to save to the uttermost them who come unto God through him." Now "coming," in the Scripture language, is another expression for *believing:* "He that cometh to God," says the apostle, "must believe." Hence it appears that faith is peculiarly necessary to those who will" be saved to the uttermost, especially a firm faith in the capital promise of the Gospel of Christ, the promise of "the Spirit of holiness" from the Father, through the Son. For "how shall they call on him, in whom they have not believed?" Or, how can they earnestly plead the truth, and steadily wait for the performance of a promise, in which they have no faith? This doctrine of faith is supported by Peter's words: — "God who knoweth the hearts [of penitent believers] bare them witness, giving them the Holy Ghost, and purifying their hearts by faith," Acts 15:8, 9. For the same Spirit of faith, which *initially* purifies our hearts when we cordially believe the pardoning love of God, *completely* cleanses them when we fully believe his sanctifying love.

10. This direction about faith being of the utmost importance, I shall confirm and explain it by an extract from Mr. Wesley's sermon, which points out the *Scripture way of salvation:* "Though it be allowed," says this judicious divine, "that both this repentance and its fruits are necessary to full salvation, yet they are not necessary either in the same sense with faith, or in the same degree. *Not in the same degree;* for these fruits are only necessary conditionally, if there be time and opportunity for them, otherwise a man may be sanctified without them. But he cannot be sanctified without faith. Likewise, let a man have ever so much of this repentance, or ever so many good works, yet all this does not at all avail; he is not sanctified till he believe. But the moment he believes, with or without those fruits, yea, with more or less of this repentance, he is sanctified. *Not in the same sense;* for this repentance and these fruits are only remotely necessary in order to the continuance of his faith, as well as the increase of it; whereas faith is immediately and directly necessary to sanctification. It remains that faith is the only condition which is immediately and proximately necessary to sanctification.

"But what is that faith whereby we are sanctified, saved from sin, and perfected in love? (1.) It is a Divine evidence and conviction, *that God hath promised it in the Holy Scriptures.* Till we are thoroughly satisfied of this, there is no moving one step farther. And one would imagine there needed not one word more to satisfy a reasonable man of this, than the ancient promise, 'Then will I circumcise thy heart, and the heart of thy seed, to love the Lord thy God with all thy heart, and with all thy soul.' How clearly doth this express the being perfected in love! How strongly imply the being saved from all sin! For as long as love takes up the whole heart, what room is there for sin therein? (2.) It is a Divine evidence and conviction, *that what God has promised he is able to perform.* Admitting, therefore, that 'with men it is impossible to bring a clean thing out of an unclean,' to purify the heart from all *sin,* and to fill it with all holiness; yet this creates no difficulty in the case, seeing 'with God all things are possible.' (3.) It is an evidence and conviction *that he is able and willing to do it* NOW. And why not? Is not a moment to him the same as a thousand years? He cannot want more time to accomplish whatever is his will. We may therefore boldly say at any point of time, 'Now is the day of salvation! Behold! all things are now ready! Come to the marriage!' (4.) To this confidence, that God is both able and willing to sanctify us now, there needs to be added one thing more, a Divine evidence and conviction *that he doth it.* In that hour it is done. God says to the inmost soul, 'According to thy faith, be it unto thee!' Then the soul is pure from every spot of sin; *it is clean from all unrighteousness.*"

Those who have low ideas of faith will probably be surprised to see how much Mr. Wesley ascribes to that Christian grace, and to inquire, why he so nearly connects our *believing that God cleanses us from all sin,* with *God's actual cleansing us.* But their wonder will cease, if they consider the definition which this divine gives of faith in the same sermon. "Faith in general," says he, "is defined by the apostle, an evidence, a Divine evidence 'and conviction [the word used by the apostle means both] of things not seen;' not visible, nor perceivable either by sight, or by any other of the external senses. It implies both a supernatural evidence of God and of the things of God. a kind of *spiritual light* exhibited to the soul, and a *supernatural sight* or perception thereof. Accordingly the Scriptures speak of God's giving sometimes light, sometimes a power of discerning it. So St. Paul, 'God who commanded light to shine out of darkness, hath shined in our hearts, to give us the light of the knowledge of the glory of God in the face of Jesus Christ.' And elsewhere the same apostle speaks of 'the eyes of our understanding being opened.' By this twofold operation of the Holy Spirit, having the eyes of our souls both opened and enlightened, we see the things which the natural 'eye hath not seen, neither the ear heard.' We have a prospect of the invisible things of God: we see *the spiritual world,* which is all round about us, and yet is no more discerned by our natural faculties, than if it had no being; and we see *the eternal world,* piercing through the veil which hangs between time and eternity. Clouds and darkness then rest upon it no more, but we already see the glory which shall be revealed."

From this striking definition of faith, it is evident that the doctrine of this address exactly coincides with Mr. Wesley's sermon; with this verbal difference only, that what he calls faith, implying a two-fold operation of the Spirit productive of *spiritual light and supernatural sight,* I have called faith, apprehending a sanctifying "baptism (or outpouring) of the Spirit." His mode of expression savours more of the rational divine, who logically divides the truth, in order to render its several parts conspicuous: and I keep closer to the words of the Scriptures, which, I hope, will frighten no candid Protestant. I make this remark for the sake of those who fancy that when a doctrine is clothed with expressions which are not quite familiar to them, it is a new doctrine, although these expressions should be as Scriptural as those of a "baptism, or outpouring of the Spirit," which are used by some of the prophets, by John the Baptist, by the four evangelists, and by Christ himself.

I have already pointed out the close connection there is between an act of faith which fully apprehends the Spirit of Christ, which makes an end of moral corruption by forcing the lingering "man of sin" *instantaneously* to breathe out his last. Mr. Wesley, in the above-quoted sermon, touches upon this delicate subject in so clear and concise a manner, that while his discourse is before me, for the sake of those who have it not at hand, I shall transcribe the whole passage, and thus put the seal of that eminent divine to what I have advanced, in the preceding pages, about sanctifying faith and the quick destruction of sin.

"Does God work this great work in the soul *gradually* or *instantaneously?* Perhaps it may be gradually wrought in some: I mean in this sense; they do not advert to the particular moment wherein sin ceases to be. But it is infinitely desirable, were it the will of God, that it should be done instantaneously; that the Lord should destroy sin by the breath of his mouth, in a moment, in the twinkling of an eye. And so he generally does; a plain fact, of which there is evidence enough to satisfy any unprejudiced person. Thou therefore look for it every moment. Look for it in the way above described; in all those good works, whereunto thou art created anew in Christ Jesus. There is then no danger: you can be no worse, if you are no better for that expectation. For were you to be disappointed of your hope, still you lose nothing. But you shall not be disappointed of your hope: it will come, and will not tarry. Look for it then every day, every hour, every moment. Why not this hour, this moment? Certainly you may look for it now, if you believe it is by faith. And by this token you may surely know whether you seek it by faith or by works: if by *works,* you want something to be done first, before you are sanctified. You think, "I must first be or do thus or thus." Then you are seeking it by works unto this day. If you seek it by *faith,* you expect it as you are, and if as you are, then expect it now. It is of importance to observe that there is an inseparable connection between these three points, — expect it *by faith,* expect it as *you are,* and expect it *now!* To deny one of them, is to deny them all: to allow one, is to allow them all. Do you believe we are sanctified *by faith?* Be true then to your principle: and look for this blessing just *as you are,* neither better nor worse: as a poor sinner, that has still nothing to plead but *Christ died.* And if you look for it as you are, then expect it now. Stay for nothing: why should you? Christ is ready; and he is all you want. He is waiting for you: he is at the door! Let your inmost soul cry out, —

> Come in, come in, thou heavenly Guest!
>   Nor hence again remove:
> But sup with me, and let the feast
>   Be everlasting love."

11. Social prayer is closely connected with faith in the capital promise of the sanctifying Spirit: and therefore I earnestly recommend that mean of grace, where it can be had, as being eminently conducive to the attaining of Christian perfection. When many believing hearts are lifted up, and wrestle with God in prayer together, you may compare them to many diligent hands, which work a large machine. At such times, particularly, the fountains of the great deep are broken up, the windows of heaven are opened, and "rivers of living water flow" into the hearts of obedient believers.

> In Christ when brethren join,
>   And follow after peace,
> The fellowship Divine
>   He promises to bless,
> His chiefest graces to bestow
> Where two or three are met below.

> Where unity takes place,
>> The joys of heaven we prove;
> This is the Gospel grace,
>> The unction from above,
> The Spirit on all believers shed,
> Descending swift from Christ their Head.

Accordingly we read, that when God powerfully opened the kingdom of the Holy Ghost on the day of pentecost, the disciples "were all with one accord in one place." And when he confirmed that kingdom, they "were lifting up their voices to God with one accord:" see Acts 2:1, and 4:24. Thus also the believers at Samaria were filled with the Holy Ghost, the Sanctifier, while Peter and John prayed with them, and laid their hands upon them.

12. But perhaps thou art alone. As a solitary bird which sitteth on the housetop, thou lookest for a companion who may go with thee through the deepest travail of the regeneration. But, alas! thou lookest in vain: all the professors about thee seem satisfied with their former experiences, and with self-imputed or self-conceited perfection. When thou givest them a hint of thy want of power from on high, and of thy hunger and thirst after a fulness of righteousness, they do not sympathize with thee. And indeed how can they? They are full already, they reign without thee, they have need of nothing. They do not sensibly want that "God would grant them, according to the riches of his glory, to be strengthened with might in the inner man, that Christ may dwell in their hearts by faith, that they, being rooted and grounded in love, may comprehend with all saints [perfected in love] what is the breadth, and length, and depth, and height, and to know the love of Christ which passeth knowledge, that they might be filled with all the fulness of God," Ephesians 3:16, &c. They look upon thee as a whimsical person, full of singular notions, and they rather damp than enliven thy hopes. Thy circumstances are sad; but do not give place to despair, no, not for a moment. In the name of Christ, who could not get even Peter, James, and John, to watch with him one hour; and who was obliged to go through his agony alone; — in his name, I say, "Cast not away thy confidence, which has great recompense of reward." Under all thy discouragements, remember that, after all, Divine grace is not confined to numbers, any more than to a few. When all outward helps fail thee, make the more of Christ, on whom sufficient help is laid for thee — Christ, who says, "I will go with thee through fire and water;" the former shall not burn thee, nor the latter drown thee. Jacob was alone when he wrestled with the angel, yet he prevailed; and if the servant is not above his master, wonder not that it should be said of thee, as of thy Lord, when he went through his greatest temptations, "Of the people there was none with him."

Should thy conflicts be "with confused noise, with burning and fuel of fire;" should thy "Jerusalem be rebuilt in troublesome times;" should the Lord "shake, not the earth only, but also heaven; should deep call unto deep at the noise of his water spouts; should all his waves and billows go over thee;" should thy patience be tried to the uttermost; remember how in years past thou hast tried the patience of God, nor be discouraged: an extremity and a storm are often God's opportunity. A blast of temptation, and a shaking of all thy foundations, may introduce the fulness of God to thy soul, and answer the end of the rushing wind, and of the shaking, which formerly accompanied the first great manifestations of the Spirit. The Jews still expect the coming of the Messiah in the flesh, and they particularly expect it in a storm. When lightnings flash, when thunders roar, when a strong wind shakes their houses, and the tempestuous sky seems to rush down in thunder showers; then some of them particularly open their doors and windows to entertain their wished-for Deliverer. Do spiritually what they do carnally. Constantly wait for full "power from on high;" but especially when a storm of affliction, temptation, or distress overtakes thee; or when thy convictions and desires raise thee above thyself, as the waters of the flood raised Noah's ark above the earth; then be particularly careful to throw the door of FAITH, and the window of HOPE as wide open as thou canst; and, spreading the arms of thy imperfect LOVE, say with all the ardour and resignation which thou art master of, —

"My heart strings groan with deep complaint,
My flesh lies panting, Lord, for thee;
And every limb, and every joint,
Stretches for perfect purity."

But if the Lord be pleased to come softly to thy help; if he make an end of thy corruption by helping thee gently to sink to unknown depths of meekness; if he drown the indwelling man of sin, by baptizing, by plunging him into an abyss of humility; do not find fault with the simplicity of his method, the plainness of his appearing, and the commonness of his prescription. Nature, like Naaman, is full of prejudices. She expects that Christ will come to make her clean with as much ado, pomp, and bustle, as the Syrian general looked for, "when he was wroth and said, Behold, I thought he will surely come out to me — and stand and call on his God — and strike his hand over the place — and recover the leper." Christ frequently goes a much plainer way to work; and by this mean he disconcerts all our preconceived notions and schemes of deliverance. "Learn of me to be meek and lowly in heart, and thou shalt find rest to thy soul," the sweet rest of Christian perfection, of perfect humility, resignation, and meekness. Lie at my feet, as she did who loved much, and was meekly taken up with "the good part, and the one thing needful." But thou frettest; thou despisest this robe of perfection; it is too plain for thee; thou slightest "the ornament of a meek and quiet spirit, which, in the sight of God, is of great price:" nothing will serve thy turn but a tawdry coat of many colours, which may please thy proud self will, and draw the attention of others, by its glorious and flaming appearance; and it must be brought to thee with lightnings, thunderings, and voices. If this be thy disposition, wonder not at the Divine wisdom which thinks fit to disappoint thy lofty prejudices; and let me address thee, as Naaman's servants addressed him: "My brother, if the prophet had bid thee do some great thing, wouldst thou not have done it? How much rather then, when he says to thee, *I am the meek and lowly Lamb of God; wash in the stream of my blood — plunge in the Jordan of my humility, and be clean!*" Instead therefore of going away from a plain Jesus in a rage, welcome him in his lowest appearance, and be persuaded that he can as easily make an end of thy sin, by gently coming in "a still, small voice," as by rushing in upon thee in "a storm, a fire, or an earthquake." The Jews rejected their Saviour, not so much because they did not earnestly desire his coming, as because he did not come in the manner in which they expected him. It is probable that some of this Judaism cleaves to thee. If thou wilt absolutely come to Mount Sion in a triumphal chariot, or make thine entrance into the New Jerusalem upon a prancing horse, thou art likely never to come there. Leave then all thy lordly misconceptions behind; and humbly follow thy King, who makes his entry into the typical Jerusalem, "meek and lowly, riding upon an ass, yea, upon a colt, the foal of an ass." I say it again, therefore, while thy faith and hope strongly insist on the blessing, let thy resignation and patience leave to God's infinite goodness and wisdom the peculiar manner of be-stowing it. When he says, "Surely I come quickly to make my abode with thee," let thy faith close in with his word; ardently and yet meekly embrace his promise. This will instantly beget power; and with that power thou mayest instantly bring forth prayer, and possibly the prayer which opens heaven, which humbly wrestles with God, inherits the blessing, and turns the wellknown petition, "Amen! Even so, come Lord Jesus!" into the well-known praises, *He is come, he is come, O praise the Lord, O my soul,* &c. Thus repent, believe, and obey; and "he that cometh will come" with a fulness of pure, meek, humble love; "he will not tarry," or if he tarry, it will be to give thy faith and desires more time to open, that thou mayest, at his appearing, be able to take in more of his perfecting grace and sanctifying power: beside, thy expectation of his coming is of a purifying nature, and gradually sanctities thee. "He that has this hope in him," by this very hope "purifies himself even as God is pure:" for "we are saved [into, perfect love] by hope as well as by faith." The stalk, as well as the root, bears "the full corn in the ear."

Up then, thou sincere expectant of God's kingdom! Let thy humble, ardent free will meet prevenient, sanctifying free grace in its weakest and darkest appearance, as the father of the faithful met the Lord, "when he appeared to him on the plain of Mamre" as a mere mortal. "Abraham lifted up his eyes and looked, and lo! three men stood by him." So does free grace (if I may venture upon the allusion) invite itself to thy tent: nay, it is now with thee in its creating, redeeming, and sanctifying influences. "And when he saw them, he ran to meet them from the tent door, and bowed himself toward the ground." Go and do likewise: if thou seest any beauty in the humbling grace of our Lord Jesus Christ, in the sanctifying love of God, and in the comfortable fellowship of the Holy Ghost, let thy free will run to meet them, and bow itself toward the ground. O for a speedy going out of thy tent, thy sinful self! O for a race of desire in the way of faith! O for incessant prostrations! O for a meek and deep bowing of thyself before thy Divine Deliverer! "And Abraham said, *My Lord, if now I have found favour in thy sight, pass not away, I pray thee, from thy servant!*" O for the humble pressing of a loving faith! O for the faith which stopped the sun, when God avenged his people in the days of Joshua! O for the importunate faith of the two disciples who detained Christ, when "he made as though he would have gone farther! They constrained him, saying, *Abide with us, for it is toward evening, and the day is far spent. And he went in to tarry with them.*" He soon indeed vanished out of their bodily sight, because they were not called always to enjoy his bodily presence. Far from promising them that blessing, he had said, "It is expedient for you that I go away: for if I go not away, the Comforter will not come unto you; but if I depart, I will send him unto you, that he may abide with you for ever. He dwelleth with you, and shall be in you." This promise is "YEA and AMEN in Christ;" only plead it according to the preceding directions, and as sure as the Lord is the true and faithful Witness, so sure will the God of hope and love soon fill you with all joy and peace, that ye may abound in pure love, as well as in confirmed hope, "through the power of the Holy Ghost." Then shall you have an indisputable right to join the believers who sing at the Tabernacle, and at the Lock Chapel, in the words of Messrs. J. and C. Wesley: —

> "MANY are we now and ONE,
> We who Jesus have put on.
> There is neither bond nor free,
> Male nor female, Lord, in thee.
> Love, like death, hath all destroy'd,
> Render'd all distinction void;
> Names, and sects, and parties fall.
> Thou, O Christ, art all in all."

In the meantime you may sing with the pious countess of Huntingdon, the Rev. Mr. Madan, the Rev. Dr. Conyers, the Rev. Mr. Berridge, Richard Hill, Esq., and the imperfectionists who use their collections of hymns: ye may sing, I say, with them all, the two following hymns, which they have agreed to borrow from the hymns of Messrs. J. and C. Wesley, after making some insignificant alterations. I transcribe them from the collection used in Lady Huntingdon's chapels, (*Bristol edition*, 1765, p. 239, &c.)

> O for a heart to praise my God!
>   A heart from sin set free:
> A heart that's sprinkled with the blood
>   So freely spilt for me:
>
> A heart resign'd, submissive, meek,
>   My dear Redeemer's throne;
> Where only Christ is heard to speak,
>   Where Jesus reigns alone:
>
> An humble, lowly, contrite heart,
>   Believing, true, and clean;
> Which neither life nor death can part
>   From him that dwells within:
>
> A heart in every thought renew'd,
>   And fill'd with love Divine;
> Perfect, and right, and pure, and good;
>   A copy, Lord, of thine!
>
> My heart, thou know'st, can never rest.
>   Till thou create my peace
> Till of my Eden repossess'd,
>   From self and sin I cease.

Doctrines of Grace and Justice

> Thy nature, gracious Lord, impart,
>> Come quickly from above;
> Write thy new name upon my heart,
>> Thy new, best name of LOVE.

Here is undoubtedly an evangelical prayer for the LOVE which restores the soul to a state of sinless rest and evangelical perfection. Mean ye, my brethren, what the good people who dissent from us print and sing, and I ask no more. Nor can ye wait for an answer to the prayer contained in the preceding hymn, in a more Scriptural manner, than by pleading "the promise of the Father" in such words as these: —

> Love Divine, all loves excelling,
>> Joy of heaven to earth come down!
> Fix in us thine humble dwelling,
>> All thy faithful mercies crown:
> Jesus, thou art all compassion,
>> Pure, unbounded love thou art;
> Visit us with thy salvation,
>> Enter every trembling heart.

> Breathe! O breathe thy loving Spirit
>> Into every troubled breast!
> Let us all in thee inherit,
>> Let us find thy promised* rest.
> Take away the power† of sinning,
>> Alpha and Omega be;
> End of faith, as its beginning,
>> Set our hearts at liberty.

> Come, Almighty to deliver,
>> Let us all thy life receive!
> Suddenly return, and never,
>> Never more thy temples leave!
> Thee we would be always blessing,
>> Serve thee as thine hosts above;
> Pray and praise thee without ceasing,
>> Glory in thy precious love.‡

> Finish then thy new creation,

---

* Mr. Wesley says, *second rest*, because an imperfect believer enjoys a first, inferior rest: if he did not, he would be no believer.

† Is not this expression too strong? Would it not be better to soften it as Mr. Hill has done, by saying, "Take away the love of [or the bent to] sinning?" Can God take away from us our *power of sinning*, without taking away our power of free obedience?

‡ Mr. Wesley says, *perfect love*, with St. John.

Pure,* unspotted may we be;
  Let us see thy great salvation,
    Perfectly restored by thee;
  Changed from glory into glory,
    Till in heaven we take our place;
  Till we cast our crowns before thee,
    Lost in wonder, love, and praise.

Lift up your hands which hang down; our Aaron, our heavenly High Priest, is near to hold them up. The spiritual Amalekites will not always prevail; our Samuel, our heavenly prophet, is ready "to cut them and their king in pieces before the Lord. The promise is unto you." You are surely called to attain the perfection of your dispensation, although you still seem afar off. Christ, in whom that perfection centres— Christ, from whom it flows, is very near, even at the door: "Behold, says he, [and this he spake to Laodicean loiterers,] I stand at the door and knock. If any man hear my voice and open, I will come in and sup with him," upon the fruits of my grace, in their Christian perfection; and he shall sup with me upon the fruits of my glory, in their angelical and heavenly maturity.

Hear this encouraging Gospel: "Ask, and you shall have; seek, and you shall find; knock, and it shall be opened unto you. For every one that asketh, receiveth; and he that seeketh, findeth; and to him that knocketh, it shall be opened. If any of you, [believers] lack wisdom — indwelling wisdom, [Christ the wisdom and the power of God dwelling in his heart by faith,] let him ask of God, who giveth to all men, and upbraideth not, and it shall be given him. But let him ask [as a believer] in faith, nothing wavering; for he that wavereth is like a wave of the sea, driven with the wind and tossed: for let not that man think that he shall receive" the thing which he thus asketh. "But whatsoever things ye desire, when ye pray, believe that ye receive them, and ye shall have them. For all things [commanded and promised] are possible to him that believeth." He who has commanded us to be perfect "in love, as our heavenly Father is perfect," and he who has promised "speedily to avenge his elect, who cry to him night and day," he will speedily avenge you of your grand adversary, indwelling sin. He will say to you, "According to thy faith, be it done unto thee; for he is able to

---

* Mr. Wesley says, indeed, *pure and sinless;* but when Mr. Hill sings *pure, unspotted,* he does not spoil the sense. For every body knows that the pure, unspotted Jesus does not differ from the sinless, immaculate Lamb of God. This fine hymn (I think) is not in Mr. Madan's collection, but he has probably sung it more than once. However, it is adopted in the Shrewsbury Collection, of which Mr. Hill is the publisher, in conjunction with Mr. De Courcy. Is it not surprising, that in his devotional warmth that gentleman should print, give out, and sing, Mr. Wesley's strongest hymns for Christian perfection; when, in his controversial heat, he writes so severely against this blessed state of heart? And may not I take my leave of him by an allusion to our Lord's words, Out of thy own mouth, thy own pen, thy own publications, thy own hymns, thy own prayers, thy own Bible, thy own reason, thy own conscience, and, (what is most astonishing!) thy own professional and baptismal vow, I will judge thy mistakes! Nevertheless, I desire the reader to impute them, as I do, not to any love for indwelling sin, but to the fatal error which makes my pious opponent turn his back upon the genuine doctrines of grace and justice, and espouse the spurious doctrines of Calvinian grace and free wrath.

do far exceedingly abundantly, far above all that we can ask or think, and of his fulness we may all receive grace for grace" — we may all witness the gracious fulfilment of all the promises, which he has graciously made, that by "them we might be partakers of the Divine nature," so far as it can be communicated to mortals in this world. You see that, with men, what you look for is impossible: but you show yourselves believers: take God into the account, and you will soon experience, that "with God all things are possible." Nor forget the omnipotent Advocate whom you have with him. Behold! he lifts his once pierced hands, and says, "Father, sanctify them through [thy loving] truth, that they may be perfected in love:" and showing to you the fountain of atoning blood, and purifying water, whence flow the streams which cleanse and gladden the hearts of believers, he says, "*Hitherto you have asked nothing in my name — what-soever you shall ask the Father in my name, he will give it you. Ask, then, that your joy may be full.*" If I try your faith by a little delay: if I hide my face for a moment, it is only to gather you with everlasting kindness. "A woman, when she is in travail, hath sorrow, because her hour is come: but as soon as she is delivered of the child, she remembereth no more the anguish for joy. Now ye have sorrow, but I will see you again, and your hearts shall rejoice, and your joy no man taketh from you." In that day ye shall ask me no question, for you shall not have my bodily presence. But my urim and thummim will be with you; and the "Spirit *of truth will himself lead you into all* [Christian] *truth.*"

O for a firm and lasting faith,
To credit all the Almighty saith,
To embrace the promise of his Son,
And feel the Comforter our own!

In the meantime be not afraid to give glory to God by "believing in hope against hope." Stagger not "at the promise [of the Father and the Son] through unbelief:" but trust the power and faithfulness of your Creator and Redeemer, till your Sanctifier has fixed his abode in your heart. Wait at mercy's door, as the lame beggar did at the beautiful gate of the temple. "Peter fastening his eyes upon him, with John, said, *Look to us:* and he gave heed to them, expecting to receive something of them." Do so too: give heed to the Father in the Son, who says, "Look unto me and be ye saved." Expect to receive "the one thing now needful" for you, — a fullness of the sanctifying Spirit: and though your patience may be tried, it shall not be disappointed. The faith and power, which, at Peter's word, gave the poor cripple a perfect soundness in the presence of all the wondering Jews, will give you, at Christ's word, a perfect soundness of heart in the presence of all your adversaries.

Faith — mighty faith, the promise sees,
    And looks to that alone,
Laughs at impossibilities,
    And cries, "It shall be done?'
Faith asks impossibilities;
    Impossibilities are given:
And I — e'en I, from sin shall cease,
    Shall live on earth the life of heaven.

Faith always "works by love," — by love of desire at least; making us ardently pray for what we believe to be eminently desirable. And if Christian perfection appears so to you, you might perhaps express your earnest desire of it in some such words as these: — How long, Lord, shall my soul, thy spiritual temple, be a den of thieves, or a house of merchandise? How long shall vain thoughts profane it, as the buyers and sellers profaned thy temple made with human hands? How long shall evil tempers lodge within me? How long shall unbelief, formality, hypocrisy, envy, hankering after sensual pleasure, indifference to spiritual delights, and backwardness to painful or ignominious duty, harbour there? How long shall these sheep and doves, yea, these goats and serpents, defile my breast, which should be pure as the holy of holies? How long shall they hinder me from being one of the worshippers whom thou seekest, — one of those who worship thee in spirit and in truth? O help me to take away these cages of unclean birds. "Suddenly come to thy temple." Turn out all that offends the eyes of thy purity; and destroy all that keeps me out of "the rest which remains for thy *Christian* people:" so shall I keep a Spiritual Sabbath, — a Christian jubilee to the God of my life. So shall I witness my share in the oil of joy with which thou anointest perfect Christians above their fellow believers; I stand in need of that oil, Lord: my lamp burns dim: sometimes it seems to be even gone out, as that of the foolish virgins; it is more like "a smoking flax" than "a burning and shining light." O! quench it not: raise it to a flame. Thou knowest that I do believe in thee. The trembling hand of my faith holds thee; and though I have ten thousand times grieved thy pardoning love, thine everlasting arm is still under me, to redeem my life from destruction; while thy right hand is over me, to crown me with mercies and loving kindness. But, alas! I am neither sufficiently thankful for thy present mercies, nor sufficiently athirst for thy future favours. Hence I feel an aching void in my soul, being conscious that I have not attained the heights of grace described in thy word, and enjoyed by thy holiest servants. Their deep experiences, the diligence and ardour with which they did thy will; the patience and fortitude with which they endured the cross, reproach me, and convince me of my manifold wants. I want "power from on high;" I want the penetrating, lasting "unction of the Holy One." I want to have my vessel (my capacious heart) full of oil, which makes the countenance of wise virgins cheerful. I want a lamp of heavenly illumination, and a fire of Divine love, burning day and night in my breast, as the typical lamps did in the temple, and the sacred fire on the altar; I want a full application of the blood which cleanses from all sin, and a strong faith in thy sanctifying word, — a faith by which thou mayest dwell in my heart, as the unwavering hope of glory, and the fixed object of my love. I want the internal oracle, — thy still, small voice, together with urim and thummim,*— "the new name which none knoweth but he that receiveth it." In a word, Lord, I want a plenitude of thy Spirit, the full promise of the Father, and the rivers which flow from the inmost souls of the believers, who have gone on to the perfection of their dispensation. I do believe that thou canst and wilt thus "baptize me with the Holy Ghost and with fire:" help my unbelief: confirm and increase my faith, with regard to this important baptism. Lord, I have need to be thus baptized of

---

* Two Hebrew words, which mean *lights and perfections.*

thee, and I am straitened till this baptism is accomplished. By thy baptisms of tears in the manger — of water in Jordan — of sweat in Gethsemane — of blood, and fire, and vapour of smoke, and flaming wrath on Calvary, baptize — O, baptize my soul, and make as full an end of the original sin which I have from Adam, as thy last baptism made of the likeness of sinful flesh, which thou hadst from a daughter of Eve. Some of thy people look at death for full salvation from sin; but, at thy command, Lord, I look unto thee. "Say to my soul, *I am thy salvation.*" and let me feel with my heart, as well as see with my understanding, that thou canst *save* from sin *to the uttermost, all that come to God through thee.* I am tired of forms, professions, and orthodox notions; so far as they are not pipes or channels to convey life, light, and love to my dead, dark, and stony heart. Neither the plain letter of thy Gospel, nor the sweet foretastes and transient illuminations of thy Spirit, can satisfy the large desires of my faith. Give me thine abiding Spirit, that he may continually shed abroad thy love in my soul. Come, O Lord, with that blessed Spirit: come thou, and thy Father, in that holy Comforter, — come to make your abode with me; or I shall go meekly mourning to my grave. Blessed mourning! Lord, increase it. I had rather wait in tears for thy fulness than wantonly waste the fragments of thy spiritual bounties, or feed with Laodicean contentment upon the tainted manna of my former experiences. Righteous Father, "I hunger and thirst after thy righteousness:" send thy Holy Spirit of promise to fill me therewith, to sanctify me throughout, and to "seal me *centrally* to the day of eternal redemption" and finished salvation. "Not for works of righteousness which I have done, but of thy mercy," for Christ's sake, "save thou me by the *complete* washing of regeneration, and the *full* renewing of the Holy Ghost." And in order to this, pour out of thy Spirit; shed it abundantly on me till the fountain of living water abundantly spring up in my soul, and I can say, in the full sense of the words, that thou "livest in me, that my life is hid with thee in God, and that my spirit is returned to him that gave it; to thee, the first and the last, — my author and my end, — my God and my all!"

SECTION XX.

An address to perfect Christians.

YE have not sung the preceding hymns in vain, O ye men of God, who have mixed faith with your evangelical requests. The God, who says, "Open thy mouth wide, and I will fill it;" the gracious God who declares, "Blessed are they that hunger after righteousness, for they shall be filled;" that faithful, covenant-keeping God has now filled you with all "righteousness, peace, and joy in believing." The brightness of Christ's appearing has destroyed the indwelling "man of sin." He who had slain the lion and the bear (he who had already done so great things for you) has now crowned all his blessings by slaying the Goliath within. Aspiring, unbelieving self is fallen before the victorious Son of David. "The quick and powerful word of God, which is sharper than any two-edged sword, has pierced even to the dividing asunder of soul and spirit." The carnal mind is cut off: the circumcision of the heart, through the

Spirit, has fully taken place in your breasts; and now "that mind is in you which was also in Christ Jesus; ye are spiritually minded." loving God with all your heart, and your neighbour as yourselves, "ye are full of goodness, ye keep the commandments," ye observe *the law of liberty*, ye fulfil *the law of Christ*. Of him ye have "learned to be meek and lowly in heart." Ye have fully "taken his yoke upon you;" in so doing ye have found a sweet, abiding rest unto your souls; and from blessed experience ye can say, "Christ's yoke is easy, and his burden is light. His ways are ways of pleasantness, and all his paths are peace. All the paths of the Lord are mercy and truth, unto such as keep his covenant and his testimonies." The beatitudes are sensibly yours: and the charity, described by St. Paul, has the same place in your breasts which the tables of the law had in the ark of the covenant. Ye are the living temples of the trinity: the Father is your life; the Son your light; the Spirit your love; ye are truly baptized into the mystery of God, ye continue to "drink into one spirit," and thus ye enjoy the grace of both sacraments. There is an end of your *Lo here!* and *Lo there!* The kingdom of God is now established within you. Christ's "righteousness, peace, and joy" are rooted in your breasts "by the Holy Ghost given unto you, as an abiding guide, and indwelling comforter. Your introverted eye of faith looks at God, who gently "guides you with his eye" into all the truth necessary to make you "do justice, love mercy, and walk humbly with your God." *Simplicity of intention* keeps darkness out of your mind, and *purity of affection* keeps wrong fires out of your breast: by the former, ye are without *guile;* by the latter, ye are without *envy*. Your passive will instantly melts into the will of God; and on all occasions you meekly say, "Not my will, O Father, but thine be done!" Thus ye are always ready to suffer what you are called to suffer. Your active will evermore says, "Speak, Lord; thy servant heareth: what wouldst thou have me to do? It is my meat and drink to do the will of my heavenly Father!" Thus are ye always ready to do whatsoever ye are convinced that God calls you to do; and "whatsoever ye do, whether ye eat, or drink, or do any thing else, ye do all to the glory of God, and in the name of our Lord Jesus Christ; rejoicing evermore; praying without ceasing; in every thing giving thanks;" solemnly *looking for* and *hasting unto* the hour of your dissolution, and the "day of God, wherein the heavens, being on fire, shall be dissolved," and your soul, being clothed with a celestial body, shall be able to do celestial services to the God of your life.

In this blessed state of Christian perfection the holy "anointing, which ye have received of him, abideth in you, and ye need not that any man teach you, unless it be as the same anointing teacheth." Agreeably, therefore, to that anointing, which teaches by a variety of means, which formerly taught a prophet by an ass, and daily instructs God's children by the ant, I shall venture to set before you some important directions which the Holy Ghost has already suggested to your pure minds: "for I would not be negligent to put you in remembrance of these things, though ye know them, and be established in the present truth. Yea, I think it meet to stir you up, by putting you in remembrance," and giving you some hints, which it is safe for you frequently to meditate upon.

I. Adam, ye know, lost his *human* perfection in paradise; Satan lost his *angelic* perfection in heaven; the devil thrust sore at Christ in the wilderness, to throw him down from his *mediatorial* perfection: and St. Paul, in the same epistles where he professes not only *Christian,* but *apostolic* perfection also, (Philippians 3:15; 1 Corinthians 2:6; 2 Corinthians 12:11,) informs us that he continued to "run for the crown of heavenly perfection" like a man who might not only lose his crown of Christian perfection, but become a reprobate, and be cast away, 1 Corinthians 9:25, 27. And, therefore, "so run ye also, that no man take your crown" of Christian perfection in this world, and that ye may obtain your crown of angelic perfection in the world to come. Still keep your body under. Still guard your senses. Still watch your own heart, and, "steadfast in the faith, still resist the devil that he may flee from you;" remembering that if Christ himself, as Son of man, had conferred with flesh and blood, refused to deny himself, and avoided taking up his cross, he had lost his perfection, and sealed up our original apostasy.

"We do not find," says Mr. Wesley, in his *Plain Account of Christian Perfection,* "any general state described in Scripture, from which a man cannot draw back to sin. If there were any state wherein this is impossible, it would be that of those who are sanctified, who are fathers in Christ, who 'rejoice evermore, pray without ceasing, and in every thing give thanks.' But it is not impossible for these to draw back. They who are sanctified may yet fall and perish, Hebrews 10:29. Even 'fathers in Christ' need that warning, 'Love not the world' 1 John 2:15. They who 'rejoice, pray, and give thanks without ceasing,' may nevertheless 'quench the Spirit,' 1 Thessalonians 5:16, &c. Nay, even they who are 'sealed unto the day of redemption,' may yet 'grieve the Holy Spirit of God,' Ephesians 5:30."*

The doctrine of the absolute perseverance of the saints is the first card which the devil played against man: — "Ye shall not surely die, if ye break the law of your perfection." This fatal card won the game. Mankind and paradise were lost. The artful serpent had too well succeeded at his first game to forget that lucky card at his second. See him "transforming himself into an angel of light on the pinnacle of the temple." There he plays over again his old game against the Son of God. Out of the Bible he pulls the very card which won our first parents, and swept the stake — paradise — yea, swept it with the besom of destruction: — "Cast thyself down," says he, "for it is written, [that all things shall work together for thy good, thy very falls not excepted,] *he shall give his angels charge concerning thee, and in their hands they shall bear thee up, lest at any time thou dash thy foot against a stone.*" The tempter (thanks be to Christ!) lost the game at that time, but he did not lose his card: and it is probable that he will play it round against you all only with some variation. Let me mention one among a thousand: — He promised our Lord that God's "angels should bear him up in their hands, if he threw himself down;" and it is not unlikely that he will promise you greater things still. Nor should I wonder if he was bold enough to hint, that when you cast yourselves down, "God himself shall bear you up in his HANDS, yea, in his ARMS of everlasting love." O ye men of God, learn wisdom by the fall of Adam. O ye anointed sons of the Most High, learn watchfulness by the conduct of Christ. If he

---

* We do not hereby deny that some believers have a testimony in their own breasts that they shall not finally fall from God. "They may have it," says Mr. Wesley, in the same tract, "and this persuasion that 'neither life nor death shall separate them from God,' far from being hurtful, may in some circumstances be extremely useful." But wherever this testimony is Divine, it is attended with that grace which inseparably connects holiness and good works, *the means,* with perseverance and eternal salvation, *the end:* and, in this respect, our doctrine widely differs from that of the Calvinists, who break the necessary connection between holiness and infallible salvation, by making room for the foulest false — for adultery, murder, and incest.

was afraid to "tempt the Lord his God," will ye dare to do it? If he rejected, as poison, the hook of the absolute perseverance of the saints, though it was baited with Scripture, will ye swallow it down as if it were "honey out of the rock of ages?" No: "through faith in Christ, the Scriptures have made you wise unto salvation:" you will not only flee with all speed from evil, but from the very appearance of evil: and when you stand on the brink of a temptation, far from "entering into it," under any pretence whatever, ye will leap back into the bosom of him who says, "Watch and pray, lest ye enter into temptation; for though the spirit is willing, the flesh is weak." I grant that, evangelically speaking, "the weakness of the flesh" is not sin; but yet the "deceitfulness of sin" creeps in at this door: and in this way not a few of God's children, "after they had escaped the pollutions of the world, through the" sanctifying knowledge of Christ, under plausible pretences, 'have been entangled again therein and overcome." Let their falls make you cautious. Ye have "put on the whole armour of God;" O keep it on, and use it "with all prayer," that ye may to the last "stand complete in Christ, and be more than conquerors through him that has loved you."

II. Remember that "every one who is perfect shall be as his Master." Now if your Master was tempted and assaulted *to the last;* if *to the last* he watched and prayed, using all the means of grace himself, and enforcing the use of them upon others; if *to the last* he fought against the world, the flesh, and the devil, and did not "put off the harness" till he had put off the body; think not yourselves above him; but "go and do likewise." If he did not regain paradise, without going through the most complete renunciation of all the good things of this world, and without meekly submitting to the severe stroke of his last enemy, death, be content to be "perfect as he was:" nor fancy that your flesh and blood can inherit the celestial kingdom of God, when the flesh and blood which Emmanuel himself assumed from a pure virgin, could not inherit it without passing under the cherub's flaming sword: I mean, without going through the gates of death.

III. Ye are not complete in wisdom. Perfect love does not imply perfect knowledge; but perfect humility, and perfect readiness to receive instruction. Remember, therefore, that if ever ye show that ye are above being instructed, even by a fisherman who teaches according to the Divine anointing, ye will show that ye are fallen from a perfection of humility into a perfection of pride.

IV. Do not confound angelical with Christian perfection. Uninterrupted transports of praise, and ceaseless raptures of joy, do not belong to Christian, but to angelical perfection. Our feeble frame can bear but a few drops of that glorious cup. In general, that *new wine* is too strong for our *old bottles;* that power is too excellent for our earthen, cracked vessels; but weak as they are, they can bear a fulness of meekness, of resignation, of humility, and of that love which is willing to "obey unto death." If God indulge you with ecstacies, and extraordinary revelations, be thankful for them: but be "not exalted above measure by them;" take care lest enthusiastic delusions mix themselves with them; and remember that your Christian perfection does not so much consist in "building a tabernacle" upon Mount Tabor, to rest and enjoy rare sights there, as in resolutely taking up the cross, and following Christ to the palace of a proud Caiaphas, to the judgment hall of an unjust Pilate, and to the top of an ignominious Calvary. Ye never read in your Bibles, "Let that glory be upon you which was also upon St. Stephen, when he looked up steadfastly into heaven, and said, *Behold! I see the heavens opened, and the Son of man standing on the right hand* of God."

But ye have frequently read there, "Let this mind be in you, which was also in Christ Jesus, who made himself of no reputation, took upon him the form of a servant, and being found in fashion as a man, humbled himself, and became obedient unto death, even the death of the cross."

See him on that ignominious gibbet! He hangs — abandoned by his friends — surrounded by his foes — condemned by the rich — insulted by the poor! He hangs— "a worm and no man — a very scorn of men, and the outcast of the people! All that see him laugh him to scorn! They shoot out their lips and shake their heads, saying, *He trusted in God, that he would deliver him; let him deliver him, if he will have him!*" There is none to help him: one of his apostles denies, another sells him; and the rest run away. "Many oxen are come about him: fat bulls of Bashan close him on every side; they gape upon him with their mouths as it were a ramping lion; he is poured out like water; his heart in the midst of his body is like melting wax; his strength is dried up like a potsherd; his tongue cleaveth to his gums; he is going into the dust of death; many dogs are come about him; and the counsel of the wicked layeth siege against him; his hands and feet are pierced; you may tell all his bones; they stand staring and looking upon him; they part his garments among them, and cast lots for the only remains of his property, his plain, seamless vesture. Both suns, the visible and the invisible, seem eclipsed. No cheering beam of created light gilds his gloomy prospect. No smile of his heavenly Father supports his agonizing soul! No cordial, unless it be vinegar and gall, revives his sinking spirits! He has nothing left except his God. But his God is enough for him. In his God he has all things. And though his soul is seized with sorrow, even unto death, yet it hangs more firmly upon his God by a naked faith, than his lacerated body does on the cross by the clenched nails. The perfection of his love shines in all its Christian glory. He not only forgives his insulting goes and bloody persecutors, but, in the highest point of his passion, he forgets his own wants, and thirsts after their eternal happiness. Together with his blood, he pours out his soul for them; and, excusing them all, he says, "Father, forgive them, for they know not what they do." O ye adult sons of God, in this glass behold all with open face the glory of your Redeemer's forgiving, praying love; and, as ye "behold it, be changed into the same image from glory to glory, by the loving Spirit of the Lord."

V. This lesson is deep; but he may teach you one deeper still. By a strong sympathy with him in all his sufferings, he may call you to "know him *every way* crucified." Stern justice thunders from heaven, "Awake, O sword, against the man who is my fellow!" The sword awakes; the sword goes through his soul; the flaming sword is quenched in his blood. But is one sinew of his perfect faith cut, one fibre of his perfect resignation injured by the astonishing blow? No; his God slays him, and yet he trusts in his God. By the noblest of all ventures, in the most dreadful of all storms, he meekly bows his head, and shelters his departing soul in the bosom of his God. "*My God, my God!*" says he, "though all my comforts have forsaken me, and all thy storms and waves go over me, yet 'into thy hands I commend my spirit. For thou wilt not leave my soul in hell; neither wilt thou suffer thy Holy One to see corruption. Thou wilt show me the path of life, in thy presence is fulness of joy, and at thy right hand [where I shall soon sit] there are pleasures for evermore.'" What a pattern of perfect confidence! O ye perfect Christians, be ambitious to ascend to those amazing heights of Christ's perfection: for hereunto are ye called; because Christ also suffered for us; leaving us an example, that we should follow his steps, who knew no sin, who, when he was reviled, reviled not again; when he suffered he threatened not, but committed himself to him that judgeth righteously." If this is your high calling on earth, rest not, O ye fathers in Christ, till your patient hope, and perfect confidence in God have got their last victory over your last enemy — the king of terrors.

"The ground of a thousand mistakes," says Mr. Wesley, "is, the not considering deeply that love is the highest gift of God, *humble, gentle, patient love:* that all visions, revelations, manifestations whatever, are little things compared to love. It were well you should be thoroughly sensible of this; the heaven of heavens is love. There is nothing higher in religion: there is, in effect, nothing else. If you look for any thing but more love, you are looking wide of the mark, you are getting out of the royal way. And when you are asking others, 'Have you received this or that blessing?' if you mean any thing but *more love,* you mean wrong; you are leading them out of the way, and putting them upon a false scent. Settle it then in your heart, that from the moment God has saved you from all sin, you are to aim at nothing *but more of that* love described in the thirteenth of the Corinthians. You can go no higher than this, till you are carried into Abraham's bosom."

VI. Love is humble. "Be therefore clothed with humility," says Mr. Wesley: "let it not only fill, but cover you all over. Let modesty and self diffidence appear in all your words and actions. Let all you speak and do show that you are little, and base, and mean, and vile in your own eyes. As one instance of this, be always ready to own any fault you have been in. If you have at any time thought, spoke, or acted wrong, be not backward to acknowledge it. Never dream that this will hurt the cause of God: no, it will farther it. Be therefore open and frank when you are taxed with any thing: let it appear just as it is; and you will thereby not hinder, but adorn the Gospel." Why should ye be more backward in acknowledging your failings, than in confessing that ye do not pretend to infallibility? St. Paul was perfect in the love which casts out fear, and therefore he boldly reproved the high priest: but when he had reproved him more sharply than the fifth commandment allows, he directly confessed his mistake, and set his seal to the importance of the duty, in which he had been inadvertently wanting. Then Paul said, "I knew not, brethren, that he was the high priest: for it is written, *Thou shalt not speak evil of the ruler of thy people.*" St. John was perfect in the courteous, humble love which brings us down at the feet of all. His courtesy, his humility, and the dazzling glory which beamed forth from a divine messenger (whom he apprehended to be more than a creature) betrayed him into a fault contrary to that of St. Paul: but, far from concealing it, he openly confessed it, and published his confession for the edification of all the Churches: "When I had heard and seen," says he, "I fell down to worship before the feet of the angel who showed me these things. Then saith he unto me, *See thou do it not, for I am thy fellow servant.*" Christian perfection shines as much in the childlike simplicity with which the perfect readily acknowledge their faults, as it does in the manly steadiness with which they "resist unto blood, striving against sin."

VII. If humble love makes us frankly confess our faults, much more does it incline us to own ourselves sinners, miserable sinners before that God whom we have so frequently offended. I need not remind you that your "bodies are dead because of sin." You see, you feel it, and therefore, so long as you dwell in a prison of flesh and blood, which death, the avenger of sin, is to pull down; so long as your final justification, as pardoned and sanctified sinners, has not taken place: yea, so long as you break the law of paradisiacal perfection, under which you were originally placed, it is meet, right, and your bounden duty to consider yourselves as sinners, who, as transgressors of the law of innocence and the law of liberty, are guilty of death, — of eternal death. St. Paul did so after he was "come to Mount Sion, and to the spirits of just men made perfect." He still looked upon himself as the chief of sinners, because he had been a daring blasphemer of Christ, and a fierce. persecutor of his people. "Christ," says he, "came to save sinners, of whom I am chief." The reason is plain. Matter of fact is, and will be matter of fact to all eternity. According to the doctrines of grace and justice, and before the throne of God's mercy and holiness, a sinner pardoned and sanctified must, in the very nature of things, be considered as a sinner; for if you consider him as a saint absolutely abstracted from the character of a sinner, how can he be a pardoned and sanctified sinner? To all eternity, therefore, but much more while death (the wages of sin) is at your heels, and while ye are going to "appear before the judgment seat of Christ, to receive" your final sentence of absolution or condemnation, it will become you to say with St. Paul, "We have all sinned, and come short of the glory of God; being justified freely [as sinners] by his grace, through the redemption that is in Jesus Christ;" although we are justified JUDICIALLY *as believers,* through faith; *as obedient believers,* through the obedience of faith; and as *perfect Christians,* through Christian perfection.

VIII. Humble love "becomes all things [but sin] to all men," although it delights most in those who are most holy. Ye may, and ought to set your love of peculiar complacence upon God's dearest children; upon "those who excel in virtue;" because they more strongly reflect the image of "the God of love, the Holy One of Israel." But, if ye despise the weak, and are above lending them a helping hand, ye are fallen from Christian perfection, which teaches us to "bear one another's burdens," especially the burdens of the weak. Imitate then the tenderness and wisdom of the good Shepherd, who "carries the lambs in his bosom, gently leads the sheep which are big with young," feeds with milk those who cannot bear strong meat, and says to his imperfect disciples, "I have many things to say to you, but ye cannot bear them now."

IX. "Where the *loving* Spirit of the Lord is, there is liberty." Keep therefore at the utmost distance from the shackles of a narrow, prejudiced, bigoted spirit. The moment ye confine your love to the people who think just as you do, and your regard to the preachers who exactly suit your taste, you fall from perfection and turn bigots. "I entreat you," says Mr. Wesley, in his *Plain Account,* "beware of bigotry. Let not your love, or beneficence, be confined to *Methodists* (so called) only; much less to that very small part of them who seem to be renewed in love; or to those who believe yours and their report. O make not this your Shibboleth." On the contrary, as ye have time and ability, "do good to all men." Let your benevolence shine upon all: let your charity send its cherishing beams toward all, in proper degrees. So shall ye be perfect as your heavenly Father, "who makes his sun to shine upon all;" although he sends the brightest and warmest beams of his favour upon "the household of faith," and reserves his richest bounties for those who lay out their five talents to the best advantage.

X. Love, pure love, is satisfied with the Supreme Good — with GOD. "Beware then of desiring any thing but him. Now you desire nothing else. Every other desire is driven out: see that none enter in again. 'Keep thyself pure: let your eye *remain* single, and your whole body shall remain full of light.' Admit no desire of pleasing food, or any other pleasure of sense; no desire of pleasing the eye or imagination; no desire of money, of praise, or esteem; of happiness in any creature. You may bring these desires back; but ye need not; you may feel them no more. 'O stand fast in the liberty wherewith Christ hath made you free!' Be patterns to all, of denying yourselves, and taking up your cross daily. Let them see that you make no account of any pleasure which does not bring you nearer to God, nor regard any pain which does; that you simply aim at pleasing him, whether by doing or suffering; that the constant language of your heart with regard to pleasure or pain, honour or dishonour, is,

> All's alike to me, so I
> In my Lord may live and die!"

XI. The best soldiers are sent upon the most difficult and dangerous expeditions: and as you are the best soldiers of Jesus Christ, ye will probably be called to drink deepest of his cup, and to carry the heaviest burdens. "Expect contradiction and opposition," says the judicious divine, whom I have just quoted, "together with crosses of various kinds. Consider the words of St. Paul, 'To you it is given in behalf of Christ,' for his sake, as a fruit of his death and intercession for you,' not only to believe, but also to suffer for his sake,' Philippians 1:23. *It is given!* God *gives* you this opposition or reproach: it is a fresh token of his love. And will you disown the giver? Or spurn his gift, and count it a misfortune? Will you not rather say, 'Father, the hour is come, that thou shouldst be glorified. Now thou givest thy child to suffer something for thee. Do with me according to thy will.' Know that these things, far from being *hinderances* to the work of God, or to your souls, unless by your own fault, are not only unavoidable in the course of Providence, but *profitable,* yea, *necessary* for you. Therefore receive them from God (not from chance) with willingness and thankfulness. Receive them from men with humility, meekness, yieldingness, gentleness, sweetness."

Love can never do, nor suffer too much for its Divine object. Be then ambitious, like St. Paul, to be made perfect in *sufferings.* I have already observed that the apostle, not satisfied to be a perfect Christian, would also be a perfect martyr; earnestly desiring to "know the fellowship of Christ's sufferings." Follow him, as he followed his suffering, crucified Lord. Your feet "are shod with the preparation of the Gospel of peace;" run after them both, in the race of obedience, for the crown of martyrdom, if that crown is reserved for you. And if ye miss the crown of those who are martyrs in *deed,* ye shall, however, receive the reward of those who are martyrs in *intention* — the crown of righteousness and angelical perfection.

XII. But do not so desire to follow Christ to the garden of Gethsemane, as to refuse following him *now* to the carpenter's shop, if Providence *now* call you to it. Do not lose *the present day* by idly looking back at *yesterday,* or foolishly antedating the cares of *to-morrow:* but wisely use every hour; spending it as one who stands on the verge of time, on the border of eternity, and one who has his work cut out by a wise Providence from moment to moment. Never, therefore, neglect using the two talents you have *now,* and doing the duty which is *now* incumbent upon you. Should ye be tempted to it, under the plausible pretence of waiting for a great number of talents:

remember that God doubles our talents in the way of duty, and that it is a maxim, advanced by Elisha Coles himself, "Use grace and have [more] grace." Therefore, "to continual watchfulness and prayer, add continual employment," says Mr. Wesley, "for grace flies a vacuum as well as nature; the devil fills whatever God does not fill." "*As by works faith is made perfect,* so the completing or destroying of the work of faith, and enjoying the favour, or suffering the displeasure of God, greatly depend on every single act of obedience." If you forget this, you will hardly do *now* whatsoever your hand findeth to do. Much less will you do it with *all* your might, for God, for eternity.

XIII. Love is modest: it rather inclines to bashfulness and silence, than to talkative forwardness. "In a multitude of words there wanteth not sin;" be therefore "slow to speak;" nor cast your pearls before those who cannot distinguish them from pebbles. Nevertheless, when you are solemnly called upon to bear testimony to the truth, and to say "what great things God has done for you;" it would be cowardice, or false prudence, not to do it with humility. Be then "always ready to give an answer to every man who [properly] asketh you a reason of the hope that is in you, with meekness [without fluttering anxiety] and with fear" [with a reverential awe of God upon your minds,] 1 Peter 3:15. Perfect Christians are "burning and shining lights," and our Lord intimates that, as "a candle is not lighted to be put under a bushel, but upon a candlestick, that it may give light to all the house;" so God does not light the candle of perfect love to hide it in a corner, but to give light to all those who are within the reach of its brightness. If diamonds glitter, if stars shine, if flowers display their colours, and perfumes diffuse their fragrance, to the honour of the Father of lights, and Author of every good gift; if without self seeking they disclose his glory to the utmost of their power, why should "ye *not* go and do likewise?" Gold answers its most valuable end when it is brought to light, and made to circulate for charitable and pious uses; and not when it lies concealed in a miser's strong box, or in the dark bosom of a mine. But when you lay out your spiritual gold for proper uses, beware of imitating the vanity of those coxcombs who, as often as they are about to pay for a trifle, pull out a handful of gold, merely to make a show of their wealth.

XIV. Love or "charity rejoiceth in the [display of an edifying] truth." Fact is fact, all the world over. If you can say to the glory of God, that *you are alive, and feel very well,* when it is so; why should you not also testify to his honour, that you "live not, but that Christ liveth in you," if you really find that this is your experience? Did not St. John say, "Our love is made perfect, because as he is, so are we in this world?" Did not St. Paul write, "The righteousness of the law is fulfilled in us, who walk after the Spirit?" Did he not, with the same simplicity, aver, that although" he had nothing, and was sorrowful, yet he possessed all things, and was always rejoicing?"

Hence it appears, that, with respect to the declaring or concealing what God has done for your soul, the line of your duty runs exactly between *the proud forwardness* of some stiff Pharisees, and *the voluntary humility* of some stiff mystics. The former vainly boast of more than they experience, and thus set up the cursed idol, SELF: the latter ungratefully hide "the wonderful works of God," which the primitive Christians spoke of publicly in a variety of languages; and so refuse to exalt their gracious benefactor, CHRIST. The first error is undoubtedly more odious than the second; but what need is there of leaning to either? Would ye avoid them both? Let your tempers and lives always declare that perfect love is attainable in this life. And when you have a proper call to declare it with your lips and pens, do it without forwardness, to the glory of God; do it with simplicity, for the edification of your neighbour; do it with godly jealousy, lest ye should show the treasures of Divine grace in your hearts, with the same *self complacence* with which King Hezekiah showed his treasures, and the golden vessels of the temple to the ambassadors of the king of Babylon, remembering what a dreadful curse this piece of vanity pulled down upon him: "And Isaiah said unto Hezekiah, Hear the word of the Lord, *Behold the days come, that all that is in thine house shall be carried into Babylon: nothing shall be left,* saith the Lord." If God so severely punished Hezekiah's pride, how properly does St. Peter charge believers to "give with fear an account of the grace which is in them!" and how careful should ye be to observe this important charge!

XV. If you will keep at the utmost distance from the vanity which proved so fatal to good King Hezekiah, follow an excellent direction of Mr. Wesley. When you have done any thing for God, or received any favour from him, retire, if not into your *closet,* into your *heart,* and say, "I come, Lord, to restore to thee what thou hast given, and I freely relinquish it, to enter again into my own nothingness. For what is the most perfect creature in heaven or earth in thy presence, but a void, capable of being filled with thee and by thee, as the air which is void and dark, is capable of being filled with the light of the sun? Grant therefore, O Lord, that I may never appropriate thy grace to myself, any more than the air appropriates to itself the light of the sun which withdraws it every day to restore it the next; there being nothing in the air that either appropriates his light or resists it. O give me the same facility of receiving and restoring thy grace and good works! I say thine, for I acknowledge that the root from which they spring is in thee, and not in me." "The true means to be filled anew with the riches of grace, is thus to strip ourselves of it; without this it is extremely difficult not to faint in the practice of good works." "And, therefore, that your good works may receive their last perfection, let them lose themselves in God. This is a kind of death to them, resembling that of our bodies, which will not attain their highest life, their immortality, till they lose themselves in the glory of our souls, or rather of God, wherewith they shall be filled. And it is only what they had of earthly and mortal, which good works lose by this spiritual death."

XVI. Would ye see this deep precept put in practice? Consider St. Paul. Already possessed of Christian perfection, he does good works from morning till night. He warns every one night and day with tears. He carries the Gospel from east to west. Wherever he stops, he plants a Church at the hazard of his life. But instead of resting in his present perfection, and in the good works which spring from it, "he grows in grace, and in the knowledge of our Lord Jesus Christ;" unweariedly "following after, if that he may apprehend that [perfection] for which also he is apprehended of Christ Jesus," — that celestial perfection, of which he got lively ideas when he was "caught up to the third heaven, and heard unspeakable words, which it is not possible for a man to utter." With what amazing ardour does he run his race of Christian perfection for the prize of that higher perfection! How does he forget the works of yesterday, when he lays himself out for God to-day! "Though dead, he yet speaketh;" nor can an address to perfect Christians be closed by a more proper speech than his. "Brethren," says he, "be followers of me — I count not myself to have apprehended [my evangelical perfection;] but this one thing I do, forgetting those things which are behind, [settling in none of my former experiences, resting in none of my good works,] and reaching forth unto those things which are before, I press toward the mark for the [celestial] prize of the high calling of God in Christ Jesus. Let us therefore, as many as are perfect, be thus minded; and if in any thing ye be otherwise minded, God shall reveal even this unto you." In the meantime you may sing the following hymn of the Rev. Mr. Charles Wesley, which is descriptive of the destruction of corrupt self will, and expressive of the absolute resignation which characterizes a perfect believer: —

> To do, or not to do; to have,
>> Or not to have, I leave to thee:
> To be or not to be, I leave:
>> Thy only will be done in me!
> All my requests are lost in one,
> "Father, thy only will be done!"
>
> Suffice that for the season past,
>> Myself in things Divine I sought;
> For comforts cried with eager haste,
>> And murmur'd that I found them not
> I leave it now to thee alone,
> Father, thy only will be done!
>
> Thy gifts I clamour for no more,
>> Or selfishly thy grace require,
> An evil heart to varnish o'er:
>> JESUS, the giver, I desire,
> After the flesh no longer known:
> Father, thy only will be done!
>
> Welcome alike the crown or cross,
>> Trouble I cannot ask, nor peace,
> Nor toil, nor rest, nor gain, nor loss,
>> Nor joy, nor grief, nor pain, nor ease,
> Nor life, nor death; but ever groan,
> "Father, thy only will be done!"

This hymn suits all the believers who are at the bottom of Mount Sion, and begin to join "the spirits of just men made perfect." But when the triumphal chariot of perfect love *gloriously* carries you to the top of perfection's hill; when you are raised far above the *common* heights of the perfect; when you are almost translated into glory, like Elijah, then you may sing another hymn of the same Christian poet, with the Rev. Mr. Madan, and the numerous body of imperfectionists who use his collection of Psalms, &c: —

> Who in Jesus confide,
> They are bold to outride
> All the storms of affliction beneath:
> With the prophet they soar

To that heavenly shore,
And outfly all the arrows of death.

By faith we are come
To our permanent home;
And by hope we the rapture improve:
By love we still rise,
And look down on the skies —
For the heaven of heavens is love!

Who on earth can conceive,
How happy we live
In the city of God, the great King?
What a concert of praise,
When our Jesus's grace
The whole heavenly company sing!

What a rapturous song,
When the glorified throng
In the spirit of harmony join!
Join all the glad choirs,
Hearts, voices, and lyres,
And the burden is mercy Divine!

But when you cannot follow Mr. Madan, and the imperfectionists of the Lock Chapel, to those rapturous heights of perfection, you need not give up your shield. You may still rank among the perfect, if you can heartily join in this version of Psalm 131: —

Lord, thou dost the grace impart!
Poor in spirit, meek in heart,
I shall as my Master be,
Rooted in humility.

Now, dear Lord, that thee I know,
Nothing will I seek below,
Aim at nothing great or high,
Lowly both in heart and eye.

Simple, teachable, and mild,
Awed into a little child,
Quiet now without my food,
Wean'd from every creature good.

Hangs my new-born soul on thee,
Kept from all idolatry;
Nothing wants beneath, above,

Resting in thy perfect love.

That your earthen vessels may be filled with this love till they break, and you enjoy the Divine object of your faith without an interposing veil of gross flesh and blood, is the wish of one who sincerely praises God on your account, and ardently prays, —

"Make up thy Jewels, Lord, and show
The glorious, spotless Church below:
The fellowship of saints make known;
And O! my God, might I be one!

O might my lot be cast with these,
The least of Jesus' witnesses!
O that my Lord would count me meet,
To wash his dear disciples' feet!

To wait upon his saints below!
On Gospel errands for them go!
Enjoy the grace to angels given;
And serve the royal heirs of heaven!"

END

Apprehending Truth Publishers
Proclaiming Truth in the Age of Deceit
AD LEGEM MAGIS ET AD TESTIMONIUM

For additional copies of this book and a list of other titles available from Apprehending Truth please visit our website:

www.ATPublishers.com

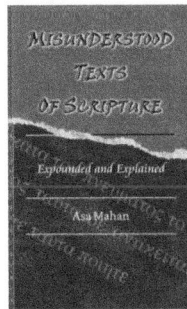

DEFINING BIBLICAL HOLINESS

John Wesley, Asa Mahan

ed. Jeffrey L. Wallace

The Biblical doctrine of "Christian Perfection" has been denied even by those who call themselves by the name of Christ. "Defining Biblical Holiness" takes a look at this all important doctrine by casting our gaze into the past, and attempting to clearly define the truth presented in this doctrine. John Wesley and Asa Mahan both had a firm grasp upon a Biblical understanding of the teaching of holiness and Christian Perfection. Their two works on the subject, along with a new introduction, are here presented in juxtaposition in order to shed light on the current antinomian trend which continues unabated in the modern professing "Church".

- ISBN: 0615444040
- EAN13: 9780615444048
- Page Count: 296
- Binding Type: US Trade Paper
- Trim Size: 6" x 9"
- Language: English
- Color: Black and White
- Related Categories: Religion / Christian Theology / Ethics

Available at ATPublishers.com and your favorite online book retailers. Ask your local bookstore to carry titles from Apprehending Truth Publishers.

www.ingramcontent.com/pod-product-compliance
Lightning Source LLC
Chambersburg PA
CBHW031231090426
42742CB00007B/149